INTRODUCING SOCIOLOGY

A COLLECTION OF READINGS

Richard T. Schaefer
Western Illinois University

Robert P. Lamm

McGRAW-HILL BOOK COMPANY

New York St. Louis San Francisco Auckland Bogotá
Hamburg Johannesburg London Madrid Mexico Milan Montreal
New Delhi Panama Paris São Paulo Singapore Sydney Tokyo Toronto

TO MY WIFE, SANDRA L. SCHAEFER
R.T.S.

IN MEMORY OF MY COUSIN,
LESLIE GOLD
R.P.L.

This book was set in Linotron by Intergraphic Technology, Inc.
The editor was Barbara L. Raab; the production supervisor
was Fred Schulte; the cover was designed by Joan E. O'Connor
Project supervision was done by Caliber Design Planning, Inc.
R. R. Donnelly & Sons Company was printer and binder.

INTRODUCING SOCIOLOGY
A Collection of Readings

1 2 3 4 5 6 7 8 9 0   DOCDOC   8 9 4 3 2 1 0 9 8 7

ISBN 0-07-055077-8

Library of Congress Cataloging-in-Publication Data

Introducing sociology.

Includes index.
1. Sociology.   2. Social Problems.   3. United States—
Social policy.   I. Schaefer, Richard T.   II. Lamm,
Robert P.
HM51.I55   1987   301   86-18604
ISBN 0-07-055077-8

CONTENTS

PREFACE

Sociology is an exciting field of study; in the 52 selections that follow, you will share in this excitement. Our selections underscore the diversity of the approaches, perspectives, and methodologies used in sociology. The readings have been selected to illustrate those concepts central to sociological thought.

As you will see, the sociological perspective is presented not only in scholarly journals and monographs but also in newsmagazines and popular periodicals. We have included both classical and more contemporary sociological studies. Thus, the contributors include pioneering theorist Max Weber and influential sociologists of recent decades, such as Peter Berger, Lewis Coser, and Erving Goffman. We have also drawn upon the work of social scientists from related disciplines, among them psychologist Sandra Bem, anthropologist Edward Hall, and political scientist Jo Freeman. Many outstanding social scientists are represented in this reader; a number have been presidents of national professional associations.

This reader may be used alone or in conjunction with an introductory sociology textbook. The readings have been selected to reflect the breadth of the discipline of sociology in terms of both substantive areas and research techniques. While providing rigorous coverage, the articles are readable and clearly present basic sociological concepts.

Introducing Sociology is divided into five parts which provide a systematic introduction to the study of human behavior. Part One focuses on sociological theories and research methods. In Part Two, students learn how social life is organized. The basic sociological concepts of culture, society, and socialization are defined and explored. Part Three addresses the persistence of social inequality in the United States and other societies. In Part Four, the critical social institutions of human societies—the family, religion, government, the economy, and education—are analyzed. Part Five emphasizes social change as a characteristic aspect of human societies.

Because of the broad range of selections, this book may be used independently or in conjunction with any basic text. However, the five-part model and the sequence of the 52 articles directly correspond to the organization of *Sociology*, 2nd edition (McGraw-Hill, 1986), written by Richard T. Schaefer in collaboration with Robert P. Lamm.

The introductions to each of the book's five parts and to each of the readings have been carefully constructed to offer insight into particular aspects of sociology. Unlike most anthologies, key terms are highlighted in the introductions and clear, concise definitions are offered. Following each article are several questions that will help students in reviewing the material. We urge students to review the introductions, key terms, and questions in order to enhance their understanding of the readings.

We wish to express our gratitude to the following sociologists, who served as reviewers for earlier drafts of this reader: Walter Clark, Morrisant Valley Community College; Eric Godfrey, Ripon College; James Jones, East Texas State University; Hugh Lena, Providence College; and Robert A. Rothman, University of Delaware.

Both of us are appreciative of the contributions made to this project by David Serbun, who first accepted the idea of this anthology, and Barbara Raab, who saw the project through to its completion. Since the genesis of the project rests with the first and second editions of our widely accepted textbook, *Sociology*, we wish to note again the important contributions of our editor, Rhona Robbin, and the conscientious academic reviewers of the text. We are also grateful to Terri Dodaro, who obtained permissions for the articles in the reader; to Karen Nelson of Western Illinois University, who assisted in manuscript preparation; and to Janis Phillips and Laura Tolley for their library research.

Richard T. Schaefer
Robert P. Lamm

INTRODUCTION

The sociologist has a distinctive way of examining human interactions. *Sociology* is the systematic study of social behavior and human groups. It focuses primarily on the influence of social relationships upon people's attitudes and behavior and on how societies are established and change. As a field of study, sociology has an extremely broad scope. Sociologists study families, gangs, business firms, political parties, schools, religions, and labor unions. They are concerned with love, poverty, conformity, discrimination, overpopulation, and community.

The 52 selections which follow will illustrate both the intellectual depth and the diversity of sociology. Each reading will help you to understand how the sociological perspective identifies underlying, recurring patterns of and influences on social behavior. You will learn how America's national pastime, baseball, has been transformed as it has become a popular sport in Japan. You will learn that sexism continues to exist in the world of education—whether it be in grade school classrooms or in the placement of MBA graduates. Even music videos, you will see, can be the subject of social scientific investigation.

In attempting to understand social behavior, sociologists rely on an unusual type of creative thinking. C. Wright Mills described such thinking as the *sociological imagination*—an awareness of the relationship between an individual and the wider society. This awareness allows people (not simply sociologists) to comprehend the links between their immediate, personal social settings and the remote, impersonal social world that surrounds them and helps to shape them. This is true whether the subject of study is the "frontier of nighttime"—as one sociologist calls it—or the reshaping of human behavior following a nuclear war.

A key element in the sociological imagination is the ability to view one's own society as an outsider, rather than from the limited perspective of personal experiences and cultural biases. Thus, instead of simply accepting the fact that movie stars are the "royalty" of American society, we could ask, in a more critical sense, why this is the case. Conceivably, an outsider unfamiliar with the United States might wonder why we are not as interested in meeting outstanding scientists, or elementary school teachers, or architects.

Sociologists do not analyze the world as a series of abstract social facts. The sociologists and other social scientists whose work is included in this volume share a commitment to organized, systematic study of social phenomena in order to enhance understanding. In a world confronted by continuing disparities between peace and war, prosperity and poverty, freedom and oppression, the sociological imagination is needed more than ever before. The intellectual curiosity, rigor, and insight evident in these 52 selections underscore the value of sociological imagination in helping us to overcome ignorance and apathy.

PART ONE

THE SOCIOLOGICAL PERSPECTIVE

Sociologists view society in different ways. Some sociologists see the world basically as stable and ongoing. They are impressed with the endurance of the family, organized religion, and other social institutions. Other sociologists see society as composed of many groups in conflict, all of them competing for scarce resources. To other sociologists, the most fascinating aspects of the social world are the everyday, routine interactions among individuals that we sometimes take for granted.

These differing perspectives of society are all ways of examining the same phenomena. Sociological imagination may employ any of a number of theoretical approaches in order to study human behavior. From these approaches, sociologists develop theories to explain specific types of behavior. The three perspectives that are most widely used by sociologists will provide an introductory look at this discipline: These are the functionalist, the conflict, and the interactionist perspectives.

Part One begins with three selections that illustrate these theoretical perspectives. Kingsley Davis ("The Sociology of Prostitution") draws upon functionalist analysis in order to explain why an aspect of society so frequently attacked can nevertheless manage to survive. Lewis Coser ("The Functions of Social Conflict") argues that conflict may serve positive functions for a group or society. Erving Goffman ("Presentation of Self in Everyday Life"), an important contributor to the interactionist perspective, examines the sometimes hidden meanings of people's unconscious social behavior.

In a general sense, sociology can be considered a science. The term *science* refers to the body of knowledge obtained by methods based upon systematic observation. Like other scientific disciplines, sociology engages in organized, systematic study of phenomena (in this case, human behavior) in order to enhance understanding. All scientists, whether they are studying mushrooms or murders, attempt to collect precise information through methods of study that are as objective as possible. They rely on careful recording of observations and accumulation of data.

An important aspect of sociological research is the decision as to how data should be collected. A *research design* is a detailed plan or method for obtaining data scientifically. Selection of a research design is a critical step for sociologists and requires creativity and ingenuity. This choice will directly influence both the cost of the project and the amount of time needed to collect the results of the research.

Sociologists regularly use experiments, surveys, unobtrusive techniques, and participant observations to generate data for their research. Murray Melbin ("Night as Frontier") draws upon the experimental approach in studying behavior in American cities during nighttime hours and possible similarities to the social patterns of the frontier. Robert Ferber, Paul Sheatsley, Anthony Turner, and Joseph Waksberg ("What Is a Survey?") examine the characteristics, purposes, and techniques of surveys. In their article, "A Content Analysis of Music Videos," Richard L. Baxter, Cynthia De Riemer, Ann Landini, Larry Leslie, and Michael W. Singletary employ a valuable technique of unobtrusive measurement in order to study an aspect of popular culture. The methodological and ethical problems sometimes faced by sociologists when they are conducting observation research are presented by Anson D. Shupe, Jr., and David G. Bromley ("Walking a Tightrope: Dilemmas of Participant Observation of Groups in Conflict") and by Laud Humphreys ("Tearoom Trade: Impersonal Sex in Public Places").

The Sociology of Prostitution

Kingsley Davis

The *functionalist perspective* of sociology emphasizes the way that parts of a society are structured to maintain its stability. For over four decades, Harvard University sociologist Talcott Parsons (1902–1979) dominated American sociology with his advocacy of functionalism. Parsons saw any society as a vast network of connected parts, each of which contributes to the maintenance of the system as a whole. Under the functionalist approach, if an aspect of social life does not contribute to society's stability or survival—if it does not serve some identifiable, useful function or promote value consensus among the members of a society—it will not be passed on from one generation to the next. The term *dysfunction* is used to refer to an element or a process of society that may actually disrupt a social system or lead to a decrease in stability.

In the following selection, sociologist Kingsley Davis, a former president of the American Sociological Assocation, analyzes prostitution from a functionalist perspective. Davis asks why a practice so widely condemned continues to display such persistence and vitality. He argues that the basic element in prostitution—the use of sex for nonsexual ends—characterizes not only prostitution but rather all societal institutions in which sex is involved, including courtship and marriage. At the same time, Davis concludes that prostitution survives as an institution because it performs certain functions that other sexual institutions cannot fully satisfy.

To the theoretical even more than to the applied sociologist, prostitution sets a profound problem: Why is it that a practice so thoroughly disapproved, so widely outlawed in Western civilization, can yet flourish so universally? Social theorists, in depicting the power of collective representations and the mores as determinants of human conduct, have at times implied that institutions are maintained only by *favorable* attitudes and sentiments. But prostitution is a veritable institution, thriving even when its name is so low in public opinion as to be synonymous with "the social evil." How, then, can we explain its vitality?

A genuine explanation must transcend the facile generalizations both of those who believe that prostitution can be immediately abolished, and of those who think vaguely that human nature and the lessons of history guarantee its immortality. In what follows I have tried to give a sociological analysis—to describe the main features of the interrelational system binding prostitution to other institutions (particularly those involving sexual relations). Such an analysis, though brief and tentative, seems to carry us a long way toward explaining not only the heedless vitality of commercial promiscuity, but also the extreme disrepute in which it and its personnel are held. . . .[1]

We cannot, however, define human prostitution simply as the use of sexual responses for an ulterior purpose. This would include a great portion of all social behavior, especially that of women. It would include marriage, for example,

[1] Disapproval of purely commercial (i.e., non-religious, non-familial) prostitution is extraordinarily widespread. Though the distinction is seldom made, disapproval of the prostitute is one thing and disapproval of the institution another. In Mongolian China, for example, prostitution was viewed with no serious disfavor, but the prostitute was treated with contempt. H. Ellis, *Studies in the Psychology of Sex,* vol. 6, p. 236.

wherein women trade their sexual favors for an economic and social status supplied by men.[2] It would include the employment of pretty girls in stores, cafes, charity drives, advertisements. It would include all the feminine arts that women use in pursuing ends that require men as intermediaries, arts that permeate daily life, and, while not generally involving actual intercourse, contain and utilize erotic stimulation.

But looking at the subject in this way reveals one thing. The basic element in what we actually call prostitution—the employment of sex for non-sexual ends within a competitive-authoritative system—characterizes not simply prostitution itself but all of our institutions in which sex is involved, notably courtship and wedlock. Prostitution therefore resembles, from one point of view, behavior found in our most respectable institutions. It is one end of a long sequence or gradation of essentially similar phenomena that stretches at the other end to such approved patterns as engagement and marriage. What, then, is the difference between prostitution and these other institutions involving sex?

The difference rests at bottom upon the functional relation between society and sexual institutions. It is through these institutions that erotic gratification is made dependent on, and subservient to, certain co-operative performances inherently necessary to societal continuity. The sexual institutions are distinguished by the fact that though they all provide gratification, they do not all tie it to the same social functions.[3] This explains why they are differently evaluated in the eyes of the mores.

The institutional control of sex follows three correlative lines. First, it permits, encourages, or forces various degrees of sexual intimacy within specific customary relations, such as courtship, concubinage, and marriage. Second, to bolster this positive control, it discourages sexual intimacy in all other situations, e.g., when the persons are not potential mates or when they are already mated to other persons.[4] Finally, in what is really a peculiar category of the negative rules, it absolutely prohibits sexual relations in certain specified situations. This last form of control refers almost exclusively to incest taboos, which reinforce the first-named (positive) control by banishing the disruptive forces of sexual competition from the family group.

These lines of control are present no matter what the specific kind of institutional system. There may be monogamy, polygyny, or concubinage; wife exchange or religious prostitution; premarital chastity or unchastity. The important point is not the particular kind of concrete institution, but the fact that without the positive and negative norms there could be no institutions at all. Since social functions can be performed only through institutional patterns, the controls are indispensable to the continuance of a given social system.

Of the numerous functions which sexual institutions subserve, the most vital relate to the physical and social reproduction of the next generation. If we ask, then, which sexual institutions in a society receive the greatest support from law and mores, we must point to those which facilitate the task of procreating and socializing the young. It follows that sanctioned sexual relations are generally those within these (or auxiliary) institutions, while unsanctioned relations are those outside them.

Marriage and its subsidiary patterns constitute the chief cultural arrangement through which

---

[2] She also contributes other services, though these are sometimes difficult to see in our middle-class society.

[3] Any institution appeals to *several* motives and performs *several* functions. Strictly speaking, therefore, there are no purely sexual institutions. Wedlock is not simply sexual, not simply procreative, not simply economic. It is all three. This linking of the sexual impulse to other things is not haphazard, but shows a high degree of structural and functional articula-

tion, demonstrable on two different but interdependent levels: the life organization of persons, and the institutional organization of society. Sex, like other elements in human nature, is drawn into the integration, and is thus controlled.

[4] For the emotional attitudes maintaining these norms see K. Davis, "Jealousy and Sexual Property," *Social Forces,* 14, March 1936, 395–405.

erotic expression is held to reproduction. It is accordingly the most respectable sexual institution, with the others diminishing in respectability as they stand further away from wedlock. Even the secondary forms of erotic behavior—flirtation, coquetry, petting, etc.—have their legitimate and their illegitimate settings. Their legitimate aspects may be subsumed under courtship, leading to marriage; but if indulged in for themselves, with no intention of matrimony, they are devoid of the primary function and tend to be disapproved. If practised by persons married to others, they are inimical to reproductive relations already established and are more seriously condemned. If practised by close relatives within the primary family, they represent a threat to the very structure of the reproductive institution itself, and are stringently tabooed. These attitudes are much more rigid with regard to actual intercourse, not solely because coitus is the essence of the sexual but because it has come to symbolize the *gemeinschaft* type of relation present in the family. With this in mind we can add that when coitus is practised for money its social function is indeterminate, secondary, and extrinsic. The buyer clearly has pleasure and not reproduction in mind. The seller may use the money for any purpose. Hence unless the money is earmarked for some legitimate end (such as the support of a family, a church, or a state), the sexual relation between the buyer and seller is illegitimate, ephemeral, and condemned. It is pure commercial prostitution.

Of course many sexual institutions besides courtship and marriage receive, in various cultures and to varying degrees, the sanction of society. These generally range themselves between marriage and commercial prostitution in the scale of social approval. They include concubinage, wife exchange, and forms of sanctified prostitution.[5] Religious prostitution, for example, not only differs from wedlock, but also from commercial prostitution; the money that passes is earmarked for the maintenance of the church, the woman is a religious ministrant, and the act of intercourse is sacred.[6] Similar considerations apply to that type of prostitution in which the girl obtains a dowry for her subsequent marriage. Whenever the money earned by prostitution is spent for a sanctified purpose, prostitution is in higher esteem than when it is purely commercial. If, for instance, prostitution receives more approval in Japan than in America, it is significant that in the former country most of the *joro* enter the life because their family needs money; their conduct thereby subserves the most sacred of all Japanese sentiments—filial piety.[7] The regulation of prostitution by governments and churches in such a way that at least some of the proceeds go towards their maintenance is control of sex behavior at a second remove. By earmarking a part of the money, the bought intercourse is made to serve a social function; but *this function is not intrinsically related to coitus in the same way as the procreative function of the family.*

In commercial prostitution both parties use sex for an end not socially functional, the one for pleasure, the other for money. To tie intercourse to sheer physical pleasure is to divorce it both from reproduction and from the sentimental primary type of relation which it symbolizes. To tie it to money, the most impersonal and atomistic type of reward possible, with no stipulation as to the use of this medium, does the same thing. Pure prosti-

---

[5] Concubinage evidently stands part way between prostitution and marrige. It resembles marriage in that it is relatively permanent, partly reproductive, and implies a *gemeinschaft* bond; but it resembles prostitution in that the woman more definitely and exclusively exists for the sexual pleasure of the master, and her social position is inferior to that of the wife. E. Westermarck, *History of Human Marriage,* 5th ed., N.Y., Allerton Book Co., 1922; D. Kulp, *Country Life in South China,* Columbia Univ. Press, 1925, chap. vi; Pearl Buck's novel, *The*

Good Earth. Wife exchange differs from marriage in that its social function appears to be, not propagation, but the cementing of solidarity within a group. W. Bogoras, *The Chukchee, Amer. Mus of Nat. Hist. Memoirs,* 7, 602–607.

[6] G. May, "Prostitution," *Ency. of Soc. Sci.;* Westermarck, *op. cit.,* vol. 1, pp. 219 *et seq.*

[7] A. M. Bacon, *Japanese Girls and Women,* Boston, Houghton Mifflin Co., 1902, pp. 175–178; D. C. McMurtrie, "Prostitution in Japan," *New York Med. Jour.,* Feb. 8, 1913.

tution is promiscuous, impersonal. The sexual response of the prostitute does not hinge upon the personality of the other party, but upon the reward. The response of the customer likewise does not depend upon the particular identity of the prostitute, but upon the bodily gratification. On both sides the relationship is merely a means to a private end, a contractual rather than a personal association.

These features sharply distinguish prostitution from the procreative sexual institutions. Within a group organized for bearing and rearing children bonds tend to arise that are cemented by the condition of relative permanence and the sentiment of personal feeling, for the task requires long, close, and sympathetic association. Prostitution, in which the seller takes any buyer at the price, necessarily represents an opposite kind of erotic association. It is distinguished by the elements of hire, promiscuity, and emotional indifference—all of which are incompatible with primary or *gemeinschaft* association.

The sexual appetite, like every other, is tied to socially necessary functions. The function it most logically and naturally relates to is procreation. The nature of procreation and socialization is such that their performance requires institutionalized primary-group living. Hence the family receives the highest estimation of all sexual institutions in society, the others receiving lower esteem as they are remoter from its *gemeinschaft* character and reproductive purpose. Commercial prostitution stands at the lowest extreme; it shares with other sexual institutions a basic feature, namely the employment of sex for an ulterior end in a system of differential advantages, but it differs from them in being mercenary, promiscuous, and emotionally indifferent. From *both* these facts, however, it derives its remarkable vitality. . . .

Where the family is strong, there tends to be a well-defined system of prostitution and the social regime is one of status. Women are either part of the family system, or they are definitely not a part of it. In the latter case they are prostitutes, members of a caste set apart. There are few intermediate groups, and there is little mobility. This enables the two opposite types of institutions to function side by side without confusion; they are each staffed by a different personnel, humanly as well as functionally distinct. But where familial controls are weak, the system of prostitution tends to be poorly defined. Not only is it more nearly permissible to satisfy one's desire outside the family, but also it is easier to find a respectable member of society willing to act as partner. This is why a decline of the family and a decline of prostitution are both associated with a rise of sex freedom. Women, released from close family supervision, are freer to seek gratification outside it. The more such women, the easier it is for men to find in intimate relations with them the satisfactions formerly supplied by harlots. This is why the unrestricted indulgence in sex for the fun of it by both sexes is the greatest enemy, not only of the family, but also of prostitution.

Not only in Soviet Russia has pleasurable sex freedom invaded and reduced prostitution, but also in America and England, where "amateur competition" is reputedly ruining the business of street-walkers and call girls.[8] This indicates that independently of communism or capitalism, due to factors more profound than mere economic organization, sex freedom can arise and, having arisen, can contribute to the decline of prostitution. Its rise seems correlated with the growth of individualization in an increasingly complex society where specialization, urbanism, and anonymity prevail—factors which are also inimical to reproductive institutions of the familial type.

But even if present trends continue, there is no likelihood that sex freedom will ever displace prostitution. Not only will there always be a set of reproductive institutions which place a check upon sexual liberty, a system of social dominance

---

[8] G. M. Hall, *op. cit.,* p. 168. "Prostitution," *Encyclopaedia Sexualis,* p. 665. J. K. Folsom, *The Family,* N.Y., Wiley, 1934, chap. xiii.

which gives a motive for selling sexual favors, and a scale of attractiveness which creates the need for buying these favors, but prostitution is, in the last analysis, economical. Enabling a small number of women to take care of the needs of a large number of men, it is the most convenient sexual outlet for an army, and for the legions of strangers, perverts, and physically repulsive in our midst. It performs a function, apparently, which no other institution fully performs.

TAKING ANOTHER LOOK

1 Why cannot prostitution be defined as the use of sex for an "ulterior purpose"?
2 According to Davis, in what way does prostitution resemble other institutions in which sex is involved, such as courtship and wedlock?
3 In what ways can prostitution be distinguished from procreative sexual institutions?
4 What happens to prostitution when the family is strong?
5 In the view of Davis, what is the relationship between prostitution and sexual freedom?

The Functions of Social Conflict

Lewis Coser

In contrast to the functionalists' emphasis on stability and consensus, conflict sociologists see the social world in continual struggle. The *conflict perspective* assumes that social behavior is best understood in terms of conflict or tension among competing groups. Such conflict need not be violent; it can take the form of labor negotiations, party politics, competition among religious groups for members, or disputes over cuts in the federal budget.

Expanding on the work of Karl Marx (who viewed struggle between social classes as inevitable, given the exploitation of workers under capitalism), sociologists and other social scientists have come to see conflict not merely as a class phenomenon but as a part of everyday life in all societies. Thus, in studying any culture, organization, or social group, sociologists want to know who benefits, who suffers, and who dominates at the expense of others. They are concerned with the conflicts between women and men, parents and children, the cities and the suburbs, whites and blacks, to name only a few. In studying such questions, conflict theorists are interested in how society's institutions (including the family, government, churches, schools, and the media) may help to maintain the privileges of some groups while keeping others in a subservient position.

Throughout most of the 1900s, American sociology was more influenced by the functionalist perspective than by the conflict perspective. However, the conflict perspective has become increasingly more persuasive since the late 1960s. It is often approached with political undertones, since its perspective is viewed as more "radical" and "activist" because of its emphasis on social change and redistribution of resources. On the other hand, the functionalist perspective, because of its focus on the stability of society, is generally seen as more "conservative." Currently, the conflict perspective is accepted within the discipline of sociology as one valid way to gain insight into a society.

In the following selection, sociologist Lewis Coser argues that the concept of social conflict is of central importance for an understanding of major areas of social relations. Whereas functionalists tend to emphasize that conflict is a negative force that tears apart a society, Coser counters that conflict may serve positive functions for a group or a society. For example, it may revitalize existent norms or contribute to the emergence of new norms. Coser concludes that the rigidity of a social structure, rather than the presence of conflict in itself, can threaten its own equilibrium by permitting "hostilities to accumulate and to be channeled along one major line of cleavage."

Conflict within a group . . . may help to establish unity or to re-establish unity and cohesion where it has been threatened by hostile and antagonistic feelings among the members. Yet, we noted that not *every* type of conflict is likely to benefit group structure, nor that conflict can subserve such functions for *all* groups. Whether social conflict is beneficial to internal adaptation or not depends on the type of issues over which it is fought as well as on the type of social structure within which it occurs. However, types of conflict and types of social structure are not independent variables.

Internal social conflicts which concern goals, values or interests that do not contradict the basic assumptions upon which the relationship is founded tend to be positively functional for the social structure. Such conflicts tend to make possible the readjustment of norms and power relations within groups in accordance with the felt needs of its individual members or subgroups.

Internal conflicts in which the contending parties no longer share the basic values upon which the legitimacy of the social system rests threaten to disrupt the structure.

One safeguard against conflict disrupting the consensual basis of the relationship, however, is contained in the social structure itself: it is provided by the institutionalization and tolerance of conflict. Whether internal conflict promises to be a means of equilibration of social relations or readjustment of rival claims, or whether it threatens to "tear apart," depends to a large extent on the social structure within which it occurs.

In every type of social structure there are occasions for conflict, since individuals and subgroups are likely to make from time to time rival claims to scarce resources, prestige or power positions. But social structures differ in the way in which they allow expression to antagonistic claims. Some show more tolerance of conflict than others.

Closely knit groups in which there exists a high frequency of interaction and high personality involvement of the members have a tendency to suppress conflict. While they provide frequent occasions for hostility (since both sentiments of love and hatred are intensified through frequency of interaction), the acting out of such feelings is sensed as a danger to such intimate relationships, and hence there is a tendency to suppress rather than to allow expression of hostile feelings. In close-knit groups, feelings of hostility tend, therefore, to accumulate and hence to intensify. If conflict breaks out in a group that has consistently tried to prevent expression of hostile feelings, it will be particularly intense for two reasons: First, because the conflict does not merely aim at resolving the immediate issue which led to its outbreak; all accumulated grievances which were denied expression previously are apt to emerge at this occasion. Second, because the total personality involvement of the group members makes for mobilization of all sentiments in the conduct of the struggle.

Hence, the closer the group, the more intense the conflict. Where members participate with their total personality and conflicts are suppressed, the conflict, if it breaks out nevertheless, is likely to threaten the very root of the relationship.

In groups comprising individuals who participate only segmentally, conflict is less likely to be disruptive. Such groups are likely to experience a multiplicity of conflicts. This in itself tends to constitute a check against the breakdown of consensus: the energies of group members are mobilized in many directions and hence will not concentrate on *one* conflict cutting through the group. Moreover, where occasions for hostility are not permitted to accumulate and conflict is allowed to occur wherever a resolution of tension seems to be indicated, such a conflict is likely to remain focused primarily on the condition which led to its outbreak and not to revive blocked hostility; in this way, the conflict is limited to "the facts of the case." One may venture to say that multiplicity of conflicts stands in inverse relation to their intensity.

So far we have been dealing with internal social conflict only. At this point we must turn to a consideration of external conflict, for the structure of the group is itself affected by conflicts with other groups in which it engages or which it prepares for. Groups which are engaged in continued struggle tend to lay claim on the total personality involvement of their members so that internal conflict would tend to mobilize all energies and affects of the members. Hence such groups are unlikely to tolerate more than limited departures from the group unity. In such groups there is a tendency to suppress conflict; where it occurs, it leads the group to break up through splits or through forced withdrawal of dissenters.

Groups which are not involved in continued struggle with the outside are less prone to make claims on total personality involvement of the membership and are more likely to exhibit flexibility of structure. The multiple internal conflicts which they tolerate may in turn have an equilibrating and stabilizing impact on the structure.

In flexible social structures, multiple conflicts crisscross each other and thereby prevent basic cleavages along one axis. The multiple group affiliations of individuals makes them participate in various group conflicts so that their total personalities are not involved in any single one of them. Thus segmental participation in a multiplicity of conflicts constitutes a balancing mechanism within the structure.

In loosely structured groups and open societies, conflict, which aims at a resolution of tension between antagonists, is likely to have stabilizing and integrative functions for the relationship. By permitting immediate and direct expression of rival claims, such social systems are able to readjust their structures by eliminating the sources of dissatisfaction. The multiple conflicts which they experience may serve to eliminate the causes for dissociation and to re-establish unity. These systems avail themselves, through the toleration and institutionalization of conflict, of an important stabilizing mechanism.

In addition, conflict within a group frequently helps to revitalize existent norms; or it contributes to the emergence of new norms. In this sense, social conflict is a mechanism for adjustment of norms adequate to new conditions. A flexible society benefits from conflict because such behavior, by helping to create and modify norms, assures its continuance under changed conditions. Such mechanism for readjustment of norms is hardly available to rigid systems: by suppressing conflict, the latter smother a useful warning signal, thereby maximizing the danger of catastrophic breakdown.

Internal conflict can also serve as a means for ascertaining the relative strength of antagonistic interests within the structure, and in this way constitute a mechanism for the maintenance or continual readjustment of the balance of power. Since the outbreak of the conflict indicates a rejection of a previous accommodation between parties, once the respective power of the contenders has been ascertained through conflict, a new equilibrium can be established and the relationship can proceed on this new basis. Consequently, a social structure in which there is room for conflict disposes of an important means for avoiding or redressing conditions of disequilibrium by modifying the terms of power relations. Conflicts with some produce associations or coalitions with others. Conflicts through such associations or coalitions, by providing a bond between the members, help to reduce social isolation or to unite individuals and groups otherwise unrelated or antagonistic to each other. A social structure in which there can exist a multiplicity of conflicts contains a mechanism for bringing together otherwise isolated, apathetic or mutually hostile parties and for taking them into the field of public social activities. Moreover, such a structure fosters a multiplicity of associations and coalitions whose diverse purposes crisscross each other, we recall, thereby preventing alliances along one major line of cleavage.

Once groups and associations have been formed through conflict with other groups, such conflict may further serve to maintain boundary lines between them and the surrounding social environment. In this way, social conflict helps to structure the larger social environment by assigning position to the various subgroups within the system and by helping to define the power relations between them.

Not all social systems in which individuals participate segmentally allow the free expression of antagonistic claims. Social systems tolerate or institutionalize conflict to different degrees. There is no society in which any and every antagonistic claim is allowed immediate expression. Societies dispose of mechanisms to channel discontent and hostility while keeping intact the relationship within which antagonism arises. Such mechanisms frequently operate through "safety-valve" institutions which provide substitute objects upon which to displace hostile sentiments as well as means of abreaction of aggressive tendencies.

Safety-valve institutions may serve to maintain both the social structure and the individual's security system, but they are incompletely functional for both of them. They prevent modification of relationships to meet changing conditions and hence the satisfaction they afford the individual can be only partially or momentarily adjustive. The hypothesis has been suggested that the need for safety-valve institutions increases with the rigidity of the social structure, i.e., with the degree to which it disallows direct expression of antagonistic claims.

Safety-valve institutions lead to a displacement of goal in the actor: he need no longer aim at reaching a solution of the unsatisfactory situation, but merely at releasing the tension which arose from it. Where safety-valve institutions provide substitute objects for the displacement of hostility, the conflict itself is channeled away from the original unsatisfactory relationship into one in which the actor's goal is no longer the attainment of specific results, but the release of tension.

This affords us a criterion for distinguishing between realistic and nonrealistic conflict.

Social conflicts that arise from frustrations of specific demands within a relationship and from estimates of gains of the participants, and that are directed at the presumed frustrating object, can be called realistic conflicts. Insofar as they are means toward specific results, they can be replaced by alternative modes of interaction with the contending party if such alternatives seem to be more adequate for realizing the end in view.

Nonrealistic conflicts, on the other hand, are not occasioned by the rival ends of the antagonists, but by the need for tension release of one or both of them. In this case the conflict is not oriented toward the attainment of specific results. Insofar as unrealistic conflict is an end in itself, insofar as it affords only tension release, the chosen antagonist can be substituted for by any other "suitable" target.

In realistic conflict, there exist functional alternatives with regard to the means of carrying out the conflict, as well as with regard to accomplishing desired results short of conflict; in nonrealistic conflict, on the other hand, there exist only functional alternatives in the choice of antagonists.

Our hypothesis, that the need for safety-valve institutions increases with the rigidity of the social system, may be extended to suggest that unrealistic conflict may be expected to occur as a consequence of rigidity present in the social structure.

Our discussion of the distinction between types of conflict, and between types of social structures, leads us to conclude that conflict tends to be dysfunctional for a social structure in which there is no or insufficient toleration and institutionalization of conflict. The intensity of a conflict which threatens to "tear apart," which attacks the consensual basis of a social system, is related to the rigidity of the structure. What threatens the equilibrium of such a structure is not conflict as such, but the rigidity itself which permits hostilities to accumulate and to be channeled along one major line of cleavage once they break out in conflict.

TAKING ANOTHER LOOK

1 According to Coser, how does the social structure provide a safeguard against conflicts that threaten to disrupt the consensual basis of social relations?

2 Why is conflict likely to be particularly intense within a group that has consistently tried to prevent expression of hostile feelings?

3 Why is it that a multiplicity of conflicts within a group can constitute a check against the breakdown of consensus?
4 How does social conflict serve as a mechanism for the adjustment of group norms?
5 According to Coser, what functions are fulfilled by a society's "safety-valve" institutions?
6 How does Coser distinguish between realistic and nonrealistic conflicts?
7 According to Coser, for which type of social structure is conflict likely to be dysfunctional?

Presentation of Self in Everyday Life

Erving Goffman

The functionalist and the conflict perspectives of sociology both analyze society at the macro level. These approaches attempt to explain society-wide patterns of behavior. However, many contemporary sociologists are more interested in social interactions at the micro level—small groups, two friends casually talking with one another, a family, and so forth. The *interactionist perspective* generalizes about fundamental or everyday forms of social interaction. It is a sociological framework for viewing human beings as living in a world of meaningful objects. These "objects" may include material things, actions, other people, relationships, and even symbols.

Sociologist Erving Goffman made a distinctive contribution by popularizing a particular type of interactionist method known as the *dramaturgical approach*. The dramaturgist compares everyday life to the setting of the theater and the stage. Just as actors present certain images, all of us seek to present particular features of our personalities while we hide other qualities: in a class, we may feel the need to project a serious image; at a party, we may feel that it is important to look relaxed and entertaining.

Early in life, the individual learns to slant his or her presentation of the self in order to create distinctive appearances and to satisfy particular audiences. Goffman refers to this altering of the presentation of the self as *impression management.* One everyday example is evident in the promotion of credit cards. Many viewers of television commercials are persuaded that they can change the presentation of their selves—and display a much more desirable social image—merely by flashing a particular credit card.

Face-work is another aspect of the self to which Goffman has drawn attention. Maintaining the proper image can be essential to continued social interaction. Face-saving behavior must be initiated if the self suffers because of embarrassment or some form of rejection. A person who leaves a party or a singles' bar alone—without having met anyone—may attempt to save face by saying: "I really wasn't in the mood" or "There wasn't anyone interesting in the entire crowd."

In the following selection, Erving Goffman argues that "when an individual appears before others he will have many motives for trying to control the impression they receive of the situation." Goffman discusses some of the common techniques that people use in order to manage impressions. He also points out that events may occur during any interaction that "contradict, discredit, or otherwise throw doubt upon" an individual's intended impression management.

When an individual enters the presence of others, they commonly seek to acquire information about him or to bring into play information about him already possessed. They will be interested in his general socio-economic status, his conception of self, his attitude toward them, his competence, his trustworthiness, etc. Although some of this information seems to be sought almost as an end in itself, there are usually quite practical reasons for acquiring it. Information about the individual helps to define the situation, enabling others to know in advance what he will expect of them and what they may expect of him. Informed in these ways, the others will know how best to act in order to call forth a desired response from him.

For those present, many sources of information become accessible and many carriers (or "sign-vehicles") become available for conveying this information. If unacquainted with the individual, observers can glean clues from his conduct and appearance which allow them to apply their previous experience with individuals roughly similar to the one before them or, more important, to apply untested stereotypes to him. They can also assume from past experience that only individuals of a particular kind are likely to be found in a given social setting. They can rely on what the individual says about himself or on documentary evidence he provides as to who and what he is. If they know, or know of, the individual by virtue of experience prior to the interaction, they can rely on assumptions as to the persistence and generality of psychological traits as a means of predicting his present and future behavior.

However, during the period in which the individual is in the immediate presence of the others, few events may occur which directly provide the others with the conclusive information they will need if they are to direct wisely their own activity. Many crucial facts lie beyond the time and place of interaction or lie concealed within it. For example, the "true" or "real" attitudes, beliefs, and emotions of the individual can be ascertained only indirectly, through his avowals or through what appears to be involuntary expressive behavior. Similarly, if the individual offers the others a product or service, they will often find that during the interaction there will be no time and place immediately available for eating the pudding that the proof can be found in. They will be forced to accept some events as conventional or natural signs of something not directly available to the senses. In Ichheiser's terms,[1] the individual will have to act so that he intentionally or unintentionally *expresses* himself, and the others will in turn have to be *impressed* in some way by him.

The expressiveness of the individual (and therefore his capacity to give impressions) appears to involve two radically different kinds of sign activity: the expression that he *gives,* and the expression that he *gives off.* The first involves verbal symbols or their substitutes which he uses admittedly and solely to convey the information that he and the others are known to attach to these symbols. This is communication in the traditional and narrow sense. The second involves a wide range of action that others can treat as symptomatic of the actor, the expectation being that the action was performed for reasons other than the information conveyed in this way. As we shall have to see, this distinction has an only initial validity. The individual does of course intentionally convey misinformation by means of both of these types of communication, the first involving deceit, the second feigning.

Taking communication in both its narrow and broad sense, one finds that when the individual is in the immediate presence of others, his activity will have a promissory character. The others are likely to find that they must accept the individual on faith, offering him a just return while he is present before them in exchange for something whose true value will not be established until after he has left their presence. (Of course, the others also live by inference in their dealings with the physical world, but it is only in the world of social interaction that the objects about which they make inferences will purposely facilitate and hinder this inferential process.) The security that they justifiably feel in making inferences about the individual will vary, of course, depending on such factors as the amount of information they already possess about him, but no amount of such past evidence can entirely obviate the necessity of

[1] Gustav Ichheiser, "Misunderstandings in Human Relations," Supplement to *The American Journal of Sociology,* LV (September, 1949), pp. 6–7.

acting on the basis of inferences. As William I. Thomas suggested:

> It is also highly important for us to realize that we do not as a matter of fact lead our lives, make our decisions, and reach our goals in everyday life either statistically or scientifically. We live by inference. I am, let us say, your guest. You do not know, you cannot determine scientifically, that I will not steal your money or your spoons. But inferentially I will not, and inferentially you have me as a guest.[2]

Let us now turn from the others to the point of view of the individual who presents himself before them. He may wish them to think highly of him, or to think that he thinks highly of them, or to perceive how in fact he feels toward them, or to obtain no clear-cut impression; he may wish to ensure sufficient harmony so that the interaction can be sustained, or to defraud, get rid of, confuse, mislead, antagonize, or insult them. Regardless of the particular objective which the individual has in mind and of his motive for having this objective, it will be in his interests to control the conduct of the others, especially their responsive treatment of him.[3] This control is achieved largely by influencing the definition of the situation which the others come to formulate, and he can influence this definition by expressing himself in such a way as to give them the kind of impression that will lead them to act voluntarily in accordance with his own plan. Thus, when an individual appears in the presence of others, there will usually be some reason for him to mobilize his activity so that it will convey an impression to others which it is in his interests to convey. Since a girl's dormitory mates will glean evidence of her popularity from the calls she receives on the phone, we can suspect that some girls will arrange for calls to be made, and Willard Waller's finding can be anticipated:

> It has been reported by many observers that a girl who is called to the telephone in the dormitories will often allow herself to be called several times, in order to give all the other girls ample opportunity to hear her paged.[4]

Of the two kinds of communication—expressions given and expressions given off—this report will be primarily concerned with the latter, with the more theatrical and contextual kind, the non-verbal, presumably unintentional kind, whether this communication be purposely engineered or not. . . .

I have said that when an individual appears before others his actions will influence the definition of the situation which they come to have. Sometimes the individual will act in a thoroughly calculating manner, expressing himself in a given way solely in order to give the kind of impression to others that is likely to evoke from them a specific response he is concerned to obtain. Sometimes the individual will be calculating in his activity but be relatively unaware that this is the case. Sometimes he will intentionally and consciously express himself in a particular way, but chiefly because the tradition of his group or social status require this kind of expression and not because of any particular response (other than vague acceptance or approval) that is likely to be evoked from those impressed by the expression. Sometimes the traditions of an individual's role will lead him to give a well-designed impression of a particular kind and yet he may be neither consciously nor unconsciously disposed to create such an impression. The others, in their turn, may be suitably impressed by the individual's efforts to

---

[2] Quoted in E. H. Volkart, editor, *Social Behavior and Personality,* Contributions of W. I. Thomas to Theory and Social Research (New York: Social Science Research Council, 1951), p. 5.

[3] Here I owe much to an unpublished paper by Tom Burns of the University of Edinburgh. He presents the argument that in all interaction a basic underlying theme is the desire of each participant to guide and control the responses made by the others present. A similar argument has been advanced by Jay Haley in a recent unpublished paper, but in regard to a special kind of control, that having to do with defining the nature of the relationship of those involved in the interaction.

[4] Willard Waller, "The Rating and Dating Complex," *American Sociological Review,* II, p. 730.

convey something, or may misunderstand the situation and come to conclusions that are warranted neither by the individual's intent nor by the facts. In any case, in so far as the others act *as if* the individual had conveyed a particular impression, we may take a functional or pragmatic view and say that the individual has "effectively" projected a given definition of the situation and "effectively" fostered the understanding that a given state of affairs obtains. . . .

When we allow that the individual projects a definition of the situation when he appears before others, we must also see that the others, however passive their role may seem to be, will themselves effectively project a definition of the situation by virtue of their response to the individual and by virtue of any lines of action they initiate to him. Ordinarily the definitions of the situation projected by the several different participants are sufficiently attuned to one another so that open contradiction will not occur. I do not mean that there will be the kind of consensus that arises when each individual present candidly expresses what he really feels and honestly agrees with the expressed feelings of the others present. This kind of harmony is an optimistic ideal and in any case not necessary for the smooth working of society. Rather, each participant is expected to suppress his immediate heartfelt feelings, conveying a view of the situation which he feels the others will be able to find at least temporarily acceptable. The maintenance of this surface of agreement, this veneer of consensus, is facilitated by each participant concealing his own wants behind statements which assert values to which everyone present feels obliged to give lip service. Further, there is usually a kind of division of definitional labor.

Each participant is allowed to establish the tentative official ruling regarding matters which are vital to him but not immediately important to others, e.g., the rationalizations and justifications by which he accounts for his past activity. In exchange for this courtesy he remains silent or noncommittal on matters important to others but not immediately important to him. We have then a kind of interactional *modus vivendi*. Together the participants contribute to a single over-all definition of the situation which involves not so much a real agreement as to what exists but rather a real agreement as to whose claims concerning what issues will be temporarily honored. Real agreement will also exist concerning the desirability of avoiding an open conflict of definitions of the situation.[5] I will refer to this level of agreement as a "working consensus." It is to be understood that the working consensus established in one interaction setting will be quite different in content from the working consensus established in a different type of setting. Thus, between two friends at lunch, a reciprocal show of affection, respect, and concern for the other is maintained. In service occupations, on the other hand, the specialist often maintains an image of disinterested involvement in the problem of the client, while the client responds with a show of respect for the competence and integrity of the specialist. Regardless of such differences in content, however, the general form of these working arrangements is the same. . . .

Given the fact that the individual effectively projects a definition of the situation when he enters the presence of others, we can assume that events may occur within the interaction which contradict, discredit, or otherwise throw doubt upon this projection. When these disruptive

---

[5] An interaction can be purposely set up as a time and place for voicing differences in opinion, but in such cases participants must be careful to agree not to disagree on the proper tone of voice, vocabulary, and degree of seriousness in which all arguments are to be phrased, and upon the mutual respect which disagreeing participants must carefully continue to ex-press toward one another. This debaters' or academic definition of the situation may also be invoked suddenly and judiciously as a way of translating a serious conflict of views into one that can be handled within a framework acceptable to all present.

events occur, the interaction itself may come to a confused and embarrassed halt. Some of the assumptions upon which the responses of the participants had been predicated become untenable, and the participants find themselves lodged in an interaction for which the situation has been wrongly defined and is now no longer defined. At such moments the individual whose presentation has been discredited may feel ashamed while the others present may feel hostile, and all the participants may come to feel ill at ease, nonplussed, out of countenance, embarrassed, experiencing the kind of anomy that is generated when the minute social system of face-to-face interaction breaks down.

In stressing the fact that the initial definition of the situation projected by an individual tends to provide a plan for the co-operative activity that follows—in stressing this action point of view—we must not overlook the crucial fact that any projected definition of the situation also has a distinctive moral character. It is this moral character of projections that will chiefly concern us in this report. Society is organized on the principle that any individual who possesses certain social characteristics has a moral right to expect that others will value and treat him in an appropriate way. Connected with this principle is a second, namely that an individual who implicitly or explicitly signifies that he has certain social characteristics ought in fact to be what he claims he is. In consequence, when an individual projects a definition of the situation and thereby makes an implicit or explicit claim to be a person of particular kind, he automatically exerts a moral demand upon the others, obliging them to value and treat him in the manner that persons of his kind have a

right to expect. He also implicitly forgoes all claims to be things he does not appear to be[6] and hence forgoes the treatment that would be appropriate for such individuals. The others find, then, that the individual has informed them as to what is and as to what they *ought* to see as the "is." . . .

To summarize, then, I assume that when an individual appears before others he will have many motives for trying to control the impression they receive of the situation. This report is concerned with some of the common techniques that persons employ to sustain such impressions and with some of the common contingencies associated with the employment of these techniques. The specific content of any activity presented by the individual participant, or the role it plays in the interdependent activities of an on-going social system, will not be at issue; I shall be concerned only with the participant's dramaturgical problems of presenting the activity before others. The issues dealt with by stagecraft and stage management are sometimes trivial but they are quite general; they seem to occur everywhere in social life, providing a clear-cut dimension for formal sociological analysis.

It will be convenient to end this introduction with some definitions that are implied in what has gone before and required for what is to follow. For the purpose of this report, interaction (that is, face-to-face interaction) may be roughly defined as the reciprocal influence of individuals upon one another's actions when in one another's immediate physical presence. An interaction may be defined as all the interaction which occurs throughout any one occasion when a given set of individuals are in one another's continuous presence; the term "an encounter" would do as well. A "performance" may be defined as all the activity of a given participant on a given occasion which serves to influence in any way any of the other participants. Taking a particular participant and his performance as a basic point of reference, we may refer to those who contribute the other performances as the audience, observers, or co-participants. The

[6] This role of the witness in limiting what it is the individual can be has been stressed by Existentialists, who see it as a basic threat to individual freedom. See Jean-Paul Sartre, *Being and Nothingness,* trans. by Hazel E. Barnes (New York: Philosophical Library, 1956), p. 365 ff.

pre-established pattern of action which is unfolded during a performance and which may be presented or played through on other occasions may be called a "part" or "routine."[7] These situational terms can easily be related to conventional structural ones. When an individual or performer plays the same part to the same audience on different occasions, a social relationship is likely to arise. Defining social role as the enactment of rights and duties attached to a given status, we can say that a social role will involve one or more parts and that each of these different parts may be presented by the performer on a series of occasions to the same kinds of audience or to an audience of the same persons.

[7] For comments on the importance of distinguishing between a routine of interaction and any particular instance when this routine is played through, see John von Neumann and Oskar Morgenstern, *The Theory of Games and Economic Behavior* (2nd ed.; Princeton: Princeton University Press, 1947), p. 49.

TAKING ANOTHER LOOK

1 According to Goffman, what two radically different kinds of sign activity are involved in the expressiveness of the individual?

2 What does Goffman mean when he asserts that "when the individual is in the immediate presence of others, his activity will have a promissory character"?

3 How does an individual project a definition of the situation when he or she appears before others?

4 What does Goffman mean when he suggests that there is usually "a kind of division of definitional labor" in an interaction?

5 According to Goffman, why is a "working consensus" often established by participants in an interaction?

6 Why does any projected definition of the situation have a distinctive moral character?

7 How does Goffman view social roles?

Night as Frontier

Murray Melbin

An important aspect of sociological research is the decision as to how data should be collected. When sociologists wish to study a possible cause and effect relationship, they may conduct experiments. An *experiment* is an artificially created situation that allows the researcher to manipulate variables. *Variables* are measurable traits or characteristics that are subject to change under different conditions. In the classic method of conducting an experiment, two groups of people are selected and compared for similar characteristics, such as age or education. One group (the *experimental* group) is exposed to an independent variable, while the other (the *control* group) is not.

In the following selection, sociologist Murray Melbin draws upon the experimental approach. Melbin argues that life in American cities during nighttime hours can be likened to social life on former land frontiers of the Old West. In his view, there are many similarities in the social patterns of night and the frontier, among them the following: (1) the population tends to be sparse and homogeneous; (2) there is a welcome solitude along with fewer social constraints; (3) government tends to be decentralized; (4) there is more lawlessness and violence; and (5) interest groups emerge focused on concerns specific to the night or the frontier.

One of Melbin's most surprising assertions is that in both the night and the frontier, there is more helpfulness and friendliness. He attempted to substantiate this view by conducting four tests of people's helpfulness and friendliness at various times during the 24-hour life cycle. In these experiments, time of day is the independent variable. The dependent variable (the variable believed to be influenced by the independent variable) is people's helpful or friendly behavior.

Humans are showing a trend toward more and more wakeful activity at all hours of day and night. The activities are extremely varied. Large numbers of people are involved. And the trend is worldwide. A unifying hypothesis to account for it is that night is a frontier, that expansion into the dark hours is a continuation of the geographic migration across the face of the earth. To support this view, I will document the trend and then offer a premise about the nature of time and its relation to space. Third, I will show that social life in the nighttime has many important characteristics that resemble social life on land frontiers. . . .

A *settlement* is a stable occupation of space and time by people and their activities. A *frontier* is a pattern of sparse settlement in space or time, located between a more densely settled and a practically empty region. Below a certain density of active people, a given space-time region is a wilderness. Above that point and continuing to a higher level of density, the presence of people in activities will make that area a frontier. Above that second cutoff point the further denseness of active people turns the area into a fully inhabited region. In a given historical period the frontier's boundaries may be stable or expanding. When expanding the frontier takes on the aspect of venturing into the unknown and is often accompanied by novelty and change. . . .

Two kinds of evidence would support the hypothesis of night as frontier. One is that the forces for expansion into the dark hours are the same as those resulting in expansion across the land. That is, a single casual explanation should account for the spread of people and their activities, whether in space or in time. I offered such an outline in another essay; it includes enabling factors, demand push, supply pull, and stabilizing feedback (Melbin, 1977). The other line of evidence is that the same important features of social life should be found both in time and in space frontiers. The rapid expansion in after-dark activity has been taking place mostly in urban areas. Therefore the culture of the contemporary urban nighttime should reveal the same patterns and moods found in former land frontiers. . . .

Because the night is a time of more violence and people feel more vulnerable then, those up and about have a similar outlook and behave toward others as pioneers did in the West. At night people are more alert to strangers when they pass on the street. Each tries to judge whether the other is potentially dangerous. Upon deciding that the other is to be trusted, one's mood shifts from vigilance to expansiveness. If not foe, then friend. Aware that they are out together in a dangerous environment, people identify with each other and become more outgoing. The sense of safety that spreads over those together at night in a diner or in a coffee shop promotes camaraderie there.

Also, on both frontiers people may be more hospitable because they have time to devote to strangers. Pioneers had plenty to do; yet often

they had nothing to do. They were not closely synchronized in daily tasks as people were in the eastern cities, and the norm of punctuality was not emphasized. One man who grew up in the West

> . . . recalled the boredom he could never escape. . . . [T]he worst time of all was Sunday afternoon, when he had nothing to do. There were no newspapers to read and no books other than the family Bible, there was no one his age to talk with, and the nearest store was miles away. (Hollon, 1974: 196)

In the city during the day, the mood of pressured schedules takes hold of folk and makes their encounters specific and short. The tempo slows markedly after midnight. The few who are out then hurry less because there are fewer places to rush to. Whereas lack of time inhibits sociability and helpfulness, available time clears the way for them.

I checked on these ideas by four tests of people's helpfulness and friendliness at various times in the 24-hour cycle. The tests are modest situations, not emergencies to which one has to respond under stress, but part of the common stream of social events. The ratings for degree of helpfulness and friendliness were established by asking sets of individuals to act as judges (ten judges for Test 3, six each for Tests 1, 2, and 4).

Test 1: Asking for directions. A male and female couple used a random sampling procedure on the street[1] to approach passersby and ask directions to a well-known location about a mile away.

---

[1] Tests 1, 2, and 3 reported in this section were carried out during each of the 166 field visits for which the sample is described in Figure 2n. A team of two researchers, always one male and one female, made a field visit. The male always asked for directions, but the two took turns attempting to secure interviews (Test 2). Tests 1, 2, and 3 were carried out in locations that were illuminated after dark, for example under a street lamp. Tests 1 and 2 both called for random sampling of passersby, and the procedure used the five-minute person-tally that contributed the data reported in Figure 2. This tally ascertained the density of the street population at that time of day, and this density number was used to set the sampling rate: if the number was greater than twenty-five, the fourth person passing from the direction would be chosen once the test was to start. If the count was from five to twenty-five, the third person would be chosen; if three or four, then the second per-

son would be chosen; and if two or fewer passed during the five-minute tally then the first person from either direction would be selected. The members of the same group passing by were counted as one person; if the group was sampled the passerby nearest the researchers was approached. A maximum of three requests for directions and eight requests for interviews was to be made during each field visit. Sometimes the attempts were fewer—especially at night—because almost no one passed by during the segment of the field-visit schedule in which these attempts were to be made. The sampling was silently carried out by one researcher, who then by nudging or an equally subtle signal told the other whom to approach. This minimized selection bias, for the researcher who was to carry out the test could not hesitate or overlook an unappealing passerby.

This is a familiar question, calling for little time and effort and one does not have to become personal in replying. Giving directions was scored one point. A nasty reaction—such as brushing by stiffly as if ignoring a panhandler, or turning and uttering an obscenity or a terse "Ask someone else," or quickly veering away from the speaker with apparent nonrecognition, or staring angrily and continuing to walk—was scored zero points. If the individual enlarged the scope of the encounter—such as by saying, in addition to giving directions, "Are you tourists here?" or "My son lives there," or "Do you need a ride? I have my car nearby"—it was scored two points. After each trial the two field researchers came to an agreement about the rating. Of 363 persons approached, 331 (91.2%) gave only directions, 21 (5.8%) enlarged the encounter, and 11 (3%) refused nastily.

Test 2: Requesting a brief interview. A male and female couple followed a random selection procedure on the street (see fn. 1) to approach passersby and ask them to answer some questions in a survey being conducted about people who are in cities. This is a less common encounter but not unfamiliar in this land of frequent polls. One is asked to give time and trust to strangers, for the interview takes several minutes and the questions are personal—concerning feelings, employment, and living situation. A nasty refusal—such as an abrupt "Not from me [do you get an interview]!" or one of the reactions listed as nasty for Test 1 above—was scored zero points. A polite refusal—such as a plausible reason: "I'm sorry, I have an appointment" or equivalent delivered courteously—was scored one point. Consent was scored two points. Of 1,129 attempts, 175 (15.5%) refused nastily, 258 (22.9%) refused nicely, and 696 (61.6%) consented to the interview.

Test 3: Finding a lost key. A key found on the street is likely to be recognized as an object of value belonging to someone the finder does not know. Would the finder care enough about the stranger who lost it to send the key back? It is an anonymous situation. One does not have to become personal with the owner in order to return the key. This is a test of whether or not there is a difference in the rate of returning keys among people who pick them up at various hours and carry them away. The idea for using a key in such an experiment was developed by Forbes, TeVault, and Gromoll (1972). At the beginning of each of the field visits (see fn. 1), the researchers placed brightly colored aluminum keys in specific well-lighted locations on the streets at the sites. Each key had a tag attached listing the name and address of someone in a city ninety miles away (Northampton) and the request "Please return." We avoided locations near store entrances since the keys might be turned in to a clerk rather than mailed directly. The keys were color-coded and notch-coded, so that we could link each returned key with a particular interval of the 24-hour period. At the end of each two-hour visit the researchers made the rounds and retrieved every key that had not been carried away.

Overall, of 326 keys carried away, 220 (67.5%) were sent back. If the key was dropped in the mailbox (from which they were delivered to Northampton and postage due charges paid), it was scored one point; 154 (47.2%) were returned in this manner. The 38 keys (11.7%) that were returned in a stamped wrapper were scored two points each. Another 25 stamped and wrapped keys (7.7%) came with a personal note enclosed and were counted three points each. Three individuals (.9%) even telephoned Northampton to say that the key was in safe hands, and were scored four points each. The reactions reflect increased degrees of giving time and investing oneself in helping a stranger. The 106 keys (32.5%) not returned were scored zero points each.

Test 4: Being sociable in the supermarket. The supermarket checkout procedure is a microcosm of city street life. People who are mostly strangers to one another make limited contact in a brief, standardized situation. Research assistants, male and female couples, followed a stratified random sampling procedure[2] to visit three 24-hour supermarkets in different parts of Boston at various hours of the day and night. They posed as customers and noted the degree of sociability between single customers and clerks at the checkout counters. Sociability is defined as "showing warmth and expanding the scope of interaction with another." In this case, smiling was taken as showing warmth. The criterion for expanding the scope of the encounter was chatting about a topic other than the transaction—such as saying to the clerk, "Are you a high school student?" or "That's a nice shirt; where'd you get it?" or reporting general news. If the customer both smiled and chatted, the encounter was scored two points. If either happened alone it was rated one point, and zero points were scored if neither took place. (Interaction between customer and clerk showed a high degree of mutuality. When one was impassive the other was too, and when one was sociable the other responded in kind. That is why this simple scoring scheme was used rather than a tally that would have included the behavior of both parties.) To what extent do people break through the confines of their roles in the supermarket checkout procedure to offer even the mildest sociability? Not much, for 562 (74.7%) of the 752 customers did not smile or talk about something other than the transaction. Smiling by itself occurred 98 times (13%), and only 66 (8.8%) both chatted and smiled.

To summarize, over 2,500 people were observed in various parts of central Boston throughout the 24-hour cycle and were rated on how they responded to four situations: giving directions when asked, consenting to be interviewed when asked, returning lost keys they found, and being

sociable with strangers during the focused moment of paying for goods at a supermarket checkout counter. Four tests were used so that several different behaviors would help define and give face validity to what is being studied. While these do not cover the entire range of helpfulness and friendliness, showing some warmth, cooperating with another's modest appeal, and expanding the scope of interaction are the initial conditions of such relationships.

The samples of people among the tests are not the same. Tests 1 and 2 used a periodic selection of passersby following a random procedure adjusted to street population density. Test 3 focused only on persons who carried keys away. Test 4 involves only single customers at the checkout register in always-open supermarkets. Nevertheless, direct *time* comparisons are appropriate, for the tests are all based on random sampling designs for the same intervals around the clock. The issue for evaluating the hypothesis will be the sizes of the differences found among times of day within each test and the consistency of results by time of day across the four tests.

The results of the tests are shown in Table 1. There is impressive consistency for three of the tests, with nighttime scores being highest. Not only does nighttime show up best in these three cases, there is no other time of day consistently second best. In some instances the differences between nighttime and its nearest competitor are not statistically significant, even though the analysis of variance yields significant results when all times are compared. Although differences among hours are small in given instances, the cumulative effect of these practices would make a noticeable difference in the social mood at various times. The overall pattern supports the prediction that

---

[2] The supermarket sample was similar to the sample for the experiments on Boston streets. . . . The same time intervals were listed in the sample frame and thirty visits were selected randomly (three, morning rush; seven, daytime; four, evening rush; seven, evening; and nine, night). The quota for nighttime visits was higher because fewer customers would be observed on each visit then. The observers were eleven pairs of students from my course on Social Interaction in the Fall,

1973; they were trained and rehearsed via earlier trials to reliability averaging .92 (between pairs of observers). One supermarket is a quarter-mile from the residential site for the street experiments; the other two markets are located in different parts of town. In each visit observers followed a systematically-varied visiting order among the three stores, for a total of 90 fifteen-minute observation periods.

TABLE 1 AGGREGATE FINDINGS OF FOUR SEPARATE TESTS FOR HELPFULNESS AND FRIENDLINESS DURING VARIOUS PHASES OF THE 24-HOUR DAILY CYCLE, IN BOSTON IN 1974

Test	Time of Day					Σ	Analysis of Variance and Significance
	Morning rush hour 0730–0929	Daytime 0930–1614	Evening rush hour 1615–1814	Evening 1815–0014	Night 0015–0729		
1. Give directions[a]	n=32[e] 1.06	n=115 .97	n=27 1.07	n=123 1.00	n=66 [1.15][e]	n=363 1.03	F=4.917, p<.001
2. Consent to interview[b]	n=93 1.17	n=366 1.45	n=81 1.46	n=363 1.50	n=226 [1.55]	n=1129 1.46	F=4.531, p<.002
3. Return lost key[c]	n=29 .93	n=113 1.00	n=26 1.04	n=94 [1.18]	n=64 .61(!)	n=326 .97	F=3.972, p<.01
4. Be sociable with stranger[d]	n=68 .24	n=212 .42	n=161 .29	n=179 .22	n=132 [.50]	n=752 .33	F=5.250, p<.001

[a] Index based on zero points for nasty response and no directions given, one point for directions given only, two points for giving directions and expanding the scope of interaction as well; summed, and divided by number of trials (persons approached) within time period. Two of six judges differed in rating a courteous refusal—e.g., "I'm sorry, I don't know"—saying it is a common way to avoid getting involved. Hence polite refusals were omitted from the analysis. A check showed this made no difference. There were thirty instances of polite refusals, scattered over the times of day, and their inclusion (one point each) yielded the same ANOVA results as their exclusion.

[b] Index based on zero points for nasty refusal, one point for polite refusal, two points for consent; summed, and divided by number of trials (persons approached) within time period.

[c] Index based on zero points if key not returned, one point if returned unwrapped, two points if returned wrapped, three points if returned wrapped with message enclosed, four points if personal contact made by telephone; summed, and divided by number of trials (keys carried away) within time period.

[d] Index based on one point for smiling only, one point for chatting only, two points for both, zero points for neither; summed, and divided by number of cases (transactions observed at the checkout counter) within time period.

[e] n = number of trials; [ ] = highest mean score for test.

nighttime is a period of more helpfulness and friendliness than other portions of the day.

In that light the outcome of the key test is surprising. The night had by far the lowest rate of helpfulness. The lowest proportion of keys were returned (50%) and the least extra effort, beyond dropping keys unwrapped into the mailbox, was made then. This finding is so clear-cut and contrary to expectations that it must be significant. Its interpretation would benefit from information still to be presented, and I will postpone comment about its bearing on the frontier hypothesis until later.

The pattern of findings for all four tests does reject a rival hypothesis: *fear* determines people's conduct toward strangers at night. We know the night is viewed as a dangerous time to be outside one's home in the city (U.S. Office of Management and the Budget, 1974:58–9, 73). If fear of criminal assault dominated social behavior then, it should be greater in face-to-face encounters than for the passive, anonymous appeal to find a key tagged "Please return." We would expect people to be more guarded towards others at night, to shun approaches by strangers, but to be more helpful in the low-risk situation of dropping a lost key into the mailbox. Table 1 tells us that just the opposite happened. Nighttimers were more helpful and friendly towards strangers face to face. And yet, of the keys picked up, they returned the fewest. . . .

DISCUSSION

The evidence bears out the hypothesis that night is a frontier. That nighttimers are *less* likely to return the keys they find also supports the idea. While the outcome of Test 3 seems to deny the claim that more help is given on a frontier, the lost-key experiment differs from the other tests in that it is the only one in which people do not meet face to face. It is a test of anonymous helpfulness. During the nighttime, strangers identify more readily with one another. A young man told me, "At 4 a.m. if someone sees you walking the streets at the same time he does, he must think, 'Gee, this guy must be part of the brethren, because no one else is awake at these times.' " However, if someone finds a key and does not know the owner, he would guess that everyone who passed that way is equally likely to have lost it. Nighttimers, knowing they are few, assume on the weight of numbers that the person who lost the key is a daytimer. . . .

CONCLUSION

What is the gain in thinking of night as a frontier? A single theoretical idea gives coherence to a wide range of events: the kind of people up and about at those hours, why they differ from daytimers in their behavior, the beginnings of political efforts by night people, the slow realization, among leaders that public policy might be applied to the time resource. Even the variety of endeavors becomes understandable—from metal smelting plants to miniature golf courses, to mayor's complaint offices, to eating places, to computerized banking terminals that dispense cash. The niche is being expanded. Bit by bit, all of society migrates there. To treat this as a sequel to the geographic spread of past centuries is to summarize the move within familiar ecological concepts of migration, settlement, and frontier. . . .

In his essay "The Frontier in American History," Frederick Jackson Turner (1893:38) reviewed the impact of the advance into western lands upon our society and remarked, "And now, four centuries from the discovery of America, at the end of a hundred years of life under the constitution, the frontier has gone." But it has not gone. During the era that the settlement of our land frontier was being completed, there began—into the night—a large-scale migration of wakeful activity that continues to spread over the world.

REFERENCES

Forbes, Gordon, B., R. D. TeVault, and H. F. Gromoll
1972 "Regional differences in willingness to help strangers: a field experiment with a new unobtrusive measure." Social Science Research 1:415–9.

Hollon, W. Eugene
1974 Frontier Violence. New York: Oxford University Press.

Melbin, Murray
1977 "The colonization of time." In T. Carlstein, D. Parkes, and N. Thrift (eds.), Timing Space and Spacing Time in Social Organization. London: Arnold.

Sumner, William Graham
[1906] Folkways. New York: New American Li-
1960 brary.

Turner, Frederick Jackson
[1893] The Frontier in American History. New
1920 York: Holt.

U.S. Office of Management and Budget
1974 Social Indicators, 1973. Washington, D.C.: U.S. Government Printing Office.

TALKING ANOTHER LOOK

1 In what ways do you think social life in the nighttime is similar to social life on land frontiers? In what ways is it different?

2 In which experiment was the highest proportion of helpfulness shown overall? In which experiment was the highest proportion of helpfulness shown at night?

3 In your view, are there any methodological problems in Melbin's four tests of helpfulness and friendliness at night?

4 What explanation does Melbin offer for the results of the one test in which people were less helpful at night than at other times?

5 Suggest one additional test that could be useful in evaluating helpfulness and friendliness at night.

6 In Melbin's view, what is the sociological gain in thinking of night as a frontier?

What Is a Survey?

Robert Ferber, Paul Sheatsley, Anthony Turner, and Joseph Waksberg

Almost all of us have responded to surveys of one kind or another. We may have been asked about what kind of detergent we use, which presidential candidate we intended to vote for, or what our favorite television program was. A *survey* is a study, generally in the form of an interview or a questionnaire, which provides sociologists with information concerning how people think and act. Among our nation's best-known surveys of opinion are the Gallup poll and the Harris poll. As anyone who watches the news during presidential campaigns knows, these polls have become an important part of political life.

In conducting surveys, sociologists do not need to question everyone in a population; rather, they can use specialized sampling techniques. A *representative sample* is a selection from a larger population that is statistically found to be typical of that population. There are many kinds of samples, of which the random sample is frequently used by social scientists. In a *random sample*, every member of an entire population being studied has the same chance of being included.

In the following selection, Robert Ferber, Paul Sheatsley, Anthony Turner, and Joseph Waksberg analyze the characteristics of surveys and discuss how a survey is carried out. They examine the purposes of surveys; various ways of classifying surveys; safeguarding the confidentiality of survey data; design of questionnaires; and sample design and selection.

CHARACTERISTICS OF SURVEYS

The Need

Any observation or investigation of the facts about a situation may be called a survey. But today the word is most often used to describe a method of gathering information from a number of individuals, a "sample," in order to learn something about the larger population from which the sample has been drawn. Thus, a sample of voters is surveyed in advance of an election to determine how the public perceives the candidates and the issues. A manufacturer makes a survey of the potential market before introducing a new product. A government agency commissions a survey to gather the factual information it needs in order to evaluate existing legislation or draft new legislation. For example, what medical care do people receive, and how is it paid for? Who uses food stamps? How many people are unemployed?

It has been said that the United States is no longer an industrial society but an "information society." That is, our major problems and tasks no longer focus merely on the production of the goods and services necessary to our survival and comfort. Rather, our major problems and tasks today are those of organizing and managing the incredibly complex efforts required to meet the needs and wishes of nearly 220 million Americans. To do this requires a prompt and accurate flow of information on preferences, needs and behavior. It is in response to this critical need for information on the part of the government, business and social institutions that so much reliance is placed upon surveys.

Surveys come in many different forms and have a wide variety of purposes, but they do have certain characteristics in common. Unlike a census, they gather information from only a small sample of people (or farms, businesses or other units, depending on the purpose of the study). In a bona fide survey, the sample is not selected haphazardly or only from persons who volunteer to participate. It is scientifically chosen so that each individual in the population has a known chance of selection. In this way, the results can be reliably projected to the larger public.

Information is collected by means of standardized questions so that every individual surveyed responds to exactly the same question. The survey's intent is not to describe the particular individuals who by chance are part of the sample, but to obtain a statistical profile of the population. Individual respondents are never identified and the survey's results are presented in the form of summaries, such as statistical tables and charts.

The sample size required for a survey will depend on the reliability needed which, in turn, depends on how the results will be used. Consequently, there is no simple rule for sample size that can be used for all surveys. However, analysts usually find that a moderate sample size is sufficient for most needs. For example, the well-known national polls generally use samples of about 1,500 persons to reflect national attitudes and opinions. A sample of this size produces accurate estimates even for a country as large as the United States with a population of over 200 million.

When it is realized that a properly selected sample of only 1,500 individuals can reflect various characteristics of the total population within a very small margin of error, it is easy to understand the value of surveys in a complex society such as ours. They provide a speedy and economical means of determining facts about our economy and people's knowledge, attitudes, beliefs, expectations, and behavior.

Who Does Surveys?

We all know of the public opinion polls which are reported in the press and broadcast media. The Gallup Poll and the Harris Survey issue reports periodically, describing national public opinion on a wide range of current issues. State polls and metropolitan area polls, often supported by a local newspaper or TV station, are reported regularly in many localities. The major broadcasting networks and national news magazines also conduct polls and report their findings.

But the great majority of surveys are not exposed to public view. The reason is that, unlike the public opinion polls, most surveys are directed to a specific administrative or commercial purpose. The wide variety of issues with which surveys deal is illustrated by the following listing of actual uses:

1 The U.S. Department of Agriculture conducted a survey to find out how poor people use food stamps.

2 Major TV networks rely on surveys to tell them how many and what types of people are watching their programs.

3 Auto manufacturers use surveys to find out how satisfied people are with their cars.

4 The U.S. Bureau of the Census conducts a survey every month to obtain information on employment and unemployment in the nation.

5 The National Center for Health Statistics sponsors a survey every year to determine how much money people are spending for different types of medical care.

6 Local housing authorities make surveys to ascertain satisfaction of people in public housing with their living accommodations.

7 The Illinois Board of Higher Education surveys the interest of Illinois residents in adult education.

8 Local transportation authorities conduct surveys to acquire information on people's commuting and travel habits.

9 Magazine and trade journals utilize surveys to find out what their subscribers are reading.

10 Surveys are used to ascertain what sort of people use our national parks and other recreational facilities.

Surveys of human populations also provide an important source of basic social science knowledge. Economists, psychologists, political scientists and sociologists obtain foundation or government grants to study such matters as income and expenditure patterns among households, the roots of ethnic or racial prejudice, comparative voting behavior, or the effects of employment of women on family life. (Surveys are also made of non-human populations, such as of animals, soils and housing; they are not discussed here, although many of the principles are the same.)

Moreover, once collected, survey data can be analyzed and reanalyzed in many different ways. Data tapes with identification of individuals removed can be made available for analysis by community groups, scientific researchers and others.

Types of Surveys

Surveys can be classified in a number of ways. One dimension is by size and type of sample. Many surveys study the total adult population, but others might focus on special population groups: physicians, community leaders, the unemployed, or users of a particular product or service. Surveys may be conducted on a national, state or local basis, and may seek to obtain data from a few hundred or many thousand people.

Surveys can also be classified by their method of data collection. Thus, there are mail surveys, telephone surveys, and personal interview surveys. There are also newer methods of data collection by which information is recorded directly into computers. This includes measurement of TV audiences carried out by devices attached to a sample of TV sets which automatically record in a computer the channels being watched. Mail surveys are seldom used to collect information from the general public because names and addresses are not often available and the response rate tends to be low, but the method may be highly effective with the members of particular groups: for example, subscribers to a specialized magazine or members of a professional association. Telephone interviewing is an efficient

method of collecting some types of data and is being increasingly used. A personal interview in a respondent's home or office is much more expensive than a telephone survey but is necessary when complex information is to be collected.

Some surveys combine various methods. Survey workers may use the telephone to "screen" for eligible respondents (say, women of a particular age group) and then make appointments for a personal interview. Some information, such as the characteristics of the respondent's home, may be obtained by observation rather than questioning. Survey data are also sometimes obtained by self-administered questionnaires filled out by respondents in groups, e.g., a class of school children or a group of shoppers in a central location.

One can further classify surveys by their content. Some surveys focus on opinions and attitudes (such as a pre-election survey of voters), while others are concerned with factual characteristics or behavior (such as a survey of people's health, housing or transportation habits). Many surveys combine questions of both types. Thus, a respondent will be asked if s(he) has heard or read about an issue, what s(he) knows about it, his(her) opinion, how strongly s(he) feels and why, interest in the issue, past experience with it, and also certain factual information which will help the survey analyst classify the responses (such as age, sex, marital status, occupation, and place of residence).

The questions may be open-ended ("Why do you feel that way?") or closed ("Do you approve or disapprove?"); they may ask the respondent to rate a political candidate or a product on some kind of scale; they may ask for a ranking of various alternatives. The questionnaire may be very brief—a few questions taking five minutes or less, or it can be quite long—requiring an hour or more of the respondent's time. Since it is inefficient to identify and approach a large national sample for only a few items of information, there are "omnibus" surveys which combine the interests of several clients in a single inteview. In such surveys, the respondent will be asked a dozen questions on one subject, half a dozen more on another subject, and so on.

Because changes in attitude or behavior cannot be reliably ascertained from a single interview, some surveys employ a "panel design," in which the same respondents are interviewed two or more times. Such surveys are often used during election campaigns, or to chart a family's health or purchasing pattern over a period of time. They are also used to trace changes in behavior over time, as with the social experiments that study changes by low-income families in work behavior in response to an income maintenance plan.

What Sort of People Work on Surveys?

The survey worker best known to the public is the inteviewer who calls on the phone, appears at the door, or stops people at a shopping center. Though survey interviewing may occasionally require long days in the field, it is normally part-time occasional work and is thus well suited for individuals who do not seek full-time employment or who wish to supplement their regular income. Previous experience is not usually required for an inteviewing job. Most research companies will provide their own basic training for the task. The main requirements are an ability to approach strangers, to persuade them to participate in the survey, and to conduct the interview in exact accordance with instructions.

Behind the interviewers are the in-house research staff who design the survey, determine the sample design, develop the questionnaire, surpervise the data collection, carry out the clerical and computer operations necessary to process the completed interviews, analyze the data, and write the reports. In most survey research agencies, the senior people will have taken courses in survey methods at the graduate level and will hold advanced degrees in sociology, statistics, marketing, or psychology, or they will have the equivalent in business experience. Middle-level supervisors and research associates frequently have similar academic backgrounds, or they have

advanced out of the ranks of clerks, interviewers or coders on the basis of their competence and experience.

Are Responses Confidential?

The privacy of the information supplied by survey respondents is of prime concern to all reputable survey organizations. At the U.S. Bureau of the Census, for example, the confidentiality of the data collected is protected by law (Title 13 of the U.S. Code). In Canada, the Statistics Act guarantees the confidentiality of the data collected by Statistics Canada, and other countries have similar safeguards. Also, a number of professional organizations that rely on survey methods have codes of ethics that prescribe rules for keeping survey responses confidential. The recommended policy for survey organizations to safeguard such confidentiality includes:

1 Using only code numbers for the identity of a respondent on a questionnaire, and keeping the code separate from that of the questionnaires.

2 Refusing to give names and addresses of survey respondents to anybody outside of the survey organization, including clients.

3 Destroying questionnaires and identifying information about respondents after the responses have been put onto computer tape.

4 Omitting the names and addresses of survey respondents from computer tapes used for analysis.

5 Presenting statistical tabulations by broad enough categories that individual respondents cannot be singled out.

HOW A SURVEY IS CARRIED OUT

As noted earlier, a survey usually has its beginnings when an individual or institution is confronted with an information need and there are no existing data which suffice. A politician may wish to tap prevailing voter opinions in his district about a proposal to build a superhighway through the county. A government agency may wish to assess the impact on the primary recipients and their families of one of its social welfare programs. A university researcher may wish to examine the relationship between actual voting behavior and expressed opinion on some political issue or social concern.

Designing a Survey

Once the information need has been identified and a determination made that existing data are inadequate, the first step in planning a survey is to lay out the objectives of the investigation. This is generally the function of the sponsor of the inquiry. The objectives should be as specific, clear-cut and unambiguous as possible. The required accuracy level of the data has a direct bearing on the overall survey design. For example, in a sample survey whose main purpose is to estimate the unemployemnt rate for a city, the approximate number of persons to be sampled can be estimated mathematically when one knows the amount of sampling error that can be tolerated in the survey results.

Given the objectives, the methodology for carrying out the survey is developed. A number of interrelated activities are involved. Rules must be formulated for defining and locating eligible respondents, the method of collecting the data must be decided upon, a questionnaire must be designed and pretested, procedures must be developed for minimizing or controlling response errors, appropriate samples must be designed and selected, interviewers must be hired and trained (except for surveys involving self-administered questionnaires), plans must be made for handling nonresponse cases, and tabulation and analysis must be performed.

Designing the questionnaire represents one of the most critical states in the survey development process, and social scientists have given a great deal of thought to issues involved in questionnaire design. The questionnaire links the information need to the realized measurement.

Unless the concepts are clearly defined and the questions unambiguously phrased, the resulting data are apt to contain serious biases. In a survey to estimate the incidence of robbery victimization, for example, one might want to ask, "Were you robbed during the last six months?" Though apparently straightforward and clear-cut, the question does present an ambiguous stimulus. Many respondents are unaware of the legal distinction between robbery (involving personal confrontation of the victim by the offender) and burglary (involving breaking and entering but no confrontation), and confuse the two in a survey. In the National Crime Survey, conducted by the Bureau of the Census, the questions on robbery victimization do not mention "robbery." Instead, several questions are used which, together, seek to capture the desired responses by using more universally understood phrases that are consistent with the operational definition of robbery.

Designing a suitable questionnaire entails more than well-defined concepts and distinct phraseology. Attention must also be given to its length, for unduly long questionnaires are burdensome to the respondent, are apt to induce respondent fatigue and hence response errors, refusals, and incomplete questionnaires, and may contribute to higher nonresponse rates in subsequent surveys involving the same respondents. Several other factors must be taken into account when designing a questionnaire to minimize or prevent biasing the results and to facilitate its use both in the field and in the processing center. They include such diverse considerations as the sequencing of sections or individual questions in the document, the inclusion of check boxes or precoded answer categories versus open-ended questions, the questionnaire's physical size and format, and instructions to the respondent or to the interviewer on whether certain questions are to be skipped depending on response patterns to prior questions.

Selecting the proper respondent in a sample unit is a key element in survey planning. For surveys where the inquiry is basically factual in nature, any knowledgeable person associated with the sample unit may be asked to supply the needed information. This procedure is used in the Current Population Survey, where the sample units are households and any responsible adult in a household is expected to be able to provide accurate answers on the employment-unemployment status of the eligible household members.

In other surveys, a so-called "household" respondent will produce erroneous and/or invalid information. For example, in attitude surveys it is generally accepted that a randomly chosen respondent from among the eligible household members produces a more valid cross section of opinion than does the nonrandomly selected household respondent. This is because a nonrandomly selected individual acting as household respondent is more likely to be someone who is at home during the day, and the working public and their attitudes would be underrepresented.

Another important feature of the survey planning process is devising ways to keep response errors and biases to a minimum. These considerations depend heavily on the subject matter of the survey. For example, memory plays an important role in surveys dealing with past events that the respondent is expected to report accurately, such as in a consumer expenditure survey. In such retrospective surveys, therefore, an appropriate choice of reference period must be made so that the respondent is not forced to report events that may have happened too long ago to remember accurately. In general, attention must be given to whether the questions are too sensitive, whether they may prejudice the respondent, whether they unduly invade the respondent's privacy, and whether the information sought is too difficult even for a willing respondent to provide. Each of these concerns has an important bearing on the overall validity of the survey results.

Sampling Aspects

Virtually all surveys that are taken seriously by social scientists and policy makers use some form of scientific sampling. Even the decennial Cen-suses of Population and Housing use sampling techniques for gathering the bulk of the data items, although 100 percent enumeration is used for the basic population counts. Methods of sampling are well-grounded in statistical theory and in the theory of probability. Hence, reliable and efficient estimates of a needed statistic can be made by surveying a carefully constructed sample of a population, as opposed to the entire population, provided of course that a large proportion of the sample members give the requested information.

The particular type of sample used depends on the objectives and scope of the survey, including the overall survey budget, the method of data collection, the subject matter and the kind of respondent needed. A first step, however, in deciding on an appropriate sampling method is to define the relevant population. This target population can be all the people in the entire nation or all the people in a certain city, or it can be a subset such as all teenagers in a given location. The population of interest need not be people; it may be wholesale businesses or institutions for the handicapped or government agencies, and so on.

The types of samples range from simple random selection of the population units to highly complex samples involving multiple stages or levels of selection with stratification and/or clustering of the units into various groupings. Whether simple or complex, the distinguishing characteristics of a properly designed sample are that all the units in the target population have a known, nonzero chance of being included in the sample, and the sample design is described in sufficient detail to permit reasonably accurate calculation of sampling errors. It is these features that make it scientifically valid to draw inferences from the sample results about the entire population which the sample represents.

Ideally, the sample size chosen for a survey should be based on how reliable the final estimates must be. In practice, usually a trade-off is made between the ideal sample size and the expected cost of the survey. The complexity of a sample plan often depends on the availability of auxiliary information that can be used to introduce efficiencies into the overall design. For example, in a recent Federal Government survey on characteristics of health-care institutions, existing information about the type of care provided and the number of beds in each institution was useful in sorting the institutions into "strata," or groups by type and size, in advance of selecting the sample. The procedure permitted more reliable survey estimates than would have been possible if a simple random selection of institutions had been made without regard to size or type.

A critical element in sample design and selection is defining the source of materials from which a sample can be chosen. This source, termed the sampling frame, generally is a list of some kind, such as a list of housing units in a city, a list of retail establishments in a county or a list of students in a university. The sampling frame can also consist of geographic areas with well-defined natural or artificial boundaries, when no suitable list of the target population exists. In the latter instance, a sample of geographic areas (referred to as segments) is selected and an interviewer canvasses the sample "area segments" and lists the appropriate units—households, retail stores or whatever—so that some or all of them can be designated for inclusion in the final sample.

The sampling frame can also consist of less concrete things, such as all possible permutations of integers that make up banks of telephone numbers, in the case of telephone surveys that seek to include unlisted numbers. The quality of the sampling frame—whether it is up-to-date and how complete—is probably the dominant feature for ensuring adequate coverage of the desired population.

Conducting a Survey

Though a survey design may be well conceived, the preparatory work would be futile if the survey were executed improperly. For personal or telephone interview surveys, interviewers must be carefully trained in the survey's concepts, definitions, and procedures. This may take the form of classroom training, self-study, or both. The training stresses good interviewer techniques on such points as how to make initial contact, how to conduct interviews in a professional manner and how to avoid influencing or biasing responses. The training generally involves practice interviews to familiarize the interviewers with the variety of situations they are likely to encounter. Survey materials must be prepared and issued to each interviewer, including ample copies of the questionnaire, a reference manual, information about the identification and location of the sample units, and any cards or pictures to be shown to the respondent.

Before conducting the interview, survey organizations frequently send an advance letter to the sample member explaining the survey's purpose and the fact that an interviewer will be calling soon. In many surveys, especially those sponsored by the Federal Government, information must be given to the respondent regarding the voluntary or mandatory nature of the survey, and how the answers are to be used.

Visits to sample units are scheduled with attention to such considerations as the best time of day to call or visit and the number of allowable callbacks for no-one-at-home situations. Controlling the quality of the field work is an essential aspect of good survey practice. This is done in a number of ways, most often through observation or rechecking of a subsample of interviews by supervisory or senior personnel, and through office editing procedures to check for omissions or obvious mistakes in the data.

When the interviews have been completed and the questionnaires filled out, they must be processed in a form so that aggregated totals, averages or other statistics can be computed. This will involve clerical coding of questionnaire items which are not already precoded. Occupation and industry categorizations are typical examples of fairly complex questionnaire coding that is usually done clerically. Also procedures must be developed for coding open-ended questions and for handling items that must be transcribed from one part of the questionnaire to another.

Coded questionnaires are keypunched, entered directly onto tape so that a computer file can be created, or entered directly into the computer. Decisions may then be needed on how to treat missing data and "not answered" items.

Coding, keypunching and transcription operations are subject to human error and must be rigorously controlled through verification processes, either on a sample basis or 100 percent basis. Once a computer file has been generated, additional computer editing, as distinct from clerical editing of the data, can be accomplished to alter inconsistent or impossible entries, e.g., a six-year-old grandfather.

When a "clean" file has been produced, the survey data are in a form where analysts can specify to a computer programmer the frequency counts, cross-tabulations or more sophisticated methods of data presentation or computation that are needed to help answer the concerns outlined when the survey was initially conceived.

The results of the survey are usually communicated in publications and in verbal presentations at staff briefings or more formal meetings. Secondary analysis is often possible to those other than the survey staff by making available computer data files at nominal cost.

TAKING ANOTHER LOOK

1 What basic characteristics do surveys have in common?

2 Why is it that most surveys are not exposed to public view?

3 Identify and briefly describe three ways in which surveys can be classified.

4 What steps do survey organizations commonly take in order to safeguard the confidentiality of survey data?

5 What activities are involved in developing the methodology for carrying out a survey?

6 What are some of the difficulties involved in designing a suitable questionnaire?

7 What is a "sampling frame"?

A Content Analysis of Music Videos

Richard L. Baxter, Cynthia De Riemer, Ann Landini, Larry Leslie, and Michael W. Singletary

The term *unobtrusive measures* is used by sociologists to refer to a variety of research techniques that have no impact on who or what is being studied. They are designated as "nonreactive," since people's behavior is not influenced. For example, Émile Durkheim's statistical analysis of suicide rates in various European nations in 1869 neither increased nor decreased human self-destruction. While subjects of experiments are often aware that they are being watched—an awareness that can influence their behavior—this is not the case when unobtrusive measures are used.

One basic technique of unobtrusive measurement is the use of statistics, as in Durkheim's work. Crime statistics, census data, budgets of public agencies, and other archival data are all readily available to the sociologist. Much of this information can be obtained at relatively low cost. However, if the researcher is forced to rely on data collected by someone else, he or she may not find exactly what is needed. Researchers studying family violence can use statistics from police and social service agencies on *reported* cases of spouse abuse and child abuse. Yet such governmental bodies have no precise data on *all* cases of abuse.

Many social scientists find it useful to study cultural, economic, and political documents, including newspapers, periodicals, radio and television tapes, scripts, diaries, songs, folklore, and legal papers, to name a few examples. In examining these sources, researchers employ a technique known as *content analysis*, which is the systematic coding and objective recording of data, guided by some rationale. Conflict theorists have found such techniques useful in detecting how the media portray women and other disadvantaged groups in a negative manner.

In the following selection, Richard L. Baxter, Cynthia De Riemer, Ann Landini, Larry Leslie, and Michael W. Singletary report the results of a content analysis of 62 Music Television Videos (MTV) in 23 content categories. Frequent occurrences were found in the categories of visual abstraction, sex, dance, violence, and crime. The researchers note that "music video sexual content may have a decidedly adolescent orientation, suited to its audience; fantasy exceeds experience and sexual expression centers primarily on attracting the opposite sex."

De Fleur and Ball-Rokeach (1982) have argued that exposure to mass media content indirectly affects behavior by shaping cultural norms. Research studies, often centered on the sexual and violent content of television, have investigated the relationship between mass media content and cultural norms. For example, the cultural indicators group (Gerbner & Gross, 1976; Gerbner, Gross, Morgan & Signorielli, 1980) have found that televised violence may cultivate perceptions of mistrust, apprehension, danger, and a "mean world." In addition, analyses of the sexual content of television (Fernandez-Collado, Greenberg, Korzenny, & Atkin, 1978; Franzblau, Sprafkin, & Rubinstein, 1977) have revealed that physical intimacy appeared most often in less sensuous forms. Kissing, embracing, and nonaggressive touching dominated the screen, while sexual behaviors such as rape and intercourse were almost never seen but often suggested. Others have studied television as a form. Wright and Huston (1983) proposed that the visual and auditory representation possible with television was a potent means of communication and "could induce active cognitive processing" (p. 841), especially for the young.

Little attention, though, has been given to the form and content of Music Television (MTV), which began in 1981. MTV airs video clips of recording artists performing their current popular music hits. The staple of MTV content is the music video, which consumes 80% of programming time (Foti, 1981). MTV does not represent the only programming service which airs music videos. Music videos also appear on USA Cable's *Nightflight* and on HBO's *Jukebox*, among other services. However, MTV often obtains the exclusive right to show a particular video first.

Critics have charged that MTV stresses sex and violence and makes rock music impersonal by removing the individual "pictures in our minds" generated by the music (Levy, 1983). In exploring both the format and the content of MTV music videos, Gehr (1983) proposed that MTV might alter the relationship between the audience and the musicians in live performances and might change how audiences hear records and radio. Gehr believed the music video separates music from visual content, resulting in " . . . discontinuity and disjunction. Gestures, actions, and intentions are nearly always divorced from systematic content" (p.39).

The content of music videos may be significant from another standpoint. Larson and Kubey (1983) found that both watching television and listening to music (as separate activities) could deeply involve adolescents. Even greater emotional involvement was reported when listening to music. The music video combines elements of both music and television in a nontraditional format. Considering that 85% of the MTV audience is estimated to be between the ages of 14 and 34 (Zimmerman, 1984), the music video has poten-

tial for contributing to the cultural norms of a relatively impressionable audience.

Given the lack of systematic content analysis of music videos, the research questions focused on how specific areas of content can be quantified. The following questions guided the research effort: (a) What are the major categories of content which emerge from observation of music videos and can these categories be analyzed systematically? (b) Do specific content categories, such as those centered on sex and violence, appear with great frequency in music videos? (c) Do music videos focus on bizarre, unconventional representations? Is androgyny present in portrayals of video characters? (d) Do symbols dealing with government, politics, and American culture and lifestyles appear with discernible frequency?

METHOD

Although previous analyses of television content are available, the coding instruments used could not be applied readily to music videos. Thus, there was a need to develop a coding form for collecting the data. The development of the coding instrument was guided by the desire to gain an exhaustive overview of music video content and not to focus on one or two areas of possible content, such as sex or violence.

A search of the literature revealed anecdotal data relating to the content of rock music and music videos. For instance, Peatman (1954) and Horton (1957) found lyrics dealt primarily with love, sex, and romance. Gehr (1983) suggested that MTV content centered on themes such as liberty, growing up, death, and fear of the loss of freedom. These suggested themes were grouped into content categories. To examine the relationship of these derived categories to actual music video content, a purposive sample of primetime MTV programming was examined, comparing content suggested by the literature with actual music video content. As a result, the content categories were expanded and each category (with two exceptions) was defined by a short descriptor and by a listing of possible actions or behaviors which could occur in that category. Defining categories by major properties was suggested by Krippendorff (1980) as a means of assuring exhaustiveness.

This preliminary coding instrument was pretested, resulting in the addition and refinement of categories. The final coding form included an "other" choice for each category so that coders could add observed elements that the researchers had overlooked. Twenty-three content categories were identified.

A random sample of 62 videos was drawn from the music videos aired on MTV during the week of April 28-May 4, 1984. One hour from each of the 7 days was recorded. The hour for each day was determined by using a table of random numbers; military time equivalents were used for the hour designates. Videos in the sample were coded only once.

The unit of analysis was the individual music video of approximately 3 minutes in duration. The length and complexity of the coding instrument influenced the researchers' decision to instruct the coders not to indicate multiple references of content in the same music video. The researchers were interested in the number of videos containing at least one reference to a content category and not in the number of times the same element appeared in a particular video.

Coders were undergraduate students trained in the use of the coding form. Each coder viewed each video twice. During the first viewing, the video was stopped every 30 seconds to allow coding of all content categories to that point. For the second viewing, the video was played nonstop and coders were allowed to make any appropriate changes on the coding form. The videos were viewed by the coders without sound, because the researchers were interested in the visual, rather than audio, content elements of the videos.

To test intercoder reliability, 21 coders recoded randomly selected videos which had already been analyzed by original coders. Coder and recoder results were analyzed using Scott's pi for nominal scale coding (Scott, 1955). A .82 reliability coefficient was obtained.

RESULTS

A total of 62 videos were analyzed for occurrences in 23 content categories. Overall percentage frequencies are found in Table 1. Content categories are listed in descending order of occurrence. Table 2 contains frequencies of the leading seven content categories with descriptive behaviors and/or actions for each category included. The researchers' decision not to code multiple occurrences of actions or behaviors in the content categories must be considered in interpreting these results.

DISCUSSION

The physical structure of the music videos studied reveals that producers rely heavily on special camera techniques, film imagery, and special effects in creating music videos. The intent may be to dazzle the eye and thus hold the attention of the largely adolescent audience. Music videos also allow the performer to dominate the action and showcasing the artist may be a prime concern.

Against the backdrop of visual structure, what other content categories appear in music videos? Consistent with Levy's (1983) observation, MTV videos stressed sexual content. However, like other studies of televised sexual content, music video sexual content was understated, relying on innuendo through clothing, suggestiveness, and light physical contact rather than more overt behaviors.

Thus, music video sexual content may have a decidedly adolescent orientation, suited to its audience; fantasy exceeds experience and sexual expression centers primarily on attracting the opposite sex. Sexual behavior, as portrayed in music videos, may reflect actual or desired adolescent courtship behavior, or the expression of attraction impulses. This issue is beyond the scope

TABLE 1 FREQUENCY OF OCCURRENCE FOR MUSIC VIDEO CONTENT CATEGORIES

Content Category	Percentages
Visual Abstraction (use of special effects to produce odd, unusual, and/or unexpected representations of reality)	90.3
Sex (portrayal of sexual feelings or impulses	59.7
Dance	56.5
Violence and/or Crime	53.2
Celebration (portrayal of happy, festive occasions)	45.2
Friendship (portrayal of relationships of mutual affection and respect)	41.9
Isolation (alone or apart from others)	41.9
Wealth (affluence, possession of valuable material objects)	38.7
Transportation (use of various types of vehicles or modes of conveyance)	35.5
Bizarre (strikingly odd in appearance or effect)	27.4
Artificial Substances (use of narcotics, stimulants, and other substances)	24.2
Physical Restraint (to hold back a person or thing from movement or action)	24.2
Androgyny (combining traditional elements of male/female appearances resulting in ambivalent or unclear gender identity)	22.6
Religion (portrayal of belief in a superhuman, controlling power)	17.7
Political Issues (overt behaviors or symbols which represent political issues, entities, or institutions)	14.5
Fitness (portrayal of physical conditioning or abilities)	14.5
Animals (use of animals)	14.5
Maturation (process of "growing up"; developmental stages associated with childhood, adolescence, and adulthood)	12.9
Death (portrayal of loss of life or rituals of death and dying)	9.7
Health (relating to medicine, medical personnel, state of well being, or illness)	1.6

Note: Frequency is the percentage of videos in the sample that contained at least one occurrence of an action or behavior from that content category. The major categories of human demographics, performance, and setting were excluded in this table because they were represented in all videos from the sample.

of this study. The study's results indicate, however, that sexually oriented, suggestive behavior is portrayed frequently in music videos. Questions regarding the impact of this portrayal on adolescent socialization, peer relationships, and modeling are raised.

The frequency of instances of violence and crime content also merits further attention. Fre-quent content elements in the violence and crime category also exhibited understated characteristics. The most frequently coded content elements were physical aggression, not the use of weapons, murder, or sexual violence. Violent action in music videos often stopped short of the fruition of the violent act.

Besides the question of *what* is on MTV, there

TABLE 2 FREQUENCIES OF ACTION/BEHAVIORS IN SEVEN LEADING MUSIC VIDEOS CONTENT CATEGORIES

Category	Action/Behavior	Percentages
Visual Abstraction	Unusual camera techniques, i.e., use of convex lens, unconventional camera angles, rapid film cuts between scenes or video segments	48
	Special lighting—varying colors and techniques	48
	Fog	32
	Superimposition imagery—filming technique which inserts persons, objects, or places onto the ongoing action of the music video although the superimposed subjects are not physically part of the action	27
	Costuming—use of clothing to portray characterizations beyond those associated with contemporary garb, e.g., cavemen, 18th century aristocrats	19
	Use of fire and flames	18
	Distortions	16
Sex	Provocative clothing	31
	Embrace or other physical contact	31
	Dance movements of sexually suggestive nature	27
	Nondance movements of sexually suggestive nature	21
	Date or courtship (male-female)	15
	Kissing	11
	Male chasing female or vice versa	11
	Use of musical instrument in sexually suggestive manner	8
	Sadomasochism	5
	Date or courtship (homosexual or lesbian)	2
	Sexual bondage	2
Dance	Group dancing—spontaneous or natural	36
	Group dancing—choreographed	16
	Couple dancing	13
	Individual or group doing jazz	10
	Individual or group doing ballet	3
	Individual or group doing tap	3
	Individual or group doing breakdancing	2
Violence and Crime	Physical aggression against people	26
	Physical aggression against objects	16
	Dance movements imitating violence	15
	Destructiveness	15
	Use of weapons (chains, guns, knives, axes, hammers, etc.)	11
	Physical aggression against self	8
	Chase	7
	Murder	3
	Victimless crime	2
Celebration	Activities which stimulate a happy or joyful reaction in participants	21
	Audience at rock concert	16
	Social gatherings or party scene with light, happy setting	18

TABLE 2 CONTINUED

Category	Action/Behavior	Percentages
Friendship	Togetherness of nonsexual variety (male-female)	24
	Comraderie—pals, girlfriends, clubs, or social groups	24
	Companionship in settings such as home, school, work, etc., where one person provides company for another	13
Isolation	Physical separation from others in indoor setting	32
	Physical separation from others in outdoor setting	12
	Desertion by loved one	5

Note: Frequency is the percentage of videos in the sample that contained at least one occurrence of an action or behavior from that content category.

is the question of *who* is on MTV. White, adult males, appearing in 96% of the videos studied, were most represented on these MTV videos. This may reflect the dominance of this group in the rock music industry. The race most depicted in this study was Caucasian (by a 2 to 1 ratio), but other races including Black, Oriental, Hispanic, and Native American were present.

At this time, most persons, from the uninitiated to the MTV fan, have little knowledge about the possible impact of music videos. Studies like the one reported here may do much to replace myth and anecdotal observation and form the basis for future empirical analysis.

REFERENCES

De Fleur, M. L., & Ball-Rokeach, S. J. (1982). *Theories of mass communication* (4th ed.). New York: Longman.

Fernandez-Collado, C. F., Greenberg, B. S., Korzenny, F., & Atkin, C. K. (1978). Sexual intimacy and drug use in TV series. *Journal of Communication, 28*(3), 30–37.

Foti, L. (1981, August 29). Punk to classics. *Billboard,* p. 4.

Franzblau, S., Sprafkin, J. N., & Rubinstein, E. A. (1977). Sex on TV: A content analysis. *Journal of Communication, 27*(2), 164–170.

Gehr, R. (1983). The MTV aesthetic. *Film Comment, 19*(4), 37–40.

Gerbner, G., & Gross, L. (1976). Living with television: The violence profile. *Journal of Communication, 26*(2), 173–199.

Gerbner, G., Gross, L., Morgan, M., & Signorielli, N. (1980). The "mainstreaming" of America: Violence profile no. 11. *Journal of Communication, 30*(3), 10–29.

Horton, D. (1957). The dialogue of courtship in popular songs. *American Journal of Sociology, 62,* 569–578.

Krippendorff, K. (1980). *Content analysis: An introduction to its methodology.* Beverly Hills: Sage.

Larson, R., & Kubey, R. (1983). Television and music: Contrasting media in adolescent life. *Youth and Society, 15* 13–31.

Levy, S. (1983, December 8). Ad nauseum: How MTV sells out rock and roll. *Rolling Stone,* p. 30.

Peatman, J. G. (1944). Radio and popular music. In P. F. Lazarsfeld & F. N. Stanton (Eds.), *Radio research, 1942–43* (pp. 335–393). New York: Duell, Sloan & Pearce.

Scott, W. A. (1955). Reliability of content analysis: The case of nominal scale coding. *Public Opinion Quarterly, 19,* 321–325.

Wright, J. C., & Huston, A. C. (1983). A matter of form: Potentials of television for young viewers. *American Psychologist, 38,* 835–843.

Zimmerman, D. (1984, March 29). Rock video's free ride may be ending. *USA Today,* Section D, pp. 1,2.

TAKING ANOTHER LOOK

1 What charges have been made by critics regarding MTV programming?
2 What methodology was used by the researchers in their content analysis of music videos?
3 In the category of sex (portrayal of sexual feelings or impulses), what types of action and behaviors were most frequently portrayed on music videos?
4 In the category of violence and crime, what types of action and behaviors were most frequently portrayed on music videos?
5 What findings are reported regarding *who* is portrayed on music videos?
6 What techniques would you use in order to conduct a content analysis of your favorite nighttime television program?

Walking a Tightrope: Dilemmas of Participant Observation of Groups in Conflict

Anson D. Shupe, Jr., and David G. Bromley

Participant observation is a research technique in which an investigator collects information through direct participation in and observation of a group, tribe, or community under study. This method allows sociologists to examine certain behaviors and communities that could not be investigated through other research techniques. In some cases, the sociologist actually "joins" a group for a period of time to get an accurate sense of how it operates.

The initial challenge that each participant observer faces is to gain acceptance into an unfamiliar group. It is no simple matter for a college-trained sociologist to win the trust of a religious cult, a youth gang, a poor Appalachian community, or a circle of skid row residents. Observation research also poses other complex challenges for the investigator. In a sense, a researcher must learn to see the world as the group sees it in order to fully comprehend the events taking place around them. Yet the sociologist must retain a certain level of detachment from the group under study, even as he or she tries to understand how members feel. If the research is to be successful, the observer cannot allow the close associations or even friendships that inevitably develop to influence the conclusions of the study.

In the following selection, sociologists Anson D. Shupe, Jr., and David G. Bromley address issues raised during a comparative participant-observation study. The two groups studied, each of which is totally antagonistic to the other, were the Unification Church of the Reverend Sun Myung Moon and an emerging network of organizations opposed to the Unification Church and other groups viewed as religious "cults."

The Unification Church was founded in South Korea in the middle 1950s by Reverend Moon, an ex-Presbyterian evangelist born in Korea in 1920. His theology is a distinctive blend of Buddhism, Taoism, and his own interpretations of the Old and New Testaments. Followers call him "Father" or acknowledge him with such grand terms as "Lord of the Second Advent" and "Master of Mankind."

Officials of the church claim that it has 10,000 members in the United States, but most outside observers estimate somewhat less than 7000. Young recruits live with other church members and generally work virtually nonstop as fund raisers. The Unification Church has come under strong attack for its deceptive methods of luring young people to weekend retreats and for its alleged brainwashing of such youths once they arrive. In 1982, Reverend Moon was convicted of filing false income tax returns; he entered federal prison in 1984 to serve an 18-month sentence.

Given the intense hostility between the Unification Church and the anticult network, Shupe and Bromley faced a difficult challenge in remaining neutral while offending neither group. They identify five key methodological problems

Author's note: This paper is the product of a joint effort. The order of authorship is random and does not imply any difference in the importance of contributions.

of participant observation that arose in the context of this study: (1) role definition and justification; (2) pressures to "go native" (abandon a neutral position and give one's allegiance to the group); (3) public pressures to take a stand; (4) evolving commitments; and (5) gaining comparable information and insights.

Much of the methodological commentary on participant observation techniques in field work focuses on the problems encountered in studying a single group. Sociologists have written extensively on the problems related to gaining entry, establishing and maintaining rapport, and disengaging once the research has been completed for the single group situation (e.g., Shaffir, Turowetz, and Stebbins, 1979; Douglas, 1972; Weinberg and Williams, 1972; Vidich, 1970). However, much less attention has been paid to the issues which develop in the conduct of comparative participant observation research.

Whether one is studying only a single group or more than one simultaneously, the researcher in either situation inevitably confronts certain basic dilemmas. On the one hand, there has been the problem of securing sufficient cooperation from informants to gain accurate, detailed information (some of which is of a confidential, sensitive nature) and becoming attuned to the informants' world views (e.g., Trice, 1970; Becker, 1952; Blum, 1952). On the other hand, researchers have tried to avoid "going native" or being subtly co-opted by the group while in the role of participant observer (Becker, 1967). As Grimshaw (1973:4) noted in his observations on the methodological skills necessary in "area" studies versus "comparative" studies:

> While the problems involved are no different in kind from those involved in domestic research, they are of such great magnitude as to constitute an almost qualitative difference for comparative, as compared to noncomparative, research.

The same could be argued for a distinction between single-group and comparative participant observation research. While we do not mean to imply in this paper that sociologists researching simultaneously two or more groups confront problems totally different from those of the more typical one-group situation, we would maintain that those problems experienced in the one-group case often combine or enlarge in the dual or multi-group case to form dilemmas that are well-nigh inescapable or at least more intricate than in the single-group case. The differences are clearly of degree, not kind. To paraphrase Grimshaw, in the multi-group situation the problems of entry, rapport maintenance, and quality control of data (among others) become so consistently manifest as to almost *seem* different to the researcher.

In this paper we shall deal with the special case of maintaining rapport with two groups, each of which was dedicated to the destruction of the other. Both were highly visible social movements of the 1970's, urban in member composition and focus of activities, and the subjects of a storm of controversy and coverage.

THE ANTAGONISTS: THE UNIFICATION CHURCH AND THE ANTI-CULT MOVEMENT

The two antagonistic groups with which the authors became involved as participant observers were (1) the controversial Unification Church of the Korean evangelist Reverend Sun Myung Moon (more popularly known as the "Moonies") and (2) the emerging network of organizations (composed primarily of families, ex-members of the Unification Church and other "new religions," and spokespersons for conventional denominations) which has actively opposed such groups as the Unification Church. The latter organizations, although less visible than the "Moonies," recently have attracted considerable attention as a result of seeking media publicity and their involvement in the practice known as "deprogramming." ("Deprogramming" is the popular term for detaining a "marginal" religion's member involuntarily and pressuring him or her, through persistent argument, to recant the new faith and return to the former lifestyle.)

The authors' involvement with these groups was typical of much participant observation in that once the project commenced new questions arose which were large unanticipated. In this case the authors initially were struck by the enormous outpouring of negative media coverage and publicity given to the Unification Church in the mid-1970's. The authors prepared a manuscript for presentation at a professional meeting which offered a speculative interpretation of this adverse social reaction (see Shupe, *et al.,* 1977). In the process of preparing this manuscript one of the authors requested information from the headquarters of the National Ad Hoc Committee—Citizens Engaged in Freeing Minds (CEFM) which, coincidentally, was located in the Dallas-Fort Worth metropolitan area. A phone call and visitation to CEFM headquarters intrigued the researcher and soon the CEFM had become a target of investigation in its own right.

At approximately the same time two relatively high ranking (state and national) representatives of the Unification Church, heading a contingent of approximately fifty missionaries, arrived in the metropolitan area and attempted to recruit university students and establish a campus student organization. One of the authors, then acting chairperson of the sociology department, was approached to serve as faculty sponsor for the campus organization after numerous refusals from other departmental chairpersons. On civil libertarian principles he agreed. Since the group planned to witness and fund raise in the metropolitan area for several weeks, we felt the situation afforded us an unusual opportunity to compare the actual activities and lifestyle of the members with the popular media image. As reciprocity for university sponsorship, over the next two months we were permitted to conduct more than forty

in-depth interviews with Church members, and engaged in a substantial amount of other observation.

Somewhat surprisingly, leaders of the anti-cult movement, although aware of the authors' research on the Unification Church, continued to provide us with information, made an effort to maintain an ongoing relationship, and later issued an invitation to participate in a closed strategy meeting of regional officers in the movement. They seemed relieved that social scientists were finally "investigating" what they perceived to be a critical problem. As a result of these contacts we gained access to personal correspondence, memos and documents, and other "insider" communications among anti-cultists by which the changes in the anti-cult movement could be monitored. One of the authors subsequently prepared several papers on the movement (Shupe, Spielmann, and Stigall, 1977a, 1977b) which members perceived as descriptively accurate and objective.

After gaining entry into both of these opposed groups, we became more deeply involved with each. Initial contacts with the Unification Church led to additional participant observation of members' activities elsewhere in Texas, frequent contacts with national Church officials, an opportunity to visit the Church's seminary and national organizational headquarters, and access to organizational files and records. Likewise the anti-cultists offered additional opportunities to attend closed strategy sessions, provided access to personal correspondence and diaries of current and former Church members, and established contacts with public officials investigating new religious groups. The deepening involvement, then, resulted in acquisition of a greater quantity of information from both sides that was at the same time more sensitive and confidential.

Much of the information which was divulged to us by each group inevitably had at least the potential for a negative impact on its opponent. As these relationships emerged over time we found ourselves confronting a unique set of problems. Rather than being participant observers of a single group, a situation involving negotiations more familiar to sociologists, we found ourselves attempting to maintain a much more delicate set of relationships, analogous to "walking a tightrope." Indeed, in a situation in which each group was devoted to the destruction of the other, any involvement with one group immediately endangered our relationship with the other. After all, from the perspective of each we were consorting with their opponents. Out of this experience we have isolated several major problems which persisted throughout the research enterprise. The way these problems were resolved had more than procedural implications. Their resolution influenced our access to additional information and the tenor of the presentation of our findings, even down to choices of wording. These problems were (1) role definition and justification; (2) pressures to go native; (3) public pressures to take a stand; (4) evolving commitments; and (5) gaining comparable information and insights.

ROLE DEFINITION AND JUSTIFICATION

In any overt participant observation situation it is necessary to explain one's presence and intentions, and this we did at the outset with each group. However, the necessity of explaining our roles tended to persist since each individual interviewed or contacted had some capacity to grant or withhold cooperation and information. Several factors reduced the barriers which groups typically maintain toward outsiders. First, the professional sociologist-researcher role carried a certain degree of legitimacy. Like most middle class Americans, our informants were accustomed to public opinion surveys and journalistic inquiries of a quasi-social science nature. Thus, although most of them lacked a precise definition of sociology per se, they were not uncomfortable with a social scientist's questioning and probing. Second, each group was seeking some type of legitimation to which it was perceived we might contribute. In the case of the Unification Church, members were quite receptive since they felt that the au-

thors' "objective" presentation of the group's lifestyle would help to dispel what they considered to be myths and stereotypes about themselves. In the case of the anti-cult movement, members were using a "brainwashing model" of how young persons came to be members of such groups as the Unification Church couched in behavioral science jargon. Since they had extremely limited knowledge of the concepts they sought to employ, the mere presence of social scientists contributed to their efforts to increase their own credibility and sophistication. Third, we gained support with leaders of each group, facilitating cooperation with rank and file members. Finally, the generally open-ended format of the interview schedules, which allowed respondents to express their own views and feelings, minimized their sense of threat.

What made the dual group situation unique was the fact that any involvement with one group automatically required an explanation of our dealings with their "enemies." Members of each group expressed puzzlement that we felt the necessity to solicit information from the other side. For example, the anti-cultists went so far as to warn us against attending dinner-lectures of the Unification Church because we might "succumb" to their alleged subtle mind control techniques. Other anti-cultists, while it was never publicly stated, were clearly concerned that our investigation of the Unification Church might not confirm their stereotypes of the group. The Church, by contrast, did not directly express reservations about our contacts with the anti-cultists, but it was evident that our association with the anti-cultists made it more difficult for the Church to locate us precisely on the supporter-opponent continuum. This was a particularly salient concern to the Church because in the past it had opened its doors to outside investigators only later to feel "burned" by the negative published accounts. (One particular investigation toward which they harbored such feelings was Stoner and Parke, 1977, in which they were lumped together with other "deviant" religions for which they felt little affinity.) Of course, the more sensitive the information to which we were given access, the more explicitly this concern was voiced. In fact, by the time we were invited to visit the Unification Church Seminary, a rather lengthy set of negotiations around just that point were required. For some time it appeared that further access would be denied because the authors' published work was perceived as not sufficiently "objective" and sensitive to the uses to which the information might be put by others.

PRESSURES TO GO NATIVE

Whenever a neutral outsider first encounters a social movement in which members are highly committed and goal oriented, there is inevitably some pressure on him or her to accept its ideology and often to involve oneself in the group's activities. In part this pressure emanates from the fact that individuals who are highly committed members of a cause believe in the rightness of their ideas and principles and tend to equate knowing and understanding with believing. In part, also, pressure occurs because social movements desire new members, and conversion of a neutral outsider constitutes a victory for the group. So while researchers may be tolerated as long as they are not a hindrance to the group, the group would much prefer a committed member to a neutral observer.

The authors experienced such pressures from each side on a belief and behavioral level. Unification Church members frequently asked our impression of the Divine Principle (the scriptural formulation of Reverend Moon's divine revelation). At first we could claim ignorance, evade such queries, and express interest in learning more. But as time went on and we had attended theological lectures, unwillingness to express personal judgements on the merits of the doctrine was increasingly viewed as implausible. In a movement which highly valued revealing one's "true heart," such professional detachment bordered on insincerity. The anti-cultists exerted their own form of pressure (i.e., to accept the

"brainwashing" model by which membership in the Unification Church was explained). This model assumed that coercive mind control techniques such as drugging, hypnosis, or outright seduction were employed by the Church to secure compliance and psychologically "enslave" members.

Pressure for behavioral participation derived from the simple fact that members of both groups were deeply involved in the day-to-day pursuit of their organizations' goals. To be with the groups meant literally to participate. For example, members of the Unification Church typically worked sixteen hour days at witnessing and fund raising, and so it was seldom possible to encounter them outside this round of activity. To observe and interview members in the course of these activities meant at least tacit approval of the latter. For example, when the authors accompanied Unification Church members on fund raising campaigns during which the members did not readily identify their affiliation, we made no attempt to correct these misrepresentations. Likewise, anti-cultists were always volunteers. A typical day in one of their houses, which served as a base of operations, saw them deluged with phone calls requesting or pledging support, and letters that had to be sorted, answered, and indexed. To stop work for a conversation or interview meant to fall several hours behind; hence as a "trade off" that also could be interpreted as tacit approval the authors had to "pitch in" and work along with informants in such activities as stuffing circulars into envelopes and copying addresses onto file cards. If this all sounds a little mundane, it must be remembered that the objective of all the group's activities was the destruction of cults. Hence, any participation, even clerical assistance, contributed to that end.

The implications of these sorts of pressures from each group took on a new significance in the dual group situation. Activities abetting either group, if known, could be interpreted by the other group (and perhaps rightfully so) as giving support to the "enemy." Thus the problem became to involve ourselves sufficiently to maintain rapport in the eyes of each group without engaging in activities so overtly partisan as to compromise our neutral image. A particularly perplexing problem arose with respect to the media. Each group requested our advocacy on local radio and television and in public meetings (e.g., church groups, PTA's, legislative hearings). Given the intense polarization of the two antagonists it was virtually impossible to discuss publicly the salient issues in any concrete detail without so offending one side or the other as to jeopardize our relationship with one or both. Explaining this dilemma openly to each side usually released us from the request but posed a further problem for them: exactly where *did* we stand on these issues?

In sum, pressures to go native were exacerbated additively by working simultaneously with two groups. Yet, as we mentioned in the previous section, each group was willing to tolerate "neutral" (i.e., non-partisan) inquiry insofar as this was useful to it, specifically in helping to eradicate myths and stereotypes about its members and lifestyle and to gain whatever prestige-by-association was available from having two social scientists on the premises. It must be admitted that likely neither group suspected we would remain non-partisan long once we had discovered the "truth," the "facts," and similar data. To reiterate, both groups subscribed to the assumption that to "really know" their respective positions was to come to believe in them.

PUBLIC PRESSURES TO TAKE A STAND

Not only were our respective informants interested in fostering a favorable public image through us, but also the various media and other interest groups solicited our opinions. Since we were viewed as among the relatively few informed experts on both sides of this conflict, it was difficult to avoid granting public interviews generated by public curiosity, fears, and rumors about the two groups. On the one hand, we knew that media coverage would be given to these events. For the

authors not to have granted interviews would have been to abdicate responsibility to less informed, more partisan individuals and to allow unfounded rumors to spread unchecked. On the other hand, any public statement ran the risk of severing laboriously built-up relationships. This problem was made more acute by virtue of the fact that the media were most interested in the spectacular and sensational and persisted in asking if such charges as "brainwashing" by the Unification Church or "kidnapping" by the anti-cultists were "really true."

Our solution to this dilemma was, first, to avoid interviews that seemed superficial, highly partisan, or exploitative, and, second, to attempt to portray the phenomena in all the complexity and to dispel obvious oversimplifications or caricatures about each group. On such an emotionally charged subject, however, it should be noted that this was at best a delicate and, from the standpoint of those who asked us, occasionally unsatisfying solution. For example, when we attempted to present an unbiased and complex view of the issues on a public affairs radio program which involved listener call-ins, we generated few call-ins and the show was terminated early by the announcer.

EVOLVING COMMITMENTS

As we have already noted in discussing the problem of role justification, information provided to us by either group had at least potentially negative implications for the other. Further, we observed that since each group valued true objectivity and neutrality only to a limited extent there was always some pressure on us to abandon our obvious detachment. However, as we sought highly sensitive "insider" information on organizational strategies and access to records and personal documents, we confronted the logical extension of the problems which we have termed the dilemma of evolving commitments. That is, as the research project with each group evolved, we discovered new sources of information of which we had previously been unaware. Further, as we acquired a more sophisticated understanding of the groups and the controversy between them we asked more probing questions. Gaining access to this more sensitive and confidential information made the authors' positions on issues and the uses to which organizational information would be put more critical to our informants. Not surprisingly, informants demanded clearer and more specific statements and assurances about the need for such sensitive data because of their greater investment in the project. As a result we found ourselves engaging in delicate negotiations concerning the details of our interpretations, walking the narrow path between revealing to informants the uses to which certain items of information would be put and allowing them to act as censors.

In the case of the Unification Church we were able to gain considerable information on the lifestyle of members by interviewing, witnessing, and fund raising teams passing though the state. However, we began to realize that it was imperative to obtain information on the national organization structure and gain access to private organizational records. Such information could be acquired only with the cooperation and consent of leaders and high ranking officials. In contrast to our initial interviewing activities, these new requests entailed greater risk, effort, and trust from them as organizational "gatekeepers." Therefore, we were required to submit an extensive list of the sorts of questions we wished to ask. Our past research on the subject (e.g., Bromley and Shupe, 1979; Shupe and Bromley, 1980) was extensively scrutinized and detailed criticisms were offered by Unification spokespersons in order to make their concerns explicit and to test our reactions. Indeed, literally dozens of phone calls and letters were needed to "clear" our visit to the Unification Theological Seminary and arrange interviews with officials in the New York City headquarters. Further, a member of the Seminary faculty was invited to campus prior to our visit in order to test fully our good will, honesty, and neutrality. Even with our elaborate efforts to achieve rapport some

factions within the Church were extremely skeptical of our intentions. This meant that those who were willing to cooperate with us really risked their own reputations. If our published work was perceived as unfavorable, their own credibility within their group would suffer. From an ethical standpoint this made us even more careful not to negotiate bargains that might be detrimental to those who cooperated with us.

With respect to the anti-cultists, we were freely sent newsletters, pamphlets, and other publications containing information on the organizational activities of the local groups. Leaders also talked openly with us at length on the phone and in person conveying details about many of their groups' meetings, activities, and strategy plans. However, other aspects of their involvements were much more private. They were particularly protective of family members who had been or currently were members of the Church. Former members usually were anxious to put their experiences behind them and hence were not easily available or receptive to interviews. Parents of current members were reluctant to reveal confidences about their son's or daughter's activities for fear of further eroding already strained relations with their offspring should their confidences somehow be made public. Anti-cultist parents thus faced a real dilemma: to withhold the intimate details of their son's or daughter's conversion reduced the persuasiveness of the allegations of "mind control," yet to reveal all the intimacies of their relationships to their son or daughter, unearthed conflicts, mistrust, and feelings of failure, was understandably difficult to share with outsiders. After a long period of building trust we were allowed to read materials such as a diary and personal family correspondence of former members. These contained the very personal reflections of the former member and the inner family conflict over Church membership. As a condition for receiving these materials we agreed to consult in advance with family members concerning any materials we wished to use and how we would use them. In these instances each informant was given the option of withdrawing their materials should they not approve of their use. We also attempted to intersperse such private materials with previously published accounts so as to camouflage the sources of the most confidential materials.

As each group began requiring more explicit assurances regarding our use of materials, we found ourselves increasingly enmeshed in a series of constraining bargains. Our deepening involvement with each group thus placed greater and greater constraints on our ability to negotiate freely with the other. For example, the anti-cultists were relatively accepting of our spending time with Church mobile fund raising and witnessing teams passing through the metropolitan area since we were perceived as simply "checking out the Moonies." However, when we invited a member of the Seminary faculty to the University in order to build rapport sufficient to gain access to national level organizational records, the anti-cultists demanded an explanation. We were, after all, providing the Church with a public forum with which to spread its message and associating our own and the University's names with the Church. Correspondingly the Church never openly questioned our contacts with the anti-cultists. However, the knowledge we obtained from the Church limited the relationship which we could maintain with the anti-cultists. We became aware of the location of a substantial number of members whose families opposed their membership in the Church and might well have made an effort to remove them from the Church had they known their whereabouts. Obviously, we could not discuss such matters with the anti-cultists without violating implicit confidences. There was no simple solution to this problem. We could only hope, by minimizing the frequency of such "deals," to conform to the pragmatic realities of researching sensitive topics with anxious people who did not always share our research goals, yet not compromising our own perspectives.

Moreover, as we gained access to increasingly more confidential information, informants on both sides were not simply concerned that *we* might

misinterpret or mishandle whatever sensitive information they gave us; they also expressed reservations that their *opponents* might use our findings, whatever our intentions, against them. This was particularly true of Unification Church leaders who regarded much of our previous research in this area, while technically "neutral" by social science standards, as nevertheless open to misinterpretation by anti-cultists. For example, the New York headquarters had previously supplied us with a national sample of almost two hundred of the most virulent "atrocity stories" told against the Church by bitter ex-members. Our content analysis of these examined the formulation and perpetuation of such tales by the media in the context of the labeling theory (see Bromley, Shupe, and Ventimiglia, 1979), but our failure to follow up our analysis with criticisms of the stories' validity was regarded as a mark against us by the Church. The anti-cultists, too, while inviting us to periodic "strategy" meetings, requested that we not mention the times and locations to others lest the Unification Church (or other groups) inadvertently find out and attempt to infiltrate them.

GAINING COMPARABLE INFORMATION AND INSIGHTS

All comparative social research confronts the problem of gathering comparable data; unless the bulk of the observations in one group have some parallel in the other group, meaningful generalizations will be difficult to formulate. In this research the two groups were alike in some important respects. Both contained numerous factions and so for both considerable effort was necessary to insure that positions attributed to the organization as a whole were in fact not just representative of local interests. Both had considerable turnover in leadership and rank and file memberships, hence strategies and activities tended to change with the composition of the group. This meant that keeping abreast of policy and personnel entailed almost constant monitoring. Both were relatively mistrustful of "outsiders," seeing themselves as underdogs in the conflict, which meant that considerable effort had to be exerted simply to gain entry and to maintain rapport.

There were also significant differences between the groups, however. Although the local groups within the Unification Church were relatively autonomous, there was an ultimate center of authority in Reverend Moon. The anti-cultists by contrast never formed a national organization which was more than a loose coalition despite considerable effort to do so. Thus we were able to obtain more information about the Unification Church by visiting its national headquarters than we were about the anti-cultists by visiting their coordinating center. Since the anti-cultists kept fewer organizational records, we were more dependent on personal communications and therefore were under greater pressure to bargain for important information. The Unificationist ideology was clearly stated in the *Divine Principle* and a host of other official Church publications. By contrast the anti-cultist ideology was less fully developed; there was no consensus on the definition of "cult," "brainwashing," "deprogramming," or other concepts crucial to their world view. Further, their writings were generally contained in what librarians refer to as "fugitive publications" (i.e., informally published, uncopyrighted pamphlets and newsletters). What this meant was that it was relatively easy to comprehend Unification thought and gauge the range of ideological diversity. By contrast it was difficult to summarize the anti-cultists' ideology or to measure the degree to which it was actually shown.

The lifestyle of anti-cultists lent itself much more readily to observation than did that of Unification Church members. For example, anti-cultists, like the authors, held conventional middle class occupations with regularly scheduled work hours. Thus free time for anti-cultists and the authors tended to coincide. By contrast, Unification Church members worked long days with unpredictable schedules and little free time. As a result we found it much more demanding to fulfill our

other role obligations and still find sufficient time for lengthy interview/observation with Unification Church members. Further, anti-cultist members had permanent residences while many Unification Church members were constantly on the move. So while it was possible, for example, with the anti-cultists to observe the lifestyle of members, changes in individuals' philosophies, and degree of commitment to the organization, such observations were much more difficult for Unification Church members.

SUMMARY AND CONCLUSIONS

Sociologists engaged in participant observation have defined a number of methodological problems in conducting investigations on single groups. In this paper we have discussed five such problems in the context of comparative participant observation: (1) role definition and justification; (2) pressures to go native; (3) public pressures to take a stand; (4) evolving commitments; and (5) gaining comparable information and insights.

Studying two groups simultaneously raised the problem of gaining comparable data on each group. Since the Unification Church and anti-cultists differ in some important respects, time and effort had to be expended differentially with the two groups to insure comparability. We also found that, since the two groups were involved in ongoing conflict, our relationships with each was a source of strain *vis-a-vis* the other. Each group had an interest in gaining our acceptance of its world view and in minimizing our involvement with the other side. A variety of other interest groups, principally among the media, wanted us to provide "expert opinion" on the highly visible controversy. We found that these pressures, although external to the research project itself, had considerable impact upon it. As we began to need more detailed and confidential information from each group, we had to negotiate more and more explicit and constraining bargains regarding its use, but our ability to agree to such bargains with either group was at least partially compromised by relationships with the other.

For most of these problems there was no single ideal solution since the problems developed along with the research project and they constantly presented themselves in new contexts. Our ongoing efforts to resolve these problems involved: developing forthright relations with both groups, participating with each group only to the extent required to remain compatible with the role definition conveyed to each group, and negotiating only those bargains requisite to obtain necessary information and protect our informants. Finally, in the absence of a pre-existing body of guidelines or theory in comparative participant observation, we were forced to develop our own ad hoc solutions to the five problems discussed. In the future as sociologists of social movements confront similar comparative problems we anticipate more attention will be given to these methodological issues.

REFERENCES

Becker, Howard
1967 "Whose side are we on?" Social Problems 14:239–47.
1958 "Problems of inference and proof in participant observation." American Sociological Review 23:652–60.

Blum, Fred H.
1952 "Getting individuals to give information to the outsider." Journal of Social Issues 8:35–42.
1979a " 'Just a few years seem like a lifetime': A role theory approach to participation in religious movements." in Louis Kriesberg (ed.), Research in Social Movements, Conflict, and Change. Greenwich, Connecticut: JAI Press.
1979b "Emerging foci in participant observation: Research as an emerging process." in W. Shaffir, A. Turowitz, and R. Stebbins (eds.), The Social Experience of Field Work. New York: St. Martin's Press.

Bromley, David G., Anson D. Shupe, Jr., and Joseph C. Ventimiglia
1979 "Atrocity tales, the Unification Church, and the social construction of evil." Journal of Communication 29(Summer):42–53.

Douglas, Jack D.
1972 "Observing deviance." Pp. 3–34 in Jack D. Douglas (ed.), Research on Deviance. New York: Random House.

Fichter, Joseph H. and William L. Kolb
1953 "Ethical limitations on sociological reporting." American Sociological Review 18: 544–50.

Grimshaw, Allen
1973 "Comparative sociology: In what ways different from other sociologies?" Pp. 3–48 in M. Armer and A. D. Grimshaw (eds.), Comparative Social Research: Methodological Problems and Strategies. New York: Wiley.

Shaffir, William, Allan Turowetz, and Robert Stebbins (eds.)
1979 The Social Experience of Field Work. New York: St. Martin's Press (in press).

Shupe, Jr., Anson D. and David G. Bromley
1980 "Some continuities in American religion: Witches, Moonies, and accusations of evil." in Thomas Robbins and Dick Anthony (eds.), In Gods We Trust: New Patterns of American Religious Pluralism. Rutgers, New Jersey: Transaction Press.

Shupe, Jr., Anson D., Robert Spielmann, and Sam Snigall.
1977a "Deprogramming: The new exorcism." American Behavioral Scientist 20:941–56.
1977b "Deprogramming and the emerging American anti-cult movement." Paper presented at the Annual Meeting of the Society for the Scientific Study of Religion.

Shupe, Jr., Anson D., Joseph C. Ventimiglia, David G. Bromley, and Sam Stigall
1977 "Political control of radically innovative religions." Paper presented at the Annual Meeting of the Association for the Scientific Study of Religion: Southwest.

Stoner, Carroll and Jo Ann Parke
1977 All Gods Children. Radnor, Penn.: Chilton.

Trice, H.M.
1970 "The 'outsider's' role in field study." Pp. 77–82 in William J. Filstead (ed.), Qualitative Sociology. Chicago: Markham.

Vidich, Arthur

1970 "Participant observation and the collection and interpretation of data." Pp. 164–73 in William J. Filstead (ed.), Qualitative Sociology. Chicago: Markham.

Weinberg, Martin S. and Colin J. Williams

1972 "Fieldwork among deviants: Social relations with subjects and others." Pp. 165–186 in Jack D. Douglas (ed.), Research on Deviance. New York: Random House.

TAKING ANOTHER LOOK

1 How did the researchers initially come to be participant-observers in Citizens Engaged in Freeing Minds (CEFM) and the Unification Church?

2 How did the professional sociologist-researcher role influence the authors' study of the Unification Church and the anticult network?

3 In what specific ways did the researchers actually participate in the group's activities?

4 In your view, did the authors of the study compromise their neutrality or objectivity in any ways?

5 What ethical problems faced the researchers as they gained sensitive information about the Unification Church and the anti-cult network?

6 Which group did the reseachers find more difficult to observe? Why?

7 What additional ethical problems would have faced the researchers had they decided to conceal their professional identities and participate in these organizations as if they were genuine members?

Tearoom Trade: Impersonal Sex in Public Places

Laud Humphreys

The *Code of Professional Ethics* published by the American Sociological Association, most recently revised in 1984, emphasizes that sociologists must maintain objectivity and integrity in research, respect the subject's right to privacy and dignity, protect subjects from personal harm, and preserve confidentiality. While no one would question these admirable general principles, many delicate ethical issues cannot be resolved simply by consulting this list.

In the following selection, a famous and highly controversial example of participant-observation research, sociologist Laud Humphreys studied casual homosexual encounters between males meeting in public restrooms in parks. Such restrooms are sometimes called "tearooms" by homosexual men. In order to study the lifestyles of men engaging in such casual sex, Humphreys served as a "lookout," warning patrons when police or other patrons approached.

Humphreys wanted to learn more about who these men were and why they took such risks. Yet most of the men in the tearooms were unaware of Humphrey's identity and would not have consented to standard sociological interviews. As a result, Humphreys decided on a research technique that some social scientists later saw as a violation of professional ethics. He recorded the license plate numbers of tearoom patrons, waited a year, changed his appearance, and then interviewed them in their homes. The interviews were conducted as part of a larger survey, but they did provide information that Humphreys felt was necessary for his work. Humphreys exerted great care in maintaining the confidentiality of his subjects. Their real identities were recorded only on a master list kept in a safe-deposit box. The list was destroyed by Humphreys after the research was conducted.

For social scientists, the ethical problem in this research was not Humphreys's choice of subject matter but, rather, the deception involved. Patrons of the tearoom were not aware of Humphreys's purposes and were further misled about the real reasons for the household interviews. However, in the researcher's judgment, the value of his study justified the questionable means involved.

Humphreys believed that, without the follow-up interviews, we would know little about the kinds of men who engage in tearoom sex and would be left with false stereotypes. Humphreys learned that most of his subjects were in their middle thirties and married. They had an average of two children and tended to have at least some years of college education. Family members appeared to be unaware of the men's visits to park restrooms for casual homosexual encounters.

At shortly after five o'clock on a weekday evening, four men enter a public restroom in the city park. One wears a well-tailored business suit; another wears tennis shoes, shorts and teeshirt; the third man is still clad in the khaki uniform of his filling station; the last, a salesman, has loosened his tie and left his sports coat in the car. What has caused these men to leave the company of other homeward-bound commuters on the freeway? What common interest brings these men, with their divergent backgrounds, to this public facility?

They have come here not for the obvious reason, but in a search for "instant sex." Many men—married and unmarried, those with heterosexual identities and those whose self-image is a homosexual one—seek such impersonal sex, shunning involvement, desiring kicks without commitment. Whatever reasons—social, physiological or psychological—might be postulated for this search, the phenomenon of impersonal sex persists as a widespread but rarely studied form of human interaction.

There are several settings for this type of deviant activity—the balconies of movie theaters, automobiles, behind bushes—but few offer the advantages for these men that public restrooms provide. "Tearooms," as these facilities are called in the language of the homosexual subculture, have several characteristics that make them attractive as locales for sexual encounters without involvement.

Like most other words in the homosexual vocabulary the origin of *tearoom* is unknown. British slang has used "tea" to denote "urine." Another British usage is as a verb, meaning "to engage with, encounter, go in against." According to its most precise meaning in the argot, the only "true" tearoom is one that gains a reputation as a place where homosexual encounters occur. Presumably, any restroom could qualify for this distinction, but comparatively few are singled out at any one time. For instance, I have researched a metropolitan area with more than 90 public toilets in its parks, only 20 of which are in regular use as locales for sexual games. Restrooms thus designated join the company of automobiles and bathhouses as places for deviant sexual activity second only to private bedrooms in popularity. During certain seasons of the year—roughly, that period from April through October that midwestern homosexuals call "the hunting season"—tearooms may surpass any other locale of homoerotic enterprise in volume of activity.

Public restrooms are chosen by those who want homoerotic activity without commitment for a number of reasons. They are accessible, easily recognized by the initiate, and provide little public visibility. Tearooms thus offer the advantages of both public and private settings. They are available and recognizable enough to attract a large volume of potential sexual partners, providing an opportunity for rapid action with a variety of men. When added to the relative privacy of these settings, such features enhance the impersonality of the sheltered interaction.

In the first place, tearooms are readily accessible to the male population. They may be located in any sort of public gathering place: department stores, bus stations, libraries, hotels, YMCAs or courthouses. In keeping with the drive-in craze of American society, however, the more popular facilities are those readily accessible to the roadways. The restrooms of public parks and beaches—and more recently the rest stops set at programmed intervals along superhighways—are now attracting the clientele that, in a more pedestrian age, frequented great buildings of the inner cities. My research is focused on the activity that takes place in the restrooms of public parks, not only because (with some seasonal variation) they provide the most action but also because of other factors that make them suitable for sociological study.

There is a great deal of difference in the volumes of homosexual activity that these accommodations shelter. In some, one might wait for months before observing a deviant act (unless solitary masturbation is considered deviant). In others, the volume approaches orgiastic dimensions. One summer afternoon, for instance, I witnessed 20 acts of fellatio in the course of an hour while waiting out a thunderstorm in a tearoom. For one who wishes to participate in (or study) such activity, the primary consideration is finding where the action is. . . .

WHAT THEY WANT, WHEN THEY WANT IT

The availability of facilities they can recognize attracts a great number of men who wish, for whatever reason, to engage in impersonal homoerotic activity. Simple observation is enough to guide these participants, the researcher and, perhaps, the police to active tearooms. It is much more difficult to make an accurate appraisal of the proportion of the male population who engage in such activity over a representative length of time. Even with good sampling procedures, a large staff of assistants would be needed to make the observations necessary for an adequate census of this mobile population. All that may be said with some degree of certainty is that the percentage of the male population who participate in tearoom sex in the United States is somewhat less that the 16 percent of the adult white male population Kinsey found to have "at least as much of the homosexual as the heterosexual in their histories." . . .

Of the bar crowd in gay (homosexual) society, only a small percentage would be found in park restrooms. But this more overt, gay bar clientele constitutes a minor part of those in any American city who follow a predominantly homosexual pattern. The so-called closet queens and other types of covert deviants make up the vast majority of those who engage in homosexual acts—and these are the persons most attracted to tearoom encounters.

Tearooms are popular, not because they serve as gathering places for homosexuals but because they attract a variety of men, a *minority* of whom are active in the homosexual subculture and a large group of whom have no homosexual self-identity. For various reasons, they do not want to be seen with those who might be identified as such or to become involved with them on a "social" basis. . . .

PEOPLE NEXT DOOR

Tearoom activity attracts a large number of participants—enough to produce the majority of arrests for homosexual offenses in the United States. Now, employing data gained from both formal and informal interviews, we shall consider

what these men are like away from the scenes of impersonal sex. "For some people," says Evelyn Hooker, an authority on male homosexuality, "the seeking of sexual contacts with other males is an activity isolated from all other aspects of their lives." Such segregation is apparent with most men who engage in the homosexual activity of public restrooms; but the degree and manner in which "deviant" is isolated from "normal" behavior in their lives will be seen to vary along social dimensions.

For the man who lives next door, the tearoom participant is just another neighbor—and probably a very good one at that. He may make a little more money than the next man and work a little harder for it. It is likely that he will drive a nicer car and maintain a neater yard than do other neighbors in the block. Maybe, like some tearoom regulars, he will work with Boy Scouts in the evenings and spend much of his weekend at the church. It may be more surprising for the outsider to discover that most of these men are married.

Indeed, 54 percent of my research subjects are married and living with their wives. From the data at hand, there is no evidence that these unions are particularly unstable; nor does it appear that any of the wives are aware of their husbands' secret sexual activity. Indeed, the husbands choose public restrooms as sexual settings partly to avoid just such exposure. I see no reason to dispute the claim of a number of tearoom respondents that their preference for a form of concerted action that is fast and impersonal is largely predicated on a desire to protect their family relationships.

Superficial analysis of the data indicates that the maintenance of exemplary marriages—at least in appearance—is very important to the subjects of this study. In answering questions such as "When it comes to making decisions in your household, who generally makes them?" the participants indicate they are more apt to defer to their mates than are those in the control sample. They also indicate that they find it more important to "get along well" with their wives. In the open-ended questions regarding marital relationships, they tend to speak of them in more glowing terms.

TOM AND MYRA

This handsome couple live in ranch-style suburbia with their two young children. Tom is in his early thirties—an aggressive, muscular and virile-looking male. He works "about 75 hours a week" at his new job as a chemist. "I am *wild* about my job," he says. "I really love it!" Both of Tom's "really close" friends he met at work.

He is a Methodist and Myra a Roman Catholic, but each goes to his or her own church. Although he claims to have broad interests in life, they boil down to "games—sports like touch football or baseball."

When I asked him to tell me something about his family, Tom replied only in terms of their "good fortune" that things are not worse:

> We've been fortunate that a religious problem has not occurred. We're fortunate in having two healthy children. We're fortunate that we decided to leave my last job. Being married has made me more stable.

They have been married for eleven years, and Myra is the older of the two. When asked who makes what kinds of decisions in his family, he said: "She makes most decisions about the family. She keeps the books. But I make the *major* decisions."

Myra does the household work and takes care of the children. Perceiving his main duties as those of "keeping the yard up" and "bringing home the bacon," Tom sees as his wife's only shortcoming "her lack of discipline in organization." He remarked: "She's very attractive . . . has a fair amount of poise. The best thing is that she gets along well and is able to establish close relationships with other women."

Finally, when asked how he thinks his wife feels about him and his behavior in the family, Tom replied: "She'd like to have me around

more—would like for me to have a closer relationship with her and the kids." He believes it is "very important" to have the kind of sex life he needs. Reporting that he and Myra have intercourse about twice a month, he feels that his sexual needs are "adequately met" in his relationships with his wife. I also know that, from time to time, Tom has sex in the restrooms of a public park.

As an upwardly mobile man, Tom was added to the sample at a point of transition in his career as a tearoom participant. If Tom is like others who share working class origins, he may have learned of the tearoom as an economical means of achieving orgasm during his navy years. Of late, he has returned to the restrooms for occasional sexual "relief," since his wife, objecting to the use of birth control devices, has limited his conjugal outlets.

Tom still perceives his sexual needs in the symbolic terms of the class in which he was socialized: "about twice a month" is the frequency of intercourse generally reported by working class men; and, although they are reticent in reporting it, they do not perceive this frequency as adequate to meet their sexual needs, which they estimate are about the same as those felt by others of their age. My interviews indicate that such perceptions of sexual drive and satisfaction prevail among respondents of the lower-middle to upper-lower classes, whereas they are uncommon for those of the upper-middle and upper classes. Among the latter, the reported perception is of a much higher frequency of intercourse and they estimate their needs to be greater than those of "most other men." . . .

STYLES OF DEVIANT ADAPTATION

. . . It should now be evident that, like other next door neighbors, the participants in tearoom sex are of no one type. They vary along a number of possible continua of social characteristics. They differ widely in terms of sexual career and activity, and even in terms of what that behavior means to them or what sort of needs it may fulfill. Act-

THE SOCIOLOGIST AS VOYEUR

The methods employed in this study of men who engage in restroom sex are the outgrowth of three ethical assumptions: First, I do not believe the social scientist should ever ignore or avoid an area of research simply because it is difficult or socially sensitive. Second, he should approach any aspect of human behavior with those means that least distort the observed phenomena. Third, he must protect respondents from harm—regardless of what such protection may cost the researcher.

Because the majority of arrests on homosexual charges in the United States result from encounters in public restrooms, I felt this form of sexual behavior to provide a legitimate, even essential, topic for sociological investigation. In our society the social control forces, not the criminologist, determine what the latter shall study.

Following this decision, the question is one of choosing research methods which permit the investigator to achieve maximum fidelity to the world he is studying. I believe ethnographic methods are the only truly empirical ones for the social scientist. When human behavior is being examined, systematic observation is essential; so I had to become a participant-observer of furtive, felonious acts.

Fortunately, the very fear and suspicion of tearoom participants produces a mechanism that makes such observation: a third man (generally one who obtains voyeuristic pleasure from his duties) serves as a lookout, moving back and forth from door to windows. Such a "watchqueen," as he is labeled in the homosexual argot, coughs when a police car stops nearby or when a stranger approaches. He nods affirmatively when he recognizes a man entering as being a "regular." Having been taught the watchqueen role by a cooperating respondent, I played that part faithfully while observing hundreds of acts of fellatio. After developing a systematic observation sheet, I recorded fifty of these encounters (involving 53 sexual acts) in great detail. These records were compared with another 30 made by a cooperating respondent who was himself a sexual participant. The bulk of information presented in *Tearoom Trade* results from these observations.

Although primarily interested in the stigmatized behavior, I also wanted to know about the men who take such risks for a few moments of impersonal sex. I was able to engage a number of participants in conversation outside the restrooms; and, eventually, by revealing the purpose of my study to them, I gained a dozen respondents who contributed hundreds of hours of interview time. This sample I knew to be biased in favor of the more outgoing and better educated of the tearoom population.

To overcome this bias, I cut short a number of my observations of encounters and hurried to my automobile. There, with the help of a tape recorder, I noted a brief description of each participant, his sexual role in the encounter just observed, his license number and a brief description of his car. I varied such records from park to park and to correspond with previously observed changes in volume at various times of the day. This provided me with a time-and-place-representative sample of 134 participants. With attrition, chiefly of those who had changed address or who drove rented cars, and the addition of two persons who walked to the tearooms, I ended up with a sample of 100 men, each of whom I had actually observed engaging in fellatio.

At this stage, my third ethical concern impinged. I already knew that many of my respondents were married and that all were in a highly discreditable position and fearful of discovery. How could I approach these covert deviants for interviews? By passing as deviant, I had observed their sexual behavior without disturbing it. Now, I was faced with interviewing these men (often in the presence of their wives) without destroying them. Fortunately, I held another research job which placed me in the position of preparing the interview schedule for a social health survey of a random selection of male subjects throughout the community. With permission from the survey's directors, I could add my sample to the larger group (thus enhancing their anonymity) and interview them as part of the social health survey.

To overcome the danger of having a subject recognize me as a watchqueen, I changed my hair style, attire and automobile. At the risk of losing more transient respondents, I waited a year between the sample gathering and the interviews, during which time I took notes on their homes and neighborhoods and acquired data on them from the city and county directories.

Having randomized the sample, I completed 50 interviews with tearoom participants and added another 50 interviews from the social health survey sample. The latter control group was matched with the participants on the bases of marital status, race, job classification and area of residence.

This study, then, results from a confluence of strategies: systematic, first-hand observation, in-depth interviews with available respondents, the use of archival data, and structured interviews of a representative sample and a matched control group. At each level of research, I applied those measures which provided maximum protection for research subjects and the truest measurement of persons and behavior observed.

ing in response to a variety of pressures toward deviance (some of which we may never ascertain), their adaptations follow a number of lines of least resistance.

In delineating styles of adaptation, I do not intend to imply that these men are faced with an array of styles from which they may pick one or even a combination. No man's freedom is that great. They have been able to choose only among the limited options offered them by society. These sets of alternatives, which determine the modes of adaptation to deviant pressures, are defined and allocated in accordance with major sociological variables: occupation, marital status, age, race, amount of education. That is one meaning of social probability.

TAKING ANOTHER LOOK

1 What led Humphreys to conclude that the tearoom participants were like "the people next door"?
2 In what ways were the subjects interviewed outside the tearooms unrepresentative of all participants?
3 What were the three ethical assumptions that guided Humphreys in studying men who engage in tearoom sex?
4 In your view, did the value of Humphreys's study justify the deception of interview subjects?

ORGANIZING SOCIAL LIFE

Sociologist Peter Berger once observed that the "sociologist is a person intensively, endlessly, shamelessly interested" in the doings of people. In Part Two, we begin our study of the organization of social life within human communities and societies.

We first examine the basic element of any society: its culture. Clyde Kluckhohn ("Queer Customs") chronicles the diversity evident in the world's cultures and emphasizes the importance of respecting cultural differences. Eldon E. Snyder and Elmer A. Spreitzer ("Baseball in Japan") show that when a society absorbs a sport from a competing culture, it will modify that sport to more closely resemble the distinctive native culture. Edward T. Hall and Mildred Reed Hall ("The Sounds of Silence") focus on the foundation of any culture—its language—and on the hidden dynamics of nonverbal communication.

We acquire the attitudes and values of a particular culture through the lifelong process of socialization. As one aspect of this learning process, children are exposed to cultural assumptions regarding sex differences. Myra and David Sadker ("Sexism in the Schoolroom of the '80s") examine differential treatment of boys and girls by their teachers. Howard S. Becker and Blanche Geer ("The Fate of Idealism in Medical School") remind us that occupational socialization continues throughout the human life cycle as people absorb the standards of appropriate behavior for specific occupations.

The term *social structure* refers to the total pattern of organization of a society into predictable relationships. This concept is central to sociological study; it focuses on how different aspects of behavior are related to one another. Culture represents the elements of a society, while social structure defines the ways and processes by which these elements are organized. Peter Berger ("The Importance of Role") focuses on social roles as a significant element of social structure. David L. Rosenhan ("On Being Sane in Insane Places") underscores the power of social structure by illustrating the impact of labeling people as mentally ill. Jean Bethke

Elshtain ("A Key to Unlock the Asylum") shows that changing the social structure, through intended social reforms, can have unexpected and unfortunate consequences.

Groups and organizations play a vital part in a society's social structure. Much of our patterned behavior takes place within groups and is influenced by the norms and sanctions established by groups. Irving L. Janis ("Groupthink") analyzes undesirable group processes evident in governmental decision-making teams. Peter Blau and Marshall W. Meyer ("The Concept of Bureaucracy") draw upon the writings of pioneering German sociologist Max Weber in order to explore the basic characteristics of formal organizations.

Not all behavior conforms to the expectations of society. However, as Martin S. Weinberg ("Sexual Modesty, Social Meanings, and the Nudist Camp") demonstrates, even people who deviate from social norms may establish their own standards of appropriate behavior. William J. Chambliss ("The Saints and the Roughnecks") points to the power of authorities to label certain individuals (and not others) as "deviant" even when their behavior is similar. Mark Fishman ("Crime Waves as Ideology") extends this type of analysis even further by suggesting that authorities can significantly influence public perceptions regarding crime and crime waves.

Queer Customs

Clyde Kluckhohn

Viewed from the perspective of sociology, *culture* is the totality of learned, socially transmitted behavior. It includes not only items such as sailboats, comic books, and birth control devices, but also the ideas, values, and customs of groups of people. In sociological terms, culture does not refer solely to the fine arts and refined intellectual taste; it consists of *all* objects and ideas within a society.

In the following selection, the noted anthropologist Clyde Kluckhohn offers a similar view of culture. He introduces vivid examples of cultural differences among peoples and emphasizes that people often feel that their cultural practices are "normal" while the customs of others are "strange" or inferior. Certainly this is true of a teacher described by Kluckhohn who fails to understand or to respect the culture of her Navaho students. Sociologists use the term *ethnocentrism* to refer to the tendency to assume that one's culture or way of life is superior to all others.

Why do the Chinese dislike milk and milk products? Why would the Japanese die willingly in a Banzai charge that seemed senseless to Americans? Why do some nations trace descent through the father, others through the mother, still others through both parents? Not because different peoples have different instincts, not because they were destined by God or Fate to different habits, not because the weather is different in China and Japan and the United States. Sometimes shrewd common sense has an answer that is close to that of the anthropologist: "because they were brought up that way." By "culture" anthropology means the total life way of a people, the social legacy the individual acquires from his group. Or culture can be regarded as that part of the environment that is the creation of man.

This technical term has a wider meaning than the "culture" of history and literature. A humble cooking pot is as much a cultural product as is a Beethoven sonata. In ordinary speech a man of culture is a man who can speak languages other than his own, who is familiar with history, literature, philosophy, or the fine arts. In some cliques that definition is still narrower. The cultured person is one who can talk about James Joyce, Scarlatti, and Picasso. To the anthropologist, however, to be human is to be cultured. There is culture in general, and then there are the specific cultures such as Russian, American, British, Hottentot, Inca. The general abstract notion serves to remind us that we cannot explain acts solely in terms of the biological properties of the people concerned, their individual past experience, and the immediate situation. The past experience of other men in the form of culture enters into almost every event. Each specific culture constitutes a kind of blueprint for all of life's activities.

One of the interesting things about human beings is that they try to understand themselves and their own behavior. While this has been particularly true of Europeans in recent times, there is no group which has not developed a scheme or schemes to explain man's actions. To the insistent human query "why?" the most exciting illumination anthropology has to offer is that of the concept of culture. Its explanatory importance is comparable to categories such as evolution in biology, gravity in physics, disease in medicine. A good deal of human behavior can be understood, and indeed predicted, if we know a people's design for living. Many acts are neither accidental nor due to personal peculiarities nor caused by supernatural forces nor simply mysterious. Even those of us who pride ourselves on our individualism follow most of the time a pattern not of our own making. We brush our teeth on arising. We put on pants—not a loincloth or a grass skirt. We eat three meals a day—not four or five or two. We sleep in a bed—not in a hammock or on a sheep pelt. I do not have to know the individual and his life history to be able to predict these and countless other regularities, including many in the thinking process, of all Americans who are not incarcerated in jails or hospitals for the insane.

To the American woman a system of plural wives seems "instinctively" abhorrent. She cannot understand how any woman can fail to be jealous and uncomfortable if she must share her husband with other women. She feels it "unnatural" to accept such a situation. On the other hand, a Koryak woman of Siberia, for example, would find it hard to understand how a woman could be so selfish and so undesirous of feminine companionship in the home as to wish to restrict her husband to one mate.

Some years ago I met in New York City a young man who did not speak a word of English and was obviously bewildered by American ways. By "blood" he was as American as you or I, for his parents had gone from Indiana to China as missionaries. Orphaned in infancy, he was reared by a Chinese family in a remote village. All who met him found him more Chinese than American. The facts of his blue eyes and light hair were less impressive than a Chinese style of gait, Chinese arm and hand movements, Chinese facial expression, and Chinese modes of thought. The biological heritage was American, but the cultural training had been Chinese. He returned to China.

Another example of another kind: I once knew a trader's wife in Arizona who took a somewhat devilish interest in producing a cultural reaction. Guests who came her way were often served delicious sandwiches filled with a meat that seemed to be neither chicken nor tuna fish yet was reminiscent of both. To queries she gave no reply until each had eaten his fill. She then explained that what they had eaten was not chicken, not tuna fish, but the rich, white flesh of freshly killed rattlesnakes. The response was instantaneous—vomiting, often violent vomiting. A biological process is caught in a cultural web.

A highly intelligent teacher with long and successful experience in the public schools of Chicago was finishing her first year in an Indian school. When asked how her Navaho pupils compared in intelligence with Chicago youngsters, she replied, "Well, I just don't know. Sometimes the Indians seem just as bright. At other times they just act like dumb animals. The other night we had a dance in the high school. I saw a boy who is one of the best students in my English class standing off by himself. So I took him over to a pretty girl and told them to dance. But they just stood there with their heads down. They wouldn't even say anything." I inquired if she knew whether or not they were members of the same clan. "What difference would that make?"

"How would you feel about getting into bed with your brother?" The teacher walked off in a huff, but, actually, the two cases were quite comparable in principle. To the Indian the type of bodily contact involved in our social dancing has a directly sexual connotation. The incest taboos between members of the same clan are as severe as between true brothers and sisters. The shame of the Indians at the suggestion that a clan brother and sister should dance and the indignation of the white teacher at the idea that she should share a bed with an adult brother represent equally nonrational responses, culturally standardized unreason. . . .

Americans are now at a period in history when they are faced with the facts of cultural differences more clearly than they can take with comfort. Recognition and tolerance of the deeper cultural assumptions of China, Russia, and Britain will require a difficult type of education. But the great lesson of culture is that the goals toward which men strive and fight and grope are not "given" in final form by biology nor yet entirely by the situation. If we understand our own culture and that of others, the political climate can be changed in a surprisingly short time in this narrow contemporary world providing men are wise enough and articulate enough and energetic enough.

TAKING ANOTHER LOOK

1 How do anthropologists use the term *culture*?
2 What does the experience of the Indiana-born youth raised in China tell us about culture?
3 Describe two examples of ethnocentrism that you have personally witnessed.
4 Why are conflict theorists especially likely to be critical of ethnocentrism?

Baseball in Japan

Eldon E. Snyder and Elmer A. Spreitzer

Sociologists use the term *diffusion* to refer to the process by which a cultural item is spread from group to group or from society to society. A culture may adopt ideas, technology, or customs from other cultures. However, diffusion of cultural traits does not occur automatically. Groups and societies resist ideas that seem too foreign or those that are perceived as threatening to their own beliefs and values. Each culture tends to be somewhat selective in what it absorbs from competing cultures. For example, Europe accepted silk, the magnetic compass, chess, and gunpowder from the Chinese, but rejected the teachings of Confucius as an ideology. Even when a society does absorb an idea or a custom from a competing culture, it often will modify the "alien" practice to more closely resemble the distinctive native culture.

In the following selection, sociologists Eldon E. Snyder and Elmer A. Spreitzer analyze the differences in American and Japanese baseball. Japanese baseball is an example of cultural diffusion; the sport originated in the United States and was introduced to Japanese students in 1873 by an American professor. Snyder and Spreitzer point out that while the structure of the game is similar in the two nations, the climate and texture of Japanese baseball have been deeply influenced by Japanese cultural values, such as self-discipline, self-sacrifice, and politeness.

The case of baseball in Japan represents an interesting example of the way in which cultural differences affect a particular sport. Although the structure of the game is basically the same as in North America, it is clear that the climate and texture of the game are very different in the two cultural settings. An American professor at Tokyo University introduced baseball to his students in 1873. The sport is now immensely popular and draws a crowd at all levels of competition. A national tournament at the high school level lasts ten days and draws about 500,000 spectators in addition to a nationwide television audience (Boersema, 1979, p. 28). At the college level, baseball is televised and draws a following akin to bigtime university rivalries in the United States. The professional baseball leagues attract about 12 million spectators in addition to huge television audiences; several games are broadcast simultaneously on weekend television. Professional baseball in Japan began in 1936 after Babe Ruth and a group of American players toured the country.

Japanese baseball is distinctive in a number of ways that Americans would find quaint. For example, the annual game of musical chairs wherein managers are "replaced" is foreign to Japan. Managers are rarely fired, and when it does take place, a stylized ritual is used to permit the former manager to save face. It is also interesting to note that in Japan baseball games can end in a tie, which is no doubt a reflection of the Japanese emphasis on *process* as well as product. Moreover, the manager and players emphasize the collective goal of winning the pennant even at the expense of individual careers. A manager may call on a star pitcher, therefore, whenever a game is critical. Star pitchers are also used for relief work which commonly results in only two days of rest between starts. Such a heavy use no doubt shortens a career. In a 1958 Japan series, one pitcher worked in six of the seven games, and he once won 42 games in a single season. His career ended at 26 years of age. Nevertheless, a player is unlikely to challenge the system since team loyalty is paramount (Boersema, 1979).

American teams have been playing regularly in Japan since 1951 on an invitational basis. During this period, the teams from America have compiled a record of 163–47–20 (won-lost-tie) against the Japanese teams. The consensus of the visitors is that the Japanese are very competitive in terms of fundamentals and basic skills but lack the strength and power of players from America (Boersema, 1979, p. 31). Two foreign players are allowed on each professional team in Japan. Most of the American players are superannuated veterans of the major leagues. The Japanese recruit the Americans with serious attention paid to personal character and personality traits. The objective is to recruit well-mannered and disciplined players who can adapt to the more structured Japanese system and who can bear the rigorous training schedule that begins in January.

It is relevant to note that sumo wrestling ranks as the second most popular sport in Japan, with baseball first. "Both are very ceremonial sports, both require of the competent spectator very minute and careful observation of the quick move made after rather long pauses for ritual and for mental preparation by the athletes" (Cleaver, 1976, p. 120). To the American observer, Japanese baseball seems authoritarian and highly ritualized; however, a brief discussion of traditional Japanese values will suggest that baseball simply mirrors the larger Japanese society. First of all, it might be noted that individualism and egotism are highly stigmatized personality traits in Japan; the following expressions illustrate the value of selflessness in Japanese society:

"Have no self."

"Be wrapped in something long."

"The nail that sticks up will be hammered down."

"If one had no selfish motives but only the supreme values, there would be no self."

"If he serves selflessly, he does not know what service is."

"If he knows what service is, he has a self."

"If you think that you work diligently, it is not true service."

"To think of merits and demerits is egotism."

"Because you do not act as you please, things will, conversely, turn out right for you."

(Minami, 1971, p. 11)

The teamwork that is evident on a Japanese baseball team is paralleled by a remarkable sense of solidarity among industrial workers in Japan (Cleaver, 1976, p. 101). There is a congruity between company policy and worker preferences that precludes alienated labor. Workers consult and advise one another on improved ways of doing a particular piece of work. Although individuals may hold disparate political views off the job, these theoretical differences do not intrude upon team efforts at work. Many leisure activities are organized through the employer as family recreation; this pattern is sometimes referred to as paternalism by Americans. Westerners continually express amazement at the work ethic of industrial workers in Japan. In 1972 an American visitor reported seeing a group of workers assembled one morning outside a factory waiting for the gates to open. While waiting they were singing the company song (Cleaver, 1976, p. 102).

One of the first character traits that Americans note in Japanese is their extreme politeness. The ceremonial and ritual etiquette associated with courtesy in Japan is expressed in a gradation of honorific language which is reflected in vocabulary as well as in grammar. La Barre's (1962) observations concerning Japanese politeness were originally published in 1945 and are therefore probably less applicable to contemporary Japan; nevertheless, his description of the Japanese character is interesting in terms of its contrast with American individualism.

By contrast, the Japanese pride themselves on their lack of selfish "individualism" and their willingness to pull together in conformity to the "Yamato spirit." Thus it is often extremely difficult in Japanese social relations . . . to get any clear idea on which side of the fence a given person stands, since everyone pretends there is no fence and since all of them seek the protective cloak of apparent conformity to public opinion. There is so much by-play and face-saving, that in the end the Japanese exasperate occidentals as being *emotionally masked* persons with no honesty of expression whatsoever, "inscrutable" and untrustworthy (p. 335).

Haring (1962, p. 389) interprets Japanese politeness as compliance with a code of behavior that specifies correct behavior vis á vis others as a means of maintaining face and one's own self-esteem. The operative question is, "Have I acted correctly?"

The Japanese concepts of self-discipline and self-sacrifice are linked with implicit assumptions concerning skill, competency, and expertness. Self-pity is a foreign concept, as is individual frustration. "In Japan one disciplines oneself to be a good player, and the Japanese attitude is that one undergoes the training with no more consciousness of sacrifice than a man who plays bridge. Of course the training is strict, but that is inherent in the nature of things" (Benedict, 1946, p. 233). Interestingly, competency drives out self-consciousness; thus when one is living in the plane of expertness, Japanese say that he or she is "living as one already dead." Through self-discipline an inherently difficult activity can be made to appear easy. This stress on "competent self-discipline" has some desirable consequences.

> They pay much closer attention to behaving competently and they allow themselves fewer alibis than Americans. They do not so often project their dissatisfactions with life upon scapegoats, and they do not so often indulge in self-pity because they have somehow or other not got what Americans call average happiness. They have been trained to pay much closer attention to the 'rust of the body' than is common among Americans (Benedict, 1946, p. 235).

The highly explicit codes of behavior in Japan account for the structured nature of the individual's response; behavior has the quality of being thoroughly planned. Spontaneous behavior is not admired. The mature individual is assumed to an-

ticipate all emergencies and to be able to meet them calmly. Display of emotion is discouraged (Haring, 1962, p. 389). Similarly, a person who is touchy or easily affronted evidences an insecure ego. In child raising the parents make it clear that claims of the individual ego are to be systematically suppressed. In order to preserve face, "there must therefore be not only a constant checking and correcting of behavior, but also an anxious concern lest any lapse be publicly noted" (LaBarre, 1962, p. 341).

This description of Japanese personality traits and cultural values explains why baseball is so different in the two countries—sport is a value receptacle for society. A respect for authority, devotion to the collectivity and self-discipline would understandably be conducive to team harmony. In Japanese baseball, doing your own thing is strongly stigmatized—salary disputes, asking for individual exemptions from team policies, temper tantrums, moodiness, complaining, clubhouse lawyers, attacking the umpire, criticizing the manager, mouthing-off to the media, bad-mouthing teammates, violation of training rules, fist fights, and *ad nauseam*. American players in Japan who have behaved in a selfish manner have experienced prompt and strong sanctions (Objski, 1975; Whiting, 1979).

Shenanigans of this type would lead to strong ostracism in a shame culture such as Japan. "Shame is a reaction to other people's criticism. A man is shamed by being openly ridiculed and rejected or by fantasizing to himself that he has been ridiculous. In either case it is a potent sanction" (Benedict, 1946, p. 233). In brief, the Japanese place a premium on the quality of the athlete's character; sport performance alone is not sufficient. Thus, the "superbrat" (the columnist Mike Royko's term) is persona non grata in Japanese baseball.

REFERENCES

Benedict, Ruth
1946 *The Chrysanthemum and the Sword: Pat-*

terns of Japanese Culture. Boston: Hough-ton-Mifflin.

Boersema, James
　1979　"Baseball: Oriental Style." *Soldiers* 34
　　　　(June): 28–31.

Cleaver, Charles G.
　1976　*Japanese and Americans: Cultural Parallels
　　　　and Paradoxes*. Minneapolis: University of
　　　　Minnesota Press, 1976.

Haring, Douglas G.
　1962　"Japanese National Character," in Bernard
　　　　Silberman (ed.), *Japanese Character and
　　　　Culture*. Tucson: University of Arizona
　　　　Press.

La Barre, Weston
　1962　"Some Observations on Character Structure
　　　　in the Orient," in Bernard Silberman (ed.),
　　　　Japanese Character and Culture. Tuscon:
　　　　University of Arizona Press.

Minami, Hiroshi
　1971　*Psychology of the Japanese People*. Toronto:
　　　　University of Toronto Press.

Obojski, Robert
　1975　*The Rise of Japanese Baseball Power*. Rad-
　　　　nor, Pa.: Chilton.

Whiting, Robert
　1979　"You've Gotta Have 'Wa.'" *Sports Illus-
　　　　trated* 51 (September 24)60–71.

TAKING ANOTHER LOOK

1 Which Japanese cultural values seem most important in shaping Japanese baseball?
2 After reflecting on the climate and the texture of Japanese baseball, which American cultural values would you say are most important in shaping American baseball?
3 What factors contribute to the impressive work ethic of industrial workers in Japan?
4 Why would the antics of an American "superbrat" athlete be unacceptable in Japanese baseball?

The Sounds of Silence

Edward T. Hall and Mildred Reed Hall

Sociologists view language as the foundation of every culture. Language includes speech, written characters, numerals, symbols, and gestures or other nonverbal communication. The interactionist perspective of sociology—a sociological framework for viewing human beings as living in a world of meaningful objects—sees language and symbols as an especially important part of human communication.

In the following selection, Edward T. Hall and Mildred Reed Hall emphasize the power of nonverbal communication. They argue that "few of us realize how much we all depend on body movement in our conversation or are aware of the hidden rules that govern listening behavior." Hall and Hall observe that most white middle-class Americans operate in four distinctive distance zones: intimate distance, personal distance, social distance, and public distance. However, as they point out, patterns of nonverbal communication vary widely from one culture to another and even among racial and ethnic groups within the same culture.

Bob leaves his apartment at 8:15 A.M. and stops at the corner drugstore for breakfast. Before he can speak, the counterman says, "The usual?" Bob nods yes. While he savors his Danish, a fat man pushes onto the adjoining stool and overflows into his space. Bob scowls and the man pulls himself in as much as he can. Bob has sent two messages without speaking a syllable.

Henry has an appointment to meet Arthur at 11 o'clock; he arrives at 11:30. Their conversation is friendly, but Arthur retains a lingering hostility. Henry has unconsciously communicated that he doesn't think the appointment is very important or that Arthur is a person who needs to be treated with respect.

George is talking to Charley's wife at a party. Their conversation is entirely trivial, yet Charley glares at them suspiciously. Their physical proximity and the movements of their eyes reveal that they are powerfully attracted to each other.

José Ybarra and Sir Edmund Jones are at the same party, and it is important for them to establish a cordial relationship for business reasons. Each is trying to be warm and friendly, yet they will part with mutual distrust and their business transaction will probably fall through. José, in Latin fashion, moved closer and closer to Sir Edmund as they spoke, and this movement was miscommunicated as pushiness to Sir Edmund, who kept backing away from this intimacy, and this was miscommunicated to José as coldness. The silent languages of Latin and English cultures are more difficult to learn than their spoken languages.

In each of these cases, we see the subtle power of nonverbal communication. The only language used throughout most of the history of humanity (in evolutionary terms, vocal communication is relatively recent), it is the first form of communication you learn. You use this preverbal language, consciously and unconsciously, every day to tell other people how you feel about yourself and them. This language includes your posture, gestures, facial expressions, costume, the way you walk, even your treatment of time and space and material things. All people communicate on several different levels at the same time but are usually aware of only the verbal dialog and don't realize that they respond to nonverbal messages. But when a person says one thing and really believes something else, the discrepancy between the two can usually be sensed. Nonverbal-communication systems are much less subject to the conscious deception that often occurs in verbal systems. When we find ourselves thinking, "I don't know what it is about him, but he doesn't seem sincere," it's usually this lack of congruity between a person's words and his behavior that makes us anxious and uncomfortable.

Few of us realize how much we all depend on body movement in our conversation or are aware of the hidden rules that govern listening behavior. But we know instantly whether or not the person we're talking to is "tuned in" and we're very sensitive to any breach in listening etiquette. In white middle-class American culture, when someone wants to show he is listening to someone else, he looks either at the other person's face or, specifically, at his eyes, shifting his gaze from one eye to the other.

If you observe a person conversing, you'll notice that he indicates he's listening by nodding his head. He also makes little "Hmm" noises. If he agrees with what's being said, he may give a vigorous nod. To show pleasure or affirmation, he smiles; if he has some reservations, he looks skeptical by raising an eyebrow or pulling down the corners of his mouth. If a participant wants to terminate the conversation, he may start shifting his body position, stretching his legs, crossing or uncrossing them, bobbing his foot or diverting his gaze from the speaker. The more he fidgets, the more the speaker becomes aware that he has lost his audience. As a last measure, the listener may look at his watch to indicate the imminent end of the conversation.

Talking and listening are so intricately intertwined that a person cannot do one without the other. Even when one is alone and talking to oneself, there is part of the brain that speaks while another part listens. In all conversations, the listener is positively or negatively reinforcing the speaker all the time. He may even guide the conversation without knowing it, by laughing or frowning or dismissing the argument with a wave of his hand.

The language of the eyes—another age-old way of exchanging feelings—is both subtle and complex. Not only do men and women use their eyes differently but there are class, generation, regional, ethnic and national cultural differences. Americans often complain about the way foreigners stare at people or hold a glance too long. Most Americans look away from someone who is using his eyes in an unfamiliar way because it makes them self-conscious. If a man looks at another man's wife in a certain way, he's asking for trouble, as indicated earlier. But he might not be ill-mannered or seeking to challenge the husband. He might be a European in this country who hasn't learned our visual mores. Many American women visiting France or Italy are acutely embarrassed because, for the first time in their lives, men really look at them—their eyes, hair, nose, lips, breasts, hips, legs, thighs, knees, ankles, feet, clothes, hairdo, even their walk. These same women, once they have become used to being looked at, often return to the United States and are overcome with the feeling that "No one ever really looks at me anymore."

Analyzing the mass of data on the eyes, it is possible to sort out at least three ways in which the eyes are used to communicate: dominance versus submission, involvement versus detachment and positive versus negative attitude. In addition, there are three levels of consciousness and control, which can be categorized as follows: (1) conscious use of the eyes to communicate, such as the flirting blink and the intimate nose-wrinkling squint; (2) the very extensive category of unconscious but learned behavior governing where the eyes are directed and when (this unwritten set of rules dictates how and under what circumstances the sexes, as well as people of all status categories, look at each other); and (3) the response of the eye itself, which is completely outside both awareness and control—changes in the cast (the sparkle) of the eye and the pupillary reflex. . . .

The eye-sparkle phenomenon frequently turns

up in our interviews of couples in love. It's apparently one of the first reliable clues in the other person that love is genuine. To date, there is no scientific data to explain eye sparkle; no investigation of the pupil, the cornea or even the white sclera of the eye shows how the sparkle originates. Yet we all know it when we see it.

One common situation for most people involves the use of the eyes in the street and in public. Although eye behavior follows a definite set of rules, the rules vary according to the place, the needs and feelings of the people, and their ethnic background. For urban whites, once they're within definite recognition distance (16–32 feet for people with average eyesight), there is mutual avoidance of eye contact—unless they want something specific: a pickup, a handout or information of some kind. In the West and in small towns generally, however, people are much more likely to look at and greet one another, even if they're strangers.

It's permissible to look at people if they're beyond recognition distance; but once inside this sacred zone, you can only steal a glance at strangers. You *must* greet friends, however; to fail to do so is insulting. Yet, to stare too fixedly even at them is considered rude and hostile. Of course, all of these rules are variable.

A great many blacks, for example, greet each other in public even if they don't know each other. To blacks, most eye behavior of whites has the effect of giving the impression that they aren't there, but this is due to white avoidance of eye contact with *anyone* in the street.

Another very basic difference between people of different ethnic backgrounds is their sense of territoriality and how they handle space. This is the silent communication, or miscommunication, that caused friction between Mr. Ybarra and Sir Edmund Jones in our earlier example. We know from research that everyone has around himself an invisible bubble of space that contracts and expands depending on several factors: his emotional state, the activity he's performing at the time and his cultural background. This bubble is a kind of mobile territory that he will defend against intrusion. If he is accustomed to close personal distance between himself and others, his bubble will be smaller than that of someone who's accustomed to greater personal distance. People of North European heritage—English, Scandinavian, Swiss and German—tend to avoid contact. Those whose heritage is Italian, French, Spanish, Russian, Latin American or Middle Eastern like close personal contact.

People are very sensitive to any intrusion into their spatial bubble. If someone stands too close to you, your first instinct is to back up. If that's not possible, you lean away and pull yourself in, tensing your muscles. If the intruder doesn't respond to these body signals, you may then try to protect yourself, using a briefcase, umbrella or raincoat. Women—especially when traveling alone—often plant their pocketbook in such a way that no one can get very close to them. As a last resort, you may move to another spot and position yourself behind a desk or a chair that provides screening. Everyone tries to adjust the space around himself in a way that's comfortable for him; most often, he does this unconsciously.

Emotions also have a direct effect on the size of a person's territory. When you're angry or under stress, your bubble expands and you require more space. New York psychiatrist Augustus Kinzel found a difference in what he calls Body-Buffer Zones between violent and nonviolent prison inmates. Dr. Kinzel conducted experiments in which each prisoner was placed in the center of a small room and then Dr. Kinzel slowly walked toward him. Nonviolent prisoners allowed him to come quite close, while prisoners with a history of violent behavior couldn't tolerate his proximity and reacted with some vehemence.

Apparently, people under stress experience other people as looming larger and closer than they actually are. Studies of schizophrenic patients have indicated that they sometimes have a distorted perception of space, and several psychiatrists have reported patients who experience their body boundaries as filling up an entire room. For these patients, anyone who comes into the room is actually inside their body, and such an intrusion may trigger a violent outburst.

Unfortunately, there is little detailed information about normal people who live in highly congested urban areas. We do know, of course, that the noise, pollution, dirt, crowding and confusion of our cities induce feelings of stress in most of us, and stress leads to a need for greater space. The man who's packed into a subway, jostled in the street, crowded into an elevator and forced to work all day in a bull pen or in a small office without auditory or visual privacy is going to be very stressed at the end of his day. He needs places that provide relief from constant overstimulation of his nervous system. Stress from overcrowding is cumulative and people can tolerate more crowding early in the day than later; note the increased bad temper during the evening rush hour as compared with the morning melee. Certainly one factor in people's desire to commute by car is the need for privacy and relief from crowding (except, often, from other cars); it may be the only time of the day when nobody can intrude.

In crowded public places, we tense our muscles and hold ourselves stiff, and thereby communicate to others our desire not to intrude on their space and, above all, not to touch them. We also avoid eye contact and the total effect is that of someone who has "tuned out." Walking along the street, our bubble expands slightly as we move in a stream of strangers, taking care not to bump into them. In the office, at meetings, in restaurants, our bubble keeps changing as it adjusts to the activity at hand.

Most white middle-class Americans use four main distances in their business and social relations: intimate, personal, social and public. Each of these distances has a near and a far phase and is accompanied by changes in the volume of the voice. Intimate distance varies from direct physical contact with another person to a distance of six to eighteen inches and is used for our most private activities—caressing another person or making love. At this distance, you are overwhelmed by sensory inputs from the other person—heat from the body, tactile stimulation from the skin, the fragrance of perfume, even the sound of breathing —all of which literally envelop you. Even at the far phase, you're still within easy touching distance. In general, the use of intimate distance in public between adults is frowned on. It's also much too close for strangers, except under conditions of extreme crowding.

In the second zone—personal distance—the close phase is one and a half to two and a half feet; it's at this distance that wives usually stand from their husbands in public. If another woman moves into this zone, the wife will most likely be disturbed. The far phase—two and a half to four feet —is the distance used to "keep someone at arm's length" and is the most common spacing used by people in conversation.

The third zone—social distance—is employed during business transactions or exchanges with a clerk or repairman. People who work together tend to use close social distance—four to seven feet. This is also the distance for conversation at social gatherings. To stand at this distance from someone who is seated has a dominating effect (for example, teacher to pupil, boss to secretary). The far phase of the third zone—seven to twelve feet—is where people stand when someone says, "Stand back so I can look at you." This distance lends a formal tone to business or social discourse. In an executive office, the desk serves to keep people at this distance.

The fourth zone—public distance—is used by teachers in classrooms or speakers at public gatherings. At its farthest phase—25 feet and beyond —it is used for important public figures. Violations of this distance can lead to serious complications. During his 1970 U.S. visit, the president of France, Georges Pompidou, was harassed by pickets in Chicago, who were permitted to get within touching distance. Since pickets in France are kept behind barricades a block or more away, the president was outraged by this insult to his person, and President Nixon was obliged to communicate his concern as well as offer his personal apologies.

It is interesting to note how American pitchmen and panhandlers exploit the unwritten, unspoken conventions of eye and distance. Both take advantage of the fact that once explicit eye contact is established, it is rude to look away, because to do so means to brusquely dismiss the other person and his needs. Once having caught the eye of his mark, the panhandler then locks on, not letting go until he moves through the public zone, the social zone, the personal zone, and finally, into the intimate sphere, where people are most vulnerable.

Touch also is an important part of the constant stream of communication that takes place between people. A light touch, a firm touch, a blow, a caress are all communications. In an effort to break down barriers among people, there's been a recent upsurge in group-encounter activities, in which strangers are encouraged to touch one another. In special situations such as these, the rules for not touching are broken with group approval and people gradually lose some of their inhibitions.

Although most people don't realize it, space is perceived and distances are set not by vision alone but with all the senses. Auditory space is perceived with the ears, thermal space with the skin, kinesthetic space with the muscles of the body and olfactory space with the nose. And, once again, it's one's culture that determines how his senses are programmed—which sensory information ranks highest and lowest. The important thing to remember is that culture is very persistent. In this country, we've noted the existence of culture patterns that determine distance between people in the third and fourth generations of some families, despite their prolonged contact with people of very different cultural heritages.

Whenever there is great cultural distance between two people, there are bound to be problems arising from differences in behavior and expectations. An example is the American couple who consulted a psychiatrist about their marital problems. The husband was from New England and had been brought up by reserved parents who taught him to control his emotions and to respect the need for privacy. His wife was from an Italian family and had been brought up in close contact with all the members of her large family, who were extremely warm, volatile and demonstrative.

When the husband came home after a hard day at the office, dragging his feet and longing for peace and quiet, his wife would rush to him and smother him. Clasping his hands, rubbing his brow, crooning over his weary head, she never left him alone. But when the wife was upset or anxious about her day, the husband's response was to withdraw completely and leave her alone. No comforting, no affectionate embrace, no attention —just solitude. The woman became convinced her husband didn't love her and, in desperation, she consulted a psychiatrist. Their problem wasn't basically psychological but cultural.

Why has man developed all these different ways of communicating messages without words? One reason is that people don't like to spell out certain kinds of messages. We prefer to find other ways of showing our feelings. This is especially true in relationships as sensitive as courtship. Men don't like to be rejected and most women don't want to turn a man down bluntly. Instead, we work out subtle ways of encouraging or discouraging each other that save face and avoid confrontations.

How a person handles space in dating others is an obvious and very sensitive indicator of how he or she feels about the other person. On a first date, if a woman sits or stands so close to a man that he is acutely conscious of her physical presence—inside the intimate-distance zone—the man usually construes it to mean that she is encouraging him. However, before the man starts moving in on the woman, he should be sure what message she's really sending; otherwise, he risks bruising his ego. What is close to someone of North European background may be neutral or distant to someone of Italian heritage. Also, women sometimes use space as a way of misleading a man and there are few things that put men off more than women who communicate contradictory messages—such as women who cuddle up and then act insulted when a man takes the next step.

How does a woman communicate interest in a man? In addition to such familiar gambits as smiling at him, she may glance shyly at him, blush and then look away. Or she may give him a real come-on look and move in very close when he approaches. She may touch his arm and ask for a light. As she leans forward to light her cigarette, she may brush him lightly, enveloping him in her perfume. She'll probably continue to smile at him and she may use what ethologists call preening gestures—touching the back of her hair, thrusting her breasts forward, tilting her hips as she stands or crossing her legs if she's seated, perhaps even exposing one thigh or putting a hand on her thigh and stroking it. She may also stroke her wrists as she converses or show the palm of her hand as a way of gaining his attention. Her skin may be unusually flushed or quite pale, her eyes brighter, the pupils larger.

If a man sees a woman whom he wants to attract, he tries to present himself by his posture and stance as someone who is self-assured. He moves briskly and confidently. When he catches the eye of the woman, he may hold her glance a little longer than normal. If he gets an encouraging smile, he'll move in close and engage her in small talk. As they converse, his glance shifts over her face and body. He, too, may make preening gestures—straightening his tie, smoothing his hair or shooting his cuffs.

How do people learn body language? The same way they learn spoken language—by observing and imitating people around them as they're growing up. Little girls imitate their mothers or an older female. Little boys imitate their fathers or a respected uncle or a character on television. In this way, they learn the gender signals appropriate for their sex. Regional, class and ethnic patterns of body behavior are also learned in childhood and persist throughout life.

Such patterns of masculine and feminine body behavior vary widely from one culture to another.

In America, for example, women stand with their thighs together. Many walk with their pelvis tipped slightly forward and their upper arms close to their body. When they sit, they cross their legs at the knee or cross their ankles. American men hold their arms away from their body, often swinging them as they walk. They stand with their legs apart (an extreme example is the cowboy, with legs apart and thumbs tucked into his belt). When they sit, they put their feet on the floor with legs apart and, in some parts of the country, they cross their legs by putting one ankle on the other knee.

Leg behavior indicates sex, status, and personality. It also indicates whether or not one is at ease or is showing respect or disrespect for the other person. Young Latin American males avoid crossing their legs. In their world of *machismo*, the preferred position for young males when with one another (if there is no dominant male present to whom they must show respect) is to sit on the base of their spine with their leg muscles relaxed and their feet wide apart. Their respect position is like our military equivalent: spine straight, heels and ankles together—almost identical to that displayed by properly brought up young women in New England in the early part of this century.

American women who sit with their legs spread apart in the presence of males are *not* normally signaling a come-on—they are simply (and often unconsciously) sitting like men. Middle-class women in the presence of other women to whom they are very close may on occasion throw themselves down on a soft chair or sofa and let themselves go. This is a signal that nothing serious will be taken up. Males, on the other hand, lean back and prop their legs up on the nearest object.

The way we walk, similarly, indicates status, respect, mood and ethnic or cultural affiliation. The many variants of the female walk are too well known to go into here, except to say that a man would have to be blind not to be turned on by the way some women walk—a fact that made Mae West rich before scientists ever studied these matters. To white Americans, some French middle-class males walk in a way that is both humorous and suspect. There is a bounce and looseness to the French walk, as though the parts of the body were somehow unrelated. Jacques Tati, the French movie actor, walks this way: so does the great mime, Marcel Marceau.

Blacks and whites in America—with the exception of middle- and upper-middle-class professionals of both groups—move and walk very differently from each other. To the blacks, whites often seem incredibly stiff, almost mechanical in their movements. Black males, on the other hand, have a looseness and coordination that frequently makes whites a little uneasy; it's too different, too integrated, too alive, too male. Norman Mailer has said that squares walk from the shoulders, like bears, but blacks and hippies walk from the hips, like cats.

All over the world, people walk not only in their own characteristic way but have walks that communicate the nature of their involvement with whatever it is they're doing. The purposeful walk of North Europeans is an important component of proper behavior on the job. Any male who has been in the military knows how essential it is to walk properly (which makes for a continuing source of tension between blacks and whites in the Service). The quick shuffle of servants in the Far East in the old days was a show of respect. On the island of Truk, when we last visited, the inhabitants even had a name for the respectful walk that one used when in the presence of a chief or when walking past a chief's house. The term was *sufan*, which meant to be humble and respectful.

The notion that people communicate volumes by their gestures, facial expressions, posture and walk is not new; actors, dancers, writers and psychiatrists have long been aware of it. Only in recent years, however, have scientists begun to make systematic observations of body motions. Ray L. Birdwhistell of the University of Pennsylvania is one of the pioneers in body-motion research and coined the term *kinesics* to describe this field. He developed an elaborate notation system to record both facial and body movement, us-

ing an approach similar to that of the linguist, who studies the basic elements of speech. Birdwhistell and other kinesicists such as Albert Shellen, Adam Kendon and William Condon take movies of people interacting. They run the film over and over again, often at reduced speed for frame-by-frame analysis, so that they can observe even the slightest body movements not perceptible at normal interaction speeds. These movements are then recorded in notebooks for later analysis. . . .

The language of behavior is extemely complex. Most of us are lucky to have under control one subcultural system—the one that reflects our sex, class, generation and geographic region within the United States. Because of its complexity, efforts to isolate bits of nonverbal communication and generalize from them are in vain; you don't become an instant expert on people's behavior by watching them at cocktail parties. Body language isn't something that's independent of the person, something that can be donned and doffed like a suit of clothes.

Our research and that of our colleagues have shown that, far from being a superficial form of communication that can be consciously manipulated, nonverbal-communication systems are interwoven into the fabric of the personality and, as sociologist Erving Goffman has demonstrated, into society itself. They are the warp and woof of daily interactions with others, and they influence how one expresses oneself, how one experiences oneself as a man or a woman.

Nonverbal communications signal to members of your own group what kind of person you are, how you feel about others, how you'll fit into and work in a group, whether you're assured or anxious, the degree to which you feel comfortable with the standards of your own culture, as well as deeply significant feelings about the self, including the state of your own psyche. For most of us, it's difficult to accept the reality of another's behavioral system. And, of course, none of us will ever become fully knowledgeable of the importance of every non-verbal signal. But as long as each of us realizes the power of these signals, this society's diversity can be a source of great strength rather than a further—and subtly power- ful—source of division.

TAKING ANOTHER LOOK

1 Describe a recent example of nonverbal communication in which you "sent" or "received" a message.
2 Why do the Halls see eye movement as an example of nonverbal communication? How does such behavior vary cross-culturally?
3 Briefly describe the four distance zones that most white middle-class Americans use in their business and social relations.
4 What is *kinesics*? What methodology is used by researchers interested in kinesics?
5 In the view of Hall and Hall, why is it difficult to consciously manipulate nonverbal communication systems?

Sexism in the Schoolroom of the '80s

Myra and David Sadker

Sociologists use the term *socialization* to refer to the process whereby people learn the attitudes, values, and actions appropriate to individuals as members of a particular culture. A critical aspect of the early socialization process is exposure to cultural assumptions regarding sex differences. *Sex roles* are behaviors, attitudes, and activities prescribed for males and females. As the primary agents of childhood socialization, parents play a central role in guiding children into those sex roles deemed appropriate in a society. However, other adults, older siblings, the mass media, and religious and educational institutions also have noticeable impact on a child's socialization into feminine and masculine norms.

In the following selection, professors of education Myra and David Sadker argue that "although many believe that classroom sexism disappeared in the early '70s, it hasn't." Their three-year study suggests that boys continue to dominate the classroom at all grade levels, in all communities, and in all subject areas. Teachers commonly engage in differential treatment of students based on gender. They praise boys more than girls and offer boys more academic help. In addition, teachers reward boys for academic assertiveness (for example, calling out answers without raising their hands) but reprimand girls for similar behavior.

If a boy calls out in class he gets teacher attention, especially intellectual attention. If a girl calls out in class, she is told to raise her hand before speaking. Teachers praise boys more than girls, give boys more academic help and are more likely to accept boys' comments during classroom discussions. These are only a few examples of how teachers favor boys. Through this advantage boys increase their chances for better education and possibly higher pay and quicker promotions. Although many believe that classroom sexism disappeared in the early '70s, it hasn't.

Education is not a spectator sport. Numerous researchers, most recently John Goodlad, former dean of education at the University of California at Los Angeles and author of *A Place Called School*, have shown that when students participate in classroom discussion they hold more positive attitudes toward school, and that positive attitudes enhance learning. It is no coincidence that girls are more passive in the classroom and score lower than boys on SAT's.

Most teachers claim that girls participate and are called on in class as often as boys. But a three-year study we recently completed found that this is not true; vocally, boys clearly dominate the classroom. When we showed teachers and administrators a film of a classroom discussion and asked who was talking more, the teachers overwhelmingly said the girls were. But in reality, the boys in the film were out-talking the girls at a ratio of three to one. Even educators who are active in feminist issues were unable to spot the sex bias until they counted and coded who was talking and who was just watching. Stereotypes of garrulous and gossipy women are so strong that teachers fail to see this communications gender gap even when it is right before their eyes.

Field researchers in our study observed students in more than a hundred fourth-, sixth- and eighth-grade classes in four states and the District of Columbia. The teachers and students were male and female, black and white, from urban, suburban and rural communities. Half of the classrooms covered language arts and English—subjects in which girls traditionally have excelled; the other half covered math and science—traditionally male domains.

We found that at all grade levels, in all communities and in all subject areas, boys dominated classroom communication. They participated in more interactions than girls did and their participation became greater as the year went on.

Our research contradicted the traditional assumption that girls dominate classroom discussion in reading while boys are dominant in math. We found that whether the subject was language arts and English or math and science, boys got more than their fair share of teacher attention.

Some critics claim that if teachers talk more to male students, it is simply because boys are more assertive in grabbing their attention—a classic case of the squeaky wheel getting the educational oil. In fact, our research shows that boys are more assertive in the classroom. While girls sit patiently with their hands raised, boys literally grab teacher attention. They are eight times more likely than girls to call out answers. However, male assertiveness is not the whole answer.

Teachers behave differently, depending on whether boys or girls call out answers during discussions. When boys call out comments without raising their hands, teachers accept their answers. However, when girls call out, teachers reprimand this "inappropriate" behavior with messages such as, "In this class we don't shout out answers, we raise our hands." The message is subtle but powerful: Boys should be academically assertive and grab teacher attention; girls should act like ladies and keep quiet.

Teachers in our study revealed an interaction pattern that we called a "mind sex." After calling on a student, they tended to keep calling on students of the same sex. While this pattern applied to both sexes, it was far more pronounced among boys and allowed them more than their fair share of airtime.

It may be that when teachers call on someone, they continue thinking of that sex. Another explanation may be found in the seating patterns of elementary, secondary and even postsecondary classrooms. In approximately half of the classrooms in our study, male and female students sat in separate parts of the room. Sometimes the teacher created this segregation, but more often, the students segregated themselves. A teacher's tendency to interact with same-sex students may be a simple matter of where each sex sits. For example, a teacher calls on a female student, looks around the same area and then continues questioning the students around this girl, all of whom are female. When the teacher refocuses to a section of the classroom where boys are seated, boys receive the series of questions. And because boys are more assertive, the teacher may interact with their section longer.

Girls are often shortchanged in quality as well as in quantity of teacher attention. In 1975 psychologists Lisa Serbin and K. Daniel O'Leary, then at the State University of New York at Stony Brook, studied classroom interaction at the preschool level and found that teachers gave boys more attention, praised them more often and were at least twice as likely to have extended conversations with them. Serbin and O'Leary also found that teachers were twice as likely to give male students detailed instructions on how to do things for themselves. With female students, teachers were more likely to do it for them instead. The result was that boys learned to become independent, girls learned to become dependent.

Instructors at the other end of the educational spectrum also exhibit this same "let me do it for you" behavior toward female students. Constantina Safilios-Rothschild, a sociologist with the Population Council in New York, studied sex desegregation at the Coast Guard Academy and found that the instructors were giving detailed instructions on how to accomplish tasks to male students, but were doing the jobs and operating the equipment for the female students.

Years of experience have shown that the best

way to learn something is to do it yourself; classroom chivalry is not only misplaced, it is detrimental. It is also important to give students specific and direct feedback about the quality of their work and answers. During classroom discussion, teachers in our study reacted to boys' answers with dynamic, precise and effective responses, while they often gave girls bland and diffuse reactions.

Teachers' reactions were classified in four categories: praise ("Good answer"); criticism ("That answer is wrong"); help and remediation ("Try again—but check your long division"); or acceptance without any evaluation or assistance ("OK" "Uh-huh").

Despite caricatures of school as a harsh and punitive place, fewer than 5 percent of the teachers' reactions were criticisms, even of the mildest sort. But praise didn't happen often either; it made up slightly more than 10 percent of teachers' reactions. More than 50 percent of teachers' responses fell into the "OK" category.

Teachers distributed these four reactions differently among boys than among girls. Here are some of the typical patterns.

Teacher: "What's the capital of Maryland? Joel?"
Joel: "Baltimore."
Teacher: "What's the largest city in Maryland, Joel?"
Joel: "Baltimore."
Teacher: "That's good. But Baltimore isn't the capital. The capital is also the location of the U.S. Naval Academy. Joel, do you want to try again?"
Joel: "Annapolis."
Teacher: "Excellent. Anne, what's the capital of Maine?"
Anne: "Portland."
Teacher: "Judy, do you want to try?"
Judy: "Augusta."
Teacher: "OK."

In this snapshot of a classroom discussion, Joel was told when his answer was wrong (criticism); was helped to discover the correct answer (remediation); and was praised when he offered the correct response. When Anne was wrong, the teacher, rather than staying with her, moved to Judy, who received only simple acceptance for her correct answer. Joel received the more specific teacher reaction and benefited from a longer, more precise and intense educational interaction.

Too often, girls remain in the dark about the quality of their answers. Teachers rarely tell them if their answers are excellent, need to be improved or are just plain wrong. Unfortunately, acceptance, the imprecise response packing the least educational punch, gets the most equitable sex distribution in classrooms. Active students receiving precise feedback are more likely to achieve academically. And they are more likely to be boys. Consider the following:

• Although girls start school ahead of boys in reading and basic computation, by the time they graduate from high school, boys have higher SAT scores in both areas.

• By high school, some girls become less committed to careers, although their grades and achievement-test scores may be as good as boys'. Many girls' interests turn to marriage or stereotypically female jobs. Part of the reason may be that some women feel that men disapprove of their using their intelligence.

• Girls are less likely to take math and science courses and to participate in special or gifted programs in these subjects, even if they have a talent for them. They are also more likely to believe that they are incapable of pursuing math and science in college and to avoid the subjects.

• Girls are more likely to attribute failure to internal factors, such as ability, rather than to external factors, such as luck.

The sexist communication game is played at work, as well as at school. As reported in numerous studies it goes like this:

• Men speak more often and frequently interrupt women.

• Listeners recall more from male speakers

than from female speakers, even when both use a similar speaking style and cover identical content.

• Women participate less actively in conversation. They do more smiling and gazing; they are more often the passive bystanders in professional and social conversations among peers.

• Women often transform declarative statements into tentative comments. This is accomplished by using qualifiers ("kind of" or "I guess") and by adding tag questions ("This is a good movie, isn't it?"). These tentative patterns weaken impact and signal a lack of power and influence.

Sexist treatment in the classroom encourages formation of patterns such as these, which give men more dominance and power than women in the working world. But there is a light at the end of the educational tunnel. Classroom biases are not etched in stone, and training can eliminate these patterns. Sixty teachers in our study received four days of training to establish equity in classroom interactions. These trained teachers succeeded in eliminating classroom bias. Although our training focused on equality, it improved overall teaching effectiveness as well. Classes taught by these trained teachers had a higher level of intellectual discussion and contained more effective and precise teacher responses for all students.

There is an urgent need to remove sexism from the classroom and give women the same educational encouragement and support that men receive. When women are treated equally in the classroom, they will be more likely to achieve equality in the workplace.

TAKING ANOTHER LOOK

1 How would conflict theorists be likely to view the persistence of classroom sexism?

2 What experiments can you identify that are referred to by the authors in their discussion of sexism?

3 According to Sadker and Sadker, in what ways are female students shortchanged in quality of teacher attention?

4 According to Sadker and Sadker, how is the "sexist communication game" played at work?

5 Why is male assertiveness not the entire explanation for teachers' talking more to male students than to female students?

The Fate of Idealism in Medical School

Howard S. Becker and Blanche Geer

The socialization process continues throughout the human life cycle. A fundamental aspect of human socialization involves learning to behave appropriately within an occupation. In the United States, working full time serves to confirm adult status; it is an indication that one has passed out of adolescence. One important phase of occupational socialization is *anticipatory socialization*, in which the individual "rehearses" for future positions, occupations, and social relationships. Children in farming families who gradually assume greater responsibility for running the farm are engaged in anticipatory socialization; so, too, is a young woman who resolves to become a dancer and focuses her adolescent years on dance training.

In the following selection, sociologists Howard S. Becker and Blanche Geer focus on anticipatory socialization in medical school settings. They examine the conventional wisdom whereby idealistic college graduates are turned into tough, hardened, unfeeling doctors by a medical school socialization process that encourages cynicism. Becker and Geer question this common view of "idealistic" medical students turning into "cynical" doctors and suggest that the growth of both idealism and cynicism are not simple developments.

It should be noted that there have been two significant changes in medical education since this classic sociological article was published in 1958. First, there has been a dramatic increase in the proportion of women entering medical school and becoming doctors. Second, some medical schools have restructured their curricula in order to narrow the gap between course work and medical practice. These schools also have encouraged earlier student interaction with patients in hospital settings.

It is also important to emphasize that anticipatory socialization continues through one's premedical and medical studies and later medical career. While this process begins in undergraduate years as students take certain classes to prepare for medical school, it continues even after medical school as doctors experience internship, residency, and then accept positions in hospitals, in private practice, or in teaching posts.

It makes some difference in a man's performance of his work whether he believes wholeheartedly in what he is doing or feels that in important respects it is a fraud, whether he feels convinced that it is a good thing or believes that it is not really of much use after all. The distinction we are making is the one people have in mind when they refer, for example, to their calling as a "noble profession" on the one hand or a "racket" on the other. In the one case they idealistically proclaim that their work is all that it claims on the surface to be; in the other they cynically concede that it is first and foremost a way of making a living and that its surface pretensions are just that and nothing more. Presumably, different modes of behavior are associated with these perspectives when

Authors' note: Revision of paper read at the annual meeting of the Midwest Sociological Society, April 5, 1957, in Des Moines, Iowa.

wholeheartedly embraced. The cynic cuts corners with a feeling of inevitability while the idealist goes down fighting. *The Blackboard Jungle* and *Not as a Stranger* are only the most recent in a long tradition of fictional portrayals of the importance of this aspect of a man's adjustment to his work.

Professional schools often receive a major share of the blame for producing this kind of cynicism—and none more than the medical school. The idealistic young freshman changes into a tough, hardened, unfeeling doctor; or so the popular view has it. Teachers of medicine sometimes rephrase the distinction between the clinical and pre-clinical years into one between the "cynical" and "pre-cynical" years. Psychological research supports this view, presenting attitude surveys which show medical students year by year scoring lower on "idealism" and higher on "cynicism."[1] Typically, this cynicism is seen as developing in response to the shattering of ideals consequent on coming face-to-face with the realities of professional practice.

In this paper, we attempt to describe the kind of idealism that characterizes the medical freshman and to trace both the development of cynicism and the vicissitudes of that idealism in the course of the four years of medical training. Our main themes are that though they develop cynical feelings in specific situations directly associated with their medical school experience, the medical students never lose their original idealism about the practice of medicine; that the growth of both cynicism and idealism are not simple developments, but are instead complex transformations; and that the very notions "idealism" and "cynicism" need further analysis, and must be seen as situational in their expressions rather than as stable traits possessed by individuals in greater or lesser degree. Finally, we see the greater portion of these feelings as being collective rather than individual phenomena.

Our discussion is based on a study we are now conducting at a state medical school,[2] in which we have carried on participant observation with students of all four years in all of the courses and clinical work to which they are exposed. We joined the students in their activities in school and after school and watched them at work in labs, on the hospital wards, and in the clinic. Often spending as much as a month with a small group of from five to fifteen students assigned to a particular activity, we came to know them well and were able to gather information in informal interviews and by overhearing the ordinary daily conversation of the group.[3] In the course of our observation and interviewing we have gathered much information on the subject of idealism. Of necessity, we shall have to present the very briefest statement of our findings with little or no support-

[1] Leonard D. Eron, "Effect of Medical Education on Medical Students," *Journal of Medical Education*, 10 (October, 1955), pp. 559–566.

[2] This study is sponsored by Community Studies, Inc., of Kansas City, Missouri, and is being carried on at the University of Kansas Medical School, to whose dean, staff, and students we are indebted for their wholehearted cooperation. Professor Everett C. Hughes of the University of Chicago is director of the project.

[3] The technique of participant observation has not been fully systematized, but some approaches to this have been made. See, for example, Florence R. Kluckhohn, "The Participant Observer Technique in Small Communities," *American Journal of Sociology*, 45 (November, 1940), pp. 331–343; Arthur Vidich, "Participant Observation and the Collection and Interpretation of Data," *ibid.*, 60 (January, 1955), pp. 354–360; William Foote Whyte, "Observational Field-Work Methods," in Maria Jahoda, Morton Deutsch, and Stuart W. Cook (editors), *Research Methods in the Social Sciences*, New York: Dryden Press, 1951, II, pp. 393–514; and *Street Corner Society* (Enlarged Edition), Chicago: University of Chicago Press, 1955, pp. 279–358; Rosalie Hankey Wax, "Twelve Years Later: An Analysis of Field Experience," *American Journal of Sociology*, 63 (September, 1957), pp. 133–142; Morris S. Schwartz and Charlotte Green Schwartz, "Problems in Participant Observation," *ibid.*, 60 (January, 1955), pp. 343–353; and Howard S. Becker and Blanche Geer, "Participant Observation and Interviewing: A Comparison," *Human Organization* (forthcoming). The last item represents the first of a projected series of papers attempting to make explicit the operations involved in this method. For a short description of some techniques used in this study, see Howard S. Becker, "Interviewing Medical Students," *American Journal of Sociology*, 62 (September, 1956), pp. 199–201.

ing evidence.[4] The problem of idealism is, of course, many-faceted and complex and we have dealt with it in a simplified way, describing only some of its grosser features.[5]

THE FRESHMEN

The medical students enter school with what we may think of as the idealistic notion, implicit in lay culture, that the practice of medicine is a wonderful thing and that they are going to devote their lives to service to mankind. They believe that medicine is made up of a great body of well-established facts that they will be taught from the first day on and that these facts will be of immediate practical use to them as physicians. They enter school expecting to work industriously and expecting that if they work hard enough they will be able to master this body of fact and thus become good doctors.

In several ways the first year of medical school does not live up to their expectations. They are disillusioned when they find they will not be near patients at all, that the first year will be just like another year of college. In fact, some feel that it is not even as good as college because their work in certain areas is not as thorough as courses in the same fields in undergraduate school. They come to think that their courses (with the exception of anatomy) are not worth much because, in the first place, the faculty (being Ph.D.'s) know nothing about the practice of medicine, and, in the second place, the subject matter itself is irrelevant, or as the students say, "ancient history."

The freshmen are further disillusioned when the faculty tells them in a variety of ways that there is more to medicine than they can possibly learn. They realize it may be impossible for them to learn all they need to know in order to practice medicine properly. Their disillusionment becomes more profound when they discover that this statement of the faculty is literally true.[6] Experience in trying to master the details of the anatomy of the extremities convinces them that they cannot do so in the time they have. Their expectation of hard work is not disappointed; they put in an eight-hour day of classes and laboratories, and study four or five hours a night and most of the weekend as well.

Some of the students, the brightest, continue to attempt to learn it all, but succeed only in getting more and more worried about their work. The majority decide that, since they can't learn it all, they must select from among all the facts presented to them those they will attempt to learn. There are two ways of making this selection. On the one hand, the student may decide on the basis of his own uninformed notions about the nature of medical practice that many facts are not important, since they relate to things which seldom come up in the actual practice of medicine; therefore, he reasons, it is useless to learn them. On the other hand, the student can decide that the important thing is to pass his examinations and, therefore, that the important facts are those which are likely to be asked on an examination; he uses this as a basis for selecting both facts to memorize and courses for intensive study. For example, the work in physiology is dismissed on both of these grounds, being considered neither relevant to the facts of medical life nor important in terms of the amount of time the faculty devotes to it and the number of examinations in the subject.

A student may use either or both of these bases of selection at the beginning of the year, before

---

[4] A fuller analysis and presentation of evidence will be contained in a volume on this study now being prepared by the authors in collaboration with Everett C. Hughes and Anselm L. Strauss.

[5] Renee Fox has shown how complex one aspect of this whole subject is in her analysis of the way medical students at Cornell become aware of and adjust to both their own failure to master all available knowledge and the gaps in current knowledge in many fields. See her "Training for Uncertainty," in Robert K. Merton, George G. Reader, and Patricia L. Kendall, *The Student Physician: Introductory Studies in the Sociology of Medical Education,* Cambridge: Harvard University Press, 1957, pp. 207–241.

[6] Compare Fox' description of student reaction to this problem at Cornell (*op. cit.,* pp. 209–221).

many tests have been given. But after a few tests have been taken, the student makes "what the faculty wants" the chief basis of his selection of what to learn, for he now has a better idea of what this is and also has become aware that it is possible to fail examinations and that he therefore must learn the expectations of the faculty if he wishes to stay in school. The fact that one group of students, that with the highest prestige in the class, took this view early and did well on examinations was decisive in swinging the whole class around to this position. The students were equally influenced to become "test-wise" by the fact that, although they had all been in the upper range in their colleges, the class average on the first examination was frighteningly low.

In becoming test-wise, the students begin to develop systems for discovering the faculty wishes and learning them. These systems are both methods for studying their texts and short-cuts that can be taken in laboratory work. For instance, they begin to select facts for memorization by looking over the files of old examinations maintained in each of the medical fraternity houses. They share tip-offs from the lectures and offhand remarks of the faculty as to what will be on the examinations. In anatomy, they agree not to bother to dissect out subcutaneous nerves, reasoning that it is both difficult and time-consuming and the information can be secured from books with less effort. The interaction involved in the development of such systems and short-cuts helps to create a social group of a class which had previously been only an aggregation of smaller and less organized groups.

In this medical school, the students learn in this way to distinguish between the activities of the first year and their original view that everything that happens to them in medical school will be important. Thus they become cynical about the value of their activities in the first year. They feel that the real thing—learning which will help them to help mankind—has been postponed, perhaps until the second year, or perhaps even farther, at which time they will be able again to act on ideal-

istic premises. They believe that what they do in the later years in school under supervision will be about the same thing they will do, as physicians, on their own; the first year had disappointed this expectation.

There is one matter, however, about which the students are not disappointed during the first year: the so-called trauma of dealing with the cadaver. But this experience, rather than producing cynicism, reinforces the student's attachment to his idealistic view of medicine by making him feel that he is experiencing at least some of the necessary unpleasantness of the doctor's. Such difficulties, however, do not loom as large for the student as those of solving the problem of just what the faculty wants.

On this and other points, a working consensus develops in the new consolidated group about the interpretation of their experience in medical school and its norms of conduct. This consensus, which we call *student culture*,[7] focuses their attention almost completely on their day-to-day activities in school and obscures or sidetracks their earlier idealistic preoccupations. Cynicism, griping, and minor cheating become endemic, but the cynicism is specific to the educational situation, to the first year, and to only parts of it. Thus the students keep their cynicism separate from their idealistic feelings and by postponement protect their belief that medicine is a wonderful thing, that their school is a fine one, and that they will become good doctors.

LATER YEARS

The sophomore year does not differ greatly from the freshman year. Both the work load and anxiety over examinations probably increase. Though they begin some medical activities, as in their at-

---

[7] The concept of student culture is analyzed in some detail in Howard S. Becker and Blanche Geer, "Student Culture in Medical School," *Harvard Educational Review* (forthcoming).

tendance at autopsies and particularly in their introductory course in physical diagnosis, most of what they do continues to repeat the pattern of the college science curriculum. Their attention still centers on the problem of getting through school by doing well in examinations.

During the third and fourth, or clinical years, teaching takes a new form. In place of lectures and laboratories, the students' work now consists of the study of actual patients admitted to the hospital or seen in the clinic. Each patient who enters the hospital is assigned to a student who interviews him about his illnesses, past and present, and performs a physical examination. He writes this up for the patient's chart, and appends the diagnosis and the treatment that he would use were he allowed actually to treat the patient. During conferences with faculty physicians, often held at the patient's bedside, the student is quizzed about items of his report and called upon to defend them or to explain their significance. Most of the teaching in the clinical years is of this order.

Contact with patients brings a new set of circumstances with which the student must deal. He no longer feels the great pressure created by tests, for he is told by the faculty, and this is confirmed by his daily experience, that examinations are now less important. His problems now become those of coping with a steady stream of patients in a way that will please the staff man under whom he is working, and of handling what is sometimes a tremendous load of clinical work so as to allow himself time for studying diseases and treatments that interest him and for play and family life.

The students earlier have expected that once they reach the clinical years they will be able to realize their idealistic ambitions to help people and to learn those things immediately useful in aiding people who are ill. But they find themselves working to understand cases as medical problems rather than working to help the sick and memorizing the relevant available facts so that these can be produced immediately for a questioning staff man. When they make ward rounds with a faculty member they are likely to be quizzed about any of the seemingly countless facts possibly related to the condition of the patient for whom they are "caring."

Observers speak of the cynicism that overtakes the student and the lack of concern for his patients as human beings. This change does take place, but it is not produced solely by "the anxiety brought about by the presence of death and suffering."[8] The student becomes preoccupied with the technical aspects of the cases with which he deals because the faculty requires him to do so. He is questioned about so many technical details that he must spend most of his time learning them.

The frustrations created by his position in the teaching hospital further divert the student from idealistic concerns. He finds himself low man in a hierarchy based on clinical experience, so that he is allowed very little of the medical responsibility he would like to assume. Because of his lack of experience, he cannot write orders, and he receives permission to perform medical and surgical procedures (if at all) at a rate he considers far too slow. He usually must content himself with "mere" vicarious participation in the drama of danger, life, and death that he sees as the core of medical practice. The student culture accents these difficulties so that events (and especially those involving patients) are interpreted and reacted to as they push him toward or hold him back from further participation in this drama. He does not think in terms the layman might use.

As a result of the increasingly technical emphasis of his thinking the student appears cynical to the non-medical outsider, though from his own point of view he is simply seeing what is "really important." Instead of reacting with the layman's horror and sympathy for the patient to the sight of

---

[8] Dana L. Farnsworth, "Some Observations on The Attitudes and Motivations of the Harvard Medical Student," *Harvard Medical Alumni Bulletin*, January, 1956, p. 34.

a cancerous organ that has been surgically removed, the student is more likely to regret that he was not allowed to close the incision at the completion of the operation, and to rue the hours that he must spend searching in the fatty flesh for the lymph nodes that will reveal how far the disease has spread. As in other lines of work, he drops lay attitudes for those more relevant to the way the event affects someone in his position.

This is not to say that the students lose their original idealism. When issues of idealism are openly raised in a situation they define as appropriate, they respond as they might have when they were freshmen. But the influence of the student culture is such that questions which might bring forth this idealism are not brought up. Students are often assigned patients for examination and follow-up whose conditions might be expected to provoke idealistic crises. Students discuss such patients, however, with reference to the problems they create for the *student*. Patients with terminal diseases who are a long time dying, and patients with chronic diseases who show little change from week to week, are more likely to be viewed as creating extra work without extra compensation in knowledge or the opportunity to practice new skills than as examples of illness which raise questions about euthanasia. Such cases require the student to spend time every day checking on progress which he feels will probably not take place and to write long "progress" notes in the patient's chart although little progress has occurred.

This apparent cynicism is a collective matter. Group activities are built around this kind of workaday perspective, constraining the students in two ways. First, they do not openly express the lay idealistic notions they may hold, for their culture does not sanction such expression; second, they are less likely to have thoughts of this deviant kind when they are engaged in group activity. The collective nature of this "cynicism" is indicated by the fact that students become more openly idealistic whenever they are removed from the influence of student culture—when they are alone with a sociologist as they near the finish of

school and sense the approaching end of student life, for example, or when they are isolated from their classmates and therefore are less influenced by this culture.[9]

They still feel, as advanced students, though much less so than before, that school is irrelevant to actual medical practice. Many of their tasks, like running laboratory tests on patients newly admitted to the hospital or examining surgical specimens in the pathology laboratory, seem to them to have nothing to do with their visions of their future activity as doctors. As in their freshman year, they believe that perhaps they must obtain the knowledge they will need in spite of the school. They still conceive of medicine as a huge body of proven facts, but no longer believe that they will ever be able to master it all. They now say that they are going to try to apply the solution of the practicing M.D. to their own dilemma: learn a few things that they are interested in very well and know enough about other things to pass examinations while in school and, later on in practice, to know to which specialist to send difficult patients.

Their original medical idealism reasserts itself as the end of school approaches. Seniors show more interest than students in earlier years in serious ethical dilemmas of the kind they expect to face in practice. They have become aware of ethical problems laymen often see as crucial for the physician—whether it is right to keep patients with fatal diseases alive as long as possible, or what should be done if an influential patient demands an abortion—and worry about them. As they near graduation and student culture begins to break down as the soon-to-be doctors are about to go their separate ways, these questions are more and more openly discussed.

While in school, they have added to their earlier idealism a new and peculiarly professional idealism. Even though they know that few doctors live up to standards they have been taught, they

[9] See the discussion in Howard S. Becker, "Interviewing Medical Students," *op.cit.*

intend always to examine their patients thoroughly and to give treatment based on firm diagnosis rather than merely to relieve symptoms. This expansion and transformation of idealism appear most explicitly in their consideration of alternative careers, concerning both specialization and the kind of arrangements to be made for setting up practice. Many of their hypothetical choices aim at making it possible for them to be the kind of doctors their original idealism pictured. Many seniors consider specialty training so that they will be able to work in a limited field in which it will be more nearly possible to know all there is to know, thus avoiding the necessity of dealing in a more ignorant way with the wider range of problems general practice would present. In the same manner, they think of schemes to establish partnerships or other arrangements making it easier to avoid a work load which would prevent them from giving each patient the thorough examination and care they now see as ideal.

In other words, as school comes to an end, the cynicism specific to the school situation also comes to an end and their original and more general idealism about medicine comes to the fore again, though within a framework of more realistic alternatives. Their idealism is now more informed although no less selfless.

DISCUSSION

We have used the words "idealism" and "cynicism" loosely in our description of the changeable state of mind of the medical student, playing on ambiguities we can now attempt to clear up. Retaining a core of common meaning, the dictionary definition, in our reference to the person's belief in the worth of his activity and the claims made for it, we have seen that this is not a generalized trait of the students we studied but rather an attitude which varies greatly, depending on the particular activity the worth of which is questioned and the situation in which the attitude is expressed.

This variability of the idealistic attitude suggests that in using such an element of personal perspective in sociological analysis one should not treat it as homogeneous but should make a determined search for subtypes which may arise under different conditions and have differing consequences. Such subtypes presumably can be constructed along many dimensions. There might, for instance, be consistent variations in the medical students' idealism through the four years of school that are related to their social class backgrounds. We have stressed in this report the subtypes that can be constructed according to variations in the object of the idealistic attitude and variations in the audience the person has in mind when he adopts the attitude. The medical students can be viewed as both idealistic and cynical, depending on whether one has in mind their view of their school activities or the future they envision for themselves as doctors. Further, they might take one or another of these positions depending on whether their implied audience is made up of other students, their instructors, or the lay public.

A final complication arises because cynicism and idealism are not merely attributes of the actor, but are as dependent on the person doing the attributing as they are on the qualities of the individual to whom they are attributed.[10] Though the student may see his own disregard of the unique personal troubles of a particular patient as proper scientific objectivity, the layman may view this objectivity as heartless cynicism.[11]

Having made these analytic distinctions, we can now summarize the transformations of these characteristics as we have seen them occurring among medical students. Some of the students' determined idealism at the outset is reaction

[10] See Philip Selznick's related discussion of fanaticism in *TVA and the Grass Roots*, Berkeley: University of California Press, 1953, pp. 205–213.

[11] George Orwell gives the layman's side in his essay, "How the Poor Die" in *Shooting an Elephant and Other Essays*, London: Secker and Warburg, 1950, pp. 18–32.

against the lay notion, of which they are uncomfortably aware, that doctors are money-hungry cynics; they counter this with an idealism of similar lay origin stressing the doctor's devotion to service. But this idealism soon meets a setback, as students find that it will not be relevant for awhile, since medical school has, it seems, little relation to the practice of medicine, as they see it. As it has not been refuted, but only shown to be temporarily beside the point, the students "agree" to set this idealism aside in favor of a realistic approach to the problem of getting through school. This approach, which we have labeled as the cynicism specific to the school experience, serves as protection for the earlier grandiose feelings about

medicine by postponing their exposure to reality to a distant future. As that future approaches near the end of the four years and its possible mistreatment of their ideals moves closer, the students again worry about maintaining their integrity, this time in actual medical practice. They use some of the knowledge they have gained to plan careers which, it is hoped, can best bring their ideals to realization.

We can put this in propositional form by saying that when a man's ideals are challenged by outsiders and then further strained by reality, he may salvage them by postponing their application to a future time when conditions are expected to be more propitious.

TAKING ANOTHER LOOK

1 Which research techniques were used by Becker and Geer in their study of idealism in medical school?

2 Briefly describe some of the expectations concerning medicine held by students who are entering medical school.

3 How does the "student culture" influence medical students?

4 Viewed from a functionalist perspective, are there ways in which the increasing cynicism of certain medical students could be said to be functional? Are there ways in which the continuing idealism of certain medical students could be said to be dysfunctional?

5 How might conflict theorists view the issue of medical students' idealism and cynicism?

The Importance of Role

Peter Berger

When we speak of an individual's "status" in casual conversation, the term usually conveys connotations of influence, wealth, and fame. However, sociologists use *status* to refer to any of the full range of socially defined positions within a large group or society—from the lowest to the highest position. Within American society, a person can occupy the status of president of the United States, fruit picker, son or daughter, violinist, teenager, resident of Minneapolis, or neighbor. Clearly, a person holds more than one status simultaneously.

Throughout our lives, we are acquiring what sociologists call *social roles*. A social role is a set of expectations of individuals who occupy a given social position or status. With each distinctive social status come particular role expectations. However, actual performance varies from individual to individual. One secretary may assume extensive administrative responsibilities, whereas another may focus on clerical duties.

Roles are a significant component of social structure. They enable us to anticipate the behavior of others and to pattern our own actions accordingly. It is important to understand social roles in terms of the distinctive characteristics of a given society. For example, in the United States the role of criminal lawyer involves developing arguments to persuade a jury, a group of persons untrained in law. Yet jury trials are virtually unknown in Europe; consequently, the role of lawyer is performed quite differently there than in the United States.

In the following selection, sociologist Peter Berger explains how people assume and play social roles. Berger suggests that roles carry with them both certain actions and the resulting emotions and attitudes. In his view, the strength of the process of assuming a role "comes precisely from its unconscious, unreflecting character." The role "forms, shapes, patterns both action and actor." Berger emphasizes that, when viewed from a sociological perspective, "identity is socially bestowed, socially sustained and socially transformed."

In this selection, Berger draws upon the work of two pioneers of sociological thought: Charles Horton Cooley and George Herbert Mead. Cooley (1864–1929), writing in the early 1900s, advanced the belief that we learn who we are by interacting with others. Our view of ourselves, then, comes not only from thinking about our personal qualities but also from our impressions of how others perceive us. Cooley used the term *looking-glass self* to emphasize that the self is the product of our social interactions with other people.

George Herbert Mead (1863–1931) is widely regarded as the founder of the interactionist perspective. Mead was interested in observing the most minute forms of communication—smiles, frowns, nodding of one's head—and in understanding how such individual behavior was influenced by the larger context of a group or society. Mead is best known for his theory of the self. According to Mead, the *self* represents the sum total of people's perceptions, beliefs, and feelings about themselves, just as it did for Cooley. However, Mead's theory of the self was shaped by his overall view of socialization as a lifelong process. As people mature, the self changes and begins to reflect greater concern about the reactions of others.

While an average individual meets up with very different expectations in different areas of his life in society, the situations that produce these expectations fall into certain clusters. A student may take two courses from two different professors in two different departments, with considerable variations in the expectations met with in the two situations (say, as between formality or informality in the relations between professor and students). Nevertheless, the situations will be sufficiently similar to each other and to other classroom situations previously experienced to enable the student to carry into both situations essentially the same overall response. In other words, in both cases, with but a few modifications, he will be able to *play the role* of student. A role, then may be defined as a typified response to a typified expectation. Society has predefined the fundamental typology. To use the language of the theater, from which the concept of role is derived, we can say that society provides the script for all the *dramatis personae*. The individual actors, therefore, need but slip into the roles already assigned to them before the curtain goes up. As long as they play their roles as provided for in this script, the social play can proceed as planned.

The role provides the pattern according to which the individual is to act in the particular situation. Roles, in society as in the theater, will vary in the exactness with which they lay down instructions for the actor. Taking occupational roles for an instance, a fairly minimal pattern goes into the role of garbage collector, while physicians or clergymen or officers have to acquire all kinds of distinctive mannerisms, speech and motor habits, such as military bearing, sanctimonious diction or bedside cheer. It would, however, be missing an essential aspect of the role if one regarded it merely as a regulatory pattern for externally visible actions. One feels more ardent by kissing, more humble by kneeling and more angry by shaking one's fist. That is, the kiss not only expresses ardor but manufactures it. Roles carry with them both certain actions and the emotions and attitudes that belong to these actions. The

professor putting on an act that pretends to wisdom comes to feel wise. The preacher finds himself believing what he preaches. The soldier discovers martial stirrings in his breast as he puts on his uniform. In each case, while the emotion or attitude may have been present before the role was taken on, the latter inevitably strengthens what was there before. In many instances there is every reason to suppose that nothing at all anteceded the playing of the role in the actor's consciousness. In other words, one becomes wise by being appointed a professor, believing by engaging in activities that presuppose belief, and ready for battle by marching in formation.

Let us take an example. A man recently commissioned as an officer, especially if he came up through the ranks, will at first be at least slightly embarrassed by the salutes he now receives from the enlisted men he meets on his way. Probably he will respond to them in a friendly, almost apologetic manner. The new insignia on his uniform are at that point still something that he has merely put on, almost like a disguise. Indeed, the new officer may even tell himself and others that underneath he is still the same person, that he simply has new responsibilities (among which, *en passant*, is the duty to accept the salutes of enlisted men). This attitude is not likely to last very long. In order to carry out his new role of officer, our man must maintain a certain bearing. This bearing has quite definite implications. Despite all the double-talk in this area that is customary in so-called democratic armies, such as the American one, one of the fundamental implications is that an officer is a superior somebody, entitled to obedience and respect on the basis of this superiority. Every military salute given by an inferior in rank is an act of obeisance, received as a matter of course by the one who returns it. Thus, with every salute given and accepted (along, of course, with a hundred other ceremonial acts that enhance his new status) our man is fortified in his new bearing —and in its, as it were, ontological presuppositions. He not only acts like an officer, he feels like one. Gone are the embarrassment, the apologetic attitude, the I'm-just-another-guy-really grin. If on some occasion an enlisted man should fail to salute with the appropriate amount of enthusiasm or even commit the unthinkable act of failing to salute at all, our officer is not merely going to punish a violation of military regulations. He will be driven with every fiber of his being to redress an offence against the appointed order of his cosmos.

It is important to stress in this illustration that only very rarely is such a process deliberate or based on reflection. Our man has not sat down and figured out all the things that ought to go into his new role, including the things that he ought to feel and believe. The strength of the process comes precisely from its unconscious, unreflecting character. He has become an officer almost as effortlessly as he grew into a person with blue eyes, brown hair and a height of six feet. Nor would it be correct to say that our man must be rather stupid and quite an exception among his comrades. On the contrary, the exception is the man who reflects on his roles and his role changes (a type, by the way, who would probably make a poor officer). Even very intelligent people, when faced with doubt about their roles in society, will involve themselves even more in the doubted activity rather than withdraw into reflection. The theologian who doubts his faith will pray more and increase his church attendance, the businessman beset by qualms about his rat-race activities starts going to the office on Sundays too, and the terrorist who suffers from nightmares volunteers for nocturnal executions. And, of course, they are perfectly correct in this course of action. Each role has its inner discipline, what Catholic monastics would call its "formation." The role forms, shapes, patterns both action and actor. It is very difficult to pretend in this world. Normally, one becomes what one plays at.

Every role in society has attached to it a certain identity. As we have seen, some of these identities are trivial and temporary ones, as in some occupations that demand little modification in the being of their practitioners. It is not difficult to change from garbage collector to night watchman. It is considerably more difficult to change from clergyman to officer. It is very, very difficult to change from Negro to white. And it is almost impossible to change from man to woman. These differences in the ease of role changing ought not to blind us to the fact that even identities that we consider to be our essential selves have been socially assigned. Just as there are racial roles to be acquired and identified with, so there are sexual roles. To say "I am a man" is just as much a proclamation of role as to say "I am a colonel in the U.S. Army." We are well aware of the fact that one is born a male, while not even the most humorless martinet imagines himself to have been born with a golden eagle sitting on his umbilical cord. But to be biologically male is a far cry from the specific, socially defined (and, of course, socially relative) role that goes with the statement "I am a man." A male child does not have to learn to have an erection. But he must learn to be aggressive, to have ambitions, to compete with others, and to be suspicious of too much gentleness in himself. The male role in our society, however, requires all these things that one must learn, as does a male identity. To have an erection is not enough—if it were, regiments of psychotherapists would be out of work.

This significance of role theory could be summarized by saying that, in a sociological perspective, identity is socially bestowed, socially sustained and socially transformed. The example of the man in process of becoming an officer may suffice to illustrate the way in which identities are bestowed in adult life. However, even roles that are much more fundamentally part of what psychologists would call our personality than those associated with a particular adult activity are bestowed in very similar manner through a social process. This has been demonstrated over and over again in studies of so-called socialization—the process by which a child learns to be a participant member of society.

Probably the most penetrating theoretical account of this process is the one given by Mead, in which the genesis of the self is interpreted as being one and the same event as the discovery of society. The child finds out who he is as he learns what society is. He learns to play roles properly belonging to him by learning, as Mead puts it, "to take the role of the other"—which, incidentally, is the crucial sociopsychological function of play, in which children masquerade with a variety of social roles and in doing so discover the significance of those being assigned to them. All this learning occurs, and can only occur, in interaction with other human beings, be it the parents or whoever else raises the child. The child first takes on roles *vis-a-vis* what Mead calls his "significant others," that is, those persons who deal with him intimately and whose attitudes are decisive for the formation of his conception of himself. Later, the child learns that the roles he plays are not only relevant to this intimate circle, but relate to the expectations directed toward him by society at large. This higher level of abstraction in the social response Mead calls the discovery of the "generalized other." That is, not only the child's mother expects him to be good, clean and truthful, society in general does so as well. Only when this general conception of society emerges is the child capable of forming a clear conception of himself. "Self" and "society," in the child's experience, are the two sides of the same coin.

In other words, identity is not something "given," but is bestowed in acts of social recognition. We become that as which we are addressed. The same idea is expressed in Cooley's well-known description of the self as a reflection in a looking glass. This does not mean, of course, that there are not certain characteristics an individual is born with, that are carried by his genetic heritage regardless of the social environment in which the latter will have to unfold itself. Our knowledge of man's biology does not as yet allow us a very clear picture of the extent to which this may be true. We do know, however, that the room for social formation within those genetic limits is very large indeed. Even with the biological questions

left largely unsettled, we can say that to be human is to be recognized as human, just as to be a certain kind of man is to be recognized as such. The child deprived of human affection and attention becomes dehumanized. The child who is given respect comes to respect himself. A little boy considered to be a *schlemiel* becomes one, just as a grown-up treated as an awe-inspiring young god of war begins to think of himself and act as is appropriate to such a figure—and, indeed, merges his identity with the one he is presented with in these expectations.

Identities are socially bestowed. They must also be socially sustained, and fairly steadily so. One cannot be human all by oneself and, apparently, one cannot hold on to any particular identity all by oneself. The self-image of the officer as an officer can be maintained only in a social context in which others are willing to recognize him in this identity. If this recognition is suddenly withdrawn, it usually does not take very long before the self-image collapses. . . .

Role theory, when pursued to its logical conslusions, does far more than provide us with a convenient shorthand for the description of various social activities. It gives us a sociological anthropology, that is, a view of man based on his existence in society. This view tells us that man plays dramatic parts in the grand play of society, and that, speaking sociologically, he *is* the masks that he must wear to do so. The human person also appears now in a dramatic context, true to its theatrical etymology (*persona*, the technical term given to the actors' masks in classical theater). The person is perceived as a repertoire of roles, each one properly equipped with a certain identity. The range of an individual person can be measured by the number of roles he is capable of playing. The person's biography now appears to us as an uninterrupted sequence of stage performances, played to different audiences, sometimes involving drastic changes of costume, always demanding that the actor *be* what he is playing.

TAKING ANOTHER LOOK

1 How does Berger define the term *role*?
2 According to Berger, how are intelligent people likely to react when faced with doubt about their roles in society?
3 How does Berger view the male role in American society?
4 What does Berger mean when he asserts that "in a sociological perspective, identity is socially bestowed, socially sustained, and socially transformed"?
5 How did George Herbert Mead use the term "significant others"?
6 According to Berger, what view of man based on his existence in society is offered by role theory?

On Being Sane in Insane Places

David L. Rosenhan

Sociologist Erving Goffman coined the term *total institution* to refer to institutions such as prisons, the military, mental hospitals, and convents that regulate all aspects of a person's life under a single authority. Individuality is often lost within total institutions. For example, upon entering prison to begin "doing time," a person may experience what Goffman calls a "mortification ceremony," as he or she is stripped of clothing, jewelry, and other personal possessions. Even the individual's self is taken away to some extent; the prison inmate loses his or her name and becomes known to authorities as a number.

In the following selection, psychologist David L. Rosenhan reports on a series of experiments that were conducted in order to assess the admissions process in residential mental institutions. He had 8 sane persons—ranging from graduate students to a pediatrician—gain admission as patients at 12 different mental hospitals. All arrived at the hospitals complaining that they had heard voices saying "empty," "hollow," and "third." However, once in the wards, the "patients" behaved normally and told psychiatrists that they felt fine.

Despite their public displays of sanity, Rosenhan's confederates were not quickly discharged. The lengths of hospitalization ranged from 7 to 52 days, and averaged 19 days. In this experiment, Rosenhan sought to explore whether a change in the independent variable (the behavior of the patients) was related to a change in the dependent variable (the staff diagnosis). His carefully conceived study demonstrated that a psychiatric label has a life of its own: the perceptions of the staff proved to be more important than the actual behavior of the 8 subjects.

Rosenhan's analysis is in line with the sociological perspective of *labeling theory*. This approach to deviance does not focus on why some individuals come to commit deviant acts; instead, it attempts to explain why certain people are *viewed* as deviant while others whose behavior is similar are not seen in such harsh terms. Similarly, rather than studying the causes of mental illness, Rosenhan focuses on how people come to be labeled as mentally ill, how they are controlled in mental hospitals, and what the possible consequences of this labeling might be. His findings are especially important given the personal, social, and legal stigmata attached to being an ex-mental patient in the United States.

If sanity and insanity exist, how shall we know them?

The question is neither capricious nor itself insane. However much we may be personally convinced that we can tell the normal from the abnormal, the evidence is simply not compelling. It is commonplace, for example, to read about murder trials wherein eminent psychiatrists for the defense are contradicted by equally eminent psychiatrists for the prosecution on the matter of the defendant's sanity. More generally, there are a great deal of conflicting data on the reliability, utility, and meaning of such terms as "sanity," "insanity," "mental illness," and "schizophrenia".[1] Finally, as early as 1934, Benedict suggested that normality and abnormality are not universal.[2] What is viewed as normal in one culture may be seen as quite aberrant in another. Thus, notions of normality and abnormality may not be quite as accurate as people believe they are.

To raise questions regarding normality and abnormality is in no way to question the fact that some behaviors are deviant or odd. Murder is deviant. So, too, are hallucinations. Nor does raising such questions deny the existence of the personal anguish that is often associated with "mental illness." Anxiety and depression exist. Psychological suffering exists. But normality and abnormality, sanity and insanity, and the diagnoses that flow from them may be less substantive than many believe them to be.

At its heart, the question of whether the sane can be distinguished from the insane (and whether degrees of insanity can be distinguished from each other) is a simple matter: do the salient characteristics that lead to diagnoses reside in the patients themselves or in the environments and contexts in which observers find them? From Bleuler, through Kretchmer, through the formulators of the recently revised *Diagnostic and Statistical Manual* of the American Psychiatric Association, the belief has been strong that patients present symptoms, that those symptoms can be categorized, and, implicitly, that the sane are distinguishable from the insane. More recently,

however, this belief has been questioned. Based in part on theoretical and anthropological considerations, but also on philosophical, legal, and therapeutic ones, the view has grown that psychological categorization of mental illness is useless at best and downright harmful, misleading, and pejorative at worst. Psychiatric diagnoses, in this view, are in the minds of the observers and are not valid summaries of characteristics displayed by the observed.[3-5]

Gains can be made in deciding which of these is more nearly accurate by getting normal people (that is, people who do not have, and have never suffered, symptoms of serious psychiatric disorders) admitted to psychiatric hospitals and then determining whether they were discovered to be sane and, if so, how. If the sanity of such pseudopatients were always detected, there would be prima facie evidence that a sane individual can be distinguished from the insane context in which he is found. Normality (and presumably abnormality) is distinct enough that it can be recognized wherever it occurs, for it is carried within the person. If, on the other hand, the sanity of the pseudopatients were never discovered, serious difficulties would arise for those who support traditional modes of psychiatric diagnosis. Given that the hospital staff was not incompetent, that the pseudopatient had been behaving as sanely as he had been outside of the hospital, and that it had never been previously suggested that he belonged in a psychiatric hospital, such an unlikely out-

[1] P. Ash, *J. Abnorm. Soc. Psychol.* **44**, 272 (1949); A. T. Beck, *Amer. J. Psychiat.* **119**, 210 (1962); A. T. Boisen, *Psychiatry* **2**, 233 (1938); N. Kreitman, *J. Ment. Sci.* **107**, 876 (1961); N. Kreitman, P. Sainsbury, J. Morrisey, J. Towers, J. Scrivener, *ibid.*, p. 887; H. O. Schmitt and C. P. Fonda, *J. Abnorm. Soc. Psychol.* **52**, 262 (1956); W. Seeman, *J. Nerv. Ment. Dis.* **118**, 541 (1953). For an analysis of these artifacts and summaries of the disputes, see J. Zubin, *Annu. Rev. Psychol.* **18**, 373 (1967); L. Phillips and J. G. Draguns, *ibid.* **22**, 447 (1971).

[2] R. Benedict, *J. Gen. Psychol.* **10**, 59 (1934).

[3] See in this regard H. Becker, *Outsiders: Studies in the Sociology of Deviance* (Free Press, New York, 1963); B. M. Braginsky, D. D. Braginsky, K. Ring, *Methods of Madness: The Mental Hospital as a Last Resort* (Holt, Rinehart & Winston, New York, 1969); G. M. Crocetti and P. V. Lemkau,

Amer. Sociol. Rev. **30**, 577 (1965); E. Goffman, *Behavior in Public Places* (Free Press, New York, 1964); R. D. Laing, *The Divided Self: A Study of Sanity and Madness* (Quadrangle, Chicago, 1960); D. L. Phillips, *Amer. Sociol. Rev.* **28**, 963 (1963); T. R. Sarbin, *Psychol. Today* **6**, 18 (1972); E. Schur, *Amer. J. Sociol.* **75**, 309 (1969); T. Szasz, *Law, Liberty and Psychiatry* (Macmillan, New York, 1963); *The Myth of Mental Illness: Foundations of a Theory of Mental Illness* (Hoeber-Harper, New York, 1963). For a critique of some of these views, see W. R. Gove, *Amer. Sociol. Rev.* **35**, 873 (1970).

[4] E. Goffman, *Asylums* (Doubleday, Garden City, N.Y., 1961).

[5] T. J. Scheff, *Being Mentally Ill: A Sociological Theory* (Aldine, Chicago, 1966).

come would support the view that psychiatric diagnosis betrays little about the patient but much about the environment in which an observer finds him.

This article describes such an experiment. Eight sane people gained secret admission to 12 different hospitals.[6] Their diagnostic experiences constitute the data of the first part of this article; the remainder is devoted to a description of their experiences in psychiatric institutions. Too few psychiatrists and psychologists, even those who have worked in such hospitals, know what the experience is like. They rarely talk about it with former patients, perhaps because they distrust information coming from the previously insane. Those who have worked in psychiatric hospitals are likely to have adapted so thoroughly to the settings that they are insensitive to the impact of that experience. And while there have been occasional reports of researchers who submitted themselves to psychiatric hospitalization,[7] these researchers have commonly remained in the hospitals for short periods of time, often with the knowledge of the hospital staff. It is difficult to know the extent to which they were treated like patients or like research colleagues. Nevertheless, their reports about the inside of the psychiatric hospital have been valuable. This article extends those efforts.

PSEUDOPATIENTS AND THEIR SETTINGS

The eight pseudopatients were a varied group. One was a psychology graduate student in his 20's. The remaining seven were older and "established." Among them were three psychologists, a pediatrician, a psychiatrist, a painter, and a housewife. Three pseudopatients were women, five were men. All of them employed pseudonyms, lest their alleged diagnoses embarrass them later. Those who were in mental health professions alleged another occupation in order to avoid the special attentions that might be accorded by staff, as a matter of courtesy or caution, to ailing colleagues.[8] With the exception of myself (I was the first pseudopatient and my presence was known to the hospital administrator and chief psychologist and, so far as I can tell, to them alone), the presence of pseudopatients and the nature of the research program was not known to the hospital staffs.[9]

The settings were similarly varied. In order to generalize the findings, admission into a variety of hospitals was sought. The 12 hospitals in the sample were located in five different states on the East and West coasts. Some were old and shabby, some were quite new. Some were research-oriented, others not. Some had good staff-patient ratios, others were quite understaffed. Only one was a strictly private hospital. All of the others were

---

[6] Data from a ninth pseudopatient are not incorporated in this report because, although his sanity went undetected, he falsified aspects of his personal history, including his marital status and parental relationships. His experimental behaviors therefore were not identical to those of the other pseudopatients.

[7] A. Barry, *Bellevue Is a State of Mind* (Harcourt Brace Jovanovich, New York, 1971); I. Belknap, *Human Problems of a State Mental Hospital* (McGraw-Hill, New York, 1956); W. Caudill, F. C. Redlich, H. R. Gilmore, E. B. Brody, *Amer. J. Orthopsychiat.* **22,** 314 (1952); A. R. Goldman, R. H. Bohr, T. A. Steinberg, *Prof. Psychol.* **1,** 427 (1970); unauthored, *Roche Report* **1** (No. 13), 8 (1971).

[8] Beyond the personal difficulties that the pseudopatient is likely to experience in the hospital, there are legal and social ones that, combined, require considerable attention before entry. For example, once admitted to a psychiatric institution, it is difficult, if not impossible, to be discharged on short notice,

state law to the contrary notwithstanding. I was not sensitive to these difficulties at the outset of the project, nor to the personal and situational emergencies that can arise, but later a writ of habeas corpus was prepared for each of the entering pseudopatients and an attorney was kept "on call" during every hospitalization. I am grateful to John Kaplan and Robert Bartels for legal advice and assistance in these matters.

[9] However distasteful such concealment is, it was a necessary first step to examining these questions. Without concealment, there would have been no way to know how valid these experiences were; nor was there any way of knowing whether whatever detections occurred were a tribute to the diagnostic acumen of the staff or to the hospital's rumor network. Obviously, since my concerns are general ones that cut across individual hospitals and staffs, I have respected their anonymity and have eliminated clues that might lead to their identification.

supported by state or federal funds or, in one instance, by university funds.

After calling the hospital for an appointment, the pseudopatient arrived at the admissions office complaining that he had been hearing voices. Asked what the voices said, he replied that they were often unclear, but as far as he could tell they said "empty," "hollow," and "thud." The voices were unfamiliar and were of the same sex as the pseudopatient. The choice of these symptoms was occasioned by their apparent similarity to existential symptoms. Such symptoms are alleged to arise from painful concerns about the perceived meaninglessness of one's life. It is as if the hallucinating person were saying, "My life is empty and hollow." The choice of these symptoms was also determined by the *absence* of a single report of existential psychoses in the literature.

Beyond alleging the symptoms and falsifying name, vocation, and employment, no further alterations of person, history, or circumstances were made. The significant events of the pseudopatient's life history were presented as they had actually occurred. Relationships with parents and siblings, with spouse and children, with people at work and in school, consistent with the aforementioned exceptions, were described as they were or had been. Frustrations and upsets were described along with joys and satisfactions. These facts are important to remember. If anything, they strongly biased the subsequent results in favor of detecting sanity, since none of their histories or current behaviors were seriously pathological in any way.

Immediately upon admission to the psychiatric ward, the pseudopatient ceased simulating *any* symptoms of abnormality. In some cases, there was a brief period of mild nervousness and anxiety, since none of the pseudopatients really believed that they would be admitted so easily. Indeed, their shared fear was that they would be immediately exposed as frauds and greatly embarrassed. Moreover, many of them had never visited a psychiatric ward; even those who had, nevertheless had some genuine fears about what might happen to them. Their nervousness, then, was quite appropriate to the novelty of the hospital setting, and it abated rapidly.

Apart from that short-lived nervousness, the pseudopatient behaved on the ward as he "normally" behaved. The pseudopatient spoke to patients and staff as he might ordinarily. Because there is uncommonly little to do on a psychiatric ward, he attempted to engage others in conversation. When asked by staff how he was feeling, he indicated that he was fine, that he no longer experienced symptoms. He responded to instructions from attendants, to calls for medication (which was not swallowed), and to dining-hall instructions. Beyond such activities as were available to him on the admissions ward, he spent his time writing down his observations about the ward, its patients, and the staff. Initially these notes were written "secretly," but as it soon became clear that no one much cared, they were subsequently written on standard tablets of paper in such public places as the dayroom. No secret was made of these activities.

The pseudopatient, very much as a true psychiatric patient, entered a hospital with no foreknowledge of when he would be discharged. Each was told that he would have to get out by his own devices, essentially by convincing the staff that he was sane. The psychological stresses associated with hospitalization were considerable, and all but one of the pseudopatients desired to be discharged almost immediately after being admitted. They were, therefore, motivated not only to behave sanely, but to be paragons of cooperation. That their behavior was in no way disruptive is confirmed by nursing reports, which have been obtained on most of the patients. These reports uniformly indicate that the patients were "friendly," "cooperative," and "exhibited no abnormal indications."

THE NORMAL ARE NOT DETECTABLY SANE

Despite their public "show" of sanity, the pseudopatients were never detected. Admitted, except in one case, with a diagnosis of schizophrenia,[10] each was discharged with a diagnosis of schizophrenia "in remission." The label "in remission" should in no way be dismissed as a formality, for at no time during any hospitalization had any question been raised about any pseudopatient's simulation. Nor are there any indications in the hospital records that the pseudopatient's status was suspect. Rather, the evidence is strong that, once labeled schizophrenic, the pseudopatient was stuck with that label. If the pseudopatient was to be discharged, he must naturally be "in remission"; but he was not sane, nor, in the institution's view, had he ever been sane.

The uniform failure to recognize sanity cannot be attributed to the quality of the hospitals, for, although there were considerable variations among them, several are considered excellent. Nor can it be alleged that there was simply not enough time to observe the pseudopatients. Length of hospitalization ranged from 7 to 52 days, with an average of 19 days. The pseudopatients were not, in fact, carefully observed, but this failure clearly speaks more to traditions within psychiatric hospitals than to lack of opportunity.

Finally, it cannot be said that the failure to recognize the pseudopatients' sanity was due to the fact that they were not behaving sanely. Where there was clearly some tension present in all of them, their daily visitors could detect no serious behavioral consequences—nor, indeed, could other patients. It was quite common for the patients to "detect" the pseudopatients' sanity. During the first three hospitalizations, when accurate counts were kept, 35 of a total of 118 patients on the admissions ward voiced their suspicions, some vigorously. "You're not crazy. You're a journalist, or a professor [referring to the continual note-taking]. You're checking up on the hospital." While most of the patients were reassured by the pseudopatient's insistence that he had been sick before he came in but was fine now, some continued to believe that the pseudopatient was sane throughout his hospitalization.[11] The fact that the patients often recognized normality when staff did not raises important questions.

Failure to detect sanity during the course of hospitalization may be due to the fact that physicians operate with a strong bias toward what statisticians call the type 2 error.[5] This is to say that physicians are more inclined to call a healthy person sick (a false positive, type 2) than a sick person healthy (a false negative, type 1). The reasons for this are not hard to find: it is clearly more dangerous to misdiagnose illness than health. Better to err on the side of caution, to suspect illness even among the healthy.

But what holds for medicine does not hold equally well for psychiatry. Medical illnesses, while unfortunate, are not commonly pejorative. Psychiatric diagnoses, on the contrary, carry with them personal, legal, and social stigmas.[12] It was therefore important to see whether the tendency toward diagnosing the sane insane could be reversed. The following experiment was arranged at a research and teaching hospital whose staff had heard these findings but doubted that such an error could occur in their hospital. The staff was informed that at some time during the following 3 months, one or more pseudopatients would at-

---

[10] Interestingly, of the 12 admissions, 11 were diagnosed as schizophrenic and one, with the identical symptomatology, as manic-depressive psychosis. This diagnosis has a more favorable prognosis, and it was given by the only private hospital in our sample. On the relations between social class and psychiatric diagnosis, see A. deB. Hollingshead and F. C. Redlich, *Social Class and Mental Illness: A Community Study* (Wiley, New York, 1958).

[11] It is possible, of course, that patients have quite broad latitudes in diagnosis and therefore are inclined to call many people sane, even those whose behavior is patently aberrant.

However, although we have no hard data on this matter, it was our distinct impression that this was not the case. In many instances, patients not only singled us out for attention, but came to imitate our behaviors and styles.

[12] J. Cumming and E. Cumming, *Community Ment. Health* **1,** 135 (1965); A. Farina and K. Ring, *J. Abnorm. Psychol.* **70,** 47 (1965); H. E. Freeman and O. G. Simmons, *The Mental Patient Comes Home* (Wiley, New York, 1963); W. J. Johannsen, *Ment. Hygiene* **53,** 218 (1969); A. S. Linsky, *Soc. Psychiat.* **5,** 166 (1970).

tempt to be admitted into the psychiatric hospital. Each staff member was asked to rate each patient who presented himself to admissions or on the ward according to the likelihood that the patient was a pseudopatient. A 10-point scale was used, with a 1 and 2 reflecting high confidence that the patient was a pseudopatient.

Judgments were obtained on 193 patients who were admitted for psychiatric treatment. All staff who had had sustained contact with or primary responsibility for the patient—attendants, nurses, psychiatrists, physicians, and psychologists—were asked to make judgments. Forty-one patients were alleged, with high confidence, to be pseudopatients by at least one member of the staff. Twenty-three were considered suspect by at least one psychiatrist. Nineteen were suspected by one psychiatrist *and* one other staff member. Actually, no genuine pseudopatient (at least from my group) presented himself during this period.

The experiment is instructive. It indicates that the tendency to designate sane people as insane can be reversed when the stakes (in this case, prestige and diagnostic acumen) are high. But what can be said of the 19 people who were suspected of being "sane" by one psychiatrist and another staff member? Were these people truly "sane," or was it rather the case that in the course of avoiding the type 2 error the staff tended to make more errors of the first sort—calling the crazy "sane"? There is no way of knowing. But one thing is certain: any diagnostic process that lends itself so readily to massive errors of this sort cannot be a very reliable one. . . .

POWERLESSNESS AND DEPERSONALIZATION

Eye contact and verbal contact reflect concern and individuation; their absence, avoidance and depersonalization. The data I have presented do not do justice to the rich daily encounters that grew up around matters of depersonalization and avoidance. I have records of patients who were beaten by staff for the sin of having initiated verbal contact. During my own experience, for example, one patient was beaten in the presence of other patients for having approached an attendant and told him, "I like you." Occasionally, punishment meted out to patients for misdemeanors seemed so excessive that it could not be justified by the most radical interpretations of psychiatric canon. Nevertheless, they appeared to go unquestioned. Tempers were often short. A patient who had not heard a call for medication would be roundly excoriated, and the morning attendants would often wake patients with, "Come on, you m-----f-----s, out of bed!"

Neither anecdotal nor "hard" data can convey the overwhelming sense of powerlessness which invades the individual as he is continually exposed to the depersonalization of the psychiatric hospital. It hardly matters *which* psychiatric hospital—the excellent public ones and the very plush private hospital were better than the rural and shabby ones in this regard, but, again, the features that psychiatric hospitals had in common overwhelmed by far their apparent differences.

Powerlessness was evident everywhere. The patient is deprived of many of his legal rights by dint of his psychiatric commitment.[13] He is shorn of credibility by virtue of his psychiatric label. His freedom of movement is restricted. He cannot initiate contact with the staff, but may only respond to such overtures as they make. Personal privacy is minimal. Patient quarters and possessions can be entered and examined by any staff member, for whatever reason. His personal history and anguish is available to any staff member (often including the "grey lady" and "candy striper" volunteer) who chooses to read his folder, regardless of their therapeutic relationship to him. His personal hygiene and waste evacuation are often monitored. The water closets may have no doors.

At times, depersonalization, reached such proportions that pseudopatients had the sense that

[13] D. B. Wexler and S. E. Scoville, *Ariz. Law Rev.* **13,** 1 (1971).

they were invisible, or at least unworthy of account. Upon being admitted, I and other pseudopatients took the initial physical examinations in a semipublic room, where staff members went about their own business as if we were not there.

On the ward, attendants delivered verbal and occasionally serious physical abuse to patients in the presence of other observing patients, some of whom (the pseudopatients) were writing it all down. Abusive behavior, on the other hand, terminated quite abruptly when other staff members were known to be coming. Staff are credible witnesses. Patients are not.

A nurse unbuttoned her uniform to adjust her brassiere in the presence of an entire ward of viewing men. One did not have the sense that she was being seductive. Rather, she didn't notice us. A group of staff persons might point to a patient in the dayroom and discuss him animatedly, as if he were not there.

One illuminating instance of depersonalization and invisibility occurred with regard to medications. All told, the pseudopatients were administered nearly 2100 pills, including Elavil, Stelazine, Compazine, and Thorazine, to name but a few. (That such a variety of medications should have been administered to patients presenting identical symptoms is itself worthy of note.) Only two were swallowed. The rest were either pocketed or deposited in the toilet. The pseudopatients were not alone in this. Although I have no precise records on how many patients rejected their medications, the pseudopatients frequently found the medications of other patients in the toilet before they deposited their own. As long as they were cooperative, their behavior and the pseudopatients' own in this matter, as in other important matters, went unnoticed throughout.

Reactions to such depersonalization among pseudopatients were intense. Although they had come to the hospital as participant observers and were fully aware that they did not "belong," they nevertheless found themselves caught up in and fighting the process of depersonalization. Some

examples: a graduate student in psychology asked his wife to bring his textbooks to the hospital so he could "catch up on his homework"—this despite the elaborate precautions taken to conceal his professional association. The same student, who had trained for quite some time to get into the hospital, and who had looked forward to the experience, "remembered" some drag races that he had wanted to see on the weekend and insisted that he be discharged by that time. Another pseudopatient attempted a romance with a nurse. Subsequently, he informed the staff that he was applying for admission to graduate school in psychology and was very likely to be admitted, since a graduate professor was one of his regular hospital visitors. The same person began to engage in psychotherapy with other patients—all of this as a way of becoming a person in an impersonal environment.

THE SOURCES OF DEPERSONALIZATION

What are the origins of depersonalization? I have already mentioned two. First are attitudes held by all of us toward the mentally ill—including those who treat them—attitudes characterized by fear, distrust, and horrible expectations on the one hand, and benevolent intentions on the other. Our ambivalence leads, in this instance as in others, to avoidance.

Second, and not entirely separate, the hierarchical structure of the psychiatric hospital facilitates depersonalization. Those who are at the top have least to do with patients, and their behavior inspires the rest of the staff. Average daily contact with psychiatrists, psychologists, residents, and physicians combined ranged from 3.9 to 25.1 minutes, with an overall mean of 6.8 (six pseudopatients over a total of 129 days of hospitalization). Included in this average are time spent in the admissions interview, ward meetings in the presence of a senior staff member, group and individual psychotherapy contacts, case presentation conferences, and discharge meetings. Clearly, patients do not spend much time in interpersonal contact with doctoral staff. And doctoral staff serve as models for nurses and attendants.

There are probably other sources. Psychiatric installations are presently in serious financial straits. Staff shortages are pervasive, staff time at a premium. Something has to give, and that something is patient contact. Yet, while financial stresses are realities, too much can be made of them. I have the impression that the psychological forces that result in depersonalization are much stronger than the fiscal ones and that the addition of more staff would not correspondingly improve patient care in this regard. The incidence of staff meetings and the enormous amount of record-keeping on patients, for example, have not been as substantially reduced as has patient contact. Priorities exist, even during hard times. Patient contact is not a significant priority in the traditional psychiatric hospital, and fiscal pressures do not account for this. Avoidance and depersonalization may.

Heavy reliance upon psychotropic medication tacitly contributes to depersonalization by convincing staff that treatment is indeed being conducted and that further patient contact may not be necessary. Even here, however, caution needs to be exercised in understanding the role of psychotropic drugs. If patients were powerful rather than powerless, if they were viewed as interesting individuals rather than diagnostic entities, if they were socially significant rather than social lepers, if their anguish truly and wholly compelled our sympathies and concerns, would we not *seek* contact with them, despite the availability of medications? Perhaps for the pleasure of it all?

THE CONSEQUENCES OF LABELING AND DEPERSONALIZATION

Whenever the ratio of what is known to what needs to be known approaches zero, we tend to invent "knowledge" and assume that we understand more than we actually do. We seem unable to acknowledge that we simply don't know. The needs for diagnosis and remediation of behavioral and emotional problems are enormous. But rather than acknowledge that we are just embarking on understanding, we continue to label patients "schizophrenic," "manic-depressive," and "insane," as if in those words we had captured the essence of understanding. The facts of the matter are that we have known for a long time that diagnoses are often not useful or reliable, but we have nevertheless continued to use them. We now know that we cannot distinguish insanity from sanity. It is depressing to consider how that information will be used.

Not merely depressing, but frightening. How many people, one wonders, are sane but not recognized as such in our psychiatric institutions? How many have been needlessly stripped of their privileges of citizenship, from the right to vote and drive to that of handling their own accounts? How many have feigned insanity in order to avoid the criminal consequences of their behavior, and, conversely, how many would rather stand trial than live interminably in a psychiatric hospital—but are wrongly thought to be mentally ill? How many have been stigmatized by well-intentioned, but nevertheless erroneous, diagnoses? On the last point, recall again that a "type 2 error" in psychiatric diagnosis does not have the same consequences it does in medical diagnosis. A diagnosis of cancer that has been found to be in error is cause for celebration. But psychiatric diagnoses are rarely found to be in error. The label sticks, a mark of inadequacy forever.

Finally, how many patients might be "sane" outside the psychiatric hospital but seem insane in it—not because craziness resides in them, as it were, but because they are responding to a bizarre setting, one that may be unique to institutions which harbor nether people? Goffman[4] calls the process of socialization to such institutions "mortification"—an apt metaphor that includes the processes of depersonalization that have been described here. And while it is impossible to know whether the pseudopatients' responses to these processes are characteristic of all inmates—they were, after all, not real patients—it is difficult to believe that these processes of socialization to a psychiatric hospital provide useful attitudes or habits of response for living in the "real world."

SUMMARY AND CONCLUSIONS

It is clear that we cannot distinguish the sane from the insane in psychiatric hospitals. The hospital itself imposes a special environment in which the meanings of behavior can easily be misunderstood. The consequences to patients hospitalized in such an environment—the powerlessness, depersonalization, segregation, mortification, and self-labeling—seem undoubtedly counter-therapeutic.

I do not, even now, understand this problem well enough to perceive solutions. But two matters seem to have some promise. The first concerns the proliferation of community mental health facilities, of crisis intervention centers, of the human potential movement, and of behavior therapies that, for all of their own problems, tend to avoid psychiatric labels, to focus on specific problems and behaviors, and to retain the individual in a relatively non-pejorative environment. Clearly, to the extent that we refrain from sending the distressed to insane places, our impressions of them are less likely to be distorted. (The risk of distorted perceptions, it seems to me, is always present, since we are much more sensitive to an individual's behaviors and verbalizations than we are to the subtle contextual stimuli that often promote them. At issue here is a matter of magnitude. And, as I have shown, the magnitude of distortion is exceedingly high in the extreme context that is a psychiatric hospital.)

The second matter that might prove promising speaks to the need to increase the sensitivity of mental health workers and researchers to the *Catch 22* position of psychiatric patients. Simply reading materials in this area will be of help to some such workers and researchers. For others, directly experiencing the impact of psychiatric hospitalization will be of enormous use. Clearly, further research into the social psychology of such total institutions will both facilitate treatment and deepen understanding.

I and the other pseudopatients in the psychiatric setting had distinctly negative reactions. We do not pretend to describe the subjective experiences of true patients. Theirs may be different from ours, particularly with the passage of time and the necessary process of adaptation to one's environment. But we can and do speak to the relatively more objective indices of treatment within the hospital. It could be a mistake, and a very unfortunate one, to consider that what happened to us derived from malice or stupidity on the part of the staff. Quite the contrary, our overwhelming impression of them was of people who really cared, who were committed and who were uncommonly intelligent. Where they failed, as they sometimes did painfully, it would be more accurate to attribute those failures to the environment in which they, too, found themselves than to personal callousness. Their perceptions and behavior were controlled by the situation, rather than being motivated by a malicious disposition. In a more benign environment, one that was less attached to global diagnosis, their behaviors and judgments might have been more benign and effective.[14]

[14] I thank W. Mischel, E. Orne, and M. S. Rosenhan for comments on an earlier draft of this manuscript.

TAKING ANOTHER LOOK

1 What evidence is there that Rosenhan attempted to study a variety of residential mental institutions?

2 What was the importance of the mental hospital's diagnosis that one of Rosenhan's pseudopatients was "in remission"?

3 In diagnosing mental illness, which of the following is more serious: a type 1 error (a false negative) or a type 2 error (a false positive)? Why?

4 In what ways were Rosenhan's findings in line with Erving Goffman's view of total institutions?

5 According to Rosenhan, what are the origins of depersonalization in mental hospitals?

6 What conclusions are offered by Rosenhan about the kinds of persons who work as staff members of residential mental hospitals and the reasons for their failures?

7 Discuss the possible ethical issues raised in this type of experiment.

A Key to Unlock the Asylum

Jean Bethke Elshtain

As noted in our discussion of David L. Rosenhan's "On Being Sane in Insane Places," a residential mental hospital is an example of a total institution in which people are removed from the larger society for an appreciable period of time. All aspects of a person's life are regulated under a single authority. In the United States, the period of the 1840s and 1850s was the "age of the asylum." Importantly, the asylum was put forward as a humanitarian and even a utopian institution that could rehabilitate the suffering and serve as a model facility for the rest of society.

By the 1960s, there was widespread criticism of this ideal; the crowding and depersonalization inherent in mental hospitals seemed to be a barrier to resolving emotional problems. The passage of the 1963 Community Mental Health Construction Act marked acceptance of the view that community-based health centers (which treat clients on an outpatient basis, thereby allowing them to continue working and living at home) provide more effective treatment than the institutionalized programs of state and county mental hospitals (which separate the mentally ill from their families and from other community supports). Consequently, community-based mental health care replaced hospitalization as the typical form of treatment.

In the following selection, political scientist Jean Bethke Elshtain critically analyzes the controversial public policy of deinstitutionalization of the mentally ill. Deinstitutionalization was often defended as a social reform that would effectively integrate the mentally ill into the outside world. Ideally, community centers, halfway houses, and therapeutic communities would be established so that released mental patients could benefit from a supportive transition period. However, as Elshtain points out, the authentic humanitarian concern behind deinstitutionalization proved to be convenient for politicians whose goal was simply cost cutting. She adds that, with former mental patients being disproportionately "dumped" into deteriorating low-income communities and neighborhoods, it is the "less well off" who are experiencing the social costs of liberal reform programs. Nevertheless, Elshtain concludes that despite possible abuses and difficulties, community mental health care remains the most desirable alternative for the majority of those in need of assistance.

The rights of mentally retarded people to decent and effective care have never received much support from an indifferent society and budget-conscious legislatures. Last month the U.S. Supreme Court tossed out as unconstitutionally vague a patients' "bill of rights" section in the Federal Developmentally Disabled Assistance and Bill of Rights Act of 1975, which provides Federal aid to state mental institutions. Upon pain of losing Federal funding under the act, the State of Pennsylvania had been ordered by a lower court to transfer patients from the Pennhurst State School, where conditions were found to be "abominable," to community-care facilities.

The callousness of the Supreme Court's ruling aside [see editorial, "Retarded Rights," *The Nation,* May 9], the case itself reflected the growing popularity of community-based therapy as an alternative to confinement in large, centralized facilities.

Deinstitutionalization has been called by its supporters a "social revolution" whose aim is to empty state hospitals for the mentally ill, the retarded, the "deviant." All such institutions will be closed down, and their patients reintegrated into the broader community. Institutionalization, once seen as a humane solution to problems of the mentally handicapped, has itself become a problem, they argue. Rather than providing therapy and care that aims at sending a well-equipped individual back into the world, institutions destroy social skills and reinforce the most destructive patterns of behavior. One advocate of deinstitutionalization, Benedict Alper, claims that "the institution as a means of coping with the problems of specific sectors of our population seems at this point to have run its course. Whether one is aged, below par intellectually or emotionally, delinquent, alcoholic, or drug-addicted, the source—and the remedy—of the problem lies in the communities where such people come from." Alper, and those who share his views, offer an alternative vision of therapeutic communities, with diverse social support facilities and halfway homes, training institutions and rehabilitative residences, that would reach out to embrace the once shunned, excluded, shut-away and ostracized.

Critics of community care argue that it is absurd to see institutions, per se, as evil, though many were and still are. Many "clients," they say, require sophisticated care available only in a total, structured setting. They insist, moreover, that deinstitutionalization programs have so far been half-baked and careless. The elderly, the mentally ill or the incompetent, juvenile offenders—all have been "dumped" into communities that are suspicious, hostile and completely unprepared for them. The result, they say, has been chaos, as the following news items attest:

Federal mental health planners envisioned the flowering of a network of support services to care for deinstitutionalized patients at the community level through the stimulus of Federal seed money. But 1,300 of the 2,000 community health centers projected for 1980 have failed to materialize and many that did have failed to service this chronically ill population. Deinstitutionalization, an ostensibly humane treatment program, has degenerated into a tragic crisis. Public scrutiny of the situation needs to begin now.
—*The New York Times,* January 26, 1980

Increasing numbers of patients discharged from mental institutions are entering nursing homes, an ironic result of the restructuring of health care financing and legislation to encourage the removal of patients from mental institutions and to promote a continuum of health care services on the community level.... An NIMH (National Institute of Mental Health) workgroup report analyzes the problems that beset the delivery of mental health services in certified nursing homes and raises serious questions about the adequacy of care received by mentally ill patients, particularly the mentally ill elderly.
—*National Health Standards Clearinghouse Information Bulletin,* August 1980

De-institutionalized mental patients have so overwhelmed the new facilities at Boston's famous Pine Street Inn that admission of guests will be limited to homeless men and women with no other options.... While the problem is not new ... the number of paients seeking shelter has increased so much ... that "they are driving out the people we were established to serve." Testifying at a State House hearing last year, Kip Tiernan, founder of Rosie's Place, a 10-bed survival home for women ... said that women mental patients were being discharged from state hospitals with "no more than a piece of paper in their hands giving out our address."
—*Boston Globe,* August 21, 1980

A brief history of how we have arrived at the current impasse is instructive. By the late eighteenth century the market relations of early capitalist society had already exerted a corrosive effect on traditional social relations, including kinship ties and communities. The reciprocal ties of the old feudal and land-based system, which dictated both dependence and aid between dominant and subordinate classes, had broken down. No longer could society rely upon this network to make provision, however inadequate, for those individuals within the community who were chronically ill, mentally incompetent, or infirm. As the numbers of dependent and "maladjusted" grew, the now fragmented traditional community could no longer cope. Social reformers hoped to solve the problem by creating institutions—workhouses, asylums, hospitals, reformatories and so on—to treat, succor, rehabilitate and punish. David Rothman, in his book *The Discovery of the Asylum,* has documented the headlong rush toward institutionalization in the America of the 1840s and 1850s. According to Rothman, "One can properly label the Jacksonian years the 'age of the asylum.'" He continues: "The asylum was to fulfill a dual purpose for its innovators. It would rehabilitate inmates and then, by virtue of its success, set an example of right action for the larger society. There was a utopian flavor to this first venture, one that looked to reform the deviant and dependent and to serve as a model for others. The well-ordered asylum would exemplify the proper principles of social organization and thus . . . insure the safety of the republic."

What went wrong? The supporters of deinstitutionalization attempt to answer that question by insisting that institutionalization per se is suspect, regardless of the quality of care, the staff-client ratio and all the rest. It is suspect, in their minds, because of its denial of individual freedom. This acute focus on "the individual," which was a prime concern of the 1960s counterculture, helped to spur widespread investigations and exposés of the abuses of total institutions. The image of the asylum as a place of refuge gave way to the image of the coercive institution that stripped individuals of their civil rights and forced them to undergo what the sociologist Erving Goffman called "rituals of degradation." They were drugged into passivity, the better to "manage" them. Some critics went so far as to deny altogether that humanitarian impulses created asylums in the first place.

Anything, these critics urged, would be better than "this." And patients, for the most part, agreed. Almost to a person, patients on the outside—those who are willing and able to convey their experiences—say that despite all the "hassles" and inadequate facilities on the "outside," they prefer this "least restrictive environment" to that most restrictive of all, the total institution. And, of course, one must agree that these patients' civil rights and liberties must have top priority in any evaluation of deinstitutionalization.

The problem with many "freedom of the patient" advocates, however, is their exclusive preoccupation with freedom *from* total control. They neglect any consideration of what freedom is *for* —what should be done to guarantee patients' employment, housing, education, therapy and decent lives. Despite this inadequate appreciation of what freedom means, there is no doubt that a genuine concern with civil and social rights has been, and remains an essential part of, the deinstitutionalization effort. Like the original advocates of institutionalization, supporters of community care also see themselves as humanitarians.

Unfortunately, the authentic humanitarian impulse behind deinstitutionalization was soon tainted by a concern with reducing expenditures for the care and support of clients. State and local governments faced with severe fiscal crises were tempted to clear out the wards of state institutions. Their already enormous labor expenditures had burgeoned with the unionization of state employees, which "virtually doubled unit costs," according to sociologist P.R. Dingman. Court decisions that forbade the use of unpaid patient labor and set minimal standards for treatment necessitated additional expenditures. Dingman claims: "Rising costs more than any other factor have made it obvious that support of state hospitals is politically unfeasible . . . that is the principal factor behind the present push to get rid of state hospitals."

Humanitarian arguments for deinstitutionalization are caricatured if they are seen as mere cover for economizing. Nonetheless, advocates of care in the community—at least in the state bureaucracies working toward dismantling institutional systems—have been forced by economic logic into a compromise position that threatens to overshadow humane considerations. Fiscal logic won the day in California's big push to deinstitutionalize while Ronald Reagan was governor, as it did during New York's disastrous early experiences under Nelson Rockefeller. The Massachusetts effort has been more complex. The state has made a serious, though wholly inadequate, attempt to create actual community support facilities. But that fiscal logic has begun to seem inexorable; as it gains wider adherence, the movement toward deinstitutionalization gains a blind momentum, like a locomotive out of control. The idea is irrestible: "Be a good guy and save money!" Recently the Massachusetts chief of Human Services, Charles Mahoney, inadvertently expressed the duality of motives behind deinstitutionalization when he commented that the alternative treatment "saves money and allows some otherwise 'hopeless' patients to make progress."

Given the current condition of the American political economy, the proliferation of taxpayer revolts, saving money becomes the overriding preoccupation, and the deinstitutionalized individual fades into the murky shadows of social concern. In the words of Andrew Scull, author of *Decarceration*:

> The promise of . . . cost savings largely explains the curious political alliance which has fostered and supported decarceration. Social policies which allegedly benefit the poorest and most desperate segments of the community do not ordinarily arouse particular enthusiasm among the so-called fiscal conservatives. The goal of returning mental patients to the community is clearly an exception, for in addition to the liberal adherents one might expect, it has attracted prominent, sometimes decisive support from their ranks.

And so the original critics of deinstitutionalization have been joined by those who have observed its effects—the plight of former clients and the pressures on communities where the deinstitu-

tionalized have been "dumped" in large numbers. These critics claim that the result has been to "warehouse" people in smaller, less centralized institutions, rather than to free them. They stress the inadequacy of current community care and point out that the communities into which former patients are supposedly integrated are themselves deteriorating.

Finally, the current critics claim the massive effort to deinstitutionalize has put enormous pressure on the poorest urban neighborhoods and on lower-income sections in smaller towns and cities. Some neighborhoods, according to a report issued by the Health Planning Council for Greater Boston, dated September 18, 1980, have become "saturated with a disproportionate number of residences while wealthier and more politically astute communities have resisted the burgeoning of such services in their areas. Resentment seems rampant in both types of communities."

To be sure, much of this resentment is sheer prejudice and fear of the unknown. But the point here is that the less well off are once again paying the social costs of liberal reform. Deinstitutionalized clients are being ghettoized in poor neighborhoods while residents in middle- and upper-middle-income communities enact restrictive zoning ordinances in order to avoid assuming their share of the social burden. Social critics Julian and Eileen Wolpert have noted that "the growing ghettoization of the returning ex-patients along with other dependent groups in the population; the growing succession of inner-city land use to institutions providing services to the dependent and needy; . . . the forced immobility of the chronically disabled within deteriorated urban neighborhoods" have all been exacerbated by deinstitutionalization.

What, then, is to be done? Despite all the possible abuses and difficulties, by any reckoning of human rights and social good, adequate community care is the preferable route for most if not all in need of special treatment and attention. But this social logic must not be undermined by market imperatives. For the truth of the matter is that if deinstitutionalization is to work as it ought, we would need a complex system of social support services that would cost *more* than the present massive institutions, with their drugged-out populations.

For deinstitutionalization to work, the following social services, minimally, on all levels and in all communities, are necessary: day care, day treatment, education of the mentally retarded and other developmentally disabled individuals, family service programs providing parent counseling, housing for family visitations, transportation allowances, health education, medical and dental rehabilitation, psychiatric and psychological services, remedial schooling, vocational training, adoption services for hard-to-place children, after-care programs, aggressive preventive medicine, community-based group homes, community liaison workers, community residences, jobs for all—juveniles through the elderly—and so on. This sort of comprehensive system, because it would rely on the therapeutic power of human compassion, would represent a complex social challenge and a great social achievement.

It is clear that current deinstitutionalization efforts, even the best, come nowhere close to this vision. If it is true that one can judge a society by how it treats its most ill, vulnerable and dependent members, our society, and the political economy that spawned it, must be judged very harshly indeed by even minimal standards of decency and justice.

TAKING ANOTHER LOOK

1 Why has the policy of deinstitutionalization been called a "social revolution" by its supporters? Why do they see institutionalization of the mentally handicapped as undesirable?

2 How do patients "on the outside" feel about deinstitutionalization?

3 Why are conflict theorists particularly concerned about the consequences of "dumping" of ex-mental patients?

4 In Elshtain's view, what kinds of social services are needed if deinstitutionalization is to work as it ought?

Groupthink

Irving L. Janis

Sociologists reserve the term *small group* to refer to a group small enough for all members to interact simultaneously, that is, to talk with each other or at least be acquainted with one another. Small groups such as work groups and families are the intermediate link between the individual and the larger society. We may think of small groups as being informal and unpatterned; yet, interactionist researchers have revealed that there are distinct and predictable processes at work in the functioning of small groups. German sociologist Georg Simmel (1858–1918) is credited as the first sociologist to emphasize the importance of interaction processes within groups.

In sociological terms, groups can serve a social-control function by introducing members to and enforcing social norms. For example, the pressure to conform in group situations can have a powerful impact on social behavior. Social psychologist Stanley Milgram defines *conformity* as going along with one's peers—individuals of a person's own status, who have no special right to direct that person's behavior.

In the following selection, psychologist Irving L. Janis argues that the group processes at work in governmental decision-making teams (especially concern with maintaining the respect of other members of the work group) may lead to a kind of *groupthink,* which prevents effective decision making. He defines groupthink as a "deterioration of mental efficiency, reality testing and moral judgment that results from in-group pressures." Janis discusses examples of groupthink in the presidential administrations of John F. Kennedy (the abortive 1961 Bay of Pigs invasion of Cuba, in which Cuban exiles trained, armed, and directed by the United States attempted to overthrow the Castro government) and Lyndon B. Johnson (the escalation of American involvement in the Vietnam War during the mid-1960s).

The idea of "groupthink" occurred to me while reading Arthur M. Schlesinger's chapters on the Bay of Pigs in *A Thousand Days.* At first I was puzzled: How could bright men like John F. Kennedy and his advisers be taken in by such a stupid, patchwork plan as the one presented to them by the C.I.A. representatives? I began wondering if some psychological contagion of complacency might have interfered with their mental alertness.

I kept thinking about this notion until one day I found myself talking about it in a seminar I was conducting at Yale on the psychology of small groups. I suggested that the poor decision-making performance of those high officials might be akin to the lapses in judgment of ordinary citizens who become more concerned with retaining the approval of the fellow members of their work group than with coming up with good solutions to the tasks at hand.

When I re-read Schlesinger's account I was struck by many further observations that fit into exactly the pattern of concurrence-seeking that has impressed me in my research on other face-to-face groups when a "we" feeling of solidarity is running high. I concluded that a group process was subtly at work in Kennedy's team which prevented the members from debating the real issues posed by the C.I.A.'s plan and from carefully appraising its serious risks.

By now I was sufficiently fascinated by what I called the "groupthink" hypothesis to start looking into similar historic fiascoes. I selected for intensive analysis three that were made during the administrations of three other American presidents: Franklin D. Roosevelt (failure to be prepared for Pearl Harbor), Harry S. Truman (the invasion of North Korea) and Lyndon B. Johnson (escalation of the Vietnam war). Each decision was a group product, issuing from a series of meetings held by a small and cohesive group of government officials and advisers. In each case I found the same kind of detrimental group process that was at work in the Bay of Pigs decision.

In my earlier research with ordinary citizens I had been impressed by the effects—both unfavorable and favorable—of the social pressures that develop in cohesive groups: in infantry platoons, air crews, therapy groups, seminars and self-study or encounter groups. Members tend to evolve informal objectives to preserve friendly intra-group relations, and this becomes part of the hidden agenda at their meetings. When conducting research on groups of heavy smokers, for example, at a clinic established to help people stop smoking, I noticed a seemingly irrational tendency for the members to exert pressure on each other to increase their smoking as the time for the final meeting approached. This appeared to be a collusive effort to display mutual dependence and resistance to the termination of the sessions.

Sometimes, even long before the final separation, pressures toward uniformity subverted the fundamental purpose. At the second meeting of one group of smokers, consisting of 12 middle-class American men and women, two of the most dominant members took the position that heavy smoking was an almost incurable addiction. Most of the others soon agreed that nobody could be expected to cut down drastically. One man took issue with this consensus, arguing that he had stopped smoking since joining the group and that

everyone else could do the same. His declaration was followed by an angry discussion. Most of the others ganged up against the man who was deviating from the consensus.

At the next meeting the deviant announced that he had made an important decision. "When I joined," he said, "I agreed to follow the two main rules required by the clinic—to make a conscientious effort to stop smoking, and to attend every meeting. But I have learned that you can only follow one of the rules, not both. I will continue to attend every meeting but I have gone back to smoking two packs a day and I won't make any effort to stop again until after the last meeting." Whereupon the other members applauded, welcoming him back to the fold.

No one mentioned that the whole point of the meetings was to help each person to cut down as rapidly as possible. As a psychological consultant to the group, I tried to call this to the members' attention and so did my collaborator, Dr. Michael Kahn. But the members ignored our comments and reiterated their consensus that heavy smoking was an addiction from which no one would be cured except by cutting down gradually over a long period of time.

This episode—an extreme form of groupthink—was only one manifestation of a general pattern that the group displayed. At every meeting the members were amiable, reasserted their warm feelings of solidarity and sought concurrence on every important topic, with no reappearance of the unpleasant bickering that would spoil the cozy atmosphere. This tendency could be maintained, however, only at the expense of ignoring realistic challenges—like those posed by the psychologists.

The term "groupthink" is of the same order as the words in the "newspeak" vocabulary that George Orwell uses in *1984*—a vocabulary with terms such as "doublethink" and "crimethink." By putting "groupthink" with those Orwellian words, I realize that it takes on an invidious connotation. This is intentional: groupthink refers to a deterioration of mental efficiency, reality testing and

ESCALATION IN VIETNAM: HOW COULD IT HAPPEN?

A highly revealing episode occurred soon after Robert McNamara told a Senate committee some impressive facts about the ineffectiveness of the bombings. President Johnson made a number of bitter comments about McNamara's statement. "That military genius, McNamara, has gone dovish on me," he complained to one Senator. To someone on his White House staff he spoke even more heatedly, accusing McNamara of playing into the hands of the enemy. He drew the analogy of "a man trying to sell his house while one of his sons went to the prospective buyer to point out that there were leaks in the basement."

This strongly suggests that Johnson regarded his in-group of policy advisers as a family and its leading dissident member as an irresponsible son who was sabotaging the family's interest. Underlying this revealing imagery are two implicit assumptions that epitomize groupthink: We are a good group, so any deceitful acts that we perpetrate are fully justified. Anyone who is unwilling to distort the truth to help us is disloyal.

This is only one of the many examples of how groupthink was manifested in Johnson's inner circle.

moral judgment that results from in-group pressures.

When I investigated the Bay of Pigs invasion and other fiascoes, I found that there were at least six major defects in decision-making which contributed to failures to solve problems adequately.

First, the group's discussions were limited to a few alternatives (often only two) without a survey of the full range of alternatives. Second, the members failed to re-examine their initial decision from the standpoint of non-obvious drawbacks that had not been originally considered. Third, they neglected courses of action initially evaluated as unsatisfactory; they almost never discussed whether they had overlooked any non-obvious gains.

Fourth, members made little or no attempt to obtain information from experts who could supply sound estimates of losses and gains to be expected from alternative courses. Fifth, selective bias was shown in the way the members reacted to information and judgments from experts, the media and outside critics; they were only interested in facts and opinions that supported their preferred policy. Finally, they spent little time deliberating how the policy might be hindered by bureaucratic inertia, sabotaged by political opponents or derailed by the accidents that happen to the best of well-laid plans. Consequently, they failed to work out contingency plans to cope with foreseeable setbacks that could endanger their success.

I was surprised by the extent to which the groups involved in these fiascoes adhered to group norms and pressures toward uniformity, even when their policy was working badly and had unintended consequences that disturbed the conscience of the members. Members consider loyalty to the group the highest form of morality. That loyalty requires each member to avoid raising controversial issues, questioning weak arguments or calling a halt to soft-headed thinking.

Paradoxically, soft-headed groups are likely to be extremely hard-hearted toward out-groups and enemies. In dealing with a rival nation, policy-makers constituting an amiable group find it relatively easy to authorize dehumanizing solutions such as large-scale bombings. An affable group of government officials is unlikely to pursue the difficult issues that arise when alternatives to a harsh military solution come up for discussion. Nor are they inclined to raise ethical issues that imply that this "fine group of ours, with its humanitarianism and its high-minded principles, could adopt a course that is inhumane and immoral."

The greater the threat to the self-esteem of the members of a cohesive group, the greater will be their inclination to resort to concurrence-seeking at the expense of critical thinking. Symptoms of groupthink will therefore be found most often when a decision poses a moral dilemma, especially

A PERFECT FIASCO: THE BAY OF PIGS

Why did President Kennedy's main advisers, whom he had selected as core members of his team, fail to pursue the issues sufficiently to discover the shaky ground on which the faulty assumptions of the Cuban invasion plan rested? Why didn't they pose a barrage of penetrating and embarrassing questions to the representatives of the C.I.A. and the Joint Chiefs of Staff? Why were they taken in by the incomplete and inconsistent answers they were given in response to the relatively few critical questions they raised?

Schlesinger says that "for all the utter irrationality with which retrospect endowed the project, it had a certain queer logic at the time as it emerged from the bowels of government." Why? What was the source of the queer logic" with which the plan was endowed? If the available accounts describe the deliberations accurately, many typical symptoms of groupthink can be discerned among the members of the Kennedy team: an illusion of invulnerability, a collective effort to rationalize their decision, an unquestioned belief in the group's inherent morality, a stereotyped view of enemy leaders as too evil to warrant genuine attempts to negotiate, and the emergence of self-appointed mind-guards.

Robert Kennedy, for example, who had been constantly informed about the Cuban invasion plan, asked Schlesinger privately why he was opposed. The President's brother listened coldly and then said: "You may be right or you may be wrong, but the President has made his mind up. Don't push it any further. Now is the time for everyone to help him all they can."

Here is a symptom of groupthink, displayed by a highly intelligent man whose ethical code committed him to freedom of dissent.

Robert Kennedy was functioning in a self-appointed role that I call being a "mind-guard." Just as a bodyguard protects the President and other high officials from physical harm, a mind-guard protects them from thoughts that might damage their confidence in the soundness of the policies which they are about to launch.

if the most advantageous course requires the policymakers to violate their own standards of humanitarian behavior. Each member is likely to become more dependent than ever on the in-group for maintaining his self-image as a decent human being and will therefore be more strongly motivated to maintain group unity by striving for concurrence.

Although it is risky to make huge inferential leaps from theory to practice, we should not be inhibited from drawing tentative inferences from these fiascoes. Perhaps the worst mistakes can be prevented if we take steps to avoid the circumstances in which groupthink is most likely to flourish. But all the prescriptive hypotheses that follow must be validated by systematic research before they can be applied with any confidence.

The leader of a policy-forming group should, for example, assign the role of critical evaluator to each member, encouraging the group to give high priority to airing objections and doubts. He should also be impartial at the outset, instead of stating his own preferences and expectations. He should limit his briefings to unbiased statements about the scope of the problem and the limitations of available resources.

The organization should routinely establish several independent planning and evaluation groups to work on the same policy question, each carrying out its deliberations under a different leader.

One or more qualified colleagues within the organization who are not core members of the policy-making group should be invited to each meeting and encouraged to challenge the views of the core members.

At every meeting, at least one member should be assigned the role of devil's advocate, to function like a good lawyer in challenging the testimony of those who advocate the majority position.

Whenever the policy issue involves relations with a rival nation, a sizable block of time should be spent surveying all warning signals from the rivals and constructing alternative scenarios.

After reaching a preliminary consensus the policy-making group should hold a "second chance" meeting at which all the members are expected to express their residual doubts and to rethink the entire issue. They might take as their model a statement made by Alfred P. Sloan, a former chairman of General Motors, at a meeting of policymakers:

"Gentlemen, I take it we are all in complete agreement on the decision here. Then I propose we postpone further discussion until our next meeting to give ourselves time to develop disagreement and perhaps gain some understanding of what the decision is all about."

It might not be a bad idea for the second-chance meeting to take place in a relaxed atmosphere far from the executive suite, perhaps over drinks. According to a report by Herodotus dating from about 450 B.C., whenever the ancient Persians made a decision following sober deliberations, they would always reconsider the matter under the influence of wine. Tacitus claimed that during Roman times the Germans also had a custom of arriving at each decision twice—once sober, once drunk.

Some institutionalized form of allowing second thoughts to be freely expressed might be remarkably effective for breaking down a false sense of unanimity and related illusions, without endangering anyone's reputation or liver. . . .

TAKING ANOTHER LOOK

1 What effects of group pressures were evident among groups of heavy smokers?
2 Identify four major defects of decision making that result from groupthink pressures.
3 According to Janis, what steps can be taken by policy-making groups to avoid the circumstances in which groupthink is most likely to flourish?
4 According to Janis, what functions are performed by a "mind-guard"?
5 How might functional theorists view the phenomenon of "groupthink"?

The Concept of Bureaucracy

Peter Blau and Marshall W. Meyer

When we think of the term "bureaucracy," a variety of images—mostly unpleasant—come to mind. Rows of desks staffed by seemingly faceless people, endless lines and forms, impossibly complex language, and frustrating encounters with red tape—all these have combined to make "bureaucracy" a dirty word and an easy target in political campaigns. However, viewed from a sociological perspective, a *bureaucracy* is a component of formal organization in which rules and hierarchical ranking are used to achieve efficiency.

In studying bureaucracy, sociologists draw on the pioneering contribution of German sociologist Max Weber (1864–1920). Weber first directed researchers to the significance of bureaucratic structure. In an important sociological advance, he emphasized the basic similarity of structure and process found in the otherwise dissimilar enterprises of religion, government, education, and business.

According to Weber, an *ideal type* is a construct, a model that serves as a measuring rod against which actual cases can be evaluated. Weber developed an ideal type of bureaucracy, which reflects the most characteristic aspects of all human organizations. In presenting this model of bureaucracy, Weber was not describing any particular business, nor was he using the term "ideal" in a way that suggested a positive evaluation. Instead, his purpose was to provide a useful standard for measuring how bureaucratic an actual organization is. Since perfect bureaucracies are never achieved, no organization will correspond exactly to Weber's ideal type. Nevertheless, Weber argued that every bureaucracy—whether its purpose is to run a day care center, a corporation, or an army—will have basic characteristics, such as division of labor, hierarchy of authority, written rules and regulations, impersonality, and security.

In the following selection, sociologists Peter Blau and Marshall W. Meyer analyze Max Weber's view of the main characteristics of a bureaucratic structure. They note that Weber's functional analysis of bureaucracy "may make the social structure appear to function more smoothly than it actually does, since he neglects the disruptions that do in fact exist." Consequently, they emphasize the importance of studying the *dysfunctions* (or potential negative consequences) of bureaucracy as well as its effective operations. Blau and Meyer conclude by discussing two misleading implications of Weber's ideal-type conception of bureaucracy.

The main characteristics of a bureaucratic structure (in the "ideal-typical" case[1]), according to Weber, are the following:

1 "The regular activities required for the purposes of the organization are distributed in a fixed way as official duties."[2] The clear-cut division of labor makes it possible to employ only specialized experts in each particular position and to make

---

[1] The "ideal type" is discussed later in this chapter.
[2] H. H. Gerth and C. Wright Mills (eds.), *From Max Weber: Essays in Sociology* (New York: Oxford University Press, 1946), p. 196. By permission.

every one of them responsible for the effective performance of his duties. This high degree of specialization has become so much part of our socioeconomic life that we tend to forget that it did not prevail in former eras but is a relatively recent bureaucratic innovation.

2 "The organization of offices follows the principle of hierarchy; that is, each lower office is under the control and supervision of a higher one."[3] Every official in this administrative hierarchy is accountable to his superior for his subordinates' decisions and actions as well as his own. To be able to discharge his responsibility for the work of subordinates, he has authority over them, which means that he has the right to issue directives and they have the duty to obey them. This authority is strictly circumscribed and confined to those directives that are relevant for official operations. The use of status prerogatives to extend the power of control over subordinates beyond these limits does not constitute the legitimate exercise of bureaucratic authority.

3 Operations are governed "by a consistent system of abstract rules . . . [and] consist of the application of these rules to particular cases."[4] This system of standards is designed to assure uniformity in the performance of every task, regardless of the number of persons engaged in it, and the coordination of different tasks. Explicit rules and regulations define the responsibility of each member of the organization and the relationships among them. This does not imply that bureaucratic duties are necessarily simple and routine. It must be remembered that strict adherence to general standards in deciding specific cases characterizes not only the job of the file clerk but also that of the Supreme Court justice. For the former, it may involve merely filing alphabetically; for the latter, it involves interpreting the law of the land in order to settle the most complicated legal issues. Bureaucratic duties range in complexity from one of these extremes to the other.

4 "The ideal official conducts his office . . . [in] a spirit of formalistic impersonality, '*Sine ira et studio,*' without hatred or passion, and hence without affection or enthusiasm."[5] For rational standards to govern operations without interference from personal considerations, a detached approach must prevail within the organization and especially toward clients. If an official develops strong feelings about some subordinates or clients, he can hardly help letting those feelings influence his official decisions. As a result, and often without being aware of it himself, he might be particularly lenient in evaluating the work of one of his subordinates or might discriminate against some clients and in favor of others. The exclusion of personal considerations from official business is a prerequisite for impartiality as well as for efficiency. The very factors that make a government bureaucrat unpopular with his clients, an aloof attitude and a lack of genuine concern with them as human beings, actually benefit these clients. Disinterestedness and lack of personal interest go together. The official who does not maintain social distance and becomes personally interested in the cases of his clients tends to be partial in his treatment of them, favoring those he likes over others. Impersonal detachment engenders equitable treatment of all persons and thus equal justice in administration.

5 Employment in the bureaucratic organization is based on technical qualifications and is protected against arbitrary dismissal. "It constitutes a career. There is a system of 'promotions' according to seniority or to achievement, or both."[6] These personnel policies, which are found not only in civil service but also in many private companies, encourage the development of loyalty to the organization and esprit de corps among its members. The consequent identification of employees with the organization motivates them to

---

[3] Max Weber, *The Theory of Social and Economic Organization,* translated by A. M. Henderson and Talcott Parsons (New York: Oxford University Press, 1947), p. 331.

[4] *Ibid,* p. 330.
[5] *Ibid,* p. 340.
[6] *Ibid.,* p. 334.

exert greater efforts in advancing its interests. It may also give rise to a tendency to think of themselves as a class apart from and superior to the rest of the society. Among civil servants, this tendency has been more pronounced in Europe, notably in Germany and France, than in the United States, but among military officers, it may be found here too.

6 "Experience tends universally to show that the purely bureaucratic type of administrative organization . . . is, from a purely technical point of view, capable of attaining the highest degree of efficiency."[7] "The fully developed bureaucratic mechanism compares with other organizations exactly as does the machine with non-mechanical modes of production."[8] Bureaucracy solves the distinctive organizational problem of maximizing organizational efficiency, not merely that of individuals.

The superior administrative efficiency of bureaucracy is the expected result of its various characteristics as outlined by Weber. For an individual to work efficiently, he must have the necessary skills and apply them rationally and energetically; but for an organization to operate efficiently, more is required. Every one of its members must have the expert skills needed for the performance of his tasks. This is the purpose of specialization and of employment on the basis of technical qualifications, often ascertained by objective tests. Even experts, however, may be prevented by personal bias from making rational decisions. The emphasis on impersonal detachment is intended to eliminate this source of irrational action. But individual rationality is not enough. As noted above, if the members of the organization were to make rational decisions independently, their work would not be coordinated and the efficiency of the organization would suffer. Hence there is need for discipline to limit the

scope of rational discretion, which is met by the system of rules and regulations and the hierarchy of supervision. Moreover, personnel policies that permit employees to feel secure in their jobs and to anticipate advancements for faithful performance of duties discourage attempts to impress superiors by introducing clever innovations, which may endanger coordination. Lest this stress on disciplined obedience to rules and rulings undermine the employee's motivation to devote his energies to his job, incentives for exerting effort must be furnished. Personnel policies that cultivate organizational loyalty and that provide for promotion on the basis of merit serve this function. In other words, the combined effect of bureaucracy's characteristics is to create social conditions which constrain each member of the organization to act in ways that, whether they appear rational or otherwise from his individual standpoint, further the rational pursuit of organizational objectives.

Without explicitly stating so, Weber supplies a *functional* analysis of bureaucracy. In this type of analysis, a social structure is explained by showing how each of its elements contributes to its persistence and effective operations. Concern with discovering all these contributions, however, entails the danger that the scientist may neglect to investigate the disturbances that various elements produce in the structure. As a result, his presentation may make the social structure appear to function more smoothly than it actually does, since he neglects the disruptions that do in fact exist. To protect ourselves against this danger, it is essential to extend the analysis beyond the mere consideration of functions, as Robert K. Merton points out.[9] Of particular importance for avoiding false implications of stability and for explaining social change is the study of *dysfunctions,* those consequences that interfere with adjustment and create problems in the structure.[10]

---

[7] *Ibid.,* p. 337.
[8] Gerth and Mills, *op. cit.,* p. 214.
[9] Robert K. Merton, *Social Theory and Social Structure,* 3rd ed. (New York: Free Press, 1968), pp. 73–138.

[10] For a general discussion of functional analysis, see Ely Chinoy, *Sociological Perspective* (New York: Random House, 1968), Chap. 5.

A reexamination of the foregoing discussion of bureaucratic features in the light of the concept of dysfunction reveals inconsistencies and conflicting tendencies. If reserved detachment characterizes the attitudes of the members of the organization toward one another, it is unlikely that high esprit de corps will develop among them. The strict exercise of authority in the interest of discipline induces subordinates, anxious to be highly thought of by their superiors, to conceal defects in operations from superiors, and this obstruction of the flow of information upward in the hierarchy impedes effective management. Insistence on conformity also tends to engender rigidities in official conduct and to inhibit the rational exercise of judgment needed for the efficient performance of tasks. If promotions are based on merit, many employees will not experience advancements in their careers. If they are based primarily on seniority so as to give employees this experience and thereby to encourage them to become identified with the organization, the promotion system will not furnish strong incentives for exerting efforts and excellent performance. These illustrations suffice to indicate that the same factor that enhances efficiency in one respect often threatens it in another; it may have *both* functional and dysfunctional consequences.

Weber was well aware of such contradictory tendencies in the bureaucratic structure. But since he treats dysfunctions only incidentally, his discussion leaves the impression that administrative efficiency in bureaucracies is more stable and less problematical than it actually is. In part, it was his intention to present an idealized image of bureaucratic structure, and he used the conceptual tool appropriate for this purpose. Let us critically examine this conceptual tool.

IMPLICATIONS OF THE IDEAL-TYPE CONSTRUCT

Weber dealt with bureaucracy as what he termed an "ideal type." This methodological concept does not represent an average of the attributes of all existing bureaucracies (or other social structures), but a pure type, derived by abstracting the most characteristic bureaucratic aspects of all known organizations. Since perfect bureaucratization is never fully realized, no empirical organization corresponds exactly to this scientific construct.

The criticism has been made that Weber's analysis of an imaginary ideal type does not provide understanding of concrete bureaucratic structures. But this criticism obscures the fact that the ideal-type construct is intended as a guide in empirical research, not as a substitute for it. By indicating the characteristics of bureaucracy in its pure form, it directs the researcher to those aspects of organizations that he must examine in order to determine the extent of their bureaucratization. This is the function of all conceptual schemes: to specify the factors that must be taken into consideration in investigations and to define them clearly.

The ideal typical model of bureaucracy, however, is not simply a conceptual scheme. It includes not only definitions of concepts but also implicit generalizations about the relationships among them, and specifically the hypothesis that the diverse bureaucratic characteristics increase administrative efficiency. If certain attributes (for example, specialization, hierarchy, rules, and impersonality) are distinctive of bureaucracy compared to other forms of administration, and if bureaucracy is the most efficient form of administration, then at least some of the attributes of bureaucracy must be conducive to efficient operations. Whereas conceptual definitions are presupposed in research and not subject to verification by research findings, hypotheses concerning relationships among factors are subject to such verification. Whether strict hierarchical authority, for example, indeed furthers efficiency is a question of empirical fact and not one of definition. But as the scientific construct Weber intended it to be, the ideal type cannot be refuted by empirical evidence. If a study of several organizations were to find that strict hierarchical authority is not related to efficiency, this would not prove that no such relationship exists in the ideal-type bureaucracy; it would show only that these organizations are not fully bureaucratized. Since generalizations about idealized states defy testing in systematic research, they have no place in science. On the other hand, if empirical evidence is taken into consideration and generalizations are modified accordingly, we deal with prevailing tendencies in bureaucratic structures and no longer with a pure type.

Two misleading implications of the ideal-type conception of bureaucracy deserve special mention. The student of social organization is concerned with the patterns of activities and interactions that reveal how social conduct is organized, and not with exceptional deviations from these patterns. The fact that one official becomes excited and shouts at his colleague, or that another arrives late at the office, is unimportant in understanding the organization, except that the rare occurrence of such events indicates that they are idiosyncratic, differing from the prevailing patterns. Weber's decision to treat only the purely formal organization of bureaucracy implies that all deviations from these formal requirements are idiosyncratic and of no interest for the student of

organization. Later empirical studies have shown this approach to be misleading. Informal relations and unofficial practices develop among the members of bureaucracies and assume an organized form without being officially sanctioned. Chester I. Barnard, one of the first to call attention to this phenomenon, held that these "informal organizations are necessary to the operations of formal organizations."[11] These informal patterns, in contrast to exceptional occurrences, . . . are a regular part of bureaucratic organizations and therefore must be taken into account in their analysis.

Weber's approach also implies that any deviation from the formal structure is detrimental to administrative efficiency. Since the ideal type is conceived as the perfectly efficient organization, all differences from it must necessarily interfere with efficiency. There is considerable evidence that suggests the opposite conclusion; informal relations and unofficial practices often contribute to efficient operations. In any case, the significance of these unofficial patterns for operations cannot be determined in advance on theoretical grounds but only on the basis of empirical investigations.

[11] Chester I. Barnard, *The Functions of the Executive* (Cambridge: Harvard University Press, 1948), p. 123.

TAKING ANOTHER LOOK

1 What is the rationale behind bureaucratic rules and regulations?

2 What is the rationale behind the impersonal detachment characteristic of bureaucracy as an ideal type?

3 In Weber's view, what factors contribute to the superior administrative efficiency of bureaucracy?

4 Why do Blau and Meyer associate Weber's view of bureaucracy with the functionalist perspective? In what ways would conflict theorists be likely to disagree with Weber's ideal type of bureaucracy?

5 Why is it that an ideal type—such as Weber's ideal type of bureaucracy—cannot be refuted by empirical evidence?

6 Briefly describe the two "misleading implications of the ideal-type conception of bureaucracy" identified by Blau and Meyer.

Sexual Modesty, Social Meanings, and the Nudist Camp

Martin S. Weinberg

For sociologists, the term *deviance* does not mean perversion or depravity. Deviance is behavior that violates the standards of conduct or expectations of a group or a society. It is a comprehensive concept that includes not only criminal behavior but also many actions not subject to prosecution. Sociologists emphasize that standards of deviance vary from group to group and over time. Consequently, deviance can only be understood within its social context. For example, in American culture it is generally acceptable to sing along at a rock or folk concert but not at the opera.

In the following selection, sociologist Martin S. Weinberg points out that members of "naturist" or nudist camps are subject to compelling social norms. If a person disrobes publicly on the street in the United States, he or she is violating widely held social norms and is thus committing a deviant act. Yet, if the same person disrobes within a nudist camp, he or she is obeying the rules and conforming to the behavior of peers. Weinberg's analysis suggests that despite the required clothing immodesty, the norms of nudist camps effectively control sexual interests and lead to patterns of modesty.

Deviant sub-systems have norms that permit, organize, and control the behavior which defines them as deviant. The nudist camp is an example of such a deviant sub-system, nudists being defined as deviant by their disregard for clothing when in the presence of others, particularly members of the opposite sex. This paper will describe the normative system of the nudist camp, its consequences for sustaining the definition of the situation common to this group, and the way it maintains those interaction patterns this sub-system shares with the outside society. . . .

THE NUDIST CAMP

The ideology of the nudist camp provides a new definition of the situation regarding nudity, which, in effect, maintains that

  1 Nudism and sexuality are unrelated
  2 There is nothing shameful about exposing the human body
  3 The abandonment of clothes can lead to a feeling of freedom and natural pleasure
  4 Nude activities, especially full bodily exposure to the sun, leads to a feeling of physical, mental, and spiritual well-being

These definitions are sustained by nudists to a remarkable degree, illustrating the extent to which adult socialization can function in changing long-maintained meanings; in this case, regarding the exposure of one's nude body in heterosexual situations. The tremendous emphasis on covering the sexual areas, and the relation between nudism and sexuality that exists in the outside society, however, suggest that the nudist definition of the situation might, at times, be quite easily called into question. The results of the field work and formal interviews indicate how the social organization of the nudist camp has developed a system of norms that contributes to sustaining the official definition of the situation. Since the major concern of this paper is modesty, we will restrict our discussion to the first two declarations of nudist ideology (i.e., that nudism and sexuality are unrelated, and that there is nothing shameful about exposing the human body). These are also the elements that lead to the classification of nudists as deviant. The normative proscriptions that contribute to the maintenance of this definition of the situation will be described.

Organizational precautions. Organizational precautions are initially taken in the requirements for admission to a nudist camp. Most camps do not allow unmarried individuals, especially single men, or allow only a small quota of singles. Those camps that do allow male-singles may charge up to 35 per cent higher rates for the single's membership than is charged for the membership of an entire family. This is intended to discourage single memberships, but, since the cost is still relatively low in comparison to other resorts, this measure is not very effective. It seems to do little more than create resentment among the singles. By giving formal organizational backing to the definition that singles are not especially desirable, it also might be related to the social segregation of single and married members that is evident in nudist camps.

An overabundance of single men is recognized by the organization as threatening the definition of nudism that is maintained. The presence of singles at the camp is suspected to be for purposes other than the "nudist way of life" (e.g., to gape at the women). Such a view may call into question the denied relation between nudity and sexuality.

Certification by the camp owner is also required before anyone is admitted on the camp grounds. This is sometimes supplemented by three letters of recommendation in regard to the character of the applicant. This is a precaution against admitting those "social types" who might conceivably discredit the ideology of the movement.

A limit is sometimes set on the number of trial visits that can be made to the camp; that is, visits made without membership in some camp or inter-camp organization. In addition, a limit is usually set on the length of time one is allowed to maintain oneself clothed. These rules function to weed out those guests whose sincere acceptance of the "nudist" definition of the situation is questionable.

Norms regarding interpersonal behavior. Norms regarding patterns of interpersonal behavior are also functional for the maintenance of the organization's system of meanings. The existence of these norms, however, should be recognized as formally acknowledging that the nudist definition of the situation could become problematic unless precautions were taken.

No staring. This rule functions to prevent any overt signs of "overinvolvement." In the words of a nonnudist who is involved in the publication of a nudist magazine, "They all look up to the heavens and never look below." This pattern of civil inattention[1] is most exaggerated among the females, who manage the impression that there is absolutely no concern or awareness that the male body is in an unclothed state. Women often recount how they expect everyone will look at them when they are nude, only to find that no one communicates any impression of concern when they finally do get up their nerve and undress. One woman told the writer: "I got so mad because my husband wanted me to undress in front of other men that I just pulled my clothes right off thinking everyone would look at me." She was amazed (and somewhat disappointed) when no one did. Thus, even though nudists are immodest in their behavior by "showing" their bodies, . . . "looking at" immodesty is controlled; external constraints prohibit staring.

(Have you ever observed or heard about anyone staring at someone's body while at camp?)[2] I've heard stories—particularly about men that stare. Since I heard these stories, I tried not to, and even done away with my sunglasses after someone said,

---

[1] See Erving Goffman, *Behavior in Public Places* (New York: The Free Press, 1963). p. 84.

[2] Interview questions and probes have been placed in parentheses.

half-joking, that I hide behind sunglasses to stare. Toward the end of the summer, I stopped wearing sunglasses. And you know what? It was a child who told me this.

No sex talk. Sex talk, or telling "dirty" jokes, is not common in the nudist camp. The owner of one of the most widely known camps in the Midwest told the writer: "It is usually expected that members of a nudist camp will not talk about sex, politics, or religion." Or, in the words of one single-male: "It is taboo to make sexual remarks here." Verbal immodesty was not experienced by the writer during his period of field work. Interview respondents who mentioned that they had discussed or talked about sex qualified this by stating that such talk was restricted to close friends, was of a "scientific" nature, or, if a joke, was of a "cute" sort. Verbal immodesty . . . is not common to the nudist camp.

When respondents were asked what they would think of someone who breached this norm, they indicated that such behavior would cast doubt on the actor's acceptance of the nudist definition of the situation:

One would expect to hear less of that at camp than at other places. (Why's that?) Because you expect that the members are screened in their *attitude for nudism*—and this isn't one who prefers sexual jokes.

They probably don't belong there. They're there to see what they can find to observe (What do you mean?) Well, their mind isn't on being a nudist, but to see so-and-so nude.

Body contact is taboo. Although the degree to which this rule is enforced varies among camps, there is at least some degree of informal enforcement. Nudists mention that one is particularly careful not to brush against anyone or have any body contact, because of the way it might be interpreted. The following quotation illustrates the interpersonal precautions taken: "I stay clear of the opposite sex. They're so sensitive, they imagine things." One respondent felt that this taboo was simply a common-sense form of modesty: "Suppose one had a desire to knock one off or feel

his wife—modesty or a sense of protocol prohibits you from doing this." When asked to conceptualize a breakdown in this form of modesty, a common response was:

They are in the wrong place. (How's that?) That's not part of nudism. (Could you tell me some more about that?) I think they are there for some sort of sex thrill. They are certainly not there to enjoy the sun.

If any photographs are taken for publication in a nudist magazine, the subjects are allowed to have only limited body contact. As one female nudist said: "We don't want anyone to think we're immoral." Outsiders' interpretations of body contact among nudists would cast doubt on the nudist definition of the situation or the characteristics set forth as the "nudist way of life."

A correlate of the body contact taboo is the prohibition of dancing in the nude. This is verbalized by nudist actors as a separate rule, and it is often the object of jest by members. This indication of "organizational strain" can be interpreted as an instance in which the existence of the rule itself brings into question the nudist definition of the situation; that is, that there is no relationship between nudism and sexuality. The following remark acknowledges this: "This reflects a contradiction in our beliefs. But it's self-protection. One incident and we'd be closed." Others define dancing in the nude as an erotic overture that would incite sexual arousal. Such rationalizations are common to the group. . . .

Alcoholic beverages are not allowed in American camps. This rule also functions in controlling any breakdown in inhibitions that could lead to "aggressive-erotic" overtures. Even those respondents who told the writer that they had "snuck a beer" before going to bed went on to say, however, that they fully favored the rule. The following quotation is representative of nudists' thoughts:

Anyone who drinks in camp is jeopardizing their membership and they shouldn't. Anyone who drinks in camp could get reckless. (How's that?) Well, when guys and girls drink, they're a lot bolder—they might get fresh with someone else's girl. That's why it isn't permitted, I guess.

Rules regarding photography. Taking photographs in a nudist camp is a sensitive matter. Unless the individual is an official photographer (i.e., one photographing for the nudist magazines), the photographer's definition of the situation is sometimes suspect, especially when one hears such remarks as the following: "Do you think you could open your legs a little more?"

There may be a general restriction on the use of cameras, and, when cameras are allowed, it is expected that no pictures will be taken without the subject's permission. Members especially tend to blame the misuse of cameras on single men. As one nudist said: "You always see the singles poppin' around out of nowhere snappin' pictures." In general, however, control is maintained, and any infractions that might exist are not blatant or obvious. Any overindulgence in taking photographs would communicate an overinvolvement in the nude state of the alters and bring doubt on the denied connection between nudism and sexuality. This like staring, . . . is controlled by the norms of the nudist camp.

The official photographers who are taking pictures for nudist magazines recognize the impression communicated by forms of immodesty other than nudity, that is, for the communication of sexuality. In regard to . . . erotic overtures . . . the following statement of an official photographer is relevant: "I never let a girl look straight at the camera. It looks too suggestive. I always have her look off to the side."

Accentuation of the body is suspect as being incongruent with the ideology of nudism. The internalization of the previously discussed principles of nudist ideology would be called into question by such accentuation. Thus, one woman who had shaved her pubic area was labeled as disgusting by those members who talked to the writer about it. Women who blatantly sit in an "unladylike" manner are similarly typed. In the words of one female nudist:

It's no more nice to do than when you are dressed. I would assume they have a purpose. (What's that?) Maybe to draw someone's attention sexually. I'd think it's bad behavior, and it's one thing that shouldn't be done, especially in a nudist camp. (Why's that?) Because it could lead to trouble or some misfortune. (Could you tell me some more about that?) It could bring up some trouble or disturbance among those who noticed it. It would not be appreciated by "true nudists."

Unnatural attempts at covering any area of the body are similarly ridiculed, since they call into question the actor's acceptance of the definition that there is no shame in exposing any area of the human body. If such behavior occurs early in one's nudist career, however, it is responded to mostly with smiles. The actor is viewed as not yet able to get over the initial difficulty of disposing of "outsiders'" definitions.

Communal toilets are also related to the ideological view that there is nothing shameful about the human body or its bodily functions. Although all camps do not have communal toilets, the large camp at which the writer spent the majority of his time did have such a facility, which was labeled "Little Girls Room and Little Boys Too." The stalls were provided with three-quarter-length doors. The existence of this combined facility helped, however, to sustain the nudist definition of the situation by the element of consistency: If you are not ashamed of any part of your body, or of any of its natural body functions, why do you need separate toilets? Thus, even the physical ecology of the nudist camp is designed in a way that will be consistent with the organization's definition of modesty.

CONSEQUENCES OF A BREAKDOWN IN CLOTHING MODESTY

In the introductory section of this paper, it was stated that common-sense actors anticipate breakdowns in clothing modesty to result in rampant sexual interest, promiscuity, embarrassment, jealousy, and shame. The field work and interview data from this study, however, indicate that such occurrences are not common to the nudist camp. The social organization of the nudist camp provides a system of meanings and norms that negate these consequences.

CONCLUSIONS

Our results make possible some general conclusions regarding modesty: (1) Covering the body through the use of clothes is not a necessary condition for a pattern of modesty to exist, nor is it required for tension management and social control of latent sexual interests. Sexual interests are very adequately controlled in nudist camps; in fact, those who have visited nudist camps agree that sexual interests are controlled to a much greater extent than they are on the outside. Clothes are also not a sufficient condition for a pattern of modesty; the manipulation of clothes and fashion in stimulating sexual interest is widely recognized. (2) Except for clothing immodesty, ... all ... forms of modesty are maintained in a nudist camp (e.g., not looking, not saying, not communicating erotic overtures). This suggests that the latter proscriptions are entirely adequate in achieving the functions of modesty when definitions regarding the exposure of the body are changed. (3) When deviance from the institutionalized patterns of modesty is limited to one cell of our typology (i.e., clothing is dispensed with), and the definition of the situation is changed, the typically expected consequence of such a breakdown in this normative pattern does not occur. Rampant sexual interest, promiscuity, embarrassment, jealousy, and shame were not found to be typical of the nudist camp.

TAKING ANOTHER LOOK

1 What is the ideology of the nudist camp?
2 Why does the presence of single men threaten nudist organizations?
3 Within the social context of the nudist camp, what kinds of behavior would be considered deviant?
4 What general conclusions are offered by Weinberg regarding modesty in nudist camps?

The Saints and the Roughnecks

William J. Chambliss

Reflecting the contribution of interactionist theorists, labeling theory emphasizes how a person comes to be labeled as deviant or to accept that label.
Sociologist Howard S. Becker, who popularized this approach, summed it up
with the statement: "Deviant behavior is behavior that people so label."
Labeling theory is also called the *societal-reaction approach,* reminding us that
it is the response to an act and not the behavior that determines deviance. For
example, a bureaucratic error can result in a financially responsible individual
being inaccurately categorized as a credit risk.

Traditionally, research on deviance has focused on those individuals who
violate social norms. In contrast, labeling theory focuses on police, probation
officers, psychiatrists, judges, teachers, employers, school officials, and other
regulators of social control. These agents, it is argued, play a significant role in
creating the deviant identity by designating certain individuals (and not others)
as "deviant." An important aspect of labeling theory is the recognition that
some persons or groups have the power to *define* labels and apply them to
others. This view recalls the conflict perspective's emphasis on the social
significance of power.

In the following selection, sociologist William J. Chambliss reports on his
participant-observation of two groups of high school males who were constantly
occupied with drinking, wild driving, truancy, petty theft, and vandalism. As
Chambliss shows, the Saints came from "good families," were active in school
organizations, expressed the intention of attending college, and received good
grades. Their delinquent acts were generally viewed as a few isolated cases of
"sowing wild oats." By contrast, the Roughnecks drove around in beaten-up
cars, were generally unsuccessful in school, and were viewed with suspicion no
matter what they did. While none of the Saints was ever arrested, every
Roughneck was continually in trouble with police and townspeople. This
differential treatment supports the argument of labeling theorists that certain
people are *viewed* as deviants, delinquents, "bad kids," "losers," and criminals,
while others whose behavior is similar are not seen in such harsh terms.

Eight promising young men—children of good,
stable, white upper-middle-class families, active
in school affairs, good pre-college students—were
some of the most delinquent boys at Hanibal High
School. While community residents and parents
knew that these boys occasionally sowed a few
wild oats, they were totally unaware that sowing
wild oats completely occupied the daily routine of
these young men. The Saints were constantly occupied with truancy, drinking, wild driving, petty
theft and vandalism. Yet not one was officially arrested for any misdeed during the two years I observed them.

This record was particularly surprising in light
of my observations during the same two years of
another gang of Hanibal High School students,
six lower-class white boys known as the Roughnecks. The Roughnecks were constantly in
trouble with police and community even though
their rate of delinquency was about equal with
that of the Saints. What was the cause of this disparity? the result? The following consideration of

the activities, social class and community perceptions of both gangs may provide some answers.

THE SAINTS FROM MONDAY TO FRIDAY

The Saints' principal daily concern was with getting out of school as early as possible. The boys managed to get out of school with minimum danger that they would be accused of playing hookey through an elaborate procedure for obtaining "legitimate" release from class. The most common procedure was for one boy to obtain the release of another by fabricating a meeting of some committee, program or recognized club. Charles might raise his hand in his 9:00 chemistry class and ask to be excused—a euphemism for going to the bathroom. Charles would go to Ed's math class and inform the teacher that Ed was needed for a 9:30 rehearsal of the drama club play. The math teacher would recognize Ed and Charles as "good students" involved in numerous school activities and would permit Ed to leave at 9:30. Charles would return to his class, and Ed would go to Tom's English class to obtain his release. Tom would engineer Charles' escape. The strategy would continue until as many of the Saints as possible were freed. After a stealthy trip to the car (which had been parked in a strategic spot), the boys were off for a day of fun.

Over the two years I observed the Saints, this pattern was repeated nearly every day. There were variations on the theme, but in one form or another, the boys used this procedure for getting out of class and then off the school grounds. Rarely did all eight of the Saints manage to leave school at the same time. The average number avoiding school on the days I observed them was five.

Having escaped from the concrete corridors the boys usually went either to a pool hall on the other (lower-class) side of town or to a cafe in the suburbs. Both places were out of the way of people the boys were likely to know (family or school officials), and both provided a source of entertainment. The pool hall entertainment was the generally rough atmosphere, the occasional hustler, the sometimes drunk proprietor and, of course, the game of pool. The cafe's entertainment was provided by the owner. The boys would "accidentally" knock a glass on the floor or spill cola on the counter—not all the time, but enough to be sporting. They would also bend spoons, put salt in sugar bowls and generally tease whoever was working in the cafe. The owner had opened the cafe recently and was dependent on the boys' business which was, in fact, substantial since between the horsing around and the teasing they bought food and drinks.

THE SAINTS ON WEEKENDS

On weekends the automobile was even more critical than during the week, for on weekends the Saints went to Big Town—a large city with a population of over a million 25 miles from Hanibal. Every Friday and Saturday night most of the Saints would meet between 8:00 and 8:30 and would go into Big Town. Big Town activities included drinking heavily in taverns or nightclubs, driving drunkenly through the streets, and committing acts of vandalism and playing pranks.

By midnight on Fridays and Saturdays the Saints were usually thoroughly high, and one or two of them were often so drunk they had to be carried to the cars. Then the boys drove around town, calling obscenities to women and girls; occasionally trying (unsuccessfully so far as I could tell) to pick girls up; and driving recklessly through red lights and at high speeds with their lights out. Occasionally they played "chicken." One boy would climb out the back window of the car and across the roof to the driver's side of the car while the car was moving at high speed (between 40 and 50 miles an hour); then the driver would move over and the boy who had just crawled across the car roof would take the driver's seat.

Searching for "fair game" for a prank was the boys' principal activity after they left the tavern. The boys would drive alongside a foot patrolman and ask directions to some street. If the policeman leaned on the car in the course of answering the question, the driver would speed away, causing him to lose his balance. The Saints were careful to play this prank only in an area where they were not going to spend much time and where they could quickly disappear around a corner to avoid having their license plate number taken.

Construction sites and road repair areas were the special province of the Saints' mischief. A soon-to-be-repaired hole in the road inevitably invited the Saints to remove lanterns and wooden barricades and put them in the car, leaving the hole unprotected. The boys would find a safe vantage point and wait for an unsuspecting motorist to drive into the hole. Often, though not always, the boys would go up to the motorist and commiserate with him about the dreadful way the city protected its citizenry.

Leaving the scene of the open hole and the motorist, the boys would then go searching for an appropriate place to erect the stolen barricade. An "appropriate place" was often a spot on a highway near a curve in the road where the barricade would not be seen by an oncoming motorist. The boys would wait to watch an unsuspecting motorist attempt to stop and (usually) crash into the wooden barricade. With saintly bearing the boys might offer help and understanding.

A stolen lantern might well find its way onto the back of a police car or hang from a street lamp. Once a lantern served as a prop for a reenactment of the "midnight ride of Paul Revere" until the "play," which was taking place at 2:00 AM in the center of a main street of Big Town, was interrupted by a police car several blocks away. The boys ran, leaving the lanterns on the street, and managed to avoid being apprehended.

Abandoned houses, especially if they were located in out-of-the-way places, were fair game for destruction and spontaneous vandalism. The boys would break windows, remove furniture to the yard and tear it apart, urinate on the walls and scrawl obscenities inside.

Through all the pranks, drinking and reckless driving the boys managed miraculously to avoid being stopped by police. Only twice in two years was I aware that they had been stopped by a Big City policeman. Once was for speeding (which they did every time they drove whether they were drunk or sober), and the driver managed to convince the policeman that it was simply an error. The second time they were stopped they had just left a nightclub and were walking through an alley. Aaron stopped to urinate and the boys began making obscene remarks. A foot patrolman came into the alley, lectured the boys and sent them home. Before the boys got to the car one began talking in a loud voice again. The policeman, who had followed them down the alley, arrested this boy for disturbing the peace and took him to the police station where the other Saints gathered. After paying a $5.00 fine, and with the assurance that there would be no permanent record of the arrest, the boy was released.

The boys had a spirit of frivolity and fun about their escapades. They did not view what they were engaged in as "delinquency," though it surely was by any reasonable definition of that word. They simply viewed themselves as having a little fun and who, they would ask, was really hurt by it? The answer had to be no one, although this fact remains one of the most difficult things to explain about the gang's behavior. Unlikely though it seems, in two years of drinking, driving, carousing and vandalism no one was seriously injured as a result of the Saints' activities.

THE SAINTS IN SCHOOL

The Saints were highly successful in school. The average grade for the group was "B," with two of the boys having close to a straight "A" average. Almost all of the boys were popular and many of them held offices in the school. One of the boys was vice-president of the student body one year. Six of the boys played on athletic teams.

At the end of their senior year, the student body selected ten seniors for special recognition as the "school wheels"; four of the ten were Saints. Teachers and school officials saw no problem with any of these boys and anticipated that they would all "make something of themselves."

How the boys managed to maintain this impression is surprising in view of their actual behavior while in school. Their technique for covering truancy was so successful that teachers did not even realize that the boys were absent from school much of the time. Occasionally, of course, the system would backfire and then the boy was on his own. A boy who was caught would be most contrite, would plead guilty and ask for mercy. He inevitably got the mercy he sought.

Cheating on examinations was rampant, even to the point of orally communicating answers to exams as well as looking at one another's papers. Since none of the group studied, and since they were primarily dependent on one another for help, it is surprising that grades were so high. Teachers contributed to the deception in their admitted inclination to give these boys (and presumably others like them) the benefit of the doubt. When asked how the boys did in school, and when pressed on specific examinations, teachers might admit that they were disappointed in John's performance, but would quickly add that they "knew that he was capable of doing better," so John was given a higher grade than he had actually earned. How often this happened is impossible to know. During the time that I observed the group, I never saw any of the boys take homework home. Teachers may have been "understanding" very regularly.

One exception to the gang's generally good performance was Jerry, who had a "C" average in his junior year, experienced disaster the next year and failed to graduate. Jerry had always been a little more nonchalant than the others about the liberties he took in school. Rather than wait for someone to come get him from class, he would offer his own excuse and leave. Although he probably did not miss any more classes than most of the others in the group, he did not take the requisite pains to cover his absences. Jerry was the only Saint whom I ever heard talk back to a teacher. Although teachers often called him a "cut up" or

a "smart kid," they never referred to him as a troublemaker or as a kid headed for trouble. It seems likely, then, that Jerry's failure his senior year and his mediocre performance his junior year were consequences of his not playing the game the proper way (possibly because he was disturbed by his parents' divorce). His teachers regarded him as "immature" and not quite ready to get out of high school.

THE POLICE AND THE SAINTS

The local police saw the Saints as good boys who were among the leaders of the youth in the community. Rarely, the boys might be stopped in town for speeding or for running a stop sign. When this happened the boys were always polite, contrite and pled for mercy. As in school, they received the mercy they asked for. None ever received a ticket or was taken into the precinct by the local police.

The situation in Big City, where the boys engaged in most of their delinquency, was only slightly different. The police there did not know the boys at all, although occasionally the boys were stopped by a patrolman. Once they were caught taking a lantern from a construction site. Another time they were stopped for running a stop sign, and on several occasions they were stopped for speeding. Their behavior was as before: contrite, polite and penitent. The urban police, like the local police, accepted their demeanor as sincere. More important, the urban police were convinced that these were good boys just out for a lark.

THE ROUGHNECKS

Hanibal townspeople never perceived the Saints' high level of delinquency. The Saints were good boys who just went in for an occasional prank. After all, they were well dressed, well mannered and had nice cars. The Roughnecks were a different story. Although the two gangs of boys were the same age, and both groups engaged in an equal amount of wild-oat sowing, everyone agreed that the not-so-well-dressed, not-so-well-mannered, not-so-rich boys were heading for trouble. Townspeople would say, "You can see the gang members at the drugstore, night after night, leaning against the storefront (sometimes drunk) or slouching around inside buying cokes, reading magazines, and probably stealing old Mr. Wall blind. When they were outside and girls walk by, even respectable girls, these boys make suggestive remarks. Sometimes their remarks are downright lewd."

From the community's viewpoint, the real indication that these kids were in for trouble was that they were constantly involved with the police. Some of them had been picked up for stealing, mostly small stuff, of course, "but still it's stealing small stuff that leads to big time crimes." "Too bad," people said. "Too bad that these boys couldn't behave like the other kids in town; stay out of trouble, be polite to adults, and look to their future."

The community's impression of the degree to which this group of six boys (ranging in age from 16 to 19) engaged in delinquency was somewhat distorted. In some ways the gang was more delinquent than the community thought; in other ways they were less.

The fighting activities of the group were fairly readily and accurately perceived by almost everyone. At least once a month, the boys would get into some sort of fight, although most fights were scraps between members of the group or involved only one member of the group and some peripheral hanger-on. Only three times in the period of observation did the group fight together: once against a gang from across town, once against two blacks and once against a group of boys from another school. For the first two fights the group went out "looking for trouble"—and they found it both times. The third fight followed a football game and began spontaneously with an argument on the football field between one of the Roughnecks and a member of the opposition's football team.

Jack had a particular propensity for fighting and was involved in most of the brawls. He was a prime mover of the escalation of arguments into fights.

More serious than fighting, had the community been aware of it, was theft. Although almost everyone was aware that the boys occasionally stole things, they did not realize the extent of the activity. Petty stealing was a frequent event for the Roughnecks. Sometimes they stole as a group and coordinated their efforts; other times they stole in pairs. Rarely did they steal alone.

The thefts ranged from very small things like paperback books, comics and ballpoint pens to expensive items like watches. The nature of the thefts varied from time to time. The gang would go through a period of systematically shoplifting items from automobiles or school lockers. Types of thievery varied with the whim of the gang. Some forms of thievery were more profitable than others, but all thefts were for profit, not just thrills.

Roughnecks siphoned gasoline from cars as often as they had access to an automobile, which was not very often. Unlike the Saints, who owned their own cars, the Roughnecks would have to borrow their parents' cars, an event which occurred only eight or nine times a year. The boys claimed to have stolen cars for joy rides from time to time.

Ron committed the most serious of the group's offenses. With an unidentified associate the boy attempted to burglarize a gasoline station. Although this station had been robbed twice previously in the same month, Ron denied any involvement in either of the other thefts. When Ron and his accomplice approached the station, the owner was hiding in the bushes beside the station. He fired both barrels of a double-barreled shotgun at the boys. Ron was severely injured; the other boy ran away and was never caught. Though he remained in critical condition for several months, Ron finally recovered and served six months of the following year in reform school. Upon release from reform school, Ron was put back a grade in school, and began running around with a different gang of boys. The Roughnecks considered the new gang less delinquent than themselves, and during the following year Ron had no more trouble with the police.

The Roughnecks, then, engaged mainly in three types of delinquency: theft, drinking and fighting. Although community members perceived that this gang of kids was delinquent, they mistakenly believed that their illegal activities were primarily drinking, fighting and being a nuisance to passersby. Drinking was limited among the gang members, although it did occur, and theft was much more prevalent than anyone realized.

Drinking would doubtless have been more prevalent had the boys had ready access to liquor. Since they rarely had automobiles at their disposal, they could not travel very far, and the bars in town would not serve them. Most of the boys had little money, and this, too, inhibited their purchase of alcohol. Their major source of liquor was a local drunk who would buy them a fifth if they would give him enough extra to buy himself a pint of whiskey or a bottle of wine.

The community's perception of drinking as prevalent stemmed from the fact that it was the most obvious delinquency the boys engaged in. When one of the boys had been drinking, even a casual observer seeing him on the corner would suspect that he was high.

There was a high level of mutual distrust and dislike between the Roughnecks and the police. The boys felt very strongly that the police were unfair and corrupt. Some evidence existed that the boys were correct in their perception.

The main source of the boys' dislike for the police undoubtedly stemmed from the fact that the police would sporadically harass the group. From the standpoint of the boys, these acts of occasional enforcement of the law were whimsical and uncalled for. It made no sense to them, for example, that the police would come to the corner occasionally and threaten them with arrest for loitering when the night before the boys had been out si-

phoning gasoline from cars and the police had been nowhere in sight. To the boys, the police were stupid on the one hand, for not being where they should have been and catching the boys in a serious offense, and unfair on the other hand, for trumping up "loitering" charges against them.

From the viewpoint of the police, the situation was quite different. They knew, with all the confidence necessary to be a policeman, that these boys were engaged in criminal activities. They knew this partly from occasionally catching them, mostly from circumstantial evidence ("the boys were around when those tires were slashed"), and partly because the police shared the view of the community in general that this was a bad bunch of boys. The best the police could hope to do was to be sensitive to the fact that these boys were engaged in illegal acts and arrest them whenever there was some evidence that they had been involved. Whether or not the boys had in fact committed a particular act in a particular way was not especially important. The police had a broader view: their job was to stamp out these kids' crimes; the tactics were not as important as the end result.

Over the period that the group was under observation, each member was arrested at least once. Several of the boys were arrested a number of times and spent at least one night in jail. While most were never taken to court, two of the boys were sentenced to six months' incarceration in boys' schools.

THE ROUGHNECKS IN SCHOOL

The Roughnecks' behavior in school was not particularly disruptive. During school hours they did not all hang around together, but tended instead to spend most of their time with one or two other members of the gang who were their special buddies. Although every member of the gang attempted to avoid school as much as possible, they were not particularly successful and most of them attended school with surprising regularity. They considered school a burden—something to be gotten through with a minimum of conflict. If they were "bugged" by a particular teacher, it could lead to trouble. One of the boys, Al, once threatened to beat up a teacher and, according to the other boys, the teacher hid under a desk to escape him.

Teachers saw the boys the way the general community did, as heading for trouble, as being uninterested in making something of themselves. Some were also seen as being incapable of meeting the academic standards of the school. Most of the teachers expressed concern for this group of boys and were willing to pass them despite poor performance, in the belief that failing them would only aggravate the problem.

The group of boys had a grade point average just slightly above "C." No one in the group failed either grade, and no one had better than a "C" average. They were very consistent in their achievement or, at least, the teachers were consistent in their perception of the boys' achievement.

Two of the boys were good football players. Herb was acknowledged to be the best player in the school and Jack was almost as good. Both boys were criticized for their failure to abide by training rules, for refusing to come to practice as often as they should, and for not playing their best during practice. What they lacked in sportsmanship they made up for in skill, apparently, and played every game no matter how poorly they had performed in practice or how many practice sessions they had missed.

TWO QUESTIONS

Why did the community, the school and the police react to the Saints as though they were good, upstanding, nondelinquent youths with bright futures but to the Roughnecks as though they were tough, young criminals who were headed for trouble? Why did the Roughnecks and the Saints in fact have quite different careers after high school—careers which, by and large, lived up to the expectations of the community?

The most obvious explanation for the differ-

ences in the community's and law enforcement agencies' reactions to the two gangs is that one group of boys was "more delinquent" than the other. Which group *was* more delinquent? The answer to this question will determine in part how we explain the differential responses to these groups by the members of the community and, particularly, by law enforcement and school officials.

In sheer number of illegal acts, the Saints were the more delinquent. They were truant from school for at least part of the day almost every day of the week. In addition, their drinking and vandalism occurred with surprising regularity. The Roughnecks, in contrast, engaged sporadically in delinquent episodes. While these episodes were frequent, they certainly did not occur on a daily or even a weekly basis.

The difference in frequency of offenses was probably caused by the Roughnecks' inability to obtain liquor and to manipulate legitimate excuses from school. Since the Roughnecks had less money than the Saints, and teachers carefully supervised their school activities, the Roughnecks' hearts may have been as black as the Saints', but their misdeeds were not nearly as frequent.

There are really no clear-cut criteria by which to measure qualitative differences in antisocial behavior. The most important dimension of the difference is generally referred to as the "seriousness" of the offenses.

If seriousness encompasses the relative economic costs of delinquent acts, then some assessment can be made. The Roughnecks probably stole an average of about $5.00 worth of goods a week. Some weeks the figure was considerably higher, but these times must be balanced against long periods when almost nothing was stolen.

The Saints were more continuously engaged in delinquency but their acts were not for the most part costly to property. Only their vandalism and occasional theft of gasoline would so qualify. Perhaps once or twice a month they would siphon a tankful of gas. The other costly items were street signs, construction lanterns and the like. All of these acts combined probably did not quite average $5.00 a week, partly because much of the stolen equipment was abandoned and presumably could be recovered. The difference in cost of stolen property between the two groups was trivial, but the Roughnecks probably had a slightly more expensive set of activities than did the Saints.

Another meaning of seriousness is the potential threat of physical harm to members of the community and to the boys themselves. The Roughnecks were more prone to physical violence; they not only welcomed an opportunity to fight; they went seeking it. In addition, they fought among themselves frequently. Although the fighting never included deadly weapons, it was still a menace, however minor, to the physical safety of those involved.

The Saints never fought. They avoided physical conflict both inside and outside the group. At the same time, though, the Saints frequently endangered their own and other people's lives. They did so almost every time they drove a car, especially if they had been drinking. Sober, their driving was risky; under the influence of alcohol it was horrendous. In addition, the Saints endangered the lives of others with their pranks. Street excavations left unmarked were a very serious hazard.

Evaluating the relative seriousness of the two gangs' activities is difficult. The community reacted as though the behavior of the Roughnecks was a problem, and they reacted as though the behavior of the Saints was not. But the members of the community were ignorant of the array of delinquent acts that characterized the Saints' behavior. Although concerned citizens were unaware of much of the Roughnecks' behavior as well, they were much better informed about the Roughnecks' involvement in delinquency than they were about the Saints'.

VISIBILITY

Differential treatment of the two gangs resulted in part because one gang was infinitely more visible than the other. This differential visibility was a direct function of the economic standing of the families. The Saints had access to automobiles and were able to remove themselves from the sight of the community. In as routine a decision as to where to go to have a milkshake after school, the Saints stayed away from the mainstream of community life. Lacking transportation, the Roughnecks could not make it to the edge of town. The center of town was the only practical place for them to meet since their homes were scattered throughout the town and any noncentral meeting place put an undue hardship on some members. Through necessity the Roughnecks congregated in a crowded area where everyone in the community passed frequently, including teachers and law enforcement officers. They could easily see the Roughnecks hanging around the drugstore.

The Roughnecks, of course, made themselves even more visible by making remarks to passersby and by occasionally getting into fights on the corner. Meanwhile, just as regularly, the Saints were either at the cafe on one edge of town or in the pool hall at the other edge of town. Without any particular realization that they were making themselves inconspicuous, the Saints were able to hide their time-wasting. Not only were they removed from the mainstream of traffic, but they were almost always inside a building.

On their escapades the Saints were also relatively invisible, since they left Hanibal and travelled to Big City. Here, too, they were mobile, roaming the city, rarely going to the same area twice.

DEMEANOR

To the notion of visibility must be added the difference in the responses of group members to outside intervention with their activities. If one of the Saints was confronted with an accusing policeman, even if he felt he was truly innocent of a wrongdoing, his demeanor was apologetic and penitent. A Roughneck's attitude was always the polar opposite. When confronted with a threatening adult authority, even one who tried to be pleasant, the Roughneck's hostility and disdain were clearly observable. Sometimes he might attempt to put up a veneer of respect, but it was thin and was not accepted as sincere by the authority.

School was no different from the community at large. The Saints could manipulate the system by feigning compliance with the school norms. The availability of cars at school meant that once free from the immediate sight of the teacher, the boys could disappear rapidly. And this escape was well enough planned that no administrator or teacher was nearby when the boys left. A Roughneck who wished to escape for a few hours was in a bind. If it were possible to get free from class, downtown was still a mile away, and even if he arrived there, he was still very visible. Truancy for the Roughnecks meant almost certain detection, while the Saints enjoyed almost complete immunity from sanctions.

BIAS

Community members were not aware of the transgressions of the Saints. Even if the Saints had been less discreet, their favorite delinquencies would have been perceived as less serious than those of the Roughnecks.

In the eyes of the police and school officials, a boy who drinks in an alley and stands intoxicated on the street corner is committing a more serious offense than is a boy who drinks to inebriation in a nightclub or a tavern and drives around afterwards in a car. Similarly, a boy who steals a wallet from a store will be viewed as having committed a more serious offense than a boy who steals a lantern from a construction site.

Perceptual bias also operates with respect to the demeanor of the boys in the two groups when they are confronted by adults. It is not simply that adults dislike the posture affected by boys of the Roughneck ilk; more important is the conviction that the posture adopted by the Roughnecks is an indication of their devotion and commitment to deviance as a way of life. The posture becomes a cue, just as the type of the offense is a cue, to the degree to which the known transgressions are indicators of the youths' potential for other problems.

Visibility, demeanor and bias are surface variables which explain the day-to-day operations of the police. Why do these surface variables operate as they do? Why did the police choose to disregard the Saints' delinquencies while breathing down the backs of the Roughnecks?

The answer lies in the class structure of American society and the control of legal institutions by those at the top of the class structure. Obviously, no representative of the upper class drew up the operational chart for the police which led them to look in the ghettoes and on streetcorners—which led them to see the demeanor of lower-class youth as troublesome and that of upper-middle-class youth as tolerable. Rather, the procedures simply developed from experience—experience with irate and influential upper-middle-class parents insisting that their son's vandalism was simply a prank and his drunkenness only a momentary "sowing of wild oats"—experience with cooperative or indifferent, powerless, lower-class parents who acquiesced to the laws' definition of their son's behavior.

ADULT CAREERS OF THE SAINTS AND THE ROUGHNECKS

The community's confidence in the potential of the Saints and the Roughnecks apparently was justified. If anything, the community members underestimated the degree to which these youngsters would turn out "good" or "bad."

Seven of the eight members of the Saints went on to college immediately after high school. Five of the boys graduated from college in four years. The sixth one finished college after two years in the army, and the seventh spent four years in the air force before returning to college and receiving a B.A. degree. Of these seven college graduates, three went on for advanced degrees. One finished law school and is now active in state politics, one finished medical school and is practicing near Hanibal, and one boy is now working for a Ph.D. The other four college graduates entered sub-managerial, managerial or executive training positions with larger firms.

The only Saint who did not complete college was Jerry. Jerry had failed to graduate from high school with the other Saints. During his second senior year, after the other Saints had gone on to college, Jerry began to hang around with what several teachers described as a "rough crowd"— the gang that was heir apparent to the Rough-necks. At the end of his second senior year, when he did graduate from high school, Jerry took a job as a used-car salesman, got married and quickly had a child. Although he made several abortive attempts to go to college by attending night school, when I last saw him (ten years after high school) Jerry was unemployed and had been living on unemployment for almost a year. His wife worked as a waitress.

Some of the Roughnecks have lived up to community expectations. A number of them were headed for trouble. A few were not.

Jack and Herb were the athletes among the Roughnecks and their athletic prowess paid off handsomely. Both boys received unsolicited athletic scholarships to college. After Herb received his scholarship (near the end of his senior year), he apparently did an about-face. His demeanor became very similar to that of the Saints. Although he remained a member in good standing of the Roughnecks, he stopped participating in most activities and did not hang on the corner as often.

Jack did not change. If anything, he became more prone to fighting. He even made excuses for accepting the scholarship. He told the other gang members that the school had guaranteed him a "C" average if he would come to play football— an idea that seems far-fetched, even in this day of highly competitive recruiting.

During the summer after graduation from high school, Jack attempted suicide by jumping from a tall building. The jump would certainly have killed most people trying it, but Jack survived. He entered college in the fall and played four years of football. He and Herb graduated in four years, and both are teaching and coaching in high schools. They are married and have stable families. If anything, Jack appears to have a more prestigious position in the community than does Herb, though both are well respected and secure in their positions.

Two of the boys never finished high school. Tommy left at the end of his junior year and went to another state. That summer he was arrested and placed on probation on a manslaughter charge. Three years later he was arrested for murder; he pleaded guilty to second degree murder and is serving a 30-year sentence in the state penitentiary.

Al, the other boy who did not finish high school, also left the state in his senior year. He is serving a life sentence in a state penitentiary for first degree murder.

Wes is a small-time gambler. He finished high school and "bummed around." After several years he made contact with a bookmaker who employed him as a runner. Later he acquired his own area and has been working it ever since. His position among the bookmakers is almost identical to the position he had in the gang; he is always around but no one is really aware of him. He makes no trouble and he does not get into any. Steady, reliable, capable of keeping his mouth closed, he plays the game by the rules, even though the game is an illegal one.

That leaves only Ron. Some of his former friends reported that they had heard he was "driving a truck up north," but no one could provide any concrete information.

REINFORCEMENT

The community responded to the Roughnecks as boys in trouble, and the boys agreed with that perception. Their pattern of deviancy was reinforced, and breaking away from it became increasingly unlikely. Once the boys acquired an image of themselves as deviants, they selected new friends who affirmed that self-image. As that self-conception became more firmly entrenched, they also became willing to try new and more extreme deviances. With their growing alienation came freer expression of disrespect and hostility for representatives of the legitimate society. This disrespect increased the community's negativism, perpetuating the entire process of commitment to deviance. Lack of a commitment to deviance works the same way. In either case, the process will perpetuate itself unless some event (like a scholarship to college or a sudden failure) external to the established relationship intervenes. For two of the Roughnecks (Herb and Jack), receiving college athletic scholarships created new relations and culminated in a break with the established pattern of deviance. In the case of one of the Saints (Jerry), his parents' divorce and his failing to graduate from high school changed some of his other relations. Being held back in school for a year and losing his place among the Saints had sufficient impact on Jerry to alter his self-image and virtually to assure that he would not go on to college as his peers did. Although the experiments of life can rarely be reversed, it seems likely in view of the behavior of the other boys who did not enjoy this special treatment by the school that Jerry, too, would have "become something" had he graduated as anticipated. For Herb and Jack outside intervention worked to their advantage; for Jerry it was his undoing.

Selective perception and labelling—finding, processing and punishing some kinds of criminality and not others—means that visible, poor, nonmobile, outspoken, undiplomatic "tough" kids will be noticed, whether their actions are seriously delinquent or not. Other kids, who have established a reputation for being bright (even though underachieving), disciplined and involved in respectable activities, who are mobile and monied, will be invisible when they deviate from sanctioned activities. They'll sow their wild oats—perhaps even wider and thicker than their lower-class cohorts—but they won't be noticed. When it's time to leave adolescence most will follow the expected path, settling into the ways of the middle class, remembering fondly the delinquent but unnoticed fling of their youth. The Roughnecks and others like them may turn around, too. It is more likely that their noticeable deviance will have been so reinforced by police and community that their lives will be effectively channelled into careers consistent with their adolescent background.

TAKING ANOTHER LOOK

1 How did police view the Saints? How did they view the Roughnecks?
2 According to Chambliss, how can we evaluate which group of boys was "more delinquent" than the other? What are the results of his evaluation?
3 According to Chambliss, how does the class structure of American society influence the differing treatment of groups such as the Saints and the Roughnecks?
4 To what degree did members of the Saints and Roughnecks turn out "good" or "bad" after high school?
5 According to Chambliss, how do the police and the community reinforce the noticeable deviance of a group such as the Roughnecks?
6 How would conflict theorists be likely to view the findings of this participant-observation study?

Crime Waves as Ideology

Mark Fishman

Crime statistics are among the least reliable social data. However, since they deal with an issue of grave concern to the public, they are frequently cited as if they were quite accurate. Such statistics do serve as an indicator of police activity, as well as an approximate indication of the level of certain crimes. Yet it would be a mistake to interpret these data as an exact representation of the incidence of crime. The most serious limitation of official crime statistics is that they include only those crimes actually *reported* to law enforcement agencies. Many crimes are not reported, including at least half of all assaults, robberies, and rapes.

With such data in mind, it becomes quite difficult to reliably determine whether a "crime wave" is taking place or not. In the following selection, sociologist Mark Fishman explores how crime waves are constructed in the mass media and how they contribute to an "ideology of crime." Fishman studies the emergence in 1976 of a major "crime wave against the elderly" in New York City. He draws upon data derived from participant observation, interviews, and content analysis of crime news as presented on a local television station and in two New York newspapers.

In examining Fishman's analysis, it is again useful to remember the contention of labeling theorists that some persons or groups have the power to *define* labels and apply them to others. Fishman emphasizes the role of journalists and police authorities in determining that a crime wave exists. News workers identify crime waves by seeing "themes" in various crime reports. A crime wave dynamic cannot occur unless journalists are supplied with a "continuous supply of incidents that can be seen as instances of the theme." Consequently, in Fishman's view, "officials with a stake in 'doing something' about crime have power over crime waves." They may use their positions to "nurture fledgling crime themes first identified by journalists" or may act to "deny the reality of crime waves."

When we speak of a crime wave, we are talking about a kind of social awareness of crime, crime brought to public consciousness. It is something to be remarked upon at the corner grocery store, complained about in a community meeting, and denounced at the mayor's press conference. One cannot be mugged by a crime wave, but one can be scared. And one can put more police on the streets and enact new laws on the basis of fear. Crime waves may be "things of the mind," but they have real consequences.

Author's note: This is a revised version of a paper presented at the 1977 Annual Meeting of the Society for the Study of Social Problems. I wish to acknowledge Ronald Vandor and David Lester, whose many hours of research assistance made this paper possible, Pamela Fishman, who helped clarify much of my thinking about crime news, and Malcolm Spector and Gaye Tuchman for their helpful comments on an earlier draft.

Crime waves are prime candidates for ideology. This study analyzes a specific crime wave that occurred in New York City in late 1976. This case both illustrates and informs my analysis that the crime waves which periodically appear in the press are constructs of the mass media and contribute to an ideological conception of crime in America.[1]

My use of the term ideology follows Dorothy Smith (1972). All knowledge is knowledge from some point of view, resulting from the use of procedures for knowing a part of the world. Ideological accounts arise from "procedures which people use as a means *not to know*" (1972:3, emphasis mine). Routine news gathering and editing involve "procedures not to know." The business of news is embedded in a configuration of institutions. These include a community of news organizations from which journalists derive a sense of "what's news now," and governmental agencies upon which journalists depend for their raw materials. Through their interactions and reliance on official sources, news organizations both invoke and reproduce prevailing conceptions of "serious crime."

Crimes Against the Elderly

In late 1976, New York City experienced a major crime wave. The city's three daily newspapers and five local television stations reported a surge of violence against elderly people. The crime wave lasted approximately seven weeks, eventually receiving national television and newspaper coverage.

One consequence of this was the public definition of a new type of crime.[2] "Crimes against the elderly" became a typical crime with typical victims, offenders, and circumstances. Reported muggers, murderers, and rapists of the elderly were usually black or hispanic youths with long juvenile records. They came from ghetto neighborhoods near enclaves of elderly whites who, for various reasons (usually poverty), had not fled the inner city. Using this scenario, journalists reported incident after brutal incident throughout November and December 1976.

The outcry against these crimes was immediate. The Mayor of New York City, who was preparing to run for re-election, criticized the juvenile justice system and the criminal courts. The New York City Police Department gave its Senior Citizens Robbery Unit (S.C.R.U.) manpower to extend plain-clothes operations. Camera crews from local news stations filmed S.C.R.U. officers dressed as old people and arresting muggers. Local police precincts held community meetings to advise the elderly how to protect themselves. New York State legislators introduced bills to make juvenile records available to a judge at the time of sentencing, to deny sixteen to nineteen year olds juvenile status if they victimized an old person, and to mandate prison sentences for crimes of violence against the aged. These proposals were passed in both the State Senate and Assembly, but were eventually vetoed

---

[1] This paper focuses on the generation of crime waves, not their effects. Thus, I infer that media crime waves contribute to existing images and fears of crime in society. To substantiate this inference would require a study of crime wave effects with a different method from that used here. There is, however, research indicating that people's fears and images of crime derive, in large part, from the news media. See, for example, Davis (1952:330) and Biderman, et al. (1967:128).

[2] While the New York City crime wave represents the first widely publicized formulation of "crimes against the elderly," the issue was not first defined by the New York media. Fredric DuBow (personal communication) has pointed out that the law enforcement establishment had formulated crimes against the elderly as a new type of crime at least two years prior to the crime wave: Since 1974 it was an important funding theme of L.E.A.A.; in 1975 it was the subject of a major conference; and in February 1976 *Police Chief* devoted a special issue to it.

These earlier law enforcement formulations probably led to the creation of the New York Police Department's Senior Citizens Robbery Unit (S.C.R.U.) well before the city's crime wave. As we shall see, S.C.R.U. played a crucial role in directing media attention to crimes against the elderly in the first stages of the crime wave. Thus, it seems that early "professional formulations" led to the establishment of a specialized agency which, in turn, enabled the media publicly to formulate a category for crimes against the elderly.

by the Governor on August 19, 1977—nine months after the crime wave had ended.

A May 1977 Harris poll suggested the crime wave also had a nation-wide effect on people's fear of crime. Moreover, it had an effect on the crime categories which the Harris organization used in its surveys; this poll included a new type of crime, crimes against the elderly, not previously present in Harris polls. Harris found that sixty percent of his respondents felt that assaults against elderly people in their home areas had been going up, and that fifty percent of those age fifty or older said they were more uneasy on the streets than they had been one year ago.[3]

It is doubtful that there really was a crime wave or any unusual surge of violence against elderly people. No one really knows, least of all the journalists who reported the crime wave. The police statistics from the N.Y.P.D. do not show a crime wave.[4] In fact, for one type of crime, homicide, the police showed a nineteen percent *drop* over the previous year's rate of elderly people murdered. This is significant because the news media began their reporting with coverage of several gruesome murders. (Twenty-eight percent of the stories reported by the three media organizations I surveyed were stories about homicides. In contrast, the police reported that homicides made up less than one percent of crimes against the elderly in 1976).

For other types of crime with elderly victims police statistics showed an increase over the previous year. Crime victimization, however, rose for all age categories in 1976. In some cases, the increases were greater for elderly victims, in others less. Robbery was up ten percent in the general population, nineteen percent for the elderly. Grand larceny was up twenty-nine percent for the general population, twenty-five percent for the

elderly. In short, police statistics substantiate only that there was a continuing increase in victimization of the elderly (as well as of the general population), not that old people were singled out, as never before. Moreover, the homicide rate contradicts the media presentation of a crime wave.

This paper, however, is not a study in the disparity between police statistics and crime news. Prior studies of crime news and crime waves (Davis, 1952; Roshier, 1973), as well as anecdotal reports (Steffens, 1931:285–291), have shown the irony of crime waves: although the public is alarmed and politicians respond to media reports of a dramatic increase in crime, such "waves" have no basis in police statistics. This study goes beyond sociological irony to examine *how and why news organizations construct crime waves.* Crime waves are taken to be waves of coverage of some topic in crime. Crime waves as *media waves* may or may not be related to something happening "on the streets" or in the police crime rates. Studying crime waves means studying processes in the mass media.

Method

I collected two kinds of data. First, two student researchers and I conducted participant observation from November 1976 to April 1977 on a New York City local television station, WAVE (a pseudonym). One student was a full-time WAVE journalist who worked as a news writer, program producer, and assignment editor. We focused on how the assignment editor assembled the daily news program by deciding what major stories would be covered for the day and assigning reporters and camera crews to these stories. In addition, we conducted interviews with journalists from WAVE and the New York *Daily News.*

Second, we kept a record of all news relating to crimes against the elderly reported from September 1976 through February 1977 in two newspapers, the New York *Daily News* and the *New*

---

[3] Reported in the *New York Post,* May 9, 1977.

[4] Thus far I have been unable to obtain a complete, month-by-month set of 1976 N.Y.P.D. crime rates. Therefore, for all but the homicide rate, the figures described below are tentative, based on partial rates for 1976.

York Post, and on WAVE, which aired a one hour newscast in the evening. This enabled us to "locate" the New York crime wave, to determine when it began and ended, and to determine the kind of coverage crimes against the elderly received before, during, and after the crime wave period.

The Crime Wave: A View From the Outside

Over the six-month period of observation the *News,* the *Post,* and WAVE presented eighty-nine stories of crimes against the elderly. Fifty-six stories or sixty-three percent occurred during the crime wave period. The weekly frequencies of news stories from all three media are shown in the appendix. This graph clearly indicates a wave of media reporting that began in the last week of October and trailed off by the second week of December. It shows a sharp, swift rise in coverage for the first two weeks, then a slow, uneven decline for the remaining five weeks.

Examining the individual patterns of coverage for each news organization reveals that prior to the crime wave each organization was reporting approximately one story of crime against the elderly every other week. After the wave, coverage in all three media was sporadic, but heavier than coverage during the prewave period, indicating that the media appear to have been sensitized to the topic.

The three individual crime waves in the *News,* the *Post,* and WAVE show that the marked increase in coverage did not coincide in all three media. The *News* had a sudden increase in the third week of October; WAVE and the *Post* did not increase their coverage until the fourth week of October. Further, in this fourth week the two "latecomers" began their increase *simultaneously.* Prior to their increased coverage, the *Post* and WAVE did not parallel each other. It was only after the *News* began reporting a wave that the others developed a synchronous pattern. This trend suggests that the other media simultaneously responded to the *Daily News'* portrayal of a wave of violence against the elderly.

All three media show different crime wave profiles. WAVE steeply increased coverage to a single peak, then had an equally steep decline (seventeen days rising and sixteen days falling). In contrast, the *Daily News* and the *Post* show bimodal curves. In the *News* there was a swift initial rise (ten days), from which coverage subsided slowly, then it turned upward to a second peak (lower than the first), and finally declined.

The unevenness of the *Daily News's* wave was echoed in the *Post.* The *Post* participated less actively in the crime wave than did the *News* or WAVE. We might even say that the *Post* did not show a crime wave, except that the period of its heaviest coverage coincided with the crime wave period in the other media. Moreover, the *Post's* pre- and post-wave patterns were similar to the other media, and during the crime wave it showed a bimodal wave which paralleled that of the *Daily News.* Thus, the *Post's* wave seems to have been a weak reflection of the *Daily News's* curve.

How can we explain these bimodal patterns? The likely reason why the *News* and *Post* reduced their coverage after the first peaks involves a major news event coinciding with this drop: the 1976 Presidential Election of November 2. The elections seem to have crowded out crimes against the elderly from the newspapers, but not from local TV news, since stations like WAVE were not trying to compete with network coverage of the Presidential race. Thus, during the slow news period after the elections, the *News* and *Post* seemed to have "rediscovered" the crime wave, which was still present in local TV news.

In other words, it seems the *News'* and the *Post's* second peak was a response to the continuing crime wave in the television media (assuming other TV stations behaved like WAVE). Just as the initial appearance of the crime wave in the *Daily News* seems to have spurred increased coverage by the *Post* and WAVE, so the continuing coverage of the crime wave on television seems to have "re-awakened" interest in the topic by the *Daily News* and the *Post.* Thus, *the behavior of each news organization during the crime wave seems to have been in response to the other media.*

Seeing Themes in Crime: A View from the Inside

How do individual crimes come to be seen as a crime wave? The answer is found in the methods by which news is organized. News workers make crime waves by seeing "themes" in the news. Crime waves are little more than the continued and heavy coverage of numerous occurrences which journalists report as a single topic (for example, "crimes against the elderly").

News themes are various: "everything Jimmy Carter did today," "the taxi cab strike," "Vietnam," "the disintegrating American family," or "labor disputes." A news theme is a unifying concept. It presents a specific news event, or a number of such events, in terms of some broader concept. For example, the mugging of an eighty-two-year-old Bronx woman can be reported as "the latest instance of the continuing trend in crimes against the elderly." A news theme allows journalists to cast an incident as an *instance* of something.

The Glasgow Media Group (1976:355) provides an interesting example of thematized news events from one British television newscast:

> The week had its share of unrest. Trouble in Glasgow with striking dustmen and ambulance controllers, short time in the car industry, no Sunday Mirror or Sunday People today and a fair amount of general trouble in Fleet Street and a continuing rumble over the matter of two builders pickets jailed for conspiracy.

As the authors point out, disparate incidents are reported together under the single theme of "unrest." Calling these things "unrest" imposes order on the events reported. Audience members are meant to see the events as unified, as instances of a single theme.

Themes give news shows and newspapers a presentational order. Items are presented in groups organized around a theme. Some themes are related to others, making it possible for groups of news stories to be placed near each other. For instance, during the crime wave against the elderly, the first ten minutes of a sixty-minute news program at WAVE was organized around interrelated themes:

1 Police apprehend three youngsters who allegedly mugged an elderly Queens couple.

2 Police and senior citizens meet at a Queens precinct to discuss fighting crimes against the elderly.

3 A feature report on the Senior Citizens Robbery Unit.

4 Police seize guns and drugs intended for warring gangs in the Bronx.

5 Two members of a youth gang are arrested for robbing someone at knife point.

6 R.O.T.C. cadet charged in the stabbing death of another cadet.

7 New York State audit finds the city police have been mishandling $9.1 million of federal funds.

8 New York City and the police union are still working on a new contract, at the same time that some layed-off firemen and subway cops will be rehired.

First, there are small groups of stories, each containing a theme that the stories in the group share in common (the first three stories are about "crimes against the elderly" and the next three about "youth crime"). Second, groups of stories are placed next to other groups, since the different themes of each group share common features (the group of crimes against the elderly and the group of youth crimes both can be seen to be about youthful perpetrators and police responses to them).

Journalists do not create themes merely to show an audience the appearance of order. News themes are very useful in newswork itself. In particular, editors selecting and organizing the day's stories need themes.[5] Every day, news editors face a glut of "raw materials" (wire service reports, press releases, police crime dispatches) out of which they must fashion relatively few news stories. This task involves a selection process which operates somewhat differently in television and newspaper newsrooms. The essentials of the process are the same: individual news items are identified and sorted according to possible themes.

The chances that any event or incident will be reported increase once it has been associated with a current theme in the news. Crime incidents are rarely reported unless news workers see them related to a past or emerging trend in criminality or law enforcement. A brief description of how the assignment editor at WAVE developed the first segment of the news show just cited illustrates this point. The assignment editor determined the top stories for the day when he noticed that several previously unrelated stories were all part of the same current newsworthy theme: crimes against the elderly. And the discovery of this theme was no coincidence: that day's program was in the midst of the crime wave period.

The assignment editor did not begin his day knowing that crime news, and, in particular, that crimes against the elderly, would receive top billing in the evening's news show. When he started work at 8:45 AM he already knew of two stories that he would most likely cover:[6] One was a feature report on the Senior Citizens Robbery Unit fighting crimes against the elderly. This feature, which eventually ran as the third story in the evening newscast, had been taped days before; it was part of a continuing series on S.C.R.U. the station had been airing for the past few weeks. The second story was a feature report on a "food fair" that afternoon in Manhattan. The editor planned to send a reporter and camera crew to cover it, but also wanted to line up, as he put it, "some better stories" for the day.

Ten minutes after he arrived in the newsroom the assignment editor began scanning his news sources for lead stories. He sifted through reams of wire service news that had collected overnight under the wire machines; he scanned the police dispatches of the previous night's and that morning's crime incidents (about ten or twelve) received through a teletype called "the police wire". He also looked to other news media for story ideas: he read the *Daily News* and *New York Times* and he listened to an all-news radio station.

In the *Daily News* he found a small story about rehiring firemen and Transit Authority police who had been laid off. He thought this would be a good story because "this indicates things may be turning around in the city." This incident became newsworthy when the assignment editor could see it as part of a current newsworthy theme (New York's fiscal crisis).

Still, the assignment editor despaired that he had "no real news," that this was "a slow news day." However, around ten AM two things happened. First, when scanning the police crime dispatches, the assignment editor found that in the 113th precinct in Queens an elderly couple had been mugged, and that one perpetrator was wounded by police. As he was clipping this dispatch, he heard over the all-news radio that the 112th precinct in Queens, very close to where the mugging occurred, was holding a crime prevention meeting with senior citizens. He now knew what his lead stories for the day would be, and he knew what he had to do to line them up:

1 He would send a reporter out to the 113th precinct to find, and get on film, whatever he could about the mugging (interviews with police, perhaps with some witnesses or with the victims themselves; and, if he was lucky, film of any suspects that were apprehended).

---

[5] The editor's use of news themes is part of the more general tendency of newsworkers to code and categorize news events in order to "routinize their unexpectedness." See Tuchman, 1973.

[6] The assignment editor started with these two stories because his superior in the newsroom had suggested that they be covered.

2 Then the reporter could go over to the nearby 112th precinct to film the police meeting with senior citizens.

3 These two reports would be followed by the pre-taped feature on S.C.R.U.

4 The story on rehiring firemen and Transit police, as well as a few other brief wire service reports relevant to crime which might come in during the rest of the day, would all follow the above three lead stories in some as yet undetermined order. The story on the "food fair" would be placed further back in the show.

Each story, seen independently, might not have merited attention. But seen together, all of them were made newsworthy by the perception of a common theme. The editor's "discovery" of the theme of crime against the elderly made the day's news come together. He knew how to assign a schedule to his reporter and camera crew; and he knew pretty much what the day's news was going to be.

The selection of news on the basis of themes is one component in the ideological production of crime news. It constitutes a "procedure not to know." This procedure requires that an incident be stripped of the actual context of its occurrence so that it may be relocated in a new, symbolic context: the news theme. Because newsworthiness is based on themes, the attention devoted to an event may exceed its importance, relevance, or timeliness were these qualities determined with reference to some theory of society. In place of any such theoretical understanding of the phenomena they report, newsworkers make incidents meaningful only as *instances of themes*—themes which are generated within the news production process. Thus, something becomes a "serious type of crime" on the basis of what is going on inside newsrooms, not outside them.

From Crime Themes to Crime Waves

Crime themes are potential crime waves. A news organization cannot make a crime wave without the collaboration of other media reporting the same crime theme. Crime waves emerge out of an interaction among news organizations.

The Indefinite Overlapping Character of News Judgments. All newsworkers depend on other media organizations for their sense of "what's news today." For example, the WAVE assignment editor began his day by reading the morning papers, the *Daily News* and *The New York Times,* and by listening to an all-news radio station. He later read the *New York Post* and watched when other TV stations aired their news. This editor told me that he did not mind using "anything, any source of news. I'm not proud. I'll steal any source of news."

In reality, stories were not stolen wholesale; rather, the other news media provided an important pool of ideas for story assignments. The noon and evening TV news shows rarely were used for this purpose because, by the time these shows were aired, most of the editor's news was set. The news on other stations mainly confirmed the assignment editor's news judgments, since his planned 10 PM news was, with few exceptions, identical to what his competitors were broadcasting. It seems his competitors were doing just what he was doing: reading the *Times* and the *News,* listening to the all-news radio, and taking stories from the same news sources (wire services, police news dispatches, and press releases).[7]

News judgments continuously overlap in space and time. Editors of afternoon and evening media look for, and are oriented by, the news in the morning media. Editors of the morning media derive their sense of news from afternoon and evening media. Since these media may be in different regions and different cities, news judgments spread throughout an indefinite expanse of territory. The wire services and a few nationally-read

---

[7] While my example of overlapping news judgments is drawn from a local television station, the same phenomenon occurs both on newspapers and national network news (Epstein, 1973:150).

newspapers, *The New York Times* and *Washington Post,* increase the diffusion of news judgments throughout the U.S.

Moreover, this overlap provides a continuity of news judgments. A specific incident or theme presented in the morning will be covered in the evening, perhaps with fresh incidents, more details, a new development or a "local angle" on the story. The process may repeat itself the next day, reproducing the theme of the previous evening.

The Crime Wave Dynamic. When journalists notice each other reporting the same crime theme, it becomes entrenched in a community of media organizations. Reporters and editors will know that "this kind of crime is news." To use Sack's (1972:333) term, journalists have established a "consistency rule": *every crime incident that can be seen as an instance of the theme, will be seen and reported as such.* The rule is used to identify the newsworthiness of certain crimes. Reporters and editors will know, for example, that a certain incident is "another one of those crimes against the elderly" and not just an incident that can be categorized in a variety of ways.

Each use of the consistency rule reestablishes the rule. Any use of the principle invites readers or viewers of the news, including other journalists, to use the same principle. In order to recognize a crime incident as an instance of a theme, readers or viewers must use the same consistency rule which was used to produce that news.

Journalists who have not yet seen a particular crime theme learn to see it simply by watching their competition. They are able, using the consistency rule, to report the same crime theme their competition taught them to see. At this point, when a crime theme is beginning to spread through more and more media organizations, the "reality" of the theme is confirmed for the media organizations who first reported it. They now see others using the theme. Moreover, as the theme persists, news organizations already using the theme will not hesitate to report new instances, because they confirm a past news judgment that "this thing really is a type of crime happening now." Thus, each use of the theme confirms and justifies its prior uses.

If it continues long enough, the process constitutes a crime wave dynamic. All crime waves begin as simple themes but by means of this dynamic can swell into waves. Crime themes constantly appear in the media and few reach the proportions of full-scale crime waves. After all, it only takes one editor with a little imagination to introduce a new theme into the news. Why is it that few crime themes go beyond a few days of coverage by one or two news organizations?

Clearly, something more than the crime wave dynamic is necessary for a theme to grow into a wave: *There must be a continuous supply of crime incidents that can be seen as instances of a theme.* Journalists may be primed to report a wave of crime incidents, but they also must know of enough incidents to report the wave. (During the period of my research, New York City journalists had been frustrated in reporting an expected "mafia war." This theme never persisted long for lack of enough incidents. Thus, "mafia war" was a hungry crime theme, starved of enough incidents to make it the crime wave it could have become.) The supply of incidents is crucial in determining the growth of crime waves. What are journalists' sources of crime news?

Perpetrators of crime could be a source, but news workers rarely learn of crimes directly from offenders. The primary source is law enforcement agencies.[8] In the newsroom of WAVE, journalists first learned of crime incidents through three sources:[9] The "police wire," the police radio, and other news organizations (wire service reports, the all-news radio station, and the *Daily News*). The first two of these were direct links to the city police. Crime news is really police news. Thus, *the media's supply of crime incidents is a function of*

---

[8] The only exception that comes to mind is the coverage of mafia news by specialized reporters on large New York publications: *The New York Times,* the New York *Daily News,* the *New York Post,* the *Wall Street Journal,* and *Newsday.*

[9] There was an occasional fourth source: phone calls from the police.

the crime reporting practices of law enforcement agencies. This reliance on law enforcement agencies constitutes another component of the ideological production of crime news. News workers will not know what the police do not routinely detect or transmit to them. What journalists do know of crime is formulated for them by law enforcement agencies.

The Pool of Potential Crime Waves

The police supply news organizations with an assortment of crime incidents every day. For media organizations in towns and small cities this assortment often consists of *all* crimes known to the police in a twenty-four-hour period. But in large urban areas there are far too many crimes known to the police for any reporter to know them all. Therefore, urban journalists depend on the police to provide a "summary" of these incidents.

In New York City, the daily summary is known as the "police wire." All the city's major media have a teletype that receives crime dispatches from the N.Y.P.D.'s Office of Public Information. In one day, this police wire types out anywhere from twelve to twenty-five messages. The crime items appearing over the police wire constitute a "crime wave pool": a collection of crime incidents known to the media and having the potential of being seen as certain crime themes. Crime themes steadily supplied with instances over the police wire can become crime waves.

While journalists may invent crime themes (I suspect the police suggest and encourage many of them), a crime wave needs enough incidents on the police wire to support it. The police have power both to veto and promote the media's construction of crime waves. The collection of crime incidents the police provide to news organizations may systematically preclude certain themes from becoming waves (the veto power). Moreover, the same collection of incidents may contain enough crime items of a certain type to allow only a restricted class of crime themes to become crime

waves (the enabling power).

For three ten-day periods from mid-February to the end of March 1977, a copy of all crime dispatches of the police wire was kept. Over this thirty-day period, 468 individual dispatches (averaging 15.6 per day) were received. Of these, I ignored ninety-seven (21%) which the police and journalists did not consider crime items. (They were mostly traffic advisories and non-suspicious fires.)

The remaining 371 crime dispatches reveal that the police wire provides journalists with a heavy and steady diet of "street crimes." Two thirds (246 items or 66.3%) of the crime items consisted of: a) robberies and burglaries (eighty-five items or twenty-three percent of all crime items), b) unspecified shootings and stabbings (156 items or forty-two percent) and c) a sprinkling of other assaults (five items or one percent —mostly rapes).

The remaining one-third of the police wire consisted of a variety of incidents: thirteen bombings; nine police suspended or arrested; six demonstrations requiring police action; five hostage situations; four raids for gambling, pornography, and drugs; three people run over by subway trains; one arson; and one hit-and-run. In addition, this third contained incidents which, I assume, the police considered "strange" and consequently of interest to the media (for example, a bus stolen, the theft of a large amount of poisons, a man threatening to set himself on fire, a person crushed by an elevator, and the discovery of a disembodied head.)

The first thing worth noting about the police wire is what it does *not* contain: incidents of price-fixing, consumer fraud, sub-standard housing, unhealthy food, environmental pollution, political bribery and corruption, and the like. None appear in this pool of crime incidents from which crime waves arise, yet all of these may occur enough to constitute a crime wave if the media were to have routine access to knowledge of their occurrence.

One reason why these do not appear over the police wire is that agencies other than the city police enforce the laws governing these kinds of crime. Because police manpower is devoted to street crimes, it is street crime reports that the police wire carries. If journalists are to report other kinds of crime, they must draw on other sources (usually the wire services and other media organizations) which provide instances of such crime only sporadically.

Moreover, in the police wire one is unable to find a number of very common crimes which local police *do* know about, but consider "uninteresting" and, thus, not worth transmitting to the media.[10] These included what journalists told me were "too common" to be news: everything from bicycle theft, liquor store stick-ups and rapes, to wife beating, child molesting and other "family matters" not resulting in homicide or hospitalization.

It is likely that a large number of the street crimes reported over the police wire were, in fact, family disputes, crimes against women, and racial conflict. But it was difficult to tell this from the information in the crime dispatches. This is particularly true of the large number of shootings and stabbings, which reporters tended to ignore.

Any descriptive features in a crime dispatch provide important clues to newsworkers looking for themes in crime. From reading the police wire, I was struck by the lack of detail. Victims, if they were identified at all, and if they were persons not businesses, were identified by sex and age. When more was told, they were described as: 1) "elderly" (for homicides and robberies), 2) policemen (for any assaults), or 3) banks (for robberies). Perpetrators (and in the police wire these were always persons, not businesses) were usually identified by sex and a specific age. When more was said, it was almost always in connection with a "youth gang" or the offender's youth. Victim-offender relationships were rarely mentioned. It was quite difficult to identify cases where the victim and offender knew each other. Thus the

police wire gives one the impression most crimes occur between strangers. Finally, the location of a crime was usually provided in terms of a specific address or intersection. But a *type* of location was mentioned only when it could be said the incident occurred in a public or semi-public place, for example, a street, a subway, a schoolyard, or an apartment hallway.

Thus, the kinds of crime items and the descriptions of them in the police wire support only special sorts of crime themes that journalists may report. Crime in public places, crimes between strangers, and crime specific to age are themes that the police wire can and does provide numerous instances of. "Crimes against the elderly" is one theme that has already blossomed into a crime wave with the help of the police wire. But other themes such as "youth gang crime," "subway crime," and "school yard crime," have an excellent chance of becoming new crime waves.

Apparently, the police who transmit crime dispatches to the media select incidents that they think will interest journalists. This criterion of selectivity has two consequences, both keeping the present image of "serious crime" from changing in the news. First, when the police perceive that the media are interested in a certain type of crime (for example, crimes against the elderly), they include instances of it in the police wire whenever they can. Thus, the police bolster emerging crime waves as long as those waves pertain to crimes the police routinely detect (that is, street crime). Second, the police decide what the media are interested in on the basis of what the media have reported before.

The police-supplied incidents that make up the media's crime wave pool all support prevailing notions of "serious crime." The crime wave pool leads the media to reproduce a common image that "real crime" is crime on the streets, crime occurring between strangers, crime which brutal-

---

[10] There were some exceptions. A handful of common crimes did appear over the police wire (e.g., four rapes in a thirty day observation period). The journalists I observed could not explain why these were there, and they ignored them.

izes the weak and defenseless, and crime perpetrated by vicious youths. Such crimes exist, but this imagery becomes *the only reality of crime* which people will take seriously because it is the only reality impressed upon them in the media. And it is the only reality newsworkers are able to report continuously as themes in crime, and periodically, as full-scale crime waves.

The Role of Authorities

I have described the crime wave pool as if it were only composed of crime incidents. This description is only partially true. During the initial phase of crime waves, media organizations mostly report crime incidents as instances of their theme-becoming-a-wave. But as soon as a crime theme looks like it is catching on and becoming a wave, journalists have another kind of news to report: the responses of politicians, police, and other officials.

The first signs of New York's crime wave against the elderly appeared in the last week of October 1976, when the city's media began reporting incidents of crime against old people. There was widespread coverage of three incidents: the murder of two aged sisters in their Bronx apartment, the rape-murder of an eighty-five-year-old Manhattan woman, and the release on fifty dollars bail of a youth who beat an elderly person. After this third incident, the first official response appeared: Mayor Beame called a news conference and, with the Police Commissioner at his side, he vowed to make the city safe for old people by beefing up the police's Senior Citizens Robbery Unit and by working for reforms in the criminal justice system. From this point on, "crimes against the elderly" became a favorite topic for political rhetoric and proposed reforms.

Starting from the very first week of the crime wave, the media could report both crimes against the elderly *and* stories of what the authorities were saying and doing about it. The entire wave was bolstered throughout its seven week course by

coverage of official statements, possible reforms of the criminal justice system, legislative debate and action, the formation of new police programs, and community conferences on the problem. These kinds of stories made up thirty-five percent of the crime-wave-related news published during the period.

Officials and authorities were willing to assume from the outset that the crime wave represented something real or, at least, they were unwilling to express any doubts in public. Thus, by making public statements and taking official action on the basis of this assumption, authorities made the wave look even more real. And they guaranteed that the wave would go on for some time. As official responses to "the problem" trailed off in mid-December, so did the number of crime incidents known to the media from the police wire and other police sources. The wave finally died.

It is clear that officials with a stake in "doing something" about crime, have power over crime waves. Whether or not they inspire crime waves, they can attempt to redirect the focus of coverage of a crime wave already being reported. Nowhere is this clearer than in the first four weeks of *Daily News* coverage of the wave of crimes against the elderly. *News* headlines during the first week emphasized "the problem," citing instance after instance. But in the next three weeks the stories (starting with the Mayor's first press conference) shifted focus to "what is being done about the problem."

Politicians and police use their news-making power to channel the coverage of social problems into a definite direction (Molotch and Lester, 1974): news of the problem becomes news of how the system is working to remedy the situation. Authorities may also use their newsmaking powers to stop certain crime themes from becoming crime waves. There is tentative data indicating that another crime theme, "crimes on the subways," was stopped from becoming a full-scale crime wave by the New York City Transit Authority.

In the third week of February 1977, the *Daily News*, the *New York Post*, and WAVE all suddenly increased their coverage of murders and muggings in subways. In the middle of that week the Police Chief of the Transit Authority told a *Daily News* reporter there was no crime wave and, soon thereafter, three senior Transit officials called a news conference to assert that the subways were safer than the city streets. From that point on, coverage of subway crime steadily decreased to its pre-wave level.

If an unwanted crime wave should arise, officials can use their newsmaking powers to deny the wave's existence or to redirect crime coverage into a "safe" direction. There is some evidence, however, that crimes against the elderly was not an "unwanted crime wave"—at least for some officials in the New York City Police Department.

The *Daily News* reporter who wrote the feature articles which turned out to be the beginning of the crime wave, told me that he received "considerable help" from the Senior Citizens Robbery Unit, whose job it was to catch muggers and murderers of the elderly (and the same unit that the Mayor expanded early in the crime wave). On October seventh, the reporter first wrote a story on two crimes with elderly victims that appeared over the police wire on the same day. This story was published October 8, two weeks before the wave. At that time, a *Daily News* editor thought it would be a good idea for the reporter to do a series of feature stories on "this kind of crime." (Such features had shown up periodically in other media organizations before.)

While he was first researching these feature stories, the reporter was in frequent contact with S.C.R.U. This police unit let him know they felt beleaguered, under-staffed, and that they were fighting a battle that deserved more attention. (According to the reporter, "They proselytized a lot.") After he had written his feature stories, police from S.C.R.U. began calling him whenever they knew of a mugging or murder of an elderly person. This enabled the reporter to follow up his

series with reports of specific crime incidents. Finally, it was S.C.R.U. which first told the reporter about the youth who was let out on fifty dollars bail after beating an elderly person. All major media in New York quickly picked up this story after the *News* reported it. At that point, the crime wave had begun.

I do not want to assert that from this brief history of one crime wave all waves are inspired by the police or politicians. It is not that simple. The crime wave against the elderly in New York seems to have resulted from a mixture of happenstance and police assistance. The history of this crime wave, however, does show that officials can and do use their positions to nurture fledgling crime themes first identified by journalists. Equally, they may use their position to deny the reality of crime waves.

SUMMARY AND CONCLUSIONS

Crime waves begin as crime themes that journalists perceive in the process of organizing and selecting news to be presented to a public. Because journalists depend on one another for their sense of "what's news," a crime theme can spread throughout a community of news organizations. As each news organization sees the theme presented by other organizations, they learn to use the theme and present it in their news.

But for this crime wave dynamic to occur, journalists must be able to associate a crime theme with a continuous supply of incidents that can be seen as instances of the theme. Media organizations know of crime almost exclusively through law enforcement agencies. The media's major source of supply for crime incidents in New York City is the N.Y.P.D.'s police wire. Crime dispatches over this wire are largely reports of street crimes: robberies, burglaries, shootings, stabbings, and other assaults. These constitute a pool of potential crime waves, excluding the possibility of certain themes. Non-street crime themes, if they were to receive massive publicity as crime waves, might challenge prevailing notions of "serious crime" in this society.

Moreover, once crime themes receive heavy coverage in the media, authorities can use their power to make news in an attempt to augment, modify, or deny a burgeoning crime wave. Thus, official sources not only control the supply of raw materials upon which crime news is based, but also the growth of crime waves.

While this study has dealt with the generation of crime waves, the news-making processes it reveals have broad implications. News plays a crucial role in formulating public issues and events, and in directing their subsequent course. Just as the interplay between local politics and local media organizations brought about New York City's crime wave, so the interplay between national elites and national media organizations may well have given rise to a number of social issues now widely accepted as fixtures in the recent American political scene.

Consider Watergate. As a few investigative reporters persisted in digging up news about the illegal activities of the Nixon administration, national elites competed among one another to halt, support, or redefine the growing Watergate news theme. Eventually, special prosecutors and Congressional committees were formed; that is, a bureaucratic apparatus was set up which began to feed the media with fresh instances of the Watergate theme. Once Nixon was deposed, this apparatus was dismantled, and so was the Watergate "news wave."

Watergate, the Bert Lance affair, the "death" of political activism of the 1960's, and many other accepted political "realities" may have been produced by the same ideological machinery that underlies crime waves.

REFERENCES

Biderman, Albert, Louise Johnson, Jennie McIntyre, and Adrianne Weir.
1967 "Report on a pilot study in the District of Columbia on victimization and attitudes toward law enforcement." Washington, D.C.: U.S. Government Printing Office.

Davis, F. James
1952 "Crime news in Colorado newspapers." American Journal of Sociology 57:325–30.

Epstein, Edward Jay
1973 News From Nowhere. New York: Random House.

Glasgow Media Group
1976 "Bad news." Theory and Society 3:339–63.

Molotch, Harvey and Marilyn Lester
1974 "News as purposive behavior: the strategic use of routine events, accidents, and scandals." American Sociological Review 39:101–12.

Roshier, Bob
1973 "The selection of crime news in the press." Pp. 28–39 in S. Cohen and J. Young (eds.), The Manufacture of News. Beverly Hills: Sage.

Sacks, Harvey
1972 "On the analyzability of stories by children." Pp. 325–45 in J. Gumperz and D. Hymes (eds.) Directions in Sociolinguistics. New York: Holt, Rinehart and Winston.

Smith, Dorothy
1972 "The ideological practice of sociology." Unpublished paper, Department of Sociology, University of British Columbia.

Steffens, Lincoln
1931 The Autobiography of Lincoln Steffens. New York: Harcourt Brace.

Tuchman, Gaye
1973 "Making news by doing work: routinizing the unexpected." American Journal of Sociology 79:110–31.

TAKING ANOTHER LOOK

1 How does Fishman use the term "crime wave"?
2 Why does Fishman assert that "it is doubtful that there really was a crime wave or any unusual surge of violence against elderly people"?

3 What methodology was used by Fishman in studying the media's coverage of the crime wave against the elderly?

4 According to Fishman how do individual crimes come to be seen as a crime wave?

5 What "consistency rule" is used by journalists in reporting incidents of crime?

6 According to Fishman, why do the police have power "both to veto and promote the media's construction of crime waves"?

7 What role can politicians play in the emergence of a crime wave?

THREE

SOCIAL INEQUALITY

Ever since people began to speculate about the nature of human society, their attention has been drawn to the differences that can be readily observed between individuals and groups within any society. The term *social inequality* describes a condition in which societal members have unequal amounts of wealth, prestige, or power. All cultures are characterized by some degree of social inequality.

When a system of social inequality is based on a hierarchy of groups, sociologists refer to it as *stratification*: a structured ranking of entire groups of people that perpetuates unequal economic rewards and power in a society. It involves the ways in which social inequalities are passed on from one generation to the next, thus producing groups of people arranged in hierarchical order.

Karl Marx was concerned with stratification in all types of human societies, beginning with primitive agricultural tribes and continuing into feudalism. But his main focus was on the effects of class on all aspects of nineteenth-century Europe. Charles H. Anderson ("Social Class and the Proletariat") offers insight into Marx's view of social class. It is important to note that contemporary societies founded upon the teachings of Marx have not necessarily achieved his socialist ideal of abolishing exploitative class relations. James R. Millar and Peter Donhowe ("The Classless Society Has a Wide Gap Between Rich and Poor") document the degree of social inequality still present in the Soviet Union some 70 years after the Russian Revolution.

The social definitions of race and ethnicity, like that of class, affect people's place and status in a society's stratification system. Sociologists use such factors to define patterns of behavior (where one lives, whom one marries, what occupations one pursues). Richard T. Schaefer ("Racial Prejudice in a Capitalist State: What Has Happened to the American Creed?") documents the dynamics of prejudice and speculates as to its impact on intergroup relations.

In American society, many minority groups have experienced prejudice and discrimination. Harry Edwards ("The Black 'Dumb Jock' ") draws our attention to harmful racial stereotypes and their impact on black youths. The precarious health of the nation's first minority, American Indians, is discussed by Tim Giago and Sharon Illoway ("Dying Too Young"). Gene Oishi ("The Anxiety of Being a Japanese-American") offers personal testimony concerning the difficulties of a minority widely regarded as "having made it." Libby Slate ("The Able Disabled: The Media Office Promotes the Country's Largest Minority") focuses on efforts to reverse negative stereotypes about persons with disabilities.

Differentiation based on sex is evident in virtually every human society about which we have information. Most Americans are socialized to hold quite different expectations for women and men. Men have traditionally been designated as the "providers" for the family, while women have been expected to assume almost total responsibility for child care and household duties. Sandra L. and Daryl J. Bem ("Case Study of a Nonconscious Ideology: Training the Women to Know Her Place") analyze the ways in which American society has socialized women to accept a subservient position. Sharon Tucker ("Careers of Men and Women MBAs: 1950–1980") highlights the difficulties of women who seek executive careers within the traditionally male business world.

Like other forms of stratification, age stratification varies from culture to culture. Samuel H. Preston ("Children and the Elderly in the U.S.") documents the similarities and differences between Americans at the beginning and at the end of the life cycle. He emphasizes that American society is not doing enough to insure the well-being of the nation's children. By contrast, Erdman Palmore ("What the USA Can Learn from Japan About Aging") explains how the United States could improve its treatment of the elderly by adapting certain practices of Japanese culture.

Social Class and the Proletariat

Charles H. Anderson

Karl Marx (1818–1883) viewed class differentiation as the crucial determinant of social, economic, and political inequality. In his view, social relations during any period of history depend on who controls the primary mode of economic production. His analysis centered on how the relationships between various groups were shaped by differential access to scarce resources. Using this type of analysis, Marx examined social relations within *capitalism*—an economic system in which the means of production are largely in private hands and the main incentive for economic activity is the accumulation of profits.

Marx focused on the two social classes that began to emerge as feudalism declined—the bourgeoisie and the proletariat. The *bourgeoisie*, or capitalist class, owns the means of production, such as factories and machinery, while the *proletariat* is the working class. In capitalist societies, the bourgeoisie maximize profit in competition with other firms. In the process, they exploit workers, who must exchange their labor for subsistence wages. With such exploitation in mind, Marx focused on the plight of the working class and felt it imperative to work for changes in the class structure of society.

In the following selection, sociologist Charles H. Anderson examines Karl Marx's views on social class. Anderson expands on Marx's writings by analyzing the role of a "surplus class" or new middle class in developed capitalist society. Anderson argues that "no hard and fast lines between proletariat and middle class can be drawn. There exists a distinctly proletarian core and an equally distinctive middle class, but the boundary lines of each are blurred and objectively uncertain."

ON CLASS

What constitutes a class under the Marxist schema? At the end of the third volume of *Capital* Marx had begun to spell out in precise terms the definition of class; but then the manuscript breaks off. We are left without a codified definition of social class from the "father" of social stratification. Marx was actually so occupied with the dynamics of the class system he evidently took for granted that his readers understood implicitly what for him constituted a class. Marx does, however, contribute some fragmentary statements on class definition. Let us try to piece together the essentials of a class in Marxist theory.

First, we are told directly and may see from the theory that the Marxist class model is in one important way dichotomous: bourgeoisie and prole-tariat, with an individual's membership in these classes being determined by his position in the organization and relations of production. According to Marx, in the objective sense of occupying a common position of being propertied or property-less, individuals may be spoken of as constituting a category or aggregate, a "class-in-itself." Although a class-in-itself is fundamentally important to the Marxist theory of conflict and change, other developments and conditions must be present for a class-in-itself to become a class-for-itself, a more substantive and socially crystallized group. Chief among these conditions for an aggregate of people with a common position in the system of production to be transformed into a viable social class is the recognition of common interests and a common class opponent. In Marxist thinking, "the separate individuals form a class only insofar as they have to carry on a common battle against another class; otherwise they are on hostile terms with each other as competitors" (Marx and Engels, 1969:65). In the capitalist epoch, this means that unless the bourgeoisie and proletariat recognize their respective internal interests vis-à-vis each other, each will engage in internal competition and conflict among themselves. Such internal competition may happen during the process of class formation, and no doubt will occur; but interclass conflict must replace intraclass conflict as the dominant fact before class formation can come to fruition.

The recognition of common interests and opponents implies the emergence of a class consciousness. Before turning to a key summary quotation from Marx, one further condition of a class-for-itself must be noted. The contradiction between the forces and relations of production in the economic base is paralleled in social structure by the conflict between capital and labor. The objective economic contradiction finds its subjective expression in the political struggle between capitalists and workers. The class struggle is a political struggle, and for the working class to wage an effective political struggle requires the existence of a political party. In brief, Marx explains that the organization of the proletariat as a class means its organization as a political party as well (Dahrendorf, 1959:17). In what is probably the most succinct definitional statement on class in the original Marx, we have from *The Eighteenth Brumaire of Louis Bonaparte*:

> In so far as millions of families live under economic conditions of existence that separate their mode of life, their interests and their culture from those of the other classes, and put them in hostile opposition to the latter, they form a class. In so far as there is merely a local interconnection among these smallholding peasants, and the identity of their interests begets no community, no national bond, and no political organisation among them, they do not form a class (Marx, 1962:334)

From this passage we may isolate the following definitional criteria of social class: (1) common position in the economic mode of production; (2) separate way of life and cultural existence; (3) conflicting and hostile interests vis-à-vis another class; (4) social relationships and social community extending across local and regional lines; (5) a societywide class consciousness; and (6) political organization. Needless to say, if all these criteria are applied, we have extremely stringent conditions to meet before we have a social class-for-itself. Yet, each must be present to a degree, and for class revolution to a very substantial degree, before we have a class in the Marxist sense. Each of these conditions tends to follow in an empirical if not logical sequence, from objective position to common interests and culture, to social community, to class consciousness, and finally to political organization.

The above does not mean, however, that social class is an all-or-nothing entity. It is a matter of degree. It is a matter of degree as to how many of the criteria will be present in a given case, and also a matter of degree with each separate criterion. The greater the number of criteria present and the greater the intensity of each, the greater is the class as revolutionary potential.

Marx recognized that within the two major classes there existed gradations; these gradations, however, do not overshadow the dichotomous relation to the means of production. Further, with the concentration of capital and the automation of production it should be expected that members of the two respective classes will become increasingly homogeneous, divided into "two hostile camps." Marx also took into consideration the fluid nature of the class throughout the capitalist epoch, though it becomes decreasingly fluid as the historic mission of capital is fulfilled. Referring to the United States' social classes, Marx (1962:405) wrote that "they have not yet become fixed, but continually change and interchange their elements in constant flux." And although the dynamic aspect of the Marxist class model is dichotomous, Marx frequently discussed the activities of other strata in the population. Perhaps we might say that his cross-sectional or descriptive view of society was multilayered and his revolutionary theoretical view dichotomous.

We are able to decipher two major trends in the shape of the class structure through the application of the Marxist economic theory of capitalist development. First, the class structure tends toward polarization between an increasingly concentrated capitalist class and an expanding proletariat (and industrial reserve army). The proletariat expands at the expense of petty capitalist, independent artisans, peasantry, and any other strata that represent outmoded productive forces or property relations. Marx (1962:118) considers the lower-middle class of independent capitalists and producers as conservative or reactionary, "for they try to roll back the wheel of history." A second trend in class structure which accompanies the first, and which as Nicolaus (1967) has stressed is a necessary aspect of the Marxist economic model, is the rise of a "surplus class" or new middle class. This introduces a third major grouping and suggests that, depending upon one's purposes, a trichotomous class model may be utilized as well as a dichotomous one. For example, descriptively speaking, the trichotomous model may at times prove to be more useful whereas in terms of revolutionary theory the dichotomy of class structure may be more powerful. The essentials of Marxist theory, however, must be grasped from the dichotomous class framework.

PROLETARIAT AND MIDDLE CLASS

A very difficult question for Marxist class theory has to do with just where the proletariat begins and the new, surplus middle class ends, and precisely what role the latter plays in developed capitalist society. We have already spoken of the proletariat as being a propertyless class. However, being propertyless is not an exhaustive criterion of proletarian status. An individual may be propertyless and still not be counted among the proletariat—e.g., a domestic servant in the employ of a capitalist. We have also referred to the proletariat as that class which produces value and surplus value as a result of its labor in the means of production. The proletariat is the producing class; it produces the material means of existence—from survival to luxury. Viewed alternatively, Engels (1962:81) states that "The proletariat is that class of society which procures its means of livelihood entirely and solely from the sale of its labour and not from the profit derived from some capital." A further mark of proletarian status, if the concept of alienation is to be of major importance here, is the performance of labor which is fragmented, which is purposeless from the individual's standpoint, over which the worker has no control, and which offers no or slight security from displacement or replacement by another worker owing to the repetitiveness of the work. In short, a proletarian is also a person who is at once both indispensable to the existence of the society and readily dispensable should another warm body be standing behind him.

Now, a pure proletarian would embody all of these traits: propertylessness, producer of means of existence, lives solely from the creation of value through labor and not at all from surplus value, and works at a fragmented and insecure job. A pure proletarian exploits no one, while he is himself exploited by others. Depending on how many of these traits or criteria we demand for inclusion in the proletariat, our proletariat will be larger or smaller, more or less solid in proletarian character (Ossowski, 1963). Let us examine the several strata of capitalist economy on the basis of this definition of the proletariat.

At the core of the proletariat is the factory worker and all those laborers who play a direct role in construction and support of the production process. Transport, installation, and maintenance of the instruments of production and the necessary labor of distribution may also be included, so long as it involves wage labor (a self-employed electrician running a shop is petit bourgeois, despite his manual labor status and function). What is the class status of technicians and engineers, the highly educated and skilled members of the production process? Are they proletarians, working class? If, say, an engineer is in the employ of capital and works at the design of automated machinery, he is propertyless and directly tied to the production of value, and hence working class. If he is paid a salary or wage that is no more than the cost of his reproduction (even though this sum would run higher than that of an assembly-line worker), he lives solely from necessary labor, and hence is proletarian in this sense as well. However, if he is paid a salary or wage over and above the cost of subsistence, and out of the surplus value or profit of capital, he is so much the less a member of the working class in this important sense. Finally, with the increasing division and specialization of engineering labor, and with the rising number of such engineers, we can imagine the engineer as being proletarian in the sense of performing fragmented and meaningless work and suffering job insecurity as well. (We may also imagine an engineer being in quite the converse work and job situation, a large and secure property owner highly placed within a major corporation.)

Marx considered the technician and engineer as natural by-products of scientifically conditioned production techniques, a highly trained or *new* working class overlaid upon the traditional factory work force: "This is a superior class of workmen [referring to engineers, mechanics, joiners, etc.], some of them scientifically educated, others brought up to a trade; it is distinct from the factory operative class and merely aggregated to it." Marx (1908a:Chapt. 15) adds that "this division of labor is purely technical" and that "it looks very like intentional misleading by statistics... when the English factory legislation excludes from its operation the class of laborer last mentioned in the text [i.e., engineers, etc.]." To a very large extent, then, technicians and engineers are working class in the Marxist model of class—individuals very critical to the increase of productivity and surplus value. Scientists, like technicians and engineers, are new working class to the

extent that their work is integral to the increase of productivity and the improvement of material support systems, and to the extent that they meet the other criteria of proletarian status. A scientist's value or cost of production is obviously much higher than the factory worker's, and thus, even if the scientist were paid a subsistence wage (as the majority are), we are able to see that the working class has within it a notable income differential. The new technological working class is not, then, in most instances a part of the surplus middle class.

We move next to a stratum that occupies a much more ambiguous status vis-à-vis labor and capital than the technological stratum, which we have seen is much closer to proletarian status than anything else, and is becoming increasingly proletarianized. This ambiguous stratum is the commercial or white-collar worker, as we would have it today. The clerical or commercial worker is similar to the proletarian in that this person is hired at a wage or salary by property owners and works at a fragmented and insecure job. The commercial worker is not proletarian in the sense of producing material means of subsistence; like the capitalist, the white-collar worker lives off the surplus value created by the producing working class. Nevertheless, the commercial worker is exploited by the capitalist in much the same way as the factory worker: the commercial worker's wages are typically less than the savings in surplus value or profit which by his efforts he helps the capitalist realize. Marx (1908b:353) puts it as follows:

The commercial laborer does not produce any surplus value directly. But the value of his labor is determined by the value of his labour-power, that is, of its costs of production, while the application of this labour-power, its exertion, expression, and consumption, the same as in the case of every other wage laborer, is by no means limited by the value of his labour-power. His wages are therefore not necessarily in proportion to the mass of profits, which he helps the capitalist to realize. What he costs the capitalist and what he makes for him are two different things. He adds to the income of the capitalist not by creating any direct surplus-value, but by helping him to reduce the costs of the realization of surplus-value. In so doing, he performs partly unpaid labor.

In the important sense of having to sell labor-power for the purpose of enhancing the surplus value and profit of the capitalist for exploitation, the commercial or white-collar worker is very much a member of the working class. To be sure, insofar as the commercial worker contributes to the ultimate expansion of productive capital, he is a member of the producing proletariat. This is not to say that *all* white-collar clerical and sales workers are members of the producing class. In the private capitalist and financial sector there has arisen a tremendous overlay of purely superfluous white-collar workers who contribute in no way to the maximization of surplus value, are totally unproductive, and live entirely off the surplus value created by the working or producing classes. The functions which they perform make sense only within the limits of capitalism and are completely dispensable to the material and social well-being of the society from a non-capitalist perspective. Insurance, real estate, credit institutions, advertising, and much of the entire financial apparatus must so be classified.

Yet from a capitalist perspective and system, these surplus consumers and other partial surplus consumers are extremely important and indispensable precisely for the reason that they help consume the surplus (in addition to their functional importance in servicing and operating the capitalist structure). As Nicolaus (1967:40) has pointed out, a class that produces more than it consumes must be balanced off by classes that consume more than they produce or the system would immediately collapse rather than simply suffer periodic crises of overproduction. Also as Nicolaus observes, Marx's theory of the surplus middle class remained embryonic, though he did refer to the constant increase of the middle classes standing between the workers and capitalists.

Also included in these unproductive, surplus-consuming, and capitalist-dependent intermediate strata are domestic and personal servants ("lackeys") and ideological employees in government, law, military, and religious functions (Marx, 1908a:487). For the most part, the functions performed here are in the service of the property-owning capitalist class. There are, however, *unproductive* workers who perform *socially necessary* functions quite separate and distinct from the prerequisites to the survival of capitalist production and organization. Most health workers belong to this unproductive but necessary class intermediate or apart from labor and capital. Educational workers, apart from those linked to the means of production, might also be included under the rubric of unproductive but socially necessary labor force. Both health and educational workers are indirectly important, even indispensable, to the continued and increased productivity of the working class per se. Their typically propertyless, employee status also links them to the proletariat, as well as does their alienating working conditions. Independent professionals, whether in medicine, education, or whatever, and professionals paid salaries beyond the cost of their labor-power are members of the bourgeoisie or middle classes either by virtue of their propertied status, predominantly surplus-derived income, or uniquely capitalist-dependent function (Caute, 1967:67–68).

No hard and fast lines between proletariat and middle class can be drawn. There exists a distinctly proletarian core and an equally distinctive middle class, but the boundary lines of each are blurred and objectively uncertain. We shall attempt further clarifications in dealing with contemporary class structure. It is enough to note here that subjective factors of culture, identification of interests, social relationships, class consciousness, and political ideology—all of those factors outlined as class criteria in the previous section—must necessarily enter into a person or group's class placement.

REFERENCES

Caute, David (ed.)
  1967 *Essential Writings of Karl Marx.* New York: Collier.
Dahrendorf, Ralf
  1959 *Class and Class Conflict in Industrial Society.* Stanford: Stanford Univ. Press.
Engels, Frederick
  1962 *Principles of Communism.* In *Collected Works*, Vol. 1. London: Lawrence & Wishart.
Marx, Karl
  1908a *Capital*, Vol. 1. Chicago: Charles H. Kerr & Company.
  1980b *Capital*, Vol 3. Chicago: Charles H. Kerr & Company.
  1962 *The Eighteenth Brumaire of Louis Bonaparte.* In *Collected Works*, Vol. 1. London: Lawrence & Wishart.
Marx, Karl, and Frederick Engels
  1969 *Selected Works*, Vol. 1. Moscow: Progress Publishers.
Nicolaus, Martin
  1967 "Proletariat and Middle Class in Marx." *Studies on the Left* 7:22–49
Ossowski, Stanislaw
  1963 *Class Structure in the Social Consciousness.* New York: Free Press.

TAKING ANOTHER LOOK

1 According to Marxist theory, what developments and conditions are necessary for a class-in-itself to become a class-for-itself?
2 Identify the six criteria that form the Marxist definition of social class.
3 Identify the two major trends in the shape of the class structure discussed by Anderson.
4 According to Marx and Engels, what traits characterize a pure proletarian?
5 How did Marx view the role of technicians and engineers within a society's class structure?
6 Why, in Anderson's view, should most commercial or white-collar workers be considered members of the working class?
7 How are health and educational workers linked to the proletariat?

The Classless Society Has a Wide Gap Between Rich and Poor

James R. Millar and Peter Donhowe

According to Karl Marx, exploitation of the *proletariat* (the working class) will inevitably lead to the destruction of the capitalist economic system. Through the guidance of revolutionary leaders, the working class will become committed to class struggle. Ultimately, the proletariat will overthrow the rule of the *bourgeoisie* (the capitalist class, comprising the owners of the means of production) and the government (which Marx saw as representing the interests of capitalists). In Marx's rather utopian view, classes and oppression will cease to exist in the postrevolutionary workers' state.

Thus far, however, a classless society has not been established in any of the nations described politically as "communist." Strictly speaking, using a very limited Marxian definition of class, the Soviet Union has eliminated the existence of social classes. The state, rather than a wealthy capitalist class, owns the means of production. Yet stratification and social inequality remain evident in the Soviet Union.

In the following selection, James R. Millar and Peter Donhowe report on the findings of a study of Soviet society, the Soviet Interview Project (SIP), which relied on interviews with nearly 2800 former Soviet citizens now living in the United States. According to these interview subjects, the Soviet Union is far from a classless society. Indeed, there is a wide gap—perhaps a growing gap—between the relatively well off and the relatively poor. Interestingly, the data from this survey suggest that those Soviet citizens who had the best housing, jobs, incomes, and education in the late 1970s tended to be the least satisfied members of that society.

The Soviet Union is a place where most people like their jobs, housing and medical care, but it is far from a classless society. A wide gap separates rich and poor, and blue-collar workers are not viewed as the heroes presented by Soviet propaganda.

It is also a society in danger of losing the support of its best and brightest.

These are among the findings of new studies of Soviet society based on interviews with nearly 2,800 former Soviet citizens now living in the United States. Perhaps the most surprising finding of the study, known as the Soviet Interview Project (SIP), is that those who were reaping the material benefits of Soviet socialist society in the late 1970s—those with the best housing, jobs, incomes and education—were in general the least satisfied members of that society.

In the early 1970s, tens of thousands of Soviet citizens, predominantly Jewish, were allowed to leave their country for the West. By 1980, more than 125,000 had been admitted into the United States. They were a diverse group, including blue- and white-collar workers, as well as doctors, lawyers, engineers and teachers. The idea of interviewing this "living archive" on Soviet society was quick to surface among scholars.

The project was funded by the National Council for Soviet and East European Research under a contract with the State Department, which backed it along with the Defense Department and the CIA.

Although the emigres interviewed obviously differed from Soviet citizens—they "voted with their feet"—the sample was constructed to reflect the adult, European population of the Soviet Union's large and medium-size cities—in short, the modern sector of the Soviet system. What is interesting are the differences that can be found according to age, income, education and sex.

Among the findings:

• Soviet society is far from a society of equals, and the discrepancies may be growing.

• Younger members of Soviet society are the most alienated from certain fundamental tenets of the Soviet system and more critical of the system's performance than their elders. Their attitudes are strikingly different from young members of Soviet society in earlier generations.

• The more education an individual had, the less likely he was to support certain aspects of the Soviet system.

• In its drive to push forward in science, technology and the production of consumer goods, the Soviet Union must rely increasingly on an educated populace. To do so, the survey suggests, is to court increasing disaffection. But in general, support for state control of major sectors of the economy declines as educational attainment increases.

A similar pattern occurs in responses to the questions that juxtaposed individual rights and the power of the state: As education advances, support for state power declines and support increases for such ideas as the right to strike or the rights of the accused.

Given that many observers believe that educational advancement and material rewards are key factors in building and maintaining support for the Soviet regime, the study's findings of disaffection among the young, the educated and the well-paid in Soviet society suggest that the drive to modernize that country's economy may be carrying with it some unsettling side effects for those who must manage Soviet society.

Evidence from a variety of sources, including the Soviets themselves, indicates that the pace of economic growth has slowed in recent years. What may be equally significant is that the way in which the Soviet pie is divided appears to have remained much the same—and not that much different fom patterns found in many western capitalist economies.

One of the project's studies concluded that in 1979 the 10 percent of households with the highest average income per household member received 33.4 percent of total household income. The share received by the lowest 10 percent was 3 percent. The highest 20 percent received 46.4 percent of total income; the lowest 20 percent received only 7.4 percent.

Soviet society is, therefore, far from achieving its stated egalitarian goals. Indeed, the gap between the relatively well-off and the relatively poor is wide—perhaps wider in 1979 than it was a decade earlier.

Additional evidence of a growing critical stance toward certain aspects of the Soviet system comes from the finding that reading *samizdat* (underground publications) and listening to foreign radio broadcasts were common among the middle elite. Among those surveyed, readership of underground publications was most common among high-level professionals (45 percent) and political leaders (41 percent) and less likely among managers (27 percent) and blue-collar workers (14 percent). However, 77 percent of the blue-collar workers listened to foreign broadcasts and 96 percent of the middle elite did so.

Moreover, efforts to avoid military service have become increasingly common over the past 30 years, the survey reveals. About 20 percent of the male respondents reported such efforts. In addition, there seems to have been an increase over time in the willingness to use *blat* or *protektsia* (bribery or influence) to get a job.

Indeed, the structure of support for the Soviet regime appears to have changed profoundly since the last time American scholars conducted a survey of Soviet emigres, in the late 1940s. Following

World War II, a small group of Harvard professors sought to gain insights into life under Joseph Stalin by interviewing Soviet emigres in camps for displaced persons in Europe.

Whereas the Harvard interviewers found the young and well-educated to be the most supportive of key elements of the Soviet system—and found older, less educated emigrants more critical—the SIP survey found the opposite to be the case.

However, SIP researchers found, as the Harvard scholars had before them, that former Soviet citizens do not unanimously reject all aspects of the Soviet socialist economy. On issues of state control of heavy industry and state provision of free medical care, the SIP respondents tended to support the approach taken in their native land. That is, 52 percent gave the strongest possible concurrence to state provision of medical care; less than 7 percent favored completely private medicine.

Even those who were strongly hostile to the Soviet system (judging from their responses to other questions on the survey) did not reject everything about that system. Those who believed, for example, that "the U.S. can learn nothing from the U.S.S.R." still stongly favored state-provided medical care (48 percent) and nearly three out of 10 reported that they favored state ownership of heavy industry.

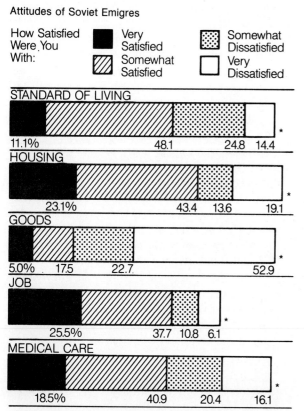

Attitudes of Soviet Emigres

How Satisfied Were You With:
- ■ Very Satisfied
- ▨ Somewhat Satisfied
- ▦ Somewhat Dissatisfied
- □ Very Dissatisfied

STANDARD OF LIVING

| 11.1% | 48.1 | 24.8 | 14.4 |

HOUSING

| 23.1% | 43.4 | 13.6 | 19.1 |

GOODS

| 5.0% | 17.5 | 22.7 | 52.9 |

JOB

| 25.5% | 37.7 | 10.8 | 6.1 |

MEDICAL CARE

| 18.5% | 40.9 | 20.4 | 16.1 |

*No category had 100% response. The 20.2% shortfall in the jobs category reflects women in the home, the unemployed and retired persons.

Clearly, the respondents were not hostile to all aspects of the Soviet system; and their willingness to endorse some key features of the Soviet regime stongly while sharply criticizing others further enhanced confidence in the validity of the survey's findings, including those that were not expected.

For example, given that those interviewed had abandoned the Soviet Union, SIP researchers were surprised to find that nearly 60 percent reported being "very satisfied" or "somewhat satisfied" with their standard of living during their "last normal period" in the Soviet Union—the five years preceding the decision to emigrate or the incident that led to that decision.

In general, the things that respondents were the most satisfied with were their jobs, housing and medical care.

Sixty-three percent were "very satisfied" or "somewhat satisfied" with their jobs—with young people having the highest levels of satisfaction. Nearly 60 percent were positive about their access to medical care. And only one-third were dissatisfied with their housing.

However, they demonstrated a real impatience with having to stand in line for goods and services that are taken for granted in the West, such as fresh vegetables, good cuts of meat and quality merchandise of all kinds. Seventy-five percent reported being "very" or "somewhat dissatisfied" with the availability of goods.

The survey also found:

• Housing was strongly linked to overall satisfaction, and a particular concern of the young, who were often required to share apartments or live in dormitories.

• Married people were more satisfied with the quality of their lives than were single people.

• Residents of smaller cities were more satisfied with their lives than those in larger ones.

• Women, particularly older women, were more satisfied than men, even though they had lower income and occupational status, and even though they agreed—as did men—that men have it better in the Soviet Union.

• Those who abandoned the Soviet Union did so for a variety of reasons—often for family rather than strictly for political reasons.

• The Marxist ideological goal of a classless society notwithstanding, blue-collar workers are seen as having relatively low status in the Soviet Union, while highly paid, well-educated professionals are held in the highest esteem.

• Low productivity in the work place is common, but workers blame the lack of incentives and the failure to reward efficiency, rather than the factors commonly cited by western scholars—alcoholism, Soviet central planning or bad management.

• Although the number of households living in poverty has declined—thanks in large measure to a recent extension of the Soviet minimum wage—it remains extensive; and, as in the United States, a "feminization of poverty" appears to be taking place, with single women and households headed by women with children accounting for an increasing share of the poor.

• Abortions were common among the 1,562 women surveyed—69 percent reported at least one abortion and nearly 70 percent of those born between 1926 and 1945 reported two or more abortions, even though abortions were technically illegal in the Soviet Union from the mid-1930s until the mid-1950s.

• Most of those interviewed hold generally favorable views about the competence of Soviet scientists, but they are pessimistic about the ability of Soviet science to solve economic problems, especially those in agriculture.

When asked why they emigrated, the reasons most often cited were "religious" or ethnic (46 percent of the respondents), family or friends (48 percent), political (43 percent) and economic (27 percent).

The significant point is that the respondents were not a like-minded group of political dissidents, each of whom was clamoring to leave the Soviet Union for the West, but instead were a much more diverse group in terms of their attitudes, interests and aspirations.

The question of bias remains a concern of the scholars involved in the project, and it was addressed in ways that yield increased confidence in the results.

Although SIP scholars have found that ethnic bias exists among those in the survey, the evidence suggests that it is a selective bias that comes into play on issues related to ethnicity and not on more general political questions.

Therefore, although the perspectives revealed by the SIP survey are not a perfect reflection of Soviet society, they still provide a unique and valuable window on that society.

The clear pattern that emerges from the survey is that the young, much more so than those who are older, judge the regime on the basis of its current performance. They are generally more critical and less inclined to accept present conditions just because they are improvements over the past.

Specifically, the young are looking for material and measureable progress, and if it does not materialize or does so only slowly and haltingly, that, too, could create problems for the Soviet leadership.

Although SIP findings show that there is a significant base of support for many aspects of the Soviet regime—especially among older, less well educated and blue-collar members of that society—it is also clear that the young and those who might be called "the best and the brightest" are restless and discontented with much that goes on around them.

TAKING ANOTHER LOOK

1 In evaluating the results of the Soviet Interview Project, what issues of bias concerned social scientists?

2 According to the data from the Soviet Interview Project, how has the structure of support for the Soviet regime changed since American scholars conducted a survey of Soviet emigres in the late 1940s?

3 In what ways did the survey respondents support certain aspects of the Soviet system?

4 What were the findings of the Soviet Interview Project regarding the position of women in Soviet society?

5 What reasons did the respondents give for emigrating from the Soviet Union?

Racial Prejudice in a Capitalist State: What Has Happened to the American Creed?

Richard T. Schaefer

When sociologists define a minority group, they are primarily concerned with economic and political power, or powerlessness, of that group. A *minority group* is a subordinate group whose members have significantly less control over their own lives than the members of a dominant or majority group have over theirs.

In American society, racial and ethnic minorities often suffer from prejudice and discrimination. *Prejudice* is a negative attitude toward an entire category of people. If you resent your roommate because he or she is sloppy, you are not necessarily guilty of prejudice. However, if your roommate is from the Magna social club, and you decide that all members of the club are sloppy because your roommate is, then that is a form of prejudice.

The biased attitudes of the prejudiced person often lead to discriminatory behavior. *Discrimination* is the process of denying opportunities and equal rights to individuals and groups because of prejudice or for other arbitrary reasons. Prejudiced attitudes should not be equated with discriminatory behavior. While the two are generally related, they are not identical, and either condition can be present without the other.

The United States, with over 28 million blacks, has the second largest black population in the world. However, despite their large numbers, blacks have long been treated as second-class citizens. Currently, by the standards of the federal government, more than one out of every three blacks—as opposed to one out of eight whites—are poor. Contemporary prejudice and discrimination against blacks are rooted in the history of slavery in the United States. As many as 15 to 20 million blacks may have come to this nation in chains.

In the following selection, sociologist Richard T. Schaefer examines the continued contrast between the egalitarian moral precepts of the "American Creed"—as described by Swedish social economist Gunnar Myrdal in his monumental 1944 study, *An American Dilemma*—and the nation's racist attitudes toward blacks. Myrdal had predicted that, in the long run, the higher values of the "American Creed" would win out over the lower ones that encouraged prejudice and discrimination. Drawing on nationwide survey data, Schaefer points out that there has been consistent and growing support among white Americans for racial integration. At the same time, he emphasizes the "resistance toward full endorsement of the American Creed" evident in white hostility to affirmative action, busing to achieve racial balance, and immigration policies sensitive to the needs of racial minorities.

Author's note: This article was presented originally at the Annual Meeting of the Society for the Study of Social Problems, Washington, D.C. August 25, 1985, and at the Faculty Forum of Western Illinois University, February 25, 1986.

It has been over 40 years since Gunnar Myrdal identified a dilemma between what he called the "American Creed," expressed in Christian ethics and the Declaration of Independence, and the continuing undemocratic behavior toward blacks. Myrdal saw this as a constant conflict that he was convinced would be resolved. The higher values of the American Creed would win out in the long run over the lower ones that encouraged discrimination and prejudice.[1] Myrdal did not specify when the victory of the American Creed would occur, but he saw this society as striving toward behavior consistent with its values.

Myrdal's notion of an American Creed that good will eventually triumph over bigotry is important, not because we may hope for its accuracy, but because this perspective reflects a naive, but widely held view of industrial society. As one witnesses progress in race relations and sees certain intolerant views cast aside, we are tempted to see tolerance, if not actual acceptance, just a decade or generation or so away. Yet, white dominance over racial minorities has been a pervasive feature of the American system.[2] Myrdal's optimism rested on the premise that the major focus of racism was in the South and that urbanization, literacy, and industrialization would eventually eradicate bigotry in the South.[3] Survey data, which are examined covering the period since this seminal work was written in 1942, offer insight into the implications and the accuracy of Myrdal's prognostication.

TRENDS IN WHITE RACIAL PREJUDICE

Nationwide surveys over the years have consistently shown growing support by whites for integration, even during the southern resistance and northern turmoil of the 1960s. Table 1 lists six questions that have appeared on several opinion polls from 1942 to 1985. All data are drawn from national adult samples and reflect white responses only. With few exceptions, they show an increase in the number of whites responding positively to hypothetical situations of increased contact with or increased acceptance of black Americans. For example, less than one-third of the whites sampled in 1942 felt that blacks should not attend separate schools (statement three), but by 1970 three-fourths supported integrated schools.

According to their responses to anonymous survey instruments, whites were also more willing to live alongside a black family. Although only 35 percent of the 1942 respondents were so willing to be neighbors to a black person of the same social class, fully 81 percent responded in that manner in 1972. Of course, this is what whites say they will do: their behavioral intention. As Andrew Greeley and Paul Sheatsley observe, "attitudes are not necessarily predictive of behavior. A man may be a staunch integrationist and still feel his neighborhood is [threatened]."[4] Attitudes are still important, apart from behavior. A change of attitude may create a context in which legislative or behavioral change can occur. This is what did, in fact, occur in certain areas during the 1960s. Changes in intergroup behavior mandated by law in housing, schools, public places of accommodation, and on the job appear to be responsible for making some new kinds of interracial contact a social reality.[5] The changes are not uniform—the bread-and-butter civil rights issues such as school desegregation and open housing are accepted and endorsed by increasing proportions of whites.

[1] Gunnar Myrdal, *An American Dilemma: The Negro Problem and Modern Democracy* (New York, 1944), p. xlvii.

[2] John Horton, "Order and Conflict Theories of Social Problems as Competing Ideologies," *American Journal of Sociology* 71 (May 1966): 708. The most recent expression of this contradiction is found in Tom W. Smith and Paul B. Sheatsley, "American Attitudes Toward Race Relations," *Public Opinion* 7 (October/November 1984): 14–15, 50–53.

[3] Myrdal, op. cit., pp. 1010–15; see also L. Paul Metzger, "American Sociology and Black Assimilation: Conflicting Perspectives," *American Journal of Sociology* 76 (January 1971): 627–647.

[4] Andrew M. Greeley and Paul B. Sheatsley, "Attitudes Toward Racial Integration," *Scientific American* 225 (December 1971): 9.

[5] Stuart Oskamp, *Attitudes and Opinions* (Englewood Cliffs, New Jersey, 1977), p. 334.

TABLE 1 ATTITUDES OF WHITES TOWARDS BLACKS, 1942–1985 (PERCENT AFFIRMATIVE)

	1942	1956	1963	1965	1966	1967	1968	1970	1972	1976	1977	1978	1980	1982	1983	1984	1985
1. Negroes/blacks have the same intelligence as white people given the same education and training.	42	77	78							72		75					
2. Negroes/blacks should not push themselves where they are not wanted.			75					84	76	71	73		68	59		59	61
3. White students and Negroes/blacks should go to the same schools, not separate ones.	30	49	63	67			60	74	86	85	86		88	91		92	93
4. Favor the busing of Negro/black children from one district to another?								14	14	13	13	18		16	21		19
5. If a Negro/black came to live next door, you would move.			45	35	34	35						13					
6. If Negroes/blacks came to live in your neighborhood, you would move.			78	69	70	71						51					

Note: Percentages indicate the proportion of the nationwide sample that agreed with the statement. The remaining respondents did not necessarily disagree: some did not answer and some expressed no opinion. The wording of the questions may change slightly from one year to the next. Questions not asked in a particular year are indicated by a blank.

Sources: Angus Campbell and Howard Schuman, *Racial Attitudes in Fifteen American Cities* (Ann Arbor, Michigan, 1958); George H. Gallup. *The Gallup Poll. Public Opinion 1935–1971* (New York, 1972); Greeley and Sheatsley, op. cit.; Herbert H. Hyman and Paul B. Sheatsley, "Attitudes Toward Desegregation," *Scientific American* 211 (July 1964); *Newsweek* "A New Racial Poll," 93 (February 26, 1979); National Opinion Research Center, *General Social Survey 1972–1985* (Chicago, 1985); Mildred A. Schwartz, *Trends in White Attitudes Towards Negroes* (Chicago, 1967); Jerome Skolnick, *The Politics of Protest* (New York, 1969); Smith and Sheatsley, op. cit.

Queries about the relative levels of white and black intelligence are not even made in national surveys because of the unanimity of the expression that racial groups are innately equal. Yet whites are still very ambivalent about busing, and the majority express concerns about blacks pushing into areas where they are not welcomed.

The trend toward tolerance was not limited to any particular subgroup of whites. The 1960s witnessed an increase in support for integration in all regions (including the South), age groups (especially those under 25), income levels, levels of education, and occupational groups. The rise of support was a nationwide phenomenon.[6] Table 2 displays still further evidence of improved attitudes toward blacks. The proportion of whites who would vote for a black presidential candidate more than doubled between 1958 and 1985. It is interesting to note the reverse in the positive trend, although a modest shift from 95 percent to 93 percent, from 1983 to 1985—a period in which the nation witnessed the Reverend Jesse Jackson's unsuccessful bid for the Democratic presidential nomination. This same table also displays the hard core of white resistance that remains. Nearly one out of every five white adults would not even vote for a qualified black person nominated by their own political party.

While white attitudes are the subject of this paper, it is worthwhile to note that the views of blacks about a black president have changed somewhat differently. The proportions of blacks endorsing such a person have been: 1974, 96 percent; 1978, 96 percent; 1982, 97 percent; 1983, 95 percent; and 1985, 99 percent. It would seem that the Jackson campaign has had a salutory effect on the view that white Americans have of a black man in the "White" house, while having a positive impact on the view of black Americans.

During the civil disorders from 1965 to 1968, many people talked about a white backlash. The

[6] Greeley and Sheatsley, op. cit.

TABLE 2 WHITE SUPPORT FOR A BLACK PRESIDENTIAL CANDIDATE, 1958–1985

Year	Percentage willing to vote for a qualified black nominated by their own political party
1958	38
1961	50
1963	47
1965	59
1967	54
1969	67
1972	67
1974	81
1975	82
1977	78
1978	83
1982	86
1983	85
1985	83

Source: Gallup, 1972, op. cit.; National Opinion Research Center, op. cit.

militancy of the Black Power movement had allegedly caused a hardening and reversal of white attitudes. The data in Tables 1 and 2 and other surveys, however, present little evidence of a reversal of attitudes on the part of previously tolerant whites. If that is the case, how did the term white backlash become so widely used? The tumult of the 1960s made race more important for whites in all regions, not just the South. Race also became important in many political issues, meaning that antiblack feelings could not just be voiced as bigoted outbursts but used as a political force in opposition to open housing, affirmative action, and school busing. Over the years, whites have shown greater resistance to continued advances by blacks but gradual acceptance of past advances. It is the new issues that have shown the old resistance, not new resistance to the old issues, as the term "backlash" seemed to convey. This seems to be verified in Table 1: whites increasingly support accomplishments of the civil rights movement while consistently agreeing that blacks should not push themselves where they are not wanted; and also whites display begrudgingly, very slow acceptance of busing. This resistance to further change came to be termed the white backlash.[7]

Two inescapable conclusions emerge from surveying white attitudes toward blacks. First, attitudes are subject to change, and in periods of dramatic social upheaval dramatic shifts can occur in one generation. Second, there is no consensus among whites.

A third area, which is less clear, is the apparent less marked progress in the last decade compared to the preceding three. This slowdown in tolerance or reluctance to accept new concerns by the oppressed minorities also comes at a time when the welfare state was slowing down. The mid-1960s were an exciting time for social welfare planners and policymakers as laws were enacted and agencies were created to address domestic ills in a manner unprecedented since the New Deal.[8] The mood of the nation was conducive to questioning old beliefs, just as it was to the questioning of old programs.

PROSPECTS FOR TOLERANCE

What are the prospects for future change in a capitalist state? Angus Campbell argues that the trend toward racial equality and racial integration will continue, but he quickly adds that the future is far from certain.[9] The movement of blacks into higher paying jobs should reduce the image that whites hold of blacks as carriers of poverty.

Sociologist Steven Tuch (1981), in a statistical analysis of some of the same data displayed in Tables 1 and 2, concurred with the observation that

levels of prejudice as measured on specific items has declined but found that the relative number of prejudiced whites remained unchanged during the 1970s and the early 1980s.[10] Fewer whites are consistently prejudiced on all issues, such as interracial marriage, school integration, support for a black for president, and neighborhood integration. However, whites are just as likely to endorse at least some antiblack statements, although perhaps not as many as they were a decade earlier. Clearly, the dominant group in the United States is far from accepting the largest racial minority.

Attitudes on virtually all questions developed in the 1960s and earlier that sought to measure prejudice of whites toward blacks appear to show a growing tolerance of the racial minority. While progress is not denied, it is observed that sizeable proportions of the dominant group hold hostile attitudes on those issues that have become articulated, particularly in the last 15 years, such as affirmative action, busing to achieve racial balance, racial quotas, and immigration policies sensitive to the needs of racial minorities. This resistance toward full endorsement of the American Creed has occurred with the tacit support of major opinion formers in the United States. Polarization of attitudes toward other minorities, recent immigrants, and potential sources of future immigration offer further evidence that there is little prospect of a significant change in white prejudice towards racial and ethnic minorities. For example, a 1977 nationwide poll showed that only 10 percent of white respondents favored hiring or admissions programs that offer preferential treatment to women and racial minorities.[11]

The paradox of both acceptance and intolerance is viewed in the social context of the greatest resistance to endorsing those issues most relevant in contemporary capitalist society, while progress has been most marked in areas with the least sig-

[7] Smith and Davis, op. cit., p. 51, on the other hand, view the change in racial attitudes as uniformly positive through 1984.

[8] Neil Gilbert, *Capitalism and the Welfare State: Dilemma of Social Benevolence* (New Haven, Connecticut, 1983), p. vii.

[9] Angus Campbell, *White Attitudes Toward Black People* (Ann Arbor, Michigan, 1971) p. 159.

[10] Steven A. Tuch, "Analyzing Recent Trends in Prejudice Toward Blacks: Insights from Latent Class Models," *American Journal of Sociology* 87 (July 1981).

[11] *Gallup Opinion Index*, "Law," 143 (June 1977): 22–23.

nificance to present-day relationships. While white America supports many principles of racial equality, there is less enthusiasm about the specific methods for implementing the lofty principles.[12] Comparison of IQ scores and the "issue" of desegregation of school districts that only have students of one race to begin with are not pressing economic issues. Job practices, such as efforts to seek out qualified minorities and seniority systems that preserve past discrimination, are economic concerns to many white Americans. The specter of institutional racism also questions what have been traditionally presented as "sound business practices" not promoted as racist ideology.

What means is there to resolve this American dilemma in the 1980s? Can we, as Myrdal and others have, view schooling as a means to end the familiar resistance to today's issues in "race relations?" Studies consistently document that increased formal education, regardless of content, is associated with racial tolerance. Considerable research data show that more educated people are more likely to indicate respect and liking for groups different from themselves. Why should more years of schooling have this effect? It could be that more education gives a more universal outlook and makes a person less likely to endorse myths that sustain racial prejudice. Formal education teaches the importance of qualifying statements and the need to at least question rigid categorizations, if not reject them altogether. Christopher Bagley suggests that "education gives training in objective and dispassionate thought, dispositions which are obviously inimical to prejudice."[13]

An alternative explanation is that education does not actually reduce intolerance but simply makes individuals more careful about revealing it. Formal education may simply instruct individuals in the proper responses, which in the case of some teachers could even be prejudiced views. Regard-

less of a clear-cut explanation, either theory suggests that the continued trend to a more educated population will contribute to a reduction of overt prejudice.[14]

Results of a comprehensive analysis by Mary R. Jackman and Michael J. Muha from a 1975 national probability sample of 1914 respondents fail to support the view either that education produces liberation from intergroup negativism or that it produces a superficial democratic commitment.[15] These data, as in some other studies, do not show that education uniformly is related to lower indications of prejudice. Greater support for individual rights seems to show closest association to education having a liberating influence. They propose a new approach that rests on different assumptions about the nature of both intergroup attitudes and educational institutions. The dominant social groups routinely develop ideologies that legitimize and justify the status quo, and the well-educated members of these dominant groups are merely the most sophisticated practitioners of their group's ideology. The well educated are but one step ahead of their peers in developing a defense of their interests that rests on qualification and individualism.

OBSERVATIONS

Intergroup attitudes may not be so much the result of individual negativism as a natural part of the dominant ideology. It must be emphasized that by dominant ideology one does not necessarily mean a belief system embraced by everyone. Clearly members of oppressed groups would be a significant exception. Survey data collected from 1972 through 1985 confirm the gap between attitudes held by blacks and whites on levels of satisfaction with family income, jobs, housing,

[12] Howard Schuman, Charlotte Steeh, and Lawrence Bobo, *Racial Attitudes in America* (Cambridge, Massachusetts, 1985).

[13] Christopher Bagley, *Social Structure and Prejudice in Five English Boroughs* (London, 1970), p. 72.

[14] Mary R. Jackman and Michael J. Muha, "Education and Intergroup Attitudes: Moral Enlightenment, Superficial Democratic Commitment, or Ideological Refinement," *American Sociological Review* 49 (December 1984): 751–769; Richard T. Schaefer, *The Extent and Content of Racial Prejudice in Great Britain* (San Francisco, 1976), pp. 127–128.

[15] Jackman and Muha, op. cit.

standard of living, and personal lives. Even black delegates to the recent presidential nominating political conventions consistently express attitudes at variance with their white counterparts.[16]

The linking of attitudes to societal belief systems or ideologies is not a novel view but has been customarily used to explain consistent differences in levels of prejudice between countries as in comparing whites in the Republic of South Africa to North American whites or in different regions of the United States.[17] The structural component of prejudice offers insights into why education does not have a clearer influence ameliorating prejudice in a capitalist state.

The dilemma for Myrdal was the difference in behavior and beliefs. While we have not examined behavior directly, we have seen selective shifts in attitudes. Whites now call upon these same high values to declare that equality and fair play does not mean special efforts on behalf of racial minorities. To be equal in this way of thinking means to be subject to no special consideration, no special remedies. More progress in attitude and behavioral change was made a generation ago.[18] True, the black community and sympathetic nonblacks were making more demands on whites than now. But more importantly, the white community is more preoccupied with its own economic welfare now than in the 1960s. The welfare state, if it has not declined, has redefined whose welfare is to be protected.

[16] *Washington Post National Weekly Edition* 2 (March 4, 1985): 38 and (January 28, 1985): 37; Diane Robinson Brown and C. Ashford Baker, "Attitude Differentiation at the 1980 Presidential Conventions: Aspects of Race and Party Identification," *Urban Research Review* 10 (No. 1, 1985): 1–3, 11.

[17] Richard T. Schaefer, *Racial and Ethnic Groups*, 2d ed. (Boston, 1984), pp. 62–63.

[18] Richard A. Apostle, et al., *The Anatomy of Racial Attitudes* (Berkeley, 1983), p. 228.

TAKING ANOTHER LOOK

1 To what extent has white support for school integration increased since 1942?

2 In Schaefer's view, why is the term "white backlash" somewhat misleading?

3 Briefly describe the "paradox of both acceptance and intolerance" reflected in white attitudes toward blacks and toward issues of special concern to blacks.

4 In what ways can education lead to greater racial tolerance?

5 According to the data discussed by Schaefer, what is the relationship between education and levels of prejudice?

The Black "Dumb Jock"

Harry Edwards

Functionalist theorists regard sports as a quasi-religious institution that uses ritual and ceremony to reinforce the common values of a society. In their view, sports "bring together" members of a community or even a nation and promote an overall feeling of social solidarity. By contrast, conflict theorists emphasize that sports reflect and even exacerbate many of the divisions of society, including those based on sex, race, and social class. As an example, sports maintain the subordinate role of blacks and Hispanics, who toil as athletes but are largely barred from supervisory positions as coaches, managers, or general managers.

In the following selection, sociologist Harry Edwards examines the impact of racial myths and stereotypes on black student athletes. *Stereotypes* are unreliable generalizations about all members of a group that do not recognize individual differences within the group. The racist stereotype of the intellectually inferior black has unquestionably contributed to prejudice and discrimination against blacks. However, according to Edwards, the myth of "innate black athletic superiority" has also been harmful to blacks. While many black youths and their families have been persuaded to view sports as a route to social and economic success, there is widespread exploitation of black student athletes. Moreover, less than 2400 black Americans are making a living in the world of professional sports. Edwards concludes that blacks must abandon their "blind belief in sport" and focus instead on the priority of educational achievement over athletic participation.

Historically, widely experienced socioeconomic hardships in this country have always had an impact on blacks *first* and almost always *worst*. The circumstances of the black student athlete in the 1980s affirm the validity of this contention.

For as long as organized sports participation has been associated with American education, the traditionally somewhat comic, not altogether unappealing "dumb jock" image of the student athlete has endured. Though over the years there have been some notable efforts by journalists, academicians, and sports activists to expose the desperately serious realities masked by this caricature, only recently has American society been jolted into recognizing the extensive and tragic implications of widespread educational mediocrity and failure among student athletes, and—no less importantly—that "dumb jocks" are not born; they are being systematically created.

The fact of negative academic outcomes, then, does not in and of itself significantly distinguish the careers of black student athletes from those of their non-black peers in sports to which blacks have access in numbers—most particularly in basketball and football. Rather, it is in the disparate character of black student athletes' educational experiences that has spawned special concern.

Black student athletes from the outset have the proverbial "three strikes" against them. They must contend, of course, with the connotations and social reverberations of the traditional "dumb jock" caricature.

But black student athletes are burdened also with the insidiously racist implications of the myth of "innate black athletic superiority," and the more blatantly racist stereotype of the "dumb

Negro" condemned by racial heritage to intellectual inferiority. Under circumstances where there exists a pervasive belief in the mutual exclusivity of physical and intellectual capability, and where, furthermore, popular sentiment and even some claimed "scientific evidence" buttress notions of race-linked black proclivities for both athletic prowess and intellectual deficiency, it should come as no surprise that the shameful situation of the black student athlete has been for so long not only widely tolerated but expected and institutionally accommodated.

But the exploitation of black student athletes is not occasioned and perpetuated merely through the unwitting interplay of sportslore and racist stereotypes. The sociological etiology of their circumstances is far more complex. Many of the social forces determining black student athletes' extraordinary vulnerability to athletic exploitation have been affecting black society generally and the black family in particular for decades.

Sports, over the last 40 years, have accrued a reputation in black society for providing extraordinary, if not exemplary, socioeconomic advancement opportunities. This perspective has its origins in black identification with the athletic exploits and fortunes of Jesse Owens, Joe Louis, Jackie Robinson, and other pre- and early post-World War II black sports heroes. In the contemporary context, blacks also find ample, if only ostensible, vindication of their overwhelmingly positive perspectives on sports. For instance, though blacks constitute only 12 percent of the U.S. population, in 1983 just over 55 percent of the players in the National Football League were black, while 25 of the 28 first round National Football League (NFL) draft choices in 1981 were black. As for the other two major professional team sports, 74 percent of the players making National Basketball Association rosters and 81 percent of the starters during the 1981–82 season were black, while blacks constituted 19 percent of America's major league baseball players at the beginning of the 1983 season.

Black representation on sports honor rolls has been even more disproportionate. For example, the last 10 Heisman Trophy awards have gone to black collegiate football players. In the final rushing statistics for the 1982 NFL season, 36 of the top 40 running backs were black. In 1982, not a single white athlete was named to the first team of a major Division I all-American basketball roster. Similarly, 21 of the 24 athletes selected for the 1982 National Basketball Association (NBA) All-Star game were black. And since 1958, whites have won the NBA's Most Valuable Player title only three times as opposed to 20 times for blacks. And, of course, boxing championships in the heavier weight divisions and "most valuable player" designations in both collegiate and professional basketball have been dominated by black athletes since the 1960s.

Black society's already inordinately positive disposition toward sport has been further reinforced through black athletes' disproportionately high visibility in the mass media compared to other high prestige occupational role models (e.g., doctors, lawyers, engineers, and college professors).

Black families' attitudes and expectations concerning sports, then, are deeply influenced by the media and by perspectives on sports held more generally in black society. Research carried out by Melvin Oliver of UCLA discloses, for example, that black families are four times more likely than white families to view their children's involvement in community sports as a "start in athletic activity that may lead to a career in professional sports."

The already heightened black emphasis upon sports achievement that is fostered through myths, stereotypes, family and community attitudes, and the media is further intensified by black youths' early educational and athletic experiences. For example, as soon as someone finds that a particular black youngster can run a little faster, throw a little harder, or jump a little higher than all of his grammar school peers, that kid becomes—as sportscaster Frank Gifford would say—something "really special." What this usually means is that, beyond sports excellence, from that point on little else is expected of him. By the time many black student athletes finish their junior high school sports eligibility and move on to high school, so little has been demanded of them academically that no one any longer even expects anything of them intellectually.

As a result of a lack of creditable academic expectations and standards, and the disproportionate emphasis placed upon developing their athletic talents from early childhood, an estimated 25–35 percent of high school black athletes qualifying for scholarships on athletic grounds cannot accept those scholarships because of accumulated high school academic deficiencies. Many of these young men eventually end up in what is called, appropriately enough, the "slave trade"—a nationwide phenomenon involving independent scouts (some would call them "flesh peddlers") who, for a fee (usually paid by a four-year college) searches out talented but academically "high risk" black athletes and places them in an accommodating junior college where their athletic skills are futher honed through participation in sports for the junior college while they accumulate grades sufficient to permit them to transfer to the sponsoring four-year school.

At the collegiate level, a systematic rip-off begins with the granting of a four-year "athletic scholarship," technically given one year at a time under existing National Collegiate Athletic Association (NCAA) rules. This means that though the athlete is committed to the school for four years, the school is committed to the athlete for only one.

Under circumstances where the grades obtained in many of the courses taken by student athletes are deficient or "automatic" or "fixed" rather than earned, there is little wonder that so many black scholarship student athletes manage to go through four years of college enrollment virtually unscathed by education. Not surprisingly either, studies indicate that as many as 65–75 percent of those black student athletes awarded col-

legiate athletic scholarships may never graduate from college (as opposed to 30–35 percent of white student athletes). Of the 25–35 percent who do eventually graduate from the schools they play for, an estimated 60–65 percent of them graduate either with physical education degrees or in "Mickey Mouse" jock majors specifically created for athletes and generally held in low repute (as compared to approximately 33 percent of white student athletes in such majors).

It was precisely these tragic circumstances that prompted Joe Paterno, 1982 Division I football "Coach of the Year" to quite candidly and succinctly exclaim in January 1983 from the floor of the NCAA convention in San Diego:

> For fifteen years we have had a race problem. We have raped a generation and a half of young Black athletes. We have taken kids and sold them on bouncing a ball and running with a football and that being able to do things athletically was going to be an end in itself.

With the end of collegiate athletic eligibility, the former student athlete faces new realities. The black "blue chipper" who completes his eligibility but is not drafted or within reasonable reach of achieving a degree tends no longer to be perceived on campus as a "big gun." Rather, he is frequently seen as a potential embarrassment to the athletic department, his former coaches, and his school. Because of his academic circumstances and his failure to be drafted, he constitutes a "loose cannon" on the deck, a potential source of disenchantment and dissension within the ranks of new recruits and student athletes still having sports eligibility. There are no more fast academic fixes, no more fancy fictions, about fame, fortune, and fat city forever. Now the hope all too often is that he will simply go away—the farther, the faster, the better, the more easily forgotten.

Even those student athletes who are drafted by the pros soon learn that the actual realities are quite different from the rumored rewards that have fueled and motivated their athletic development. Approximately 8 percent of the draft-eligible student athletes in collegiate basketball, baseball, and football are actually drafted by professional teams each year. Of the black athletes drafted most are *not* offered professional contracts. Among these, a minority will return to school to complete degrees. But far too many of these former aircraft carriers degenerate into athletic "Flying Dutchmen," season after season drifting pathetically from one professional tryout to another, victims of a dream that has become a perpetual nightmare of futility and disappointment, holding to the hope of professional stardom until age and despair compel them to face the realities of life after sports.

Unlike the white student athlete, the black student athlete tends to have a less economically viable background and tends to come from a more transient community. The latter is also less likely than the former to secure financial support for post-eligibility college matriculation. The result is that there is a much lower social and financial "safety net" under the black collegiate athlete than under the white athlete. When the black collegiate athlete fails to graduate or sign a professional contract, he is therefore much more likely than the white athlete to find himself on the street. This has contributed to the fact that among this group, expressions of "disengagement trauma" sometimes have been severe to the extreme—including antisocial behavior, substance abuse, "nervous breakdowns," and even suicides.

Only 2 percent of the athletes drafted will ever sign a professional contract, and just over 60 percent of these are back on the street within 3–4 years. In the National Football League, where blacks constitute 55 percent of the players and where the average athlete will play only four-and-a-half years, according to NFL figures between 70 and 80 percent of the players have no college degree. Among athletes in the National Basketball Association, where 74 percent of the players are black and where the average playing career lasts only 3.2 years, the graduation figures are equally dismal.

It is simply not understood in black society that despite the fact that 74 percent of the players in professional basketball are black, 55 percent in professional football, and 19 percent in professional baseball, there are still just over 1,400 black people (up from about 1,100 before the establishment of the United States Football League) making a living as professional athletes in these three major sports today. And if one added to this number all the black athletes making a living as professionals in all other American sports, all the blacks making a living in minor and semiprofessional sports leagues, and all the black trainers, coaches, and doctors making a living in professional sports, there would still be less than 2,400 black Americans making a living in professional athletics today. . . .

Black communities, black families and black student athletes themselves also have critically vital roles to play in efforts to remedy the disastrous educational consequence of black sports involvement. The undeniable fact is that through its blind belief in sport as an extraordinary route to social and economic salvation, black society has unwittingly become an accessory to, and a major perpetuator of, the rape, or less figuratively put, the disparate exploitation of the black student athlete. We have in effect *set up our own children* for academic victimization and athletic exploitation by our encouragement of, if not insistence upon, the primacy of sports achievement over all else. We have then sold them to the highest bidders among collegiate athletic recruiters, and literally on the average received nothing in return for either our children or ourselves. It would, therefore, constitute a fraudulent rationalization and a dangerous delusion for blacks to lay total responsibility for correcting this situation upon educational institutions and sports governing bodies.

But even Rip Van Winkle eventually woke up. As a people, we have responsibility to learn about the realities of black sports involvement—its liabilities as well as its opportunities—and to teach our children to deal with these realities intelligently and constructively. As a people, we can no longer permit many among our most competitive and gifted youths to sacrifice a wealth of personal potential on the altar of athletic aspiration, to put playbooks ahead of textbooks. We must also recognize that, in large part, the educational problems of black student athletes will be resolved not on the campus, but *in the home.* Black parents must insist upon the establishment and enforcement of creditable academic standards at all educational levels, and they must instill black youths with values stressing the priority of educational achievement over athletic participation and even proficiency. We must understand that having "graduated" is not synonymous with being "educated." Thus, it is not sufficient to rely upon grades alone. Standards imply testing for skills development. If this tack is taken, I am convinced young black student athletes will rise to the occasion in academics no less than they have in the realm of athletics.

And finally, it must be made unequivocally clear that in the last analysis, it is black student athletes themselves who must shoulder a substantial portion of the responsibility for improving their own circumstances. Education is an activist pursuit and cannot in reality be "given." It must be obtained "the old fashion way"—*one must earn it!* Black student athletes, therefore, must insist upon educational discipline no less than athletic discipline among themselves, and they must insist upon educational integrity in athletic programs rather than, as is all too often the case, merely seeking the most parsimonious academic route to maintaining athletic eligibility. The bottom line here is that if black student athletes fail to take an active role in establishing and legitimizing a priority upon academic achievement, nothing done by any other party to this American sports tragedy will matter—if for no other reason than the fact that *a slave cannot be freed against his will.*

TAKING ANOTHER LOOK

1 How would conflict theorists be likely to view the analysis of sports offered by Harry Edwards?

2 What three burdens do black student athletes have to bear?

3 What role does the mass media play in reinforcing black society's disposition toward sports?

4 According to Edwards, what is the contemporary "slave trade"?

5 Why are black athletes more likely than white athletes to end up "on the street" after failing to graduate from college or to sign a professional sports contract?

Dying Too Young

Tim Giago and Sharon Illoway

To the outsiders who came to the United States—European settlers and their descendants—the native people came to be known as American Indians. By the time that the Bureau of Indian Affairs (BIA) was organized as part of the War Department in 1824, Indian-white relations had already included three centuries of mutual misunderstanding. Many bloody wars took place in the nineteenth century, and a significant part of the nation's native American population was wiped out. By the end of the nineteenth century, schools for Indians operated by the BIA or by church missions, often segregated, prohibited the practice of Indian cultures. Yet such schools did little to make the children effective competitors in white society.

It should be noted that more than any other segment of the population, with the exception of the military, today's reservation Indians find their lives determined by the federal government. From the condition of the roads to the level of fire protection to the quality of the schools, reservation life is effectively controlled by the federal government and such agencies as the BIA and the Public Health Service. Indian tribes and their leaders are consulted more than in the past, but the ultimate decisions rest in Washington, D.C., to a degree that is not true for the rest of the civilian population.

In the following selection, Tim Giago and Sharon Illoway document the fact that life remains difficult for native Americans both in the nation's cities and on the reservations. Giago is a member of the Oglala Sioux Tribe and is editor and publisher of the *Lakota Times*, the weekly newspaper that serves the Pine Ridge and Rosebud Reservations of South Dakota. Illoway, a *washicu* (white), is a correspondent and investigative reporter for the *Lakota Times*.

Giago and Illoway focus on the health-related problems evident among native Americans. For example, the death rate of Navajo babies over 18 weeks old is 2½ times that of the overall American population. The distressing data presented in their article reminds us that stratification indeed does make a difference in people's lives. In American society, health care is often a privilege rather than a right. Partly as a result, both social class and race appear to be factors in the differential incidence of disease within the United States.

Words will not give my people health or save my people's lives.

Chief Joseph of the Nez-Perce Tribe

The Indian is the most misunderstood, and least understood, of all Americans.

John F. Kennedy

Just as it has done with many sovereign nations, the United States signed treaties with Native American tribes pledging a new alliance. In exchange for the vast rich lands controlled by Indians, the Federal government solemnly promised, among other things, to provide health care and hospitals for Native American people. Yet Native Americans in the United States today are on average dying younger than any other population group in the country—20 years younger in the case of the Navajo people....

In spite of the significant drop in infant death

rates on U.S. reservations, for example, the death rate of Navajo babies over 18 weeks old is *two and a half times* that of the overall population, according to Dr. Taylor McKenzie, hospital administrator in Window Rock, Arizona. White Americans would no doubt find that statistic and the factors contributing to it intolerable in their own communities.

Pneumonia and diarrhea are the two main problems for Navajo babies this age. These problems start after the baby stops coming to the "well-baby" clinic, the Navajo doctor said. The fact is that too many Navajo parents lack the means to drive the distances back and forth to these clinics for their baby's checkups. "I would say it's a nutritional problem—tied in with the low standard of living. Families just don't have the financial means to provide a healthful diet or living situation."

An inadequate water supply or poor sewage control also increase the chance of disease. When this situation occurs, the weakest in the family have the greater chance of becoming ill—that means the very young or the very old. Yet, according to Dr. Thomas Lowe, a health care administrator with the Navajo, 40 percent of Navajo families have no piped-in water. And despite these almost life and death aspects of water and sewage systems, Federal plans for 10,800 units of housing include no sanitary or water facilities. How could the government plan to put up housing—and simply leave out water and sanitary facilities? Dr. Lowe wasn't surprised. "Government doesn't always do things with forethought. Things just get overlooked in appropriations."

A supreme irony confronting Indians today is that, with all of the deserved attention being given to the lengthening life spans of Americans, death still comes at an early age for Native Americans. Across the country, the average life span of the U.S. non-Indian population is 65.1 years. Yet, the average life for the Navajo people ends more than 22 years earlier at age 42.4.

One IHS statistician argues that because the Indian birth rate is higher than the national rate,

this figure does not give a fair picture of Indian health. There are more people at risk age because of the high birth rate, he says. New life expectancy figures, which are projected for people being born now, are more accurate, he maintains. Navajo Indians born today are expected to live 64.9 years, Indians in general 65.1 years, and the rest of the U.S. population 70.9 years—a gap of some six years.

But others argue that the average age of death, which is startlingly low for the Navajo, is more accurate—since it is based on actual cases, rather than projected figures. In either case, the rates show that Indians are dying younger than any other population group in the country.

The IHS network of hospitals has managed to reduce the rate of deadly diseases, like tuberculosis, from 55.1 deaths per 100,000 in 1955 to 7.7 deaths per 100,000 in 1975. But there are other diseases with rising rates which are killing Native Americans at far higher rates than for others in the U.S.

Twice as many 25 to 34 year old Indians die from diabetes, for example. Deaths from cirrhosis of the liver soared 217 percent from 1955 to 1975 for Indian men and women. Once again, it is the 25 to 34 year olds, the people who should be the backbone of their tribes, who suffer the most. Cirrhosis of the liver hits them 14.5 times as often as the 4.2 death rate for all other U.S. races in this age group.

Problems of alcohol addiction among Indians are not well understood by most Americans, observes Dr. Lowe. "The Anglo-Saxon population in this country has tended to blame the Indian for drinking. That becomes an excuse for not dealing with the situation, or for dealing only with the symptoms, rather than the root causes," he notes.

According to one theory, Dr. Lowe said, there may be a factor, like an enzyme, that is genetically lacking in Indians. If this is the case, as it seems to be for several Asian groups who are genetically related in various degrees to Native Americans, the ability to clear alcohol from the system would be greatly reduced. That would reduce tolerance for alcohol and make it easier to become physically dependent on it, he explains.

Sugar is a factor in both diabetes and alcohol addiction. Most Indians who drink heavily get addicted to a very sweet Muscatel wine nicknamed "Green Lizard." Few Americans are aware that a high preponderance of Indians cannot metabolize lactose from milk. Ironically, those who are not genetically allergic to milk often lack access to stores selling it. Both of these factors contribute to the early and concentrated use of sugar-laden soft drinks. The step from sweet soda to sweet port or tokay is not a large one in Indian country.

Experts are beginning to look into the drastic change of diet Indians went through in moving from independence to dependence on white society, a "dietary bottleneck" through which not all could pass. The Plains Indians, for example, changed from a very high protein diet (meat, wild turnips, chokecherries) to a diet loaded with starch and sugar. The monthly dole of "commodities" given out by the Federal government, which includes a high number of starches, would make any person committed to a balanced daily diet flinch in horror. It contains flour, macaroni, spaghetti, sugar, rice, beans, canned vegetables, canned fruit juices, canned meat stew (nicknamed "Alpo" by some reservation wisecrackers), canned pork, powdered milk, butter and one five-pound box of fresh cheese. The milk, butter and cheese often become food for the animals in Navajo country because of their lactose intolerance.

Despite the extreme gravity of alcohol addiction, there are very few detoxification programs on U.S. reservations. And some of the small efforts at combatting it are being cut back. "We need a full-blown alcoholism program, starting with detoxification," says Leonard Little Finger, assistant administrator at the Pine Ridge IHS hospital. "But we are not able to receive funding for new programs."

And in nearby Rosebud, Pat Eagle Elk, the director of the tribe's alcoholism programs, recently warned that the local Little Hoop Treatment Lodge may have to close down for lack of funds.

Eagle Elk calls alcoholism the "most devastating disease" on the Rosebud Reservation, urging that the treatment lodge remain open to try to deal with it.

Cirrhosis of the liver is not the only killer that is tied to alcohol addiction. High motor vehicle accident rates and high suicide rates, two of the major causes of death for Native Americans, are both connected with drinking in a majority of cases. Newborn babies, as well, can suffer from "fetal alcohol syndrome" if their mothers drink even moderately during pregnancy.

"Of mothers (of all population groups) who drink heavily during pregnancy, about 44 percent give birth to babies with birth defects," warns David Rooks in an article in the *Lakota Times*, the Pine Ridge Reservation newspaper. These babies are born with brain damage, heart defects, or weak muscle, bone and skin development. Rooks pointed out they also have difficulty forming emotional bonds with their mothers at birth, and with other people later on. Birth defects can have other causes as well, including poor nutrition for the mother while she is carrying the child.

Reports from the Center for Disease Control in Atlanta, Georgia show there are a large number of birth defects in babies born on the Pine Ridge Reservation, home of the Oglala Sioux. A controversy started over this two years ago, when Women of All Red Nations (WARN), an organization with members from many tribes, publicly raised the issue over whether high radiation levels in the water were a major cause of birth defects. The Disease Control Center maintained radiation levels were not too high for safety, disagreeing with WARN's tests which declared they were unsafe. WARN is unconvinced.

Pregnancy complications, accidents, respiratory diseases and digestive diseases are the four most prevalent reasons for hospitalization for Native Americans in this country. The fifth most frequent cause may surprise some people. It is mental illness.

This certainly belies the romanticized image many people hold about the Native American.

According to this image, mainly ground out in Hollywood, the Indian is calm and unruffled—a being with a strong profile and steady nerves.

Suicide rates for Native Americans have increased, not declined, since the '50s. While there are differences between the tribes and nations with regard to rates and incidence of alcoholism and suicide, a study in the '70s showed the overall suicide rate for Native Americans 15 to 24 years old was four times as high as the national rate for the same age group of other races. Dr. Philip A. May, now at the University of New Mexico, lived on the Pine Ridge Oglala Sioux Reservation for three years. He noted that, in one very severe year on this reservation, there was a suicide attempt once every four days. Many of the people who tried to kill themselves were drinking at the time. And some of those who tried to kill themselves were as young as seventh, eighth, and tenth grade children.

Dr. May emphasizes that this horrifying loss of life is not going to stop until overall economic and social conditions on the reservation change. "There is a large segment of the society," he stressed, "virtually denied access to the few steady jobs or roles available. Individuals then become casualities with feelings of frustration, hopelessness, and fatalism."

When life becomes purposeless and painful, when there is no way to find gainful employment despite repeated attempts, the next step is often escape. Dr. May notes this by saying that a large number of people "escape from reality—through drinking, carelessness and accidents, suicide attempts and suicide." Moreover, "A negative self-image of Americans Indians portrayed vividly to them in the surrounding border towns and through the media" only increases low self-esteem and feelings of lack of direction and purpose, he explains. Males are especially affected since their role as provider is under attack while females have continuity in their lives as mothers and they experience less drug and alcohol dependency.

Francis Montileaux, a psychiatric social worker who directs human services at Pine Ridge Hospital and is himself a Sioux, observes, "We see a lot of people come in frustrated because they have no work, no training. They're not able to provide for their families.

"This can easily lead to family tension, with the wife throwing it up in her husband's face that he's not a good provider. Then he'll often go out and get drunk to forget." The problem has become much more pronounced in the last two or three years, since a number of the few jobs available on the reservation were eliminated by decisions in Washington, he said.

"There's also a lot of stress from overcrowding in the homes," said another counselor. "People have to move in with another family because they don't have housing of their own." Forty-six percent of Indian families at Pine Ridge live in one or two room houses. That compares with only five percent of non-Indians who have to live in homes that small.

One 27-year-old woman with three children had to move in with her parents after her husband died. Her sister, who also had children, also shared the house. So she watched her sister's children along with her own, and drove her mother to Rapid City several times a week for medical care for a kidney disease. What this woman really wanted was a home and job of her own. Neither was available. One evening, after an argument with her brother, "something snapped"—and she ran into the bathroom, grabbed a razor blade and slashed her wrists. This young woman survived the suicide attempt. But there are others who will not.

The Bureau of Indian Affairs (BIA) estimates that the Pine Ridge Reservation, where this young woman lives, has a 75 percent unemployment rate (local estimates are higher). But the bleak outlook for finding jobs does not affect Pine Ridge alone. Both the Yankton Sioux and the Standing Rock Sioux Reservations in the Dakotas have unemployment rates of 79 percent. The BIA's conservative statistics show 53 percent unemployment for the Shoshone Tribe in Idaho and the Blackfoot in Montana. Indeed, the only state in the country that seems to show a high *employment* rate for Indian Tribes is Oklahoma, where renewed oil development is creating a very different situation than that experienced by other Indian peoples.

"Only a long-term economic development program can eliminate some of the basic causes of poor physical health," concludes the report, *That These People May Live*, prepared in 1970 by the U.S. Department of Health, Education and Welfare. Eileen Maynard and Gayla Twiss, authors of the report, show that the rate of health problems among Indians is twice as high as among non-Indians living in the same geographical area. But, they add, public health service alone cannot change this. The health problems are too interwoven with the total socio-economic situation.

"Congressmen who live near Indians tend to understand their problems and be supportive. But the people back east who never see Indians don't have a lot of understanding about what's going on," observes Dr. Lowe in Arizona. "I don't think it's malice [that causes the under-funding], I think it's lack of understanding."

The hospital in Pine Ridge had positions for seven doctors and 32 nurses 12 years ago, in 1970. "Since then our patients have doubled—and our doctors and nurses remain the same," says administrator Terry Pourier. "Out here, when someone's dying, you go 100 miles an hour to get to the hospital 100 miles away—and hope to get there on time!" commented one member of the tribe. The National Congress of American Indians has been urging Congress to allocate a mere $45,000 for a clinic in Kyle, at the opposite end of the reservation, as well as funds for clinics on South Dakota and Montana reservations.

There are some serious misapprehensions about Indians held by non-Indians. One of these is the feeling that Native Americans receive huge sums of Federal money—more than anyone else. Congressman Morris Udall's research showed that, in fact, the opposite is the case. Average per capita government spending for all U.S. citizens was $3,688 in 1980. The total amount of aid going

to Indians the same year was $2,948. Concluded Udall, "The Indian people, whom all people generally concede are the most impoverished in this country, have been receiving 20 percent *less* in governmental services than the national population."

Most Americans may also be unaware of the fact that 10,000 Navajo and Hopi people are slated for "relocation" in the next several years. They are to be moved, by congressional decision, from rural homes where they live quietly traditional lives herding sheep and cattle, and put in the middle of border towns—with all the concomitant noise, red tape, gadgets and complicated loan and payment systems. The few already moved have become confused and disoriented, with some experiencing physical illness from the drastic change.

The ruthless treatment of people, with no consideration of their feelings and lifeways, is bound to result in severe health problems in the future. One cannot expect doctors and nurses to rush in and "cure" people with bandages where deep psychic wounds have been made. Instead, the government should reconsider such drastic and inhuman programs, and avert problems before they start. Just how ill-conceived the plans for this relocation are can be measured in the words of Relocation Commissioner Hawley Atkinson: "They'd better be out by July, 1986," he declared. "Or else we'll go in with guns and Federal marshals—just as we did with stock reduction."

Urban Indians, as well, are largely overlooked by fellow city residents who may not even be aware they have Apache, Navajo, or Cherokee neighbors. In New York City, for example, there are almost 12,000 Indians of different tribes in the five boroughs. A tiny clinic at 842 Broadway serves this population. Unless funds are voted this winter, this clinic will have to close. The Public Health Service Hospital on Staten Island, where many Indians went for medical care, closed last year.

Those living off the reservation (which means most Native Americans at one time or another in their lives) run into other kinds of discrimination. The widow of Kenneth Porcupine brought suit against a hospital in Scottsbluff, Nebraska for denying medical care to her husband. They sent him to Pine Ridge Hospital, 140 miles away, even though that facility had no neurosurgeon, and no "CAT-scanner" to check for blood clots or hematoma. The deathly sick man arrived at Pine Ridge, where staff had to immediately send him off again to Rapid City where hospitals had the same equipment he could have been treated with in Scottsbluff. He died before reaching Rapid City.

One staff member working in Washington for the BIA summarizes the overall situation wryly: "Health professionals and Native Americans poured into this city to give testimony to the House and Senate back in '78. They documented the fact, thoroughly, that health care to the Indian is the lowest of any segment of the population." But that has not done much to raise the level of funding, he adds, noting that it's easy to play with statistics to make things look better than they are. For example, "You need $100, and someone gives you $20. The next year you need $200, and they give you $40, saying well, we've doubled your budget."

"That's the way it's been with Indian health programs. They were under-funded right from the beginning. So people may say money was increased every year, but if the base was low in the beginning, it doesn't mean anything." He chuckled ironically. "I've watched this since I was a child, growing up on a reservation myself. It's not really funny. It's pathetic."

As Americans reach for the last of the popcorn while watching those recurring movie images of a Sioux chief with a gloriously feathered bonnet riding into the sunset, they are oblivious to the fact that the great great grandchild of that same chief may be enduring multiple traumas on the reservation. The maddening part of it all is that many of the conditions causing that plight *can* be addressed—if enough Americans only knew more about the actual lives America's first people are leading today and insisted on honoring long-standing Federal government pledges to Native Americans.

TAKING ANOTHER LOOK

1 How might the reservation system be viewed by functionalist theorists and conflict theorists?

2 How do the economic and social conditions of reservation life contribute to the ill health of Indians?

3 What factors contribute to the high proportion of birth defects found among babies born on the Pine Ridge reservation?

4 According to Giago and Illoway, what misapprehensions about Indians are held by non-Indians?

5 According to Dr. Philip A. May, what factors contribute to the high suicide rates evident among young native Americans?

The Anxiety of Being a Japanese-American

Gene Oishi

There are approximately 700,000 Japanese-Americans in the United States. As a people, they are relatively recent arrivals to this nation. In 1880 there were only 148 Japanese immigrants in the United States, but by 1920 there were over 110,000. The early Japanese immigrants, the *Issei*, were usually males seeking employment opportunities in America. Along with Chinese immigrants, they were seen as a "yellow peril" by many white Americans and faced widespread prejudice and discrimination.

In 1941, the attack on Pearl Harbor by Japan had severe repercussions for Japanese-Americans. The federal government decreed that all Japanese-Americans on the west coast must leave their homes and report to "evacuation camps." They became, in effect, scapegoats for the anger that other Americans felt concerning Japan's role in World War II. In an unprecedented application of guilt by virtue of ancestry, 113,000 Japanese-Americans were forced to live in hastily built camps by August 1943.

Financially, the Federal Reserve Board placed the losses of evacuation for Japanese-Americans at nearly $0.5 billion, or more than $4500 per person ($27,000 per person in today's dollars). Moreover, the psychological effect on these citizens including the humiliation of being labeled as "disloyal," was immeasurable. Eventually, the American-born Japanese, the *Nisei*, were allowed to enlist in the army and serve in a segregated combat unit in Europe. Others resettled in the east and midwest to work in factories.

In 1983, the Federal Commission on Wartime Relocation and Internment of Civilians recommended government payments of $20,000 to each of the 60,000 surviving Japanese-Americans who were held in detention camps during World War II. These payments and other forms of compensation, expected to total some $1.5 billion, were endorsed as an "act of national apology" for a "grave injustice." The Commission, established by Congress in 1980, reported that the detention was motivated by "race prejudice, war hysteria, and a failure of political leadership." It added that "no documented acts of espionage, sabotage, or fifth-column activity were shown to have been committed" by Japanese-Americans. The panel proposed passage of a congressional resolution offering formal apology to the Japanese-American citizens and resident aliens who were relocated and detained during the war, roughly half of whom are now deceased. Thus far, however, Congress has neither adopted such a resolution nor authorized the recommended payments to Japanese-Americans.

In the following selection, Gene Oishi, managing editor of *Action Line*, a publication of the Maryland State Teachers Association, offers a vivid personal account of the fear and anger associated with being a Japanese-American who experienced the World War II internment. While noting that many Japanese-Americans of the Nisei generation are prosperous, well-educated members of the American middle class, Oishi nevertheless suggests that fear rules the lives of these seemingly well-assimilated citizens. He also traces the continuing impact of the internment on the *Sansei*, the third generation of Japanese living in the United States.

My base camp was the Hyatt Regency Hotel, an imposing fortresslike structure towering above downtown Phoenix. My room on the 12th floor looked south over the desert, dotted with flat-topped buttes that looked like bombed-out Mount Fujis. Somewhere out there was the site of the Gila River Relocation Center, the internment camp in which I spent an important part of my childhood during World War II.

As I looked out over the desert from my well-appointed hotel room I could feel traces of a nagging fear, and I began to sense why it had taken me nearly 40 years to revisit the scene of my wartime internment.

It was last April that I made the trip to Arizona, ostensibly to complete my research for an article dealing with the assimilation of Japanese into the American mainstream. Actually, I went there in the hope of overcoming a writer's block.

Much has been written about the internment of Japanese during World War II, and so I had not intended to dwell on that aspect of Japanese-American history. But as I began to write the article, it became clear to me that there was much more that needed to be said about the experience.

I recalled the hearings held in 1981 by the Commission on Wartime Relocation and Internment of Civilians. The commission was created by Congress, in the wake of renewed demands for reparations, to re-examine the internment of Japanese during World War II. Hundreds of Japanese came forth to testify, and many feel that those hearings constituted the most significant event that has occurred in the Japanese community since the internment itself.

The commission concluded its work in the summer of 1983 with a list of five recommendations, including one that calls for a $1.5 billion fund to be used to provide a one-time compensatory payment of $20,000 to each of the approximately 60,000 remaining survivors of the internment. There was a bill in the last Congress —and action on a reintroduced version is expected in the current session—that would implement the commission's recommendations.

Regardless of the fate of that bill, the commission hearings had a permanent impact on the Japanese community.

At the hearings, the usually reticent and undemonstrative nisei—second-generation Japanese-Americans—choked back tears or let them flow as they told their stories. Many of the spectators wept, too, as they listened, and it seemed as if a dam had burst and the community was at long last truly mourning its past. The sansei—third-generation Japanese-Americans, most of whom were too young to have experienced the internment—were astonished. "I never saw nisei act that way before," said a sansei afterward.

It was not *what* the witnesses said that was so remarkable, for most of them simply described the economic and physical hardships they endured. What was remarkable was that they spoke at all. I, too, spoke to the commission at a pre-hearing briefing seminar in June 1981. My throat and chest suddenly felt so constricted that I thought I was coming down with an attack of bronchitis. It took all the strength I had to get through my talk and to keep from breaking into tears.

The reasons for the severity of my reaction, and that of the other witnesses, long remained a mystery to me. Even in the spring of 1983, when I traveled around the country interviewing Japanese of all ages and in a wide variety of occupations, I had not yet plumbed the emotional depths of the internment experience. Nor did I start out with the intention of doing so. My plan was to flesh out what social scientists had been saying for the last two decades: that Japanese-Americans are an extraordinarily successful ethnic group.

As a group (there are about 700,000 Japanese in the United States), they are for the most part prosperous, well-educated and are rapidly joining the mainstream of middle-class life. But in the course of my interviews I began to notice in myself as well as in those I interviewed an intense discomfort with the "model minority" theme.

Chris Iijima, a teacher and politically oriented folk singer in New York, first articulated this discomfort for me in a rational way. Every stereotype, he said, has a "flip side." Hard-working can become ruthless. Resourceful and ingenious can become diabolical. Friendly can become sneaky. Dedicated can become fanatical. What Iijima said struck a chord in me, for within my own lifetime I have seen the Japanese stereotype among the American public turn from negative to positive, and there are signs that as a result of economic competition with Japan it might flip again as more Americans view Japan as a threat to their livelihood.

Later, as I thought about Iijima's observation and my reaction to it, I began to understand that the reason for my near-breakdown before the Congressional commission was fear. I was speaking to a commission that represented in my mind the same type of officialdom that in 1942 could not see past the color of our skin and hair and the shape of our eyes and noses and concluded that we were actual or potential enemies.

It was in Arizona, at the scene of my wartime internment, that I began to suspect that our discomfort with stereotypes, even positive ones, was rooted in fear. For the first time, I began to get a sense of how fear had ruled much of my life and perhaps the lives of most Japanese of my generation.

I was surprised by the ease with which I found the old campsite in the Gila River Indian Reservation, about 30 miles south of Phoenix. The barracks were gone, but the concrete foundation blocks, with twisted and rusted steel flanges clinging to them, were still there, as were the large slabs of concrete that once were the floors of the mess halls. From the top of a butte I had often climbed as a child, I could see a cattle farm and greening fields of wheat in the distance. None of this had existed when I first was here. At that time, there was nothing but desert wilderness as far as the eye could see. I felt high indignation; they were ruining my desert, encroaching on that precious isolation that had provided a measure of safety for me as a child. I realized then that I had

not wanted to leave the camp. The desert, with its primitive desolation and extremes of weather, can be frightening at times, but it was not as frightening to me as the uncertainties and ambiguities of the world from which I had been ejected.

For the first nine years of my life my home had been Guadalupe, a small farming community in California's Santa Maria Valley. My father, who was a prominent farmer and civic leader in the Japanese community, was arrested early in the morning on Dec. 8, 1941, within 24 hours after the Japanese attack on Pearl Harbor. Though he was never charged with any crime, he thought he was going to be executed and so he wrote a letter of farewell to his family from a cell in the Santa Barbara County Jail.

Although my father and other community leaders arrested with him were not killed, many of the older Japanese feared they were being sent to extermination camps as the general "evacuation" began on the West Coast several months later. These fears I learned of much later, but I got a hint of them at the time from my mother's perpetually furrowed brow, from the sound of her crying at night and from her hair, which seemed to have turned gray overnight.

The roots of the fear went back to the late 19th century, when Japanese first started coming to this country in significant numbers. Like the Chinese before them, Japanese were subjected to intense racial hatred and vilification. Every effort was made to keep them from becoming woven into the social and economic fabric. They were not allowed naturalization privileges. Most Western states passed laws forbidding Asians from owning land. Antimiscegenation and other racially discriminatory laws were enacted. There was pressure put on Congress to stop further immigration from the Far East. In 1882, immigration from China was stopped, and in 1924 the ban was extended to Japan.

With the Japanese attack on Pearl Harbor, racial animosity flared with renewed ferocity. It was a time when racism was not universally condemned as it is today publicly, and members of

Congress and newspaper columnists and editors openly expressed racial hatred for the Japanese. Ultimately, in February 1942, President Franklin D. Roosevelt signed Executive Order 9066, which enabled the Government to remove 110,000 Japanese—71,000 of them American citizens—from the West Coast and to place them in internment camps in the interior.

The first camp we were sent to was an "assembly center" built at the county fairgrounds in Tulare, Calif. My memories are of heat, dust and a pervasive, sickening smell of the tar paper with which the barracks were covered. There were two barbed-wire fences surrounding the camp. This was not simply an "assembly center"; it was a prison. Soldiers with fixed bayonets patrolled the area between the two fences, and if you had any further doubts about what this camp was, there were guard towers along the perimeter, each equipped with a machine gun and searchlight.

Tulare was a hateful place, and I suppose anyone who spent time there would find his own reasons for finding it so. Mine never had any coherent pattern. First of all, my mother got sick and I had the feeling that she had deserted me. The food tasted tinny, maybe because it was served on metal trays. Juices from the canned vegetables, canned frankfurters and melting Jell-O flowed together to form a tepid, mildly sweet soup. The latrines were dirty and smelly and swarmed with flies. I still have unpleasant dreams about toilets filled and smeared with human feces. The barracks were crowded and noisy. Our family of six was assigned one small compartment that was barely large enough to hold our cots. The couple in the next compartment were always quarreling, and you could hear every word, even those they whispered.

During the day, I roamed with a band of children who resembled a pack of domestic dogs gone wild. We tried to make friends with the soldiers patrolling the camp, but they were sullen, even a little hostile, so we gave up. I don't know about the other children, but I never held it against the soldiers. Instead, I began to resent the Japanese they were guarding.

The camp in Arizona had no fence. None was needed, situated as we were in the middle of the wilderness. I recall being inordinately afraid of rattlesnakes. I was afraid to go out of the barracks at night for fear that one would come slithering out of the crawl space under the building. It is only in recent years that I have begun to realize that the state of panic in which I lived during the first few months in Arizona was in some way connected with being a Japanese. At the weekly movie, an American war film played that ended with the sinking of a Japanese battleship. As American bombs began exploding on the deck of the ship, Japanese sailors began to panic and leap into the sea. The children and young adults in the audience began to giggle, and as the battleship sank they broke into cheers and applause. I cheered and applauded, too, knowing full well that our parents in the crowd were deeply pained that their children were turning against Japan and perhaps even against them. By late 1943, those who had pledged their loyalty to the United States were allowed to leave. Most of those who remained were children—or older folk who had been born in Japan and who, under the law, were not allowed to become citizens. They knitted, sculptured ironwood, grew morning glories, built rock gardens, or sat in the shade, fanning themselves and squinting against the heat. Life remained pretty much that way until the war ended and we were told to leave.

I recall the first words spoken to me when I met a former schoolmate upon our return to Guadalupe. He had been a friend before the war and I had often gone to his house to play. "Hi, Norman," I said. "Remember me? I'm Gene." Norman stared for some time. I waited for a smile of recognition that never came. Instead, he tilted his head back a little and asked with a sniff, "*All you Japs coming back?*"

I eventually got over Norman's rude welcome. I graduated from high school, served in the Army, went to college, got married to a Swiss woman, moved to the East Coast and began a career as a newspaper reporter. I lived in a white neighborhood, had white friends and for long stretches of time would forget I was Japanese. I would feel extremely uncomfortable when inevitably I would be reminded of it.

For years I thought I was unusual in my reactions, but as I interviewed Japanese around the country, I discovered I was more typical than not of the generation of so-called nisei who grew up in the 1930's and 40's and were interned with their immigrant parents.

Dwight Chuman, a Los Angeles journalist and sansei, or third-generation Japanese, called the nisei "confused young men who succeeded by selling their self-hatred and disappearing into the mainstream mentality." It is difficult to be lectured by a member of the younger generation, but I found myself agreeing with Chuman and with most of the sansei activists I interviewed.

Feelings of self-hatred and shame are well documented among victims of aggression and abuse, such as raped women, abused children and prisoners of war. But until recently, I had not thought of myself as a victim and had not allowed myself to feel fear or anger about the internment. As I interviewed Japanese around the country, I found others who were better able to articulate their feelings.

Bebe Toshiko Reschke, a psychiatric social worker at an adult outpatient clinic in California, was a child during the internment. She recalled that while in camp three military policemen came into her family's compartment to search for contraband.

"I had such a feeling of being violated," she said. "I still have a problem with that, of trusting authority.... That anyone can have such control over you, and it can happen so fast."

"When I read these stories dealing with Japan," she continued, referring to coverage of Japanese competition with the United States, "I still get that emotional reaction. I think, 'Oh my God, the American public is turning against us again.' This time I'm not going. That's my line. This time

I'm going to fight. I've joined the American Civil Liberties Union. That's my way of coping with my fears about what happened."

Her comment is an indication of the anger suppressed by many nisei that is only now beginning to bubble to the surface. The more fortunate Japanese-Americans, in my view, are those who in one way or another expressed their anger at the time. Minoru Yasui, a lawyer and former executive director of the Denver Community Relations Commission, is one of them.

A trim elegant man with a lively twinkle in his eyes, Yasui does not strike one as a stubborn fighter. In fact, as a young lawyer in Portland Ore., in 1942, he had no intention of turning himself into a test case. "But we couldn't find anyone else to do it." he said. "You were laying your career, your life, your record on the line.... It was scary. If you were convicted, you didn't know whether you were going to come out of prison alive."

Despite his fear, Yasui refused to obey a curfew imposed on Japanese-Americans after the outbreak of World War II and refused to leave his home voluntarily when ordered to evacuate. He was arrested and served nine months in the Multnomah County Jail in Portland. Yasui appealed his conviction all the way to the Supreme Court, which upheld it.

Yasui and others who fought for their constitutional rights in court were the exceptions. The Japanese American Citizens League, which assumed leadership within the Japanese community in 1942, discouraged even legal challenges and urged cooperation with the authorities. After an initial protest, league leaders accepted the position of authorities that the evacuation of all Japanese from the West Coast was a military necessity. They cooperated with the authorities in getting Japanese into camps. Once they were there, the league lobbied Washington successfully to allow nisei to volunteer for the armed forces and to be subject to the draft. At one point, Mike Masaoka, a league leader, was reported to have urged the formation of an all-Japanese "suicide battalion." Masaoka today says he does not recall having used the words "suicide battalion," and goes on to say that even if he had he did not have in mind anything like the kamikaze units formed later in the war by the Japanese enemy.

Passions were whipped raw during the first months of internment. In some camps, Japanese American Citizens League leaders were attacked and beaten. But on the whole, the league position was supported. About 75 percent of Japanese-American males responded "yes" to a loyalty questionnaire that made them subject to the draft. Ultimately, more than 33,000 Japanese-Americans, including women, volunteered or were drafted into the armed forces during the war. In the Pacific, they served as interpreters and translators; and in Europe, the all-Japanese 100th Battalion and the 442nd Regimental Combat Team were two of the most decorated and bloodied units of the war.

Thus, Japanese in the United States paid with blood the price of acceptance as Americans. But there are many of us who feel that we are continuing to pay a price.

Amy Iwasaki Mass, a nisei who is a clinical social worker and an instructor at Whittier College, in Whittier, Calif., has worked with many nisei as a therapist and concludes that the internment experience continues to be "a real attack on our sense of well being and our self esteem."

The reaction of many nisei, she said, was much like that of some hostages who start to identify with their captors. "Identification with the aggressor makes us feel safer and stronger," she said.

She observed, as others have, that some nisei have shed their ethnic identity and have merged into the white mainstream. "What is sacrificed is the individual's own self-acceptance," she said. "It places an exaggerated emphasis on surface qualities, such as a pleasant non-offensive manner, neat grooming and appearance, nice homes, nice cars, and well behaved children."

A further misfortune, she said, is that many nisei have passed on their basic insecurity to their sansei children.

Some sansei, however, have managed to break out of such a nisei mold. One of them is Steve Nakajo, a familiar figure on the streets of San Francisco's Japantown. His generous girth decked out in jeans and sneakers, he walks the streets with a swagger reminiscent of a sumo wrestler. He founded Kimochi Inc. to help the people of Japantown. One of the first projects was a movie escort service. Sansei, wearing yellow and black happi coats, walked or drove issei—first-generation immigrants—to and from Japanese movie theaters. This proved to be a popular service because of the old people's fear of street crime. Later, the Kimochi (which means "feeling") Lounge was opened, where issei could congregate, find reading materials, take up handicrafts and receive counseling for social services. A nutrition program was started as part of the federally financed meal program. Kimochi's crowning achievement, so far, is a $1.3 million, 20-bed facility for elderly Japanese. It was built entirely with private contributions, mostly from individuals, but with some corporate and foundation grants.

There are those who say that the internment benefited the Japanese by dispersing them throughout the country and making them more familiar and acceptable to other Americans. Such people ignore the damage done to the Japanese sense of family and to generational ties that sansei like Nakajo are trying to restore.

I am one of those whose trauma was real, and in recent years I have struggled with the thought of my father's humiliation and downfall. After coming to this country in 1903 at the age of 19, he established himself as a successful farmer in Guadalupe. A flamboyant man, he drove a big Buick, wore tailored suits, smoked cigars and sent two sons to Stanford University. With his arrest by Federal Bureau of Investigation agents and the internment of his family, he lost everything he had worked for and achieved in 40 years.

When we returned to Guadalupe after the war, he and my mother went to work as field laborers.

Contrary to the Japanese stereotype, my father was a man who freely vented his feelings. A devotee of the Kabuki theater, he would be moved to tears by tales of death, sacrifice and downfall. Yet he never complained about his own economic ruin and loss of status. He carried on as if none of that really mattered. It is only in recent years, long after his death, that I have grown to appreciate his courage and to understand that if the authorities indeed wanted to emasculate him, they did not succeed. When I am able to accept that, perhaps my long night of fear will finally come to an end.

TAKING ANOTHER LOOK

1 Why were the *Sansei* surprised at the reactions of the *Nisei* during the hearings of the Commission on Wartime Relocation and Internment of Civilians?
2 What did folk singer Chris Iijima mean when he suggested that every stereotype has a "flip side"?
3 How did the United States treat Japanese immigrants during the late nineteenth century?
4 Briefly describe Oishi's experiences at the internment camp in Tulare, California.
5 How does social worker Amy Iwasaki Mass view the continuing impact of the internment on Japanese-Americans? How does she view the attempt of some *Nisei* to merge into the white mainstream?
6 How would conflict theorists be likely to view the internment of Japanese-Americans during World War II?

The Able Disabled: The Media Office Promotes the Country's Largest Minority

Libby Slate

Like blacks, native Americans, and Japanese-Americans, disabled persons are a minority group subject to prejudice and discrimination. However, following the lead of other minorities, a growing movement for "disabled rights" has emerged across the United States. Activists in this movement have lobbied to end employment practices that discriminate against those with disabilities and to eliminate architectural barriers that deny the handicapped access to public buildings.

A key priority of the disabled rights movement has been to integrate the disabled into educational institutions. Current policy toward the handicapped in American schools was shaped by the passage in 1975 of Public Law 94–142 (Education for All Handicapped Children Act), which took full effect in 1980. With few exceptions, this law calls for local school districts to provide a separate individualized education program (IEP) for every handicapped child. In addition, Public Law 94–142 holds that states wishing to receive federal funds to educate the handicapped must place these students within the "least restrictive environment." In other words, handicapped children must be educated in the atmosphere most suitable to a regular classroom that is suitable for them.

The practice of promoting maximum integration of handicapped children with nonhandicapped children is known as *mainstreaming*. An important goal of mainstreaming is to break down societal prejudices regarding handicapped individuals. Viewed from the perspective of labeling theory, mainstreaming is an attempt to remove the stigma attached to children with disabilities. It is hoped that, through day-to-day interactions with handicapped children, nonhandicapped peers (as well as parents and teachers) will become more accepting of those with disabilities.

In the following selection, Libby Slate discusses the work of the Media Office, a unique liaison between the entertainment industry and the disabled community. Just as mainstreaming represents an attempt to offset the stigma attached to disabilities, the Media Office hopes to reverse negative stereotypes of disabled persons—partly by promoting increased employment of disabled performers and other professionals. As the executive director of the Media Office points out, television is an especially powerful agent of socialization and has an important impact on people's perceptions of disabled Americans.

"There are thirty-six million people with disabilities in the United States. That makes them this country's largest minority, aside from men."

So says Tari Susan Hartman, who, as executive director of the Media Office, has good reason to care about such statistics. Since its establishment in June 1980, the Media Office has served as a unique liaison between the media/entertainment industry and the disability community, working to change the general public's conception of people with disabilities by reversing negative stereotypes, eliminating attitudinal and other barriers, and providing increased employment opportunities for disabled performers and other industry professionals.

"People's values, attitudes, and perceptions are based not only on their real-life experiences but on the perceptions created and shaped by the media, primarily television," explains Hartman, a former actress who holds a master's degree in social work from the University of Southern California. "We've found, for instance, that negative stereotypes are perpetuated by telethons, which raise money by guilt and pity. Disabled people are depicted as childlike ('Jerry's kids'), asexual, incompetent, nonproductive, a drain on the taxpayers and the economy. They don't show the mobility and all the other positive aspects."

Originally recognized more for its administration of the annual Media Access Awards of the California Governor's Committee for Employment of the Handicapped, the Media Office has developed—primarily since Hartman signed on almost four years ago—a multitude of programs, services, lobbying efforts to more actively pursue its goals. It now boasts a Steering Committee and Board of Advisors numbering well over one hundred studio, union, and network executives, casting directors, producers, and performers, as well as leaders of the disability civil rights movement. At press time, the Media Office was in the process of setting up its own nonprofit foundation; created as a project of the California Governor's Committee for Employment of the Handicapped, it had more recently been under the auspices of the nonprofit California Foundation on Employment and Disability.

One of the Media Office's major roles, according to Hartman, is its function as the official casting clearing house for disabled performers. It has been sanctioned for this purpose by the Interguild Committee of Performers with Disabilities, representing SAG, AFTRA, SEG, and American Federation of Musicians, Local 47. The program includes provisions for disabled performers' special needs, such as sign language interpreters, wheelchair access, Braille scripts, audiotapes, and special education teachers for children.

"We got our first collection of names from the 1978 SAG Skills and Talents Survey," Hartman recalls. "There was a file marked Handicapped, which had never been pulled from the master computer. Then-SAG President William Schallert and I weeded out a lot of illegitimate stuff—people had listed Bald, Ugly Toes, Overweight. We found we had a nice amount left, including little people, deaf, blind, and amputees." There are now more than three hundred individuals on file. Last year, more than 150 television and film roles were filled by disabled performers—a 400 to 500 percent increase, in the estimation of one casting director, since the Media Office's inception.

The Media Office, needless to say, encourages the hiring of disabled performers to play disabled characters but takes a realistic approach to the matter. "The producers' bottom line is talent. Ours is access," says Hartman. "Sometimes they meet and sometimes they don't. We don't demand that a producer hire a disabled performer, because we're aware of creative and other considerations. But we encourage them to open auditions to our performers. For the upcoming midseason replacement series *Mr. Sunshine*, for instance, a sitcom about a blind college English professor, several blind actors were tested before sighted actor Jeffrey Tambor was cast. I've found little discrimination but much lack of education, so I go by the premise that it's lack of awareness."

Her point is born out by Rick Husky, supervising producer of *T.J. Hooker*, who this year won two Media Access Awards, as Outstanding Media Employer and for Series as a Whole. "A few years ago I had no idea the Media Office existed. We did a show with a role for a blind woman and had already hired a sighted actress. There was a scene with the woman teaching blind kids, so we needed a technical advisor and the kids. I was referred to Tari Hartman. Before that it never entered my mind that there were blind actresses available; had I known, I would have read them. The next time there was an opportunity, we hired a deaf actress—Hooker, on a stakeout, had no court order for wiretapping to eavesdrop, so we had a deaf woman watch the suspects with binoculars and read their lips. We've used a lot of disabled performers since then, hired just as any other actor. It's a pleasure working with the Media Office. There's no pressure; if you feel a nondisabled performer is better for the role, you know you're not going to have anybody picketing you."

The audition process, a trying experience for any performer, often places added pressures on disabled actors and actresses.

"When I go in for a reading, I always get amazed looks from the casting people, like 'Oh, my God, she can read!' " relates actress Christopher Templeton, who for the past two and a half years has played secretary Carol Robbins on *The Young and the Restless*. "My favorite cold reading was for *T.J. Hooker*—I decided I would play the character off-the-wall. They all roared, and William Shatner said, 'Take it further,' so I did. They all roared again. I also got to do a little stunt [she uses a leg brace and cane as a result of polio] and convinced them I'm not a delicate little flower, that I work out two or three times a week."

Adds wheelchair-user Hugh Farrington, now in his third season as Detective Lieutenant Pete O'Brien on *T.J. Hooker*, "You have to make your own opportunities. When I was up for *Quincy*, they offered me a role in a hospital bed, which I didn't want. So Jack Klugman asked, 'Do you see something you like?' and I said, 'Yes, the doctor.' Jack said, in terms of the storyline, 'You could never get the victim's body in the trunk of a car.' I told him, 'Take a good look at me—the arms, the shoulders. If I wanted to put someone in a trunk, I certainly *would* be able to!' "

While Hartman says her policy regarding casting is "consultation, not confrontation," occasionally the Media Office will take a more active stance, notifying the trades after meeting with producers, such as when no deaf actresses were auditioned for a remake of *Johnny Belinda*, nor disabled actors read for a postpolio role on

Quincy. On the other hand, this year the soap *Capitol* won a Media Access Award for its positive depiction of disabled character Dr. Thomas McCandless, who is played by able-bodied actor Michael Catlin.

Performers with disabilities enact two kinds of roles: those revolving around the disability—"gimp of the week," as some actors sardonically term them—and vastly preferred "nonspecific" parts in which the characters just happen to be disabled.

"Those nonspecified roles are so important to us," declares Templeton. "Disability causes fear in able-bodied people. Kids learn from their parents 'Don't touch, don't ask questions.' We have to educate people that it's OK to touch; they're not going to get cooties. If viewers see us on television portrayed as normal people, they'll be more apt to accept us."

In addition to Templeton's and Farrington's roles, nonspecified regular or recurring series roles have included Templeton's nurse in *Ryan's Four*, Lou Ferrigno's ambulance driver and Alan Toy's anesthesiologist in *Trauma Center*, Les Jankey's bartender in *Tales of the Gold Monkey*, Jonathan Hall Kovacs' brother and son in *The Second Family Tree*, Geri Jewell's comedienne in *The Facts of Life*, and Victoria Ann-Lewis's secretary in *Knots Landing*.

Ann-Lewis, who walks with a polio-induced limp, is in her second season on *Knots*. "My character, Peggy, is very much a part of the office scene. She's not subservient," she says. "She's a real person, not a glamour puss. I feel very warmly accepted. I'm glad they're not going with the disability as the character's defining point, because that boxes you in." (As part of her resistance to being "boxed in," Ann-Lewis developed and co-starred in two television disability-themed musical documentaries, *Tell Them I'm a Mermaid*, which won twelve national awards, and the recent *Who Parks in These Spaces?*, soon to be broadcast nationally, which she also coproduced.)

Besides facilitating employment opportunities for disabled performers, the Media Office provides technical assistance and consultation to producers and networks to ensure the accuracy of disability portrayal and issues. Its Community Relations Subcommittee (CRS)—which also conducts programs for the nonentertainment industry disability community—has developed language guidelines for use by writers, standards and practices executives, and others. Notes Hartman, "Just as you wouldn't say 'kike' or 'nigger,' there are certain words to avoid. 'Crippled,' which is derogatory, 'wheelchair-bound' and 'confined to a wheelchair'; wheelchairs provide added independence and mobility, so it's a misnomer to say they're physically confining. We say, 'People who use wheelchairs.' " The Office also shuns the term "handicapped"; the word dates back to the seventeenth century, when deformed people were forced to walk the streets, begging with caps in hands.

The media's portrayal of the disabled community has changed over the years, according to CRS chairman Paul K. Longmore, a program specialist in the Program in Disability and Society at USC. Disability, he notes, has long been associated with criminality (Captain Hook, Captain Ahab) or monstrosity (*The Hunchback of Notre Dame, The Phantom of the Opera*, and other horror film characters). Since World War II, and the return to American society of numerous disabled veterans, the most frequent characterization has been that of the angry, embittered war veteran, with the disability conveyed as an emotional as well as physical adjustment. The disability community's cause was aided by the establishment of the President's and Governor's Committees for Employment of the Handicapped in 1947 and by the passage of federal anti-discrimination legislation in the 1970s. A landmark in the portrayal of people with disabilities was the 1978 feature film *Coming Home*, which depicted a Vietnam veteran as attractive and sexual. (Ironically, there have been few film breakthroughs since then, a situation that Hartman hopes to rectify.)

"The newest theme is that it's possible to accept and learn to live with the disability," says

Longmore, a Ph.D. in history whose polio left him without the use of his arms. "It's progressive, but still inaccurate; there's a lot more to disability than just coping. We're a non-ethnic minority group. We're the objects of social prejudice, and by making the point of the drama the emotional coping, we're taking society off the hook. Only a few shows have touched on prejudice: on *Quincy* a teenager with Down's syndrome encountered prejudice when attempting to live independently, and on *St. Elsewhere* a woman with Elephant Man's disease talked with a black orderly about the prejudice they both experienced." On daytime television, *Capitol* has also tackled the issue with such storylines as a father not wanting Dr. McCandless to operate on his son.

Certain roles are still more common than others, according to Longmore, among them Vietnam veterans and patients on medical shows. And certain stereotypes persist—the disabled person as being noble or inspirational or else being embittered about the disability until shown the light by an able-bodied character. When it comes to choosing roles, then, actors face dilemmas not encountered by their nondisabled peers.

"I'm often called in to read for what turn out to be embarrassing parts," says Alan Toy, a postpolio partial paraplegic whose credits include a recurring role on *Trauma Center* and guest shots on *Simon & Simon* and *Highway to Heaven*. "You're in the position of thinking, 'I'm a relatively unknown person in this town; do I take the politically horrible thing because it's work and it's credit and who knows where it will lead, or do I tell them to stick it because it's something that demeans both me as a person and a whole class of people I'm representing whenever I get work.' It's tough. I've taken one or two roles I'm not proud of. I've also chosen not to read for things."

Toy says he has encountered difficulties even with his nonstereotypical parts, such as an aide to attorney general candidate Angie Dickinson in the television movie *A Touch of Scandal*.

"When it came time to work, the director studiously tried to cover up my disability by using shots where my crutches didn't show because he felt he didn't have time to explain it. With smaller roles, you don't need to know why someone is disabled. In *Scandal* it really bothered me, not just physically, but because it would make sense that a political candidate would want that area of her constituency represented. On the other hand, it didn't bother me when I played a bartender on *WRKP in Cincinnati*. I was standing behind the bar, and there was no need for my crutches to show."

Frustration of a different nature is expressed by Templeton regarding her role on *The Young and the Restless*. "The times they've used me have been built mostly around disability issues, and they've done some wonderful things. And when scenes are questionable or offensive, I've always been able to change them. The exposure for me has been wonderful, but there's so much more that could be done. It's time to move past the disability issues, but they seem to be stuck."

Longmore points out that stereotypes also exist in nonfiction programs, such as *Real People* and *That's Incredible!*, and the news. "Stories usually have to do with the heroic overcoming of a disability—climbing a mountain, wheeling across the U.S. People are interviewed about coping and say they want to be inspirational to others. We're covered as human interest but rarely as hard news—job discrimination, architectural inaccessibility. Disabled people are not characterized as a social minority with civil rights but as victims of a tragic fate."

The one area which has shown progress in the past year or so, says Longmore, is that of television commercials. Advertisers are now beginning to recognize the disabled community as consumers, and fears are somewhat dissipating that disabled actors will "turn off" potential customers. McDonald's has aired its third commercial with disabled performers; others are featured in spots for Levi Strauss, Chrysler, Kodak and *People* magazine.

In addition to its casting and consultation functions, the Media Office produces showcases so that the work of disabled performers, writers, and directors can be seen by industry professionals. Performers are auditioned by a blue ribbon panel to ensure high-caliber talent. Says Mark Malis, Universal's vice-president of television casting and unofficial chairman of the showcase committee, "The industry people who come aren't expecting much, and when they see the scenes, they're knocked out. The performers immediately start to get work."

For less advanced actors and actresses, the Media Office awards scholarships for performing-related expenses; it also coordinates the annual Wallis Annenberg Scholarships for disabled California college students with media-related majors at any accredited California college.

Perhaps the enterprise's most visible activity remains the annual Media Access Awards, which recognize the contribution of producers, individuals, and corporations toward accurate portrayal of the disabled community in television, film, radio, theater, and print. The awards, which actually predate the Media Office, were developed in 1978 by producer Fern Field, then fresh from an Academy Award nomination for the disability-themed short *A Different Approach*. Under her guidance, and later, that of then-Showtime executive Loreen Arbus, the event has grown from a sparsely attended luncheon to a fund-raising, celebrity-studded evening supported by industry professionals and press. (The awards ceremony is the major source of Media Office funding, but fund-raising continues to be a challenge for the nonprofit endeavor.) This year's Seventh Annual Awards ceremony was highlighted by a speech by presenter Aaron Spelling, who said that prior to the evening he had erroneously thought his company had been fully utilizing the talents of the disabled community; he promised to do so in the future.

As for the Media Office's own future, Hartman and company hope to make greater strides in existing programs and branch out in new directions, such as working more with children, becoming involved with both the television and motion picture academies, and conducting research. Having been instrumental in creating the Writers Guild Committee on Disabilities, Hartman plans to implement programs for disabled writers and then directors, eventually encompassing every industry position. Lobbying activities, which this July resulted in the establishment of National Disabilities in Entertainment Week, will continue, as will efforts to make studios more accessible; there is now a permanent ramp to the MTM casting office and a dressing room with lift at Universal.

Actor Alan Toy—who is one of the better known disabled performers but who worked only one day as a SAG actor in the first nine months of this year—stresses that still more performance doors must open. "When you become disabled at an early age, it makes you more insightful—and isn't that what we're looking for in actors?" he asks rhetorically. "It makes you more intelligent in some respects, because you have to learn ways around things, and it makes you more sensitive, and doesn't the industry want intelligence and sensitivity in its actors?"

There are still attitudinal barriers, which can create more problems than the actual disability, to be alleviated. "As sensitized as I am, I've still had problems with my attitude regarding [using disabled people] in my own projects," acknowledges Fern Field. "We have to recognize the fact that we're going to feel uncomfortable about the concept, and realize that that's OK. Otherwise, you feel so guilt-ridden, so ashamed of being uncomfortable that you never get past that to deal with the people themselves."

And finally, reminds Christopher Templeton, "What able-bodied people have to realize is that they are only one accident away from being disabled themselves. If they did become disabled, would they want to be treated the way they've been treating us?"

TAKING ANOTHER LOOK

1 Why are activists in the disabled rights movement often critical of telethons, such as those run by Jerry Lewis, which raise money for charities serving the disabled?

2 Why are "nonspecific" parts so important for disabled actors? How does employment of disabled actors in "nonspecific" parts help to combat stereotypes associated with disabilities?

3 In the view of the Media Office, why should Americans avoid use of such terms as "crippled" and "handicapped"?

4 Why are disabled persons sometimes critical of the media's focus on the heroic overcoming of a disability?

5 Are there physical or other barriers at your college that create difficulties for students, professors, or employees with disabilities?

6 After reading Slate's article, are you more aware of stereotypes that you have held about persons with disabilities? Discuss.

Case Study of a Nonconscious Ideology: Training the Woman to Know Her Place

Sandra L. and Daryl J. Bem

The second wave of American feminism emerged in the 1960s and came into full force in the 1970s. In part, the movement was inspired by the publication of two pioneering books for women's rights: Simone de Beauvoir's *The Second Sex* and Betty Friedan's *The Feminine Mystique*. In addition, the general political activism of the 1960s led women (many of whom were working for black civil rights or against the war in Vietnam) to reexamine their own powerlessness as women. The sexism often found within allegedly progressive and radical political circles made many women decide that they needed to establish their own movement for "women's liberation."

More and more women became aware of sexist attitudes and practices—including attitudes they themselves had accepted through socialization into traditional sex roles—and began to challenge male dominance. A sense of "sisterhood," much like the class consciousness that Karl Marx hoped would emerge in the proletariat, became evident. No longer were women "happy" in submissive, subordinate roles ("false consciousness" in Marxist terms).

This new sense of group solidarity and loyalty was fostered within feminist consciousness-raising groups. In these small discussion groups, women shared their personal feelings, experiences, and conflicts. Many discovered that their "individual" problems were shared by other women and often reflected sexist conditioning and powerlessness. Such awareness of common oppression is a precondition for social change. Consciousness does not always lead to efforts to transform social conditions, but it is essential in mobilizing a group for collective action.

In the following selection, psychologists Sandra L. Bem and Daryl J. Bem argue that American society has maintained a powerful "nonconscious ideology" of traditional sex-role assumptions, which has motivated subtle practices that keep women in subservient positions. Bem and Bem suggest that this nonconscious ideology militates against the goal of self-fulfillment for women; they also criticize the "ideological rationalization" that men and women hold complementary but equal positions in society.

Early in their article, Bem and Bem discuss the importance of *reference groups* in socializing youths into the nonconscious ideology of sexism. Sociologists use the term *reference groups* when speaking of any group that individuals use as a standard for evaluating themselves and their own behavior.

We have seen what happens when an individual's reference groups conflict. Alternative ideologies are suddenly brought into his awareness, and he is forced to select explicitly his beliefs and attitudes from among the competing alternatives. But what happens when all his reference groups agree, when his religion, his family, his peers, his teachers, and the mass media all disseminate the same

Authors' note: The order of the authors' names was determined by the flip of a coin.

message? The consequence is a nonconscious ideology, a set of beliefs and attitudes which he accepts implicitly but which remains outside his awareness because alternative conceptions of the world remain unimagined. As we noted earlier, only a very unparochial and intellectual fish is aware that his environment is wet. After all, what else could it be? Such is the nature of a nonconscious ideology.

A society's ability to inculcate this kind of ideology into its citizens is the most subtle and most profound form of social influence. It is also the most difficult kind of social influence to challenge because it remains invisible. Even those who consider themselves sufficiently radical or intellectual to have rejected the basic premises of a particular societal ideology often find their belief systems unexpectedly cluttered with its remnants.

In our view, there is no ideology which better exemplifies these points than the beliefs and attitudes which most Americans hold about women. Not only do most men and women in our society hold hidden prejudices about the woman's "natural" role, but these nonconscious beliefs motivate a host of subtle practices that are dramatically effective at keeping her "in her place." Even many liberal Americans, who insist that a black skin should not uniquely qualify its owner for janitorial and domestic service, continue to assume that the possession of a uterus uniquely qualifies its owner for precisely that.

Consider, for example, the first student rebellion at Columbia Unversity, which took place in the spring of 1968. You will recall that students from the radical left took over some administration buildings in the name of equalitarian ideals which they accused the university of flouting. Here were the most militant spokesmen one could hope to find in the cause of equalitarian ideals. But no sooner had they occupied the buildings than the male militants blandly turned to their sisters-in-arms and assigned them the task of preparing the food, while they—the menfolk—would presumably plan further strategy. The reply they received was the reply they deserved, and the fact that domestic tasks behind the barricades were desegregated across the sex line that day is an everlasting tribute to the class consciousness of the ladies of the left.

But these coeds are not typical, for the nonconscious assumptions about the woman's "natural" role are at least as prevalent among women as they are among men. Philip Goldberg (1968) demonstrated this by asking female students to rate a number of professional articles from each of six fields. The articles were collated into two equal sets of booklets, and the names of the authors were changed so that the identical article was attributed to a male author (e.g., John T. McKay) in one set of booklets and to a female author (e.g., Joan T. McKay) in the other set. Each student was asked to read the articles in her booklet and to rate them for value, competence, persuasiveness, writing style, and so forth.

As he had anticipated, Goldberg found that the same article received significantly lower ratings when it was attributed to a female author than when it was attributed to a male author. He had predicted this result for articles from professional fields generally considered the province of men, such as law and city planning, but to his surprise the female students also downgraded articles by female authors drawn from the fields of dietetics and elementary school education. In other words, these women rated the male authors as better at everything, agreeing with Aristotle that "we should regard the female nature as afflicted with a natural defectiveness." We repeated this experiment informally in our own classrooms and discovered that male students show the same implicit prejudice against female authors that Goldberg's female students showed. Such is the nature of a nonconscious ideology!

It is significant that examples like these can be drawn from the college world, for today's college generation has the least investment in perpetuating the established ways of looking at most issues, including the role of women. As we noted in our discussion of sexual conduct, today's college students have been quick to reject those attitudes of their parents which conflict explicitly with the students' major values. But as the above examples suggest, they will find it far more difficult to shed some of the more subtle aspects of a sex-role ideology which—as we shall now attempt to demonstrate—conflicts just as surely with their existential values as any of the explicit parental commands to which they have so effectively raised objection. It is thus by examining America's sex-role ideology within the framework of values held by the most aware and sensitive of today's youth that we can best illustrate the power and pervasiveness of the social influences that produce non-conscious ideologies in a society.

THE IDEOLOGY VERSUS THE VALUE OF SELF-FULFILLMENT

The dominant values of today's student culture concern personal growth, on the one hand, and interpersonal relationships, on the other. Accordingly, one subset of these values emphasizes the importance of individuality and self-fulfillment; the other stresses openness, honesty, and equality in all human relationships.

The major corollary of the self-fulfillment value is that each human being, male or female, is to be encouraged to "do his own thing." Men and women are no longer to be stereotyped by society's definitions. If sensitivity, emotionality, and warmth are desirable human characteristics, then they are desirable for men as well as for women. (John Wayne is no longer an idol of the young, but their pop satire.) If independence, assertiveness, and serious intellectual commitment are desirable human characteristics, then they are desirable for women as well as for men. The major prescription of this college generation is that each individual should be encouraged to discover and fulfill his own unique potential and identity, unfettered by society's presumptions.

But society's presumptions enter the scene much earlier than most people suspect, for parents begin to raise their children in accord with popular stereotypes from the very beginning.

Boys are encouraged to be aggressive, competitive, and independent, whereas girls are rewarded for being passive and dependent (Barry, Bacon, & Child, 1957; Sears, Maccoby, & Levin, 1957). In one study, six-month-old infant girls were already being touched and spoken to more by their mothers than were infant boys. When they were thirteen months old, these girls were more reluctant than the boys to leave their mothers; they returned more quickly and more frequently to them; and they remained closer to them throughout the entire session. When a physical barrier was placed between mother and child, the girls tended to cry and motion for help; the boys made more active attempts to get around the barrier (Goldberg & Lewis, 1969). There is no way of knowing for sure to what extent these sex differences at the age of thirteen months can be attributed to the differences in the mothers' behavior at the age of six months, but it is hard to believe that the two are unconnected.

As children grow older, more explicit sex-role training is introduced. Boys are encouraged to take more of an interest in mathematics and science. Boys, not girls, are given chemistry sets and microscopes for Christmas. Moreover, all children quickly learn that mommy is proud to be a moron when it comes to mathematics and science, whereas daddy knows all about those things. When a young boy returns from school all excited over a biology class, he is almost certain to be encouraged to think of becoming a physician. A girl with similar enthusiasm is told that she might want to consider nurse's training later so she can have "an interesting job to fall back upon in case —God forbid—she ever needs to support herself." A very different kind of encouragement. And a girl who doggedly persists in her enthusiasm for science is likely to find her parents as horrified by the prospect of a permanent love affair with physics as they would be by the prospect of an interracial marriage.

These socialization practices have their effect. By the ninth grade, 25% of the boys, but only 3% of the girls, are considering careers in science and engineering. (In the Soviet Union, approximately 35% of the engineers are women.) When they apply for college, boys and girls are about equal on verbal aptitude tests—about 60 points higher on the College Board examinations, for example (Brown, 1965, p. 162). Those who would attribute such differences to feminine hormones should know that girls improve their mathematical performance if problems are reworded so that they deal with cooking and gardening, even though the abstract reasoning required for their solutions remains the same (Milton, 1958). It would appear that both motivation and ability have been affected.

The effects in mathematics and science are only part of the story. A girl's long training in passivity and dependence appears to exact a similar toll from her overall motivation to achieve, to search for new and independent ways of doing things, and to welcome the challenge of new and unsolved problems. Psychologists have found that elementary school girls are more likely to try solving a puzzle by imitating an adult, whereas boys are more likely to search for a novel solution not provided by the adult (McDavid, 1959). Furthermore, when given the opportunity to return to puzzles a second time, girls are more likely to rework those they had already solved, whereas the boys are more likely to try puzzles they had been unable to solve previously (Crandall & Rabson, 1960). One almost expects to hear an audible sigh of relief when a woman marries and retires from the outside world of novel and unsolved problems. This, of course, is the most conspicuous outcome of all: the majority of American women become full-time homemakers.

Such are the consequences of a nonconscious ideology.

But how does all of this militate against the goal of self-fulfillment? First of all it should be clear that the value of self-fulfillment is not necessarily being violated just because some people may regard the role of homemaker as inferior to other roles. That is not the point. Rather, the point is that our society is managing to consign a large segment of its population to the role of homemaker solely on the basis of sex just as inexorably as it has in the past consigned individuals with black skin to the roles of janitor and domestic. It is not the role itself which is at issue here, but the fact that, in spite of their unique identities, the majority of America's women end up in the *same* role.

Even if this is so, however, there are several arguments which can be advanced to counter the claim that America's socialization of its women violates the value of self-fulfillment. The three most common arguments invoke respectively (1) free will, (2) biology, and (3) complementarity.

1 The free will argument proposes that a 21-year-old woman is perfectly free to choose some other role if she cares to do so; no one is standing in her way. But this argument overlooks the fact that society, which has spent twenty years carefully marking the woman's ballot for her, has nothing to lose in the twenty-first year by pretending that she may cast it for the alternative of her choice. Society has controlled not her alternatives, but her motivation to choose any but one of those alternatives. The so-called freedom to choose is illusory and cannot be invoked when the society controls the motivation to choose.

2 The biological argument suggests that there may really be physiological differences between men and women in, say, aggressiveness or mathematical ability. Or that there may be biological factors (beyond the fact that women can become pregnant and nurse children) which uniquely dictate that women, but not men, should stay home all day and shun serious outside commitment. Maybe female hormones really are somehow responsible. One difficulty with the argument is that female hormones would have to be different in the Soviet Union, where women comprise 75% of the physicians and, as noted above, about 35% of the engineers, and where only one married woman in twenty is a full-time homemaker. Female physiology is different, and it may account for some of the psychological differences between the sexes, but most psychologists, including us, continue to believe that it is America's sex-role ideology which causes so few women to emerge from childhood with the motivation to seek out any role other than the one that society has dictated.

But even if there really were biological differences between the sexes along these lines, the biological argument would still be irrelevant. The reason can best be illustrated with an analogy.

Those who subscribe to the value of self-fulfillment would be outraged, we submit, if every black American boy were to be socialized to become a jazz musician on the assumption that he has a "natural" talent in that direction, and if black parents should subtly discourage their sons from other pursuits because it is "inappropriate" for black men to become physicians or physicists. But suppose that it *could* be demonstrated that black Americans, *on the average*, did possess an innate better sense of rhythm than white Americans. Would that change outrage to acquiescence? Would that argue that a *particular* black youngster should have his unique characteristics ignored from the very beginning and that he should be specifically socialized to become a musician? We don't think so. Similarly, as long as a woman's socialization does not nurture her uniqueness, but treats her only as a member of a group on the basis of some assumed *average* characteristic, she will not be prepared to realize her own potential in the way that the values of today's college students imply she should.

The irony of the biological argument is that it does not take biological differences seriously enough. That is, it fails to recognize the range of biological differences between individuals within the same group category. Thus, recent research has revealed that biological factors help determine many personality traits. For example, the personality traits of dominance and submissiveness have been found to have large inheritable components; that is, biological factors have the potential for partially determining how dominant or submissive an individual male or female, will

turn out to be. But this potential is realized more frequently in males (Gottesman, 1963). Apparently, only the males in our culture are raised with sufficient flexibility, with sufficient latitude given to their biological differences, for their "natural" or biologically determined potential to shine through. The females, it would appear, are subjected to a socialization which so ignores their unique attributes that even the effects of biology are swamped. In sum, the biological argument for continuing America's homogenization of its women gets hoist with its own petard.

3 Many people recognize that most women do end up as full-time homemakers because of their socialization and that these women exemplify the failure of our society to raise girls as unique individuals. But, they point out, the role of homemaker is not inferior to the role of the professional man: it is complementary but equal.

This argument is usually bolstered by pointing to the joys of taking care of small children. Indeed, mothers *and* fathers find child-rearing rewarding. But the argument appears weak when one considers that the average American woman now lives to age 74 and has her last child in her late twenties; thus, by the time the woman is 33 or so, her children all have more important things to do with their daylight hours than spend them entertaining an adult woman who has nothing to do during the second half of her life-span. As for the other "joys" of homemaking, many writers (e.g., Friedan, 1963) have persuasively argued that the role of the homemaker has been glamorized far beyond its intrinsic worth. This charge becomes plausible when one considers that the average American homemaker spends the equivalent of a man's working day, 7.1 hours, in preparing meals, cleaning house, laundering, mending, shopping, and doing other household tasks. In other words, 43% of her waking time is spent in work that commands an hourly wage on the open market well below the federally set minimum wage for menial industrial work.

The point is not how little she would earn if she did these things in someone else's home, but that this use of time is virtually the same for home-makers with college degrees and for those with less than a grade school education, for women married to professional men and for women married to blue-collar workers. Talent, education, ability, interests, motivations—all are irrelevant. In our society, being female uniquely qualifies an individual for domestic work.

It is true, however, that the American home-maker has, on the average, 5.1 hours of leisure time per day, and it is here, we are told, that each woman can express her unique identity. Thus, politically interested women can join the League of Women Voters; women with humane interests can become part-time Gray Ladies; women who love music can raise money for the symphony; and so forth.

But politically interested men run for Congress. Men with humane interests become physicians or clinical psychologists; men who love music play in the symphony; and so forth. In other words, in our society a woman's unique identity most often determines only the periphery of her life rather than its central core.

Again, the important point is not that the role of homemaker is necessarily inferior, but that the woman's unique identity has been rendered irrelevant. Consider the following "predictability test." When a boy is born, it is difficult to predict what he will be doing 25 years later. We cannot say whether he will be an artist or a doctor or a college professor because he will be permitted to develop and to fulfill his own unique identity, particularly if he is white and middle-class. But if the newborn child is a girl, we can usually predict with confidence how she will be spending her time 25 years later. Her individuality doesn't have to be considered because it will be irrelevant.

The socialization of the American male has closed off certain options for him too. Men are discouraged from developing certain traits such as tenderness and sensitivity just as surely as women are discouraged from being assertive and "too bright." Young boys are encouraged to be incom-petent at cooking and child care just as surely as young girls are urged to be incompetent at mathematics and science.

One of the errors of the early feminist movement in this country was that it assumed that men had all the goodies and that women could attain self-fulfillment merely by being like men. But that is hardly the utopia that today's college students envision. Rather, the logical extension of their value of self-fulfillment would require that society raise its children so that some men might emerge with the motivation, the ability, and the opportunity to stay home and raise children without bearing the stigma of being peculiar. If home-making is as glamorous as the women's magazines portray it, then men too should have the option of becoming homemakers. Even if homemaking isn't all that glamorous, it would probably still be more fulfilling for some men than the jobs in which they now find themselves.

And if biological differences really do exist between men and women in "nurturance," in their innate motivations to care for children, then this will show up automatically in the final distribution of men and women across the various roles: relatively fewer men will choose to stay at home. The value of self-fulfillment, therefore, does not imply that there must be equality of outcome, an equal number of men and women in each role. It does imply that there should be the widest possible variation in outcome consistent with the range of individual differences among people, regardless of sex. At the very least, the value of self-fulfillment would seem to imply that the society should raise its males so that they could fulfill their own identities in activities that might be less remunerative than those being pursued by their wives without feeling that they were "living off their wives." One rarely hears it said of a woman that she is "living off her husband."

Thus, it is true that men's options are also limited by our society's sex-role ideology, but as the "predictability test" reveals, it is still the women in our society whose identities are rendered irrelevant by America's socialization practices. In 1954 the United States Supreme Court declared that a fraud and hoax lay behind the slogan "separate but equal." It is unlikely that any court will ever do the same for the more subtle motto that successfully keeps the woman in her place: "complementary but equal."

THE IDEOLOGY VERSUS THE VALUE OF INTERPERSONAL EQUALITY

The ideological rationalization that men and women hold complementary but equal positions in society appears to be a fairly recent invention. In earlier times—and in more conservative company today—it was not felt necessary to provide the ideology with an equalitarian veneer. Indeed, the basic assumptions of the ideology have frequently been stated quite explicitly. There is certainly nothing subtle or non-conscious about the moral to be drawn from what happened In the Beginning:

> In the beginning God created the heaven and the earth .... And God said, Let us make man in our image, after our likeness; and let them have dominion over the fish of the sea, and over the fowl of the air, and over the cattle, and over all the earth .... And the rib, which the Lord God had taken from man, made he a woman and brought her unto the man.... And the Lord God said unto the woman, What is this that thou has done? And the woman said, The serpent beguiled me, and I did eat.... Unto the woman he [God] said, I will greatly multiply thy sorrow and thy conception; in sorrow thou shalt bring forth children; and thy desire shall be to thy husband, and he shall rule over thee. (Gen. 1, 2, 3)

> For a man .... is the image and glory of God; but the woman is the glory of the man. For the man is not of the woman, but the woman of the man. Neither was the man created for the woman, but the woman for the man .... Let your women keep silence in the churches; for it is not permitted unto them to speak, but they are commanded to be under obedience, as also saith the law. And if they will learn anything, let them ask their husbands at home, for it is a shame for women to speak in the church.

> (1 Cor. 11, 14)

> Wives, submit yourselves to your own husbands, as unto the Lord. For the husband is the head of the wife, even as Christ is the head of the church; and he is the savior of the body. Therefore, as the church is subject unto Christ, so let the wives be to their own husbands in everything. (Eph. 5)

> Let the woman learn silence with all subjection. But I suffer not a woman to teach, nor to usurp authority over the man, but to be in silence. For Adam was first formed, then Eve. And Adam was not deceived, but the woman, being deceived, was in the transgression. Notwithstanding, she shall be saved in childbearing, if they continue in faith and charity and holiness with sobriety. (1 Tim. 2)

And lest it be thought that only Christians have this rich heritage of ideology, consider the morning prayer of the Orthodox Jew:

> Blessed art Thou, oh Lord, our God, King of the Universe, that I was not born a gentile.
> Blessed art Thou, oh Lord our God, King of the Universe, that I was not born a slave.
> Blessed art Thou, oh Lord our God, King of the Universe, that I was not born a woman.

Or the Koran, the sacred text of Islam:

> Men are superior to women on account of the qualities in which God has given them pre-eminence.

The sex-role ideology in these passages is hardly ambiguous, and many young people are horrified to learn that such radical inequality between the sexes is advocated in the theological literature of their own religion. Because they value equalitarian relationships generally, they are quick to reject this traditional view of the male-female relationship, and an increasing number of them even plan to enter marriages very much like the following hypothetical example.

> Both my wife and I earned Ph.D. degrees in our respective disciplines. I turned down a superior academic post in Oregon and accepted a slightly less desirable position in New York where my wife could obtain a part-time teaching job and do research at one of the several other colleges in the area. Al-

though I would have prefered to live in a suburb, we purchased a home near my wife's college so that she could have an office at home where she would be when the children returned from school. Because my wife earns a good salary, she can easily afford to pay a maid to do her major household chores. My wife and I share all other tasks around the house equally. For example, she cooks the meals, but I do the laundry for her and help her with many of her other household tasks.

Without questioning the basic happiness of such a marriage or its appropriateness for many couples, we can legitimately ask if such a marriage is, in fact, an instance of the interpersonal equality so many young people claim to value these days. Have all the hidden assumptions about the woman's "natural" role really been eliminated? Has the traditional ideology really been exorcised?   There is a very simple test. If the marriage is truly equalitarian, then its description should retain the same flavor and tone even if the roles of the husband and wife were to be reversed:

Both my husband and I earned Ph.D. degrees in our respective disciplines. I turned down a superior academic post in Oregon and accepted a slightly less desirable position in New York where my husband could obtain a part-time teaching job and do research at one of the several other colleges in the area. Although I would have preferred to live in a suburb, we purchased a home near my husband's college so that he could have an office at home where he would be when the children returned from school. Because my husband earns a good salary, he can easily afford to pay a maid to do his major household chores. My husband and I share all other tasks around the house equally. For example, he cooks the meals, but I do the laundry for him and help him with many of his other household tasks.

It seems unlikely that many men or women in our society would mistake this marriage as either equalitarian or desirable, and thus it becomes apparent that the ideology about the woman's "natural" role nonconsciously permeates the entire fabric of such marriages. The point here is not that such marriages are bad or that their basic as-

sumptions of inequality produce unhappy, frustrated women. Quite the contrary. It is the very happiness of the wives in such marriages that reveals society's success in socializing its women. It is a measure of the distance our society must yet traverse toward the goals of self-fulfillment and interpersonal equality that such marriages are widely characterized as utopian and fully equalitarian. It is a mark of how well the woman has been kept in her place that the husband in such a marriage is often idolized by women, including his wife, for permitting her to squeeze a career into the interstices of their marriage so long as his own career is not unduly inconvenienced. Thus is the white man blessed for exercising his power benignly while his "natural" right to that power remains forever unquestioned.

Such is the subtlety of a nonconscious ideology!

The existential values of today's young people would seem to require marriages in which the careers or outside commitments of both partners carry equal weight when important decisions are to be made and in which the division of labor satisfies what might be called a "roommate test." That is, the labor is divided just as it is when two men or two women room together in college or set up a bachelor apartment together. Errands and domestic chores are assigned by preference, agreement, flipping a coin, given to hired help, or —as is frequently the case—left undone.

It is significant that today's young people, many of whom live this way prior to marriage, seem to find that this kind of arrangement within marriage is foreign to their thinking. Consider an analogy. Suppose that a white male college student decided to room or set up a bachelor apartment with a black male friend. Surely the typical white student would not blithely assume that his black roommate was to handle all the domestic chores. Nor would his conscience allow him to do so even in the unlikely event that his roommate would say, "No, that's okay. I don't mind the domestic chores. In fact, I'd be happy to do them." We suspect that the typical white student would still not be comfortable if he took advantage of this offer, if he took advantage of the fact that his roommate had been socialized to be "happy" with such an arrangement. But change this hypothetical black roommate to a female marriage partner and somehow the student's conscience goes to sleep. At most it is quickly tranquilized by the thought that "she is happiest when she is ironing for her loved one." Such is the power of a nonconscious ideology.

Of course, it may well be that she *is* happiest when she is ironing for her loved one.

Such, indeed, is the power of a nonconscious ideology!

REFERENCES

Barry H., III, Bacon, M. K., and Child, I. L. A cross-cultural survey of some sex differences in socialization. *Journal of Abnormal and Social Psychology*, 1957, *55*, 327–332.

Brown, R. *Social psychology*. New York: Free Press, 1965.

Crandall, V. J., and Rabson, A. Children's repetition choices in an intellectual achievement situation following success and failure. *Journal of Genetic Psychology*, 1960, *97*, 161–168.

Friedan, B. *The feminine mystique*. New York: Norton, 1963.

Goldberg, P. Are women prejudiced against women? *Transaction*, April 1968, *5*, 28–30.

Goldberg, S., and Lewis, M. Play behavior in the year-old infant: Early sex differences. *Child Development*, 1969, *40*, 21–31.

Gottesman, I. I. Heritability of personality: A demonstration. *Psychological Monographs*, 1963, *77* (Whole No. 572).

McDavid, J. W. Imitative behavior in preschool children. *Psychological Monographs*, 1959, *73* (Whole No. 486).

Sears, R. R., Maccoby, E. E., and Levin, H. *Patterns of child rearing*. Evanston, Ill.: Row, Peterson, 1957.

TAKING ANOTHER LOOK

1 What were the findings of Philip Goldberg's study of students' assumptions about female and male authors?

2 How do Bem and Bem counter the "free will argument" as it applies to women?

3 How do Bem and Bem counter the biological argument that there may really be physiological differences between men and women in such areas as aggressiveness or mathematical ability?

4 How do Bem and Bem respond to the argument that the position of homemaker is "complementary but equal" to that of the professional man?

5 How would functionalist theorists be likely to view the arguments made by Bem and Bem?

6 How would conflict theorists be likely to view the arguments made by Bem and Bem?

Careers of Men and Women MBAs: 1950–1980

Sharon Tucker

American women are participating increasingly more frequently in the nation's paid labor force. No longer is the adult woman being confined solely to the role of homemaker. Instead, millions of women (married and single, with children and childless) are working outside the home. In fact, a greater proportion of women are seeking and obtaining paid employment than ever before in American history. By 1984, more than 54 percent of adult American women held jobs outside the home, as compared with 43 percent in 1970. A majority of women in 1984 were members of the paid labor force, not full-time homemakers.

Women continue to be underrepresented in occupations historically defined as "men's jobs," which often carry much greater financial rewards and prestige than traditional "women's jobs." For example, in 1982 women accounted for roughly 43 percent of the nation's paid labor force. Yet, they represented only 6 percent of all engineers, 7 percent of all artisans, 15 percent of all physicians and dentists, and 15 percent of all lawyers and judges.

In 1981, women held only 6 percent of all managerial positions in the United States, and many of these women reported to higher-level male executives. In addition, women own only 7 percent of all businesses in the United States, and these firms account for less than 7 percent of all business receipts. Despite these dismal statistics, women now account for more than one-fourth of all students pursuing a master of business administration (MBA) degree.

In the following selection, sociologist Sharon Tucker reports on her study of men and women who received an MBA degree between 1950 and 1978. Tucker hoped to examine how the careers of female MBAs had changed over the last three decades and also how the careers of male MBAs compared to women during this time period. Relying on intensive interviewing of a small sample, Tucker found that "careers for men and women unfolded differently in every decade. Women of all decades lagged behind men in salary and authority." Moreover, women rarely held positions in business firms; they were more likely to be found in alternate settings, such as universities.

I'm not unhappy. I mean I think that [my business] has done very well. You might say we're not going to be the biggest in the world, but we're not small. You might say a rewarding life. Things could be worse, a lot worse. [partner in a small business, MBA '55, male]

I really didn't have a career goal, say 20 years ago, for myself. I was willing to do this or willing to do that, so you might say that I've just done things as they've come along. [high school teacher, MBA '57, female]

I'm very satisfied .... I would think that the next position would be president of our division. I think that is a reasonable bet. [vice president, MBA '66, male]

Author's Note: I wish to thank Walter R. Nord, Seymour Sarason, and two anonymous reviewers for their comments on an earlier draft of this article. This research was funded by a grant from Washington University in St. Louis.

I began going to different corporations, and I was repeatedly told to take typing tests .... I had been really naive. I thought I would be in demand .... I ended up going to an employment agency, which was unheard of for an MBA. [management consultant, MBA '66, female]

I'm a little concerned about my future with this large company. In the department I'm in .... an education is not stressed, and also my growth channels are not well defined. So I'm not really sure what my next position would be with this company. [investment analyst, MBA '71, male]

They have come right out and told me because I am a woman I was better off staying in a staff position, because women move better [in staff rather than line positions]. My whole problem is that I don't want to stay in a staff position [accounting liaison, MBA '74, female].

These quotes from men and women who received the MBA between 1950 and 1978 illustrate the changing experiences of men and women who came of age at different times in history. The purpose of this research was to explore first how the careers of female MBAs changed over the last three decades and second how the careers of men compared to women's over this time period. Research on doctors and lawyers who received degrees prior to 1974 found that women tended to work in different settings than their male counterparts, being concentrated in teaching institutions and public organizations rather than private practice (Yohalem, 1979:60). One important question was whether this pattern would hold for women with MBAs.

Whether or not female MBAs enter, remain, and experience success in business firms is important for two reasons. First, MBA programs are designed primarily to train business managers. Students who enter graduate business schools generally expect to get a union card that will allow them access to the higher echelons of the coporate world or smaller businesses. Failure to get that access is often a defeat. Second, business firms, es-

pecially large corporations, offer opportunities for personal income that have not been available in settings traditionally staffed by women. Management success has the potential for reducing the income gap between men and women.

In undertaking this research there was reason to believe that women of the 1970s would have very different career experiences than earlier cohorts. The Civil Rights Act of 1964 guaranteed legal equality to women in the work place. By the 1970s, suits had reached the Supreme Court and the EEOC had gained enforcement powers (Burstein, 1979). In addition, women had increasingly accepted the appropriateness of working while raising a family (Mason et al., 1976). More recent data indicate a tapering off of social change, though gender role attitudes are still more liberal than they were prior to the 1960s (Cherlin and Walters, 1981).

On the other hand, research published in the seventies did not find major improvements in career opportunities for women. Kanter (1977) observed that women were more likely than men to be blocked in career advancement, and a large body of research found discrimination against women in hiring (Shaw, 1972; Rosen and Jerdee, 1974, 1975; Dipboye et al., 1975; Haefner, 1977), in pay (Wolf and Fligstein, 1979; Terborg and Ilgen, 1975; Taylor, 1979), and in promotion (Day and Stogdill, 1972; Rosen and Jerdee, 1975), particularly in promotion to positions of authority(Wolf and Fligstein, 1979).

If men's and women's careers unfolded differently over the last three decades, discrimination may have been one cause. A second cause may have been women's family responsibilities. Mortimer, Hall, and Hill (1978) described a number of structural aspects to a husband's career that interfere with his wife's career. Ferber and Loeb (1974) found that married, female professors earned substantially less than single women. In a similar vein, Pfeffer and Ross (1982) found that men with employed wives earned less than men with homemaker wives. They argued that a nonemployed wife is an additional resource to the organization for which the husband is compensated. Because career women almost never have "wives," their careers may be expected to suffer if they are married and have children.

This study was an effort to extend current knowledge by following the career paths of men and women who had prepared for business management—both those who succeeded and those who failed—tracking the experience of the different graduating cohorts.

METHOD

The method used for this study was intensive interviewing of a small sample of men and women to explore their career experiences. The intent was to elicit descriptions of the ways these people saw the world and then to look for patterns in their very personal experiences. There were two reasons for choosing this method. First, the study was exploratory. Although there are data demonstrating liberalizing of the female work role, little is yet known about the particular experiences of career women. It was premature to test hypotheses on a large sample. Second, the open-ended qualitative nature allowed men and women to tell their own stories without the contraints of response categories. This made it possible to know not only what happened to people, but also in glowing terms to know how they felt about their careers and how they made sense of what had happened to them.

Sample

Respondents were drawn from a population of men and women who received the MBA from Washington University in St. Louis between 1950 and 1978 and were listed in the alumni records. All degrees were generalist; there were no majors in this particular MBA program. A total of 10 men and 10 women were randomly selected from each decade of graduates. There were only five women in the fifties and ten women in the sixties who received MBAs. All of these women were

contacted. In comparison, there were 187 men who received MBAs in the fifties and 575 men who received MBAs in the sixties. In the seventies, 910 men received MBAs compared to 121 women. Sampling with replacement was used in the three male categories and in the seventies female category, yielding a final sample of 46 respondents from 66 selected. Of the 66, 13 were never contacted either because they were not locatable or were not a home when the interviewer called. There was a 7.3% refusal rate among those contacted, with men making up three-fourths of those who refused. Three interviews were discarded due to malfunctions in the tape recording process. In all, there were 5 women and 8 men who graduated in the fifties, 7 women and 9 men who graduated in the sixties, and 8 women and 9 men who graduated in the seventies.

Even though the research was exploratory, random selection of the sample was important because it reduced the probability that the experiences of these individuals were different in any systematic way from the experiences of other Washington University MBAs. Most of those not located were men (69%) and most of the refusals (75%) were by men. Therefore, the male respondents may have been somewhat less mobile and more willing to discuss their work lives than were the total group of male MBAs. The women interviewed should have been very much like the total population of women.

Most of the sample had been employed continuously since receiving the MBA. The median time out of the workforce for women was five months, so that women had slightly less experience than men. The interviews were done in 1980, making the amount of experience range from 30 years for the earliest fifties graduates to 2 years for the latest seventies grads.

Although the sample was drawn with the intent of making these respondents similar to the entire pool of Washington University MBAs, no claims of generalizability are made. Rather, the qualitative method was used to specify the particular experiences of a group of people and to develop hypotheses that could be tested on other samples drawn from other populations.

Interviews

Each respondent was interviewed by telephone using an interview guide consisting of open-ended questions designed to explore a variety of career, work quality, and job outcomes issues. Respondents were guaranteed anonymity to increase the likelihood that their responses would be valid. The interviews were conversational and exploratory in nature, yielding a set of rich personal perceptions, descriptions, and anecdotes. Each interview lasted from 30 minutes to an hour.

Data Analysis

Interviews were content analyzed for patterns or themes that distinguished one group from another. Nearly all of the analysis was purely qualitative, scanning the interviews for the commonalities and differences in the perceptions of the individuals studied. Some simple statistical procedures, reported in the findings section, were used to examine salary and authority data. All names used in the findings section are pseudonyms.

FINDINGS

Women's Careers

There were striking and important differences in the career outcomes of the women graduating in the three decades. A career is here defined as a sequence of jobs associated with certain positions in the labor force (Spillerman, 1977), in particular the positions in business usually occupied by people who have the MBA.

Despite their professional training, women of the fifties were likely to be unconcerned about a career. Five women were interviewed. Of these five women who were the entire group of female MBAs to graduate in the fifties, only two had ca-

reer ambitions. As might be expected, the three without ambitions had not had definable careers. One sold residential real estate, one was a high school teacher who had spent a number of years helping her husband in his job as a manufacturer's representative, the third was in retail sales in a department store. The real estate agent described her work experiences.

> Well, I don't really much look upon it as a career. The times they are a changing, and what is looked upon as a career today is really a full time idea. . . . I really suspect I have the best of all possible worlds, because I have the ability to work at something when I want to. . . . I think of a career as being something very high powered.

Two women had very clear career ambitions. One of these women had been able to climb to a high rank in her corporation. She had held a number of management positions, had been promoted regularly, and had a salary in excess of $50,000 a year. The other woman, however, had gone into industrial sales and had found tremendous barriers for women. In spite of the fact that she had been willing to transfer 9 or 10 times at the company's request, she had never been promoted to a management position and her salary after 25 years of service was under $30,000. Out of all the fifties women who got MBAs, only one out of five had advanced up a corporate ladder and become a manager, even though the major purpose of the degree is preparation for management.

There were ten women who received the MBA during the sixties; seven of them were interviewed. Women who graduated in the sixties had a very difficult time establishing their careers. Only two of them had continued to work in a corporate setting, even though all of them had entered corporations after receiving their degrees. Of those two, one was a stockbroker who had had great difficulty getting initial jobs and who had switched to an independent consulting position within a brokerage. The other believed she had not been on the same career track as men and had not been promoted. At age 50 she was earning

$23,000 as a market researcher. Of the remaining five sixties graduates, three left the corporation for independent work in consulting, teaching, or as an entrepreneur. Their corporate experiences ranged from traumatic to acceptable but without a future. One sixties grad, Linda McKenzie, who finally became an independent management consultant, described her early career experiences.

> Anyway, we went through two years of graduate school. At the end of that, I was looking for a job, of course, and it was the height of the Vietnam War, and I had met Jack there, who is now my husband. Jack was going on interviews, flying all over the country being interviewed. I had sent my resume all over the country likewise, and I did not get one offer, not one. And I have this feeling, I'm babysitting his cat while he is going all over the country on these interviews. . . . I came back to City X, which is my home. I began going to corporations. I was repeatedly told to take typing tests. . . . I had really been naive. I thought I would be in demand. Still in City X and not one job. I ended up going to an employment agency, which was unheard of for an MBA. . . . I was working for Corporation XXX and I worked for them for four months and was fired. [She reports that sexual harassment was involved] . . . . Then Jack was living in City Y, and we decided to get married. I moved to City Y and I began the whole process anew of looking for a job and not being able to find one, then going to another employment agency and then finding a job in marketing. My concentration was in marketing. . . . I quit there because I did not have a very good work experience there.

Linda's experience was very similar to all of the other sixties graduates who found getting first jobs in their fields nearly impossible or who were blocked soon after they began their careers.

The remaining two sixties graduates had negative corporate experiences and were out of the workforce raising families. Both expressed a value of being at home with young children and did not say that their choice to quit work was related to unfulfilling work experiences. But neither had any definite plans to return to work. They had worked for a number of years before starting families, and clearly their work experiences had been negative enough that the incentives to return to work were weak. Roberta Jackson described her time in a corporation.

> I went into retailing with the WWW Company, and I would assume that I probably worked five years with them. . . . I left for two reasons. First, I didn't like the kind of person I was becoming in it, and secondly I was out and out told by the personnel man that I could earn no more money because I was a single female. It made no difference that I had a better work record and a much better profit record than the man in linens who had six kids. and I felt that there was no reason that his incompetency or lack of birth control information should affect my salary. . . . And the third reason was . . . they told me my next move was to buy training bras, junior lingerie. And I said that they had to be kidding. That was a department that was just not my field.

Both women who were out of the workforce raising children reported great frustration in their work lives prior to their choice to quit work.

Women who graduated in the seventies did not choose careers in corporations in great numbers. Of the nine women interviewed, four started in corporations, a smaller percentage than in the sixties. Of those, one has already dropped out with hopes of starting her own company, though she is now unemployed. One has recently started a job in personnel and feels positive about her future. The remaining two have questions about whether they will be promoted. One has been told she cannot be promoted in the line positions she desires. The other, a public accountant, is bothered by the time she spends away from her children and wants to cut back to part-time. She fears that working part-time will destroy her career.

Five of the women never attempted a corporate career. One is an accountant for a university, so her career experiences might be similar to those entering corporations. However, she received her

MBA late in her life and expects no further advancement. Two seventies graduates entered less complex organizational settings. One is a management recruiter for a small firm; the other is an MBA admissions director in a university who would need a Ph.D. to advance in that setting. Finally, two women have not worked outside the home since receiving their degrees. One brought a severely handicapped child home from an institution during her work on her MBA and has since stayed home to attend to the child's needs. The other will begin work when both of her children are in school.

In sum, there has been very little movement among this sample of female MBAs toward management positions that have the potential for large rewards in income and power. In fact, a smaller percentage of women in the seventies started out in management tracks than in the sixties.

In these cohorts, none of the women who achieved responsible management positions was less family oriented than the women who attempted management careers but were blocked. In the fifties, both women who went into corporations had husbands who strongly supported their careers to the extent of transferring, agreeing to live apart, and performing social duties for the company. Yet one reached upper middle management and the other never became a manager. Sixties women who remained in the corporation and those who left were equally likely to be married with children, divorced with children, or single. No one in this group reported either strong support or great demands from their families. The two who left their careers for homemaking had either very negative or mildly frustrating corporate experiences for many years prior to becoming parents. Among seventies graduates a single woman felt stuck in a corporation, a married woman optimistic about her corporate career, a remarried divorcee with children left corporate employment and planned to start her own business. Of the employed women who never worked in corporations, one was single, one was divorced without children, one was married without children. In sum, for no

cohort does family orientation explain career differences.

Men's Careers

Like the women, male graduates of the fifties tended not to choose corporate careers, but as a group they attained positions of authority and reasonably high income (see Tables 1 and 2). Three of the eight in this group had been unusually successful, attaining positions as corporate vice presidents and earning $100,000 or more. The other five did not work in corporate settings. One had spent most of his working life in a single corporation but had taken early retirement, apparently because he was aligned with a losing political faction within the firm. Two were in family businesses, and two taught in universities. There was considerable variance among fifties men in the amount of authority and income accorded them, but the range for the men began at a much higher level that it did for the women. Therefore, using the standards of power and income, men were far more successful than women who graduated in the fifties.

In contrast to sixties women and even fifties men, nearly all of the male graduates of the sixties entered corporate careers and made acceptable progress as they started. Only one did not begin in a corporate setting, and he made his career in the armed services, an organizational setting as complex and stratified as any corporation. The paths careers took after the outset diverged somewhat. After steady promotion, one had become a vice president over half of his company. Another was the financial vice president for a small firm. Similarly, the military man had made steady progress up the ladder, and though he was not near the top, he saw no limit to his advancement.

Three others had been promoted and given increasingly more responsibility when they were younger but had plateaued and expected no further advancement. They did not plan to leave the corporate setting even though their futures were blocked. Jim Martin illustrates the experience of early success that plateaued.

I: Did [the MBA] pay off?

JM: I was chosen for positions that would lead to management very early, and subsequently I've been in management really since 1963. I was in a staff position in 1961, so within a year of my graduation, my success, such as it's been, started almost immediately.

I: What would you have to do to get promoted to the position directly above yours?

JM: Move to City Y, which I am not willing to do. . . . The job of the man I report to is located in headquarters, and if I were interested in getting the position that would be the first requirement. . . . I was in corporate headquarters for 4 years and then came out here . . . really on my own direction. When I left City Y . . . I had decided to substantially limit my career.

Unlike Jim, the others who had plateaued had not made the choice to trade career advancement for a certain lifestyle. They had simply reached a point where they were no longer being promoted.

Finally, the last three left the corporation, two to head their own firms and one to go back to school to train for a new job. All three of these people expressed a preference for the independence of being one's own boss. In contrast to the sixties women who chose consulting or unemployment as an alternative to organizational constraints, the men who headed companies had found a way to be independent and yet be part of a firm that provided a high income and authority over others.

In sum, male graduates of the sixties as a group had very successful careers at least until they reached responsible middle management positions. None of them had been blocked early in their careers; all but one had authority over others for at least part of their careers, and their incomes were reasonably high. In marked contrast, sixties women had found corporate life a great struggle and usually without reward. Their incomes as a group were low, and only one of them was a manager (see Tables 1 and 2).

Seventies men all started out in corporations, though three of the nine have either become more independent or have moved to a smaller firm. Of the five now in corporations, four have made good progress in their careers; two think they will continue to advance, and three believe they are stuck. Only one of this group dreams of getting out of a corporate job. The others plan to stay. Two of the seventies graduates felt burdened by organizational constraints and so struck out on their own. At this point their new careers are unestablished and their incomes modest. Unlike the two sixties entrepreneurs, neither plans to head a firm. Rather, they seek greater autonomy without strings. George Mathias talked about his reasons for changing.

I would have to say that I left [accounting consulting] because I didn't think I'm cut out for the corporate structure at all. . . . The main goal of [the insurance program I'm entering] is to put someone in their own agency somewhere in about five or six years, which sounds awful damned appealing to me. Immense people responsibilities, immense P & L responsibilities, albeit your independence is somewhat restricted in that kind of environment. But the opportunity to shape and mold an organization into what you would really like it to be, that I think is really the most independent form of work in the world. . . . That is awful appealing to me.

As with women there was no evidence of a relationship between family orientation and management success. Some very successful men adapted their work to their families by limiting transfers and business expansion; some single men had many career difficulties. There was a clear trend over the three decades for men to become more and more family oriented. One fifties graduate said, "I was transferred a lot. I told my wife she could come if she wanted, but I was going. She always trailed along." In less extreme form, all but one of the fifties graduates indicated that their wives followed and sacrificed for their husband's careers. By the seventies, three of the ten respondents reported a 50-50 division of household chores and another also reported a 50-50 division of child care responsibilities. Still, these data do not reveal a relationship between career outcomes and family orientation.

Over the decades, the contrasts between men and women are clear. In the fifties, the MBA was not in great demand by corporations, and consequently neither men nor women went to corporate settings in large numbers. By the sixties, corporations had begun heavy recruiting of MBAs. Men of the sixties and seventies flocked to the major corporations, but women found their experience in the corporate setting frustrating and painful. By the seventies, women had still not chosen or been chosen by corporations and were using their MBAs to carve out alternative careers.

Salary and Authority Differences over the Decades

The sample was drawn for the purposes of exploring the career experiences of men and women and is therefore necessarily small and not well suited to statistical analysis. However, a presentation of the reported salaries and number of people supervised provides a graphic demonstration of the differences in job outcomes for men and women over the last three decades.

The data on salaries with those unemployed removed from the analysis show wide differences between men and women who graduated in the fifties and a trend toward closing that gap for more recent grads (Table 1).

Because the study was not longitudinal it was not possible to discern whether women were catching up with men or whether men and women started with similar salaries but diverged as they progressed in their careers. Longitudinal research at Stanford (Harrell and Harrell, 1980) found men and women graduates of the seventies starting with equal salaries but diverging over time. The differences in 1980 salaries for this sample were clear. Women who received their degrees in the fifties earned about 41% of the salaries of men who graduated in the same decade. Graduates of the sixties earned 64%, and 1970s grads earned 81% of their female counterparts' salaries. This difference might be attributed to the discontinuities in some women's careers that arise from child rearing absences from the work force. However, the correlation between months out of the work force and income was low and nonsignificant ($r = -.14$, $df = 33$). A point biserial correlation between gender and income with months out of the work force controlled yielded a fairly large and significant coefficient ($r = -.40$, $df = 33$, $p < .05$, 1 = female, 0 = male), leading to the conclusion that factors other than time out of the work force were responsible for the differences. These findings of salary differences replicate those of Harlan (1978) at Harvard, Zappert and Weinstein (1981), and Harrell and Harrell (1980) at Stanford.

Similarly, there were clear differences between men and women on the number of people supervised (see Table 2). The distributions for both men and women were positively skewed toward zero by the number of people who had no supervisory responsibilities. The median number of people supervised by women and men combined was only one person, though the number ranged from 0 to 1,000. Chi-square, used to compare men and women on whether or not they were below the median (supervised no one), was computed with decade categories collapsed (see Table 3).

TABLE 1 1980 INCOME DIFFERENCES BETWEEN WOMEN AND MEN BY DECADE

Decade	Women		Men		t	df	p
	x̄	S	x̄	S			
All	$28,700	11,652	$50,250	32,408	2.16	29	.05
1950's	$27,375	13,790	$66,875	44,154	1.6	10	ns
1960's	$31,333	6,342	$48,924	23,208	1.16	8	ns
1970's	$28,180	11,989	$34,781	9,024	1.04	11	ns

TABLE 2   NUMBER OF PEOPLE SUPERVISED BY GENDER AND DECADE

	Women			Men		
	50's	60's	70's	50's	60's	70's
Below Median	3	4	5	3	3	3
Median Above	1	1	3	4	5	6

Note: Median = 1.

The median test indicates that women were disproportionately distributed in the category of nonsupervisors, those who had no authority over anyone. Moreover, although each cohort of men increased in the proportion who were supervisors, sixties women made no advances over fifties women, and seventies women's advances still left them with supervisory responsibilities only half as frequent as their male counterparts. Again, a possible explanation for women's lack of supervisory responsibility is that they dropped out of the work force to raise children, putting them behind in career advancement. However, there is no correlation between the number of people supervised and months out of the work force ($r = -.03$). Harlan (1978) and Zappert and Weinstein (1981) report similar findings at Harvard and Stanford.

These quantitative data support the qualitative findings that careers for men and women unfolded differently in every decade. Women of all decades lagged behind men in salary and authority. One possible explanation for the differences is that women diverted more energy into their families than did men. Although the findings do indicate that more women than men report child care

TABLE 3   SUPERVISORY RESPONSIBILITIES OF MEN AND WOMEN

	Women	Men
Below Median	12	9
Median and Above	5	15

Note: Median = 1. $\chi^2 = 4.38$, df = 1, $p < .05$.

responsibilities, there are no systematic differences in child care responsibilities between women who were more or less successful. Therefore, family orientation is unlikely to be a major cause of the differences between men and women. Another explanation is that these women were less qualified than the men. Harrell and Harrell (1974) found second year MBA grades a good predictor of earnings. This research did not investigate grade point, though competence differences are an unlikely explanation because admission standards at least in the earlier decades probably favored men, and the sample was randomly drawn.

DISCUSSION

How does it happen that women with the same degrees as men and increasingly positive attitudes toward a career end up in very different settings from men? Obviously at one time, simple sex discrimination affected the settings in which women worked. Studies of managers prior to 1970 found very negative attitudes toward women executives (Bowman et al., 1965; Bass et al., 1971). But even after legal changes prohibiting such overt discrimination, large numbers of women with MBAs are not in business management. The following is a set of explanations consistent with the data and prior research and theory that might explain the de facto segregation of men's and women's business careers.

Research on organizational commitment provides some guidance in understanding women's lack of commitment to business management as a career. Findings from this line of study indicate that long tenure (Hrebniak and Alutto, 1972; Lee, 1971), job challenge and job satisfaction (Berlew and Hall, 1966; Lee, 1971; Hall and Schneider, 1972; Buchanan, 1974), and social support and peer attitudes (Evan, 1963; Sheldon, 1971; Lee, 1971; Buchanan, 1974; Steers, 1977) are related to commitment to an organization. Commitment declines when there is role tension, dissatisfaction with the bases of promotion (Hrebniak and

Alutto, 1972), or disconfirmed expectations (Buchanan, 1974). These are among the factors that influence women's choices to enter and remain in business management careers.

Proposition 1. Entry into an organizational setting is constrained by socially shared norms about the appropriateness of that setting to one's gender role, even for women entering nontraditional careers.

In the fifties, the majority of the women interviewed simply did not consider corporate careers, even though they had professional business degrees. Corporate business, with its orientation toward money and success, was certainly incompatible with female role prescriptions for nurturance and self-sacrifice (Schein, 1973, 1974). Women MBAs of the sixties clearly felt the corporate setting was appropriate for them. However, widely shared changes in the definition of women's roles were slower in coming, so that female sixties MBAs did not find social support for their attempts to redefine their roles once they entered the corporate world. By the mid-seventies female MBAs were much greater in number, probably resulting in a greater diversity of ambitions and career expectations among those getting the degree. This time period seems to mark an increase in the numbers of women committed to business but an accompanying increase in entry into positions and settings more compatible with traditional female roles.

Proposition 2. Sustained commitment to a career in a particular organizational setting for both men and women is facilitated by receiving (1) rewards that meet expectations for a fair exchange between the organization and the individual and (2) more rewards than are available in alternative settings [Thibaut and Kelly, 1959].

Women of the fifties who entered business firms had low expectations. Therefore, when one of the two failed to be promoted to a management position, she was not faced with a serious disconfirmation of her beliefs about fair treatment and so stayed in the corporate setting. Women of the sixties had unrealistically high expectations given

the social norms of the times. They used MBA men as a reference group for evaluating their careers rather than comparing themselves to other women. The jobs they got, although better than the traditional female jobs, were often not challenging and/or they offered little potential for advancement, leading to an experience of relative deprivation (Merton, 1957) compared to men and generally in a loss of commitment to the corporate setting. In contrast, most male graduates of the fifties and sixties found early confirmation of their career expectations, and therefore developed an enduring commitment to business as a work place. By the seventies the situation had changed for men and women. Nearly half of the men and three quarters of the women have already left the corporation or are considering such a move.

Proposition 2a: When expectations for fair rewards are disconfirmed very early in the career, alternative settings will be sought.

Both men and women who were blocked early moved out of corporations very quickly. The most dramatic example was sixties women, whose expectations were dashed beginning with the job interviewing process. As a group, these women sought more rewarding alternatives in independent careers or in the home where their fates were not so highly controlled by others. These findings are supported by Smith's (1979) investigation of promotional patterns and turnover in the civil service in the sixties.

Proposition 2b: When the blocks to careers come near midlife, the commitment to the career setting has been made and usually will not change.

The men in this sample, most of them sixties graduates, who found they were blocked at the age of 40 and 45 did not leave the corporation. Some became more involved in outside activities, devoting less emotional energy to their work, but they did not change settings. Undoubtedly, the costs of changing settings at this age are extraordinarily high, making the likely choice decreasing the importance of work rather than changing settings.

Proposition 3: Social support is a necessary but insufficient condition for enduring commitment to an organizational setting.

This proposition cannot be derived directly from these data alone; however, the convergence of the experiences reported here along with previous research findings lead one to suspect that social support plays a very significant role in the choice to remain in a setting. In particular, people need personal acceptance and access to informal information channels in order to receive the rewards of advancement and challenging positions (Kanter, 1977). Moreover, acceptance and support is valued for itself because it provides affirmation for the individual (Rogers, 1961). Sheldon (1971) found social involvements to be very important in producing organizational commitment among professionals who also had commitments to their profession. Many times workers fail to receive support from their superiors, but they have peers who meet this need. Those who can receive acceptance and support from neither peers nor superiors can be expected to seek alternative settings that are more ego gratifying. Women who entered business in the sixties and still in the seventies found social support very difficult to obtain. In all probability, the conflict between what they perceived to be their appropriate role and what male managers perceived to be their appropriate role frequently resulted in the drawing of battle lines. Such postures made it difficult or impossible for women to receive support from men, and typically there were no women managers in the organization to provide that acceptance.

In sum, there are three likely contributors to commitment to an organizational setting. They are (1) the compatibility of the gender role with the setting, (2) confirmation of expectations for fair rewards and alternative sources of rewards, and (3) social support provided in the setting. Women had none of the above and so were generally not committed to corporate careers.

SUMMARY

For a couple of decades, women have been redefining their roles to include professions in business. The most recent trend for the graduates studied here is for many more women to seek the MBA but to work in settings other than business firms that are more compatible with traditional gender roles. Two probable reasons for the movement away from business firms are disconfirmed expectations of equality with male MBAs and a lack of positive interpersonal relationships. Among these respondents, family responsibilities very infrequently accounted for the choice to work outside a business firm. In sum, although larger numbers of women are entering graduate business programs, the majority of them are not entering or remaining in business, particularly in corporations. This fact may account for the increasing male-female earnings gap that occurred over time among graduating cohorts at Stanford and that probably also occurred among the graduates in this research.

REFERENCES

Bass, B. M., J. Krussell, and R. A. Alexander (1971) "Male managers' attitudes toward working women." Amer. Behavioral Scientist 15: 221–236.

Berlew, D. E. and D. T. Hall (1966) "The socialization of managers: effects of expectations on performance." Admin. Sci. Q. 11: 207–223.

Bowman, G., B. N. Wortney, and S. H. Greyser (1965) "Are women executives people?" Harvard Business Rev. 43: 14–28, 164–178.

Buchanan, B. (1974) "Building organizational commitment: the socialization of managers in work organizations." Admin. Sci. Q. 19: 533–546.

Burstein, P. (1979) "Equal employment opportunity legislation and the income of women and non-whites." Amer. Soc. Rev. 44: 367–391.

Cherlin, A. and B. M. Walters (1981) "U.S. men's and women's sex role attitudes." Amer. Soc. Rev. 46.

Cooper, M. R., B. S. Morgan, P. M. Foley, and L. B. Kaplan (1979) "Changing employee values: deepening discontent?" Harvard Business Rev. 59 (January-February): 117–125.

Day, D. R. and R. M. Stogdill (1972) "Leader behavior of male and female supervisors: a comparative study." Personnel Psychology 25: 353–360.

Dipboye, R. L., H. Fromkin, and L. Wilbach (1975) "Relative importance of applicant sex, attractiveness and scholastic standing in evaluation of job applicant resumes." J. of Applied Psychology 60: 39–43.

Evan, W. M. (1963) "Peer group interaction and organizational socialization: a study of employee turnover." Amer. Soc. Rev. 28: 436–440.

Ferber M. A. and J. W. Loeb (1974) "Professors, performance, and rewards." Industrial Relations 13: 69–77.

Haefner, J. E. (1977) "Race, age, sex, and competence as factors in employee selection of the disadvantaged." J. of Applied Psychology 62: 199–202.

Hall, D. T. and B. Schneider (1972) "Correlates of organizational identification as a function of career pattern and organizational type." Admin. Sci. Q. 17: 340–350.

Harlan, A. (1978) "A comparison of careers for male and female MBAs." A paper presented at the annual meetings of the Academy of Management.

Harrell, T. W. and M. S. Harrell (1980) "Careers of women, minority, and white male MBAs." Research Paper No. 558, Stanford University.

———(1976) "Predicting compensation and the attainment of a general management position among MBA graduates." Research Paper No. 298, Stanford University.

———(1974) "Relation of second year MBA grades to business earnings." Personnel Psychology 27: 487–491.

Hrebniak, L. G. and J. A. Alutto (1972) "Personal and role related factors in the development of organizational commitment." Admin. Sci. Q. 17: 555–572.

Kanter, R. M. (1977) Men and Women of the Corporation. New York: Basic Books.

Lee, S. M. (1971) "An empirical analysis of organizational identification." Academy of Management J. 14: 213–226.

Mason, K. O., J. L. Czajka, and S. Arber (1976) "Change in U.S. women's sex role attitudes: 1964–1974." Amer. Soc. Rev. 41 (August): 573–596.

Merton, R. K. (1957) Social Theory and Social Structure. (Rev. ed.) Glencoe, IL: Free Press.

Mortimer, J., R. Hall, and R. Hill (1978) "Husbands' occupational attributes as constraint on wives' employment." Sociology of Work and Occupations 5: 285–313.

Pfeffer, J. and J. Ross (1982) "The effects of marriage and a working wife on occupational and wage attainment." Admin. Sci. Q. 27 (March): 66–80.

Rogers, C. R. (1961) On Becoming a Person. Boston: Houghton Mifflin.

Rosen, B. and T. H. Jerdee (1975) "Effects of applicant's sex and difficulty of job on evaluations of candidates for managerial positions." J. of Applied Psychology 60: 442–445.

———(1974) "Sex stereotyping in the executive suite." Harvard Business Rev. (March–April): 45–58.

Schein, V. E. (1975) "Relationships between sex role stereotypes and requisite management characteristics among female managers." J. of Applied Psychology 60: 340–344.

———(1973) "The relationship between sex role stereotypes and requisite management characteristics." J. of Applied Psychology 57: 95–100.

Shaw, E. A. (1972) "Differential impact of negative stereotyping in employee selection." Personnel Psychology 25: 333–338.

Sheldon, M. E. (1971) "Investments and involvements as mechanisms producing commitment to the organization." Admin. Sci. Q. 24: 362–381.

Smith, C. B. (1979) "Influence of internal opportunity structure and sex of worker on turnover patterns." Admin. Sci. Q. 24: 362–381.

Sofer, C. (1970) Men in Mid-Career: A Study of British Managers and Technical Specialists. New York: Cambridge Univ. Press.

Spillerman, S. (1977) "Careers, labor market structure, and socioeconomic achievement." Amer. J. of Sociology 83, 3: 551–593.

Steers, R. M. (1977) "Antecedents and outcomes of organizational commitment." Admin. Sci. Q. 22: 46–56.

Taylor, P. A. (1979) "Income inequality in the federal civilian government." Amer. Soc. Rev. 44: 468–479.

Terborg, J. R. and D. R. Ilgen (1975) "A theoretical approach to sex discrimination in traditionally masculine occupations." Organizational Behavior and Human Performance 13: 352–376.

Thibaut, J. W. and H. H. Kelley (1959) The Social Psychology of Groups. New York: John Wiley.

Wolf, W. C. and N. D. Fligstein (1979) "Sex and authority in the workplace." Amer. Soc. Rev. 44: 235–252.

Yohalem, A. M. (1979) The careers of professional women. Montclair, NJ: Allanheld Osmun.

Zappert, L. T. and H. M. Weinstein (1981) "Sex differences in adaptation to work: physical and psychological differences." A paper presented at the annual
meetings of the American Psychological Association, Montreal.

TAKING ANOTHER LOOK

1 What reasons does Tucker offer for choosing the methodology used in this study?

2 Briefly summarize the differences in the career outcomes of women respondents who graduated with MBA degrees in the 1950s, the 1960s, and the 1970s.

3 Briefly summarize the career outcomes of male respondents who graduated with MBA degrees in the 1950s, the 1960s, and the 1970s.

4 What quantitative data are reported by Tucker to support the qualitative findings that careers for men and women unfolded differently in every decade?

5 According to Tucker, what are the three likely contributors to commitment to an organizational setting?

6 According to Tucker, what are the probable reasons for women MBAs' movement away from business firms?

Children and the Elderly in the U.S.

Samuel H. Preston

Social scientists and journalists have used the term "the graying of America" to refer to the fact that an increasing proportion of the American population is composed of elderly citizens. Individuals 65 years of age and over constituted only 4.1 percent of the nation's population in the year 1900, but by 1980 this figure had risen to 11.2 percent. It is currently projected that in the year 2000 there will be some 31.8 million elderly Americans; they will constitute 12.2 percent of the population of the United States.

It should be noted that the fastest-growing segment of the elderly population is the "old old." In 1950, less than one-third of elderly Americans were 75 years old and over. Yet by the year 2000, 45 percent of the elderly may fall into that age category. This projected rise in the old old is particularly worrisome for the nation's legislators, since it may necessitate a dramatic increase in many social service programs. Clearly, the "graying of America" is a phenomenon that can no longer be ignored, either by social scientists or by government policymakers.

In the following selection, Samuel H. Preston analyzes the impact of the nation's changing age structure on its elderly population and on its children. He argues that "since the early 1960s the well-being of the elderly has improved greatly whereas that of the young has deteriorated." Preston draws on measures of health care, educational achievement, and poverty status in order to support his surprising assessment. He concludes that the United States is not devoting sufficient resources to ensure the quality of education and psychological well-being of children.

In the 1960's and 1970's two developments that had not been expected by demographers changed the age structure of the U.S. population in a dramatic way. The first was a decrease in the number of children. From 1960 to 1982 the number of children younger than 15 fell by 7 percent. The decline was mainly due to the drop in the birth rate that followed the "baby boom."

The second development was a rapid increase in the number of elderly people. Between 1960 and 1980 the number of people 65 or older grew by 54 percent. The increase was caused mainly by a sharp reduction in the death rate among older people, acting on a population that already was large because of the large number of babies born between 1890 and 1915. As a result, during the 1970's the elderly population of the U.S. increased at a higher rate than the total population of India.

One might expect such a change in age structure to help the young and hurt the old. Fewer children should mean less competition for resources in the home and greater per capita availability of social services such as public schools. More old people, on the other hand, should put great pressure on resources such as hospitals, nursing homes and social security funds. I believe, however, that exactly the opposite has happened. Since the early 1960's the well-being of the elderly has improved greatly whereas that of the young has deteriorated. Demographic trends underlie these changes: in the family, in politics and in industry the growing number of older people and the declining number of children have worked to the advantage of the group that is increasing in size.

In order to account for what has happened to children and older people in the U.S. it is first

In order to account for what has happened to children and older people in the U.S. it is first necessary to document the changes in living conditions among the two groups. The measures that are commonly used by social scientists to measure the well-being of large groups include levels of income, health, educational achievement and reports of satisfaction with life.

One of the most straightforward ways to compare children with the elderly is to measure the fraction of the two groups that live in poverty. Since children generally do not have independent incomes, one cannot directly compare personal income. One can, however, measure the incomes of the families in which the children live and compare the incomes to a minimum standard of need. The Bureau of the Census uses an Economy Food Plan drawn up by the Department of Agriculture as the basis of such a standard. Families that have an income equal to an amount less than three times the cost of the food plan are said to be living in poverty.

By this standard there have been remarkable changes in the proportion of children who live in poverty compared with the corresponding proportion of the elderly. In 1970, 16 percent of those under 14 lived in poverty compared with 24 percent of those older than 65. By 1982 the situation had been reversed: 23 percent of children lived in poverty compared with 15 percent of the elderly. . . .

Monetary income is not the only measure of material well-being. Non-cash transfer payments such as food stamps and Medicare have a strong influence on the condition of society's dependents. The Census Bureau estimated that in 1982 the market value of non-cash transfers was $98 billion, much of it in medical payments to the elderly. If this sum is taken into account, the disparity in poverty status between children and the elderly is increased further. The fraction of the elderly living in poverty in 1982 falls from 15 to 4 percent. The corresponding reduction for children is only from 24 to 17 percent.

An examination of public outlays as a whole reinforces the idea that the elderly have done better than children at society's hands in recent years. Mary Jo Bane of Harvard University concluded that in 1960 the average government expenditure (including Federal, state and local funds) on each elderly person was about three times the expenditure on each child. Both types of spending increased rapidly in the succeeding decades; hence the ratio remained about the same through 1979. Because the expenditure on the elderly started from a higher level, however, the absolute gain for each elderly person was much larger than the gain for each child.

Since 1979 there has been a sharp break in the pattern of government expenditure that kept the ratio of per capita outlays for the two groups roughly constant. Many public programs for children have been cut back while those for older people have been expanded. For example, the Aid to Families with Dependent Children (AFDC) program has been substantially reduced. In 1979, out of every 100 children in poverty 72 were enrolled in AFDC. By 1982 only 52 out of 100 were in the program. In comparison, Medicare outlays rose from $3.4 billion in 1967 to $57.4 billion in 1983, and it has been estimated that they will rise to $112 billion by 1988.

The Federal Office of Management and Budget has recently begun estimating the fraction of all Federal benefits that are directed to those who are 65 or older. Older people got $44 billion in Federal funds in 1971 and $217 billion in 1983. The 1983 figure is equivalent to about $7,700 per person who is older than 65 and is a sum larger than the total spent on national defense in that year.

Federal expenditures on children are harder to calculate, but I have attempted to do so from budget documents. The total Federal outlay on the major child-oriented programs (AFDC, Head Start, food stamps, child health, child nutrition and aid to education) is about $36 billion for 1984; this is about a sixth of the total spending on the elderly. Because there are more children than old people, the expenditure per child through these programs is less than a tenth the expenditure per older person. These figures are not strictly comparable to the data collected by Bane, but they do give a sense of the increasing disparity between public outlays on the young and those on the old.

The gulf in well-being that separates the old and the young has been widened still further by the fact that public spending on the young has become less effective. The largest portion of public money spent on the young goes to public schools. Many indicators suggest the quality of public schooling has declined drastically in the past two decades.

The sum of the scores in the verbal and mathematics sections of the Scholastic Aptitude Test (S.A.T.) declined by 90 points from 1963 through 1980. The Wirtz Commission, which was the most authoritative group to investigate this trend, concluded that about half of the decline was due to the fact that a wider range of students now take the test than took it in the 1960's. About half of the decline, however, represents an actual decline among students with qualifications similar to those taking the test earlier. Most of the real decline took place in the early 1970's. In addition there has been a decrease in the proportion of U.S. teen-agers who finish high school. In 1965 the fraction was 76.3 percent; by 1980 it had fallen to 73.6 percent.

Education is the principal public service for the young; health care is the principal service for the old. Some 69 percent of the medical bills of people 65 or older are paid for with public funds. The Congressional Budget Office estimates that in 1984 the Federal Government will spend an average of $2,948 on health care for each person 65 or older.

A good index of the effectiveness of public spending on health care is the mortality rate. Between 1968 and 1980 mortality rates improved in all age groups in the U.S. The improvements, however, were not equally distributed between the young and the old. Demographers employ statistical standards called "model life tables" to compare the relations of death rates in different age groups with the relations that would be expected from international and historical experience. If model life tables are used to analyze the recent changes in mortality in the U.S., it can be shown that the greatest improvements in the death rate have occurred in the older age groups. By normal standards of progress, children and young adults gained the least. . . .

Thus according to several measures, including health, educational achievement and poverty status, the elderly appear to be doing better than the young. The elderly are not oblivious to the improvement in their welfare. A Gallup poll made in 1982 found that 71 percent of those 65 or older reported they were highly satisfied with their standard of living, by far the greatest level of satisfaction in any age group. The proportion of the elderly who scored "Very high" on a psychological scale of anxiety fell from 22 to 15 percent between 1957 and 1976, while the corresponding proportion of younger adults rose sharply. Furthermore, since 1960 there have been reductions in the suicide rate among the elderly, which also seems to suggest increased well-being.

Although suicide is rare among children, the trend appears to be upward. Other indicators also suggest that a deterioration has occurred in the mental health of children. The U.S. Health Examination Survey asked parents whether "anything had ever happened to seriously upset or disturb your child?" The fraction of parents who answered in the affirmative rose from 27 percent in 1963–65 to 37 percent in 1976.

The major reason for the increased emotional disturbance among children, as reported by parents, seems to be the intensification of marital discord. Indeed, changes in the structure of the family appear to be closely connected to what has happened to both children and the elderly in recent years.

One reason that changes in family structure can have such a strong effect on the status of dependent groups is that the family is an important vehicle for the transfer of society's resources. James N. Morgan of the University of Michigan estimated that roughly a third of the U.S. gross national product takes the form of transfers from income earners to nonearners within family groups that live together.

As a result, any change in the family's capacity to care for its dependents has powerful consequences for those who are being taken care of. These consequences are more significant for children than they are for the elderly because the family has relinquished to the state an increasing share of responsibility for elderly dependents. Hence older people are to some extent protected against changes in family structure.

The situation is very different for children. The government assumes a much smaller share of support for the young than it does for the elderly. The conjugal family is the chief source of support for children. In recent years it has begun to divest itself of its responsibility for the young, just as earlier it abandoned much of its responsibility for the elderly. Absent fathers are the main factor in this divestiture. In 1960 only 5.3 percent of births were out of wedlock. By 1980 the figure had risen to 18.4 percent. The rate of illegitimacy has a strong influence on resources available for children because in most out-of-wedlock births the father takes no lasting responsibility for his child.

Even for children born in wedlock, the situation has deteriorated. According to Larry Bumpass of the University of Wisconsin at Madison, persistence of the divorce rates that prevailed at the end of the 1970's will mean that 43 percent of the children born in wedlock will experience parental separation before they are 16. If the rate of increase in divorce of the past decade continues, the proportion could reach two-thirds. Furthermore, fathers contribute little on the average to the support of children from previous marriages. A recent study by the Census Bureau found that fewer than half of all children living with their mother after a divorce were supported by payments from their father. The immediate consequence is that the economic condition of mothers and children deteriorates after a divorce. Morgan and his colleague Greg J. Duncan conclude that in divorces occurring from 1972 through 1978, 72 percent of the affected children experienced a reduction in their family's income in relation to the minimum standard of need.

It is obvious that the economic consequences of marital disruption have much to do with the increase in the number of children who live in poverty. Census Bureau data show that 69 percent of the increase in the number of children living in poverty from 1970 through 1982 occurred in households headed by women. Evidence suggests that the instability of the nuclear family is also responsible for some of the decline in educational achievement.

The main vehicle other than the family for transferring resources to dependents is the state. In a pluralistic democracy such as that of the U.S. the formation of public policy is strongly influenced by the relative power of interest groups. In recent decades the old have become a far more powerful interest group, while the constituency for children has declined in power.

In exerting their political influence the elderly draw on support from three overlapping but substantial groups. The first group consists of the elderly members themselves. The second consists of members of the under-65 population acting on behalf of elderly family members who are currently or potentially in need of financial assistance. The third consists of the entire under-65 population acting on behalf of themselves in their own (future) old age. The elderly, unlike some other special interests, make up a group we all expect, or at least hope, to join eventually. Most government programs for those more than 65 years old are to some extent perceived as a social contract enabling middle-aged adults to transfer resources to themselves later in life.

Children have only one of these three sources of political influence. Young people cannot vote.

Furthermore, adults cannot agitate to improve conditions in their own childhood, since that is the past. Children's only remaining source of political influence is parents acting on behalf of their progeny.

Because of the imbalance between the sources of political support available to older people and the sources available to children, the change in age structure can have a "multiplier" effect on public policy. The sharp mortality decline in the older age groups has led not only to an increase in the number of voters older than 65 but also to an increase in the number of middle-aged adults who have living parents and an increase in the number of years beyond 65 that the average adult can expect to live.

The most significant of these changes is probably the increase in the number of elderly. In the past decade the increase has been combined with a high level of political participation. In the 1982 congressional elections 65 percent of those aged 65 through 74 voted. This was the highest percentage of any age group and more than twice the rate among people aged 20 through 29. Once again the trend reverses earlier patterns: in the congressional elections of 1966 the voting rate for those older than 65 was lower than it was for any age group between 35 and 64.

The elderly probably have also come to exercise a stronger claim on the political allegiance of those younger than 65. I estimate that in 1980 the average 40-year-old couple had 2.59 living parents and 2.72 living children. If present fertility and mortality rates persist, however, the average 40-year-old couple would eventually have 2.88 living parents and 1.78 living children. It would not be until age 52 that the average couple would have as many living children as they would have living parents.

When parents are 52, of course, most children have left home. It turns out that under current fertility and mortality rates there is no stage in the life cycle when the average married couple will have more children under the age of 20 than they will have surviving parents. The dependency con-

cerns of the middle-aged are thus shifting toward the elderly, at least in numerical terms.

None of this would matter if people of different ages and in different domestic circumstances saw public issues in the same light. But they do not. For example, the 1983 Gallup Poll of Public Attitudes toward the Public Schools asked whether people would vote to raise taxes for schools if asked to do so by the local school board. Those younger than 50 were evenly split; those older than 50 were opposed by 62 to 28 percent.

The foregoing discussion of politics deals only with the part of political behavior that is motivated by self-interest. What about altruism? Altruism is not a negligible motive in human affairs, particularly altruism directed toward people with whom an individual shares some corporate identity. I suspect, however, that W. Norton Grubb and Marvin Lazerson, then at the University of California at Berkeley, were at least partially correct in proposing that we have drifted toward a form of society and government based mainly on self-interest and adversarial relations between groups. Grubb and Lazerson argue that in U.S. society there has never been a strong sense of collective responsibility for other people's children. Furthermore, the wide availability of effective contraception could well have exaggerated this split between private and collective concerns. Reliable contraceptives give a married couple a high degree of control over whether they have children. Since children are now the result of a private decision rather than of chance, many people today think the parents should bear the cost of child rearing. On the other hand, we do not choose to have parents and so there is no equivalent motive for insisting that parents be privately supported.

A second factor that probably helps to suppress altruism toward other people's children is the fact that these children are increasingly from minority groups with whom the majority have trouble identifying: 24 percent of those younger than 15 are black or Hispanic, compared with only 11 percent of those older than 65.

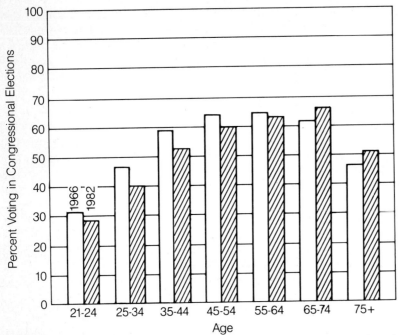

VOTER PARTICIPATION is one of several factors that have made the elderly an increasingly influential group in U.S. politics. The chart shows the proportion of each age group who voted in the congressional elections of 1966 (white) and 1982 (gray). Between the two elections voting became more common among the old and less common among the young. Hence in 1982 the highest voter-participation rate was among those from 65 through 74 years old.

Both in the family and in politics demographic mechanisms have improved the situation of older people in relation to that of the young. A third, quite subtle, mechanism operates to the same effect in the industries that provide services to the two dependent groups.

For the young, the most important service is education. The most significant recent trend in education has been the decline in enrollment. Between the early 1970's and the early 1980's public elementary school enrollment fell 11 percent and secondary school enrollment fell 18 percent. I think a persuasive argument can be made that the decrease in enrollment is one reason for the apparent decline in the quality of U.S. schools. On a casual examination the evidence seems to be to the contrary. Between the early 1970's and the early 1980's the total expenditure per pupil in constant dollars increased by 22.5 percent. The student-teacher ratio fell from 22 to 18. The average amount of professional experience of teachers rose, as did the fraction of teachers who had master's degrees. The problem is that none of these variables has been shown to be related to students' academic performance. Eric A. Hanushek of the University of Rochester recently reviewed 130 studies of factors affecting achievement in school. Hanushek concludes that the only reasonably consistent finding in the studies is that students' academic achievement increases with the intelligence of the teacher.

Since the quality of teachers is such an important variable and since better salaries would be ex-

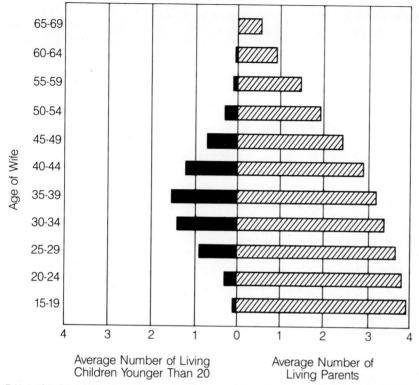

Age of Wife

65-69
60-64
55-59
50-54
45-49
40-44
35-39
30-34
25-29
20-24
15-19

4 3 2 1 0 1 2 3 4

Average Number of Living
Children Younger Than 20

Average Number of
Living Parents

BALANCE OF DEPENDENTS has shifted toward the elderly because of decreases in both
birth and death rates. The chart shows the number of living parents and children under age
20 that the average working-age couple will have at each stage in life. Husbands and wives
are assumed to be the same age. The data are based on the assumption that the fertility
and mortality rates of the early 1980's will persist. Under this assumption there is no point
when the couple will have more children than they will have living parents. Such trends have
probably caused increasing concern among working-age couples about supporting dependent elderly parents.

pected to attract better teachers, the work of
Hanushek and others focuses attention on working
conditions for teachers. Hence it is surprising to
note that teachers have not shared in the increased expenditures on schools. From 1973
through 1983 teachers' real incomes declined by
12.2 percent. Moreover, reductions in teachers'
incomes are correlated with decreases in school
enrollment. I used state enrollment and salary
data to compare changes in teachers' salaries with
changes in enrollment over the period from 1972
through 1982. The correlation suggests that in the

1970's for each decline of 10 percent in school enrollment teachers' salaries decreased about 1.2
percent.

The outcome of a reduction in average salary is
predictable: the brightest workers, who can readily get other jobs, leave a field or do not enter it in
the first place. This is what has happened in
teaching. The decline in S.A.T. scores among all
high school students is quite sharp, but the decline in S.A.T. scores among those intending to
major in education has been even more acute. In
1973 future education majors scored 59 points

lower than the national average on the combined S.A.T.; by 1982 they scored 82 points lower. The negative selection of those going into teaching has been aggravated by negative selection among those already in the field. The 1972 National Longitudinal Survey of high school seniors shows that the mean S.A.T. score for those who enter the field of teaching and then leave it is 42 points higher than the score of those who enter and stay. Those who remain permanently in the profession have a combined S.A.T. score 118 points lower than the score of those who have never taught.

The most plausible interpretation of these very unsettling data is that the demand for teachers was reduced by the decrease in the number of school-age children. The reduction in demand led to a lower average wage for teachers. Therefore a disproportionate number of the brightest teachers (who get the best results) left the field and many potentially good teachers avoided the field altogether. This result is clearly incompatible with the hypothesis that school districts would use funds liberated by falling enrollments to raise salaries and find better teachers. Quite the opposite has apparently taken place.

Medical care is a service as crucial to the elderly as teaching is crucial to the young. The medical profession, however, requires less discussion because it is manifestly robust. Whereas the number of teachers has remained constant and their salaries and quality have declined, in medicine the opposite has been true. Applicants to U.S. medical schools are so outstanding that the system for choosing among them has been described as a lottery.

It is also notable that large amounts of capital have flowed into the health-care industry in the past decade. These investments have been converted into advances in equipment and improvements in the training of medical personnel. Capital has been attracted to the industry by a sharp increase in the demand for health-care services. The growth of demand is due in turn to an increase in the number of elderly and the expansion of entitlement programs that enable older people to afford more and better medical treatment. Thus the elderly, whose number has grown quickly, have been far better served by their specialized industry than the young, whose number has declined.

Some readers may be disturbed by the fact that in demonstrating the existence of the demographic mechanisms affecting the elderly and the young, age has been emphasized to the exclusion of other traditional demographic variables, including race. In discussing the changing status of children and the elderly in the U.S., however, I see no reason to analyze the races separately. For those who think the current problems of children are confined to racial minorities it should be pointed out that there is not one trend described above that does not apply to both blacks and whites. On the contrary, in the case of some of the most significant trends, including rising illegitimacy rates and declining school achievement, the changes have been much greater among whites than they have among blacks.

In summarizing the lessons to be learned from recent demographic trends I do not want to paint the elderly as the villains of the piece. I am primarily concerned about the fate of children and in that context the elderly serve largely for comparison. Nevertheless, it is unrealistic simply to wish away the possibility that there is direct competition between the young and the old for society's resources.

Even if the young and the old are to some extent competitors, however, the elderly alone do not decide where society's resources are to be expended. That is a collective, political decision that society makes. It is certainly reasonable to ask whether such decisions in recent decades have taken us along a useful course. There is surely something to be said for a system in which conditions improve as we pass through life.

On the other hand, the failure to devote resources to children cannot be defended so easily. Whereas expenditure on the elderly can be thought of mainly as consumption, expenditure on the young is a combination of consumption and investment. The quality of education and the psychological well-being of children are crucial to the future productive capacity of the U.S.

If we care about our collective future rather than simply about our futures as individuals we are faced with the question of how best to safeguard the human and material resources represented by children. These resources have not been carefully guarded in the past two decades. Rather than as-suming collective responsibility, as has been done in the case of the elderly, U.S. society has chosen to place almost exclusive responsibility for the care of children on the nuclear family. Marital instability, however, has much reduced the capacity of the family to care for its own children. Hence insisting that families alone care for the young would seem to be an evasion of collective responsibility rather than a conscious decision about the best way to provide for the future.

TAKING ANOTHER LOOK

1 How has the pattern of government expenditures for children and for the elderly changed since 1979?

2 According to Preston, in what ways has public spending for the young become "less effective"?

3 What is the primary reason for the increased emotional disturbance among children, as reported by parents?

4 Compare the sources of political influence available to children and to the elderly.

5 According to Preston, what factors contribute to American society's diminished sense of altruism toward other people's children?

6 Why does Preston place such emphasis on comparisons between educational and health-care services?

7 How might functionalist theorists be likely to view the nation's differing treatment of children and the elderly?

What the USA Can Learn from Japan About Aging

Erdman Palmore

Age, like race and sex, is an ascribed status that forms the basis for social differentiation. Like other forms of stratification, age stratification varies from culture to culture. One society may treat the elderly with great reverence, while another sees them as "unproductive" and "difficult." It is understandable that all societies have some system of age stratification and associate certain social roles with distinct periods in one's life. However, as is the case with stratification by sex, age stratification in the United States goes far beyond the physical constraints of human beings at different ages. Physician Robert N. Butler coined the term *ageism* to refer to prejudice and discrimination against the elderly.

One explanation of the impact of aging, *disengagement theory*, contends that society and the aging individual mutually sever many of their relationships. Implicit in disengagement theory is the view that society *should* help older people to withdraw from their accustomed social roles. Those elderly citizens who sever their social ties are considered to be the best adjusted. By contrast, *activity theory*—often seen as an opposing approach to disengagement theory— argues that the elderly person who remains active will be best adjusted. Advocates of activity theory point out that the activities of one's life are constantly changing. Therefore, the older person—like people at earlier stages of the life cycle—should have the option of replacing earlier activities with new pursuits. Whereas disengagement theorists argue that the elderly find satisfaction in withdrawal from society, proponents of activity theory find such withdrawal harmful for both the elderly and the larger society.

In the following selection, sociologist and gerontologist Erdman Palmore analyzes the position of the elderly within Japanese society. Palmore observes that the Japanese maintain a high level of respect for their elders and a high level of integration of the elderly in the family, work force, and community. In line with the findings of activity theorists regarding older Americans, Palmore sees important benefits stemming from the participation of Japan's elderly in the paid labor force, in housework and child care duties, and in educational, recreational, and political activities. He identifies numerous practices of Japanese culture that could be adapted by the United States and other western societies in an effort to improve their treatment of the elderly.

STATUS AND INTEGRATION

Aging in Japan is almost a mirror image of aging in the United States. Despite high levels of industrialization and urbanization, the Japanese have maintained a high level of respect for their elders and a high level of integration of their elders in the family, work force, and community. While there is considerable prejudice and discrimination against the aged in America (Palmore, 1969, 1973), old age is recognized by most Japanese as a source of prestige and honor. The most common word for the aged in Japanese, *Otoshiyori*, literally means "the honorable elders." Respect for the elders is shown in the honorific language used in speaking to or about the elders; rules of etiquette which give precedence to the elders in seating arrangements, serving order, bathing order, and going through doors; bowing to the elders; the national holiday called Respect for Elders Day; giving seats on crowded public vehicles to the elders, and the authority of the elders over many family and household matters.

The high level of their integration into Japanese society is demonstrated by the following facts. Over 75% of all Japanese aged 65 years or more live with their children (Office of the Prime Minister, 1973) in contrast to 25% in the United States (Epstein and Murray, 1967). The majority of Japanese men over 65 continue to be in the labor force (Japan Census Bureau, 1965), compared to 29% of men in the United States over 65 (Palmore, 1964). Most of the Japanese elders who are not actually employed continue to be useful in housekeeping, child care, shopping, and gardening, often freeing their daughters or daughters-in-law for employment outside the home. The vast majority of Japanese elders also remain active in their communities through Senior Citizens Clubs, religious organizations, and informal neighborhood groups. And, most surprising of all, there appears to have been little decline in these high levels of integration during the past 20 or 30 years (Palmore, 1975).

This high status and integration of the elders has roots in the "vertical" structure of the society and in the religious principles of filial piety. Japan has often been called a "vertical society" because most relationships tend to be hierarchical rather than horizontal or egalitarian (Nakane, 1970). Age grading is one of the most important dimensions determining who is above or below. The principles of filial piety go back to both Confucian precepts and ancestor worship, "the real religion of Japan" (Hearn, 1955). The principles of filial piety specify that respect and duty toward parents is one of the most important virtues of all.

Thus, the most general thing we can learn about aging from the Japanese is that high status and integration can be maintained in a modern industrialized society.

SUGGESTIONS FOR THE UNITED STATES AND THE WEST

Obviously, many of the practices and attitudes of Japanese toward their elders are not likely to be imported as such. However, many of these practices do suggest ways in which the situation of older Americans in the United States as well as the Western world could be improved.

1 Respect for the Elders Day is a popular national holiday and apparently succeeds in encouraging respect for the elders and a great awareness in encouraging respect for the elders and a great awareness of their problems, as well as actions to reduce these problems. . . .

2 The Japanese also use the 61st birthday as an occasion to honor the elders and to express affection for them. In the United States, Americans sometimes use the 21st birthday as an occasion to recognize the new adult. Other rites of passage for the young are christening, confirmation or bar mitzvah, graduation, and marriage ceremonies. There are few such ceremonies for older persons. . . .

3 In an egalitarian society, it is unlikely the West would adopt forms of deference toward older people such as bowing or honorific language. Nevertheless, we do have a weak tradition of "age before beauty" when going through doors and when serving people. This saying, unfortunately, implies that the aged are not beautiful. However, it may be that strengthening and extending the tradition of precedence for older persons would help restore more respect for elders and more self-respect among older persons themselves.

4 The United States also has a weak tradition of giving seats to elders on crowded public transportation. This could be reinforced, as the Japanese have done, by regulations which give priority to older persons for a certain number of seats in each bus or train. In addition to recognizing special privileges for elders, this would facilitate the ease of travel of older persons, more of whom must rely exclusively on public transportation.

5 All older Japanese are eligible for a minimum income payment from the government. While this amounts to little more than pocket money at present, the principle of a minimum income guaranteed by the government for older persons is a good one. . . .

6 Several cities in Japan have established programs in which elders living alone are visited or called on a daily basis in order to see if they are all right or need anything. Such a program in the United States, which is sporadically conducted instead of being universal, would not only reduce the fears of older persons living alone that they might have some kind of accident or even die before anyone could be reached, but it would also reduce their isolation. There is evidence that isolation can lead to mental and even physical deterioration among the aged (Lowenthal, Berkman, Brisette, Buehler, Pierce, Robinson, and Trier, 1967; Roth and Kay, 1962).

7 It is a widespread practice for Japanese of all ages to begin their day with some kind of group exercise. This is carried over into homes for the aged in which the day typically begins with a combination of group exercise and folk dance in rhythm to music. Such morning exercise is widely recognized as an excellent way to preserve physical and mental functioning. When it is done on a group basis, there is the added satisfaction of social support and interaction. Instituting such programs of exercise for older people in the West should improve their physical and mental health (Palmore, 1970; Palmore and Luikart, 1972).

8 The Japanese government encourages and subsidizes sports day for the elders. Generally, this takes the form of various track and field events which are not too strenuous for healthy older persons. . . .

9 Another program to improve the health of Japanese elders is the free annual health examination, which is followed by more detailed examinations and treatments for those who need it. The present Medicare program in the United States does not cover such routine examinations. . . .

10 Starting in 1973, the Japanese government began providing completely free medical care to most Japanese over age 70. Some cities provide free medical care to their residents between the ages of 65 and 70. . . .

11 Perhaps the most important single idea the United States could benefit by is the provision of more employment opportunities for older persons. Japanese older persons are not only permitted, but are *expected*, to continue working or doing housework of some kind as long as they are able. . . . The Japanese believe that voluntary employment of older persons contributes to their physical and mental health, to their satisfaction, to their financial independence, and to the nation's productivity. There is considerable evidence in Japan and in the USA that they are correct in this belief (Palmore, 1972).

12 Another idea with potentially great benefit is more integration of older persons in the families of their children and grandchildren. It appears unlikely that USA citizens will greatly increase the proportions of older persons living with their children. But it may be feasible and desirable for more older Americans to live near enough to their children and grandchildren to contribute more fully to their household activities. On the one side, this would decrease the isolation and inactivity of many older persons, and on the other side it would reduce the mother's and father's burdens of child care, housekeeping, and household maintenance.

13 The Japanese have a nation-wide system of government-supported Elders Clubs, to which about half the elders belong. These clubs function not only to provide community service, group study, and recreation, but also, provide mutual support and self-pride among the elders. The USA has some Senior Citizens Clubs and some yet modest government support. But, compared to Japan, these clubs are few and weak. . . .

14 A related program in Japan is the building of welfare centers for the aged, where various educational, recreational, and consultation services are provided with little or no charge. The centers are subsidized by the government and now exist in most large communities. Again, while the USA

has a few such centers, they are rare compared to the Japanese.

15 Perhaps most important in terms of getting these and other recommendations implemented is organized political action and demonstrations by the aged. In Japan, the elders are a recognized political force. This is true not only because they themselves constitute a sizeable proportion of the voters, but because they exert a strong influence over the votes of their family and younger friends. Furthermore, because of the high level of organization and self-pride among the elders, they are able to mount massive demonstrations and other forms of political pressure to get the government to meet their needs better. There are signs in the USA that more of the aged are beginning to realize the necessity for developing more political "clout." . . .

16 Finally, the most complex and yet fundamental way in which one could learn from the Japanese relates to respect for elders and self-respect among the elders. Respect for Japanese elders is rooted in the basic social structure of their "vertical society" and in their religion of ancestor worship and filial piety. But the very idea of a vertical society and of ancestor worship would seem alien, if not completely repugnant to most USA citizens. Yet it appears that respect for the aged is the key element which can maintain the status and integration of the aged in modern industrial societies. Therefore, in order to improve the status and integration of older Americans, it is necessary to improve respect for the aged somehow. Instead of the vertical society, perhaps one could use egalitarian ideology that all persons are entitled to respect because they are humans, regardless of race, sex, *or age*. . . .

The commentary above is not intended to propose a culture which assumes the aged are superior simply because they are old (as was true in old Japan). Nor is this intended to be an argument for a gerontocracy in which the aged have most of the power and rewards of the society (as in ancient Japan). It is intended, instead, to suggest that stereotypes and prejudices in the USA and other Western countries should be overcome to provide the elderly equal respect with all other humans; and, therefore, in the USA discrimination against the aged in employment, in our families, and in our communities should be stopped so that they can regain an equal share of power and rewards.

Those who agree with these ideals may be able to learn something from the land of "The Honorable Elders."

REFERENCES

Epstein, L., and Murray, J. *The aged population of the United States*, USGPO, Washington, 1967.

Hearn, L. *Japan: an interpretation*. Charles E. Tuttle, Rutland, Vt., 1955.

Japan Census Bureau. *1965 population census*. Japan Census Bureau, Tokyo, 1965.

Lowenthal, M. F., Berkman, P. L., Brisette, G. G., Buehler, J. A., Pierce, R. C., Robinson, B. C., and Trier, M. L. *Aging and mental disorder in San Francisco*. Jossey-Bass, San Francisco, 1967.

Nakane, C. *Japanese society*. Univ. of California Press, Berkeley, 1972.

Office of the Prime Minister. *Public opinion survey about problems of old age*. Office of the Prime Minister, Tokyo, 1973.

Palmore, E. "Work experience and earnings of the aged in 1962." *Social Security Bulletin*, 1964, **27**, 3–15.

Palmore, E. "Sociological aspects of aging." In E. W. Busse & E. Pfeiffer (Eds.), *Behavior and adaptation in late life*. Little Brown, Boston, 1969.

Palmore, E. "Ageism compared to racism and sexism." *Journal of Gerontology*, 1973, **28**, 363–369.

Palmore, E. "Health practices and illness among the aged." *Gerontologist*, 1970, **10**, 313–316.

Palmore, E. "Compulsory versus flexible retirement." *Gerontologist*, 1972, **12**, 343–348.

Palmore, E. *The honorable elders*. Duke Univ. Press, Durham, N.C., 1975.

Palmore, E., and Luikart, C. "Health and social factors related to life satisfaction." *Journal of Health & Social Behavior*, 1972, **13**, 68–80.

Roth, M., and Kay, D. "Social, medical and personality factors associated with vulnerability to psychiatric breakdown in old age." *Gerontologica Clinica*, 1962, 147–160.

TAKING ANOTHER LOOK

1 In what ways are the elderly integrated into Japanese society?
2 What does the term *vertical society* mean when applied to Japan?
3 In what ways does the Japanese government attempt to assist the elderly and improve their lives?
4 List five Japanese practices that could be adapted in order to improve the situation of the elderly in the United States.
5 How would conflict theorists be likely to view the position of the elderly in the United States?

PART FOUR

FOUR

SOCIAL INSTITUTIONS

The mass media, the government, the economy, the family, and the educational system are all examples of social institutions found in American society. *Social institutions* are organized patterns of beliefs and behavior centered on basic social needs. Institutions are organized in response to particular needs such as replacing personnel (the family) and preserving order (the government).

By studying social institutions, sociologists gain insight into the structure of a society. For example, the institution of religion adapts to the segment of society that it serves. Church work has a very different meaning for ministers who serve a skid row area, a naval base, and a suburban middle-class community. Religious leaders assigned to a skid row mission will focus on tending to the ill and providing food and shelter. By contrast, clergy in affluent suburbs will be occupied with counseling those who are considering marriage and divorce, arranging youth activities, and overseeing cultural events.

The family as a social institution is present in all cultures. Sociologists use the term *family* to refer to a set of persons related by blood, marriage (or some other agreed-upon relationship), or adoption who share the primary responsibility for reproducing and caring for members of society. Historically, the most consistent aspect of American family life has been the nation's high rate of marriage. In recent decades, however, there have been significant changes both in American family life and in the ways in which sociologists view the American family.

Philip Blumstein and Pepper Schwartz ("Couples: Job Satisfaction, Ambition, and Success") examine issues of job satisfaction and success as they affect four types of American couples: married couples, cohabiting couples, gay male couples, and lesbian couples. Letty Cottin Pogrebin ("Are Men Discovering the Joys of Fatherhood?") suggests that more American males are becoming caring, involved fathers. Linda Haas ("Role-Sharing Couples: A Study of Egalitarian Marriages") reports on families in which husbands and wives share traditionally male and female family responsibilities. James M. Makepeace ("Courtship Violence Among College Students") sheds light on a distressing aspect of American family life—domestic violence—by showing that courtship violence is far from rare.

Émile Durkheim was perhaps the first sociologist to recognize the critical importance of religion in human societies. He saw its appeal for the individual, but more important he stressed the *social* impact of religion. In Durkheim's view, religion is a collective act and includes many forms of behavior in which people interact with others. Durkheim initiated sociological analysis of religion by defining *religion* as a "unified system of beliefs and practices relative to sacred things." In his formulation, religion involves a set of beliefs and practices that are uniquely the property of religion—as opposed to other social institutions and ways of thinking.

Saul V. Levine ("Radical Departures") sheds light on the relationship between religious commitment and family life by examining young people who join communal groups and religious cults. Dean M. Kelley ("Why Conservative Churches Are Still Growing") attempts to account for the remarkable growth of fundamentalist religious denominations in the last 20 years. Calvin Goldscheider ("Social Change and Jewish Continuity") focuses on the stong ethnic, religious, and communal identification of American Jews.

The term *political system* refers to a recognized set of procedures for implementing and obtaining the goals of a group. In their study of politics and political systems, sociologists are concerned with social interactions among individuals and groups. The term *economic system* refers to the social institution through which goods and services are produced and distributed. As with social institutions such as the family, religion, and government, the economic system shapes other aspects of the social order and is, in turn, influenced by them.

In a classic piece, "On Authority," Max Weber discusses three ideal types of authority: traditional, legal-rational, and charismatic. Reflecting a more contemporary and empirical approach to the study of power, Harold R. Kerbo and L. Richard Della Fave ("The Empirical Side of the Power Elite Debate: An Assessment and Critique of Recent Research") assess the controversial question of whether a small elite of Americans actually runs the country. Donald F. Roy (" 'Banana Time,' Job Satisfaction and Informal Interaction") focuses on the relationships among members of a small work group.

In a sense, education is an aspect of *socialization*—the lifelong process of learning the attitudes, values, and behavior appropriate to individuals as members of a particular culture. When such learning is explicit and formalized—when people consciously teach while others adopt the social role of learner—this process is called *education*. Christopher J. Hurn ("Theories of Schooling and Society: The Functional and Radical Paradigms") contrasts the views of schooling offered by functionalist and conflict theorists. Jomills Henry Braddock II, Robert L. Crain, and James M. McPartland ("A Long-Term View of School Desegregation: Some Recent Studies of Graduates as Adults") assess the impact of desegregation on social relations in the United States.

Couples: Job Satisfaction, Ambition, and Success

Philip Blumstein and Pepper Schwartz

Traditionally, when Americans have thought of "couples," they have thought of married couples or of heterosexual couples preparing for marriage. However, in recent decades, there have been significant changes in American family life. One of the most dramatic trends has been the tremendous increase in male-female couples who choose to live together without marrying, thus engaging in what is known as *cohabitation*. The number of such households rose sixfold in the 1960s and quadrupled between 1970 and 1985. Increases in unmarried coupling have also been found in France, Sweden, Denmark, and Australia.

In studying American couples, it is important to remember that not all couples are heterosexual. According to estimates, homosexual men and lesbians together constitute perhaps 10 percent of the nation's population. Their lifestyles vary greatly. Some live alone; others live with roommates. Some live in long-term, monogamous relationships with a lover and with children from former marriages; others remain married and have not acknowledged their homosexual identities.

In the following selection, sociologists Philip Blumstein and Pepper Schwartz examine the issues of job satisfaction and success as they affect the lives of American couples. In their extensively researched 1983 study, *American Couples*, the two sociologists personally interviewed 400 couples. These included married couples, cohabiting couples, gay male couples, and lesbian couples. Among the conclusions reported by Blumstein and Schwartz are the following: (1) for employed wives, the happier they are with their jobs, the happier they are with their marriages; (2) husbands enjoy their work more than cohabiting men do; (3) gay men seem happier with their work if they are open about their sexual preference; (4) cohabiting men are too competitive with their partners for the women's success to enhance the relationship; and (5) a working wife makes her husband more ambitious.

Most people like to think that their partners will love them no matter what kind of work they do or how successful they become. Ideally, marriage or an intimate relationship functions as a refuge from the world of work—a place where each person is loved and admired for who he or she is, rather than for what he or she achieves. But some social thinkers hold to the view that modern society has become so judgmental that spouses and lovers now evaluate one another according to how well they do at their jobs. In his book *Haven in a Heartless World*, Christopher Lasch writes with bitterness that the working world has invaded family life and that personal relationships are no longer immune from being judged by its standards.[1] He goes on to say that unconditional love is no longer possible because partners and relationships are graded in the same way job performance is.

Is success on the job related to the way partners feel about each other? Are people who spend all day in a work environment appraising others for their skills and ability to produce able to put such measures aside when they return home? Can one partner be too successful and invoke competi-

[1] Christopher Lasch, *Haven in a Heartless World: The Family Besieged* (New York: Basic Books, 1977).

tive feelings in the person he or she lives with? Now that so many men and women are in the labor force we are eager to see how both sexes respond to a partner's success or lack of it in work. As work comes to dominate the time of so many American couples, do they know how to form emotional boundaries that keep it from affecting their personal lives?

For employed wives, the happier they are with their job, the happier they are with their marriage[2]

We interpret this to mean that wives allow their relationships to affect their jobs and their jobs to affect their relationships. When things are not going well at work, they are likely to bring their concerns home, and when they feel upset with their husbands, it is difficult for it not to affect how they feel about work. As one wife in her fifties told us:

I was very good at my job and I enjoyed it . . . but looking back on it, I also gloss over how hard it was to keep going when he and I were having problems, especially problems with our oldest daughter. We built our whole life around her and this took its toll on everything. There would be some mornings I would be at work and all I would be doing was thinking about if she [was doing all right]. . . . I would want to discuss these things with my husband, but he would be too tired in the morning and then he would say he was too tired at night and finally it was, "I don't want to talk about it because it produces too much tension." . . . I would be under a lot of tension myself and it was impossible for me to hide it from everyone. I had too many friends at the office, so that really became a very important emotional outlet

for me as well as a professional one.

Stacey and Glenda have been married for six years. Stacey, thirty-two, is a music teacher, and Glenda, thirty, is a graphic artist. Glenda reported:

When I have had a bad day I'm afraid I am grumpy and he's very good at getting me out of it by offering advice so that I don't ruin our whole evening. . . . I'm afraid I store up a lot of frustration and I am likely to take it out on him because I can't take it out on the people who deserve it. . . . He's very good about deflecting it and pointing out to me what I'm doing. . . . He never does the same thing back to me. I sometimes wish he would, so it would be tit for tat —but he rarely mentions anything but good news or maybe some office gossip. I have to dig to get information and he just has to watch me walk through the door and I unload on him.

From the questionnaires and interviews we get a picture of how intertwined work and home life can be for employed wives. When married couples fight about the wife's work, their conflict can compromise the pleasure she derives from her job as well as from her marriage.[3] Wives often want more time and attention from their husbands than they are able to get. Some seek stimulation in a job. We believe that when they work—and enjoy it—they indeed satisfy many of their needs. Consequently they can place fewer demands on their husbands and are more content with their marriage. We also feel that when they are happy in their marriage, they bring fewer anxieties and tensions to their job, hence the more they are able to enjoy it. As one wife, thirty-one, who works as a textile designer, told us:

[2] Among wives who are employed part time, 77 percent of those who are satisfied with their work are very satisfied with their marriage ($N = 401$), as compared to 73 percent of those who feel neutral about their work ($N = 308$), and 66 percent of those who dislike their work ($N = 87$). The comparable figures for wives who are employed full time are 75 percent ($N = 696$), 66 percent ($N = 519$), and 66 percent ($N = 152$). [The partial correlation between satisfaction with work and satisfaction with the relationship is .153 (controlling dura-

tion, age, and whether she has been previously married). For the other groups in the study the comparable partials are less than .100. Satisfaction with work is measured by item 3 of the Statistical Information part of the questionnaire.]

[3] [Partial correlations were computed between the amount of conflict the couple has over the effect of the wife's job on their relationship, and her satisfaction both with her work and with her marriage (controlling the same variables as in the preceding note). The correlations are $-.141$ and $-.212$.]

It's important to have at least one thing going well at a time. Because I can count on my marriage, I feel my energies are released for my work. It would be terrible if I had to worry about two things at once. But he is my support and my deep strength and having him there allows me to handle my day and get a lot accomplished. I don't think I could do what I do —or do it as well—if it wasn't for his support. He gets a great amount of pleasure from my being able to be in business and the fact that I enjoy it so much is something he can appreciate.

Thus we see that for wives, a good relationship and a good job can be mutually enhancing.

This does not seem to be as true for the other women. Many cohabiting women are in the process of defining their relationships so we think they are cautious about burdening them with worries from work. It is likely that they also take care to protect their work lives from the ups and downs of their private lives, and they do not wish to endanger the job in the event the relationship breaks up. They probably feel less free to allow a relationship to intrude into a work situation because their employers and co-workers may not consider cohabitation as serious an arrangement as marriage.

Much of what we think about female cohabitors we believe of lesbians as well. Lesbians may be inhibited even further from allowing a relationship to affect them on the job because they may have concealed its existence entirely and therefore be unable to display stress that comes from that quarter. Kathy and Liz have lived together for nine years. Kathy, forty, is a psychiatrist, and Liz, thirty-six, is a school psychologist. Liz told us:

It's been tough at times. . . . Last year when she and I were going through a trial separation and it looked like we were going to break up—and she was living with another woman—I was in pain every day and I dreaded going to work and having to make light con-

versation. I kept thinking in my head that my whole life was cracking up but all I could do was look like nothing special was happening. I think that was a terrible strain on me and I know she experienced the same kind of thing later when she was going through tough times and she couldn't talk about it.

Another lesbian, in a six-year relationship, told us about having to hide her emotions at work:

The absolute worst was one day I came in after being up all night crying because we were having another of our "should we stay together" conversations. My face was all blotchy and my eyes were puffy and several people tried to be nice, and asked me if anything was the matter. And I had to lie to them, 'cause I couldn't open up then—after all those years—and I told them that a very close relative had died and so everyone gave me their condolences over that. . . . It was really shitty.

One lesbian, a hospital administrator, explained that she felt just as constrained about her private life even though she is not in the closet:

People know I'm gay but still I think that if I were going to bring up my issues when we were talking at the office, that some people wouldn't think it was in good taste.

Men try to segregate their emotional lives from their work lives. Historically, since men were expected to be the breadwinners, they could not allow themselves the luxury of letting their home lives influence how they did their jobs. This meant not letting their true feelings manifest themselves. For the most part, the world of work is not a therapeutic community. It teaches those who greatly invest themselves in it the absolute necessity of separating personal problems from the demands of the job. Those who learn this lesson well are likely to be rewarded professionally. We feel that when people orient themselves to their work and consider it essential for their survival, the more the division of the personal and the professional will occur.

Husbands enjoy their work more than cohabiting men do.[4]

What makes cohabiting men different from husbands? We think it is that cohabitors do not take the provider role as a central identity. Work may be important in their lives, but it is a source of personal accomplishment rather than an obligation to support a cherished partner. It could be argued that husbands have an extra burden because of the people dependent upon them, and that they should be more alienated from their work and worn down because of serious obligations. But we find that husbands actually enjoy their work more than cohabiting men do. We feel that providing for other people infuses their work with greater meaning, so that even a tedious job can reward them. Perhaps this is the truth behind the conventional wisdom frequently given to a young man—that marriage is good for him. The responsibilities of caring for a family may help him focus his efforts and cause him to be more serious about making himself a success. This may be part of the reason why many employers display a marked preference for married men.

Gay men seem happier with their work if they are open about their sexual preference.

There is a debate among psychologists, sociologists, and gay activists over whether it is psychologically harmful for gay people to keep their sexual preference a secret. In the interviews men told us about the compromises they had to make at work because they were "in the closet," and it seemed to us it diminished their satisfaction with their jobs. One reason a man chooses to stay in the closet is fear of losing his job or imperiling his relationship with his co-workers.[5] Being able to be open has distinct advantages—if a man survives the disclosure or has chosen a profession where his sexuality is not a concern to anyone. Dmitri and Walter have lived together for seventeen years. Dmitri is a nightclub singer and Walter is an executive for an automobile-manufacturing company. Dmitri told us how fortunate he is to have a job that allows him to admit that he is gay:

> We have a bone to pick over how "out" one or both of us should be. I am in the entertainment field and I picked that field because I refuse to live a lie, and I challenge anyone not to accept me for exactly who and what I am. . . . He is in the most conservative environment imaginable and he doesn't dare say anything about his home or me. . . . He can't take me to social events, whereas I take him to all of mine. . . . He gets upset with me because I am so open and I frankly think he suffers stress because of how he has to live. You'd think an employee of fourteen years' good work would not have to depend on such things to keep his job. . . . I think it is demoralizing for him and I would never never do such a thing.

Another gay man, who works as a flight attendant, has similar feelings:

> I have very lovely relations with the people I work with. I don't talk about being gay any more than they talk about their sexual needs, but everyone knows and I don't think anyone cares. . . . I suppose if I wanted a big promotion it might hurt me somewhere, but I don't think about that. . . . The price of pretending to be something I'm not is too high, and I have a much more pleasant day each day because I can let Andrew's name slip or mention that we are having people for dinner.

---

[4] Among husbands under twenty-six years of age, 44 percent are very satisfied with their work ($N = 258$) as compared to 39 percent of male cohabitors of the same age ($N = 116$). For men between the ages of twenty-six and forty, the percentages are 52 percent ($N = 1,832$) versus 46 percent ($N = 397$); and for men over forty they are 64 percent ($N = 1,298$) versus 52 percent ($N = 90$). It may also be true that a man who feels good about his work is more confident of his future and more willing to make a commitment to marry. Such a man may also be more attractive to a woman seeking a husband. We believe, however, that it gives people pleasure to be responsible for the welfare of others, and for husbands this is expressed in satisfaction with their jobs. In the interviews with husbands, we often sensed this.

[5] Twenty-seven percent of our gay men ($N = 1,887$) feel they have had problems on the job because they were known to be, or suspected of being, gay. A somewhat larger number of lesbians (32 percent) report the same experience ($N = 1,514$). [See Lifestyle question 16a.]

Gay men, like heterosexual men, do not want their private lives to affect their work. But some are keenly aware of the possible risk to their careers if their homosexuality is disclosed and this worry colors how at ease they can feel. In order to make exposure less likely, some may even create an imaginary heterosexual life. These men may hesitate to share casual banter with their co-workers for fear of saying something revealing, and co-workers, unaware of their sexual preference, may unwittingly make jokes or derogatory remarks about homosexuals. If it were known that they were gay, they might be spared these experiences.

If a lesbian is not open about her sexual preference, her satisfaction with her work seems to be affected less. Not only do lesbians prize privacy more than our gay men, we think that people ask fewer questions about their personal lives.[6] A single woman, or a woman living with another woman, is not as readily assumed to be homosexual and so she is not likely to feel she has to give an account of her private life to anyone. Sheila and Mia have been living together for seventeen years. Sheila, forty-one, is head of neighborhood planning in a city government, and Mia, forty-three, is a dietician. Sheila believes strongly in the virtues of being in the closet:

No one asks about my private life and if someone did, I could give them a few leads to send them in the wrong direction and that would be that. ... I don't see any reason to tell anyone anything. I don't think it's anyone else's business and I don't think it would help my work any. I have my friends and my private life and it works well to just let *those* people know. ... You never know what people could use against you, or let fall even if they weren't meaning

to. ... I argue with her about this, because she would like to be more open, but I insist on discretion.

Another lesbian, fifty, an attorney in a federal agency, expressed the same attitude:

Lesbians of my age do not believe in all this rhetoric about coming out. The young gals do, because they think discrimination is something you can change. ... Well, I don't, and furthermore, I think that people ought to be able to discriminate between who they want to be with and who they don't, at least on a personal basis. ... I get along perfectly well with the people at work and that is based on professional business, which is fine. They respect my work and I respect theirs. There is no reason for them to have to evaluate me on other grounds.

Wives, husbands, and cohabiting women are happier in their relationships if their partners are successful in their jobs.

Male cohabitors are too competitive with their partners for the women's success to enhance the relationship.

Traditionally, a wife was assumed to take pleasure in her husband's career as though it were her own. If her husband was successful, a wife then considered herself successful. She would be treated in society on the basis of her husband's accomplishments. We are not surprised to find that this tradition still endures: When a wife has a successful husband she is more satisfied with her relationship.[7] We learned in interviews that when a wife feels that her husband is a success, she feels he is fulfilling the classic requirements of being a good spouse. He earns her respect as he has earned it in the outside world. She is pleased to be married to such a man and more content with their marriage.

---

[6] The lesbians in our study are somewhat more closeted than the gay men. Twenty-eight percent of the women under twenty-six want few or no heterosexuals to know they are lesbians ($N = 319$), and this is also true for 36 percent of those between twenty-six and forty ($N = 1,025$), and 44 percent of those over forty ($N = 208$). The comparable figures for gay men are: 16 percent $N = 245$), 20 percent ($N = 1,244$), and 35 percent ($N = 430$). It is impossible to infer from these data that lesbians are more closeted than gay men in general. The

very closeted are likely to have avoided participating in our study. Indeed, the very closeted may even avoid being part of a couple. [See Lifestyle question 18.]

[7] [The partial correlation between a wife's assessment of her husband as accomplished in his work and her happiness with her relationship in general is .216. The control variables are duration, both spouses' ages, both incomes, and both educational levels. The measure of the wife's perception of the husband as a success is Relationship question 19f.]

Alexandra and Whit have been married sixteen years. Alexandra, forty, is a homemaker, and Whit, forty-two, owns a plumbing-supply store. According to Alexandra:

> He has done better than I ever expected when we first started out. . . . All I wanted was security and a nice home, not having to worry about money, that sort of thing. . . . He has succeeded beyond my fantasies, and while it was not necessary for our marriage, I am grateful for the ability to live as well as we do. . . . He may not have been a "catch" to my mother when we first married but I think she thinks of him as one now!

Another wife, married almost fifty years, expressed her pleasure about her husband's success as a building contractor:

> I always tell my children how lucky we are to have him. Particularly when I read in the paper about these men who desert their families, or don't work, or I hear about somebody not helping their kid with his education or, you know, deadbeat stuff. I tell them about what a good provider their father has been and how generous he is with them. . . . He has always worked very hard for a living and done a good job and I think he ought to be given credit for what he's accomplished for us.

It is not surprising that a wife is happier with her marriage when her husband is a success. What is surprising is that husbands feel the same way about their wives. Sociologists often imply that husbands do not derive any glory from a wife's

success.[8] This is not generally true for the husbands in our study. Husbands with successful wives are happier with their marriages.[9] These are usually men who have chosen to be in a marriage where the woman is free to pursue her career fully, and neither partner is threatened at the prospect of sharing the provider role.[10] Milo and Estelle have been married for eighteen years. Milo, forty-one, is an engineer, and Estelle, thirty-nine, is an urban planner. Milo is proud of Estelle:

> Some of the guys in my company asked me if I was upset when she was promoted . . . last year. . . . I was shocked. Why would I be upset? Then I realized these guys would be upset if their wife started to get ahead and I began to wonder why, and I decided it must be because they are feeling crummy about themselves or are having some kind of trouble in the company. That's all I could think of. I was totally behind her working from the beginning—although I have to admit I was glad she waited till the kids were in kindergarten. . . . I want her to get as far as she wants to go. I think it helps us both out and it makes me proud of her.

Another married couple are both actors. They are in their mid-twenties and have been married less than two years. The husband takes pride in his wife's accomplishments:

> I respect her as an artist. I also respect the fact that she gets off her keister and gets out there and contributes to the mundane financial worries that we have. . . . I think the best thing that could happen is

---

[8] It is commonly held among sociologists that wives derive their position in society from their husbands' social standing or occupational status. For example, Robert F. Winch wrote in 1971: "It is generally the case in Western societies that a woman . . . assumes the socioeconomic status . . . of her husband. The recognition that the woman takes her socioeconomic status from her husband is of course the crux of the interest of single girls, and their parents, in the 'prospects' of their young men. Popenoe [another family sociologist] has telescoped much discussion into the remark that a man marries a wife but a woman marries a standard of living." (*The Modern Family*, 3rd ed. [New York: Holt, Rinehart & Winston, 1971]. pp. 230–231.) There is never any mention in these discussions of the husband deriving his position in society from his wife's accomplishments.

[9] [The partial correlation between the husband's rating of

his wife as accomplished at her job (only for employed wives) and his overall satisfaction with the relationship is .191 (same controls as in Note 7).]

[10] Among husbands who endorse the notion that both spouses should share the responsibility for earning a living to support the household, 91 percent have employed wives ($N = 1,118$), as compared to 78 percent of husbands who have neutral or mixed feelings on this issue ($N = 1,255$), and 57 percent of husbands who reject the idea ($N = 1,209$). Another factor in the finding of a correlation between happiness with the relationship and having a partner who is a success at work is that a successful partner is probably a happier person, and this may make him or her easier to live with. A person whose business is failing or who is not meeting his or her own goals at work is probably difficult to live with.

that we both make it and can arrange work together or help out each other's careers some of the time. . . . In the beginning, we worried that we might resent it if one of us got a call-back or got asked to read and the other didn't. But I think we are genuinely happy for one another when some good news happens. . . . We think as a team.

Women who are in living-together arrangements feel the same way wives do. Even without a marriage contract, they take pleasure in their partner's accomplishments.[11] But male cohabitors are not like the husbands: Their partner's success or lack of it does not affect the way they feel about the relationship.[12] We think this may have something to do with competitiveness between the two partners.[13] Phil and Judi have been living together for nine years. Phil, thirty-four, teaches sculpture, and Judi, thirty-one, is a painter. Judi described what she sees as Phil's competitiveness:

Sometimes I feel like he is looking over my work looking for flaws. I don't always trust his criticisms. I think this is particularly true when he's feeling frustrated or blocked. If I think he is taking his frustrations out on me, I tell him so, and we can get into a pretty good row about it. . . . I sometimes wish we were doing work that was more different from one another than it is. Sometimes the collaboration is great and creative, but when he gets competitive, I get offended and then I get depressed.

Another male cohabitor, in his early twenties, complained to us about his relationship and his partner's success at work:

She makes a lot more money than I do, which I must admit is touchy with us. . . . I would like her to cut back. I don't think we need the money so much, and we could use the time together. I think she is driven to work in ways that are not flattering to her.

It is ironic that male cohabitors hold to the belief that their partners should be independent—and they have partners who are eager to oblige—yet they are not happier when their partners have dramatically proved their ability to be self-reliant. Some male cohabitors are inclined to construe a partner's drive as competition with him, rather than dedication to her work.

A working wife makes her husband more ambitious.[14]

In our study we talked to many husbands who are not only happy that their wives work but derive great pleasure from their success. They do not, however, want their wives to take over the provider role. Instead, we feel a wife's accomplishments spur a husband to set higher goals for himself. He may not wish to do better than his wife, but he certainly does not want to do less well. Even most modern-day egalitarian husbands do not want to play a secondary role to their wives, either in their own eyes, their wives' eyes, or the eyes of the world. The wife of such a man may receive mixed messages. Her husband encourages her to achieve great things, but he is likely to become competitive if she begins to surpass what he has done.[15] Some competition is

---

[11] [The partial correlation between the female cohabitor's rating of her partner as accomplished at his job and her overall satisfaction with the relationship is .182 (same control variables as in Note 7).]

[12] [The partial correlation between the male cohabitor's rating of his partner as a success on her job and his satisfaction with their relationship is .102 (same control variables as in Note 7).]

[13] Cohabitors are more competitive with each other than any of the other kinds of couples. Twenty-six percent of the men describe themselves as competitive ($N = 651$), and 23 percent of the women feel the same ($N = 648$). This is in contrast to 16 percent of husbands($N = 3,627$), 18 percent of wives ($N = 3,627$), 20 percent of gay men ($N = 1,928$), and

20 percent of lesbians ($N = 1,557$). [See Relationship question 20j.]

[14] Among couples where the wife works full time, 45 percent of the husbands say they are very ambitious($N = 1,367$), as compared to 42 percent of those where the wife works part time ($N = 800$), and 39 percent where she is a full-time homemaker ($N = 894$). It is possible that ambitious men are more likely to marry women who wish to work in the labor force or that these men are more likely to encourage their wives to work. However, we find no correlation between a man's ambition and his attitudes toward his wife's working. [The ambition item is Relationship question 20m.]

[15] When their wives are employed full time, 19 percent of husbands describe themselves as competitive with her ($N =$

quite common, but if it becomes excessive the couple may start to take less pleasure in each other. We find that couples who say they suffer a lot of competition are less happy in their marriage.[16]

Only gay men judge their success by comparing it to what their partners have achieved.

All partners in all four kinds of couples feel successful when they earn a high income.[17] But only gay men feel even more successful if their partner's income is lower.[18] We believe that when men evaluate their success they look for someone to measure themselves against. The likely comparisons have traditionally been other men—co-workers, people in similar jobs, friends, or neighbors. Gay men have another man close to them—their partner—who can become a basis for comparison. Heterosexual men do not feel especially successful when their female partners make little money. They have not been accustomed to competing with women because it is difficult for women to achieve the same level of earning power as men do in our society.

Heterosexual women do not use their partner's success as a point of comparison. They are more likely to want him to succeed because his attain-

ment will reflect favorably on them. While women no longer define themselves *only* by what their male partners have achieved, our society still categorizes a woman according to her husband's status. It is therefore impossible to imagine a heterosexual woman feeling better about herself if her partner is a failure, or earning little money. And finally, lesbians, like other women, have learned to want an accomplished partner.[19]

A man's sense of his worth is stongly affected by how he performs at work. He might like to compartmentalize his life, keeping the frustrations and setbacks of his job separate from his life at home, and to some extent he is able to do this. But work can intrude into his home environment in a number of subtle ways. For example, when he arrives home from work, he may very well be greeted by a partner who also works. And no matter how well he is doing in his career, his partner may be doing even better. He may think, as most people do, that he judges himself by the standards set by the marketplace. A promotion, a raise, or a special compliment from a supervisor are the clear and established signs of accomplishment. But these pleasures may be short-lived if he discovers that his own achievement pales in comparison to someone else's. In two-paycheck couples, the person he chooses to compare himself with

1,368), as compared to 16 percent of the husbands of part-time employed women ($N = 798$), and 13 percent of the husbands of women who are full-time homemakers ($N = 893$). Part of the husbands' competitiveness may be in reaction to competitiveness on the part of their wives. We find that when wives are employed, both they and their husbands tell us the women are more competitive. Twenty-one percent of wives employed full time say they are competitive with their husbands ($N = 1,368$), as compared to 17 percent of those employed part time ($N = 797$), and 15 percent of those who are full-time homemakers ($N = 892$). [Perception of one's partner's competitiveness is measured by Relationship question 19e.]

[16] Among husbands who describe their wives as competitive, 65 percent are very satisfied with their relationship($N = 670$), as compared to 77 percent of those who say she is not competitive ($N = 1,679$). The comparable figures for wives are 60 percent ($N = 599$), versus 80 percent ($N = 2,033$).

[Partial correlations were computed between ratings of one's partner's competitiveness and satisfaction with the relationship, controlling for duration, both partners' ages, educa-

tion levels, and incomes. The association is stronger for wives ($-.242$) than for husbands ($-.146$). The same partials were computed for commitment to the future of the relationship, and again we find that the wife is more strongly affected by her partner's competitiveness. The partial for wives is $-.161$, while for husbands it is only $-.082$.]

[17] [Zero-order correlations between income level and an individual's rating of himself or herself as accomplished are: husbands: $r = -.278$; wives: $r = -.171$; male cohabitors: $r = -.391$; female cohabitors: $r = -.316$; gay men: $r = -.382$; lesbians: $r = -.261$. A negative correlation means that people with higher incomes feel more accomplished.]

[18] [The partial correlation between gay men's self-rating as accomplished and their partner's income, controlling for their own income, is .149. A positive correlation means that the higher the partner's income, the *less* accomplished a gay man feels.]

[19] Twenty percent of lesbians feel it is extremely important to have an accomplished partner($N = 1,558$). The comparable figure for female cohabitors is 23 percent($N = 648$).

may be his partner.

The American occupational structure has traditionally conspired to reduce the prospect of such competition between men and women. When women worked, they were employed in different occupations, almost always of a lower status, and they earned significantly lower wages. For example, a man might have begun work as a stockboy, but he could entertain the not too improbable dream of moving up. If a woman began as a clerk, she might be praised for doing her job well, but no one in the firm would mark her for a more responsible position. Now that women are more interested in and able to have careers, their mobility is not so impeded, and so there is a greater chance that both partners will have similar jobs with similar chances for success. Thus opportunities for comparison can present themselves, even among intimates, and gradually create tension in the relationship. A wife's success pleases her husband only if he is doing well himself. With a working wife, his home may become less of a haven and just another reminder of what he perceives to be his inadequacies.

We might have suspected that the tensions created by work would be magnified when both partners are men. Work is likely to be valued by both partners, both have access to similar kinds of jobs, and comparisons can be made more readily. We find, however, that while gay male couples do compete some of the time, their struggles are not worse than those of married couples with a successful working wife.[20] We think men grow more accustomed to competing with other men and they learn that sometimes they will lose. That is the nature of the game in the work place. When one gay man is more successful than his partner, he may gain some status. This may indeed cause competition in the relationship, but unlike the situation where the wife outdistances the husband, the less successful partner is not seen as having failed as a provider.

Lesbians may want their partners to be successful and ambitious, but they do not make invidious comparisons. Lesbians prize the same qualities in their partners that heterosexual women do. And they confront the same expectations from their partners that heterosexual men do. Yet, unlike heterosexual men, lesbians do not become competitive with a partner whose career is going well. This makes us think it is not women's working and achieving that causes problems between partners. Rather, the source is the difficulty men have in accepting female equality.

---

[20] Eighteen percent of gay men say they are competitive with their partners($N = 1,926$), compared with 19 percent of husbands and 21 percent of wives in couples where the wife is employed full time($N = 1,368$).

TAKING ANOTHER LOOK

1 What arguments about changes in American family life were made by Christopher Lasch in his book *Haven in a Heartless World?*

2 Why are work and home life so intertwined for working wives?

3 According to Blumstein and Schwartz, what makes cohabiting men different from husbands?

4 How do members of lesbian couples feel about their partners' success?

5 According to Blumstein and Schwartz, how does men's difficulty in accepting female equality affect married and cohabiting couples?

Are Men Discovering the Joys of Fatherhood?

Letty Cottin Pogrebin

American society is increasingly geared toward specialization of labor. However, we do not have specialization of parental labor in the same sense that we have it within the educational system or on the assembly line. We expect all parents to become expert in dealing with newborn babies, inquisitive young children, and rebellious adolescents. Clearly, the socialization of children is essential to the maintenance of our culture. Consequently, parenthood is one of society's most important (and most demanding) social roles.

The changing sex roles of American society are reshaping the institution of parenthood. Those women who opt for motherhood are often sharing the moment of birth with their husbands, who assist their wives in the delivery room as coaches. Motherhood is not viewed as the only legitimate occupation for an adult woman, and family specialists no longer counsel against mothers working outside the home. As women become increasingly involved in the paid labor force, men will have an opportunity to become more involved in the care and socialization of children.

In the following selection, Letty Cottin Pogrebin (an editor of *MS.* magazine and author of *Growing Up Free*, a blueprint for nonsexist child-rearing) argues that "fathering is becoming a new kind of verb—an active verb," as American men are "affirmatively taking off time to be with their children." Pogrebin notes that the traditional sex-role socialization to be a "real man" actually ran counter to the qualities and activities essential to being a good father. However, in her view, while the typical American father "has a long way to go to achieve parity parenthood," an increasing number of men are becoming caring, involved fathers.

I have been thinking a lot about fatherhood.

I'd swear everyone is. Since the publication of *Growing Up Free*, my book on nonsexist child-rearing, I have made the round of some 30 cities doing lectures, interviews, and talk shows where listeners call in to register their views. The subject that comes up most often and arouses the most passion is not, as one might expect, sex after sex roles, or tips for an egalitarian marriage, but how men can be better fathers.

• "My father never knew me," said an intense male voice over a Grand Rapids phone-in show. "I don't want to make the same mistakes. I'm trying to learn how to father my own kids while there's still time."

• "I'll never forget what happened when I was ten years old. My mother had just died and my sister and I were standing beside the casket bawling," recalled a San Francisco man of 70. "When my father saw my tears, he grabbed me by the shoulders and said, 'We're *men*; we're not going to cry. We're going to be strong.' I've swallowed my tears for sixty years and all I've got to show for it is a lifelong lump in my throat and mean memories of my father."

• A New York City cabdriver told me forthrightly: "Being a father is more important to me than being black, being a Baptist, or being a man."

• "When our son said he was coming home from college on the day of my husband's office Christmas party, my husband asked him to come straight to the office," said a woman in Washington, D.C. "The boy bounded in, saw his father across the roomful of people, ran and threw his arms around my husband's neck and hugged and kissed him. At first I was embarrassed for my husband, but then I heard one man after another come up to him and say, 'I'd give the world if my son would do that with me.' "

Things seem to be changing. Fathering is becoming a new kind of verb—an active verb—that describes a new kind of role and a new set of behaviors. Men are affirmatively taking off time to be with their children. They are talking to one another about fathering, learning the parenting trade, and exchanging ideas and impressions the way mothers have for centuries. ... They are looking to women, not as emotional surrogates and stand-ins for the too-busy dad, but as expert counselors in the art of parent-child intimacy.

All over America, people are thinking about the fathers we have or the fathers we are, and fatherhood is being redefined, reinvented, and redeemed.

The one line in my book that many men have singled out as the most resonant is this bit of advice: *Don't be the man you think you should be, be the father you wish you'd had.*

American men grow up under powerful sex-role pressures to achieve that heralded state called "manhood." Many spend their lives trying to *prove* their manhood. Or to *earn* it by establishing the number of ways in which they are different from women. Primary in this proof-of-manhood-by-contrast-with-womanhood is the relationship each sex is "supposed" to have with babies and children.

It begins with the topsy-turvy notion that doll play makes boys into "sissies." If this homophobic equation did not cloud men's minds, they would recognize that when a boy plays with a doll, he is simply modeling the parent-child relationship he has known himself: he is pretending to be his own father. Presumably, in most cases, his own father is heterosexual. Thus, odd as it may sound, doll play for boys is homage to the husband-father role envisioned in the future of every heterosexual male.

More importantly, by making doll play off-limits to boys and by squelching their interest in "playing house," or caring for small children, *our culture creates an aversion to the very activities that make a man a good father.*

The way to resolve this absurd no-win situation is to reconcile the two contradictory paradigms— the "real man" and the "good father"—so that both embody the same admirable human values. ... Although a "real man" need not be a father, one who *is* a father must be able to feel his manhood enlarged and not depleted by active, caring fatherhood.

The language gives away the bias: "to father" a child refers to the momentary act of impregnation; "to mother" a child means to give succor and self-sacrifice for years.

We cannot watch a man kiss, rock, feed, bathe, or comfort a child, and exclaim: "Look at how he fathers that child!"—without feeling somehow as though we have misrepresented the scene. Needing to say "He mothers that child" is like needing to say "Those sisters exhibited real brotherhood toward one another." But the new "sisterhood" and the new "fatherhood" are returning those words to use with refreshed and refurbished meaning.

A child who grows up without a mother is said to be suffering maternal "deprivation" (dictionary definition: "loss, dispossession, bereavement"). Life without father, however, is merely father "absence" ("a state of being away"). The difference between "deprivation" and "absence" as value-packed concepts has allowed men routinely to walk out on their families and be bad guys at worst, while women who do so are unnatural monsters.

When a man is the "head of household," our society calls the family "traditional," but when a woman is the "head of household," the family is called "matriarchal" (as in the Moynihan Report on what's "wrong" with black families in America).

Patriarchy means "power of men." Matriarchy has come to mean "power of mothers." Patriarchy is the name of a social system in which men rule over women. Matriarchy is the name of a house without a father.

"Kramer vs. Kramer" mined the emotional truth of single parenthood, a long-ignored theme, but turned upside down the statistical reality of who leaves whom: Hollywood found the one story that made the mother the "heavy."

Nevertheless, the emotional residue the film leaves behind is profoundly radical: "Kramer vs. Kramer" subversively taught us what real fatherhood feels like, and what happens to a man who feels it. It showed us that a father who is deeply involved in the dailiness of his child's life, a father who is forced to be the buck-stops-here parent, to give routine and constant care, to *be* there, to witness the heart-stopping injuries, not just hear about them over dinner—that kind of father is unable to let his child go. (It is my hunch that such a father could not send his child to war with sanguine bravado, either.)

Dustin Hoffman did not fight for his son just to win or just to keep the boy from Meryl Streep. He fought because *he could not imagine life without his child*. He could not go back to fathering the way he used to, the way most men are fathers, and certainly not the way most men with visitation rights are fathers.

While a faculty member was introducing me to a college lecture audience, the hushed auditorium was pierced by a tiny child's high voice imitating a fire-engine siren. There was much rustling as heads turned toward the back where a man was trying to silence a baby of 18 months or so. The baby responded with "wrrooooeeeee," just as the introducer spoke my name. I sensed the collective embarrassment, watched the father hustle toward the exit, child in arms, nervously patting the child to keep it still.

From the podium, I called after him: "To the father in the back row, please remain with us. If your baby begins squealing during my speech, I will make an extra effort to be heard and the audience will listen a little harder. Although you happen to be a man, you are in the position of millions of women who, because of their sole responsibility for their children, exempt themselves from public events, or are excluded from places of education or entertainment.

"When we assume some of that responsibility," I continued, "we help parents remain in our midst. If we have learned to work, think, speak, and listen to one another over the sounds of male technology—over the air conditioners, phones, jet planes, stock market tickers, photocopiers, wire service machines, and computers—we can make an accommodation for the human sound of one baby in a college auditorium."

The audience roared their approval. The father stayed in his seat. I delivered my speech and eventually the baby fell asleep.

A few days later, my husband and I attended a concert in Manhattan. When a baby started mewing in the balcony, its father stayed, but its mother carried it from the concert hall.

Perhaps when more fathers are caretakers of children and more mothers are in control of the podium, family needs will be accommodated in public life.

I'm still hearing a lot about "bonding," that mystical connection that some say is forged between mother and child when, moments after birth, the baby is placed against the mother's chest. Supposedly, the amount of skin-to-skin touching and face-to-face cooing and eye contact determines how close mother and child will be for years to come.

This is typical of the Madonna-and-child mentality that isolates the twosome and puts the child's proper place at Mama's breast and in Mama's arms. "Mother and baby are doing fine," we say.

Where's Poppa? Out of the picture. Made to feel like an intruder in the charmed circle, he learns to stand at a slight distance gazing proudly as if at a precious possession—proprietary and concerned, but not crucial to the scene.

According to some bonding experts, "the first hours may have a lot to do with shaping the mother's attitude toward the child, the strength of her commitment to him [sic], and her capacity for mothering."

Might not the same be said for those first hours' potential to "attach" fathers to their children? The bonding proponents seem to be saying that without a strong early push in the baby's direction, the fabled "maternal instinct" might not emerge. Where are they when it comes to the father-infant bond, which is in far more desperate need of repair, since it hangs by a thread: paternity and little more?

Have you ever wondered why there are so few men in child care and so many men in the Right-to-Life movement? Or why a man who testifies so passionately about "unborn babies" is usually mute and impassive about child abuse, children's health problems, or children living in poverty?

The problem is that on public issues, men act as men, not as fathers. Until and unless men are full and involved buck-stops-here fathers, children can be meaningful only as symbols of patriarchal survival, not as fresh new lives needing nourishment and support.

Perhaps masculinist thinking divides life into dualities and dichotomies so that men can get the half that suits them. Children *per se* have been divided into the concept and the reality. Men are in charge of the concept of the child (they decide when life begins, or which child is "illegitimate," for example), while women are in charge of the reality (morning sickness, toxemia, breech births, cracked nipples, three meals a day, fevers, snowsuits, bathtimes, nightmares, and diapers).

As men become more familiar with the reality —through deeper forms of fatherhood—they may agree with mothers that many of the concepts have been wrong. Without dualities and dichotomies, both women and men might see children and childhood clearly from all directions for the first time.

If you doubt whether institutions can change, check the old and new editions of Dr. Spock's *Baby and Child Care*. After 27 years and sales in the tens of millions, Benjamin Spock rewrote portions of his "baby bible" to make important non-sexist improvements, including this bit about fathers:

Original: *A man can be a warm father and a real man at the same time. . . . Of course I don't mean that the father has to give just as many bottles or change just as many diapers as the mother. But it's fine for him to do these things occasionally. He might make the formula on Sunday.*

Revised: *I think that a father with a full-time job—even where a mother is staying home—will do best by his children, by his wife and himself if he takes on half or more of the management of the children (and also participates in the housework when he gets home from work and on weekends).*

In traditional households, there are two kinds of fathers: the father of sons and the father of daughters. These two kinds of fathers sometimes coexist in one and the same man. For instance, Daughter's Father kisses his child good-night, strokes her hair, hugs her warmly. This same man goes into the next room where he becomes Son's Father who says in a hearty voice perhaps accompanied by a firm pat on the shoulder: "Goodnight, son; see you in the morning."

Rather than be the best, most loving, most natural father he can be, this man screens his behavior. He relates to girls and boys in different ways, according to prescriptive notions of the father's role in helping each child's proper sexual identification. He has infused male-to-male affection with so many negative innuendoes that father-son love is tainted with perversion. So he holds back, is not as demonstrative as he might want to be, worries about toughening up his son for a man's world.

On the other side of the ledger, father-daughter relations are idyllic when the girl is young and neuter. But the more his daughter physically resembles a full-grown woman, the more the father loses sight of everything else she is as a person, and the more he cools his affection so that their relationship not seem "provocative" or "suggestive."

Although much has been written about the silence surrounding sexual abuse in troubled families, few have spoken of the millions of ordinary families who have suffered from the sexist sexualization of *normal* father-daughter relations.

In terms of *time* alone, the typical American father has a long way to go to achieve parity parenthood. One famous study found that the average father interacts with his baby for less than 38 seconds a day. In 38 seconds, you cannot even change a crib sheet or sing three verses of "The Farmer in the Dell." The *most* that any father in this sample devoted to his infant in one day was 10 minutes, 26 seconds—barely time enough for a bottle and a burp.

Other fathers studied have logged up to 15 minutes a day feeding their babies, compared to one and a half hours daily for mothers; almost half these fathers said that they had *never* changed the baby's diapers, and three out of four had no regular care-giving responsibilities whatsoever. With one-year-olds, fathers spend between 15 and 20 minutes per day, and although no one is quite sure how to measure father involvement with older children, we have only to look at children's survey responses to learn that it is not enough. In one study:

- half the preschool children questioned preferred the TV to their fathers;
- one child in 10 (age seven to 11) said that the person they fear most is their father;
- half the children wished their fathers would spend more time with them;
- among children of divorce, only one third said that they see their fathers regularly.

While reassuring harassed working mothers that what counts isn't the quantity but the quality of time they spend with their children, for the newly involved father, the challenge is to increase both quality *and* quantity.

After centuries—even millennia—of neglect, children are discovering their "other parent." And men are discovering their other selves.

Fathers are coming out of the closet: out of the still-stiff patriarchal collars of *their* fathers; out from the shadows of mothers' preeminence in the nursery; out of the office and factories where they have spent their lives being paid more the more they stayed away from their families.

As Ari Korpivaara shows in his account of life in a father-child play group . . . involved, creative fathering can be learned, and in the process a man can learn something unexpected about himself.

This then is the new father. We've been waiting for him for a long, long time.

TAKING ANOTHER LOOK

1 What does Pogrebin mean when she tells American males: "Don't be the man you think you should be, be the father you wish you had."

2 In Pogrebin's view, how does making doll play off-limits to boys and squelching their interest in "playing house" affect their later performance as fathers?

3 According to Pogrebin, what impact did the Hollywood film "Kramer vs. Kramer" have on the public's view of fatherhood?

4 According to traditional sex-role socialization, how do the fathers of sons differ from the fathers of daughters?

5 How do conflict theorists view the feminist critique of traditional sex-role socialization?

Role-Sharing Couples: A Study of Egalitarian Marriages

Linda Haas

In the traditional nuclear family, the husband serves as the sole breadwinner, while the wife confines herself to the roles of mother and homemaker. However, an increasing proportion of American couples are rejecting this model for a "dual-career" lifestyle. Currently, the majority of all married couples have two partners active in the paid labor force. In one-fourth of couples, both partners are "permanently committed" to their careers in that they have worked for at least five years.

In a sense, members of dual-career couples must undergo a process of *resocialization* (the process of discarding former behavior patterns and accepting new ones as part of a transition in one's life). A newly married couple may intend to have a "two-career household" and share child care in an egalitarian manner. Their parents, however, may have followed the conventional nuclear family pattern described earlier. Thus, neither of the newlyweds may have had useful role models of a dual-career lifestyle. Each may have had to overcome previous socialization into traditional expectations regarding marriage and the "proper" roles of husbands and wives.

In the following selection, sociologist Linda Haas examines a new style of marriage called "role-sharing" in which husbands and wives share traditionally male and female family responsibilites. A selected sample of 31 egalitarian couples was interviewed intensively over a six-month period. Haas reports that "almost all of the couples . . . revealed that they adopted role-sharing not as a result of an ideological commitment to sexual equality, but rather as a practical way of obtaining certain benefits which they perceived could not be realized in a traditional marriage with segregated husband-wife roles." She traces both the benefits and difficulties of role-sharing arrangements and concludes that this lifestyle demands "the wholeheartedly and enthusiastic willingness of both spouses to participate."

Many observers of changes in family roles have discussed the completely egalitarian or role-sharing arrangement as a theoretical possibility (Bailyn, 1978; Bernard, 1973; Bott, 1971; Garland, 1972; Nye, 1976; Scanzoni, 1972; Young & Willmont, 1973). The purpose of this paper is to report some results of a detailed empirical study of couples who have attempted role-sharing and generally succeeded in putting it into practice. The goals of the study were to discover the reasons couples adopted this alternative family lifestyle, the problems they had adjusting to it, and the solutions they developed to combat the problems encountered.

A marriage style based on the equal sharing of traditionally sex-segregated roles is very rarely

Author's Note: The author wishes to thank Sally Weiler and Rose Gartner for help with interviewing, and Ain Haas, Russell Middleton, Bert Adams, Bill Strahle and Colin Williams for comments on an earlier version of this paper. This research was partially supported by a traineeship and a small research grant from the NIMH Social Organization Training Program, University of Wisconsin—Madison, 1975–76.

found in practice and subsequently has been generally unstudied by social scientists. There have been several studies of dual-career families, but these families generally do not practice role-sharing. While the wife is committed to a career, her basic family responsibilities typically remain intact and her husband's career has precedence over hers (Bryson, Bryson & Johnson, 1978; Holmstrom, 1973; Poloma & Garland, 1971; Rapoport & Rapoport, 1977). Studies have also been done on American parents who shared the child-care role (DeFrain, 1975; 1979) and Norwegian couples where both spouses chose part-time work (Grønseth, 1976; 1978). Yet even in these studies, the role-sharing arrangement was only partly in evidence: DeFrain's androgynous parents did not share housework or breadwinning equally and Grønseth's work-sharing couples did not share housework or childcare evenly. Sociologists have also paid some attention to discovering the actual division of labor and its determinants in the general population (e.g., Nye, 1976), but their samples have not been large enough to incorporate many role-sharing families, and thus have given us little insight into the role-sharing lifestyle.

As distinct from the partial steps toward sex-role equality discussed above, fully developed role-sharing can be defined as the sharing by husband and wife of each of the traditionally segregated family roles, including:

The breadwinner role. The husband and wife are equally responsible for earning family income; the wife's employment is not considered more optional or less desirable than the husband's. Consequently, the spouses' occupations are equally important and receive equal status, or at least the occupation which has more status is not determined by notions of the intrinsic supremacy of one sex over the other.

The domestic role. The husband and wife are equally responsible for performing housekeeping chores such as cooking, cleaning, and laundry.

The handyman role. The husband and wife are equally responsible for performing traditionally masculine tasks such as yardwork and repairs.

The kinship role. The husband and wife are equally responsible for meeting kinship obligations, like buying gifts and writing letters, which have traditionally been the wife's responsibility.

The childcare role. The husband and wife are equally responsible for doing routine childcare tasks and for rearing and disciplining of children.

The major/minor decision-maker roles. The spouses have generally equal influence on the making of major decisions which males have traditionally dominated and the minor decisions traditionally delegated to the female.

Specialization within any of these roles (e.g., husband cooks, wife launders) would be compatible with role-sharing, as long as specific tasks are not assigned to a spouse *on the basis of sex* (i.e., because they are deemed more appropriate for someone of his/her gender) and as long as the over-all responsibility for the duties of *each* role is evenly shared.

STUDY DESIGN

Since past studies of the family imply that role-sharing couples make up a very tiny proportion of the general population, a random sampling design could not be employed in this study without a great amount of expense and time. Therefore, a type of purposive or strategic sampling technique was employed (cf. Glaser & Strauss, 1967). In the liberal university community of Madison, Wisconsin, 154 couples were identified who had been referred by others or by themselves as sharing fairly evenly the responsibilities of breadwinning, housekeeping, childcare, and decision-making. Their names were obtained through contacts in various local institutions and associations (e.g., a daycare center, a chapter of the National Organization for Women, a liberal religious group, university organizations) and through announcements published in local newsletters and newspapers.

Each of these couples was contacted by telephone during January, 1976. Whoever answered the phone was asked several questions designed to ascertain in a rough fashion whether or not his or her relationship was characterized by role-sharing, as reputed. To be included for further study, both spouses had to be engaged in, looking for, or preparing for work and spending roughly the same number of hours per week on work or school-related pursuits. The wife's employment could not be seen as something less permanent than the husband's, and an unequivocally affirmative answer had to be given to the question, "Would you say that each of you has roughly the same amount of influence over family decisions?" When asked, "What percent of all the housework that's done in your household do you think you do?", the answer had to be in the 40–60% range, as did the answer to a similar question about childcare.

In the group of couples who were initially contacted by phone and willing to be interviewed, nearly half turned out not really to practice role-sharing in their marriages, according to the rough preliminary measures. Among the remaining couples who were tentatively labeled as role-sharers, some types were not included in the study. One type consisted of couples who hired outside help for housecleaning. Since being able to afford cleaning help is not available to all economic classes and I was primarily interested in studying the factors which promise to increase role-sharing among couples on a widespread basis, a decision was made to exclude those having housecleaning help. Another group of role-sharing couples not picked for further study were those not legally married since they might have unique arrangements that I was not prepared to study in detail. Several other couples were eliminated for miscellaneous reasons, such as living too far out of town for convenient interviewing.

After eliminating couples on such grounds, there were 31 remaining who qualified on the various criteria and were willing to participate in the study. The sample was fairly homogeneous, despite efforts to recruit a variety of types for the study. For the most part, the people in the sample were training themselves for or engaged in jobs in professional fields, usually in social service or the humanities. The sample couples tended to be young, with a majority of them being 26 to 30 years old. The mean number of years they had been married was six. Nearly half of them had children, most of which were not yet old enough to go to school.

Both the husband and wife in each of the 31 couples were interviewed three times from January through June of 1976. Averaging 1–1/2 hours each, these interviews usually took place in the couples' homes and were tape-recorded. The spouses were interviewed separately during most of the questioning. After the interviews, written forms were left with the individuals to be filled out and returned by mail. These included a time-budget and an attitudinal questionnaire.

The great majority of the 31 couples were later found to be generally as egalitarian as the preliminary phone measures suggested, when the extent and ways in which couples shared breadwinning, housekeeping, childcare, kinship obligations, and handyman chores were investigated. The family power structure was also studied by obtaining information on the process and outcome of several recent and hypothetical decision-making activities. Any departures from equality were spread out, with no couples falling short on more than a small proportion of the numerous and fairly stringent standards for meeting an ideal of total role-sharing. Even those who failed to meet every last one of these standards showed themselves to be aspiring towards an ideal of marital equality not strived for by the general population or even by most dual-career couples. (See Haas, 1977, for a full description of all the indicators for role-sharing and specifics on how these couples measured up.)

RESULTS AND DISCUSSION

Motivations for Role-Sharing Behavior

In replies to open-ended questions about why they shared the responsibilities of bread-winning, decision-making, and domestic chores, each couple gave several motives for role-sharing. In the results which follow, couples are listed as giving a certain reason if either spouse reported it, but spouses usually answered the same way. Almost all of the couples in the sample revealed that they adopted role-sharing not as a result of an ideological commitment to sexual equality, but rather as a practical way of obtaining certain benefits which they perceived could not be realized in a traditional marriage with segregated husband-wife roles. The vast majority of couples said they became pessimistic about traditional marriage roles after trying a traditional pattern in their marriage in its early years. Over one-third of the individuals said they were also predisposed to attempt a non-traditional role pattern because they felt their parents had been constrained by the traditional familial division of labor. Finally, a handful of the respondents had been married previously and complained that conflict over sex-role expectations had been a major factor in their divorces.

The benefits attainable through role-sharing usually occurred to the wife first and more often aided her than the husband. However, a considerable part of the motivation to try a non-traditional pattern also involved a desire to liberate the husband from the confines of his traditional family role.

Benefits for the Individual One anticipated benefit for both spouses was a greater opportunity to develop their abilities and pursue personal interests without being limited by traditional role expectations. Over four-fifths of the sample adopted role-sharing so the wife could satisfy her desire to work outside the home for personal fulfillment. One-fifth of the couples reported picking the role-sharing lifestyle so that each spouse would have the freedom to quit outside employment for a time and pursue other interests.

Another motive for role-sharing was relief from the stress and overwork that results from having primary responsibility for a broad area of family life. Almost three-fourths of the couples wanted to eliminate the overload dilemmas faced by working women who remain primarily responsible for housework and childcare. This benefit of role-sharing did seem to have been realized, according to time-budget data collected in individual diaries for a week between the first and second interviews. Wives in the sample averaged 16.0 hours per week at housework, while men averaged 16.2.

Mothers in the study averaged 12.2 hours per week at specific childcare tasks, while fathers spent 10.4. The general equality of the workload was also evident in the finding that the women spent 26.8 hours per week at hobbies, watching television, socializing, organizational meetings, etc., compared to the men's average of 26.2 hours of leisure activities. In contrast, time-budget studies of the general population show employed husbands averaging almost 6–1/2 more hours of free-time activities a week than employed wives (Szalai, 1972).

Over half of the couples mentioned that the role-sharing lifestyle was adopted so that the husband would not be burdened more than the wife with the provider responsibility and its concomitant anxiety and stress. While this benefit was fully achieved by the majority of couples in the study, at least one partner in one-third (10) of the couples (usually the male) reported a little difficulty in completely letting go of the traditional idea that the man is more responsible for earning income than the wife, or that the wife was less obligated to work to provide family income. In most of these cases, it was the wife's newer or lesser interest in a career that was used as an explanation for the partial retention of this traditional sex-role expectation for men. These 10 couples said, however, that this was an idea they no longer wanted to believe in and certainly would not act on.

Another major motive for role-sharing cited by these couples was greater independence of the husband and wife. While the role-sharers in the study neither desired nor actually led completely independent lives within marriage, over one-fourth of them initiated role-sharing to avoid the economic dependence wives traditionally have had on husbands, while one-sixth wanted to avoid the dependence most husbands experience when it comes to getting domestic chores done—e.g., cooking, laundry, mending.

Benefits for the Family Several people who were happier because of new opportunities for self-fulfillment and relief from one-sided burdens reported themselves to be better marriage partners as a side benefit, however there were other ways in which couples tried to improve their family life directly through role-sharing. For instance, almost two-thirds of the couples cited a desire to cut down on the resentment and conflict that they saw resulting from husbands having more power in marriage. Generally, a shared decision-making pattern was the first aspect of role-sharing to be tried, and the one aspect that was relatively easy to establish. Several individuals commented that a positive but unanticipated consequence of a shared decision-making pattern was that it called for a considerable amount of discussion and this communicating in turn brought greater intimacy between husband and wife.

Another way couples thought role-sharing would improve husband-wife relations, reported by one-fifth of the couples, was in giving them more in common—with both spouses working and both having domestic responsibilities. Several individuals reported that having so much in common caused them to appreciate and sympathize with each other more. Each could appreciate problems the other had at work or school because they came up against the same things, and they were less likely to nag at each other if a task went undone because they personally knew how hard it was to get around to doing an undesirable chore. Several people also said the role-sharing gave them the opportunity to do more things together, increasing interaction and thus enhancing husband-wife closeness. A few couples were in the same occupational field, so they could profitably discuss their work and occasionally work on projects together. The spouses also had occasion to be together while domestic chores were being performed. Since the work hours of husbands and wives were approximately even and their work schedules were often similar, the couples had occasion to spend a lot of their free time together.

Besides an improvement in husband-wife relations, another major benefit of role-sharing cited for the family was improvement in parent-child relations. This was not a factor in the initial decision to adopt role-sharing, but it became a reason for continuing the arrangement. Five of the twelve women with children at home felt they had become better mothers because they worked outside the home and shared childcare with their husbands. They felt they were less bored, less hassled with managing two roles, and not resentful about shouldering the entire burden of childcare. Three of the 24 parents mentioned that sharing childcare meant that the children got to know their father better than they would in a traditional family, and three parents thought children benefited by being exposed to more than just the mother's outlook on things.

The final major benefit for the family that couples wanted to achieve with role-sharing was greater financial security. One-fourth of the couples said they chose a dual-earner arrangement to provide the family with more income on a permanent basis. Incidentally, the vast majority of couples pooled their incomes, and in all of the couples the wife's income was not saved for extras but was used for family expenses as much as was the husband's.

PROBLEMS WITH ROLE-SHARING

While these couples' efforts to implement role-sharing brought the benefits they anticipated, several difficulties with this arrangement were reported in responses to questions about problems with role-sharing. Some of these problems appeared to result from certain personal obstacles related to vestiges of traditional sex roles in the family. Others seemed to come from trying to transcend sex roles within family units in the context of a larger more traditional society. Still other problems seemed to be inherent in the role-sharing lifestyle itself.

Problems Sharing the Domestic Role   Of all the areas of role-sharing, couples reported problems most often in the establishment of an egalitarian division of domestic chores. These problems can be grouped into four types, listed here in order of their frequency: disinclination to do non-traditional tasks, discrepancies in housekeeping standards, wife's reluctance to delegate domestic responsibility, and lack of non-traditional domestic skills.

The most common type of problem in sharing domestic chores, reported by over half of the couples, was that one or both spouses lacked the inclination to do some non-traditional tasks for which they had skills or for which no special skill was required. About one-third of the couples with this problem mentioned that it was hard to break with the traditional pattern they had observed in their parents' households. Over one-third claimed that it often seemed more efficient to let the traditional spouse perform the chore in the face of the other partner's inexperience, busy schedule, or laziness.

Couples had different solutions for this problem. Most often, the spouse who felt over-worked (usually the wife) complained and threatened to stop doing the chore or some other task until the lazy spouse resolved to do better. Sometimes a temporary system of rotation was agreed upon to get the recalcitrant spouse into the right habit. Occasionally the lazy spouse would develop more of a liking or tolerance for the chore or become so experienced at it that the problem would be solved. Some couples ended up agreeing to some specialization in order to avoid further conflict, especially if each spouse wanted to avoid certain non-traditional chores that the other spouse did not mind doing.

Another frequent problem in overcoming the traditional chore pattern involved the standards spouses had for housekeeping. Over half of the couples reported that at an earlier time in their marriage the wives had generally advocated a much higher standard of orderliness and cleanliness in the household than their husbands. This did not produce any conflict as long as the woman was in charge of getting the chores done, but when the decision to share responsibility for chores was reached, wives pushed for chores to be done as often as they wanted to see them done and in the manner they preferred. They fretted about the condition of the house all the time and experienced embarrassment if someone dropped in unexpectedly. Husbands, on the other hand, wanted to do the chores according to their own ideas on how often they needed to be done and in the manner (often unconventional) that appealed most to them. Husbands consistently felt wives were too finicky and wives regarded husbands as too sloppy.

Most of the couples coped with this discrepancy in standards by simultaneously having wives lower their expectations and husbands raise theirs. This change was usually precipitated by wives being busy with their jobs or schoolwork and it was accompanied by many heated discussions and practical experiments. Both spouses generally professed to be happier with the new standard, but the wives still tended to believe in a somewhat higher standard than their husbands. When asked, "Do you think that housework is done as often and as well as you want it to be?" almost one-half of the wives (but less than one-third of the husbands) expressed discontent with the level or orderliness and cleanliness of their homes. Wives were also more likely to mention spontaneously that they would like to hire outside help, while most of their husbands opposed hiring an outsider to do domestic chores.

Since both the husband and wife were busy with jobs or schoolwork, it is not surprising that many individuals felt anxious about their housekeeping standard. On the other hand, there was little evidence that their homes were in fact being neglected, for their homes generally seemed neat and clean to the interviewers. The actual number of hours spent at traditional housekeeping tasks (around 20 hours a week per couple) was still rather high, though not in the 30–40 hour range for working couples or the 50–70 range for house-wives found in other studies (Robinson & Converse, cited in Babcock, 1975; Walker, 1970). Either the role-sharing couples were correct in their belief that they had a low housekeeping standard, in ways not apparent to a casual visitor, or they skipped a lot of unnecessary housework and kept house more efficiently than traditional couples.

A third problem, mentioned by half the couples, was the wife's reluctance to give up her traditional authority over many domestic chores. For all but one of these couples, this problem had been overcome by the time of the study. One-third of the women in the study reported that they expected to do all the traditionally female domestic chores when they got married because of socialization—their mothers had done them and they had learned it was the woman's duty to do those chores. Some of the women in the sample mentioned that they had actually enjoyed the challenge of trying to be simultaneously a great housewife and a successful professional.

The change to a more even sharing of domestic chores was not easy. Not only did the wives have to contend with the husband's disinclination to do chores, they also had to cope with guilt feelings about abandoning their traditional role and with the mixed feelings they had seeing their husbands do non-traditional tasks. As their strong interest in a profession consumed more and more of their mental and physical energy over the years, however, housework seemed increasingly tedious rather than challenging. In addition, the women's movement led them to believe that doing double work is unfair and made them feel better about sharing domestic chores with their husbands.

The last type of problem couples had in sharing domestic chores was a lack of skills on the part of one or the other of the spouses. Over one-third of the couples cited this as an impediment to the realization of equality. For half of these couples it was the husband's lack of expertise in areas such as cooking or sewing which had caused problems, and in the other half of the cases it was the wife's inability to do things like make repairs or handle the car which had inhibited an equal sharing of responsibility.

Couples sought to cope with this type of problem by having the more knowledgeable spouse teach the other one the new skill, or by having the incapable spouse develop the necessary ability on his or her own. This solution often failed to work out, for the spouse without a certain skill often lacked a desire to persist through the frustration and disappointment accompanying the learning experience. Other individuals claimed they were too busy with their careers or hesitated giving up valuable leisure time to learn a new skill and it seemed more efficient to let the expert spouse do the task. Many tasks also came up only in a crisis (stopped-up drain, faulty car brakes, popped-off button) and many individuals felt that this was not a good time to learn. Normalcy would be restored quicker if the expert fixed things up. Finally, in cases such as wives trying to learn car maintenance and home repairs, they had to interact with skeptical and hostile outsiders in the pursuit of these skills (e.g., hardware store personnel, garage mechanics). As a result, wives tended to shrink away from this type of contact and avoid learning the task.

Wives were generally less successful at acquiring the skills required for the husband's traditional chores than vice versa. Husbands on the average spent the same amount of hours doing traditionally feminine domestic chores as wives but wives spent less time on the average than husbands on "male" chores such as interior home repairs and yardwork (1.3 hours per week vs. 2.9, according to time-budget data). The figures are small, but they do suggest that the wives, who typically were the instigators of role-sharing, hadn't put much effort into sharing all of the husband's traditional family responsibilities. Interestingly, most of the couples did not perceive this difference to be a problem, perhaps because masculine domestic chores take up so little time compared to other types of domestic chores.

A few couples had succeeded in getting one spouse to pick up a skill once possessed only by the other. Husbands learning how to mend was the situation most often cited. In these cases it seemed that learning was aided by the wife restraining herself from nagging the husband to learn, and by her giving him positive verbal reinforcement of non-condescending type.

Conflicts Involving Jobs   Besides problems in sharing domestic responsibilities, couples also described several difficulties associated with having two jobs in the sample family. One serious problem was conflict between the spouses' jobs or studies. All but three of the couples felt that conflicts between jobs could be a problem in the future, when asked about a hypothetical situation where one spouse would be offered a job in a city different from that in which his or her spouse already worked. Most couples had already settled on strategies for dealing with this situation. A strategy most of them planned to employ was to give the spouse who had the *less* marketable skills or the poorer job opportunities their choice when a conflict arose. (Husbands' jobs were not any more likely to be given priority in the total sample than were wives'.) The next most common plan was establishing a long-distance marriage—that is, both spouses accepting their job offers, living in different cities, and visiting each other regularly. This possibility was mentioned by over half of the couples, most of whom did not yet have children. For the most part, couples did not like the idea of separating but were willing to consider it as a way to maintain a dual-career marriage. Another solution mentioned by some couples was for husband and wife to take turns holding the job of their choice. Finally, a few couples mentioned that one spouse's job offer in another city might be regarded as an opportunity for the other to do free-lance work, engage in independent research, or start a business. Several couples hoped to avoid

making a decision about job priority by only looking for jobs at the same time in the same geographic area. This solution was only available to couples in which the husband and wife were at comparable stages in their careers, which was not common, since husbands tended to be older than wives.

Another common problem was conflict between jobs and family responsibilities. This was reported by over half of the total sample, by husbands a little more often than wives (in contrast to typical dual-career couples, where the wife usually reports job-family conflicts). Most of those individuals reporting job-family conflicts mentioned that their jobs interfered with family responsibilities in various ways: housework didn't get done, they lacked energy and patience to interact well with their children, or they did not have enough leisure time to spend with their families. About one-third of those reporting conflicts mentioned that family duties interfered with their job performance: they had to cut down on overtime work, had trouble doing job-related work at home, had to rearrange their schedules when children became ill, or had little time to attend job-related meetings in the evenings and on weekends.

The couples' strategies for dealing with job-family conflicts usually involved adjusting housework. The most common strategy, employed by over one-third of the couples, was to cut down on housework or at least give it a very low priority—after meeting job or school responsibilities and after spending free time with family members. Next most common was for couples to maintain a regular schedule of housekeeping so it never got out of hand. Several couples mentioned that almost daily they engaged in negotiation and discussion regarding who would assume responsibility for the various family chores that would come up that day. By careful planning they were able to save considerable time while also assuring that chores got done. The two couples with the oldest children had encouraged their offspring to take care of themselves to a great extent (e.g., wash their own clothes) and to assume regular responsibility for some household chores.

Several couples mentioned that they tried to cut down on their jobs' interference with family life by segregating the two as much as possible. Both husbands and wives tried not to bring work home and tried to reserve weekends and evenings for family activities. It was not clear whether role-sharing put these individuals at a real career disadvantage, although some observers have suggested that it would (Hunt & Hunt, 1977). Many of the role-sharers in the study were noticeably productive in their fields, so perhaps a role-sharing lifestyle contains some compensations that allow an individual to do well at a career (e.g., interaction with spouse on professional matters, more efficient time-use).

CONCLUSION

The problems and pitfalls experienced by the role-sharers in this study suggest that role-sharing is a lifestyle demanding the wholeheartedly and enthusiastic willingness of both spouses to participate. Both partners have to take into account each other's job and leisure activities when planning things that impinge on each other. For these couples, this kind of commitment to role-sharing seemed to derive from the expectation that the arrangement would produce benefits for both spouses which would outweigh the costs of implementing a new style of marriage.

REFERENCES

Babcock, B., Freedman, A., Norton, E., & Ross, S. *Sex discrimination and the law—causes and remedies.* Boston: Little, Brown, 1975.

Bailyn, L. Accommodation of work to family. In R. Rapoport & R. Rapoport (Eds.), *Working couples.* New York: Harper & Row, 1978.

Bernard, J. *The future of marriage.* New York: Bantam, 1973.

Bott, E., *Family and social network.* New York: Free Press, 1971.

Bryson, R., Bryson, J., & Johnson, M. Family size, satisfaction, and productivity in dual-career couples. *Psychology of Women Quarterly,* 1978, **3**, 66–77.

DeFrain, J. *The nature and meaning of parenthood.* Unpublished doctoral dissertation, University of Wisconsin-Madison, 1975.

DeFrain, J. Androgynous parents tell who they are and what they need. *The Family Coordinator,* 1979, **28**, 237–243.

Garland, T. N. The better half? The male in the dual profession family. In C. Safilios-Rothschild (Ed.), *Toward a sociology of women.* Lexington, MA: Xerox, 1972.

Glaser, B. G., & Strauss, A. L. *The discovery of grounded theory: Strategies for qualitative research.* Chicago: Aldine, 1967.

Grønseth, E. Work-sharing families. In A. G. Kharchev & M. B. Sussman (Eds.), *Liberation of women, changing sex roles, family structure and dynamics.* New York: 1976.

Grønseth, E. Work sharing: A Norwegian example. In R. Rapoport & R. Rapoport (Eds.), *Working couples.* New York: Harper & Row, 1978.

Haas, L. *Sexual equality in the family: A study of role-sharing couples.* Unpublished doctoral dissertation, University of Wisconsin-Madison, 1977.

Holstrom, L. *The two-career family.* Cambridge, MA: Schenkman, 1973.

Hunt, J., & Hunt, L. Dilemmas and contradictions of status: The case of the dual-career family. *Social Problems,* 1977, **24**, 404–416.

Nye, F. *Role structure and analysis of the family.* Beverly Hills: Sage, 1976.

Poloma, M., & Garland, T. N. The myth of the egalitarian family: Familiar roles and the professionally employed wife. In A. Theodore (Ed.), *The professional woman.* Cambridge, MA: Schenkman, 1971.

Rapoport, R., & Rapoport, R. *Dual career families re-examined.* New York: Harper & Row, 1977.

Scanzoni, J. *Sexual bargaining.* Englewood Cliffs, NJ: Prentice-Hall, 1972.

Szalai, A. *The use of time.* Paris: Mouton, 1972.

Walker, K. Time-use patterns for household work related to homemakers' employment. U.S. Department of Agriculture, Agricultural Research Service, 1970.

Young, M., & Willmont, P. *The symmetrical family.* New York: Pantheon, 1973.

TAKING ANOTHER LOOK

1 Identify five of the traditionally segregated family roles that are shared in a role-sharing couple.
2 Why was it undesirable to use a random sampling design in this study of role-sharing couples?
3 In the view of role-sharing couples, what benefits for the individual can result from such arrangements? What benefits for the family can result?
4 What problems were reported by couples in sharing domestic chores?
5 What problems were reported by couples involving conflict between the spouses' jobs?
6 How might functionalist theorists view the findings of this study of role-sharing couples?
7 How might conflict theorists view the findings of this study of role-sharing couples?

Courtship Violence Among College Students

James M. Makepeace

Wife battering, child abuse, abuse of the elderly, and other forms of domestic violence are an ugly reality of American family life. Sociologist Murray Straus has estimated that at least 8 million Americans are assaulted every year by family members. However, it is difficult to measure precisely the prevalence of domestic violence, since many Americans are reluctant to call the police or to bring charges against family members. Lois Haight Herrington, chair of the attorney general's Task Force on Family Violence, admits that "family violence is an enormous problem, but we have no idea how enormous."

In a sense, domestic violence may even begin before marriage in the form of violent behavior within dating and courtship relationships. Violence during dating resembles other assaults in that it may involve pushing, slapping, punching, hitting with a weapon, and choking. Yet its consequences differ in one important respect: while assaults or rapes by strangers leave victims wary of being alone, an attack by an acquaintance often causes the victim to become fearful of trusting someone again and frightened of close relationships.

In the following selection, sociologist James M. Makepeace reports the results of a survey of 202 college students concerning the extent and nature of courtship violence. More than three-fifths (61.5 percent) of the respondents personally knew of someone who had been involved in courtship violence; more than one-fifth (21.2 percent) had had at least one direct personal experience. Makepeace concludes that "violence is a common, albeit neglected, aspect of premarital heterosexual interaction." He calls for further research on courtship violence and for the development of social policies to deal with this disturbing problem.

In recent years sociologists and social practitioners have devoted increasing attention to the occurrence of violent behavior within familial contexts. Goode (1971) and Steinmetz and Straus (1973) have presented general theoretical analyses of the use of force and violence in the family that have influenced much subsequent work. This has been complemented by work by others that has been focused on more particular forms of family violence. Interest in parent-child violence, for example, has been expressed by Gil (1971), Chase (1975), Steinmetz and Straus (1974), and others have focused on inter-spousal including Straus (1978), Gelles (1972), and Martin (1976).

Although there are reviews of the general literature of family violence (Gelles, 1979; Renvoize, 1978; Straus, Gelles, & Steinmetz, 1980), little attention has been devoted to the occurrence of violent behavior within the context of dating and courtship relationships. This seems to be a significant hiatus in the literature because the premarital relationship is so typically viewed as the context in which actors are socialized into later marital roles. Instead of focusing on the premarital period as one of socialization into spousal violence, however, researchers consistently seem to have focused instead on a link with violence in the family of orientation (Flynn, Note 1; Gelles, 1972; Langley & Levy, 1977; Owens & Straus, 1975; Steele & Pollock, 1968; Straus et al., 1980). The potential mediating link that courtship violence might play between violence in the family of orientation and violence in the later family (the family of procreation) appears to have been overlooked.

The present study constitutes an initial approach to the problem of courtship violence. It is an exploratory study for which the following goals were delineated: to develop and refine an instrument for measuring and studying courtship violence, to estimate the incidence of courtship violence in a sample of college students, to describe variations in the forms that courtship violence takes, and to identify basic social correlates of the phenomenon.

METHODS

The research was conducted at a medium size midwestern state university in the spring of 1979. A questionnaire exploring various dimensions of courtship violence was distributed to students enrolled in several sections of introductory sociology and family sociology. The questionnaires were anonymous, took about 20 minutes to complete, and were administered during regularly scheduled class periods.

The sample consisted of 202 respondents, 49% of whom were men and 51% of whom were women. Respondents were predominantly freshmen and sophomores (81.3%), from rural and small town backgrounds (only 30.5% were from communities over 25,000), middle income (62% from families in the $10,000–30,000 range), and predominantly Protestant and Catholic (78.4%).

RESULTS

Prevalence

The incidence of both actual and threatened courtship violence was examined; also, respondents were questioned both about direct personal experiences and about the violent experiences of people that they personally knew. The phenomenon was sufficiently common that the majority of the students responding (61.5%) had personally known of someone who had been involved in courtship violence, and one-fifth (21.2%) had had at least one direct personal experience. Of the 39 students who had been personally involved, 25 had had such an experience on only one occasion; one person had had such experiences on 8 separate occasions.

The particular form in which the force was manifested varied. The respondents were presented with a list of specific forms that violence might take and asked to check those in which they had been involved. The specific forms of violence contained on the checklist ranged from threat to assault with a lethal weapon. It is recognized that the various forms of violence studied do not necessarily represent consistent degrees of severity or brutality. Clearly, a threat of assault with a weapon could be construed as the use of a greater measure of force than a mild shove, and similarly, repeated brutal shoves against a concrete wall constitute a greater measure of force than a one time swipe with a small hand bag. Furthermore, the social context in which the violence occurs and the relationship of the aggressor to the victim greatly influence the "meaning" of the means of violence employed. The order of the forms on the checklist represents, thus, not a consistent characteristic of the forms themselves, but a preconception regarding the seriousness which each form represents "most of the time."

[1]Flynn, J. *Spouse assault: Its dimensions and characteristics in Kalamazoo Co., Mich.* Unpublished field studies in research and practice. School of Social Work, Western Michigan University, Kalamazoo, MI, 1975.

The results of this phase of the inquiry are displayed in Table 1. As would be expected, the incidence of courtship violence "known of" greatly exceeded that which was directly experienced, and the forms that ordinarily are thought of as more extreme, such as assault with an object or weapon, were less common than the milder forms such as "pushing" or "slapping." Beyond the existence of a differential in incidence, there appears to be a clustering effect among the different forms. Thus, choking and assault with a lethal weapon were alike in that they were directly experienced in a relatively small number of cases, whereas punching and striking with an object were three to four times as common, threatening was twice again as common, and pushing-shoving and slapping were both about one and one-half times again as common.

Description of the Experiences

In view of the variety of purposes for which violence may be employed—as Goode (1971) has said, it is one of the four "major resources by which people can move others to serve their ends" —it would be expected that there would be significant variations in the particular ways in which it is manifested. Not unexpectedly, the most frequent reason cited as the source of the disagreement that sparked the violence was jealousy of one partner in the relationship over the real or perceived involvement of the other with another man or woman (27.2%). Disagreements over drinking behavior and anger over sexual denial were the other two most frequently mentioned sources that precipitated disagreement. The most frequent place of occurrence was a residence (51.3%; a home, a dormitory, or an apartment), but a significant percentage of the incidents also occurred in vehicles (21.6%) and out-of-doors (21.6%).

The perception of who was the victim and who the aggressor would, more than most of the questions, seem likely to be influenced by the subjective perceptions of those involved. The self reports of actors involved in a violent courtship situation would, like those involved in other situations where the "social desirability" bias (Edwards, 1957) would operate, tend to depict "self" in a relatively favorable way and "other" in a relatively negative way. It is probably for this reason that when asked, "Would you consider yourself the victim or the aggressor in the incident?," the respondents were more likely to report themselves to have been the victim (71.1% vs. 28.9%).

Finally, the involvement of alcohol in courtship violence was explored briefly. Respondents were asked whether they themselves, and whether the other person involved, were under the influence of alcohol at the time of the occurrence of the incident. No attempt was made to quantify the degree of intoxification. Rather, the respondents were allowed to refer to their own understanding of the terms "under the influence of alcohol" in answering the question.

As with the foregoing item of victim/aggressor status, some social desirability bias probably influenced the responses to this question producing an underestimate of the percentage of respondents and an overestimate of the percentage of the "others" who were under the influence of alcohol. About one-third (31.6%) of the respondents re-

TABLE 1 EXPERIENCE OF COLLEGE STUDENTS WITH VARIOUS TYPES OF COURTSHIP VIOLENCE, DIRECT AND INDIRECT

| Type of Violence | Incidence of Experience | | | |
| | Indirect | | Direct | |
	n	%	n	%
Threat	72	35.6	17	8.4
Pushed	84	41.9	28	13.9
Slapped	98	48.5	26	12.9
Punched	47	23.3	8	4.0
Struck with Object	32	15.8	7	3.5
Assault with Weapon	16	7.9	2	1.0
Choked	15	7.4	3	1.5
Other	13	6.4	6	3.0

ported that they had been drinking, whereas 50% indicated that the other person had been drinking.

Selected Sex Differences

One of the striking findings of Straus, Gelles, and Steinmetz's recent study of family violence was the lack of a significant difference between males and females in the extent of their use of violence. Overall, there were about the same number of wives who had attacked their husbands (11.6%) as husbands who had attacked their wives (12.1%). They cautioned, however, that this should not be interpreted to mean that husbands are as seriously victimized by intra-spousal violence as are wives—indeed, "Even though wives are also violent, they are in the weaker, more vulnerable position in respect to violence in the family" (Straus et al., 1980, p. 44).

Although this study did not include an investigation of the relative extent of violence by sex, it appeared that, as with intra-spousal violence, the female partner was more likely to be victimized, or at least to feel victimized, than was the male. Thus, whereas the majority of the male respondents (69.2%) reported that they were the "aggressor," the females overwhelmingly (91.7%) perceived of themselves as victims (see Table 2).

Also shown in Table 2 are two other variables that were expected to be sex linked: (a) whether the respondent was under the influence of alcohol, and, (b) whether legal authorities were notified. It was expected that because males were more

often the "aggressors," and because being under the influence of alcohol has some acceptance as an excuse for "letting off steam" in our culture, that the males would be more likely to report this to have been the case. Although the result was in line with this expectation, the difference was not statistically significant.

Finally, it was expected that because there would be considerably more likelihood of ridicule of a male who reported having been assaulted by a female than vice-versa, males would be significantly less likely to report such an incident to legal authorities. The difference, again, is in the direction anticipated—in fact, not a single male made such a report. However, the difference, and the sample sizes, simply were not large enough to yield statistical significance. Additional research on these questions may yield significant results if more extensive samples are employed.

Subsequent Developments

Data concerning the following aspects of the subsequent development of the relationship were collected: (a) whether the individuals continued their involvement with one another, (b) whether law enforcement authorities were notified, and, (c) whether the respondents were involved in further courtship violence with one another on a subsequent occasion. It would seem reasonable to expect that most individuals who had been subjected to or threatened with violence in a courtship relationship would avoid seeing the other person again, and that some, especially those who were subjected to more severe violence, would notify legal authorities. Previous research (Gelles, 1976; Langley & Levy, 1977) on spousal abuse has found, however, that, for a variety of reasons many individuals subjected to violence will continue their relationship with their assailant even when the abuse has been very brutal.

Many of the constraints that are assumed to explain the continued involvement of victims in relationships with their assailants do not, however, seem particularly pertinent to violence in court-

TABLE 2   SEX DIFFERENCES ON SELECTED FEATURES OF COURTSHIP VIOLENCE

Feature	Male		Female	
	n	%	n	%
Perceived self as victim	4	30.8	22	91.7*
Under influence of alcohol	6	46.2	6	35.3
Notified authorities	0	00.0	3	13.0

*p < .01.

ship situations. The factors of economic hardship, need of their children for a father's economic support, desire to avoid the stigma of divorce, and the difficulty that women with children have in finding work, simply are not particularly germaine to the situations of unmarried victims. It might, therefore, be expected that the outcome would be different. The present results, however, do not support such an interpretation.

In half (18 of 37) of the cases examined, violence occurred on multiple occasions, and in several cases (8%) it occurred 5 or more times. Only about half of the relationships "broke off" (55.3%); the other half either were still involved with the other person in the same capacity (15.8%) or had actually become more deeply involved (28.9%) by the time the survey was conducted. It should be pointed out that this gives an overestimate of the relationships that broke off immediately in response to the violent incident (the question asked about the status of their relationship to the other person at the time of the administration of the questionnaire). Many of the 55.3% who eventually broke off could have continued their relationship for a considerable period of time after the occurrence of violence.

In only 5.1% of the cases were legal authorities such as police or sheriff's department personnel notified. In view of these results, it seems pertinent to ask just what social controls are operating in the situations of actors involved in courtship violence to maintain their relationships and to prevent the reporting of their experiences to authorities.

DISCUSSION

It appears that violence is a common, albeit neglected, aspect of premarital heterosexual interaction. If our results are typical of college students in general, more than one student in 5 has had direct personal experience in courtship violence and a majority have personally known someone else who has been involved in it. Although the percentages of students who have experienced the more serious forms of violence may seem small, the students actually suggest a serious social problem. Thus, if the 4% incidence of assault with closed fists is typical, then 800 of the students on a 20,000 student campus would have experienced this form of violence. Similarly, if the 1% and 1 1/2% incidences of assault with a weapon and choking/strangulation are typical, then several hundred students would have been involved in forms of violence that are potentially life-threatening. Extending these figures to students and young people nation-wide suggests the existence of a major hidden social problem. We do not know, of course, if these results are typical of other campuses or of young people in general. However, it is indicated by these findings that the problem exists to some extent; thus, further investigations are warranted.

Apparently, both popular and professional conceptions of dating and courtship relationships are idealized and unrealistic, or at best, one-sided. Although there may be a few people today who would accept the traditional romantic love interpretations as literally accurate accounts of what courtship relationships are typically like in American society, there is, nonetheless, almost a total neglect of consideration of the negative aspects of courtship, and particularly of the existence of courtship violence.

Premarital heterosexual relationships consistently are depicted in popular songs, books, films, and TV programs as inordinately blissful or, at worst, bittersweet. In the media, where there is trouble in a relationship it takes the form of a conflict between the couple and their parents or between the young man and woman. Young couples consistently overcome nearly insurmountable obstacles to achieve a successful relationship in spite of their parents' and other adults' reservations to the surprise and wonderment of all. In other cases, the forlorn, youthful lovers cope with their frustrations, rejections, and surreptitious foibles with remarkable insight and maturity. For the stresses and strains inherent in the relationships to exceed the coping abilities of the young intimates and to result in eruptions of aggression and violence is patently unheard of.

If premarital interaction is characterized by highly idealized conceptions and systematic neglect of violence in popular literature, the same can be said of the literature of family sociologists. From the accounts in this literature, one gained the impression that young people in dating and courtship relations are busily engaged in anticipatory socialization for marital roles: narrowing the field of eligibles, constructing ideal mate images, and revolving on the wheel of love. This is not to say that the potential for the expression of antisocial behaviors within the dating context has been overlooked entirely. It has not. The competitive and exploitative potential inherent in dating and courtship relationships has been recognized (Kanin, 1967; Waller, 1937; Berger & Wenger, Note 2).

The existence of a substantial amount of courtship violence suggests the need for further research and for the development of social policies. Certainly, there is some awareness among helping professionals of the existence of such violence, and, certainly, the victims of such violence are assisted by some current social programs. However, treatment is usually an incidental feature of programs that have other main purposes; the special causes and dynamics of this phenomenon have not received the focused attention they deserve. Cases are typically dealt with as isolated individual aberrations rather than as persistent and patterned features of American courtship and without systematic procedures for the processing and therapy of victims and aggressors.

[2] Berger, D. G., & Wenger, M. C. *The ideology of virginity.* Paper presented at the annual meeting of the National Council on Family Relations, Portland, OR, 1972.

REFERENCES

Chase, N. F. *A child is being beaten.* New York: McGraw-Hill, 1975.

Edwards, A. L. *The social desirability variable in personality assessment and research.* New York: Dryden, 1957.

Gelles, R. J. *The violent home: A study of physical aggression between husbands and wives.* Beverly Hills: Sage, 1972.

Gelles, R. J. Abused wives: Why do they stay? *Journal of Marriage and the Family,* 1976, **38**, 659–668.

Gelles, R. J. *Family violence.* Beverly Hills: Sage, 1979.

Gil, D. G. Violence against children. *Journal of Marriage and the Family,* 1971, **33**, 644–648.

Goode, W. J. Force and violence in the family, *Journal of Marriage and the Family,* 1971, **33**, 624–636.

Kanin, E. J. An examination of sexual aggression as a response to sexual frustration. *Journal of Marriage and the Family,* 1967, **29**, 428–433.

Langley, R., & Levy, R. C. *Wife beating.* New York: Pocket Books, 1977.

Martin, D. *Battered wives.* New York: Simon & Schuster, 1976.

Owens, D. M., & Straus, M. A. The social structure of violence in childhood and approval of violence as an adult. *Aggressive Behavior,* 1975, **1**, 193–211.

Renvoize, J. *Web of violence.* London: Routledge & Kegan Paul, 1978.

Steele, B. F., & Pollock, C. B. A psychiatric study of parents who abuse infants and small children. In R. E. Heifer & C. H. Kempe (Eds.), *The battered child.* Chicago: University of Chicago Press, 1968.

Steinmetz, S. K., & Straus, M. A. The family as cradle of violence. *Society,* 1973, **10**, 50–56.

Steinmetz, S. K., & Straus, M. A. *Violence in the family.* New York: Harper & Row, 1974.

Straus, M. Wife beating: How common and why? *Victimology,* 1978, **2**, 443–458.

Straus, M. A., Gelles, R. J., & Steinmetz, S. K. *Behind closed doors.* Garden City, NY: Anchor, 1980.

Waller, W. The rating and dating complex. *American Sociological Review,* 1937, **2**, 727–734.

TAKING ANOTHER LOOK

1 In what ways could Makepeace's sample be viewed as representative of all American college students? In what ways could the sample be viewed as unrepresentative?

2 What were the most frequently reported reasons cited as the sources of disagreement that led to courtship violence?

3 To what extent did male and female respondents view themselves as the aggressors in incidents of courtship violence? To what extent did male and female respondents view themselves as victims of such incidents?

4 In what ways could traditional sex-role socialization influence the incidence of courtship violence and the likelihood of reporting such violence to legal authorities?

5 Why is Makepeace critical of the mass media's treatment of premarital heterosexual relationships?

6 In Makepeace's view, why are current social programs to assist victims of courtship violence somewhat inadequate?

Radical Departures

Saul V. Levine

Some people are not satisfied with traditional marriage and family arrangements and prefer to live in some form of community with others. In a sense, they wish to create entirely new families, not necessarily including blood relatives or a spouse, with which they will live. The term *commune* is used to describe a small, self-supporting community joined voluntarily by persons dedicated to cooperative living. Communes are perhaps the best known and least understood of alternative lifestyles. Currently, there may be some 2000 to 3000 communes in the United States. They are found primarily in rural areas of the country, though occasionally they are established in urban centers.

Many Americans join communes in order to escape the sense of alienation and isolation that they encounter in the "straight" (conventional) world. Some communes have strict moral codes that sharply restrict sexual behavior and prohibit the use of drugs. Others have few rules; each member is free to do whatever he or she pleases within general standards established by the group.

In certain instances, communal living arrangements involve members of a religious sect or cult. A *sect* can be defined as a relatively small religious group that has broken away from some other religious organization. Sects are fundamentally at odds with society and do not seek to become established national religions. It is difficult to distinguish sects from cults. As psychotherapist Irvin Doress and sociologist Jack Nusan Porter have suggested, the word *cult* has taken on a negative meaning in contemporary American society and is used as a means of discrediting religious minorities. They note that some groups, such as the Hare Krishna, are labeled as "cults" because they come from foreign (often nonwestern) lands and have customs perceived as "strange." Doress and Porter suggest that a cult tends to have a powerful and charismatic leader, a rather mystical nature, a millenial vision of "saving the world," a proselytizing spirit, and a deep feeling of alienation from the larger culture.

It has been estimated that as many as 2 to 3 million Americans—primarily between the ages of 18 and 25—belong to religious sects and cults. Older cults are generally based on more established forms of Christianity; more recent sects and cults reflect the growing influence of Hinduism and Buddhism in the United States. The majority of the newer cults are less than 20 years old, which suggests that they may depend for survival on the emotional appeal of a charismatic leader.

In the following selection, psychiatrist Saul V. Levine reports on his research involving more than 400 people who joined (and, in most cases, eventually left) communal groups or religious cults. He identifies factors that lead young people to join and later to leave these groups. Levine's findings run counter to many sensationalistic press reports regarding the types of youths who join such communal groups, the alleged "brainwashing" responsible for recruitment, and the feelings of departers toward the groups to which they once belonged. Interestingly, Levine views participation in such groups as a "rehearsal for separation, preparation for the real task of growing up" and entering full adulthood.

June 27, 1983, was a cloudy, breezy day in the San Francisco Bay area. Around a breakfast table in the Thomas home in an affluent suburb, good-humored conversation was interrupted by the honk of a horn. Mark got up from the table and made for the door to join his friends waiting in the car.

His father stopped him. Pressing a $20 bill into Mark's hand, he rested his arm on his son's shoulder for a moment and made an embarrassed joke about the money. "Just in case you get in trouble in the big city," he winked. He could afford to make such jokes. Mark, as clean-cut a blond as any middle-class family could hope for, had never been in trouble in his life. He was willing and reliable, the kind of boy who had been given responsibilities since elementary school.

After kissing his mother good-bye, Mark strode out the door to the waiting car. It was the Monday after high school graduation, and Mark and his friends were on their way to celebrate for a day in San Francisco. When the group returned that evening, Mark wasn't with them. His friends had last seen him late that afternoon in Golden Gate Park, where they had gone to share a six-pack of beer and watch the sun go down. The Thomases weren't worried. He had probably missed his train; he would call them from the station shortly.

But Mark didn't call his parents that night, nor the next night. After 72 hours, the Thomases finally heard from Mark. They weren't to worry, he told them during the collect call from Oregon. He said he was fine. Mark had joined the followers of Bhagwan Shree Rajneesh. He had made a "radical departure."

Every year thousands of young people abruptly turn their backs on family, friends and future to join one or another of an estimated 2,500 communal groups in North America whose values, dress and behavior seem totally alien to everything the joiner has stood for. Practitioners of Rajneeshism wear clothes in the "sunrise colors." Around their necks hang pendants bearing a portrait of their enlightened Master. When the Thomases next saw

their son, he was on a street corner in Portland chanting in a circle dance, robed in red. He refused to acknowledge his father's greeting; indeed, he showed no sign of recognizing his parents.

Mark Thomas is a composite of several young men among the hundreds I have studied since the late 1960s (see the "Questions and Answers" box). In my book, *Radical Departures*, I follow nine such young men and women through their journeys into and out of communal groups.

Radical departures are a fact of life, a cultural phenomenon that has inspired more fear, agony, anger, disgust—and misinterpretation—than almost any other. When I started my studies, most people agreed that the groups were hostile to the fundamental standards of middle-class conduct, but beyond that judgment there was a lot of confusion. Were the joiners troubled, academic failures; loners from embattled homes; drug addicts? Certainly there was a subpopulation of such dropouts, and mental-health professionals were quick to indict all radical departures as a manifestation of pathology. The most charitable judgment was that kids who joined charismatic fringe groups were gullible innocents who had been brainwashed.

Given this widespread sentiment, I was surprised to find, as my research got under way, that these young people, massed in urban communes or converted to a variety of intensely ideological groups, came right off the cover of *The Saturday Evening Post*. There were no more signs of pathology among them than among any group of youngsters. They came from warm, concerned families that had given them every material, social and intellectual benefit. They were, in short, Mark Thomases—good kids with everything to look forward to.

Those who followed press reports on these "cults," as they were invariably called, were treated to a first impression much like what I at first perceived. Such groups were controlled by a charismatic leader who used his power to enrich himself unconscionably. The beliefs he perpetrated were counterfeit, and those who followed him had been duped into serving against their will. They might be held captive by force, deprived of financial means to escape and prevented from communicating with their families.

The details varied from group to group, but the press reports were uniformly negative. One cult censored incoming and outgoing mail and prevented privacy through an intrusive "buddy system." It used the words of the Bible, "For I am come to set a man at variance against his father, and the daughter against her mother," to turn children against their parents. Young girls were encouraged to be "happy hookers in Christ"—that is, to seduce new members sexually.

Another group practiced "heavenly deception," begging donations in public places by selling flowers to benefit a fictional home for the retarded or some other nonexistent cause. Their tactic was to bar the way of hurried travelers with smiling entreaty, making it clear that it would be easier to reach for some change than to brush them off.

Other cults practiced extreme asceticism, foisting inadequate nutrition, clothing and housing on their converts. A zealous leader of one group considered five hours of sleep a night sufficient for members, some of them still growing children.

As I gradually became involved in the study of communal groups, first in the United States, and later in Europe, Israel and my native Canada, I found that the reality of the ones I dealt with simply did not accord with press sensationalism. I have seen bad things, but in the hundreds of groups I know of firsthand, I have never seen excesses worthy of the perjorative label of "cult." Furthermore, not all of these intense groups are religious; some are political, therapeutic or social in nature.

Because these groups don't easily lend themselves to existing terminology, I have chosen the rather inexact term "radical" to describe both the groups and the joining that makes them possible. It is a relative term: To the families of joiners,

their children's beliefs and behavior seem radically opposed to the families' own intellectual, spiritual and social standards.

Although there is an underlying structure that makes these groups similar—the fantasized omniscience of leaders, rigid belief systems opposed to the outside world and a studied strangeness—the earmark of a radical departure is less the specific characteristics of the group than the rapid, total transformation of the joiner. Mark Thomas could not say when, if ever, he would return. His previous plans for college no longer meant a thing to him. Similarly, voracious readers stop reading; musicians abandon their instruments; athletes stop exercising. There is an ominous narrowing of horizons, and their absolute commitment is, they believe, for the rest of their lives.

I have worked among radical departers and their families since 1969, throughly studying more than 400 subjects in 15 groups. In no case was the sudden leave-taking expected by those who knew them best. These departures are called "out of character" by people who can make no sense of them; the radical departers appear to have taken leave of their senses.

I have come to realize how much sense radical departures make, despite their appearance of irrationality, as desperate attempts to grow up in a society that places obstacles in the way of normal youthful yearnings. The strangeness that unnerves, the hostility that enrages and even the euphoria that puzzles are expressions of belief and belonging that adolescents use as catalysts in growing up.

To understand what this means, we must consider the entire history of a radical departure, beginning with the months just prior to it, then the moment of first approach, the screening process the groups employ and on through life in the group during the peak period of commitment. This history helps us understand the remarkable endings to radical departures: More than 90 percent end in a return home within two years, and virtually all joiners eventually abandon their groups. Most important, they resume their previous lives and find gratification in the middle-class world they had totally abjured. In short, they use their radical departures to grow up.

Radical departers share certain characteristics. While there are exceptions, the majority are between 18 and 26 years of age, unmarried, affluent, well-educated, white and from intact families. But only a few such adolescents make radical departures; to understand what makes them different, one must examine what normally happens during these years.

The school years up to about age 12 are ordinarily a time of smooth progress. By each birthday, a child has grown taller, reads at a grade level higher and acts with measurably greater sophistication. But in the following six years, adolescents' bodies change so radically and rapidly that they must constantly look in the mirror to see who they are and how they like it. Nature dumps on adolescents the makings of adulthood but doesn't tell them what to make of it.

In our middle-class culture, we strongly believe that during these years, children must separate from their families and establish their individuality both practically and psychologically. No radical departer I have known has been able to separate gradually to everyone's satisfaction. All of them are still so closely tied to their parents that I tend to refer to joiners as children despite their true age.

Normally, as children become teenagers, parents begin to diminish control. They no longer try to supervise homework or to act as constant chaperones. Even if they wish to, they can no longer control their children's aggressiveness and sexual impulses, so adolescents are forced to a degree of independence. At the same time, parents also make it clear to high school students that adult responsibilities loom ahead. They are asked to think about college and to make tentative career choices; most are expected to leave home. These challenges, unlike most challenges of childhood, smack of permanence.

At the same time that parents withdraw control, their children withdraw the unconditional love and faith that typify childhood. But because they cannot proceed into adulthood without love and without faith, they seek intimacy with friends and lovers.

That is the normal course. But of the radical departers I have studied, few have been involved in relationships that were more than exploitive or tentative. None felt committed to a value system at the time of joining.

Joiners look to belief as a way to avoid their personal dilemma. Feeling so little self-esteem, they can't shoulder the responsibility of perhaps making a wrong moral choice and thereby feeling even more worthless. They are looking for ideology that will bolster whatever is admirable in them and purge whatever is bad.

Everyone must experience self-doubt, disillusion and loneliness on the way to adulthood. Radical departers are notable not only for the degree of their pain, but for the fact that everything seems to hit them at once. Too much has been put off, and confluence of unfaced dilemmas causes a developmental logjam. They open the dam of their own development by the abrupt and violent breaking away that is a radical departure.

The final ingredient is often an accident. At just this critical period in their lives, they are offered what seems a magical solution: separation without accompanying pain. It is very common to make a radical departure while away from home, sometimes for the first time. These children wish to be back at home, safe from the frightening freedom of travel, but then how can they be separate? Separate, they feel empty—a word frequently used by radical departers—as if there is not enough to fill them. The departure is a compromise solution to this conflict.

Despite the public perception that teenagers are somehow tricked into joining radical groups, the initial encounter is actually only the beginning of a screening process that will sort out those who do belong from those who might be alien to the group. The process varies from group to group, but it often involves three basic steps.

The first step is for a member of the group to

approach a youth of about the same age and background as the members themselves. Anyone may be the target of propaganda or solicitation, but approaches are made only to those who appear interested, who ask questions or linger longer than most passersby. Friendly conversation leads quite naturally to an invitation to spend an evening with the group.

Only about 5 of every 100 approached in this way feel so attracted to these new friends that they consent to the first visit. Direct proselytizing is rare, but members and candidate are indirectly checking one another's values for a match. Those who are not screened out by the group or themselves are invited for a two- or three-day retreat.

The retreat is usually held in a secluded, rural and often strikingly beautiful spot away from the busy city that surrounds most groups' central meeting place. There is ordinarily no television, radio or telephone. It is as though there were no outside—no appointments, no hassles to endure, no criticism to answer, no worldly chores, schedules, deadlines or expectations.

Joiners have told me that during the retreat, the group's ideology, which seemed mere background noise before, suddenly makes immense sense. They feel a new clarity to their thoughts; the words they hear seem rich with significance and truth. Meaning dawns: This is the way that they and the world are to be seen. Interestingly, as gripping as the euphoria is, fewer than 10 percent of those who attend the first retreat decide to stay within the group. Indeed, the screening process is so accurate that, while only 1 in 500 of those originally approached chooses to join, those who do usually stay at least six months.

I have spent hundreds of hours reading the voluminous works of all the many ideological groups I've studied in an effort to understand what their beliefs are and why radical departers should be so moved by them. The vocabulary is theological, political or therapeutic, depending on the avowed nature of the group, but they all sound the same. They are replete with tautologies ("Being here as a group brings us together") and truisms ("Life can be difficult"). Mostly the beliefs are incomprehensible to outsiders and, I suspect, to most members as well. But in a curious way, it doesn't matter. There is even relief in not understanding, comfort in knowing that there are those at the top who do understand.

One common characteristic of these various belief systems is that they closely match the ideals of the joiner's family. One young woman who joined the Children of God could just as well have joined two other sects whose teachings echoed perfectly the Sunday School lessons of her childhood. Beneath the verbiage there inevitably lie the goals all mankind has always wished for, but the rationale for achieving this peace and unity is lost in anti-intellectualism. To me, this smacks of the innocence of early childhood when, in union with one's parents who need not be understood to be trusted utterly, prayers are answered and endings are always happy.

Belonging is the heart of radical departure. They are a unity, all doing the same things, believing the same beliefs, speaking the same stock phrases, eating the same food, wearing the same clothes and working for the same cause. For the period of their commitment, they give up the usual adolescent struggle to form an independent self and instead participate with relief in a flawless group self.

But this is by no means a complete retreat from growing up. The departers have taken a giant step. Because the group self is vehemently not bound up with that of the parents, psychological separation from them has begun. For these children, however, separation can be accomplished only within the safety of joining. Or perhaps rejoining is more accurate, because these groups are built along the lines of an exaggerated and idealized family. Careful attention is given to serving good, nutritious food, for example, an emphasis that closely echoes a mother's care in assuring that her children have a wholesome diet. Health in general is high on the list of most groups' concerns, and in

QUESTIONS AND ANSWERS

In the 15 years I have been studying radical departures, I have developed a methodology that balances the need for objective data with an equal need for subjective impressions. I first meet with the local leader of a group to ask permission to study the membership, making clear that my purpose is to understand, not to pass judgment on the group's beliefs or activities. No leader has ever turned down my request.

Individual participation is voluntary. To screen out members who aren't fully committed to a group, I study only individuals who have belonged for at least six months. I usually meet most members first during the height of their commitment, then as their intensity and single-mindedness begin to give way to doubt and, finally, within the first six months of their return home. For many, I have brief follow-ups some years later.

I first take a demographic profile: age, education, residence, parents' occupations and marital status, siblings, prior religious training and previous interests. The interview proper starts with rather formal questions that usually elicit pat answers as to why they joined this group, what they feel to be significant about their activities and so on. As members gradually begin to feel more comfortable with me, I can usually investigate further for their feelings in the months before their departure, how they are getting along now with their parents and their relationships within the group. Subsequent meetings explore similar territory in relation to later phases of membership or the return to their families. Altogether, I usually spend about five hours talking to each person during the course of the study.

When I first started, I also gave several standard psychological inventories to check my personal impressions of members' mental health. I no longer do so for two reasons: There was never a discrepancy between test results and my own assessment, and the young people considered the testing so nefarious that it interfered with a trusting relationship.

If a participant agreed, I also interviewed their families. When possible, I spent some time with other relatives and with peers who had been close friends of the joiner.

Using this technique, I have thoroughly studied a total of 15 radical groups ranging from the drug cults of the 1960s to the religious, political and therapeutic groups most active today.

In addition, because of my interest and expertise in this area (I served on a government commission that examined the issue), I have received letters and referrals from hundreds of people in Western Europe, the British Isles, North America and Israel. Through these contacts, I have been involved with members of at least 100 other groups—a total of more than 1,000 individuals in all.

fact my studies revealed a bunch of unusually healthy youngsters, who are free from stress, anxiety and depression.

I don't believe, however, that these radical departers are happy in the way that happiness is generally understood. As much as I have looked at beatific faces and witnessed gushes of joy, something has always prevented me from being swept up. Again and again, with hundreds of committed group members, I have felt that theirs is a performance, a case of bad acting in which the actor is himself carried away by the ringing truth of his role yet fails to convince the audience.

It is this spurious air, I think, that leads parents to the mistaken conclusion that their children have been brainwashed and to the public perception that joiners were weird to begin with. They are not brainwashed or weird, but neither are they quite whole. The happy face that joiners wear is uncontagious precisely because it does not accurately represent their inner dynamics. Conflict, fear and resentment may have the weight of bad baggage, but these feelings cannot be dumped so easily outside the mind. They can, however, be put temporarily in the unconscious while the radical departer goes through the psychological adjustment necessary for dealing with those feelings.

One of the most fascinating findings about radical departures, given the impenetrable commitment of group members, is that nine out of ten members leave their group within two years. After a period of some months, subtle but unmistakable changes begin. Dogmatic attitudes relax;

there are fewer unequivocal opinions and less inflexible faith. This is quickly followed by a siege of doubt about the perfection of the group and its leader, an upwelling of longing for the family and, finally, a return to the world.

Some joiners are able to identify the specific event that triggered or crystallized their doubts. Others describe instead a gradual creeping of ambiguity into a faith that had been absolute. During this period of doubt, criticism of the group by the family and society that previously had been ignored is suddenly reheard. In many ways this echoes the joiners' period of self-doubt just prior to their radical departures. The leader of the group, once perceived to be as perfect as the child supposes his parents to be, is revealed as flawed. Beliefs, once accepted with childlike faith and lack of understanding, begin to seem less significant, then hypocritical, finally nonsensical. Formerly committed members now entertain rebellious thoughts and contemplate another departure, with an important difference: This time they know what they are doing and feel the conflict of impending separation.

What has happened to create this difference? I'm convinced that a radical departure is a rehearsal for separation, practice for the real task of growing up. While the departers appear to be passively frozen into their narrow mold of commitment, they are actively rehearsing for their coming out. The new perceptions that intrude upon them during this second period of doubt mark the reentry into their conscious minds of the unwanted feelings that were cast out during the time of commitment. They are now psychologically fortified to deal with conflict.

The fact that the original departure is never accompanied by conflict gives away its play-like nature. Now the young people are ready to come out of rehearsal and try the painful thrust of adulthood for real. All the fears and failures that had prevented them from taking a more direct path earlier now come back to trouble them.

The most overwhelming feeling the returnees have to deal with is guilt, not about making the departure but about how they treated family and friends. They sometimes say that if they had it to do over again they would handle departures differently—less suddenly and with more careful explanations—but they rarely feel that joining was a mistake. Former members seldom vilify the group to which they once belonged or look back on the experience with shock and distaste. I have found quite the opposite: Former members almost always extract from their experience permanent values which they integrate into their present lives.

To understand this, it is important to appreciate the voluntary nature of both the radical departure and the return. Going back to the very beginning, we have seen that the percentage of potential joiners who drop out at each escalation of group pressure also escalates; of every 500 youngsters who are approached, only one actually joins. If recruitment techniques are so sinister, why do they so rarely work? The answer is that very few children are looking for what radical groups have to offer. They don't buy it because they don't want it. Those who do usually get what they want.

This doesn't mean that radical groups don't use group-pressure techniques to assure conformity. They do. But so do corporations intent on whipping up the enthusiasm of the sales force, preachers who seek generous donations from their congregation and football coaches eager for a winning season. The short-term outcome of a young person's recruitment into a group is not likable, and some mental-health professionals even consider the characteristic "symptoms," from tunnel vision to uncontagious bliss, to be pathological. But such judgments are inaccurate. Mourning takes extreme forms in many societies, but it would be inaccurate to label such a crucial period of psychological reorganization pathological. Radical departure, like mourning, is in the end therapeutic, although excesses can occur in both.

Just as the original departure is voluntary, so must the return be. In my experience, if there is no voluntary homecoming, physical or emotional, the joiner who has left a group is merely "between jobs" and has not set for himself the task of resolution. Some radical departers stay with a group not because they are able to use it in a true resolution of their problems, but because any resolution at all has been cut off by the brutality of the parents' response.

One dramatic, and rare, kind of brainwashing I have come upon during 15 years of research is that practiced by deprogrammers. Frustrated by their children's departure, thousands of parents have resorted to kidnapping and deprogramming, practices that are expensive, illegal and developmentally harmful. Designed to whip away the group member's defenses with duplicity and duress, the method does just that; and whether it "works" or fails, it can cause permanent psychological damage.

More often, deprogramming does not work. Or, more accurately, it works against the possibility that the joiners will resolve their conflicts, leave the group and rejoin their families in the kind of mature relationship that cements generations. Deprogramming interferes with the natural rhythm of a radical departure, and it can drive young people back into their group, or into a pattern of cult-hopping, for years. The grotesque experience of young adults suing their parents for unlawful acts of deprogramming has been played out too often.

When deprogramming works—brings the joiner back to the family—the loss is even greater. Halted before they have been able to utilize the group self in their own behalf, former members are thrown back upon their psychological dependency on parents. The more clearly they perceive

their "mistake," the less trust former members have in their own ability to make wise choices and the more dangerous freedom seems to them.

Like other reformed "sinners," successfully deprogrammed group members feel great hostility toward the group they once found congenial and now preach against it with the same fervor with which they once proselytized for it. They exhibit exactly the alarming traits of intolerance, rigidity and closed-minded hostility that society finds unsettling in the groups themselves.

This can be avoided only by letting radical departures run their course. Although many returning group members experience severe emotional upheaval in the first few months, my experience indicates that a reassuring majority have not been damaged. To be certain, there is a cost: Families suffer extreme pain, some relationships suffer irrevocably and time lost from school and other goals may be irretrievable. To say that nine out of ten children who make radical departures return within a few years to pick up the threads of their lives successfully is not to wish a radical departure on anyone. It is a desperate move.

But by understanding what it is that joiners seek, why they find commitment gratifying and—most important—how the experience is of genuine psychological use to them, we are in a better position to judge what we as a society should do. While most radical groups disappear within a few years, new groups spring up to supplant them. This cultural phenomenon may be telling us what we can and should be doing as a society to enable our youth to emancipate themselves and find meaning in their lives.

TAKING ANOTHER LOOK

1 According to Levine, what types of youths tend to join communal, religious, and ideological groups?

2 In Levine's view, what is the earmark of a radical departure? What types of behavior changes are evident as this process begins?

3 According to Levine, what are radical departers looking for as they join communal groups? What are they avoiding?

4 Briefly describe Levine's methodology in studying radical departures. Which research methods does he use?

5 In Levine's view, what leads parents to the mistaken conclusion that their children have been "brainwashed" by communal groups and cults?

6 Why does Levine place such emphasis on the voluntary nature of both the radical departure and the return?

Why Conservative Churches Are Still Growing

Dean M. Kelley

In the late 1960s, something rather remarkable took place in the world of organized religion. For the first time in American history, most of the major Christian denominations began to shrink in size. The Presbyterians, Lutherans, Methodists, and Episcopalians all decreased in membership, while Roman Catholics remained stable primarily because of an influx of practicing Catholics from Latin America. However, not all religious faiths were in decline. During this same period, groups such as the Southern Baptist Convention, the Assemblies of God, the Mormons, the Jehovah's Witnesses, and the Seventh-Day Adventists began overflowing with vitality. These groups share a conservative, "back-to-basics" approach to religion and stress literal interpretation of the Bible.

This religious revival was termed *resurgent fundamentalism* by theologian Martin Marty. It has been accompanied by noticeable growth among evangelical and Pentecostal faiths. *Evangelical faiths* are Christian faiths that place great emphasis on a personal relationship between the individual and God and believe that each adherent must spread the faith and bear personal witness by openly declaring their religion to nonbelievers. *Pentecostal faiths* hold many of the same values but also believe in the infusion of the Holy Spirit into services and in such religious experiences as faith healing and "speaking in tongues."

Interestingly, as Marty points out, this fundamentalist revival has surprised many observers of American religious life. It had been widely assumed that, in the face of increasing secularization, the only religions likely to survive would be those that were least demanding and most tolerant of differences in religious interpretation. Instead, people seem anxious to return to traditional sources of collective religious feeling that have long been viewed as fundamental to religion's role in society.

What has led to this dramatic change in religious life? In the following selection, Dean M. Kelley, an executive with the National Council of Churches and an authority on religious behavior, argues that Americans do not wish their clergy to focus on social action at the expense of pastoral and comfort-bringing activities. Moreover, Kelley suggests that "the quality which makes one system of ultimate meaning more convincing is not its content but its seriousness/costliness/strictness." In his view, mainline ecumenical churches have not communicated their seriousness as effectively as have fundamentalist churches.

For at least a century the dominant national religious bodies in the United States have been increasing in membership with the nation's increase in population, coasting up the population escalator with the momentum of procreation. Then, in the mid-1960's, they reversed the trend, turned

Author's Note: Revised from a paper presented at the annual meeting of the Society for the Scientific Study of Religion, 1976.

around, and descended the "up" escalator, which was still ascending at a rate of 1.4% per year—not an easy thing to do.

At the same time, a number of other religious bodies continued to increase at a rate not inferior to the population increase but significantly greater, suggesting not just the momentum of procreation but the impetus of significant attractiveness. These bodies appear to represent a different category from the first group, not only in respect to membership trends but in other respects as well, which are not easy to characterize in one word, but which form a pattern easily recognizable to those familiar with the religious scene in America. Perhaps the least perjorative label would be "non-ecumenical."

For better or worse, one of the first to call attention to this curious and highly interesting contrast in membership trends—at least in hardcover publications—was the book *Why Conservative Churches Are Growing*, which excited a certain amount of controversy, if not actual scandal, among those who thought such things were better off unannounced. Since then, and perhaps due in part to the aforesaid book, the statistical phenomenon referred to has become a matter of a rather general awareness, penetrating even the austere pages of the *Scientific American.*[1]

During the intervening four years, the membership trends have continued much as they had been characterized in that volume, with three possible exceptions, which were heralded by Ted Fiske on the front page of the N.Y. *Times* with the headline "Conservative Churches have *Stopped* Growing!" The churches referred to, of course, were the Presbyterian Church in the U. S., the Lutheran Church—Missouri Synod, and the Christian Reformed Church, which were reported in that year to have shown membership losses for the first time. (The former two were undergoing incipient schisms, and the pre-1972

curves of all three suggested that their growth was slowing and about to peak.)

No such decline, however, marks the rapidly-growing churches, whose rate was significantly greater than the population increase; the Southern Baptist Convention, the Church of Jesus Christ of Latter-day Saints, Jehovah's Witnesses, Seventh-Day Adventists, Church of the Nazarene, Salvation Army, etc. They continue to expand at rates that pose a marked contrast to the "mainline" or ecumenical churches.

The data from 1975 reported to the *Yearbook of American and Canadian Churches* for the 1977 edition, show a continuation of present growth trends. (There is an error in the reporting of the Mormon Church in the 1976 Yearbook: its membership in that year was 2,267,866 rather than the reported 2,683,573, making a curve more consistent with the latest figure, 2,336,715.[2]) These reported figures for 1975 will be reflected in the updated graphs which appear in the paperback edition of *Why Conservative Churches Are Growing*.

Though many people—and even some social scientists and scholars of religion—are not aware of the curious contrasts in membership trends that occurred during the past decade, no one has come up with a satisfactory explanation of (1) why it happened to these particular religious bodies and (2) why it happened at this particular time in history.

I would like to think that I offered a persuasive, or at least provocative, answer to the first question: that the denominations which grow are, by and large, those which do a better job at the essential function of religion, which I characterized as "making life meaningful in ultimate terms" (a characterization I believe was used by C. Wright Mills in his lectures at Columbia University in 1950, though I cannot find it in my notes, and Phil Hammond could not place its ori-

[1] See Nelkin (1976) where a graph appears at p. 36 comparing the membership trends of twelve national denominations, but on a scale which does not do justice to the contrasts of the past decade. The data of the chart are not referred to in the text.

[2] Letter of Archivist to Editor, *Yearbook of American and Canadian Churches, 1977*. Constante H. Jacquet, Jr. (Ed.). Nashville, Tenn., Abingdon.

gin when I wrote him to ask about it twenty years later; it was a rather endemic concept around the Sociology Department at that time).

I am less satisfied with my answer to the second question. Since the qualities I suggested accounted for the religious ineffectuality of the declining denominations had been present for some time before the decline set in. This discrepancy would require some kind of protractive mechanism to prolong the period of growth—or at least of relative stasis—after the effective discharge of the religious function had deteriorated.

I suggested that membership growth in the ecumenical churches continued for some time as a result of the secular trend of "religiosity," and that that trend ended, or severely declined, in the early 1960's, either as a result of the general and increasing distrust of received institutions of all kinds, or as a result of the disillusionment of Roman Catholics with their Church, which relaxed many of its historic demands at Vatican Council II, and when this firm "anchor" church gave way, many less rigorous churches lost credibility as well. If the church which was thought to be most serious about its business suddenly abandoned its insistence on auricular confession, abstaining from meat on Fridays, nonrecognition of other religious bodies, and veneration of a whole array of saints, then why should anyone continue to be awed by its mandates, let alone those of churches which were seen to be less serious to begin with?

It is with this quality of "seriousness" that the book has mostly to do. The title has been a source of much misunderstanding. It is not really about "conservative" churches (whatever *they* are) or church growth, as such. In a way, the two opening chapters on church membership rates serve the same purpose as the 2 by 4 with which the farmer struck his mule in order to "get his attention." They pose the question of which churches are really to be taken seriously—those which have en-

joyed traditional esteem while looking down their noses at the "sects" in the store-fronts and Kingdom Halls *or* those which are drawing new members while the former are not. They point out the embarrassing contrast between the two sets of churches with the object of getting the formerly rather self-satisfied ecumenical churches to engage in some rudimentary self-evaluation which had previously not seemed necessary.

The editors at Harper & Row chose the title of the book to speak to people who hadn't yet read it.[3] If the title were to sum up the book, it would be something more like "Why Strict Churches Are Strong—whether "liberal" or "conservative" —whether growing in members at the time or not. That is the basic message of the book, which—I hope—will remain, regardless of what happens to denominational membership trends, since it is not dependent upon them.

For some time I have been wishing that someone would come along to do for religion what Freud did for sex: to show that it has its own elemental drives, dynamics, and necessities, and is not to be "explained" in terms of other (e.g., economic, demographic, or political) factors, at least not entirely. I still hope someone will do so. Some of the explanations of current trends in church membership do not measure up to this hope.

To attribute decline in Presbyterian or Methodist or Episcopalian membership to the increase in family camping or other week-end attractions, or to "backdoor" losses of members losing interest, is not to explain much. Why do P, E, or M members go camping or golfing instead of to church, but Southern Baptists and Adventists apparently are able to resist this temptation? If Mormons and Jehovah's Witnesses have some way of minimizing defections, is that not another indication of their vigorousness as effective religious bodies? The declining birth-rate may have hit Episcopalians harder than the Church of the Naz-

---

[3] With some success; the book has brought in some $20,000 in royalties to the National Council of Churches, mostly from Southern Baptists, Missouri Synod Lutherans, and other non-ecumenical purchasers who would not normally contribute to the NCC—a fitting irony. The NCC paid my salary during a 3-month sabbatical, as well as typing and photocopying costs, when it was not yet apparent whether the book would sell—or even whether there would be one.

arene or the Assemblies of God, but is that the kind of "explanation" with which we should be content?

Have we no more to learn from this fascinating conundrum that there is class differentiation among denominations? (How, then, to account for the rapid growth of the Evangelical Convenant Church, which is comprised mainly of managerial and professional people? "Because they're mostly Swedish." That is to substitute one "extraneous" explanation for another. What is it about the *religious* qualities of the Evangelical Convenant Church that make it a magnet while the Episcopal Church seems to be opposite?)

I do not mean to suggest that class or ethnic or age or sex factors do not play a part, but do they exhaust the variance? Or is it that we simply do not yet know how to identify and quantify the *religious* factors? I suspect that studies of religion based on the techniques of public-opinion polling will probably not yield information of much greater value than public-opinion polls do. What profound insights into religious behavior do we gain by learning that 48.6% of respondents *say* they believe that the Son is of the *same* substance as the Father, 36.3% *say* they believe that the Son is of *like* substance to the Father, and 15.1% are undecided? What difference does it make? Back in the days when wars were fought over the iota of difference between *homo-ousion* and *homoi-ousion*, it may have mattered. But today it costs nothing to *say* one or the other—or actually to *believe* it.

The most revealing data about religious behavior (or any other behavior) is not to be found in respondents' assertions of assent to intellectual propositions formulated by the interviewer but in action that *costs* something in money (which is a relatively cheap level of cost), time, effort, anguish, involvement, or sacrifice. It simply *costs* more to be an Adventist than an Episcopalian, not just proportionately but absolutely and not just in money but in the much costlier materials of human life! (But then, that's easily understandable, since Episcopalians are richer, and it is well-

known that the wealthier the membership of a denomination, the lower the level of per capital contributions.)

One of the most cogent criticisms of *Why Conservative Churches Are Growing* is that which contends that a particular class-linked mode of religious behavior has been taken as the norm and all others subordinated to it (i.e., the religious style of lower-class sect-members). The implication of the critic is that this is an unfair comparison; that Episcopalians are just as religious as Adventists, albeit they show it in a different and less demonstrative way. In the eyes of God, that may be true, since only He knows the inner devotion of the heart. But to any outward observer, there is no comparison. In the double tithe, the time spent, the efforts made, the witnessing overtures to non-members, the constant preoccupation with the faith, the average Adventist so far outshines the average Episcopalian that they are not even in the same category of magnitude. If this is indeed the case, it suggests that religious behavior is actually more intensive (and extensive) among lower-class people (or at least among religious groups attracting such people), and that is a significant datum in itself.

A less cogent criticism is directed toward making Church membership statistics so central to the book's thesis, as though numbers were the main objective and criterion of the kingdom. This is an understandable mis-perception of the book, but still a mis-perception. Membership trends are seen as a crude but informative index of the vitality of a church (or other institution), particularly in a free-market competition among exclusivist rival faith-groups. The church-growth people have seized upon it as a resource, but in my view as well as R. Hudnut's, *church growth is not the point.* It is a *by-product* of a church that is vigorously meeting people's religious needs.

To other critics, that notion of what churches should be doing is even more deplorable. Somehow to them it smacks of pandering for the church to be concerned about meeting people's religious needs. They seem to view such a process as akin to "stroking" souls with mystical introspection, turning them inward, away from each other and the world's needs. They see the church's needing to choose between two mutually-exclusive alternatives, in the words of the title of a recent work by Glock and Stark, "To Comfort *or* to Challenge" (emphasis mine).

The Churches are tempted to settle for "comforting" people when they should be "challenging" them—a thankless task at best. And, according to this school of thought—reflected in works by Glock, Stark, Hadden, Quinley, and McFaul—it was the ecumenical churches' recent efforts to "challenge" their members to engage in social action that precipitated the departure of disgruntled members who wanted to be comforted rather than challenged. Or worse, they dominated the local churches and drove out the prophetic young preachers and those who sympathized with them, refusing to contribute to the support of church programs that emphasized social action.

The supposition that church members want to be comforted rather than challenged, and that they will withhold support or drive out the minister or leave the church if they are challenged rather than comforted is a gross calumny upon the laity, perpetrated in large part by the clergy (with the help of some social-science researchers who have relied on interviews with a sample composed almost entirely of clergy and drawn almost entirely from Northern California, i.e., Quinley).

A more reliable understanding is gained from the North American Interchurch Study, which reports interviews with over 3500 church people, laity *and* clergy, in the U. S. and Canada. It offers a much more charitable, and credible, view of what lay people expect of the church, and indicates a serious misunderstanding of their expectations by the clergy.

The clergy seem to believe that the laity does not want them to engage in social action, but they will go ahead and do so anyway, even into martyrdom, because it is their Christian duty! But that is not what the laity thinks at all. They said in interviews that a social witness is an essential part of the church's mission, and that they would consider it improper to withhold contributions just because they happened to disagree with the views of church leaders on such issues. Their dissatisfaction with the church was at another point, best indicated by the rank-order of the respondents' expectations of the local church (Cornell & Johnson, 1972, p. 80).

With surprising unanimity among clergy and laity—at least in the top choices—the following preferences were expressed:

A {
1 winning others to Christ
2 provide worship for members
3 provide religious instruction
4 provide ministerial services
5 provide for sacraments
}

B {
6 help the needy
7 support overseas missions
8 serve as social conscience to the community
9 provide fellowship activities
10 maintain facilities for congregation
11 support denomination
12 support minority groups
13 influence legislation
14 build low-cost housing
}

If one were to divide this series into two sections (which the researchers did not), with the first five items in group A and the remaining in group B, then one might characterize group A as the activities by which ultimate meaning is promulgated, inculcated, and nurtured; group B as the activities by which it is embodied, exercised, and practiced—once it has been acquired. The lay respondents did not *reject* the B activities, indeed felt they were *necessary*—perhaps more on the national or regional level than the local—but placed them in a position of *secondary* urgency. They did not *object* to the clergy giving attention to such things; *what they objected to was the clergy's doing them in preference to, in exclusion of, almost as a substitute for, the A group.*

That is another way of putting the thesis of *Why Conservative Churches Are Growing.* Ecumenical churches are losing members, not because they are engaging in the B group of activities, but because they are muffing the A group. Non-ecumenical churches are flourishing because they are effective at the A group. (It might be charged that they are weak on the B group, but that is not necessarily true; they must have a different way of doing the B group—opposing drinking, smoking, gambling, pornography, etc.—which may not be congenial to "liberal" social-gospel leaders, but is no less effective in fulfilling the religious function. In fact, it is possible that the religious function could be fulfilled fairly well without any B activities at all. It would be Christian heresy, but still an effective religious organization: the Jehovah's Witnesses are a case in point.)

The purpose of the church is not, and should not be, to "comfort" or to "challenge," "to meet people's religious needs" or "to explain the ultimate meaning of life," but to " preach the Gospel" and "win others to Christ." If it does that effectively, it will both comfort and challenge, it will meet people's religious needs by making life meaningful in ultimate terms, and—sooner or later—it will attract new members as well as retaining present members: it will grow.

In four years of giving talks around the country, reading reviews and correspondence, I have not encountered much disagreement with the first main point of the book: that the basic business of religion is to explain the ultimate meaning of life. The second main point has not been as fortunate: that the quality which makes one system of ultimate meaning more convincing is not its content but its seriousness/costliness/strictness. That is an ungracious notion that falls discordantly upon the debonair, modern "liberal" churchperson, producing such prodigies of Humpty-dumptyism as the Unitarian who declared that, "we are very strict about permitting individual diversity!"—thus substituting for the object of strictness its functional opposite.

"Strictness" is usually caricatured as invariably authoritarian, harsh, punitive, irrational, etc. We are all captives of our historical experience, and it is a pity that almost the only experiences of strictness in Western culture have been marked by heresy-trials, inquisitions, excommunications, auto-da-fe's, persecutions, crusades, and pogroms; and that the only content about which it is thought possible to be strict is some kind of fundamentalism.

That need not be the case. The Anabaptists, being poor, could not afford the luxury of priests or preachers to tell them what to do, so they had to figure it out for themselves in a way that was the very essence of democracy. The difference between their mode and the modern church-meeting is that, once they reached a consensus, it was binding on all members. There's the rub! We resist the notion of "bindingness" in church affairs, and as a result they are seen—by members and outsiders—as not very serious, and therefore not very convincing.

Could not a modern congregation sit down together and search the Scriptures and ask themselves: What is it we are prepared—in obedience to God—to be serious about—if anything? What are we prepared—in obedience to God—to die for —if anything? If nothing, then the air would be cleared, and they would realize that theirs was not really a church but a clubhouse-with-a-steeple, and they could quit pretending to be a religious, and everyone would be much relieved, including God, who could then turn her/his attention to more serious devotees. It should not require any very profound insight to suspect that people interested in religious help would be more drawn to a congregation or a denomination that was trying to be serious about its task than to one that was merely playing at it.

If ecumenical churches feel that they are as serious about what they believe as fundamentalists are, then it behoves them to find appropriate ways to exercise and communicate that seriousness. Why should the devil have all the good tunes?

One form of strictness mentioned in the book is

rigorous membership standards. A couple of indications have caused me to wonder whether that is as central as I had supposed: the United Presbyterian study, which found no correlation between strictness of membership standards and gain or loss of members, and a report on a dozen fast-growing "body-life" churches in the Southwest, which make no special emphasis on membership standards at all. The church "membership" consists of whoever was in attendance at the booming services last Sunday.

In preparing the paperback edition of *Why Conservative Churches Are Growing*, I have been asked if I would make any changes. Essentially, I would not. I am unrepentant and unreconstructed. The curves are continuing much as they were, except for a slight flattening at the lower end of some downward arcs (becoming ogival, going from convex to concave, perhaps "bottoming out?" Let us hope so). . . .

Just as there are many ways to articulate and inculcate ultimate meaning, so there are many ways in which seriousness can be expressed and evoked. Rather than exhausting the subject or saying the last word on it, I have hoped to stimulate others to explore it further, to compare the effectiveness of various modes of the meaning-enterprise, to develop and assess new and better ways of being serious about it. This seems to me a wide-open field for religious research.

REFERENCES

Cornell, George and Douglas Johnson
   1972 *Punctured Preconceptions.* New York, Friendship Press.

Glock, Charles Y. and
   1967 *To Comfort or to Challenge.* Berkeley: University of California Press.

Hadden, Jeffrey K.
   1969 *The Gathering Storm in the Churches.* Garden City, N. Y.: Doubleday.
   1974 *Gideon's Gang.* Philadelphia: United Church Press.

Hadnut, Robert K.
   1975 *Church Growth Is Not the Point.* New York: Harper & Row.

Kelly, George
   1976 *Religious News Service* 10 (11): 11.

McFaul, Thomas R.
   1974 " 'Strictness' and church membership." *Christian Century* 3: 281–284.

Nelkin, Dorothy
   1976 "The science-textbook controversies." *Scientific American* 234 (33): 36.

Quinley, Harold E.
   1974 *The Prophetic Clergy.* New York: Wiley.

TAKING ANOTHER LOOK

1 Summarize the trends in the membership of American religious denominations in the last two decades.
2 In Kelley's view, why did the disillusionment of Roman Catholics after Vatican Council II have such an effect on other Christian denominations?
3 What does Kelley mean when he asserts that "it simply *costs* more to be an Adventist than an Episcopalian"?
4 According to Kelley, how important are membership trends in assessing the vitality of a church?
5 Why is Kelley so critical of the supposition that church members wish to be comforted rather than challenged?
6 According to the survey of laity and clergy conducted by the North American Interchurch Study, what activities should be the highest priorities of churches?
7 In Kelley's view, can nonfundamentalist denominations meet a standard of religious "strictness"?

Social Change and Jewish Continuity

Calvin Goldscheider

Jews constitute almost 3 percent of the American population. They play a prominent role in the worldwide Jewish community because the United States has the world's largest concentration of Jews. Like the Japanese-Americans, many Jewish immigrants came to this country and became white-collar professionals. But again, as in the case of the Japanese-Americans, Jewish achievements have come despite prejudice and discrimination.

Anti-Semitism, that is, anti-Jewish prejudice, in the United States has often been vicious, although rarely as widespread and never as formalized as in Europe. In many cases, Jews have been used as scapegoats for other people's failures. Jews have not achieved equality in American society. Despite high levels of education and professional training, they are still conspicuously absent from the top management of large corporations (except for the few firms founded by Jews). Until the late 1960s, many prestigious universities maintained restrictive quotas that limited Jewish enrollment. Social clubs and fraternal groups frequently limit membership to gentiles (non-Jews), a practice upheld by the Supreme Court in the 1964 case of *Bell v. Maryland.*

Interestingly, Jews in the United States can be viewed both as an ethnic minority and as a religious denomination. Many people in the United States consider themselves to be culturally Jewish—and are seen by others as Jewish—even though they do not participate in Jewish religious life. As is true of other minorities, American Jews face the choice of maintaining ties to their long religious and cultural heritage or becoming as indistinguishable as possible from gentiles. Many Jews have sought to assimilate, as is evident from the rise in marriages between Jews and Christians. This trend worries Jewish religious leaders, who fear that the long-term future of the Jewish faith is in jeopardy.

In the following selection, sociologist Calvin Goldscheider analyzes the changing forms of religious and ethnic cohesion evident in the American Jewish community. Goldscheider draws on social surveys of the Boston-Jewish community (and of Boston's non-Jews) in 1965 and 1975. While he points to a "decline in religiosity" in the Jewish community, he adds that "there remains a strong sense of religious identification among Jews." Goldscheider suggests that the Jewish community is characterized by "multiple bases of cohesion" and that social and economic changes have reinforced (rather than diminished) ethnic-communal identification among Jews. He concludes that the Jewish community in the United States "has emerged as a dynamic source of networks and resources binding together family, friends, and neighbors, ethnically and religiously."

Religion and ethnic factors are particularistic features of the Jewish community. They are the defining quality of American Jewish life and the source of communal consensus. The secularization of Judaism and Jews has long been observed in America. The critical issue, however, is whether alternative sources of group cohesion have emerged as religious centrality has declined. Religious and ethnic forms of Jewishness have changed in America. Interpreting these changes and understanding their link to the future of the American Jewish community are a key analytic concern.

The data from Boston surveys document the changing manifestation of religious forms of cohesion. They also clearly indicate how forms of religious and ethnic cohesion provide a wide range of options for Jews at different points in the life cycle. For some, religion in its Americanized form is of central importance in their Jewishness; for most Jews, social, communal, ethnic, and religious dimensions of Jewishness are combined. It is most problematic to specify and measure the "quality" of Jewish life, since there is no theoretical or empirical consensus about it. Nevertheless, it is clear that the decline in religiosity per se must be viewed in the context of the emergence of these alternative forms of Jewishness. Secularization in the religious sense is not necessarily equal to the decline of the Jewish community, to its assimilation or demise. By treating Jews as members of a community in the broad sense, we recognize religion as one dimension of the total array of factors, but not as equivalent to the whole.

Despite the evidence of secularization, there remains a strong sense of religious identification among Jews. Fully three-fourths of Boston Jewry define themselves denominationally, attend synagogue sometimes during the year, and observe some personal religious rituals. This high level of religious identification is not matched by formal membership in religious institutions. Hence, membership per se is not an adequate indicator of religious identification. Life cycle- and family-related factors determine membership patterns. Nonmembership does not seem to imply the lack of commitment to Jewish continuity.

These patterns characterize the younger as well as the older generations, men and women, and appear to be a pervasive feature throughout the Jewish community. In particular, there are no clear relationships between educational level and religiosity or between other social class indicators and

Jewishness. Hence, neither the attainment of high levels of education nor upward mobility can be viewed as a "threat" to Jewish continuity.

For recent generations, there are high levels of religious denominational continuity, albeit in less traditional and usually less intense forms. Similarities in affiliation across generations forge bonds of interaction and reduce conflict over religious issues. Even those not affiliated denominationally are similar in background to the denominational, thereby not splitting them from their age peers. The increasing generational homogeneity in religious denominational affiliation, in which three-fourths of the younger generation have the same denominational affiliation as their parents, while three-fourths of the older generation were "downwardly" religiously mobile, is an additional source of cohesion in the community.

This generational continuity in religious denominational affiliation parallels the continuity in social class and family life. Over and above the effects of religious affiliation on Jewish continuity, generational continuity per se has become an additional basis of Jewish cohesion. This socioeconomic, family, and religious continuity implies high levels of consensus between generations in lifestyle, interests, kin networks, economic linkages, values, and norms. It also implies fewer sources of generational conflict. Again, we argue that the more the bases of cohesion, the stronger the community and the firmer the anchors for continuity. This continuity takes on particular significance, since it characterizes the young and most-educated, the future of the American Jewish community.

These indicators of religious continuity and the importance of religion as one distinguishing feature of Jewish communal life are reinforced by ethnic-communal forms of Jewish cohesion. Jewish networks have emerged which are based not on traditional modes of behavior but on lifestyle, jobs, residence, education, and family ties—cemented by religious observance and identification. The new forms of Jewishness are family- and community-based. While religion has lost its centrality and dominance in the Jewish world, it continues to play a supportive role in linking educational, family, economic, and lifestyle issues to broader communal issues.

Among those who are religiously anchored and who share family, social-class, and residential ties with other Jews, the issues of continuity are not problematic. In this context, the question of the future of the nondenominational, those not affiliated or identified religiously, has been raised. Most of the conclusions in previous research about the nondenominational have been inferential: if Jews do not identify religiously, they are lost to the community. Nondenominationalism is an indicator of (or a first step toward) total assimilation.

The evidence does not confirm this inference. The causal connections between nondenominationalism and other social processes are difficult to establish. In particular, nondenominationalism is linked to life cycle changes. Hence, higher rates among the young do not necessarily imply generational decline, but life cycle effects which will change as the young marry and have children. Most important, there is no systematic relationship between nondenominationalism and the variety of communal and ethnic ties characteristic of the Jewish community.

The incomplete and limited data which we have analyzed together with the body of previous cumulative research lead to the overall conclusion that there is much greater cohesiveness in the Jewish community than is often portrayed. It is consistent with the data (although beyond its power to confirm fully) that the Jewish community is characterized by multiple bases of cohesion. On both quantitative and qualitative grounds, the American Jewish community of the late twentieth century has a variety of sources of continuity. The changes and transformations over the last several decades have resulted in greater ties and networks among Jews. These connect Jews to each other in kinship relationships, jobs, neighborhoods, lifestyles, and values. Change—whether referred to as assimilation or acculturation—has reinforced ethnic-communal identification. The modernization of American Jews has been so far a challenge, not a threat, to continuity.

The longer-range question is whether these social networks and the emerging constellation of family, ethnic, and religious ties will persist as bases of cohesion for the Jewish community in the twenty-first century. How much secularization and erosion of traditional religious practices can occur without having a major impact on the Jewishness of the younger generation? Are the new forms of Jewish ethnicity able to balance secularization? Will the "return" to Judaism or the development of creative expressions of Jewish religious fellowship become the new core of generational continuity? These questions emerge from our study, although they cannot be addressed with any data available.

Nevertheless, the response to modernization as threatening, as the road to total assimilation and the end of the Jewish people, is not consistent with the evidence. The Jewish community in America has changed, indeed has been transformed. But in that process, it has emerged as a dynamic source of networks and resources binding together family, friends, and neighbors, ethnically and religiously. As a community, Jews are surviving in America, even as some individuals enter and leave the community. Indeed, in every way the American Jewish community represents for Jews and other ethnic minorities a paradigm of continuity and change in modern pluralistic society.

TAKING ANOTHER LOOK

1 How does Goldscheider view the impact of secularization on the American-Jewish community?

2 To what extent is the high level of religious identification of American Jews matched by

formal membership in religious institutions?

3 According to Goldscheider, what relationships have been found between social class indications and Jewishness?

4 Summarize the factors identified by Goldscheider as important sources of cohesion for the American-Jewish community.

5 According to Goldscheider, what is the relationship between nondenominationalism among Jews (Jews' nonaffiliation to religious denominations such as Orthodox, Conservative, or Reform Judaism) and Jewish assimilation?

6 According to Goldscheider, what is the relationship between modernization and Jewish continuity?

Types of Authority

Max Weber

Power is at the heart of a political system. Sociologist Max Weber defined *power* as the ability to exercise one's will over others. To put it another way, if one party in a relationship can control the behavior of the other, that individual or group is exercising power. Power relations can involve large organizations, small groups, or even people in an intimate association, such as members of a family.

Weber made an important distinction between legitimate and illegitimate power. In a political sense, the term *legitimacy* refers to the belief of a citizenry that a government has the right to rule and that a citizen ought to obey the rules and laws of that government. Of course, the meaning of that term can be extended beyond the sphere of government. Americans typically accept the power of their parents, teachers, and religious leaders as legitimate. By contrast, if the right of a leader to rule is not accepted by most citizens (as is often the case when a dictator overthrows a popularly elected government), the regime will be considered illegitimate. When those in power lack legitimacy, they usually resort to coercive methods in order to maintain control over social institutions.

The term *authority* refers to power that has been institutionalized and is recognized by the people over whom it is exercised. Sociologists commonly use the term in connection with those who hold legitimate power through elected or publicly acknowledged positions. It is important to stress that an individual's authority is limited by the constraints of a particular social position.

Max Weber provided a classification system regarding authority that has become one of the most useful and frequently cited contributions of early sociology. In the following selection, written in 1922, he discusses three ideal types of authority: traditional, legal-rational, and charismatic. Weber did not insist that particular societies fit exactly into any one of these categories. Rather, all of these categories can be present in a society, but their relative degree of importance varies.

According to Weber, in a political system based on *traditional authority,* legitimate power is conferred by custom and accepted practice. The orders of one's superiors are felt to be legitimate because "this is how things have always been done." For example, a king or a queen is accepted as ruler of a nation simply by virtue of inheriting the crown. For the traditional leader, authority rests in custom, not in personal characteristics, technical competence, or even written law.

Power made legitimate by law is known as *legal-rational authority.* Leaders of such societies derive their authority from the written rules and regulations of political systems. Generally, in societies based on legal-rational authority, leaders are conceived as servants of the people. They are not viewed as having divine inspiration, as are the heads of certain societies with traditional forms of authority. The United States, as a society that values the rule of law, has legally defined limits on the power of government.

Weber also observed that power can be legitimized by the charisma of an individual. The term *charismatic authority* refers to power made legitimate by a leader's exceptional performance or emotional appeal to his or her followers. Charisma allows an individual to lead or to inspire without relying on set rules or traditions. Since it rests on the appeal of a single individual, charismatic authority is necessarily much more short-lived than either traditional or legal-rational authority.

All ruling powers, profane and religious, political and apolitical, may be considered as variations of, or approximations to, certain pure types. These types are constructed by searching for the basis of *legitimacy,* which the ruling power claims. Our modern 'associations,' above all the political ones, are of the type of 'legal' authority. That is, the legitimacy of the power-holder to give commands rests upon rules that are rationally established by enactment, by agreement, or by imposition. The legitimation for establishing these rules rests, in turn, upon a rationally enacted or interpreted 'constitution.' Orders are given in the name of the impersonal norm, rather than in the name of a personal authority; and even the giving of a command constitutes obedience toward a norm rather than an arbitrary freedom, favor, or privilege.

The 'official' is the holder of the power to command; he never exercises this power in his own right; he holds it as a trustee of the impersonal and 'compulsory institution.' This institution is made up of the specific patterns of life of a plurality of men, definite or indefinite, yet specified according to rules. Their joint pattern of life is normatively governed by statutory regulations.

The 'area of jurisdiction' is a functionally delimited realm of possible objects for command and thus delimits the sphere of the official's legitimate power. A hierarchy of superiors, to which officials may appeal and complain in an order of rank, stands opposite the citizen or member of the association. Today this situation also holds for the hierocratic association that is the church. The pastor or priest has his definitely limited 'jurisdiction,' which is fixed by rules. This also holds for the supreme head of the church. The present concept of [papal] 'infallibility' is a jurisdictional concept. Its inner meaning differs from that which preceded it, even up to the time of Innocent III.

The separation of the 'private sphere' from the 'official sphere' (in the case of infallibility: the *ex cathedra* definition) is carried through in the church in the same way as in political, or other, officialdoms. The legal separation of the official from the means of administration (either in natural or in pecuniary form) is carried through in the sphere of political and hierocratic associations in the same way as is the separation of the worker from the means of production in capitalist economy: it runs fully parallel to them.

No matter how many beginnings may be found in the remote past, in its full development all this is specifically modern. The past has known other bases for authority, bases which, incidentally, extend as survivals into the present. Here we wish merely to outline these bases of authority in a terminological way.

1 In the following discussions the term 'charisma' shall be understood to refer to an *extraordinary* quality of a person, regardless of whether this quality is actual, alleged, or presumed. 'Charismatic authority,' hence, shall refer to a rule over men, whether predominantly external or predominantly internal, to which the governed submit because of their belief in the extraordinary quality of the specific *person.* The magical sorcerer, the prophet, the leader of hunting and booty expeditions, the warrior chieftain, the so-called 'Caesarist' ruler, and, under certain conditions, the personal head of a party are such types of rulers for their disciples, followings, enlisted troops, parties, et cetera. The legitimacy of their rule rests on the belief in and the devotion to the extraordinary, which is valued because it goes beyond the normal human qualities, and which was originally valued as supernatural. The legitimacy of charismatic rule thus rests upon the belief in magical powers, revelations and hero worship. The source of these beliefs is the 'proving' of the charismatic quality through miracles, through victories and other successes, that is, through the welfare of the governed. Such beliefs and the claimed authority resting on them therefore disappear, or threaten to disappear, as soon as proof is lacking and as soon as the charismatically qualified person appears to be devoid of his magical power or forsaken by his god. Charismatic rule is not managed according to general norms, either traditional or rational, but, in principle, according to concrete revelations and inspirations, and in this sense, charismatic authority is 'irrational.' It is 'revolutionary' in the sense of not being bound to the existing order: 'It is written—but I say unto you . . . !'

2 'Traditionalism' in the following discussions shall refer to the psychic attitude-set for the habitual workaday and to the belief in the everyday routine as an inviolable norm of conduct. Domination that rests upon this basis, that is, upon piety for what actually, allegedly, or presumably has always existed, will be called 'traditionalist authority.'

Patriarchalism is by far the most important type of domination the legitimacy of which rests upon tradition. Patriarchalism means the authority of the father, the husband, the senior of the house, the sib elder over the members of the household and sib; the rule of the master and patron over bondsmen, serfs, freed men; of the lord over the domestic servants and household officials; of the prince over house- and court-officials, nobles of office, clients, vassals; of the patrimonial lord and sovereign prince (*Landesvater*) over the 'subjects.'

It is characteristic of patriarchical and of patrimonial authority, which represents a variety of the former, that the system of inviolable norms is considered sacred; an infraction of them would re-

sult in magical or religious evils. Side by side with this system there is a realm of free arbitrariness and favor of the lord, who in principle judges only in terms of 'personal,' not 'functional,' relations. In this sense, traditionalist authority is irrational.

3 Throughout early history, charismatic authority, which rests upon a belief in the sanctity or the value of the extraordinary, and traditionalist (patriarchical) domination, which rests upon a belief in the sanctity of everyday routines, divided the most important authoritative relations between them. The bearers of charisma, the oracles of prophets, or the edicts of charismatic war lords alone could integrate 'new' laws into the circle of what was upheld by tradition. Just as revelation and the sword were the two extraordinary powers, so were the two typical innovators. In typical fashion, however, both succumbed to routinization as soon as their work was done.

With the death of the prophet or the war lord the question of successorship arises. This question can be solved by *Kürung*, which was originally not an 'election' but a selection in terms of charismatic qualification; or the question can be solved by the sacramental substantiation of charisma, the successor being designated by consecration, as is the case in hierocratic or apostolic succession; or the belief in the charismatic qualification of the charismatic leader's sib can lead to a belief in hereditary charisma, as represented by hereditary kingship and hereditary hierocracy. With these routinizations, *rules* in some form always come to govern. The prince or the hierocrat no longer rules by virtue of purely personal qualities, but by virtue of acquired or inherited qualities, or because he has been legitimized by an act of charismatic election. The process of routinization, and thus traditionalization, has set in.

Perhaps it is even more important that when the organization of authority becomes permanent, the staff supporting the charismatic ruler becomes routinized. The ruler's disciples, apostles, and followers became priests, feudal vassals and, above all, officials. The original charismatic community lived communistically off donations, alms, and the booty of war: they were thus specifically alienated from the economic order. The community was transformed into a stratum of aids to the ruler and depended upon him for maintenance through the usufruct of land, office fees, income in kind, salaries, and hence, through prebends. The staff derived its legitimate power in greatly varying stages of appropriation, infeudation, conferment, and appointment. As a rule, this meant that princely prerogatives became *patrimonial* in nature. Patrimonialism can also develop from pure patriarchalism through the disintegration of the patriarchical master's strict authority. By virtue of conferment, the prebendary or the vassal has as a rule had a personal *right* to the office bestowed upon him. Like the artisan who possessed the economic means of production, the prebendary possessed the means of administration. He had to bear the costs of administration out of his office fees or other income, or he passed on to the lord only part of the taxes gathered from the subjects, retaining the rest. In the extreme case he could bequeath and alienate his office like other possessions. We wish to speak of *status* patrimonialism when the development by appropriation of prerogatory power has reached this stage, without regard to whether it developed from charismatic or patriarchical beginnings.

The development, however, has seldom stopped at this stage. We always meet with a *struggle* between the political or hierocratic lord and the owners or usurpers of prerogatives, which they have appropriated as status groups. The ruler attempts to expropriate the estates, and the estates attempt to expropriate the ruler. The more the ruler succeeds in attaching himself a staff of officials who depend solely on him and whose interests are linked to his, the more this struggle is decided in favor of the ruler and the more the privilege-holding estates are gradually expropriated. In this connection, the prince acquires administrative means of his own and he keeps them firmly in his own hands. Thus we find political rulers in the Occident, and progressively from Innocent III to Johann XXII, also hierocratic rulers

who have finances of their own, as well as secular rulers who have magazines and arsenals of their own for the provisioning of the army and the officials.

The *character* of the stratum of officials upon whose support the ruler has relied in the struggle for the expropriation of status prerogatives has varied greatly in history. In Asia and in the Occident during the early Middle Ages they were typically clerics; during the Oriental Middle Ages they were typically slaves and clients; for the Roman Principate, freed slaves to a limited extent were typical; humanist literati were typical for China; and finally, jurists have been typical for the modern Occident, in ecclesiastical as well as in political associations.

The triumph of princely power and the expropriation of particular prerogatives has everywhere signified at least the possibility, and often the actual introduction, of a rational administration. As we shall see, however, this rationalization has varied greatly in extent and meaning. One must, above all, distinguish between the *substantive* rationalization of administration and of judiciary by a patrimonial prince, and the *formal* rationalization carried out by trained jurists. The former bestows utilitarian and social ethical blessings upon his subjects, in the manner of the master of a large house upon the members of his household. The trained jurists have carried out the rule of general laws applying to all 'citizens of the state.' However fluid the difference has been—for instance, in Babylon or Byzantium, in the Sicily of the Hohenstaufen, or the England of the Stuarts, or the France of the Bourbons—in the final analysis, the difference between substantive and formal rationality has persisted. And, in the main, it has been the work of *jurists* to give birth to the modern Occidental 'state' as well as to the Occidental 'churches.' We shall not discuss at this point the source of their strength, the substantive ideas, and the technical means for this work.

With the triumph of *formalist* juristic rationalism, the legal type of domination appeared in the Occident at the side of the transmitted types of domination. Bureaucratic rule was not and is not the only variety of legal authority, but it is the purest. The modern state and municipal official, the modern Catholic priest and chaplain, the officials and employees of modern banks and of large capitalist enterprises represent, as we have already mentioned, the most important types of this structure of domination.

The following characteristic must be considered decisive for our terminology: in legal authority, submission does not rest upon the belief and devotion to charismatically gifted persons, like prophets and heroes, or upon sacred tradition, or upon piety toward a personal lord and master who is defined by an ordered tradition, or upon piety toward the possible incumbents of office fiefs and office prebends who are legitimized in their own right through privilege and conferment. Rather, submission under legal authority is based upon an *impersonal* bond to the generally defined and functional 'duty of office.' The official duty—like the corresponding right to exercise authority: the 'jurisdictional competency'—is fixed by *rationally established* norms, by enactments, decrees, and regulations, in such a manner that the legitimacy of the authority becomes the legality of the general rule, which is purposely thought out, enacted, and announced with formal correctness.

TAKING ANOTHER LOOK

1 According to Weber, which type of authority is generally evident in our modern political associations?
2 Briefly explain Weber's view of the nature of charismatic authority.
3 According to Weber, what is *patriarchalism*?
4 Briefly explain Weber's view of the routinization of charismatic authority.
5 Do you agree with Weber that bureaucratic rule is the purest variety of legal authority? Discuss.

The Empirical Side of the Power Elite Debate: An Assessment and Critique of Recent Research

Harold R. Kerbo and L. Richard Della Fave

Who really holds power in the United States? Do "we the people" genuinely run the country through elected representatives? Or is there a small elite of Americans that governs behind the scenes? It is difficult to determine the location of power in a society as complex as the United States. In exploring this critical question, social scientists have developed two basic views of our nation's power structure: the elite and pluralist models.

Like others who hold an *elite model* of power relations, Karl Marx believed that society is ruled by a small group of individuals who share a common set of political and economic interests. In Marx's view, government officials and military leaders were essentially servants of the capitalist class and followed their wishes. Therefore, any key decisions made by politicians inevitably reflected the interests of the dominant bourgeoisie.

In his pioneering work, *The Power Elite,* written in 1956, sociologist C. Wright Mills described the existence of a small ruling elite of military, industrial, and government leaders who controlled the fate of the United States. Power rested in the hands of a few, both inside and outside of government—the *power elite.* A key element in Mills's thesis is that the power elite not only has relatively few members but also operates as a self-conscious, cohesive unit.

Sociologist G. William Domhoff agreed with Mills that American society is run by a powerful elite. But, rather than fully accepting Mills's power elite model, Domhoff argued that the United States is run by a socially cohesive upper class that forms a ruling class through its dominant role in the economy and government. In his view, members of this class dominate powerful corporations, foundations, universities, and the executive branch of government. They control presidential nominations and the political party process through campaign contributions. Like Mills and other advocates of elite models of power, Domhoff suggested that the masses of American people have no real influence on the decisions of the powerful.

Several social scientists have questioned these elite models and insisted that power in the United States is more widely shared. In their view, a pluralist model more accurately describes the American political system. According to the *pluralist model,* many conflicting groups have access to public officials and attempt to influence policy decisions. Certain community studies of power, such as a famous investigation of decision making in New Haven, Connecticut, by political scientist Robert Dahl, have supported the pluralist model.

In the following selection, sociologists Harold R. Kerbo and L. Richard Della Fave assess the debate over elite domination of American society by critically examining the empirical evidence. They note that different researchers use

Author's note: Revision of a paper presented at the annual meeting of the American Sociological Association, San Francisco, September, 1978. We thank Hermann Strasser, Richard Shaffer, and Kathy Kerbo for their helpful comments on this work, and Diane Goldman for her editing and typing of the manuscript.

differing methodologies, definitions, and indicators of elite status, which presents serious problems for social scientists who wish to weigh the conflicting data. Kerbo and Della Fave focus on four areas of quantitative research concerning elites: elite backgrounds; elite interlock (the situation in which an individual simultaneously holds two or more elite positions); elite unity or cohesiveness; and elite influence on government policy. They conclude that, in terms of the debate between elite theorists and pluralists regarding the distribution of power in the United States, "the weight of evidence appears to fall on the side of the elitists."

One of the longest running debates in the social sciences is over the nature of power stratification, a debate that can be traced back at least to the works of Marx, Mosca, Pareto, and others. Since the writings of C. Wright Mills (1956), however, the debate has become even more heated. And with the increased interest since the 1960s the opposing positions in the debate have become more complex. But, contrary to what we might expect, the new interest in the nature of power stratification, until recently, has not brought with it an increased level of systematic empirical research. We can suggest at least two reasons for the modest volume of research: first, the reality under study is often simply inaccessible (Mills, 1956:363); and second, the question is so politically significant that theorists too often have been influenced more by political values than by empirical research (Bachrach, 1967; Dye, 1976; Mankoff, 1970). The result has been ambiguous theories that make empirical research difficult.

In the past decade, however, we have witnessed a shift in the power elite controversy from a debate dominated almost completely by theory to one striking a more equitable balance between theory and empirical research. Like the shift toward pluralism which occurred in the 1950s, allegedly due to changing value assumptions (see Bachrach, 1967; Walker, 1966), the changing assumptions in the late 1960s and early 1970s have led to an increased interest in elites (see Lowi, 1973:vii–ix). With an increase in the volume of empirical research, however, we find nearly as much disagreement on indicators, definitions, and parameters to be used in empirical studies of na-

tional elites as we do with respect to theory. As the debate becomes more focused on empirical questions, the old problem of differing elite concepts and indicators (Zuckerman, 1977) becomes more evident.

The present work is primarily devoted to a critical examination of recent *quantitative* research on the existence and power of national elites focusing on four key areas: elite backgrounds, elite interlock, elite unity, and elite influence on public policy. In each of these areas we will compare the findings, attempting to explain differences and contradictions. Finally, we will summarize the overall picture of elites suggested by the several sets of data, discuss the theoretical implications, and outline future research needs.

RESEARCH ON ELITE BACKGROUNDS

Social class ties and other background characteristics of elites have been of interest. Much research has been concerned with religious, racial, sex, regional, and educational backgrounds of elites (for example, Prewitt and McAllister, 1976; Zweigenhaft, 1975), but the most important questions have involved the extent to which the top is open or closed to those from non-elite backgrounds, and the extent to which one segment of the society (such as an upper class) dominates elite positions. Though the correspondence between background, on the one hand, and attitudes, values, and behavior, on the other, is far from perfect, research has shown sufficiently strong correlations to make this line of research worthwhile (Edinger and Searing, 1967; Dye, 1976:149).

G. William Domhoff (1967, 1970) was one of the first to take up the research tradition left by the death of C. Wright Mills. The basis of Domhoff's (1967:143) model of a "governing class" is found in his "sociology of leadership method," which attempts to show that one of the most important means of upper class dominance is through holding key institutional positions in the society. Thus, much of his work involves identifying the class backgrounds of individuals in such positions. Domhoff specifies five major indicators of upper class membership (Domhoff 1970: 21-27; also see Domhoff 1967:33-37): (1) a listing in one of the various blue books or the *Social Register*; (2) any male member of the family attending one of the elite prep schools; (3) any male member of the family belonging to one of the elite social clubs; (4) any female member of the family belonging to an elite club or attending an elite prep school; (5) and finally, upper class membership is assumed if the "father was a millionaire entrepreneur or $100,000-a-year corporation executive or corporation lawyer" *and* the person attended an elite prep school or belonged to an exclusive club on an extended list of these schools and clubs. Identification with any one of these five categories places an individual on Domhoff's list of upper class membership.

Much of Domhoff's work is not systematic. Only with respect to a few positions has he been able to determine overall percentages of individuals from the upper class. Table 1 shows that among the top 15 to 20 financial, industrial, transportation, utility, and merchandising corporations, Domhoff (1967:51) found an overall majority of the directors of these corporations to be members of the upper class as defined by his indicators. For the government sector, he examined "key" cabinet posts. Covering a period from 1932-1964, Domhoff (1967:97-99) found five of eight Secretaries of State and the Treasury, and eight of thirteen Secretaries of Defense to be members of the upper class.

Recent work by Mintz (1975) and Freitag (1975) shows an impressive amount of systematic data concerning the corporate and social class ties of individuals in the executive branch of the Federal government. They compiled information on the background characteristics of all cabinet members serving thirteen Presidents from 1897 to 1973 (a total of 205 individuals and 358 positions). In terms of their indicators of business elite backgrounds, "an individual was considered a member of the business elite if he/she held a position as a director or officer of a major industrial corporation or non-industrial corporation (such as a bank, insurance company, utility, or transportation company) in the United States"; *or* an individual was considered a member of the business elite if "(1) the person was listed as a member of a corporate law firm in the *Martindale-Hubbell* law directory; (2) the person was listed in a biographical source as having been a member of such a corporate law firm; or (3) a biographical narrative stated that the individual had served as a lawyer representing a major U.S. corporation" (Freitag, 1975:150). Mintz's (1975: 133) indicators of upper class membership were similar to, but broader than, those used by Domhoff: "An individual was defined as a member of the social elite if he was listed in the *Social Register*; had attended one of an extremely small set of exclusive preparatory academies; had attended Harvard, Yale, or Princeton; was a member of one of the 105 social clubs listed in the front of the *Social Register*."

Freitag and Mintz report (see Table 1) that "Nearly 90% of all cabinet officials who held office in the period 1897-1973 were members of either the social or business elite ..." (Mintz, 1975:135). It should be noted that this figure includes those belonging to the business elite before or after the cabinet position. Further analysis shows that 54.6 percent were members of both, 63.4 percent were members of the business elite before the cabinet position, 76.1 percent were members of the business elite before or after, and 66 percent were members of the upper class before joining the cabinet (Mintz, 1975:135; Freitag, 1975:151). In addition, if the criterion of cor-

TABLE 1 FINDINGS ON CORPORATE AND GOVERNMENT ELITE BACKGROUNDS

Study	% Upper Class Membership	% Business Elite	% Business Elite or Upper Class	% Members of Exclusive Clubs	% Previous Corporate Elite***
1. Domhoff					
Corporate Elite					
Directors of top					
20 industrials	54				
15 banks	62				
15 insurance	44				
15 transportation	53				
15 utilities	30				
Government Elite (1932–1964)					
Secretaries of State	63*				
Secretaries of Defense	62				
Secretaries of Treasury	63				
2. Mintz and Freitag					
Cabinet Secretaries (from 1897–1973)					
all cabinet	66.0				
Democrats	60.4				
Republicans	71.3				
all cabinet (with business elite only before cabinet)		63.4			
all cabinet (with business elite before or after)		76.1			
Democrats		73.6			
Republicans		78.1			
all cabinet (this includes business elite before or after cabinet)			90.0		
all cabinet (this includes business before and after)			54.6		
3. Dye					
Government Elite**	25				
Corporate Elite	30				
Government Elite				6	
Corporate Elite				44	
Government Elite					26.7

* Listing in *Social Register* indicating upper class membership
** More expanded definition of government and corporate elite than Domhoff.
*** Dye's corporate elite excludes corporate lawyer, Mintz and Freitag's business elite includes corporate lawyers.

porate lawyer is excluded, the number in the cabinet with business elite backgrounds before and after the cabinet position only drops to 62 percent (Freitag, 1975:141). These studies show a steady increase in business elite backgrounds (before and after) for cabinet members and little difference between Democrat and Republican administrations (Freitag, 1975:142–44). And a breakdown by cabinet posts shows *all* to have had a majority from the business elite—ranging from a high of 100 percent to a low of 53.8 percent for Secretaries of Labor (Freitag, 1975:147).

Thomas Dye's (1976; Dye and Pickering, 1974; and Dye, DeClercq, and Pickering, 1973) massive study of institutional elites in the United States provides an interesting contrast to the works of Domhoff, Freitag, and Mintz. We must begin with Dye's (see Dye and Pickering, 1974:901–5) indicators and measures of institutional elites. Included among the corporate elite are the directors and presidents (3,572 individuals) of the top corporations that control one-half of the corporate assets in the nation (i.e., beginning with the top corporation and working down until one-half of the assets are included). This is done with industrial corporations, banks, insurance companies, utilities, communications, and transportation. For the government elite, Dye (1976:12) selects "the president and vice-president; secretaries, under-secretaries, and assistant secretaries of all executive departments; White House presidential advisors and ambassadors-at-large; congressional committee chairpersons and ranking minority committee members in the House and Senate; House and Senate majority and minority party leaders and whips; Supreme Court Justices; members of the Federal Reserve Board and the Council of Economic Advisors." In addition Dye includes top military officers and secretaries in the government elite for most of his analysis (total of 286 individuals in all, with 59 of these from the military).

Using the above indicators, Dye presents the following findings: 26.7 percent of the members of the government elite have held positions in the corporate elite (Dye, 1976:136); 16.6 percent of the government elite list their principle occupation as being in the corporate elite (Dye, 1976:159); 83.5 percent of the government elite have held a previous position in the government elite; 39.6 percent of the corporate elite have held previous positions in the government elite; and another 56.1 percent of the government elite have held positions in top law firms. Using indicators of upper class similar to those of Domhoff, Dye (1976:152) found 30 percent of the corporate elite and 25 percent of the non-military government elite to have upper class origins. Looking only to membership in exclusive upper class clubs from a list similar to Domhoff's, Dye (1976:164) found 44 percent of the corporate elite and 6 percent of the non-military government elite to be members.

In comparing these studies, their comparability must be considered. Beginning with the indicators of upper class membership, Domhoff's and Mintz's are broadly similar. The main difference is that Mintz includes attendance at Harvard, Yale, and Princeton and an expanded list of exclusive social clubs (see Mintz, 1975:133). Dye's indicators of upper class membership, however, present greater problems of comparability. While Dye (1976:151) claims to use Domhoff's basic indicators, he also includes parents' elite institutional position as an indicator of upper class membership. In another respect, however, Dye has a more exclusive definition of upper class membership. In the use of exclusive social clubs as an indicator, Domhoff includes four clubs not used by Dye (see Dye, 1976:164; Domhoff, 1970:23). Finally, Domhoff's listing of elite prep schools is slightly more inclusive than Dye's listing—37 versus 33 (Domhoff, 1970:22–33; Dye, 1976:154). It is impossible to estimate precisely the importance of Dye's differing indicators of upper class membership, but the differences do not appear large enough to prevent our arriving at some fairly firm conclusions.

Turning to indicators of corporate elite status, Dye and Domhoff differ in that Domhoff looks only to the 15 or 20 wealthiest corporations while Dye (1976:20) looks to all of those controlling half of the assets in the particular area (100 of the top industrial corporations; 33 of the top corporations in transportation, communications, and utilities; the top 50 banks; and the 18 top insurance companies). This is not a serious problem, however, and in fact gives us an opportunity to compare the backgrounds of those at different "levels" of corporate elite status. Another difference is with Dye's inclusion of corporation directors *and* presidents in the business elite because Domhoff includes only the directors of the corporations. The most serious obstacles to comparability, however, are with the work of Mintz and of Freitag who include all top corporations (though they never say exactly how many they include in the top—see Freitag, 1975:140) and consider the elite to consist of the directors and "officers" of these corporations (again, they do not mention how far they go in including officers—see Freitag, 1975:140). Also, Mintz and Freitag include corporate lawyers in the business elite while Dye and Domhoff do not. The effects of the inclusion of corporate lawyers by Mintz and Freitag, and their exclusion by Dye, cannot be determined (mainly because of Dye's larger definition of the government elite). We can see that this has only a minimal effect on Mintz and Freitag's findings, however, when we note that the cabinet ties to the business elite dropped only from 76.1 percent to 62 percent when corporate lawyers are excluded (Freitag, 1975:141).

Finally, we must consider the differing indicators of membership in the government elite. While Domhoff looks only at a few cabinet positions (from 1932 to 1964), Freitag and Mintz include the entire cabinet (from 1897 to 1973), while Dye has an inclusive definition. These differences should not concern us because they refer to differing levels within the government elite. The only significant problem in our estimation, is that Dye's indicator is too broad, including the military elite as part of the government elite throughout most of his analysis. There are clear differences in the recruitment patterns and background of military as compared to civilian leaders (Dye, 1976:152, 154, 159). Thus, because the military makes up 21 percent of his total government elite when possible we have dropped the military from the figures presented here.

Despite these problems, we can draw the following conclusions about the backgrounds of corporate and government elites: (1) Domhoff's estimation of a high proportion of cabinet members having upper class background is reinforced by Mintz's study; (2) As the corporate elite is defined in more restrictive terms, the higher the percentage recruited from upper class backgrounds (this was suggested, but not followed up by earlier studies of elite backgrounds—for example, see Keller, 1963:209–10, 319); (3) Viewing the President's Cabinet as the top of the government elite, Mintz's data show a high percentage of individuals from the upper class (66 percent to 25 percent in Dye's expanded government elite). Thus, upper class backgrounds increase as more limited indicators of a government elite are used; (4) When looking to corporate elite backgrounds among members of the government elite corporate backgrounds appear more prevalent the more restrictive the definition of the government elite is (63.4 percent to 26.7 percent with Dye's larger government elite), and the more inclusive the definition of the corporate elite is (i.e., Freitag's definition).

ELITE INTERLOCK

Elite interlock can be described as the situation in which an individual simultaneously holds two or more elite positions. This is different from the study of elite backgrounds because in the case of elite backgrounds we are dealing with the previous characteristics of, or institutional positions held by, an elite individual (a dynamic view); but with the study of elite interlock we are concerned with the overlap between elite positions at one point in time (a static view). An examination of elite interlocks is a subject of major concern for students of national power distribution because the more numerous the interlocks, the greater the number of key positions held by the same individuals; thus, the more power is concentrated in the hands of a few individuals or positions.

Dye (1976:134) examined the extent of interlock between the government and other elite positions and greatly emphasized the fact that only 19.4 percent of the government elite positions in his study are so interlocked. Most of these positions (91.2 percent) are in what he calls the public interest sector. This is hardly surprising when we consider that government officials are prevented from holding other positions which will result in conflicts of interest. To study ties between government and corporate elites, one must, therefore, examine elite backgrounds (or dynamic interlocks) as has been done by some of the researchers discussed in the previous section of this paper. For this reason we will restrict our concern in this section to interlocks within the economic sector.

As Sonquist and Koening (1975:196) put it, "It is important to focus attention on the specific nature of interlocks because an understanding of the relationships between interlocking firms can tell us much about the dynamics of power and control in the U.S. political economic system." This is especially critical when we consider the extent to which the economy is dominated increasingly by a smaller number of giant corporations. For example, as Dye's (1976:20) data show, in 1970, more than 50 percent of the industrial assets are controlled by 100 of the more than 200,000 corporations. The greater importance of interlocks with top corporations is also indicated by research which shows that the corporations on top today, contrary to those on top in the past, are more likely to stay on top (Mermelstein, 1969:536). Also important in this question of economic concentration is the new data showing that just 21 corporate investors are found in the top 5 stockholders in over half of the top 122 corporations (Subcommittee of Governmental Affairs, 1978:1). Thus, the number of interlocks among

these top corporations becomes increasingly important.

Turning first to Dye's (1973, 1974, 1976) recent research, we note that "44% of all top corporate positions were interlocked with other top positions" (see Table 2). Most of the interlocks involving incumbents of top corporate positions were *within* the corporate sector (72 percent) rather than with other sectors. Though they would be interesting, no figures are given by Dye on how many *individuals* account for this 44 percent interlock in positions. What we do know is that while 40 percent of all *positions* (government, corporate, and public interest sectors) are interlocked, only 20 percent of the 4,101 individuals account for these interlocked positions; and there is a lifetime average of 11.1 elite positions held by corporate elite individuals (Dye, 1976:130, 135). Because Dye's data include only the top 100 corporations, he cannot say how many of the corporate elite are interlocked with corporations *below* the top 100. In addition, it would be interesting to know the amount of interlock among corporate directors only (excluding corporate presidents), and the pattern and types of interlocks among the various corporations.

A recent study by Allen (1974) answers a few of these questions. Allen (1974:399) examined the amount of interlock among the directors of the 200 largest nonfinancial corporations and 50 largest financial institutions and found (see our Table 2) that these corporations and financial institutions had an average of 10.41 interlocks in 1970. This was divided to show that the average was 16.92 for the financial institutions, 9.62 for the industrial corporations, and 7.41 for the remaining nonindustrial corporations. Also of interest is that the amount of assets held was strongly correlated with the number of interlocks (.57), even when the differing size of the directorate is controlled (.49, larger corporations having more interlocks). (See Allen, 1978 which was in press simultaneously with this paper.)

Another interesting study is Dooley (1969:314) who collected data on the interlocks

TABLE 2 ECONOMIC ELITE INTERLOCK (STATIC VIEW)

Study	Findings
1. DYE	
Total Corporate Interlocks* (positions with interlocks)	44.0 %
Of Total Interlock	
percent to other corporate positions	72.7 %
percent to public interest positions	25.9 %
percent to government positions	0.2 %
2. ALLEN (1970 Data)**	
Average interlocks of corporations	10.41
Average interlocks of financial institutions	16.92
Average interlocks of industrial corporations	9.62
Average interlocks of non-industrial corporations	7.41
3. DOOLEY (1965 Data)**	
Average interlocks of corporations	9.9
Average interlocks of financial institutions	15.2
Average interlocks of industrial corporations	9.1
Average interlocks of non-industrial corporations	8.6
Average interlocks to size of corporation***	
less than .5 billion assets	6.0
1.0 to 1.4 billion assets	6.8
1.5 to 1.9 billion assets	9.2
3.0 to 3.9 billion assets	16.4
5.0 and over billion assets	23.7

* Top 100 industrial, 50 banks, 18 insurance, 33 transportation, communication, and utilities in 1970 (board of directors and presidents).
** Top 200 non-financial and top 50 financial corporations (board of directors).
*** Selected categories from Dooley's table.

among the boards of directors in the top 250 corporations (200 non-financial and 50 financial). By comparing his data from 1965 with a similar set for 1935, Dooley found that the number of interlocks were about the same (225 in 1935 and 223 in 1965, Dooley, 1969:315). In comparing Dooley's data with Allen's (for 1970) we find that larger corporations have more interlocks than smaller ones (see our Table 2). Dooley (1969:316) lists a progressively increasing number of interlocks from smaller to larger corporations (see our Table 2). Thus, much like the findings on the upper-class backgrounds of elites, as we move closer to the top we find more interlocks. Also of interest is Dooley's (1969:317) finding that by excluding board members who also hold executive positions within the corporation, the average number of interlocks with re-

maining board members is greatly increased. Soref's (1976) findings confirm that these men whose power comes through ownership, rather than executive position in the corporation, are more likely to have upper class backgrounds, are more concerned with major decisions, and are able to spread a web of influence to a larger number of corporations. We are, however, nowhere near solving the debate between those who argue that the board of directors have more power (see Soref, 1976:360) and those who argue that the executive officers hold more power (see Pfeffer, 1972; also see Zald, 1969; Seider, 1977).

Finally, Dooley's (1969:316) findings show the number of interlocks involving financial institutions are much higher for financial (15.2) than for industrial (9.1). Allen's (1974:399) 1970 data show even more extensive financial interlocks

(16.9 average), with the 1935 financial interlocks least frequent (14.8 average). This seems to indicate the growing importance of financial institutions in the economy (see Subcommittee on Governmental Affairs, 1978). Allen (1974:399) argues, however, that this is related to the greater size (in terms of assets) of the financial institutions. But, the fact remains that their sphere of influence is greater. In identifying 15 "tight-knit" groups (in terms of number of interlocks) in his 1965 data, Dooley (1969:320) finds these groups have a recurring pattern: at the centers or hubs are found top financial institutions. And also of interest is the recent findings on what can be called "indirect interlocks" (Bunting, 1976a,b), a situation in which two corporations are tied, not directly but through interlocks to a common third corporation. These are found to be increasing recently, and with a majority of the host corporations (third corporation or midpoint) in the financial sector (Bunting, 1976a:34).

In related research, Sonquist and Koening (1975:204) began their work with *Fortune's* top 797 corporations in 1969 (including 11,290 directorships), but later reduced this number to 401 corporations by including only those with at least double interlocks. Using Levine's (1972) sociometric method, four types of corporations were identified: isolates, trivial dyad members, satellite cliques, and central cliques (Sonquist and Koening, 1975:206). Of the last, 32 major central cliques were identified for further analysis (details on all of these are contained in their appendix). Of special interest are the financial cliques. These tend to expand outward toward satellite cliques, while the non-financial cliques were more self-contained. One of the most important recent findings on the increasing power of financial institutions in the economy shows that financial institutions have influence not only through interlocks with other corporations but also through the control of voting shares of stock in major corporations (Subcommittee on Governmental Affairs, 1978). The proportion of stock ownership by institutions is increasing rapidly, and it is financial corpora-

tions who often hold voting rights with this stock. In 1976, banks, investment companies, and insurance companies held 34.8 percent of the voting rights of all corporate stock in the United States (Subcommittee on Governmental Affairs, 1978:14). This of course brings up an interesting question of who controls the voting stock in the major banks. In their study, the Subcommittee on Governmental Affairs (1978:260) found, "the principal stock voters in large banks are—large banks." The most important seems to be Morgan and Company which is the number one stock voter in five of the top banks in the nation (Bankamerica, Citicorp, Manufacturers Hanover, Chemical N.Y. Corporation, and Bankers Trust N.Y.).

In comparing these studies we find few problems with incompatible indicators such as those encountered with the elite background research (with the exception of Dye's research which includes corporate executives with directors). The most significant findings relating to the nature of corporate interlocks include the following: (1) The extent of interlock among corporate directors is fairly high, and has remained so through this century; (2) Directors who are not also executives in the corporation are more likely to be involved in these interlocks; (3) The larger the corporation the more interlocks; (4) A few powerful and important cliques can be identified within this mass of interlocks, with large financial institutions often at the center of these cliques; and (5) The average number of interlocks leading from financial institutions has been growing steadily, at least since 1935.

ELITE UNITY

The existence of elite unity or cohesiveness is of central importance for those who argue from a ruling class or "governing class" position. Given this importance we would expect much research on the question, but that is not the case. We might conclude that some basis for unity exists when recalling the findings showing the upper class backgrounds of many elite individuals. But both sides agree that common background alone is not enough. With the exception of a few case studies (for example Baltzell, 1958), little has been done empirically on the question until the recent work of Domhoff.

Domhoff's (1974) most noted research in this area, in which he uses qualitative and quantitative methods, is contained in his study of San Francisco's Bohemian Club and Retreat. He attempts to demonstrate the upper class nature of this organization. Through an examination of the membership he finds 27 percent to be members of the "most exclusive club" in San Francisco, the Pacific Union Club. He argues that 38 percent of the resident members belong to the upper class. In addition, Domhoff (1974:30) found 45 percent of the 411 "nonresident regular members" listed in other upper class "blue books." And finally, Domhoff (1974:31) interprets as a tie to the corporate elite the figures which show "that at least one officer or director from 40 of the 50 largest industrial corporations in America was present" at the Bohemian Grove retreat in one year, along with directors of 20 of the top 25 commercial banks, 12 of the top 25 life insurance companies, 10 of the top 25 in transportation, and 8 of the 25 top utilities. In total, 29 percent of *Fortune's* top 797 corporations "were 'represented' by at least one officer or director" (Domhoff, 1974:32).

Domhoff attempts to show, through qualitative methods, that the members of these organizations gather not only to relax and socialize, but also to devote their time to shaping "consensus" on common business and political problems (see for example, 1974:15–18). More interesting for our purposes, however, are his attempts to show membership interlock between the various clubs and upper class organizations (Domhoff, 1974:105; 1975:178). With a statistical method for measuring the "centrality" of a club or organization in the total matrix (i.e., the extent to which an organization interlocks with many other organizations), he is able to list what he claims are the most important upper class clubs and organiza-

tions in the United States. By using this listing of top organizations he finds that 673 of *Fortune's* top 797 corporations have at least one connection to at least one of just 15 clubs and upper class organizations. In Domhoff's (1975:179) words, "this finding is even more impressive when we consider only the top 25 corporations in each category. Here we see that 25 of 25 industrials, 25 of 25 banks, 23 of 25 insurance companies, 24 of 25 transports, 24 of 25 utilities, 19 of 25 retails, and 18 of 25 conglomerates are connected."

Not everyone is convinced by Domhoff's work, however. One of the skeptics is Thomas Dye (1976:164; also our Table 1) whose data also show a great deal of membership in social clubs in general (75 percent), and 37 elite clubs in particular (44 percent). But his data also show that only 38 percent of the non-military government elite belong to these clubs, with only 6 percent belonging to any of the 37 exclusive clubs. In reflecting on these findings, and those of Domhoff, Dye (1976:163) writes, "It is our judgment that club membership is a result of top position-holding in the institutional structure of society rather than an important independent source of power . . . the clubs merely help facilitate processes that occur anyway." Dye (1976:163) believes the low membership of the government elite "undercuts the importance attributed to club membership by many 'power elite' writers."

In assessing Dye's position, it is difficult to see how he can dismiss the significance of club memberships by saying that this is only a "process that would occur anyway." Domhoff has never maintained that club membership is an "independent source of power." Rather, Domhoff's argument is only that such membership is a source of unity and consensus formation. Finally, although Dye finds that the government elite lacks participation in elite clubs, a close reading of Domhoff's (1974:18) list of speakers at the 1970 gathering at the Bohemian Grove suggests that though the government elite may not be members of these organizations, they do have an important role.

Domhoff's most serious error is his overestimation of the significance of his findings (see Domhoff, 1974:87; 1975:175). First, his study of the Bohemian Grove is only one piece to the puzzle. Also, his data often are not impressive (see McNall, 1977) in terms of the percentages of overlap in these clubs (see Domhoff, 1974:105). The most important question, of course, is how much unity and consensus is actually *created* and *maintained* through these organizations? This, no doubt, is difficult to measure, and all Domhoff is able to do at this point is suggest that the findings from psychological studies on how group solidarity is formed support his conclusions (Domhoff, 1974:89–90). What we need are more direct measures of the effects of participation in these elite organizations.

ELITE INFLUENCE ON GOVERNMENT POLICY

In this section we consider the economic elite's ability to shape government policy. Much of the research we have already discussed assumes that the relationships are important because of their effects on government policy. But, it is argued, the economic elite has other means of influence. It is here that we find a stress on upper class "policy forming organizations" such as the Council on Foreign Relations, the Committee for Economic Development, the Business Council, and others such as wealthy foundations and elite sponsored research in major universities (see Domhoff, 1974). For as Dye (1976:191) points out, it is by these means that "corporate and personal wealth provides both the financial resources and the overall direction of policy research, planning and development."

The first question involves the upper class and corporate elite membership and interlock in these "policy forming organizations." Domhoff attempts to demonstrate their elite membership in two ways. First he shows the upper class status of particular organizations. Domhoff (1970:116) finds that half of the 1400 members of the Council on Foreign Relations (CFR) are listed in the *Social Register*. But with the other organizations

Domhoff is content mainly with showing their interlock with upper class clubs. His matrix of overlapping members (see Domhoff, 1975:178) shows (to name a few) the Business Council (.63, .57, .44, .49), the Committee for Economic Development (.58, .49, .46, .47), and the Council on Foreign Relations (.37, .34, .24, .64), to have a great deal of overlap with just four elite clubs (Pacific Union, Bohemian Club, California Club, and Centurary Association). One of these organizations (the Business Council) is selected for special attention. Domhoff (1974:107) finds that 154 members of this organization (those members listed in *Who's Who* for 1971–72) hold 730 directorships in 435 banks and corporations. And finally, with a method to determine the "centrality" of several clubs and organizations (Domhoff, 1975:177–78), five of these policy organizations are listed in the top ten (with the Business Council listed as number one).

For upper class ties to the major foundations, Domhoff (1967:65) finds that of the top 13 (in terms of assets), two-thirds of their trustees are members of either the upper class (51 percent) or boards of major corporations (15 percent). For the universities, Domhoff (1967:78–79) is able only to present findings from another study done in the mid-1930s showing that one-third of the trustees of 30 "major" universities were listed in the *Social Register* and another 45 percent were directors or executives in major corporations.

In attempting to assess Domhoff's work on the question of how these organizations are able to influence government policy we must be aware that he is able to rely on a few "case studies." An example of one type of research needed in this area can be found in the work of Shoup (1975), who provides an historical analysis of the Council on Foreign Relations, how the CFR was established by upper class individuals, and its impact on major decisions during WW II and later.

But for quantitative data in this area we return again to Thomas Dye (1976:216) who argues that the pluralist view has been too simplistic: "The federal law-making process involves bargaining, competition, and compromise, as generally set forth in 'pluralist' political theory. But this interaction occurs *after* the agenda for policy-making has been established and the major directions of policy changes have already been determined." It is interesting to note that Dye rejects Domhoff's ruling class type theory. Although Dye claims not to be working from any particular model or theory of elites, several statements by Dye clearly suggest that he accepts a model very close to Keller's (1963) "strategic elites" (for example, see Dye, 1976:3–6).

With Dye's massive data on elite backgrounds and interlock we find an ambiguous category of elites he calls the "public interest" sector, which includes individuals from top law firms, directors of major foundations, trustees of elite universities, directors of "civic organizations" (such as the Council on Foreign Relations, the Committee for Economic Development, the Brookings Institution, and cultural organizations such as the Metropolitan Museum of Art) and presidents and directors of the major mass media. Dye's data contains a division in this sector which enables us to look at his findings on foundations, elite universities, and "civic" organizations separately. Dye creates a problem by including "cultural organizations" such as the Metropolitan Opera in this "civic organization" category, and because he does not tell us how many of the individuals examined in this category come from the "cultural organizations," we cannot estimate the bias produced.

The total interlock between directors of these organizations and other elites is quite high. With other elite positions, there is a 52.9 percent interlock with foundation directors, 32.9 percent with university trustees, and 42.9 percent with directors of civic organizations. Overall, the interlocks from these institutions are with corporate elites (58.8 percent), other public interest positions (60.4 percent), and government positions (4.7 percent according to Dye, 1976:134). It must be noted that these figures included individuals from top law firms as well as foundations, universities,

and civic organizations. Among foundation directors, there is an average of 5.2 previous positions in the corporate elite, while the figure for university trustees is 3.6, and for civic organization directors it is 4.4 (Dye, 1976:136). Finally, Dye (1976:152) finds 42 percent of the directors from the foundations, 25 percent from the elite universities, and 40 percent from the civic organizations to be members of the upper class, and 50 percent of the directors from the foundations, 62 percent from the elite universities, and 66 percent from the civic organizations were members of at least one of the 37 exclusive clubs listed by Dye (1976:164).

Assessing the recent research in the area of elite influence on government policy, there are at least five major questions that need consideration: (1) the extent of elite control of "policy forming institutions"; (2) how the ideas or policy recommendations from these institutions get to the government; (3) funding sources of these institutions; (4) the general policies of these institutions themselves; and (5) how often the ideas and policy recommendations produced by these institutions are put into practice or written into law by the government. As the research discussed in this section shows, we have some useful data on question 1, some limited information (mainly from Domhoff, 1967; 1970) on question 3, much discussion, but little data on question 2, and almost nothing on questions 4 and 5.

DISCUSSION

Though much additional research is needed, and we have not been able to consider research on many points in the power elite debate, we believe some important conclusions can be drawn from the data. A major question is this: Do the findings lend more support to the pluralist or the elitist side of the debate? Despite Dye's (1976:11, 145) repeated statements that his data can be used to support either side, by refining his indicators of elite status and combining his findings with those from other works reviewed here, the weight of evidence appears to fall on the side of the elitists. It is important to recognize, however, that there is a variety of elite theories, ranging from "conservative" to "critical." The present evidence is certainly not sufficient to offer unequivocal support for either of these elite theories.

It is safe to say that no matter how elite status is measured, not only are persons of elite background found in key positions far out of proportion to their representation in the population, but in some cases, for example the cabinet posts studied by Freitag, they comprise a majority of the incumbents. Clearly discernible patterns of intercorporate interlock and influence centering around major financial institutions have been discovered. So have widespread linkages between major corporations and several exclusive clubs, as well as patterns of disproportionate elite input into policy formulating organizations that have the ear of government.

Still, the meaning of these findings is not altogether clear. For instance, the pluralists claim that governmental decision making is a complex process that involves the interplay of countervailing pressure groups. The crucial question is whether or not the extent of elite overrepresentation in high governmental positions and policy formulating organizations, corporate interlock and involvement in exclusive social clubs is sufficient to upset the power balance among competing interests. Is it sufficient to insure that an elite (or a coalition of three elites in the case of Mills' thesis) can and does have its way on decisions it considers vital to its interests even against the opposition of a broad range of pressure groups representing the interests of the majority of the population?

This question immediately gives rise to others. How much elite overrepresentation would it take to insure such dominance? Do those of elite background who occupy high-level posts act on behalf of ingroup interests or do they act in a neutral manner in keeping with their official, governmental role obligations? In some of the most vital policy areas such as foreign affairs and the management of the economy, exactly which policies benefit which segments of the population? If elites do dominate, how does one explain the rise of reforms which, at least ostensibly, are opposed by elites (see Mintz et al., 1976; Mollenkopf, 1975)? None of these questions can be answered by the findings reviewed in this paper. Nevertheless, they are central to the larger debate over the distribution of power in American society, and thus a few suggestions as to how they might be attacked will be taken up later.

In our view, the patterns of interlock and overrepresentation that appear repeatedly in the studies reviewed here are sufficient to cast serious doubt upon the pluralist view of power in America. Given the conflict oriented assumptions of the pluralists (Kerbo, 1975, 1976) concerning human nature, it is incumbent upon them to explain how and why any group would not use to the fullest extent the opportunities offered by disproportionate representation in key positions. While this does not imply that an elite exercises total dominance, it suggests that if opposition is to have any hope of being effective, it would have to be extremely broadbased and highly mobilized, conditions that are met only infrequently.

A similar burden of proof is on the pluralists with respect to elite interlock and unity of purpose. The patterns of interlock, both those cutting across industries and centering about commercial banks (Subcommittee on Governmental Affairs, 1978; Levine, 1972) as well as those among "competitors" within a single industry (Scheuerman, 1975) raise serious questions about the role of competition versus coincidence of interest among segments of the business community. Research on the National Association of Manufacturers (Burch, 1973) and the U.S. Chamber of Commerce (Collins, forthcoming) suggests that there is a strong disagreement between big business and small to medium-sized firms over such basic issues as the extent of government intervention in the economy. The former is much more tolerant than the latter, because big business would find it easier to turn such intervention to its own advantage. And we are still left with big business equipped with extensive networks of interlock. Again, it is necessary for pluralists to explain why these networks would not be used to promote the collective interests of big business. Specifically, they could be used to generate and maintain tacit understandings that would lead to distribution of shares of the market, consequent suppression of aggressive price competition, cooperation in pressing the government to minimize the tax burden on industry (see Salamon and Siegfried's 1977 findings) and those with large property holdings, and channeling government intervention in the economy to favor the largest firms in particular industries. All of these things would promote the concentration of purchasing power away from the general public by preventing competitive pressures to lower consumer prices. They would also make it easier for business to pass on cost increases to the consumer in the form of higher prices and frustrate any move toward an effectively progressive tax system. We are arguing, again using the pluralists' own assumptions, that it is in the interests of major corporations to neutralize the disciplinary pressures of the market upon them. Extensive interlocks could greatly facilitate the effective pursuit of such interests (Herman, 1973).

This brings us directly to the issues that divide the two principal types of elite theorists, the "conservatives" (Dye, 1976; Putnam, 1976; Prewitt and Stone, 1973; Keller, 1963; Baltzell, 1958) and "critical" theorists (Anderson, 1974; Birnbaum, 1969; Bottomore, 1966; Domhoff, 1974, 1970, 1967; Miliband, 1969; Mills, 1956). Unlike the pluralists (i.e., Dahl, 1961, 1967; and Rose, 1967), both of these approaches acknowledge the centralization of political and economic power. Where they disagree is on the issue of in whose interests that control is exercised, and on whether or not such concentration of power is inevitable (Kerbo, 1975). Disputes between those two schools of elite theory often center around the question of whether one should focus upon collective issues as opposed to distributive ones. "Con-

servatives" see inequality as an inevitable aspect of complex societies, stemming from their functional needs of organization, and not the result of conspiratorial or capricious elite decision making. The "critical" theorists maintain, however, that such inequality is not inevitable, at least not on a scale anywhere close to what presently exists.

But here we come to a division within the critical elitist camp itself. On the one hand, there are the instrumentalists (Domhoff, 1974, 1970, 1967; Freitag, 1975; Mintz, 1975) who focus their attention on the question of *who* occupies powerful positions and *who* is linked with them, research that we have been reviewing in this paper. On the other hand, there are the structuralists (Harrington, 1976, 1970; Parkin, 1971; Poulantzas, 1975) who argue that it matters little who makes the decisions. As long as the economic system is based upon private ownership and the criterion of the profitability of the individual firm, and as long as there is public pressure from all strata on politicians to keep the economy thriving, the range of decisions that any "realistic" and "responsible" politician can make is restricted narrowly to those which promote the profitability of business. This, the structuralists argue, explains not only why the distribution of income has remained relatively constant throughout this century in both the United States and in Western Europe, but also why such inequality will necessarily be perpetuated in the future. Only a transformation of the economy into one based upon providing for human needs rather than profitability (in Marx's terms, use values instead of exchange values) is seen as capable of eliminating the gross inequalities that exist.

If present disagreements between "conservative" and "critical" elite theorists and between instrumentalists and structuralists within the "critical" camp are to be submitted to an empirical test, we must devise new research strategies. Especially if we are to compare *what* is with *what could be* we must turn to more sophisticated historical and comparative methods. Domhoff (1970) has attempted to use historical methods in a limited way, and Putnam (1976) has attempted to use comparative data. Both have been hampered, however, by numerous problems, especially a lack of comparable data.

PROGRAM FOR FUTURE RESEARCH

We need to consider what must be done if the debate over the distribution of power on a national level is to progress beyond the state in which we now find it. It will be helpful if we explore generally the problems of theory building and testing.

Hage (1972:13) believes that little intellectual progress was made in fields such as biology until that "field shifted from non-variable to general variable concepts." Hage (1972:10) uses the example of democracy: "Democracy is an either-or phenomenon, a specific non-variable of categorical concept—regardless of the number of indicators we might have, the concept categorizes a society or political system as being democratic or not democratic." It is obvious that at present, the power stratification debate has been viewed in precisely these terms. A first step is to conceptualize the debate in terms of *degrees* of elite domination. Second, we must keep in mind several dimensions or aspects of elite domination or pluralist competition, four of which we have treated in this paper, and each of which must be treated as a continuum.

This type of research, however, will only be able to tell us what presently exists (i.e., degree of elite membership in the upper class, degree of elite unity, etc.). It can tell us little about the inevitability of elite rule or the outcome of degrees of elite domination. For answers to these questions we must turn eventually to historical and comparative analysis. And once we have moved to general variable concepts, we will be in a better position to benefit from comparative analysis. At the same time, once we have come to some agreement and have perfected our indicators for the dimensions involved in the debate (as we have attempted in this paper), we will be able to generate comparable data across societies.

An example of what we are suggesting here is in order. Let us take the issue of ties between corporate and governmental elites. If the degree of elite concentration makes little or no difference in the degree of inequality, then the structuralist argument gains credence. If, however, there is an inverse correlation between these variables, then the instrumentalist position is strengthened. Such findings also would be relevant to the "conservative"–"critical" controversy among elite theorists though not so clearly as in the case of the structuralists and instrumentalists. For example, if the degree of elite concentration shows little or no correlation with the degree of inequality, "conservatives" could argue that it demonstrates that elites are not especially exploitative, and that the inequality that exists probably constitutes an irreducible minimum for advanced industrial societies. If, however, a positive correlation between elite concentration and inequality is discovered, the "critical" theorists could claim support for their position.

No doubt the type of research described above will not be without problems. One of the greatest difficulties will be finding societies that are comparable in most respects, so that we know that variance found in one factor, such as class differences in income or working conditions, is at least partially explained by the variance in the extent of corporate and government elite ties. But until attempts are made in perfecting this type of analysis, we will have little chance of resolving many of the issues separating the various sides in the debate.

REFERENCES

Allen, Michael, 1974. "The structure of interorganizational elite cooptation: interlocking corporate directorates." American Sociological Review 39:393–406.

———. 1978. "Continuity and change within the core corporate elite." The Sociological Quarterly 19:510–21.

Anderson, Charles H. 1974. The Political Economy of Social Class. Englewood Cliffs, N.J.: Prentice-Hall.

Bachrach, Peter. 1967. The Theory of Democratic Elitism. Boston: Little, Brown.

Baltzell, E. Digby. 1958. Philadelphia Gentlemen. New York: Free Press.

Birnbaum, Norman, 1969. The Crisis of Industrial Society. New York: Oxford University Press.

Bottomore, Thomas B. 1966. Classes in Modern Society. New York: Vintage Books.

Bunting. David. 1976a. "Corporate interlocking, part II: the modern money trust." Directors and Boards 1:28–36.

————. 1976b. "Corporate interlocking, part IV: a new look at interlocks and legislation." Directors and Boards 1:39–47.

Burch, Philip. 1973. "The N.A.M. as an interest group." Politics and Society 4:97–130.

Collins, Robert M. (forthcoming). "Positive business responses to the new deal: the roots of the Committee for Economic Development, 1933–1942." Business History Review.

Dahl, Robert. 1961. Who Governs? New Haven: Yale University Press.

————. 1967. Pluralist Democracy in the United States. Chicago: Rand McNally.

Domhoff, G. William. 1967. Who Rules America? Englewood Cliffs, N.J.: Prentice-Hall.

————. 1970. The Higher Circles. New York: Random House.

————. 1974. The Bohemian Grove and Other Retreats. New York: Harper.

————. 1975. "Social clubs, policy-planning groups, and corporations: a network study of ruling-class cohesiveness." The Insurgent Sociologist 5:173–84.

Dooley, Peter. 1969. "The interlocking directorate." American Economic Review 59:314–23.

Dye, Thomas R. 1976. Who's Running America? Englewood Cliffs, N.J.: Prentice-Hall.

Dye, Thomas R., Eugene Declercq, and John Pickering, 1973. "Concentration, specialization, and interlocking among institutional elites." Social Science Quarterly 54:8–28.

Dye, Thomas R. and John Pickering. 1974. "Governmental and corporate elites: convergence and differentiation." Journal of Politics 36:900–925.

Edinger, Lewis, and Donald Searing. 1967. "Social background in elite analysis: a methodological inquiry." American Political Science Review 61:428–45.

Freitag, Peter. 1975. "The cabinet and big business: a study of interlocks." Social Problems 23:137–52.

Hage, Jerald, 1972. Techniques and Problems of Theory Construction in Sociology. New York: Wiley.

Harrington, Michael. 1970. Socialism. New York: Saturday Review Press.

————. 1976. The Twilight of Capitalism. New York: Simon and Schuster.

Herman, Edward, 1973. "Do bankers control corporations." Monthly Review 25:12–29.

Keller, Suzanne. 1963. Beyond the Ruling Class. New York: Random House.

Kerbo, Harold R. 1975. "Paradigms of social stratification: the contemporary power elite debate." Unpublished Ph.D. dissertation, Virginia Polytechnic Institute and State University.

————. 1976. "Pluralism or ruling class: a case of paradigm conflict." Paper presented at the annual meeting of the American Sociological Association, New York City.

Levine, Joel. 1972. "The sphere of influence." American Sociological Review 37:14–27.

Lowi, Theodore J. 1973. "Foreword." Pp. vii–xii in Kenneth Prewitt and Alan Stone (eds.), The Ruling Elites. New York: Harper and Row.

Mankoff, Milton. 1970. "Power in advanced capitalistic society: a review essay on recent elitist and Marxist criticism of pluralist theory." Social Problems 17:418–30.

McNall, Scott. 1977. "Does anybody rule America?: a critique of elite theory and method." Paper presented at the annual meetings of the American Sociological Association, Chicago.

Mermelstein, David. 1969. "Large industrial corporations and asset shares." American Economic Review 59:531–41.

Miliband, Ralph. 1969. The State in Capitalist Society. New York: Basic Books.

Mills, C. Wright. 1956. The Power Elite. New York: Oxford University Press.

Mintz, Beth. 1975. "The president's cabinet, 1897–1972: a contribution to the power structure debate." Insurgent Sociologist 5:131–48.

Mintz, Beth, Peter Freitag, Carol Hendricks, and Michael Schwartz. 1976. "Problems of proof in elite research." Social Problems 23:314–24.

Mollenkopf, John. 1975. "Theories of the state and power structure research." Insurgent Sociologist 5:245–64.

Parkin, Frank. 1971. Class Inequality and Political Order. New York: Praeger.

Pfeffer, Jeffrey. 1972. "Size and composition of corporate boards of directors: the organization and its environment." Administrative Science Quarterly 17:218-28.

Poulantzas, Nicos. 1975. Political Power and Social Classes. Atlantic Highlands, N.J.: Humanities Press.

Prewitt, Kenneth, and William McAllister. 1976. "Changes in the American executive elite, 1930-1970." Pp. 105-32 in Heinz Eulau and Moshe Czudnowski (eds.), Elite Recruitment in Democratic Politics. New York: Halsted Press.

Prewitt, Kenneth, and Alan Stone. 1973. The Ruling Elites. New York: Harper and Row.

Putnam, Robert. 1976. The Comparative Study of Elites. Englewood Cliffs, N.J.: Prentice-Hall.

Rose, Arnold M. 1967. The Power Structure. New York: Oxford University Press.

Salamon, Lester and John Siegfried. 1977. "Economic power and political influence: the impact of industry structure on public policy." American Political Science Review 71:1026-43.

Scheuerman, William. 1975. "Economic power in the United States: the case of steel." Politics and Society 5:337-66.

Seider, Maynard. 1977. "Corporate ownership, control and ideology: support for behavioral similarity." Sociology and Social Research 62:113-28.

Shoup, Laurence. 1975. "Shaping the postwar world: the Council of Foreign Relations and U.S. war aims during WW II." Insurgent Sociologist 5:9-52.

Sonquist, John, and Thomas Koening. 1975. "Interlocking directorates in the top U.S. corporations: a graph theory approach." Insurgent Sociologist 5:196-229.

Soref, Michael. 1976. "Social class and a division of labor within the corporate elite: a note on class, interlocking, and executive committee membership of directors of U.S. firms." The Sociological Quarterly 17:360-68.

Subcommittee on Governmental Affairs (U.S. Senate). 1978. Voting Rights in Major Corporations. Washington, D.C.: U.S. Government Printing Office.

Walker, Jack. 1966. "A critique of the elitist theory of democracy." American Political Science Review 60:285-95.

Zald, Mayer. 1969. "The power and functions of boards of directors: a theoretical synthesis." American Journal of Sociology 75:97-111.

Zuckerman, Alan. 1977. "The concept of political elite: lessons from Mosca and Pareto." Journal of Politics 39:324-44.

Zweingenhaft, Richard. 1975. "Who represents America." Insurgent Sociologist 5:119-30.

TAKING ANOTHER LOOK

1 Identify the five major indicators of upper-class membership specified by G. William Domhoff.

2 What conclusions are drawn by Kerbo and Della Fave regarding the backgrounds of corporate and government elites?

3 According to Kerbo and Della Fave, which are the most significant findings regarding the nature of corporate interlocks?

4 Why is the existence of elite unity or cohesiveness of central importance for those who argue from a ruling class or "governing class" position?

5 On what grounds are Kerbo and Della Fave critical of the pluralist view of power?

6 Briefly summarize the suggestions of Kerbo and Della Fave regarding future research on elite domination of American society.

7 How would conflict theorists be likely to view the debate between elite theorists and pluralists over the distribution of power in the United States?

"Banana Time": Job Satisfaction and Informal Interaction

Donald F. Roy

Many pioneers of sociological thought were concerned that changes in the workplace resulting from the Industrial Revolution would have a negative impact on workers. Émile Durkheim argued that as labor becomes more and more differentiated, individuals experience *anomie,* or a loss of direction. Workers cannot feel the same fulfillment from performing one specialized task in a factory as they do when they are totally responsible for creating a product. Max Weber suggested that impersonality is a fundamental characteristic of bureaucratic organizations. One result is the cold and uncaring feeling often associated with contemporary bureaucracies. However, the most penetrating analysis of the dehumanizing aspects of industrialization was offered by Karl Marx.

Marx believed that as the process of industrialization advanced within capitalist societies, people's lives became increasingly devoid of meaning. While Marx expressed concern about the damaging effects of many social institutions, he focused on what he saw as a person's most important activity: labor. For Marx, the emphasis of the Industrial Revolution on specialization of factory tasks contributed to a growing sense of alienation among industrial workers.

The term *alienation* refers to a feeling of disassociation or estrangement from the surrounding society. The division of labor increased alienation because workers were channeled into monotonous, meaningless repetition of the same tasks. However, in Marx's view, an even deeper cause of alienation is the powerlessness of workers in a capitalist economic system. Workers have no control over their occupational duties, the products of their labor, or the distribution of profits.

In the following selection, sociologist Donald F. Roy examines workers' alienation through a two-month period of participant observation within a small work group of factory machine operatives. Drawing on the interactionist perspective, Roy carefully records the social interactions among members of the work group, including many structured "times" and "themes" designed to break up long days of simple, repetitive work. He concludes that his observations "seem to support the generally accepted notion that one key source of job satisfaction lies in the informal interaction shared by members of a work group."

This paper undertakes description and exploratory analysis of the social interaction which took place within a small work group of factory machine operatives during a two-month period of participant observation. The factual and ideational materials which it presents lie at an intersection of two lines of research interest and should, in their dual bear-ing, contribute to both. Since the operatives were engaged in work which involved the repetition of very simple operations over an extra-long work-day, six days a week, they were faced with the problem of dealing with a formidable "beast of monotony." Revelation of how the group utilized its resources to combat that "beast" should merit the attention of those who are seeking solution to the practical problem of job satisfaction, or employee morale. It should also provide insights for those who are trying to penetrate the mysteries of the small group.

Convergence of these two lines of interest is, of course, no new thing. Among the host of writers and researchers who have suggested connections between "group" and "joy in work" are Walker and Guest, observers of social interaction on the automobile assembly line.[1] They quote assembly-line workers as saying, "We have a lot of fun and talk all the time,"[2] and "If it weren't for the talking and fooling, you'd go nuts."[3]

My account of how one group of machine operators kept from "going nuts" in a situation of monotonous work activity attempts to lay bare the tissues of interaction which made up the content of their adjustment. The talking, fun, and fooling which provided solution to the elemental problem of "psychological survival" will be described according to their embodiment in intra-group relations. In addition, an unusual opportunity for close observation of behavior involved in the maintenance of group equilibrium was afforded by the fortuitous introduction of a "natural experiment." My unwitting injection of explosive materials into the stream of interaction resulted in sudden, but temporary, loss of group interaction.

My fellow operatives and I spent our long days of simple, repetitive work in relative isolation from other employees of the factory. Our line of machines was sealed off from other work areas of the plant by the four walls of the clicking room. The one door of this room was usually closed. Even when it was kept open, during periods of hot weather, the consequences were not social; it opened on an uninhabited storage room of the shipping department. Not even the sounds of work activity going on elsewhere in the factory carried to this isolated work place. There were occasional contacts with "outside" employees, usu-

ally on matters connected with the work; but, with the exception of the daily calls of one fellow who came to pick up finished materials for the next step in processing, such visits were sporadic and infrequent.

Moreover, face-to-face contact with members of the managerial hierarchy were few and far between. No one bearing the title of foreman ever came around. The only company official who showed himself more than once during the two-month observation period was the plant superintendent. Evidently overloaded with supervisory duties and production problems which kept him busy elsewhere, he managed to pay his respects every week or two. His visits were in the nature of short, businesslike, but friendly exchanges. Otherwise he confined his observable communications with the group to occasional utilization of a public address system. During the two-month period, the company president and the chief chemist paid one friendly call apiece. One man, who may or may not have been of managerial status, was seen on various occasions lurking about in a manner which excited suspicion. Although no observable consequences accrued from the peculiar visitations of this silent fellow, it was assumed that he was some sort of efficiency expert, and he was referred to as "The Snooper."

As far as our work group was concerned, this was truly a situation of laissez-faire management. There was no interference from staff experts, no hounding by time-study engineers or personnel men hot on the scent of efficiency or good human relations. Nor were there any signs of industrial democracy in the form of safety, recreational, or production committees. There was an international union, and there was a highly publicized union-management cooperation program; but actual interactional processes of cooperation were carried on somewhere beyond my range of observation and without participation of members of my work group. Furthermore, these union-man-

[1] Charles R. Walker and Robert H. Guest, *The Man on the Assembly Line,* Harvard University Press, Cambridge, 1952.

[2] *Ibid.,* p. 77.
[3] *Ibid.,* p. 68.

agement get-togethers had no determinable connection with the problem of "toughing out" a twelve-hour day at monotonous work.

Our work group was thus not only abandoned to its own resources for creating job satisfaction, but left without that basic reservoir of ill-will toward management which can sometimes be counted on to stimulate the development of interesting activities to occupy hand and brain. Lacking was the challenge of intergroup conflict, that perennial source of creative experience to fill the otherwise empty hours of meaningless work routine.[4]

The clicking machines were housed in a room approximately thirty by twenty-four feet. They were four in number, set in a row, and so arranged along one wall that the busy operator could, merely by raising his head from his work, freshen his reveries with a glance through one of the three large barred windows. To the rear of one of the end machines sat a long cutting table; here the operators cut up rolls of plastic materials into small sheets manageable for further processing at the clickers. Behind the machine at the opposite end of the line sat another table which was intermittently the work station of a female employee who performed sundry scissors operations of a more intricate nature on raincoat parts. Boxed in on all sides by shelves and stocks of materials, this latter locus of work appeared a cell within a cell.

The clickers were of the genus punching machines; of mechanical construction similar to that of the better-known punch presses, their leading features were hammer and block. The hammer, or punching head, was approximately eight inches by twelve inches at its flat striking surface. The descent upon the block was initially forced by the operator, who exerted pressure on a handle attached to the side of the hammer head. A few inches of travel downward established electrical connection for a sharp, power-driven blow. The hammer also traveled, by manual guidance, in a

horizontal plane to and from, and in an arc around, the central column of the machine. Thus the operator, up to the point of establishing electrical connections for the sudden and irrevocable downward thrust, had flexibility in maneuvering his instrument over the larger surface of the block. The latter, approximately twenty-four inches wide, eighteen inches deep, and ten inches thick was made, like a butcher's block, of inlaid hardwood; it was set in the machine at a convenient waist height. On it the operator placed his materials, one sheet at a time if leather, stacks of sheets if plastic, to be cut with steel dies of assorted sizes and shapes. The particular die in use would be moved, by hand, from spot to spot over the materials each time a cut was made; less frequently, materials would be shifted on the block as the operator saw need for such adjustment.

Introduction to the new job, with its relatively simple machine skills and work routines, was accomplished with what proved to be, in my experience, an all-time minimum of job training. The clicking machine assigned to me was situated at one end of the row. Here the superintendent and one of the operators gave a few brief demonstrations, accompanied by bits of advice which included a warning to keep hands clear of the descending hammer. After a short practice period, at the end of which the superintendent expressed satisfaction with progress and potentialities, I was left to develop my learning curve with no other supervision than that afforded by members of the work group. Further advice and assistance did come, from time to time, from my fellow operatives, sometimes upon request, sometimes unsolicited.

THE WORK GROUP

Absorbed at first in three related goals of improving my clicking skill, increasing my rate of output, and keeping my left hand unclicked, I paid

---

[4] Donald F. Roy, "Work Satisfaction and Social Reward in Quota Achievement: An Analysis of Piecework Incentive."

American Sociological Review, XVIII (October, 1953), 507–514.

little attention to my fellow operatives save to observe that they were friendly, middle-aged, for-
eign-born, full of advice, and very talkative. Their
names, according to the way they addressed each
other, were George, Ike, and Sammy.[5] George, a
stocky fellow in his late fifties, operated the machine at the opposite end of the line; he, I later
discovered, had emigrated in early youth from a
country in Southeastern Europe. Ike, stationed at
George's left, was tall, slender, in his early fifties,
and Jewish; he had come from Eastern Europe in
his youth. Sammy, number three man in the line,
and my neighbor, was heavy set, in his late fifties,
and Jewish; he had escaped from a country in
Eastern Europe just before Hitler's legions had
moved in. All three men had been downwardly
mobile as to occupation in recent years. George
and Sammy had been proprietors of small businesses; the former had been "wiped out" when his
uninsured establishment burned down; the latter
had been entrepreneuring on a small scale before
he left all behind him to flee the Germans. According to his account, Ike had left a highly
skilled trade which he had practiced for years in
Chicago.

I discovered also that the clicker line represented a ranking system in descending order from
George to myself. George not only had top seniority for the group, but functioned as a sort of
leadman. His superior status was marked in the
fact that he received five cents more per hour
than the other clickermen, put in the longest
workday, made daily contact, outside the workroom, with the superintendent on work matters
which concerned the entire line, and communicated to the rest of us the directives which he received. The narrow margin of superordination was
seen in the fact that directives were always relayed in the superintendent's name; they were on
the order of, "You'd better let that go now, and
get on the green. Joe says they're running low on
the fifth floor," or, "Joe says he wants two boxes
of the 3-die today." The narrow margin was also

seen in the fact that the superintendent would
communicate directly with his operatives over the
public address system; and, on one occasion, Ike
or Sammy would leave the workroom to confer
with him for decisions or advice in regard to work
orders.

Ike was next to George in seniority, then
Sammy. I was, of course, low man on the totem
pole. Other indices to status differentiation lay in
informal interaction, to be described later.

With one exception, job status tended to be
matched by length of workday. George worked a
thirteen-hour day, from 7 a.m. to 8:30 p.m. Ike
worked eleven hours, from 7 a.m. to 6:30 p.m.; occasionally he worked until 7 or 7:30 for an eleven
and a half- or a twelve-hour day. Sammy put in a
nine-hour day, from 8 a.m. to 5:30 p.m. My twelve
hours spanned from 8 a.m. to 8:30 p.m. We had a
half hour for lunch, from 12 to 12:30.

The female who worked at the secluded table
behind George's machine put in a regular plant-
wide eight-hour shift from 8 to 4:30. Two women
held this job during the period of my employment; Mable was succeeded by Baby. Both were
Negroes, and in their late twenties.

A fifth clicker operator, an Arabian *emigré*
called Boo, worked a night shift by himself. He
usually arrived about 7 p.m. to take over Ike's machine.

THE WORK

It was evident to me, before my first workday
drew to a weary close, that my clicking career was
going to be a grim process of fighting the clock,
the particular timepiece in this situation being an
old-fashioned alarm clock which ticked away on a
shelf near George's machine. I had struggled
through many dreary rounds with the minutes and
hours during the various phases of my industrial
experience, but never had I been confronted with
such a dismal combination of working conditions
as the extra-long workday, the infinitesimal cerebral excitation, and the extreme limitation of
physical movement. The contrast with a recent

---

[5] All names used are fictitious.

stint in the California oil fields was striking. This was no eight-hour day of racing hither and yon over desert and foothills with a rollicking crew of "roustabouts" on a variety of repair missions at oil wells, pipe lines, and storage tanks. Here there were no afternoon dallyings to search the sands for horned toads, tarantulas, and rattlesnakes, or to climb old wooden derricks for raven's nests, with an eye out, of course, for the telltale streak of dust in the distance which gave ample warning of the approach of the boss. This was standing all day in one spot beside three old codgers in a dingy room looking out through barred windows at the bare walls of a brick warehouse, leg movements largely restricted to the shifting of body weight from one foot to the other, hand and arm movements confined, for the most part, to a simple repetitive sequence of place the die, —— punch the clicker, —— place the die, —— punch the clicker, and intellectual activity reduced to computing the hours to quitting time. It is true that from time to time a fresh stack of sheets would have to be substituted for the clicked-out old one; but the stack would have been prepared by someone else, and the exchange would be only a minute or two in the making. Now and then a box of finished work would have to be moved back out of the way, and an empty box brought up; but the moving back and the bringing up involved only a step or two. And there was the half hour for lunch, and occasional trips to the lavatory or the drinking fountain to break up the day into digestible parts. But after each momentary respite, hammer and die were moving again: click, —— move die, —— click, —— move die.

Before the end of the first day, Monotony was joined by his twin brother, Fatigue. I got tired. My legs ached, and my feet hurt. Early in the afternoon I discovered a tall stool and moved it up to my machine to "take the load off my feet." But the superintendent dropped in to see how I was

"doing" and promptly informed me that "we don't sit down on this job." My reverie toyed with the idea of quitting the job and looking for other work.

The next day was the same: the monotony of the work, the tired legs and sore feet and thoughts of quitting.

THE GAME OF WORK

In discussing the factory operative's struggle to "cling to the remnants of joy in work," Henri de Man makes the general observations that "it is psychologically impossible to deprive any kind of work of all its positive emotional elements," that the worker will find *some* meaning in any activity assigned to him, a "certain scope for initiative which can satisfy after a fashion the instinct for play and the creative impulse," that "even in the Taylor system there is found luxury of self-determination."[6] De Man cites the case of one worker who wrapped 13,000 incandescent bulbs a day; she found her outlet for creative impulse, her self-determination, her meaning in work by varying her wrapping movements a little from time to time.[7]

So did I search for *some* meaning in my continuous mincing of plastic sheets into small ovals, fingers, and trapezoids. The richness of possibility for creative expression previously discovered in my experience with the "Taylor system"[8] did not reveal itself here. There was no piecework, so no piecework game. There was no conflict with management, so no war game. But, like the light bulb wrapper, I did find a "certain scope for initiative," and out of this slight freedom to vary activity, I developed a game of work.

The game developed was quite simple, so elementary, in fact, that its playing was reminiscent of rainy-day preoccupations in childhood, when attention could be centered by the hour on

[6] Henri de Man, *The Psychology of Socialism,* Henry Holt and Company, New York, 1927, pp. 80–81.

[7] *Ibid.,* p. 81.
[8] Roy, *op. cit.*

colored bits of things of assorted sizes and shapes. But this adult activity was not mere pottering and piddling; what it lacked in the earlier imaginative content, it made up for in clean-cut structure. Fundamentally involved were: a) variation in color of the materials cut, b) variation in shapes of the dies used, and c) a process called "scraping the block." The basic procedure which ordered the particular combination of components employed could be stated in the form: "As soon as I do so many of these, I'll get to do those." If, for example, production scheduled for the day featured small, rectangular strips in three colors, the game might go: "As soon as I finish a thousand of the green ones, I'll click some brown ones." And, with success in attaining the objective of working with brown materials, a new goal of "I'll get to do the white ones" might be set. Or the new goal might involve switching dies.

Scraping the block made the game more interesting by adding to the number of possible variations in its playing; and, what was perhaps more important, provided the only substantial reward, save for going to the lavoratory or getting a drink of water, on days when work with one die and one color of material was scheduled. As a physical operation, scraping the block was fairly simple; it involved application of a coarse file to the upper surface of the block to remove roughness and unevenness resulting from the wear and tear of die penetration. But, as part of the intellectual and emotional content of the game of work, it could be in itself a source of variation in activity. The upper left-hand corner of the block could be chewed up in the clicking of 1,000 white trapezoid pieces, then scraped. Next, the upper right-hand corner, and so on until the entire block had been worked over. Then, on the next round of scraping by quadrants, there was the possibility of a change of color or die to green trapezoid or white oval pieces.

Thus the game of work might be described as a continuous sequence of short-range production goals with achievement rewards in the form of activity change. The superiority of this relatively complex and self-determined system over the technically simple and outside-controlled job satisfaction injections experienced by Milner at the beginner's table in a shop of the feather industry should be immediately apparent:

> Twice a day our work was completely changed to break the monotony. First Jennie would give us feathers of a brilliant green, then bright orange or a light blue or black. The "ohs" and "ahs" that came from the girls at each change was proof enough that this was an effective way of breaking the monotony of the tedious work.[9]

But a hasty conclusion that I was having lots of fun playing my clicking game should be avoided. These games were not as interesting in the experiencing as they might seem to be from the telling. Emotional tone of the activity was low, and intellectual currents weak. Such rewards as scraping the block or "getting to do the blue ones" were not very exciting, and the stretches of repetitive movement involved in achieving them were long enough to permit lapses into obsessive reverie. Henri de Man speaks of "clinging to the remnants of joy in work," and this situation represented just that. How tenacious the clinging was, how long I could have "stuck it out" with my remnants, was never determined. Before the first week was out this adjustment to the work situation was complicated by other developments. The game of work continued, but in a different context. Its influence became decidedly subordinated to, if not completely overshadowed by, another source of job satisfaction.

INFORMAL SOCIAL ACTIVITY OF THE WORK GROUP: TIMES AND THEMES

The change came about when I began to take serious note of the social activity going on around me; my attentiveness to this activity came with growing involvement in it. What I heard at first, before

[9] Lucille Milner, *Education of An American Liberal*, Horizon Press, New York, 1954, p. 97.

I started to listen, was a stream of disconnected bits of communication which did not make much sense. Foreign accents were strong and referents were not joined to coherent contexts of meaning. It was just "jabbering." What I saw at first, before I began to observe, was occasional flurries of horseplay so simple and unvarying in pattern and so childish in quality that they made no strong bid for attention. For example, Ike would regularly switch off the power at Sammy's machine whenever Sammy made a trip to the lavatory or the drinking fountain. Correlatively, Sammy invariably fell victim to the plot by making an attempt to operate his clicking hammer after returning to the shop. And, as the simple pattern went, this blind stumbling into the trap was always followed by indignation and reproach from Sammy, smirking satisfaction from Ike, and mild paternal scolding from George. My interest in this procedure was at first confined to wondering when Ike would weary of his tedious joke or when Sammy would learn to check his power switch before trying the hammer.

But, as I began to pay closer attention, as I began to develop familiarity with the communication system, the disconnected became connected, the nonsense made sense, the obscure became clear, and the silly actually funny. And, as the content of the interaction took on more and more meaning, the interaction began to reveal structure. There were "times" and "themes," and roles to serve their enaction. The interaction had subtleties, and I began to savor and appreciate them. I started to record what hitherto had seemed unimportant.

Times

This emerging awareness of structure and meaning included recognition that the long day's grind was broken by interruptions of a kind other than the formally instituted or idiosyncratically developed disjunctions in work routine previously described. These additional interruptions appeared in daily repetition in an ordered series of informal interactions. They were, in part, but only in part and in very rough comparison, similar to those common fractures of the production process known as the coffee break, the coke break, and the cigarette break. Their distinction lay in frequency of occurrence and in brevity. As phases of the daily series, they occurred almost hourly, and so short were they in duration that they disrupted work activity only slightly. Their significance lay not so much in their function as rest pauses, although it cannot be denied that physical refreshment was involved. Nor did their chief importance lie in the accentuation of progress points in the passage of time, although they could perform that function far more strikingly than the hour hand on the dull face of George's alarm clock. If the daily series of interruptions be likened to a clock, then the comparison might best be made with a special kind of cuckoo clock, one with a cuckoo which can provide variation in its announcements and can create such an interest in them that the intervening minutes become filled with intellectual content. The major significance of the interactional interruptions lay in such a carryover of interest. The physical interplay which momentarily halted work activity would initiate verbal exchanges and thought processes to occupy group members until the next interruption. The group interactions thus not only marked off the time; they gave it content and hurried it along.

Most of the breaks in the daily series were designated as "times" in the parlance of the clicker operators, and they featured the consumption of food or drink of one sort or another. There was coffee time, peach time, banana time, fish time, coke time, and, of course, lunch time. Other interruptions, which formed part of the series but were not verbally recognized as times, were window time, pickup time, and the staggered quitting times of Sammy and Ike. These latter unnamed times did not involve the partaking of refreshments.

My attention was first drawn to this times business during my first week of employment when I was encouraged to join in the sharing of two peaches. It was Sammy who provided the peaches; he drew them from his lunch box after making the announcement, "Peach time!" On this first occasion I refused the proffered fruit, but thereafter regularly consumed my half peach. Sammy continued to provide the peaches and to make the "Peach time!" announcement, although there were days when Ike would remind him that it was peach time, urging him to hurry up with the mid-morning snack. Ike invariably complained about the quality of the fruit, and his complaints fed the fires of continued banter between peach donor and critical recipient. I did find the fruit a bit on the scrubby side but felt, before I achieved insight into the function of peach time, that Ike was showing poor manners by looking a gift horse in the mouth. I wondered why Sammy continued to share his peaches with such an ingrate.

Banana time followed peach time by approximately an hour. Sammy again provided the refreshments, namely, one banana. There was, however, no four-way sharing of Sammy's banana. Ike would gulp it down by himself after surreptitiously extracting it from Sammy's lunch box, kept on a shelf behind Sammy's work station. Each morning, after making the snatch, Ike would call out, "Banana time!" and proceed to down his prize while Sammy made futile protests and denunciations. George would join in with mild remonstrances, sometimes scolding Sammy for making so much fuss. The banana was one which Sammy brought for his own consumption at lunch time; he never did get to eat his banana, but kept bringing one for his lunch. At first this daily theft startled and amazed me. Then I grew to look forward to the daily seizure and the verbal interaction which followed.

Window time came next. It followed banana time as a regular consequence of Ike's castigation by the indignant Sammy. After "taking" repeated references to himself as a person badly lacking in morality and character, Ike would "finally" retaliate by opening the window which faced Sammy's machine, to let the "cold air" blow in on Sammy.

The slandering which would, in its echolalic repetition, wear down Ike's patience and forbearance usually took the form of the invidious comparison: "George is a good daddy! Ike is a bad man! A very bad man!" Opening the window would take a little time to accomplish and would involve a great deal of verbal interplay between Ike and Sammy, both before and after the event. Ike would threaten, make feints toward the window, then finally open it. Sammy would protest, argue, and make claims that the air blowing in on him would give him a cold; he would eventually have to leave his machine to close the window. Sometimes the weather was slightly chilly, and the draft from the window unpleasant; but cool or hot, windy or still, window time arrived each day. (I assume that it was originally a cold season development.) George's part in this interplay, in spite of the "good daddy" laudations, was to encourage Ike in his window work. He would stress the tonic values of fresh air and chide Sammy for his unappreciativeness.

Following window time came lunch time, a formally designated half-hour for the midday repast and rest break. At this time, informal interaction would feature exchanges between Ike and George. The former would start eating his lunch a few minutes before noon, and the latter, in his role as straw boss, would censure him for malobservance of the rules. Ike's off-beat luncheon usually involved a previous tampering with George's alarm clock. Ike would set the clock ahead a few minutes in order to maintain his eating schedule without detection, and George would discover these small daylight saving changes.

The first "time" interruption of the day I did not share. It occurred soon after I arrived on the job, at eight o'clock. George and Ike would share a small pot of coffee brewed on George's hot plate.

Pickup time, fish time, and coke time came in the afternoon. I name it pickup time to represent the official visit of the man who made daily calls to cart away boxes of clicked materials. The arrival of the pickup man, a Negro, was always a noisy one, like the arrival of a daily passenger train in an isolated small town. Interaction attained a quick peak of intensity to crowd into a few minutes all communications, necessary and otherwise. Exchanges invariably included loud depreciations by the pickup man of the amount of work accomplished in the clicking department during the preceding twenty-four hours. Such scoffing would be on the order of "Is that all you've got done? What do you boys do all day?" These devaluations would be countered with allusions to the "soft job" enjoyed by the pickup man. During the course of the exchanges news items would be dropped, some of serious import, such as reports of accomplished or impending layoffs in the various plants of the company, or of gains or losses in orders for company products. Most of the news items, however, involved bits of information on plant employees told in a light vein. Information relayed by the clicker operators was usually told about each other, mainly in the form of summaries of the most recent kidding sequences. Some of this material was repetitive, carried over from day to day. Sammy would be the butt of most of this newscasting, although he would make occasional counter-reports on Ike and George. An invariable part of the interactional content of pickup time was Ike's introduction of the pickup man to George. "Meet Mr. Papeatis!" Ike would say in mock solemnity and dignity. Each day the pickup man "met" Mr. Papeatis, to the obvious irritation of the latter. Another pickup time invariably would bring Baby (or Mable) into the interaction. George would always issue the loud warning to the pickup man: "Now I want you to stay away from Baby! She's Henry's girl!" Henry was a burly Negro with a booming bass voice who made infrequent trips to the clicking room with lift-truck loads of materials. He was reputedly quite a ladies' man among the colored population of the factory. George's warning to "Stay away from Baby!" was issued to every Negro who entered the shop. Baby's only part in this was to laugh at the horseplay.

About mid-afternoon came fish time. George and Ike would stop work for a few minutes to consume some sort of pickled fish which Ike provided. Neither Sammy nor I partook of this nourishment, nor were we invited. For this omission I was grateful; the fish, brought in a newspaper and with head and tail intact, produced a reverse effect on my appetite. George and Ike seemed to share a great liking for fish. Each Friday night, as a regular ritual, they would enjoy a fish dinner together at a nearby restaurant. On these nights Ike would work until 8:30 and leave the plant with George.

Coke time came late in the afternoon, and was an occasion for total participation. The four of us took turns in buying drinks and in making the trip for them to a fourth floor vending machine. Through George's manipulation of the situation, it eventually became my daily chore to go after the cokes; the straw boss had noted that I made a much faster trip to the fourth floor and back than Sammy or Ike.

Sammy left the plant at 5:30, and Ike ordinarily retired from the scene an hour and a half later. These quitting times were not marked by any distinctive interaction save the one regular exchange between Sammy and George over the former's "early washup." Sammy's tendency was to crowd his washing up toward five o'clock, and it was George's concern to keep it from further creeping advance. After Ike's departure came Boo's arrival. Boo's was a striking personality productive of a change in topics of conversation to fill in the last hour of the long workday.

Themes

To put flesh, so to speak, on this interactional frame of "times," my work group had developed various "themes" of verbal interplay which had become standardized in their repetition. These topics of conversation ranged in quality from an extreme of nonsensical chatter to another extreme of serious discourse. Unlike the times, these themes flowed one into the other in no particular sequence of predictability. Serious conversation could suddenly melt into horseplay, and vice versa. In the middle of a serious discussion on the high cost of living, Ike might drop a weight behind the easily startled Sammy, or hit him over the head with a dusty paper sack. Interaction would immediately drop to a low comedy exchange of slaps, threats, guffaws, and disapprobations which would invariably include a ten-minute echolalia of "Ike is a bad man, a very bad man! George is a good daddy, a very fine man!" Or, on the other hand, a stream of such invidious comparisons as followed a surreptitious switching-off of Sammy's machine by the playful Ike might merge suddenly into a discussion of the pros and cons of saving for one's funeral.

"Kidding themes" were usually started by George or Ike, and Sammy was usually the butt of the joke. Sometimes Ike would have to "take it," seldom George. One favorite kidding theme involved Sammy's alleged receipt of $100 a month from his son. The points stressed were that Sammy did not have to work long hours, or did not have to work at all, because he had a son to support him. George would always point out that he sent money to his daughter; she did not send money to him. Sammy received occasional calls from his wife, and his claim that these calls were requests to shop for groceries on the way home were greeted with feigned disbelief. Sammy was ribbed for being closely watched, bossed, and henpecked by his wife, and the expression "Are you man or mouse?" became an echolalic utterance, used both in and out of the original context.

Ike, who shared his machine and the work schedule for it with Boo, the night operator, came in for constant invidious comparison on the subject of output. The socially isolated Boo, who chose work rather than sleep on his lonely night shift, kept up a high level of performance, and George never tired of pointing this out to Ike. It so happened that Boo, an Arabian Moslem from Palestine, had no use for Jews in general; and Ike, who was Jewish, had no use for Boo in particular. Whenever George would extol Boo's previous

night's production, Ike would try to turn the conversation into a general discussion on the need for educating the Arabs. George, never permitting the development of serious discussion on this topic, would repeat a smirking warning, "You watch out for Boo! He's got a long knife!"

The "poom poom" theme was one that caused no sting. It would come up several times a day to be enjoyed as unbarbed fun by the three older clicker operators. Ike was usually the one to raise the question, "How many times you go poom poom last night?" The person questioned usually replied with claims of being "too old for poom poom." If this theme did develop a goat, it was I. When it was pointed out that I was a younger man, this provided further grist for the poom poom mill. I soon grew weary of this poom poom business, so dear to the hearts of the three old satyrs, and knowing where the conversation would inevitably lead, winced whenever Ike brought up the subject.

I grew almost as sick of a kidding theme which developed from some personal information contributed during a serious conversation on property ownership and high taxes. I dropped a few remarks about two acres of land which I owned in one of the western states, and from then on I had to listen to questions, advice, and general nonsensical comment in regard to "Danelly's farm."[10] This "farm" soon became stocked with horses, cows, pigs, chickens, ducks, and the various and sundry domesticated beasts so tunefully listed in "Old McDonald Had a Farm." George was a persistent offender with this theme. Where the others seemed to be mainly interested in statistics on livestock, crops, etc., George's teasing centered on a generous offering to help with the household chores while I worked in the fields. He would drone on, *ad nauseam,* "when I come to visit you, you will never have to worry about the housework,

---

[10] This spelling is the closest I can come to the appellation given me in George's broken English and adopted by other members of the group.

Danelly. I'll stay around the house when you go out to dig the potatoes and milk the cows, I'll stay in and peel potatoes and help your wife do the dishes." Danelly always found it difficult to change the subject on George, once the latter started to bear down on the farm theme.

Another kidding theme which developed out of serious discussion could be labelled "helping Danelly find a cheaper apartment." It became known to the group that Danelly had a pending housing problem, that he would need new quarters for his family when the permanent resident of his temporary summer dwelling returned from a vacation. This information engendered at first a great deal of sympathetic concern and, of course, advice on apartment hunting. Development into a kidding theme was immediately related to previous exchanges between Ike and George on the quality of their respective dwelling areas. Ike lived in "Lawndale," and George dwelt in the "Woodlawn" area. The new pattern featured the reading aloud of bogus "apartment for rent" ads in newspapers which were brought into the shop. Studying his paper at lunchtime, George would call out, "Here's an apartment for you, Danelly! Five rooms, stove heat, $20 a month, Lawndale Avenue!" Later, Ike would read from his paper, "Here's one! Six rooms, stove heat, dirt floor. $18.50 a month! At 55th and Woodlawn." Bantering would then go on in regard to the quality of housing or population in the two areas. The search for an apartment for Danelly was not successful.

Serious themes included the relating of major misfortunes suffered in the past by group members. George referred again and again to the loss, by fire, of his business establishment. Ike's chief complaints centered around a chronically ill wife who had undergone various operations and periods of hospital care. Ike spoke with discouragement of the expenses attendant upon hiring a housekeeper for himself and his children; he referred with disappointment and disgust to a teen-age son, an inept lad who "couldn't even fix his own lunch. He couldn't even make himself a sandwich!"

Sammy's reminiscences centered on the loss of a flourishing business when he had to flee Europe ahead of Nazi invasion.

But all serious topics were not tales of woe. One favorite serious theme which was optimistic in tone could be called either "Danelly's future" or "getting Danelly a better job." It was known that I had been attending "college," the magic door to opportunity, although my specific course of study remained somewhat obscure. Suggestions poured forth on good lines of work to get into, and these suggestions were backed with accounts of friends, and friends of friends, who had made good via the academic route. My answer to the expected question, "Why are you working here?" always stressed the "lots of overtime" feature, and this explanation seemed to suffice for short-range goals.

There was one theme of especially solemn import, the "professor theme." This theme might also be termed "George's daughter's marriage theme"; for the recent marriage of George's only child was inextricably bound up with George's connection with higher learning. The daughter had married the son of a professor who instructed in one of the local colleges. This professor theme was not in the strictest sense a conversation piece; when the subject came up, George did all the talking. The two Jewish operatives remained silent as they listened with deep respect, if not actual awe, to George's accounts of the Big Wedding which, including the wedding pictures, entailed an expense of $1,000. It was monologue, but there was listening, there was communication, the sacred communication of a temple, when George told of going for Sunday afternoon walks on the Midway with the professor, or of joining the professor for a Sunday dinner. Whenever he spoke of the professor, his daughter, the wedding, or even of the new son-in-law, who remained for the most part in the background, a sort of incidental like the wedding cake, George was complete master of the interaction. His manner, in speaking to the rank-and-file of clicker operators, was indeed that of master deigning to notice his underlings. I came to the conclusion that it was the professor connection, not the straw-boss-ship or the extra nickel an hour, which provided the fount of George's superior status in the group.

If the professor theme may be regarded as the cream of verbal interaction, the "chatter themes" should be classed as the dregs. The chatter themes were hardly themes at all; perhaps they should be labelled "verbal states," or "oral autisms." Some were of doubtful status as communication; they were like the howl or cry of an animal responding to its own physiological state. They were exclamations, ejaculations, snatches of song or doggerel, talkings-to-oneself, mutterings. Their classification as themes would rest on their repetitive character. They were echolalic utterances, repeated over and over. An already mentioned example would be Sammy's repetition of "George is a good daddy, a very fine man! Ike is a bad man, a very bad man!" Also, Sammy's repetition of "Don't bother me! Can't you see I'm busy? I'm a very busy man!" for ten minutes after Ike had dropped a weight behind him would fit the classification. Ike would shout "Mamariba!" at intervals between repetition of bits of verse, such as:

Mama on the bed,

Papa on the floor,

Baby in the crib

Says giver some more!

Sometimes the three operators would pick up one of these simple chatterings in a sort of chorus. "Are you man or mouse? I ask you, are you man or mouse?" was a favorite of this type.

So initial discouragement with the meagerness of social interaction I now recognized as due to lack of observation. The interaction was there, in constant flow. It captured attention and held interest to make the long day pass. The twelve hours of "click, —— move die, —— click, —— move die" became as easy to endure as eight hours of varied activity in the oil fields or eight hours of playing the piecework game in a machine shop.

The "beast of boredom" was gentled to the harmlessness of a kitten.

BLACK FRIDAY: DISINTEGRATION OF THE GROUP

But all this was before "Black Friday." Events of that dark day shattered the edifice of interaction, its framework of times and mosaic of themes, and reduced the work situation to a state of social atomization and machine-tending drudgery. The explosive element was introduced deliberately, but without prevision of its consequences.

On Black Friday, Sammy was not present; he was on vacation. There was no peach time that morning, of course, and no banana time. But George and Ike held their coffee time, as usual, and a steady flow of themes was filling the morning quite adequately. It seemed like a normal day in the making, at least one which was going to meet the somewhat reduced expectations created by Sammy's absence.

Suddenly I was possessed of an inspiration for modification of the professor theme. When the idea struck, I was working at Sammy's machine, clicking out leather parts for billfolds. It was not difficult to get the attention of close neighbor Ike to suggest *sotto voce,* "Why don't you tell him you saw the professor teaching in a barber college on Madison Street? . . . Make it near Halsted Street."

Ike thought this one over for a few minutes, and caught the vision of its possibilities. After an interval of steady application to his clicking, he informed the unsuspecting George of his near West Side discovery; he had seen the professor busy at his instructing in a barber college in the lower reaches of Hobohemia.

George reacted to this announcement with stony silence. The burden of questioning Ike for further details on his discovery fell upon me. Ike had not elaborated his story very much before we realized that the show was not going over. George kept getting redder in the face, and more tight-lipped; he slammed into his clicking with increased vigor. I made one last weak attempt to keep the play on the road by remarking that barber colleges paid pretty well. George turned to hiss at me, "You'll have to go to Kankakee with Ike!" I dropped the subject. Ike whispered to me, "George is sore!"

George was indeed sore. He didn't say another word the rest of the morning. There was no conversation at lunchtime, nor was there any after lunch. A pall of silence had fallen over the clicker room. Fish time fell a casualty. George did not touch the coke I brought for him. A very long, very dreary afternoon dragged on. Finally, after Ike left for home, George broke the silence to reveal his feelings to me:

> Ike acts like a five-year-old, not a man! He doesn't even have the respect of the niggers. But he's got to act like a man around here! He's always fooling around! I'm going to stop that! I'm going to show him his place!
>
> . . . Jews will ruin you, if you let them. I don't care if he sings, but the first time he mentions my name, I'm going to shut him up! It's always "Meet Mr. Papeatis! George is a good daddy!" And all that. He's paid to work! If he doesn't work, I'm going to tell Joe! [The superintendent.]

Then came a succession of dismal workdays devoid of times and barren of themes. Ike did not sing, nor did he recite bawdy verse. The shop songbird was caught in the grip of icy winter. What meager communication there was took a sequence of patterns which proved interesting only in retrospect.

For three days, George would not speak to Ike. Ike made several weak attempts to break the wall of silence which George had put between them, but George did not respond; it was as if he did not hear. George would speak to me, on infrequent occasions, and so would Ike. They did not speak to each other.

On the third day George advised me of his new communication policy, designed for dealing with Ike, and for Sammy, too, when the latter returned to work. Interaction was now on a "strictly business" basis, with emphasis to be placed on raising the level of shop output. The effect of this new

policy on production remained indeterminate. Before the fourth day had ended, George got carried away by his narrowed interests to the point of making sarcastic remarks about the poor work performances of the absent Sammy. Although addressed to me, these caustic depreciations were obviously for the benefit of Ike. Later in the day Ike spoke to me, for George's benefit, of Sammy's outstanding ability to turn out billfold parts. For the next four days, the prevailing silence of the shop was occasionally broken by either harsh criticism or fulsome praise of Sammy's outstanding workmanship. I did not risk replying to either impeachment or panegyric for fear of involvement in further situational deteriorations.

Twelve-hour days were creeping again at snail's pace. The strictly business communications were of no help, and the sporadic bursts of distaste or enthusiasm for Sammy's clicking ability helped very little. With the return of boredom, came a return of fatigue. My legs tired as the afternoons dragged on, and I became engaged in conscious efforts to rest one by shifting my weight to the other. I would pause in my work to stare through the barred windows at the grimy brick wall across the alley; and, turning my head, I would notice that Ike was staring at the wall too. George would do very little work after Ike left the shop at night. He would sit in a chair and complain of weariness and sore feet.

In desperation, I fell back on my game of work, my blues and greens and whites, my ovals and trapezoids, and my scraping the block. I came to surpass Boo, the energetic night worker, in volume of output. George referred to me as a "day Boo" (day-shift Boo) and suggested that I "keep" Sammy's machine. I managed to avoid this promotion, and consequent estrangement with Sammy, by pleading attachment to my own machine.

When Sammy returned to work, discovery of the cleavage between George and Ike left him stunned. "They were the best of friends!" he said to me in bewilderment.

George now offered Sammy direct, savage crit

icisms of his work. For several days the good-na-tured Sammy endured these verbal aggressions without losing his temper; but when George shouted at him "You work like a preacher!" Sammy became very angry, indeed. I had a few anxious moments when I thought that the two old friends were going to come to blows.

Then, thirteen days after Black Friday, came an abrupt change in the pattern of interaction. George and Ike spoke to each other again, in friendly conversation:

> I noticed Ike talking to George after lunch. The two had newspapers of fish at George's cabinet. Ike was excited; he said, "I'll pull up a chair!" The two ate for ten minutes. . . . It seems that they went up to the 22nd Street Exchange together during lunch pe-riod to cash pay checks.

That afternoon Ike and Sammy started to play again, and Ike burst once more into song. Old themes reappeared as suddenly as the desert flow-ers in spring. At first, George managed to main-tain some show of the dignity of superordination. When Ike started to sing snatches of "You Are My Sunshine," George suggested that he get "more production." Then Ike backed up George in pressuring Sammy for more production. Sammy turned this exhortation into low comedy by calling Ike a "slave driver" and by shouting over and over again, "Don't bother me! I'm a busy man!" On one occasion, as if almost overcome with joy and excitement, Sammy cried out, "Don't bother me! I'll tell Rothman! [the com-pany president] I'll tell the union! Don't mention my name! I hate you!"

I knew that George was definitely back into the spirit of the thing when he called to Sammy, "Are you man or mouse?" He kept up the "man or mouse" chatter for some time.

George was for a time reluctant to accept fruit

when it was offered to him, and he did not make a final capitulation to coke time until five days after renewal of the fun and fooling. Strictly speaking, there never was a return to banana time, peach time, or window time. However, the sharing and snitching of fruit did go on once more, and the window in front of Sammy's machine played a more prominent part than ever in the renaissance of horseplay in the clicker room. In fact, the "rush to the window" became an integral part of in-creasingly complex themes and repeated se-quences of interaction. This window rushing became especially bound up with new develop-ments which featured what may be termed the "anal gesture."[11] Introduced by Ike, and given backing by an enthusiastic, very playful George, the anal gesture became a key component of fun and fooling during the remaining weeks of my stay in the shop:

> Ike broke wind, and put his head in his hand on the block as Sammy grabbed a rod and made a mock rush to open the window. He beat Ike on the head, and George threw some water on him, playfully. In came the Negro head of the Leather Department; he remarked jokingly that we should take out the ma-chines and make a playroom out of the shop.

Of course, George's demand for greater pro-duction was metamorphized into horseplay. His shout of "Production please!" became a chatter theme to accompany the varied antics of Ike and Sammy.

The professor theme was dropped completely. George never again mentioned his Sunday walks on the Midway with the professor.

CONCLUSIONS

Speculative assessment of the possible signifi-cance of my observations on information interac-

---

[11] I have been puzzled to note widespread appreciation of this gesture in the "consumatory" communication of the work-ing men of this nation. For the present I leave it to clinical psychologists to account for the nature and pervasiveness of this social bond and confine myself to joining offended readers in the hope that someday our industrial workers will achieve such a level of refinement in thought and action that their be-havior will be no more distressing to us than that of the college students who fill out our questionnaires or form groups for lab-oratory experimentation.

tion in the clicking room may be set forth in a series of general statements.

Practical Application

First, in regard to possible practical application to problems of industrial management, these observations seem to support the generally accepted notion that one key source of job satisfaction lies in the informal interaction shared by members of a work group. In the clicking-room situation the spontaneous development of a patterned combination of horseplay, serious conversation, and frequent sharing of food and drink reduced the monotony of simple, repetitive operations to the point where a regular schedule of long work days became livable. This kind of group interplay may be termed "consumatory" in the sense indicated by Dewey, when he makes a basic distinction between "instrumental" and "consumatory" communication.[12] The enjoyment of communication "for its own sake" as "mere sociabilities," as "free, aimless social intercourse," brings job satisfaction, at least job endurance, to work situations largely bereft of creative experience.

In regard to another managerial concern, employee productivity, any appraisal of the influence of group interaction upon clicking-room output could be no more than roughly impressionistic. I obtained no evidence to warrant a claim that banana time, or any of its accompaniments in consumatory interaction, boosted production. To the contrary, my diary recordings express an occasional perplexity in the form of "How does this company manage to stay in business?" However, I did not obtain sufficient evidence to indicate that, under the prevailing conditions of laissez-faire management, the output of our group would have been more impressive if the playful cavorting of three middle-aged gentlemen about the barred windows had never been. As far as achievement of managerial goals is concerned, the most that could

[12] John Dewey, *Experience and Nature,* Open Court Publishing Co., Chicago, 1925, pp. 202-206.

be suggested is that leavening the deadly boredom of individualized work routines with a concurrent flow of group festivities had a negative effect on turnover. I left the group, with sad reluctance, under the pressure of strong urgings to accept a research fellowship which would involve no factory toil. My fellow clickers stayed with their machines to carry on their labors in the spirit of banana time.

Theoretical Considerations

Secondly, possible contribution to ongoing sociological inquiry into the behavior of small groups, in general, and factory work groups, in particular, may lie in one or more of the following ideational products of my clicking-room experience:

1 In their day-long confinement together in a small room spatially and socially isolated from other work areas of the factory the Clicking Department employees found themselves ecologically situated for development of a "natural" group. Such a development did take place; from worker inter-communications did emerge the full-blown sociocultural system of consumatory interactions which I came to share, observe, and record in the process of my socialization.

2 These interactions had a content which could be abstracted from the total existential flow of observable doings and sayings for labelling and objective consideration. That is, they represented a distinctive sub-culture, with its recurring patterns of reciprocal influencings which I have described as times and themes.

3 From these interactions may also be abstracted a social structure of statuses and roles. This structure may be discerned in the carrying out of the various informal activities which provide the content of the sub-culture of the group. The times and themes were performed with a system of roles which formed a sort of pecking hierarchy. Horseplay had its initiators and its victims, its amplifiers and its chorus; kidding had its attackers and attacked, its least attacked and its most attacked, its ready acceptors of attack and its strong resistors to attack. The fun went on with the participation of all, but within the controlling frame of status, a matter of who can say or do what to whom and get away with it.

4 In both the cultural content and the social structure of clicker group interaction could be seen the permeation of influences which flowed from the various multiple group memberships of the participants. Past and present "other-group" experiences or anticipated "outside" social connections provided significant materials for the building of themes and for the establishment and maintenance of status and role relationships. The impact of reference group affiliations on clicking-room interaction was notably revealed in the sacred, status-conferring expression of the professor theme. This impact was brought into very sharp focus in developments which followed my attempt to degrade the topic, and correlatively, to demote George.

5 Stability of the clicking-room social system was never threatened by immediate outside pressures. Ours was not an instrumental group, subject to disintegration in a losing struggle against environmental obstacles or oppositions. It was not striving for corporate goals; nor was it faced with the enmity of other groups. It was strictly a consumatory group, devoted to the maintenance of patterns of self-entertainment. Under existing conditions, disruption of unity could come only from within.

Potentials for breakdown were endemic in the interpersonal interactions involved in conducting the group's activities. Patterns of fun and fooling had developed within a matrix of frustration. Tensions born of long hours of relatively meaningless work were released in the mock aggressions of horseplay. In the recurrent attack, defense, and counterattack there continually lurked the possibility that words or gestures harmless in conscious intent might cross the subtle boundary of accepted, playful aggression to be perceived as real assault. While such an occurrence might incur

displeasure no more lasting than necessary for the quick clarification or creation of kidding norms, it might also spark a charge of hostility sufficient to disorganize the group.

A contributory potential for breakdown from within lay in the dissimilar "other group" experiences of the operators. These other-group affiliations and identifications could provide differences in tastes and sensitivities, including appreciation of humor, differences which could make maintenance of consensus in regard to kidding norms a hazardous process of trial and error adjustments.

6 The risk involved in this trial and error determination of consensus on fun and fooling in a touchy situation of frustration—mock aggression —was made evident when I attempted to introduce alterations in the professor theme. The group disintegrated, *instanter.* That is, there was an abrupt cessation of the interactions which constituted our groupness. Although both George and I were solidly linked in other-group affiliations with the higher learning, there was not enough agreement in our attitudes toward university professors to prevent the interactional development which shattered our factory play group. George perceived my offered alterations as a real attack, and he responded with strong hostility directed against Ike, the perceived assailant, and Sammy, a fellow traveler.

My innovations, if accepted, would have lowered the tone of the sacred professor theme, if not to "Stay Away From Baby" ribaldry, then at least to the verbal slapstick level of "finding Danelly an apartment." Such a downgrading of George's reference group would, in turn, have downgraded George. His status in the shop group hinged largely upon his claimed relations with the professor.

7 Integration of our group was fully restored after a series of changes in the patterning and quality of clicking-room interaction. It might be said that reintegration took place *in* these changes, that the series was a progressive one of step-by-step improvement in relations, that reequilibration was in process during the three weeks that passed between initial communication collapse and complete return to "normal" interaction.

The cycle of loss and recovery of equilibrium may be crudely charted according to the following sequence of phases: a) the stony silence of "not speaking"; b) the confining of communication to formal matters connected with work routines; c) the return of informal give-and-take in the form of harshly sarcastic kidding, mainly on the subject of work performance, addressed to a neutral go-between for the "benefit" of the object of aggression; d) highly emotional direct attack, and counter-attack, in the form of criticism and defense of work performance; e) a sudden rapprochement expressed in serious, dignified, but friendly conversation; f) return to informal interaction in the form of mutually enjoyed mock aggression; g) return to informal interaction in the form of regular patterns of sharing food and drink.

The group had disintegrated when George withdrew from participation; and, since the rest of us were at all times ready for rapprochement, reintegration was dependent upon his "return." Therefore, each change of phase in interaction on the road to recovery could be said to represent an increment of return on George's part. Or, conversely, each phase could represent an increment of reacceptance of punished deviants. Perhaps more generally applicable to description of a variety of reunion situations would be conceptualization of the phase changes as increments of reassociation without an atomistic differentiation of the "movements" of individuals.

8 To point out that George played a key role in this particular case of re-equilibration is not to suggest that the homeostatic controls of a social system may be located in a type of role or in a patterning of role relationships. Such controls could be but partially described in terms of human interaction; they would be functional to the total configuration of conditions within the field of influence. The automatic controls of a mechanical system operate as such only under certain achieved and controlled conditions. The human body recovers from disease when conditions for such homeostasis are "right." The clicking-room group regained equilibrium under certain undetermined conditions. One of a number of other possible outcomes could have developed had conditions not been favorable for recovery.

For purposes of illustration, and from reflection on the case, I would consider the following as possibly necessary conditions for reintegration of our group: a) Continued monotony of work operations; b) Continued lack of a comparatively adequate substitute for the fun and fooling release from work tensions; c) Inability of the operatives to escape from the work situation or from each other, within the work situation. George could not fire Ike or Sammy to remove them from his presence, and it would have been difficult for the three middle-aged men to find other jobs if they were to quit the shop. Shop space was small, and the machines close together. Like a submarine crew, they had to "live together"; d) Lack of conflicting definitions of the situation after Ike's perception of George's reaction to the "barber college" attack. George's anger and his punishment of the offenders was perceived as justified; e) Lack of introduction of new issues or causes which might have carried justification for new attacks and counter-attacks, thus leading interaction into a spiral of conflict and crystallization of conflict norms. For instance, had George reported his offenders to the superintendent for their poor work performance; had he, in his anger, committed some offense which would have led to reporting of a grievance to local union officials; had he made his anti-Semitic remarks in the presence of Ike or Sammy, or had I relayed these remarks to them; had I tried to "take over" Sammy's machine, as George had urged; then the interactional outcome might have been permanent disintegration of the group.

9 Whether or not the particular patterning of interactional change previously noted is somehow typical of a "re-equilibration process" is not a ma-

jor question here. My purpose in discriminating the seven changes is primarily to suggest that re-equilibration, when it does occur, may be described in observable phases and that the emergence of each succeeding phase should be dependent upon the configuration of conditions of the preceding one. Alternative eventual outcomes may change in their probabilities, as the phases succeed each other, just as prognosis for recovery in sickness may change as the disease situation changes.

10 Finally, discrimination of phase changes in social process may have practical as well as scientific value. Trained and skillful administrators might follow the practice in medicine of introducing aids to re-equilibration when diagnosis shows that they are needed.

TAKING ANOTHER LOOK

1 What social roles did George, Ike, and Sammy play within the work group?

2 How did Roy search for meaning within his repetitive work tasks?

3 In Roy's view, what was the importance of "peach time," "banana time," and other special "times" observed during the workday of the clicker operators?

4 Select one of the "themes" of verbal interplay discussed by Roy and analyze its importance for the group.

5 What happened on "Black Friday"? How was this crisis eventually resolved?

6 Based on Roy's findings, what is the relationship between informal interactions among members of a work group and the group's output?

7 Which problems of participant observation as a research method are evident in this study?

Theories of Schooling and Society: The Functional and Radical Paradigms

Christopher J. Hurn

As in the study of other social institutions, the functionalist and conflict perspectives of sociology diverge sharply in their view of education. Functionalists emphasize that schooling performs many functions that are essential in maintaining the stability of society. Among these are the transmission of knowledge, the transmission of culture, the bestowal of status, the maintenance of social control, and the promotion of social and political integration.

By contrast, conflict theorists are much more critical of education. They argue that the educational system socializes students into values dictated by the powerful, that schools stifle individualism and creativity in the name of maintaining order, and that the level of social change promoted by education is relatively insignificant. From a conflict perspective, the inhibiting effects of education are apparent in the creation of standards for entry into occupations, the differential way in which status is bestowed, and the existence of a dual system of private and public schools.

In the following selection, sociologist Christopher J. Hurn compares two theories of schooling: the *functional paradigm* (which offers both an explanation and a justification for the role of schools in society) and the *radical paradigm* (which is closely related to the conflict perspective's view of education). Hurn attempts to define these paradigms and weigh their merits and weaknesses. In his analysis of the functional paradigm, he emphasizes that it portrays the major features of contemporary society in "fundamentally benign terms." In his analysis of the radical paradigm, Hurn emphasizes that it "sees schools as serving the interests of elites, as reinforcing existing inequalities. . . ." He devotes particular attention to the theories of education offered by social critic Ivan Illich and by radical social scientists Samuel Bowles and Herbert Gintis.

The word "theory" often triggers some degree of anxiety in the layman. Theory suggests to some people a high degree of abstraction and complexity and an intricate structure of logically related propositions. The theories I shall discuss in this chapter, however, need provoke no great anxiety. These ideas are neither highly complex nor particularly esoteric. Sociological theories of schooling, indeed, are closely related to implicit common sense ideas about education and its function in modern society—a group of more or less coherent ideas, rather than a set of tightly knit theoretical propositions.

Until ten years ago discussion of theories of schooling in modern society would have made little sense. The contest between groups of competing ideas, each claiming to offer an explanation of what schools do and why they do it, is fairly recent. Until a decade or so ago one major interpretation of the role of schooling in modern society prevailed almost unchallenged. This theory, which I shall call the *functional paradigm,* offers both an explanation and a justification for the role of educational institutions. In simplest terms, the functional paradigm argues that schools are essential institutions in modern society because they perform two crucial functions: first, schools represent a rational way of sorting and selecting talented people so that the most able and motivated attain the highest status positions; second, schools teach the kind of cognitive skills and norms essential for the performance of most roles in a society increasingly dependent upon knowledge and expertise. The functional paradigm is largely an elaboration of these two apparently straightforward propositions.

Although these beliefs are still very widely held, still constituting the core of what might be called the liberal orthodoxy in educational thought, they have lost some of the taken-for-granted character that they possessed a decade or so ago. Most obviously, the image of constantly expanding schooling meeting the needs of an increasingly complex and knowledge-dependent society (an image implicit in some of the cruder formulations of the functional paradigm) has been questioned in recent years. Not only has schooling (at least in the United States) ceased to expand, projections for college enrollments suggest there may be fewer students in college in the late 1980s than at present. The titles of two recent books—*The Case Against College* and *The Overeducated American*—suggest a new skepticism about the benefits and necessity of high levels of schooling.[1] They convey a picture of a society with far more schooling than it needs, where investment in higher education no longer yields the benefits previously taken for granted. Such skepticism is not confined to higher education. The many unsuccessful efforts at educational reform in the last fifteen years—attempts to create schools that unleash the natural intelligence or creativity of students and attempts to reduce class and race differences in educational performance —have led more and more educators and social scientists to question the optimistic assumptions about the direction of educational change that lie

at the heart of the functional paradigm.

Most fundamentally, however, this dominant theory of schooling and society has recently been challenged by a new, much less sanguine account. This theory, which I shall call the *radical paradigm,* portrays schools not as more or less rational instruments for sorting and selecting talented people, but as institutions that perpetuate inequality and convince lower class groups of their inferiority. In the radical paradigm what is important about schooling is not the cognitive and intellectual skills schools teach, but the class-related values and attitudes that they reinforce. In this view, schools are instruments of elite domination, agencies that foster compliance and docility rather than independent thought and humane values.[2] The debate between these two paradigms or theories of schooling underlies virtually all the issues I shall discuss in this book: from the study of inequality to the problem of what schools teach; from the expansion of schooling in this century to the issue of how to change and reform schools. In this chapter I define these two paradigms in some detail and begin to examine their merits and limitations.

THE FUNCTIONAL PARADIGM OF SCHOOLING

The functional paradigm of schooling is not the work of any one individual theorist, nor does it consist exclusively of the ideas of sociologists. In its most general form the functional paradigm has long been part of the conventional wisdom of liberal intellectuals in Western society and, to a large extent, part of the working assumptions of the great majority of all who have thought and written about schooling in Western societies until quite recently. Many of its assumptions are found in commencement addresses and political speeches on the benefits of education, as well as in textbooks on the sociology of education.[3]

---

[1] See note 5, Chapter 1.
[2] The clearest statements of this argument are in Samuel Bowles and Herbert Gintis, *Schooling in Capitalist America* (New York: Basic Books, 1976); Martin Carnoy, ed., *School-*

ing in a Corporate Society* (New York: McKay, 1975), pp. 1–37; Maurice Levitas, *Marxist Perspective in the Sociology of Education* (London: Routledge and Kegan Paul, 1974).
[3] For example, Wilbur Brookover, *A Sociology of Educa-*

Modern Society—The Functional View

At the heart of the functional paradigm is an analysis of what adherents to the model see as the unique character of the modern Western world and the crucial role that schooling plays in that world. The paradigm sees modern Western societies differing from most previous societies in at least three crucial respects.

The Meritocratic Society First, in modern societies occupational roles are (and should be) achieved rather than ascribed. Contemporary intellectuals have long regarded the inheritance of occupational roles, and more broadly the inheritance of social status, as anathema. People believe high status positions should be achieved on the basis of merit rather than passed on from parent to child. The children of the poor should have equal opportunity to achieve high status with more privileged children. And in all Western societies, particularly since World War II, governments have responded to this belief by trying to increase equality of opportunity: by expanding higher education, introducing universalistic rules for employment intended to discourage nepotism, and legislating elimination of discrimination on the basis of religion, race, and sex. The functional paradigm, therefore, sees modern society as *meritocratic:* a society where ability and effort count for more than privilege and inherited status. And while there is disagreement about just how far along this road to a perfectly meritocratic social order we have traveled, there is agreement that modern society is at least more meritocratic than most societies of the past.

In part this contention is a moral argument. It is simply wrong, we believe, that doctors or members of elite groups should enjoy overwhelming advantages in passing on inherited status to their children.[4] But besides the moral argument, underlying the meritocratic thesis is a conviction that achievement is a far more rational way of allocating status than ascription. The theory maintains that modern society demands and requires far larger percentages of highly skilled people than ever before. The percentage of professionals in the United States labor force, for example, has multiplied about ten times since 1900. It is essential, therefore, that the most talented individuals be recruited for these demanding occupations. The health and the economic well-being of a society depends on the degree to which it can find and place its most talented individuals in the most demanding occupations. An increasingly meritocratic society is not only morally justified, but it is also a more rational and efficient society.

The Expert Society A second distinctive feature of the contemporary social order is closely related to these ideas about talent, efficiency, and rationality. The functional paradigm sees modern society as an "expert" society: one that depends preeminently on rational knowledge for economic growth, requiring more and more highly trained individuals to fill the majority of occupational positions. Schools perform two crucial functions in this view of society. The research activities of universities and colleges produce the new knowledge that underpins economic growth and social progress. And extensive schooling both equips individuals with specialized skills and provides a general foundation of cognitive knowledge and intellectual sophistication to permit the acquisition of more specialized knowledge. Extensive education, therefore, becomes an increasingly necessary feature of any modern society. Skills that were primarily acquired on the job must now be acquired in specialized educational institutions. If schools cannot always teach the highly specific knowledge and skills required by an increasing number of

---

tion (New York: American Book Company, 1955); Robert Havighurst and Denise Neugarten, *Society and Education* (Boston: Allyn and Bacon, 1975). If these books appear to be a-theoretical, concerned with presenting concepts rather than testing explanations, they still implicitly share most of the functional assumptions.

[4] Michael Young's book, *The Rise of Meritocracy* (Baltimore: Penguin Books, 1967), is one of the few attempts to challenge the idea that a more meritocratic society is necessarily a better society.

jobs, they do provide a foundation of general cognitive skills that alone permits effective learning of more specialized knowledge.[5] And since occupational skills change or rapidly become obsolete in contemporary society, individuals need an extensive general education as a foundation to learn new skills. They may also require later retooling educational programs long after adolescence. Some progressive accounts of this argument, indeed, see schooling as "lifelong learning" and the whole society as a "learning society." The crucial function of schools is not so much to teach specific useful vocational skills, but to teach people how to learn.[6]

The Democratic Society Finally, the functional paradigm portrays contemporary society as a democratic society moving gradually toward the achievement of humane goals: toward social justice, a more fulfilling life for all citizens, and the acceptance of diversity. Implicit in the functional paradigm, therefore, is a particular kind of political liberalism; a view that does not deny the evils and inequities of the present society, but does believe that progress has been made and will continue to be made. Increasing levels of education are at the core of this conception of progress. An educated citizenry is an informed citizenry, less likely to be manipulated by demagogues, more likely to make responsible and informed political decisions and to be actively involved in the political process. Education reduces intolerance and prejudice, and increases support for civil liberties; it is, in other words, an essential bulwark of a democratic society dedicated to freedom and justice. And a more educated society, finally, will be a better society in another sense: a society dedicated not only to economic growth and material wealth, but also to the pursuit of social justice.

The educated society is concerned with the quality of life and the conditions that make individual fulfillment possible.

Schooling and Society

In this general form, then, the functional paradigm is an account of what are the most distinctive and important features of modern society and a set of assertions about the role schooling plays in sustaining and supporting these features. At the same time it is the theory of what schools do, how schools are changing and will change in the future, and a justification for high levels of society commitment to schooling.[7] This model views the close relationship between schooling and future status in contemporary society as an essentially rational process of adaptation: a process where the needs of the increasingly complex society for talented and expert personnel are met by outputs from the educational system in the form of cognitive skills and the selection of talented individuals.[8] And if only the most uncritical supporters of the paradigm would assert that such a process of social selection in schools is perfectly meritocratic or that disadvantaged groups have identical opportunities to those afforded to more privileged students, there is some general confidence that the direction of educational change has been in a meritocratic direction. From this perspective the net effect of the expansion of schooling has been to increase the percentage of poor but talented students who reach high status positions, with the assumption that further expansion of schooling will move us closer toward a society of equal opportunity. What schools teach is also, although imperfectly, a functional adaptation to the needs of the social order. As the nature of the modern economy increasingly demands (even in middle or

---

[5] Burton Clark's *Educating the Expert Society* (San Francisco: Chandler, 1962) states these arguments very clearly.

[6] For the learning society argument, see Alvin Toffler, *Future Shock* (New York: Bantam Books, 1971), chapter 18.

[7] See the justifications for educational expansion given in Clark Kerr, et al., *Industrialism and Industrial Man* (New

York: Oxford, 1964).

[8] The "schooling is rational as well as moral" argument is best represented in the reports of the Carnegie Commission on Higher Education, Clark Kerr, ed., *A Digest of Reports of the Carnegie Commission on Higher Education* (New York: McGraw-Hill, 1974).

lower status occupations) more sophisticated cognitive skills and flexibility and adaptability in the work force, so pedagogical techniques and curricula shift away from rote memorization and moral indoctrination to concern with cognitive development and intellectual flexibility. In this respect the functional paradigm is not necessarily traditional and politically conservative, as critics sometimes allege. ... People often use functional paradigm arguments to attack traditional schools and to call for a new more rational school system to better meet the needs of the contemporary world.

But if the functional paradigm is not necessarily politically conservative, it certainly does portray the major features of contemporary society in fundamentally benign terms.[9] Inequality, for example, is often seen as a necessary device for motivating talented individuals to achieve high status positions. And while it is recognized by most observers that the correlation between ability and high status is far from perfect, they see the problem of inequality in contemporary society as one of raising barriers to the mobility of talent rather than as a problem of redistributing wealth from high status positions to low status positions.[10] That talent in turn tends to be conceived as one dimensional, underlying both success in school and success in life. And if many liberals within this tradition argue that there are "vast reserves of untapped talent" among disadvantaged groups, others more pessimistically conclude that such talent is inherently scarce. ...

THE RADICAL PARADIGM

I have shown that the model of schooling and society that dominated much thought about education until quite recently is beset with serious difficulties. Schools do undoubtedly teach cognitive skills and increase the intellectual sophistica-

tion of their students, but it is not clear that it is these skills that explain the relationship between schooling, occupational status, and earnings. The available evidence does not suggest that United States society is substantially more meritocratic than in the past. Nor is there much evidence to indicate that increased resources devoted to schooling have resulted in more favorable opportunities for the talented children of disadvantaged parents to obtain high status positions. Simply put, the expansion of schooling does not seem to have worked in the way the functional paradigm suggests that it should work.

The radical paradigm offers a very different interpretation of schooling in its relationship to society. Like the functional paradigm, the radical paradigm sees schools and society as closely linked—and I, shall argue, too closely linked—but it stresses the links between schools and the demands of elites rather than the needs of the whole society. It also stresses the connection between schooling and the learning of docility and compliance rather than the acquisition of cognitive skills. If the functional paradigm sees schools as more or less efficient mechanisms for sorting and selecting talented people and for producing cognitive skills, the radical paradigm sees schools as serving the interests of elites, as reinforcing existing inequalities, and as producing attitudes that foster acceptance of this status quo.

The Intellectual Background

The functional paradigm took shape at a time when the climate of intellectual opinion was predominantly optimistic about the main features of contemporary society and its likely future evolution. Modern society was viewed as increasingly rational and meritocratic, a society where prejudice, racism, intolerance, and the ignorance that fostered these evils would gradually disap-

---

[9] Much of what I have called the *functional paradigm* is described as the *progressive paradigm* by Phillip Wexler in *The Sociology of Education: Beyond Equality* (Indianapolis: Bobbs Merrill, 1976).

[10] See Wexler, *Sociology of Education,* for an excellent discussion of how the central problem of early research in the sociology of education was conceived as one of erasing barriers to the mobility of talent.

pear. Schools taught, sustained, and nurtured essentially modern cosmopolitan values and attitudes. Schools, at least the best schools, worked to emancipate children from parochialism, from an unreflecting respect for the traditions of the past, and from ignorance and prejudice. The new mathematics of the late 1960s, with its stress on understanding the principles of logic rather than the mere acquisition of immediately useful skills, and the new English curriculum, with its use of modern novels that invited frank discussion of contemporary moral issues, both symbolized a commitment to modern, liberal, and cosmopolitan ideals. The best schools, at least, taught rationality; they developed the ability to handle moral complexity and to tolerate ambiguity. If the prisons of ignorance, prejudice, and unthinking respect for the past prevented many parents from entering this new world, schools were agencies of emancipation for the next generation. In the modern world, schools do not merely reproduce the values, attitudes, and skills of the past, they are "active agents" in creating a more liberal, a more rational, and a more humane society.[11]

The attack on these ideas in the later 1960s and 1970s reflected a broader critique of their view of society, a disenchantment with the liberal vision of the modern world, and a rejection of the optimism of that world view. The ten years from 1965 to 1975 were a time of increasing skepticism about the benefits of science and technology and an increasing cynicism about the good intentions and moral purposes of established authority. The liberal model of modern society—a world admittedly full of serious imperfection, but nevertheless moving in a fundamentally progressive direction—was replaced, for more and more intellectuals, by a model of society requiring urgent and wholesale surgery to avoid disaster. The new, more skeptical vision saw greedy business corporations intent on destroying the environment, cynical and corrupt politicians concerned with their own power and privilege, and entrenched racism and sexism in virtually every social institution. Instead of a model of society where authority was based on expertise and competence, this radical vision defined a society where powerful elites manipulate public opinion to preserve their own entrenched position. Such elites might make symbolic or token concessions to pressures for reform, but such evils as racism, poverty, and sexism could only be eliminated by changing the distribution of power in the society.

The rejection of the liberal model of society implied a more skeptical interpretation of what schools teach and the role that schooling plays in modern society. Instead of teaching the values and attitudes essential to the functioning of a modern liberal democratic policy, schools were seen as institutions that teach middle class morality—unthinking patriotism, good work habits, good manners. Rather than teaching students to think for themselves, schools teach conformity to business values. Instead of teaching the cognitive skills needed by the complex nature of modern occupations, schools teach a narrow technocratic vision of the world.[12] Successful students are not more creative or more intelligent than others; they are successful because they have learned to play by the official rules of the game. They have learned to work the system to their own advantage, to conform to the officially established definitions of knowledge and truth.

None of these ideas, perhaps, is distinctively radical. The observation that institutions subvert the aims that they profess is not necessarily radical nor even particularly novel. Nor can all those who complain that schools teach passivity and compliance be regarded as radical theorists. The boundaries between the functional and the radical paradigm, therefore, are not always clear-cut. Per-

---

[11] The phrase "active agent" comes from Burton Clark, *Educating the Expert Society.*

[12] For clear statements of this ideology see Ivan Illich, *Deschooling Society* (New York: Harper, 1971); Charles Reich, *The Greening of America* (New York: Random House, 1970).

haps most distinctive, however, is the radical paradigm's attribution of the source of schools' failings. The radical paradigm assumes that the failure of schools is inevitable because of the organization of contemporary capitalist society. Schools are not imperfect institutions in the process of gradual transformation toward new and more humane ends. The defects of schooling, rather, are a reflection of a social order demanding repression and requiring the perpetuation of inequality. Instead of conceiving of the traditional school as obsolete, soon to be replaced by a school better adapted to the needs of the present social order, the radical paradigm sees the repressive character of schooling as intimately associated with the repressive character of the society as a whole.

Within these general guiding assumptions are important disagreements among radical theorists. On the one hand some writers (many of the popular school critics fall into this category) imply that a fundamental reconstruction of schooling is conceivable within existing capitalist society. School reform can, in this view, serve as a catalyst of broader social change because a reconstructed school system will produce individuals intolerant of exploitation, repression, and racism.[13] Many of the progressives in the early decades of this country made such an argument, though in less strident form.

A second, and often specifically Marxist argument, asserts that revolutionary social change must precede the reconstruction of educational institutions.[14] From this perspective any attempt to create a more "humane" and liberated school will inevitably be extinguished or emasculated by the vested interests that elites have in preventing such outcomes. These elites may tolerate or even encounter such innovations as new or more "rational" curricula, open classrooms, or nondirective teaching styles, but more fundamental changes in

the social organization of schools that affect the whole population rather than only a privileged minority are not possible in contemporary capitalist society. The theories of Ivan Illich and the theories of Samuel Bowles and Herbert Gintis are perhaps the two most important exemplars of the radical paradigm. They illustrate different approaches toward the problem of repressive schooling in a repressive society.

Ivan Illich's Theory of Schooling

The publication of Ivan Illich's *Deschooling Society* in the *New York Review of Books* in 1969 was a watershed in thought about schooling in Western society.[15] Before Illich, of course, radical criticism of schools had become fashionable among many intellectuals. Throughout the late 1960s books calling for the reform of United States schools by John Holt, James Herndon, Herbert Kohl, and others were enthusiastically received. Illich's work, however, is distinctive in calling for the abolition of schooling rather than reform. Illich argues that societies should not require compulsory schooling in any form and maintains that legislation should forbid employers from hiring individuals on the basis of the amount of their schooling. Illich calls not for new and better schooling but for deschooling society, for a revolution that would break the link between schooling and future employment.

Central to Illich's thesis is a powerful (though I believe ultimately misleading) metaphor between schooling and the Catholic church and between education and religion. For Illich contemporary faith in schooling is closely equivalent to the medieval faith in salvation through the Catholic church. Schooling, perhaps, is the one almost unchallengeable universal good in modern society. For the individual it is the road to personal fulfillment as well as to material afflu-

---

[13] See, for example, Neil Postman and Charles Weingartner, *Teaching as a Subversive Activity* (New York: Dell, 1969), chapter 1.

[14] This is essentially Bowles and Gintis's argument.
[15] Later published by Harper and Row in 1971.

ence; for society more and better schooling is the key to a better, more humane and just social order. And as Illich points out, schooling is almost universally seen in poor countries as a key to their entry into the modern world and an end to their "backwardness." A high priority of virtually every poor country is a rapid expansion of schooling, and most people view universal compulsory schooling as an essential feature of any modern society. Its benefits—literacy, increasing tolerance and sophistication, equality of opportunity—are presumed to be self-evident.

Illich calls for an abandonment of this faith in universal schooling on several grounds. He argues that there is no conceivable way that poor countries can close the schooling gap between themselves and rich countries. To place faith in schooling is, for a poor country, to be condemned to perpetual inferiority. Most poor countries in Asia, Africa, and Latin America simply do not have the resources to provide five years of elementary schooling for all students, let alone universal secondary schooling. And if the idealistic goal of universal schooling is chimerical, the pursuit of that goal actually heightens inequalities and increases the sense of inferiority that many people in poor countries experience. The effect of educational expansion in poor countries is to close opportunities to those who have little or no schooling. The most important knowledge that children who attend school in Brazil for two years will learn, Illich suggests, is a sense of their own inadequacy and inferiority. The child will learn that mobility, success, and self-worth require more schooling than most children can achieve. Rather than seeing compulsory schooling as indispensable for the creation of literacy in the population, Illich sees schooling as a status symbol of modernization that will condemn much of the world's population to a sense of their own lack of self-worth.[16]

Illich makes a sharp distinction between what

[16] These arguments are stated somewhat less polemically by Everett Reimer in *School Is Dead* (New York: Doubleday, 1971).

he regards as the goals of education—the acquisition of useful skills, cognitive growth, and intellectual autonomy—and the effects of schooling. Schools, he says, do not achieve these goals, but rather teach a bureaucratic, corporate world view. They teach students to value economic growth and material goods; they teach technical know-how; and most importantly, they teach students to recognize that worthwhile knowledge requires further dependence on teachers and experts. Just as the Catholic church before the Reformation claimed a monopoly on salvation, contemporary schools and universities claim a monopoly on knowledge. The message of schools to students is that nothing can be learned that is of any worth without school attendance and the corresponding dependence on teachers. Such messages, Illich believes, are extraordinarily powerful. They are reinforced by the fact that schools have the power to issue certificates or credentials that are tickets to future high status positions. Throughout the world, people increasingly confuse this particular form of school knowledge gained in a particular way with all knowledge.

Like most radical critics, Illich sees schools as very effective institutions in transmitting ideas and values he dislikes and very ineffective in transmitting ideas and values of which he approves. Schools effectively teach a particular narrow, technological vision of the world, where problems can only be solved by bureaucracy and large-scale technology. Schools effectively make people recognize their own ignorance and teach them that only by more and more schooling can they solve the problems they face in their environment.

But in other respects, schools are very ineffective institutions. The basic skills of literacy and numbers-learning do not need to be acquired in schools. Indeed, they may be more readily acquired in special skill centers designed for that specific purpose. With the Brazilian educator Paulo Freire, Illich argues that compulsory schooling for children is a very inefficient way of increasing the literacy of a population in poor countries.[17] Far from increasing cognitive development and rationality schools undermine intellectual autonomy—the capacity to think for oneself or to act intelligently in one's environment. Such intellectual autonomy can only be achieved outside the confines of compulsory schooling.

The solution for rich and poor countries alike is to abolish compulsory schooling and to set up alternative "convivial" institutions to foster true educational goals. The state must cease to require that children go to school, and equally important, employers must be forbidden inquiry into a person's scholastic experience—grades, examination results, degrees, and so on. Instead employers must hire people on the basis of competence for a particular job. To replace schools, a network of alternative institutions must be established and individuals given vouchers permitting them to purchase units of instruction at whatever centers they choose to attend. They can attend skill centers teaching literacy, computational skills, or specific vocational skills. The resources of computer technology can be used to assemble groups of people with similar interests who wish to exchange ideas and information. Individuals who wish to discuss a particular play of Shakespeare, for example, will be put in touch with other individuals with the same interests. Those who wish to acquire the most recent knowledge in agricultural technology can be matched with those who wish to teach.[18] Illich believes that attendance at these convivial institutions must not be made a condition for future employment or future status. The link between educational credentials and occupational status must be broken.

Illich's work stands the liberal conventional wisdom about the effects of schooling on its head. The expansion of schooling in the modern world

heightens inequalities between nations and between individuals within society. The close connection between educational attainment and occupational status characteristic of the modern world is not a sign that our society has become more rational and more competence based. Rather, the connection reflects a misplaced conviction that schooling is synonymous with education and that scholastic credentials indeed certify competence. Finally, the belief that the expansion of schooling underlies any just, humane, and democratic order is altogether incorrect. Western societies, despite their professed principles, are fundamentally undemocratic and inhumane. They are dedicated to the pursuit of material affluence, where decisions are increasingly made by individuals with technical knowledge rather than by elected officials, and individual lives are increasingly governed by large bureaucracies over which people have no control. Schools teach the inevitability of this present social order; they are essential props of the bureaucratic and technological world view of Western society. They may encourage questioning and dissent within that world view—questions about means and methods rather than ends—but they have the effect of discouraging alternative and more democratic visions of society.[19]

The Neo-Marxist Theories of Bowles and Gintis

The work of Bowles and Gintis, while making many of the same substantive assertions about the effects of schooling, differs profoundly in methods and procedures from Illich's analysis. Illich is not a social scientist. He cites virtually no empirical evidence for the sweeping conclusions that he draws. He gives no footnotes, making it virtually impossible to know the basis for many of his gen-

---

[17] Paulo Freire, *Pedagogy of the Oppressed* (New York: Herder and Herder, 1970).

[18] It is not clear how Illich, who is opposed to any kind of "institutionalized values," proposes to prevent these alternative "convivial" institutions from developing the "dry rot" that

afflicts existing institutions.

[19] As he writes, "School is the advertising agency which makes you believe you need the society as it is." Ivan Illich, *Deschooling*, p. 163.

eralizations. He exaggerates deliberately, perhaps in an effort to provoke the reader to question the conventional wisdom. Bowles and Gintis, by contrast, are highly competent social scientists. Their book *Schooling in Capitalist America* is packed with charts and tables and careful reasoning on the basis of empirical evidence.

Bowles and Gintis' central thesis is that schools serve the interests of the capitalist order in modern society. Schools "reproduce" the values and personality characteristics necessary in a repressive capitalist society. Although all schools must repress and coerce students to secure a compliant and efficient adult labor force, different schools accomplish this function in different ways. The values and qualities required by an efficient manual worker on the production line are different from the values and qualities needed by an executive of a large corporation. While the manual worker must be taught punctuality, the ability to follow instructions, and some degree of respect for his superiors, the executive needs some degree of flexibility, an ability to tolerate ambiguity, and favorable attitudes toward change and innovation.

Therefore, schools whose graduates enter predominantly low status occupations stress rule following, provide minimal discretion in choice of tasks, and teach obedience to constituted authority. Schools and universities that prepare students for elite positions, by contrast, encourage students to develop some capacity of sustained independent work, to make intelligent choices among many alternatives, and to internalize norms rather than to follow external behavioral rules. If we compare junior colleges with elite universities, for example, or the college preparatory tracks of a suburban high school with the vocational curriculum, we will find not only differences in curriculum, but also differences in the social organization of instruction. In junior colleges and in the lower tracks of a high school students will be given more frequent assignments, have less choice in how to carry out those assignments, and will be subject to more detailed supervision by the teaching staff.

By contrast, the college preparatory tracks of many suburban high schools and elite universities have an educational environment a great deal more open and flexible. Such differences mirror both different class values (the preference of working class parents for stricter educational methods and the preference of professional parents for schooling that encourages initiative and independence) and the different kinds of qualities of personality needed for good performance in high and low status occupations. The social organization of particular schools—the methods of instruction and evaluation, the amount of choice and discretion permitted the students—reflects the demands of the particular occupations that their graduates will eventually obtain.[20]

Reinforcing Inequality Bowles and Gintis' major argument, therefore, is that the educational system reinforces class inequalities in contemporary society. Different social classes in America tend to attend different neighborhood schools. Both the value preferences of parents and the different financial resources available to different communities mean that schools catering to working class students will teach different values and different personal qualities than schools serving higher status populations. These latter schools are not "better" or "freer" in any absolute sense, but high status schools communicate to their students the distinctive values and attitudes required by high status occupations in modern capitalist societies. The great majority of occupations in contemporary society, Bowles and Gintis believe, require a loyal and compliant work force to perform tasks with little responsibility and discretion. Most schools, therefore, teach their students to follow orders reliably, to take explicit directions, to be punctual, and to respect the authority of the teacher and of the school. Such schools, which satisfy the preference of most parents for disci-

---

[20] This differentiated analysis is, I think, what makes their analysis superior to more conventional Marxist critiques of schooling.

pline and good manners in their children, channel students to manual and lower level white-collar occupations. But schools serving more elite groups are only superficially less repressive. Such schools encourage students to work at their own pace without continuous supervision, to work for the sake of long-term future rewards, and to internalize rules of behavior rather than depend on specific and frequent instructions. These qualities are essential to effective performance in middle or high status positions in large organizations. But work in such organizations permits only limited freedom and autonomy. Workers may question specific procedures, but not the purpose of the organization; employees may be flexible and innovative, but they must be loyal. The capitalist society requires that all schools teach the values of individual achievement, material consumption, and the inevitability of the present social order. Free schools are therefore impossible in a repressive society.[21]

Bowles and Gintis decisively reject the meritocratic hypothesis, with its assumption that schools are efficient ways of selecting talented people. Instead schools work to *convince* people that selection is meritocratic. It is essential for the legitimacy of the capitalist order that the popula-

tion be convinced that people in high status positions do deserve these positions, that they are more talented and harder workers than others. Schools are an essential prop of this legitimacy. Selection for particular tracks within a school must appear to be made on the basis of ability and intelligence, and such purportedly objective criteria as IQ and grades serve this function. But these criteria mask the fact that success in schooling, and of course success in later life, is strongly related to social class and shows no indication of becoming less closely related over time. The correlation between college graduation and social class in the last twenty years, they report, has remained unchanged despite the rapid expansion of higher education. Schools remain institutions that reproduce and legitimate existing inequalities between social classes. This state of affairs will continue indefinitely in capitalist societies unless capitalism itself is abolished. Reforms in the educational system alone cannot reduce inequalities in the life chances of different social classes. The premise of liberal educational reform—that educational expansion and improved schooling can create equality of opportunity—is false. Schools that liberate, diminishing rather than reinforcing the handicaps of inequality, can only be achieved after a revolution in the distribution of power and the ownership of the means of production in contemporary capitalist society.

[21] See their comments on the free school movement, Bowles and Gintis, *Schooling,* p. 254.

TAKING ANOTHER LOOK

1 According to Hurn, which two "straightforward propositions" are at the heart of the functional paradigm?
2 According to the functional paradigm, in what important ways do modern western societies differ from previous societies?
3 What does it mean to suggest that modern society is *meritocratic*?
4 According to Hurn, what particular kind of political liberalism is implicit in the functional paradigm?
5 According to the radical paradigm, why is the failure of schools inevitable?

6 Briefly summarize Ivan Illich's theory of schooling.
7 According to Samuel Bowles and Herbert Gintis, in what ways do schools serve the interests of the capitalist order? On what grounds do Bowles and Gintis reject the meritocratic hypothesis?

A Long-Term View of School Desegregation: Some Recent Studies of Graduates as Adults

Jomills Henry Braddock II, Robert L. Crain, and James M. McPartland

A turning point in the struggle for black equality in the United States came in the unanimous Supreme Court decision in the 1954 case of *Brown v. Board of Education of Topeka, Kansas.* The Court outlawed segregation of public school students, ruling that "separate educational facilities are inherently unequal." In the wake of the *Brown* decision, there was a surge of activism on behalf of black civil rights, including boycotts of segregated bus companies and sit-ins at restaurants and lunch counters that refused to serve blacks.

If it is unconstitutional to keep black and white pupils apart, can the Constitution require busing to bring them together when they live in different neighborhoods? In 1971 the Supreme Court ruled in the *Swann* case that busing was "a normal and accepted tool of educational policy." However, many white parents bitterly opposed the busing of their children into black neighborhoods—or the busing of black children into white neighborhoods—in order to achieve racial balance. Some blacks and Mexican-Americans also questioned the use of busing, particularly if it would not lead to an improvement in educational quality. Busing advocates suggest that such measures may be the only realistic way of ending school segregation that results from segregated housing patterns. Opponents counter that busing will destroy the nation's neighborhood school system and have a harmful impact on youths sent to schools that are far from their homes.

In the following selection, Jomills Henry Braddock II, Robert L. Crain, and James M. McPartland—all associated with the Center for Social Organization of Schools, Johns Hopkins University—argue that the debate over the merits of school desegregation has focused too heavily on the academic achievement of school children. They point out that the test scores of minority students rise after desegregation is implemented. However, in the view of these researchers, "the real test is whether desegregation enables minorities to join other Americans in becoming well-educated, economically successful, and socially well-adjusted adults." After reviewing a wealth of studies, they conclude that school desegregation leads to desegregation in several areas of adult life—in college, in social situations, and on the job.

The case for or against desegregation should not be argued in terms of academic achievement. If we want a segregated society, we should have segregated schools. If we want a desegregated society, we should have desegregated schools.[1]

[1] Christopher Jencks et al., *Inequality* (New York: Basic Books, 1972), p. 106.

In 1984, the 30th anniversary of *Brown* v. *Board of Education,* it is important to keep in mind this elegantly blunt statement by Christopher Jencks. Social scientists and educators are mistaken, if they assume that the only point—or even the main point—of the *Brown* decision was to insure that black students are given equal opportunities to learn the basic skills. Schools have a broader mission than that. Writing for the Supreme Court in *Brown*, Chief Justice Earl Warren noted:

> Today, education is perhaps the most important function of state and local governments. . . . It is the very foundation of good citizenship. . . . [It] is a principal instrument in awakening the child to cultural values, in preparing him for later professional training, and in helping him to adjust normally to his environment. In these days it is doubtful that any child may reasonably be expected to succeed in life if he is denied the opportunity of an education.[2]

Warren's view is widely shared by both scholars and policy makers. A major goal of public education in the U.S. has always been to facilitate the assimilation of minorities; indeed, school desegregation may be the most significant example of a national policy using educational reform to achieve this end.

Yet the debate over the merits of school desegregation has virtually ignored the goal of assimilation, focusing instead on such narrow issues as whether achievement test scores rise or fall after desegregation. The evidence suggests that the test scores of minority students rise after desegregation, but this outcome is not the real test of the value of desegregating the schools. The real test is whether desegregation enables minorities to join other Americans in becoming well-educated, economically successful, and socially well-adjusted adults.

Clearly, we cannot evaluate school desegregation as if it were simply another educational innovation, akin to "new" math or to an innovative technique of individualizing reading instruction. Schools do more than teach academic skills; they also socialize the young for membership in adult society. School desegregation is not simply an educational reform; it also reforms the socialization function of the schools. For this reason, U.S. society cannot avoid the pain of decisions about school desegregation simply by improving the quality of segregated schools. Desegregation puts

majorities and minorities together so that they can learn to coexist with one another, not so that they can learn to read.

Data from our work at the center for Social Organization of Schools and from the research of a few colleagues elsewhere suggest that school desegregation is leading to desegregation in several areas of adult life. Table 1 lists the relevant studies. These studies, which have typically followed large groups of students through school and into adulthood, are few in number because of their high cost.

Without exception, the studies listed in Table 1 show that desegregation of schools leads to desegregation in later life—in college, in social situations, and on the job. One of the most dysfunctional aspects of racial segregation is its tendency to become self-perpetuating. Racial segregation gives birth to and nurtures a form of avoidance learning that helps to maintain the separation of blacks and whites.[3]

Prior to the *Brown* decision, blacks were educated in a dual school system that offered them putatively inferior training, especially in the South. When schools in the South began to desegregate, blacks were legally entitled to attend formerly all-white elementary and secondary schools. However, in part because of anticipated hostility from whites and in part because of the belief that prior differences in educational preparation might place them at a competitive disadvantage in desegregated schools, many blacks in the South were ambivalent about and reluctant to take full advantage of this hard-won educational opportunity.

For this reason, the Supreme Court ruled that "freedom of choice"—that is, offering blacks the opportunity to leave segregated schools for desegregated ones—is inconstitutional. The Court recognized that a century of segregation had created enormous social inertia that would, given the opportunity, maintain segregated schools far into the future.

---

[2] *Brown* v. *Board of Education*, 347 U.S. 483 (1954).
[3] Thomas Pettigrew, "Continuing Barriers to Desegregated

Education in the South," *Sociology of Education*, Winter 1965, pp. 99-111.

TABLE 1 SUMMARY OF RECENT RESEARCH EVIDENCE ON THE EFFECTS OF DESEGREGATION

Study	Data	Independent Variable
Braddock (1980)	Survey in 1972 of black students attending four colleges in Florida (N = 253)	High school racial composition
Braddock and McPartland (1982)	Black subsample of the National Longitudinal Study (NLS) High School Class of 1972 (N = 3,119)	Elementary/secondary school racial composition
Braddock, McPartland, and Trent (1984)	Black and white subsamples of the NLS Class of 1972 merged with survey data from their 1976 and 1979 employers (blacks = 1,518; whites = 1,957)	High school and college racial composition
Crain and Weisman (1972)	Survey in 1966 of blacks living in North and West (N = 1,651)	Elementary/secondary school racial composition
Braddock and McPartland (1983)	Two-year follow-up of black subsample of NLS 1980–81 Youth Cohort (N = 1,074)	High school racial composition
Green (1981; 1982)	Ten-year follow-up of 1971 black college freshmen surveyed by American Council on Education (N = 1,400)	High school and college racial composition
Crain (1984a)	Survey in 1982 of Project Concern participants (N = 660)	Elementary/secondary school racial composition
Crain (1984b)	Survey of employers of NLS respondents (N = 4,080)	Inner-city school vs. suburban school
Pearce (1980)	14 communities	Change in school segregation indices
Pearce, Crain, and Farley (1984)	25 large cities	Change in school segregation indices

Dependent Variable	Control Variables	Findings
Racial composition of college	Socioeconomic status, sex, high school grades, college costs and reputation, financial aid, and proximity to college	Black students from majority-white high schools are more likely to enroll at majority-white four-year colleges.
Racial composition of college	Socioeconomic status, sex, high school grades and test scores, region, and proximity to college	Black students from majority-white elementary/secondary schools are more likely to enroll in and persist at majority-white two- and four-year colleges.
Racial composition of employing firm	Sex, age, public vs. private employment, educational attainment, region, and community racial composition	Blacks and whites from desegregated elementary/secondary schools are more likely to work in desegregated firms; blacks from predominantly white colleges are also more likely to work in desegregated firms.
Interracial contact, neighborhood racial composition, racial composition of occupation	Socioeconimic status, age, sex, region of birth	Blacks from desegregated elementary/secondary schools are more likely to have white social contacts, live in integrated neighborhoods.
Racial composition of co-worker groups and attitudes toward white supervisors and white co-workers	Sex, age, public vs. private employment, job status, and community racial composition	Northern blacks from majority-white high schools are more likely to have white co-workers. In the South, this relationship is also positive but confounded with community racial composition. Desegregated blacks evaluate white co-workers and supervisors more positively than do segregated blacks.
Racial composition of co-worker and friendship groups	Sex, high school grades, college major, etc.	Black adults who graduated from majority-white high schools or majority-white colleges and who grew up in majority-white neighborhoods are more likely to have white work associates and friends.
Interracial contact and neighborhood racial composition	Socioeconomic status, age, and test scores	Blacks who attend desegregated schools are more likely to move into integrated neighborhoods and to have a greater number of white friends.
Employment decisions about applicants	Race, age, sex, education, and how applicant came to firm	Employers give preference to blacks from desegregated (i.e., suburban) schools.
Change in degree of desegregation in housing and in marketing policies in housing	Communities matched by size, region, racial composition	Communities with a communitywide school desegregation plan have more integration in housing and less "racial steering" by the real estate industry.
Change in housing segregation indices	City size, racial composition, previous level of segregation	Central cities where schools are desegregated have more desegregation in housing.

Just as blacks who grew up in segregated schools are reluctant to send their children to desegregated schools, so they are also reluctant to place themselves in desegregated adult settings. As contact theory would predict, blacks have learned to avoid and to withdraw from interracial situations that might cause them pain or indignity. Even though the situation has changed, and the pain and indignity have lessened or disappeared altogether, many blacks remain reluctant to test the new arrangements.

Thus, as we have already pointed out, historic patterns of de jure and de facto segregation have generated a social inertia that sustains blacks' isolation from major social institutions. And this long-standing isolation of blacks has perpetuated patterns of avoidance learning and social behavior among whites that cause them to resist desegregation in the schools and in other social settings. Desegregation of elementary and secondary schools would help the U.S. to replace a self-perpetuating cycle of segregation with a self-perpetuating cycle of desegregation.

The first two research studies listed in Table 1 found that minority students who have been educated in desegregated elementary and secondary schools are more likely than their counterparts from segregated schools to attend predominantly white colleges and universities.[4] Blacks who have attended segregated schools in the South tend to perpetuate their segregation by enrolling in traditionally black four-year colleges. Blacks who have attended segregated schools in the North are more likely than their counterparts from desegregated schools to enroll in predominantly black community colleges located in urban areas.

The third study listed in Table 1 found that both blacks and whites who have attended desegregated schools are more likely than their counterparts from segregated schools to be working in desegregated settings.[5] The fourth study, by Robert Crain and Carol Weisman, used data collected in the 1960s by the U.S. Commission on Civil Rights; this study showed that blacks educated in desegregated schools are more likely than those educated in segregated ones to have white social contacts and to live in integrated neighborhoods.[6] The fifth study listed in Table 1 showed that blacks from desegregated schools are more likely than their counterparts from segregated schools to work in desegregated settings.[7]

The sixth and seventh studies listed in Table 1 found that blacks who have attended desegregated schools are more likely to work in desegregated settings, more likely to live in racially mixed neighborhoods, and more likely to have cross-racial friendships.[8] (The seventh study, conducted by Robert Crain and funded by the National Institute of Education, was a 15-year follow-up evaluation of an experimental desegre-

---

[4] Jomills Henry Braddock II, "The Perpetuation of Segregation Across Levels of Education: A Behavioral Assessment of the Contact-Hypothesis," *Sociology of Education,* July 1980, pp. 178-86; and Jomills Henry Braddock II and James M. McPartland, "Assessing School Desegregation Effects: New Directions in Research," in Ronald Corwin, ed., *Research in Sociology of Education and Socialization, Vol. 3* (Greenwich, Conn.: JAI, 1982), pp. 259-82.

[5] Jomills Henry Braddock II, James M. McPartland, and William Trent, "Desegregated Schools and Desegregated Work Environments," paper presented at the annual meeting of the American Educational Research Association, New Orleans, 1984.

[6] Robert L. Crain and Carol Weisman, *Discrimination, Personality, and Achievement* (New York: Seminar Press, 1972). See also U.S. Commission on Civil Rights, *Racial Isolation in the Public Schools, Vols. I and II* (Washington, D.C.: U.S. Government Printing Office, 1967).

[7] Jomills Henry Braddock II and James M. McPartland, *More Evidence on Social-Psychological Processes That Perpetuate Minority Segregation: The Relationship of School Desegregation and Employment Segregation,* Report No. 338 (Baltimore: Center for Social Organization of Schools. Johns Hopkins University, 1983).

[8] Kenneth Green, "Integration and Attainment: Preliminary Results from a National Longitudinal Study of the Impact of School Desegregation," paper presented at the annual meeting of the American Educational Research Association, Los Angeles, 1981; idem, "The Impact of Neighborhood and Secondary School Integration on Educational Achievement and Occupational Attainment of College-Bound Blacks" (Doctoral dissertation, University of California-Los Angeles, 1982); and Robert L. Crain, "Desegregated Schools and the Non-Academic Side of College Survival," paper presented at the annual meeting of the American Educational Research Association, New Orleans, 1984.

gation program in Hartford, Connecticut.)

The eighth study in Table 1, also conducted by Crain, showed that a national sample of employers gives preference in hiring to black graduates of desegregated high schools.[9] And the last two studies in Table 1, which looked at entire communities, showed that those cities with desegregated schools are also more likely to have integrated neighborhoods.[10]

The studies in Table 1 show strong and consistent effects: members of minority groups who have been educated in segregated schools will generally move into segregated niches in adult society. If they have had no childhood experience with whites, members of minority groups will tend to avoid dealing with whites as adults. Sometimes they practice avoidance because they expect rejection. But this avoidance may also be explained by the fact that they have had no chance to develop effective ways of interacting and coping with whites; moreover, they have lacked opportunities in competitive situations to test their abilities against those of whites. We think it is likely, too, that the same mechanism that produces prejudice among whites from segregated backgrounds will produce prejudice among blacks who have had no contact with whites.

It seems intuitively obvious that, among blacks, the social and psychological barriers to seeking or sustaining memberships in desegregated groups should be greater for those individuals who unrealistically expect hostile reactions from whites, who have little confidence that they can function successfully in interracial situations, or who have trouble dealing with the strains that

may accompany interpersonal contacts across racial lines. And indeed, Crain found, in his study of participants in the Hartford desegregation program, that minority males who had graduated from segregated schools perceived more racism, both in college and in business settings, than did males who had graduated from desegregated schools.[11] If childhood experiences in desegregated settings help blacks to break down these social and psychological barriers, the logical outcome would seem to be less avoidance or withdrawal from integrated situations in adulthood.

School desegregation also changes the attitudes and behavior of whites, by reducing racial stereotypes and removing whites' fears of hostile reactions in interracial settings. Using data on racial attitudes derived from national surveys, Richard Scott and James McPartland found that attending desegregated schools improves the attitudes of both blacks and whites toward future interracial situations.[12]

Similarly, mainstream institutions respond to school desegregation by providing more opportunities for blacks to associate with whites. Cities that have desegregated schools develop a larger quantity of desegregated housing than do cities with segregated school systems. Corporations also react more positively to black applicants who come to them from desegregated schools. Thus, even if the attitudes and behaviors of minority and majority students did not change, school desegregation would still make white-controlled institutions more open to members of minority groups, thereby creating greater opportunities for adult desegregation.

Nowhere is this result more apparent than in the two studies of the impact of schools on local

---

[9] Robert L. Crain, *The Quality of American High School Graduates: What Personnel Officers Say and Do About It*, Report No. 354 (Baltimore: Center for Social Organization of Schools, Johns Hopkins University, 1984).

[10] Diana Pearce, *Breaking Down the Barriers: New Evidence on the Impact of Metropolitan School Desegregation on Housing Patterns* (Washington, D.C.: National Institute of Education, 1980); and Diana Pearce, Robert L. Crain, and Reynolds Farley, "Lessons Not Lost: The Effect of School De-

segregation on the Rate of Residential Desegregation in Large Central Cities," paper presented at the annual meeting of the American Educational Research Association, New Orleans, 1984.

[11] Crain, "Desegregated Schools. . . ."

[12] Richard Scott and James M. McPartland, "Desegregation as National Policy: Correlates of Racial Attitudes," *American Educational Research Journal*, vol. 19, 1982, pp. 397-414.

housing markets.[13] We tend to think of schools simply as educational settings, but they are also major employers and respected social institutions in their communities. As such, the schools exert a powerful influence on local real estate values, and the choice of a school site is one of the most powerful city-planning tools available to local government. Cities that locate their schools and assign students to them in a manner that promotes segregation will find that they are also segregating their housing market.

An old argument, which has recently resurfaced, suggests that separate-but-equal is as good for the society as integrated-and-equal. Where the schools are concerned, at least, that argument is wrong.

Segregation in elementary and secondary schools leads to segregation in adult life—which inevitably means inequality of opportunity with regard to higher education, employment, and housing. If they wish to attend college, for example, high school graduates who are members of minority groups often have no choice but to attend a predominantly white institution. But if they have been ill-prepared by their elementary and secondary schools to cope with whites, they have been ill-prepared to cope with higher education.

Meanwhile, high school and college graduates who are members of minority groups must deal with an employment market dominated by white-owned institutions. If they lack the credentials that impress white personnel directors, these graduates are not likely to receive job offers. Moreover, researchers have found that blacks from segregated schools who have white supervisors in the workplace have more negative feelings about those supervisors than do blacks from desegrated schools.[14] Thus blacks educated in segregated schools are probably less likely to keep their jobs with white employers and to earn promotions.

Finally, in today's economy, the major portion of the average family's net worth is tied up in the family home. But those blacks who reside in the inner city have purchased homes characterized by declining property values, and they suffer serious economic losses as a consequence.

The perpetuation of segregation from childhood into adulthood might not be economically and socially harmful to minorities in a society in which minority-owned institutions provided ample opportunities for economic and social success. But U.S. society does not provide such opportunities. Therefore, segregation is harmful, because most minority-group members must find their ways into desegregated institutions if they are to achieve success as adults.

Some of the studies we have completed lend support to this statement. For example, a 1981 study by Jomills Braddock and Marvin Dawkins showed that blacks educated in desegregated high schools made better grades both in historically black colleges and in predominantly white ones.[15] Similarly, Robert Crain, Rita Mahard, and Ruth Narot found in 1983 that black males educated in segregated junior high schools in the South had much lower test scores as students in desegregated high schools than did black males educated in desegregated junior high schools in the South.[16]

By the same token, a 1978 study by Crain and Mahard showed that in the North, which has very few predominantly black four-year colleges, blacks educated in desegregated elementary and secondary schools are more likely than blacks in the South to graduate from college.[17] This seems

[13] Pearce, *Breaking Down the Barriers. . . .*, and Pearce, Crain, and Farley, "Lessons Not Lost. . . ."

[14] Braddock and McPartland, *More Evidence on Social-Psychological Processes. . . .*

[15] Jomills Henry Braddock II and Marvin Dawkins, "Predicting Black Achievement in Higher Education," *Journal of Negro Education,* vol. 50, 1981, pp. 319-27.

[16] Robert L. Crain, Rita Mahard, and Ruth Narot, *Making Desegregation Work* (Cambridge, Mass.: Ballinger, 1983).

[17] Robert L. Crain and Rita Mahard, "School Racial Composition and Black College Attendance and Achievement Test Performance," *Sociology of Education,* vol. 51, 1978, pp. 81-101.

to be the case partly because blacks in the North are more likely to choose to attend a four-year college, partly because they make higher grades there, and partly because they are less willing to drop out. Braddock and McPartland reported similar findings in 1982.[18] And Kenneth Green, in his analysis of data on black college freshmen collected by the American Council on Education, found that blacks from desegregated schools tended to make higher grades in college and to have higher college graduation rates than blacks from segregated schools.[19]

We are also beginning to accumulate some evidence that black graduates of desegregated schools have better employment opportunities than do their counterparts from segregated schools. In a study done nearly 20 years ago, Crain and Weisman found that black males from desegregated schools had better jobs and higher incomes than their peers from segregated schools.[20] Analyses by Braddock,[21] Braddock and McPartland,[22] Mickey Burnim,[23] and Harold Brown and David Ford,[24] using four different samples of data, all showed that black graduates of predominantly white colleges and universities enjoyed some degree of income advantage over their counterparts who had graduated from predominantly black institutions. If we combine these findings with those of Crain, from his study of employer stereotypes of blacks from segregated schools,[25] and with those of Diana Pearce in 1980 and of Pearce, Crain, and Reynolds Farley in 1984 on housing opportunities in cities that have desegregated schools,[26] we have considerable evidence that school desegregation is a necessary step to insure equality of economic opportunity to minorities in U.S. society.

Additional research remains to be done, however. We need more studies of how whites relate to blacks as a result of their own segregated or desegregated schooling. Nor is there yet a good study, using up-to-date data, to replicate the Crain and Weisman finding that black graduates of desegregated elementary and secondary schools enjoy higher incomes than their counterparts from segregated schools.

Nonetheless, the evidence already in hand tells us that the initial conception of the impact of school desegregation, as expressed in 1954 in the *Brown* decision, has been borne out. The schools are the place in which a society socializes its next generation of citizens. The research findings that we have presented here suggest that the U.S. cannot afford segregated schools, if this nation is genuinely committed to providing equality of opportunity to every citizen.

---

[18] Braddock and McPartland, "Assessing School Desegregation Effects. . . ."

[19] Green, "The Impact of Neighborhood and Secondary School Integration. . . ."

[20] Crain and Weisman, *Discrimination, Personality, and Achievement.*

[21] Jomills Henry Braddock II, "College Race and Black Occupational Attainment," paper presented at the annual meeting of the American Sociological Association, Detroit, 1983.

[22] Jomills Henry Braddock II and James M. McPartland, "Some Costs and Benefits for Black College Students of Enrollment at Predominantly White Institutions," in Michael Nettles and Robert Thoeny, eds., *Qualitative Dimensions of Desegregation in Higher Education* (San Francisco: Jossey-Bass, forthcoming).

[23] Mickey Burnim, "The Earnings Effect of Black Matriculation in Predominantly White Colleges," *Industrial and Labor Relations Review,* vol. 33, 1980, pp. 518-24.

[24] Harold Brown and David Ford, "An Exploratory Analysis of Discrimination in the Employment of Black MBA Graduates," *Journal of Applied Psychology,* vol. 62, 1977, pp. 50-56.

[25] Crain, "The Quality of American High School Graduates. . . ."

[26] Pearce, *Breaking Down the Barriers. . . .,* and Pearce, Crain, and Farley, "Lessons Not Lost. . . ."

TAKING ANOTHER LOOK

1 Briefly summarize the view of public education held by the late Earl Warren, who was Chief Justice of the Supreme Court at the time of the *Brown* decision.

2 What do the authors consider to be one of the most dysfunctional aspects of racial segregation?
3 How does school desegregation reshape the socialization function of American schools?
4 How would conflict theorists be likely to view resistance to busing and other efforts to achieve school desegregation?
5 How does school desegregation change the attitudes and behavior of blacks? How does it change the attitudes and behavior of whites?

CHANGING SOCIETY

Throughout this book, we have been reminded that sociologists are vitally concerned with changes in cultures, social institutions, and social behavior. Part Five focuses more directly on change as a characteristic aspect of human societies.

Human ecologists have long been interested in how the physical environment shapes people's lives (rivers can serve as a barrier to residential expansion) and also in how people influence their surrounding environment. While human ecology is concerned with the interrelationship between people and their environment, *urban ecology* focuses on such relationships as they emerge in urban areas. It has often been suggested that life is healthier in rural areas than in the nation's cities, but C. R. Creekmore ("Cities Won't Drive You Crazy") challenges this stereotype and offers a more positive view of urbanization and its impact on community life.

World population growth vitally concerns anyone who wishes to confront the social problems of the 1980s. In addition to its size, the composition and distribution of the American population have an important influence on many issues of social policy. Joseph A. McFalls, Jr. ("Where Have All the Children Gone?"), examines social, economic, and health-related factors that contribute to the declining birthrate of the United States. Paul R. and Anne H. Ehrlich ("What Happened to the Population Bomb?") focus on the continued threats posed by world population growth.

Sociologists consider the study of collective behavior to be an important part of understanding social change. David L. Miller, Kenneth J. Mietus, and Richard A. Mathers ("A Critical Examination of the Social Contagion Image of Collective Behavior: The Case of the Enfield Monster") study people's participation in a rather unusual event: an alleged sighting of a monster. Jo Freeman ("The Origins of the Women's Liberation Movement") traces the evolution of a controversial and influential social movement. James W. Vander Zanden ("Resistance and Social Movements") analyzes countermovements that attempt to *resist* social change.

In studying social change, social scientists often find it useful to speculate on future events or alterations in social patterns. Andrew Cherlin and Frank F. Furstenberg, Jr. ("The American Family in the Year 2000"), examine the future of the American family as a social insititution. Bem P. Allen ("After the Missiles: Sociopsychological Effects of Nuclear War") questions what survivors could expect after the most devastating experience of "social change" imaginable.

Cities Won't Drive You Crazy

C. R. Creekmore

One of the most profound social changes evident throughout American history has been urbanization. Currently, three-quarters of the American population is concentrated in a mere 1.5 percent of the nation's land area. In 1984 some 180 million Americans, or 76 percent of the nation's people, lived in metropolitan areas. Of these, about 40 percent lived in central cities, while the balance of metropolitan area residents were found in the suburbs.

Sociologists have long been concerned about the impact of urban life on city residents. In his notable 1938 article, "Urbanism as a Way of Life," American sociologist Louis Wirth argued that a relatively large and permanent settlement leads to distinctive patterns of behavior, which he called *urbanism*. He identified three critical factors contributing to urbanism: the size of the population, population density, and the heterogeneity (variety) of the population. Each of these factors has particular implications for the nature of relations among people within an urban environment. Size prevents residents from getting to know most of the people in the community. It also facilitates spatial (or physical) segregation based on race, ethnicity, social class, and lifestyle.

A frequent result of urbanism, according to Wirth, is that we become insensitive to events around us and restrict our attention to primary groups, such as our immediate family, roommates, or coworkers, to which we are emotionally attached. Thus, residents of large cities may walk by winos passed out on the street without offering any assistance. As far back as 1902, German sociologist Georg Simmel observed in a lecture that it is impossible to carry on a social relationship with each person that one encounters in an urban area. Therefore, the size of an industrial city contributes to a certain distancing in personal relationships outside one's primary groups.

In the following selection, C. R. Creekmore critically examines the stereotype that "the dirty, crowded, dangerous city must gradually destroy an urbanite's psyche." Drawing on a large body of research conducted by social scientists from various disciplines, Creekmore suggests that in many important respects life is healthier in the cities than in rural areas. Indeed, he concludes by quoting a statement of author Brendan Gill about New York City's psychic energy in which Gill contends that the true urbanite "rejoices in stress" and through it reaches "a state of euphoria in which the loftiest of ambitions seems readily attainable."

Trapped in one of those Olympian traffic jams on the Garden State Parkway in New Jersey, I waited to pay my toll for the Newark exit. Horns, insults and exhaust fumes had settled in a noisy, dark-tempered cloud. As I finally reached the end of the exact-change line, I faced a sudden dilemma. There was the automatic toll collector, side-by-side with a human toll taker standing in his little booth. I stared into the impersonal mouth of the collection machine, then at the person, and chose him. The man looked shocked. He regarded the quarter I thrust at him as if it were a bug. "Grow up!" he screamed at me with a sense of indignation that I assumed was generated by a life dedicated to the parkway system. "Grow up and use the machine!"

To me, the incident has always summed up the essence of what cities are: hotbeds of small embarrassments, dehumanizing confrontations, monetary setbacks, angry people and festering acts of God.

Many Americans agree with this stereotype and believe firmly that the dirty, crowded, dangerous city must gradually destroy an urbanite's psyche. This belief has a corollary: Rural life, haven of natural purity, wholesome values and the spirit of self-reliance, is the wellspring of physical and mental health.

A large body of research, conducted in the past 15 years by a diverse group of social scientists, challenges these heartfelt prejudices. These studies conclude that metropolitan living is more than OK. In many ways, researchers have found, city pavements outshine the sticks as healthy places to live and work.

Jonathan Freedman, chairperson of the psychology department at the University of Toronto, is an authority on how cities affect those who live in them. On the physical side, he believes that life expectancy is higher for people in urban areas and infant mortality rates are lower. The potentially unhealthy aspects of city life, such as pollution, stress and crime, are more than offset by better medical care, better water supplies and sewage systems and better systems for handling emergencies of all kinds.

What about mental illness? Surely the fabled rat race must eventually sap mental endurance and lead to breakdowns. Not according to mental-health statistics. In a now classic study of the subject, *Mental Health in the Metropolis: The Midtown Manhattan Study*, sociologist Leo Srole and five colleagues compared mental-health statistics in Manhattan with those in small towns. They concluded that small towns have a slightly higher rate of mental illness.

This doesn't mean that cities are easy to live in. Manhattan psychiatrist Herbert E. Walker and C. Ray Smith, a writer on urban planning, point out

in an article that certain environmental stress comes with the urban territory: automobile traffic, air pollution, high noise levels, lack of privacy and such architectural faults as poor lighting, tight spaces and inadequate seating.

With all this to contend with, why don't cities drive more people around the bend? One answer is that we learn to cope with the multiple problems. "It's not a bad environment, just a very complex one," says Gerda McCahan, chairperson of the department of psychology at Furman University in Atlanta, who once worked as a clinical psychologist in New York City. "An effect of living in the big city is that with time people learn to insulate themselves in a psychological sense. They learn not to allow a lot of stimuli to impinge on their consciousness. They sift out things that do not concern them."

Another answer is that mental illness goes deeper than environmental stress. "Severe mental illness is not caused by the kinds of environmental stimuli characteristic of a city—loud noises, noxious odors, density of population and high levels of activity, for instance," Freedman explains. "Rather, it is caused by complex human and social problems such as genetic defects, interpersonal relationships and the stresses of dealing with one's needs. And these problems are carried wherever you go. City stimuli might affect your mood temporarily, but they are unlikely to cause real mental illness."

Crowding is perhaps the most studied problem of city living. As urbanites do battle with blitzing cabdrivers, crammed subway cars, the frustrations of traffic and deadly competition for parking spaces, they have one big thing going for them. As McCahan suggests, their saving grace is superior adaptability.

Take some of the ways city folk deal with common crowding situations. They live on many levels, so the entire population is not constantly milling together on the ground. They have complex social rules (walk on the right; stop at red lights; wait in line for services) for pedestrian traffic. Cities now install bicycle, horse and foot paths that connect parks and open space and make movement safer and more pleasant. Freeways are built to travel to and from downtown faster. And planners use a variety of methods (rotaries, coordinated traffic lights, one-way roads) to improve traffic flow in the most crowded areas.

Other improvements are on the way. "One feature now becoming standard on urban expressways is noise barriers," says Dorn McGrath Jr., a professor of urban and regional planning at George Washington University. "That's because research carried on over the last 15 years has determined that highway noise is not only annoying to nearby residents, but can be psychologically and physiologically harmful."

This type of human adaptability is one reason Freedman is skeptical about the relevance of experiments that test the effect of crowding on rats and other animals—research that typically shows heightened levels of aggression, competitiveness, infant neglect and early death. Freedman feels that these findings can't be usefully applied to human crowding conditions. "Humans are much more adaptable creatures than other animals," he explains. Additionally, "the level of density you are talking about with laboratory animals is extraordinary, a level that would never appear in the real world."

Other researchers are less certain about the harmlessness of crowding to humans. For example, psychologists Janice Zeedyk-Ryan and Gene F. Smith report that crowding took its toll when 16 undergraduates volunteered to stay in a 12-foot-by-18-foot civil-defense shelter for 18 hours. Compared to a group of six students who occupied the same shelter in a second test, the densely packed students became markedly more hostile and anxious as the hours passed.

In another experiment, psychologists Yakov M. Epstein, Robert L. Woolfolk and Paul M. Lehrer created an environment that approximated the close conditions found in rush-hour mass-transit systems. They then compared the students' reactions under these conditions to what happened when they were put with the same number of strangers in a normal-sized room. The researchers found that the crowded students had higher blood pressure, reported that they felt unfriendlier and less in control and were rated by the strangers (who were actually working with the experimenters as observers) as tenser and more uncomfortable and annoyed than the uncrowded students.

Studies such as these suggest that crowding cramps the style of city dwellers and produces stress. Freedman has another interpretation. "Density intensifies people's reactions to events around them," he explains. "If you get people who are feeling aggressive for other reasons—who have been angered at home or work, for instance—and you put them under high-density conditions, they are likely to be more aggressive. On the other hand, if the same people are feeling good and cooperative, density will also intensify that."

Freedman uses loud music as an analogy. If people like the music being played, turning it up usually enhances the experience. If they don't, increased volume makes the experience even more unpleasant.

Thus, when crowding occurs in situations normally considered negative, such as commuting to work or waiting in line for service in a bank or store, it intensifies those negative feelings. But place the same crowds in an amusement park, at a cocktail party or in a basketball arena, and crowding enhances the fun.

One recent study indicates that under the right conditions, population density can actually improve relations in a neighborhood. Sociologists Lois M. Verbrugge and Ralph B. Taylor explained how this worked in a study they did in Baltimore. As population density increases, some environmental resources diminish and people start to compete for limited space, ease of movement, services and other resources.

The ultimate result of this competition, however, is that people adapt. They add services, make adjustments in how they live and increase social interaction to make up for scarce resources.

Think of the Guardian Angels, patrolling neighborhoods to augment police services. Or consider those neighborhood characters who direct people to vacant parking spaces and act as traffic cops for alternate-side-of-the-street parking changes. In adaptive ways of this kind, neighbors get together.

"Local social resources actually increase," Verbrugge and Taylor point out. "High density provides opportunities for informal contact and assistance because people are more accessible. . . . It is very possible that increasing density enhances social ties."

Crowding aside, it seems obvious that other stimuli peculiar to cities can be harmful to many people. In their article on urban stress, Walker and Smith list anxiety, depression, back pain, ulcers and heart attacks as diseases that can be traced to the high level of environmental stress in the city. "But for those people equipped to handle it," McCahan argues, "the city is the absolute optimum habitat." And, she adds, people can find their share of stress in the country as well. The boredom, lack of variety and low level of stimulation can be just as stressful as city living for those not accustomed to it.

Cities can also provide ties that help inhabitants handle stress better than their country cousins do. Home economist David Imig of the University of Missouri investigated the impact of life stress on 37 rural and 64 urban families with similar economic and educational backgrounds. He discovered that when the families suffered unemployment, money problems, relocation, illness and divorce, the city people suffered considerably less disruption in family relationships than did the rural families.

The difference seems to lie in the support systems that influence people's perception of stress. Urban families, Imig says, usually have closer connections to their social environment. They operate within a wide-ranging network of secondary relationships that may not involve close kinship or friendship, but which do offer informal support and exchange of services. You take my kid to dance class; I take yours to the ball game.

By contrast, rural families usually limit their support networks to a few close primary ties. This means that urban families have more outlets to diffuse stress. "Rural families don't have the large support system that urban families do," Imig believes. "They don't have anyone to turn to, to fall back on, when stress concentrates on their few close ties."

Another popular urban myth was depicted humorously in the movie *Terms of Endearment*. In one scene, an Iowa banker chastises a rude and insensitive cashier by noting, "You must be from New York."

Many studies contradict this stereotype of the cold, impersonal city. We have already seen that dense population can improve social ties, and that the city support network often works better than that in the country. In a study reported in *Psychology Today* (April 1981) environmental psychologist Karen Franck and two colleagues at the City University of New York found that although good friends come slowly in the city, friendships there eventually seem to become more intimate and more highly valued than those in nonurban settings. City friendships also tend to be more varied, broadening people's perspectives and opportunities.

"You have access to people at your own level in intellectual pursuits, sports, artistic interests—any area that you select," McCahan explains. "And you can seek out people at or above your own level who stimulate your growth."

Another measure of an area's elusive sense of warmth and personality is whether its inhabitants help one another in times of need. Do people help less in cities than in the country? The jury is still out on that one.

"A majority of studies find more help in rural areas," says Erwin Staub, a professor of psychology at the University of Massachusetts who has studied helping behavior extensively. "But some find no difference. And a minority even find more help in urban areas.

"The more confusing a situation, the more complex the stimuli, the more people's attention tends to be distracted," Staub says. "So the complexity of a city situation might distract people from helping." But, he points out, some areas also feature helping networks that can spur onlookers to come to the aid of victims.

People living in an urban neighborhood with a strong sense of identity—a Little Italy, a Chinatown or a rehabilitated neighborhood, for example —see emergency situations as their responsibility. After all, it's their turf. Cities also have concentrations of people with special helping skills such as CPR expertise, civil-defense training or medical backgrounds, and these people help in emergencies because they are conditioned to do so.

One of the most important mechanisms for triggering a person's helping response, Staub proposes, is a "prosocial orientation," previous experience being helpful. Since cities are the regional centers for charitable causes, social campaigns and reform efforts, many people learn to be helpers.

Thus, the whole process of solving city problems is part of a healthy cycle of activity. "If you want to look for problems that need addressing," says urban planner McGrath, "cities are the places where they tend to accumulate." Among the problems that he lists are "the awesome fabric of despair and difficulty" that covers our ghettos; bad traffic flow with its accompanying pollution and psychological frustration; noise; pollution of the environment; and frightening rises in already frightening urban crime rates.

"As one consequence, there are people drawn to deal with these problems. The whole process acts to revitalize a city," McGrath continues. "And the very problems that accumulate also serve to get meaning and satisfaction into the lives of the people who live there by giving them causes."

McGrath's viewpoint is another indication that the key to living in a city is adaptability. Stress is in the eye and mind of the beholder. An urbanite must be able to take apparently unpleasant stimuli and use them to his or her advantage.

Can people learn this psychological backflip?

Yes, according to Walker and Smith, who tell in their article how to manipulate city stress. "Urban stress should be seen as a stimulus," they say. And to relieve pressure, they advise exercising regularly in enjoyable, varied places, attending a wide range of entertainments, living in a pleasant, well-lighted space, being assertive when a situation demands it and adopting a positive attitude about the city and its complexity.

"To flourish in the city, you must have a good sense of self-esteem and be able to tolerate competition," McCahan adds. "You must be able to pit yourself against the best and, win or lose, learn something positive about yourself. And you must be relatively assertive. If you are a shy person, the city can eat you up."

The city can also do you in if you are saddled with competitive handicaps; if you are financially, socially, physically or mentally restricted from competing. But for those geared to compete, city life can be a horn of plenty. "I always think of living in the city as a potential growth center for human beings," McCahan says. "One reason is that cities attract the best of everything."

There are good jobs. The city offers the opportunity, according to McCahan, of "seeking your own milieu" and level of competence, whatever your calling. You can see good plays and artsy movies. Professional and collegiate sports abound. You can go to street fairs and ethnic festivals in the park. Take your pick of music, art galleries and cultural exhibits. Or you can spend your days wandering among various periods of architecture, testing Lewis Mumford's observation that "In the city, time becomes visible."

And, of course, you can always take advantage of a city's most notable amenity—going out for Chinese food at 3 a.m.

All of this activity is what makes a city go: a great, roiling, collective energy. "It is as if, far down in the rocky bowels . . . some vast, secret turbine were generating an extra source of power, capable of being shared by all the inhabitants of the city," wrote author Brendan Gill about New York's psychic energy. "It is a power that gives them the means of meeting the city on its own fierce terms of constant stress. And it is profoundly the case that your true (urbanite) rejoices in stress; the crowds, the dirt, the stench, the noise. Instead of depressing him, they urge him onto an unexpected 'high,' a state of euphoria in which the loftiest of ambitions seems readily attainable."

TAKING ANOTHER LOOK

1 What stereotype do many Americans hold regarding rural life?
2 According to the research of sociologist Leo Srole and his colleagues, how do rates of mental illness in Manhattan compare with the rates found in small towns?
3 Briefly summarize the research on crowding described in Creekmore's article.
4 In what ways can population density actually *improve* relations in a neighborhood?
5 Contrast the types of support systems available to urban and rural residents during times of stress.
6 According to social scientists, how can urban residents most effectively deal with the stresses of city life?

Where Have All the Children Gone?

Joseph A. McFalls, Jr.

Demography is the scientific study of population. It draws upon several components of population, including size, composition, and territorial distribution in order to understand the social consequences of population. Demographers study geographical variations and historical trends in their effort to develop population forecasts. In addition, they analyze the structure of a population in terms of the age and sex of its members.

Demographers employ the distinctive terminology of their science in analyzing and projecting population trends. Population facts are communicated with a language derived from the basic elements of human life—birth and death. The *birthrate* (also known as the *crude birthrate*) is the number of live births per 1000 population in a given year. This figure provides information on the actual reproductive patterns of a society. By contrast, the biological potential for reproduction in a society is called *fecundity*. It is very unusual for women—and unknown for any society as a whole—to reach this potential. Millions of couples across the world cannot conceive as many children as they wish. Demographers use the term *subfecundity* to refer to a limited or a diminished ability to reproduce.

Demographers use the term *zero population growth* to refer to the state of a population with a growth rate of zero, which is achieved when the number of births plus immigrants is equal to the number of deaths plus emigrants. As of the mid-1980s, 37 of the world's nations, including the United States, had achieved or were approaching zero population growth (ZPG). Collectively, these countries account for about one-fourth of the world's people. If the United States achieves ZPG in the first half of the twenty-first century, there will be relatively equal numbers of persons in each age group, and the median age of Americans could rise as high as 37 (compared with 29 in 1975).

In the following selection, demographer Joseph A. McFalls, Jr., predicts that the United States will reach ZPG by about the year 2020. He identifies various factors as contributing to the declining birthrate of the nation, among them: the rising cost of bearing and raising children; the declining proportion of Americans who marry and the rising rate of divorce; the increasing options open to women other than marriage and motherhood; greater availability of contraceptive methods, legal abortions, and sterilization procedures; and subfecundity stemming from stress factors and contaminating chemicals. McFalls suggests that, by the year 2000, the United States will follow the lead of various European countries in subsidizing reproduction within the family.

In the year 2000, only the rich will be able to afford large families unless the government decides to heavily subsidize childbearing. Large families would be a form of conspicuous consumption, a new status symbol for those wealthy enough to absorb the prohibitive cost of raising more than two children. Moreover, only wealthy women would be able to eschew the then almost universal norm of female employment by opting for the relatively luxurious lifestyle of being solely a housewife and mother. Foregoing the family's second income to devote full time to raising children would be financially out of the question for most couples. In fact, a recent study by the Joint Center for Urban Studies of MIT and Harvard University reports that the proportion of all households that are one-worker husband/wife types will fall from an already low 1975 figure of 25% to 14% in 1990, and could dip below 10% by the year 2000.

Today, it is estimated that the average middle-class family spends between $50,000 and $100,000 to raise a child, depending mostly on the kind of education provided. This sum includes expenditures for such necessities as housing, clothing, medical services, and education. One study found that a single child may consume more than 40% of a family's income. The validity of these estimates was impressed upon the author, whose recent baby cost over $6,000 even before coming home from the hospital—$1,000 for prenatal care and delivery, $4,500 for the mother's and infant's hospital stays, and $500 for the home nursery equipment. In the past, these childrearing costs were offset, at least in part, by the income-producing activity of adolescents and by the economic security children provided parents during old age. Today, however, this is no longer true, and the government has largely assumed the latter function by underwriting such programs as Social Security and Medicare.

The cost of children is one of many reasons why the birth rate is now at an all-time low in the U.S. and why it will probably plummet even further by the year 2000. Currently, couples are reproducing at a rate that will yield an average of 1.8 births, which is shy of the 2.1 births needed to replace their generation in the population. Many demographers predict that average family size will fall to about 1.5 children by the turn of the century. Barring substantial increases in immigration, either figure would lead to the achievement of zero population growth sometime during the first third of the 21st century and then to an absolute decline in the size of the U.S. population.

Needless to say, these demographic trends would be accompanied by profound social change.

In addition to the rising cost of childbearing, another reason for the falling American birth rate is that individuals are spending increasingly less of their prime reproductive lives in a stable marital union, the place where most childbearing occurs. Fewer individuals are marrying and more of those who do are postponing the event until after sizeable chunks of their reproductive lives have elapsed. The proportion of those not married by ages 20–24 rose from about 25% in 1960 to 50% in 1980 and could well approach 70% by the year 2000. Moreover, an increasing proportion of those who do marry do not stay married. The divorce rate in the U.S. is at an all-time high and is expected to increase in the future. Experts predict that 40% of those who married in 1980 will eventually become divorced. Finally, fewer divorced persons remarry than in the past and, for those that do, the divorce rate is even higher than for first marriages. Thus, fewer individuals marry, there is more postponement, more divorce, and less remarriage—all trends that are prejudicial to childbearing.

Another reason for low rates of childbearing now and in the future is that women are achieving growing economic independence from men. In pre-industrial America, most women had virtually no occupational alternative to being a farmer or housewife. If they did not marry and assume these roles, they had no choice but to live in a relative's home with a status somewhere between that of a servant and a child. However, by the 20th century, women had gained access to an increasing number of occupations, and now fully 60% participate in the labor force during their prime reproductive years. Moreover, while most working women today have part-time or part-year jobs or work intermittently over a period of years, recent trends indicate that increasing numbers of women, especially young women, are developing more substantial and permanent attachments to work and are filling more year-round, full-time, and continuous positions. As demographer Charles Westoff notes, increasing proportions of women will not have to trade companionate, sexual, household, and maternal services for the status, income, and security emanating from a man's employment. Women can now secure these things themselves. Thus, unlike in the past, women have a practical and viable alternative to marriage and motherhood. In addition, society's views toward working women and childless women have liberalized tremendously, making it easier for women to opt toward these roles. Due in part to these changing attitudes and roles, some demographers expect that as many as one-third of all women being born today may remain childless.

CONTRACEPTION AND ABORTION

Another reason why the birth rate is low today and should be even lower in the future is that unplanned pregnancies are less common than in the past. The post-World War II baby boom that lasted until the early 1960's, for instance, was due in part to an increase in accidental pregnancies and unintended births that occurred because of inefficient and sloppy contraceptive practices. Unplanned births are less common today because the birth control techniques available now are more efficient and do not require skill on the part of the user. The pill is virtually foolproof if used properly, and the IUD is relatively immune to user error. Moreover, legalized induced abortion can neutralize contraceptive error for those willing to use it. This means that, for a substantial portion of the population, an unintended birth is almost always avoidable. In addition, sterilization for contraceptive purposes is now commonly used to avert unintended births once desired family size has been achieved. It is estimated that about 75% of once-married white couples in the U.S. will obtain contraceptive sterilization within 15 years after their last wanted birth. Surprisingly, equal proportions of husbands and wives undergo the procedure. It is true that adolescents are still

having a considerable amount of unplanned births, but these too should decline in the future as sex education in the schools improves and expands.

The recent Supreme Court ruling that the Federal government is not obliged to fund abortions for poor women will probably not substantially increase the number of unwanted children actually born, at least in the long run. A study conducted in 1978 when the Hyde Amendment was in force found that only about 20% of women who would have previously been eligible for a Medicaid-funded abortion were not able to obtain one through alternative financing and therefore carried the unwanted pregnancy to term. It is also possible that family planning organizations will set up low-cost clinics with volunteer medical personnel to accommodate these remaining indigent women, or redouble their efforts to teach contraception so that fewer of these unwanted pregnancies occur. Moreover, some states chose to continue paying for abortions to Medicaid-eligible women from their own funds.

The reasons discussed above for the low birth rate—the high cost of children, the decreasing time spent in marriage, new opportunities and roles for women, and the more sophisticated and versatile birth control technology—are not the only ones at work. Other factors are operating, such as the decline in religious authority and the expansion of education for women, both trends being powerful anti-natalist forces. (Today, for instance, more women attend college than men.) For the birth rate to rise in the future, many of these trends must be reversed, but there seems little likelihood of that. It is safe to say, for instance, that the cost of raising children will not decline.

Rather than these trends reversing, it is far more likely that they will continue. Contraception, for instance, will be even more sophisticated and versatile in the future, with available methods including easily reversible sterilization and long-term pills or injections. Depo Provera, a contraceptive injection that is effective for three months, is already being marketed successfully outside the U.S., and it is only a matter of time before it or something similar is introduced here. Contraceptive methods currently under investigation include vaccination against the pregnancy hormone, synthetic steroid implants in the arm or the buttocks, vaginal rings and intracervical devices, contraceptive bracelets to be worn at night, and, yes, even pharmacologic contraception for males.

NEW FORMS OF REPRODUCTIVE TECHNOLOGY

Not only is it likely that causes of the declining birth rate will continue, but they will be joined by other forces acting in the same direction. For instance, new forms of reproductive technology will exert downward pressure on childbearing. One form is sex selection—the ability to determine the sex of offspring. Within the last year, clinics have opened in major cities where a couple can increase the chances of having a boy from 50% to 75%, and it is simply a matter of time before techniques are developed to raise the probability to near 100% for acquiring both male and female offspring. Thus, if a couple wants a boy and a girl, the new technology will make it possible for the parents to achieve this through two pregnancies. There will be fewer couples having a third and higher order child in hope that the sex that have eluded them will turn up. Thus, the number of births as a whole would decline. However, the full force of this technology on the birth rate probably will not be exerted since government will likely limit the practice to avoid a large generational sex imbalance. Men and women in the U.S. prefer to have male offspring (a 1975 study found that twice as many women preferred boys as did girls, and that their husbands preferred boys over girls by as much as three or four to one). If many individuals actually availed themselves of this technology (and this could occur in a society where couples are economically and socially limited to one or two children), a generation would be born with substantially more males than females. Such an imbalance would create many social problems for society and especially for the surplus males. Most felonies are committed by unmarried men, for instance, and such sexual deviations as prostitution and homosexuality could also increase. More importantly, if a generation splits 60% male/40% female, for instance, one-third of the men would not have the opportunity to marry, which obviously would create a tremendous personal and emotional hardship. Women, on the other hand, would certainly have the upper hand in the marriage mart, with benefits including the increased marriageability of older women to younger men. (Such unions are usually associated with few births.) To avoid such sex imbalances and their attendant social problems, the government will almost certainly intervene, probably by licensing the procedure to assure that equal numbers of boys and girls are selected.

Sex selection is not the only new form of reproductive technology that can lower the birth rate. Another trend is the freezing of sperm, ova, and even embryos for future use, techniques already widely used in animal breeding. The second "test tube" baby born in India was frozen at the embryonic stage for nearly two months before implantation in its mother's uterus. A New York City firm, one of the nation's leading suppliers of semen for artificial insemination, already is laying plans to offer women the service of freezing embryos for reimplantation later in life. This service provides insurance for those individuals who wish to postpone childbearing, but do not want to run the risk of becoming unable to conceive in the future. While this service would tend to increase births by undercutting the effect of any conceptive failure, it would also tend to decrease births because married couples who divorce in the interval will not have the embryo implanted. Children who otherwise would have been born early in the marriage would never come to be. Since it is far more likely that a couple will divorce than be unable to bring about a conception, the net effect on the birth rate will be negative.

Nevertheless, many couples do experience conceptive failure or some other type of reproductive dysfunction, and this is likely to increase in the future. Indeed, subfecundity (diminished reproductive potential) is yet another force exerting downward pressure on the birth rate. The causes of subfecundity are varied, and include psychopathological factors, malnutrition, disease, genetics, and environmental factors. In *Psychopathology and Subfecundity* (Academic Press), the author recently discussed the negative effects of psychological stress on coital ability, conceptive ability, and the ability to carry a pregnancy to a successful conclusion. Stress causes from 50 to 75% of impotence, for example, and it is no surprise to psychiatric experts that impotence increases during periods of inflation and economic difficulties. It is likely that such economic conditions will continue between now and the year 2000. Other new and powerful threats to the reproductive ability of the U.S. population include, for instance, an alarming number of chemicals, particularly pesticides, herbicides, and those used in the manufacture of plastics, that are now identified as causing serious reproductive health problems. About 50,000 chemicals are now widely used in the U.S., with an additional 1,000 being introduced every year. The air Americans breathe, the water they drink, the food the eat, and even the clothes they wear are becoming increasingly contaminated with chemicals capable of threatening reproduction. PCB's, widely used industrial chemicals now identified as powerful carcinogens, are believed to lower sperm count. They are present in the tissue of virtually every animal and are thought to be among the principal factors responsible for the steady decrease in the human sperm count which has been observed over the last several decades. Also, the exposure of millions of male children to the flame-retardant chemical TRIS in their sleepwear may be a cause of reproductive dysfunction when these individuals reach adult life, since the chemical is now known to have adverse effects on the male reproductive system. Other causes of subfecundity that will continue to increase include radiation exposure and diseases such a gonorrhea, genital herpes, and non-gonococcal urethritis.

In sum, there are many forces marshalled against reproduction, and both their number and intensity are likely to increase in the future. The birth rate, already substantially below replacement, will probably continue to fall. Barring increased immigration, which is unlikely, or government intervention, the U.S. will achieve zero population growth around 2020, and thereafter the number of individuals in the U.S. will actually decline.

SUBSIDIZED REPRODUCTION

Few societies face negative population growth with equanimity. Regardless of their objective circumstances, they believe it is in their interest, if not to grow, at least to remain stable in size. The family institution is almost always assigned the task of reproduction. If the family is not able to accomplish this task satisfactorily, the society has two alternatives: it can farm out the task in whole or in part to another institution such as the economic institution by making reproduction there more attractive.

The latter alternative has already been tried by several populations who are at or near zero population growth. East and West Germany, Austria, Luxembourg, and Britain have already reached zero population growth and depopulation, and others—Czechoslovakia, Hungary, Denmark, Norway, and Sweden, to mention just a few—are on the verge of zero population growth or at least nearer to it than the U.S. is. The governments of many of these nations have already intervened in many ways to encourage couples to have more children, including interest-free credit of $10,000 excused entirely on the birth of the third child; reducing a mother's work week, but not her pay; preference on housing; child bonuses; paid maternity and paternity leave; supplementary income for working mothers; child, marriage, and housing allowances; free maternity and child health services; free day care centers and school lunches;

and guaranteed job security for women workers who marry and become pregnant. In Sweden, despite many of these programs, the birth rate for citizens fell below replacement in the 1970's and deaths have exceeded births since 1975. These programs have been more successful in Eastern Europe, however, where there has also been a tightening of abortion laws, a powerful pro-natalist tactic. So, the results have been mixed, leaving most sociologists convinced that most governments will either be forced to raise the financial ante substantially and/or wipe out legal and illegal induced abortion. The force of the latter tactic can not be underestimated, for some societies presently have more induced abortions than births. It is estimated that the Soviet Union, for instance, has had years when abortions have outnumbered live births by four to one. Since Russians within the Soviet Union have higher rates of abortion than non-Russian minorities, and hence a much lower birth rate, it is no accident that by the end of this century the Russians themselves will be a minority—a prospect they find quite unsettling.

The precedents are clear—the U.S. government will be heavily subsidizing reproduction within the family by the year 2000. By then, European countries will have worked out the most cost-effective formula and the U.S. will profit from their experience. Actually, some might argue that subsidizing reproduction in the U.S. is nothing new, that it is being done now through such programs as Aid to Dependent Children, at a direct and indirect cost of many thousands of dollars per child. These children will tend to disappear in the future, however, as the birth rates of the poor and minorities continue to converge on the total U.S. rate and the unmarried teenage childbearing problem is solved. Black fertility is already near replacement, is falling faster than white fertility, and may even be lower than the latter by the year 2000.

If, in the future, societies find that they are unable to subsidize childbearing enough to encourage the family to perform this task satisfactorily, then, of course, there is the second alternative mentioned above—*i.e.*, assigning the task to the political or the economic institutions. Corporations could be commissioned to produce children of the state. In the short run, this could be accomplished through artificial insemination of surrogate mothers or even embryo implantation of host mothers. For a while, many women could find employment as baby makers or "incubators." There is already movement in the U.S. to strip away the socio-legal impediments to these services and there apparently is an abundant supply of applicants if the price is right.

Ultimately, genetic selection and engineering together with fetuses developing in precisely controlled laboratory environments will make even the surrogate mother obsolete. This may sound like science fiction to many, but so did sex selection, fertilization outside the mother, and frozen embryos only yesterday. Mankind is now in the vestibule of a brave new world of reproduction—a world ready to rush into any vacuum left by attenuating traditional and natural processes. Children of the state, whether born to surrogate mothers or in laboratory devices, could be raised in childcare centers or in the homes of paid "socializers." It all sounds very cold-blooded indeed, but, in the view of some sociologists, it is not inconsistent with the way industrial societies have been moving inexorably since the beginning of the Industrial Revolution. This view points to the shattering of traditional family ties and other primary group influences, and the increasing attachment of individuals to large, impersonal, and rational organizations. In such a world, why would reproduction and socialization elude the forces of rationalism and social and biological engineering?

TAKING ANOTHER LOOK

1 According to McFalls, how is women's growing economic independence from men likely to reshape American childbearing patterns?

2 In what ways will new forms of reproductive technology exert downward pressures on childbearing?
3 According to McFalls, what are some of the major causes of subfecundity in the United States?
4 What steps have European governments already taken to encourage couples to have more children?
5 Which issues raised by McFalls would be of greatest concern to conflict theorists?

What Happened to the Population Bomb?

Paul R. and Anne H. Ehrlich

In his still controversial work, *Essays on the Principle of Population*, first published in 1798, the Reverend Thomas Robert Malthus suggested that the world's population was growing more rapidly than the available food supply. According to his analysis, the gap between the food supply and the population will continue to grow over time. Even though the food supply will increase, it will not increase nearly enough to meet the needs of an expanding world population. Malthus saw population control as an answer to the gap between rising population and food supply, yet he explicitly denounced artificial means of birth control because they were not sanctioned by religion. For Malthus, the appropriate way to control population was to postpone marriage. He argued that couples must take responsibility for the number of children they choose to bear; without such restraint, the world would face widespread hunger, poverty, and misery.

Karl Marx, who was a contemporary of Malthus, strongly criticized the British theorist's views on population. Marx saw the nature of economic relations in Europe's industrial societies as the central problem. He could not accept the Malthusian notion that rising world population, rather than capitalism, was the cause of social ills. In Marx's opinion, there was no special relationship between world population figures and the supply of resources (including food). If society were well ordered, increases in population should lead to greater wealth, not to hunger and misery.

The insights of Malthus and Marx regarding population issues have come together in what is termed the *neo-Malthusian view*. Best exemplified by Paul R. Ehrlich—a professor of population studies and author of the 1968 book, *The Population Bomb*—neo-Malthusians agree with Malthus that world population growth is outstretching natural resources. However, in contrast to the British theorist, they insist that birth control measures are needed to regulate population increases. Neo-Malthusians have a Marxist flavor in their condemnation of developed nations, which, despite their low birthrates, consume a disproportionately large share of world resources. These theorists stress that birth control and sensible use of resources are essential responses to rising world population.

In the following selection, Paul R. Ehrlich and research biologist Anne H. Ehrlich discuss the slowing of population growth in the United States and some other countries during the last decade. While encouraged by this trend, they add that "all less developed countries must look forward to vastly increased populations over the next century and to the array of horrendous problems that such growth entails." Ehrlich and Ehrlich warn that the inequities and hazards of the world food supply system could lead to widespread famine. They call for "profound transformations in our systems of economics and social justice," yet at the same time they emphasize that population control is essential to the well-being of the planet.

Ten years ago, when *The Population Bomb* was written, the United States population explosion was alive and well—and projected to get even healthier. Virtually all demographers thought that the early 1970s would be a time of rising birth rates in the United States and that it would take decades, at the very least, for fertility to decline to replacement reproduction (an average family size at which each generation just replaces itself). We agreed with them; their reasoning made sense.

But we were all dead wrong. In the early 1970s the women who had been born in the postwar baby boom were in their early 20s, their prime reproductive years. Because a high proportion of the population were young people at an age when they would be having families, demographers had predicted a surge in the birth rate (conventionally expressed as the number of babies born per 1,000 people in the population per year). But contrary to all expectations, the birth rate plunged dramatically from 18.4 in 1970 to around 15 by 1973, and it has remained there ever since.

Correspondingly, the net reproductive rate in the United States has fallen to just below one and has stayed there. The net reproductive rate is a measure of the relative reproduction of generations. A rate of one is replacement reproduction—technically, each female baby born alive in one generation is replaced by exactly one female baby born alive in the next. A rate of two theoretically indicates a population that roughly doubles each generation; a rate of .5, a population that halves each generation. In the mid 1970s the net reproductive rate in the United States was about .9, a little below replacement. If this level of fertility continued and if there were no immigration, population would decline.

Why were the experts confounded by the people? How could there have been a lowering of desired family size so drastic that it overwhelmed the effect of the increased number of women of childbearing age? In retrospect there may have been several factors involved. One was a tight job market for young people as the expansive 1960s gave way to the economically troubled 1970s. An-

other was the women's liberation movement, which made it increasingly acceptable for women to seek fulfillment in ways other than by producing numerous offspring. A third was increased public awareness of the problems of further population growth—an awareness generated in part by citizen action groups like Zero Population Growth (ZPG) and by books like *The Population Bomb*. Finally, as reasons for having smaller families became widely discussed, effective means for preventing birth became more accessible. The pill and IUDs became available during the 1960s, family planning services were provided for low-income groups, and between 1967 and 1973 abortion was progressively legalized.

Above all, the demographic surprise of the early 1970s showed that, when conditions are right, social change can occur with astounding rapidity. In our view this is the most cheering event since the end of World War II, because it raises the hope that other social transformations necessary to assure the survival of civilization could occur with equal speed.

Unfortunately, the drop of fertility to below replacement level has been widely misinterpreted as meaning the end of population growth in the United States. Newspaper and television commentators proclaimed that the United States had "reached ZPG," membership in population organizations plummeted, and people in general relaxed because "the population explosion is over." But when a previously growing human population reaches a net reproductive rate of one, its growth does not halt immediately. It continues to expand because human beings of several generations live simultaneously (a generation spans about 25 years). A growing population has disproportionately more people in the high birth-rate, low death-rate younger generation than in the low birth-rate, high death-rate older generations. This means that for a while, even at a net reproductive rate of one or less, the more numerous young adults who are just replacing themselves will generate more births than the relatively few older people will contribute deaths. And as long as births exceed deaths, a population will increase.

This tendency for a population to grow even after replacement reproduction is reached is often referred to as "the momentum of population growth." In the United States that momentum means that, *if completed family sizes remain about where they are now*—which is slightly below replacement—the population will stop its natural increase in about 50 years with a peak population of about 250 million, about 30 million more than today. After that a slow decline will set in. (These estimates include continued legal immigration at current rates, but do not include illegal immigration, for which no solid information exists.)

The slowing of population growth in the United States over the past decade no doubt has already had significant social and economic effects, some of which have gone largely unrecognized. It has, of course, been blamed in part for the sluggishness of economic growth in the 1970s that has plagued most overdeveloped countries. Some problems, such as higher unemployment rates due to the sudden increase of women in the work force, clearly are traceable to the rapid social change of which lower birth rates are a part.

But if our population had continued to expand at rates like those prevailing in the early 1960s, the increased demand for food, energy, and housing, to name a few important examples, would probably have severely strained the social order. All three have been subject to supply shortages and spiraling prices during the 1970s. Even though political factors have played a part, especially for energy, pressures generated by a large, growing, affluent population must bear a large measure of responsibility. A good case can be made for the proposition that the economic troubles of the 1970s (and those we can expect in the 1980s and beyond) would be considerably worse if the birth rate had not been reduced. Conversely, a further reduction in population growth would result in less pressure by affluent Americans on the world's threatened resource base.

What about the population explosion in the rest of the world? Many other overdeveloped countries have also experienced birth-rate declines in the past decade. Several countries in western Europe that have had relatively low birth rates for one or two generations now have passed their population peaks and begun to decline, notably the two Germanies, Luxembourg, and the United Kingdom. (In the latter, emigration has been an important factor in hastening ZPG.) In these comparatively densely populated countries, already heavily dependent on imports of food, energy, and raw materials to maintain high living standards, the ending of population growth can hardly be considered anything but beneficial. The sooner it can be accomplished for over-developed countries that are still growing, the better.

According to the latest projections by the U.S. Census Bureau, population momentum ensures that, if present fertility rates persist, the industrialized world as a whole (including the United States) will expand from 1.13 billion people to about 1.33 billion by the year 2000, and slackening growth will continue into the next century. Population projections for the overdeveloped world may seem less alarming than they did a decade ago, but nonetheless the population explosion of the rich countries is far from over. In view of these countries' greatly disproportionate impact on resources and global ecological systems, *any* growth in their populations must be seen as a future threat.

Turning to the less developed countries, we find even less cause for complacency. There the projected effects of population momentum are far more spectacular than in the overdeveloped countries. In 1970 Harvard demographer Nathan Keyfitz predicted that if a typical less developed country reduced fertility to replacement level by the year 2000 (which is unlikely for most), its population nevertheless would continue to grow for a century, soaring to two and a half times its 1970 size. If India, with a 1970 population of about 600 million, were to achieve a birth-control miracle and reach a net reproductive rate of one in the year 2000, its peak population size would be about 1.5 billion people (assuming no rise in death rates). That is more than the present population of Africa, South America, North America, Oceania, and Europe combined.

The most recent demographic estimates anticipate that the world's population will grow from its current size of slightly over four billion to about 6.2 billion at the end of the century. Momentum is expected to carry the population to an ultimate peak of somewhere between nine and 12 billion in the 22nd Century. Such projections make ecologists wish the population-control movement had caught on 50 years ago. With any humane method of stopping population growth, the "braking distance" is long indeed.

Family planning programs have been established in the majority of less developed countries in the last 15 years. But, except for a handful of small, relatively prosperous, and "advanced" countries (such as Hong Kong, Singapore, Taiwan, South Korea, Costa Rica, and Trinidad and Tobago), hardly a dent has been made in their birth rates. Many of their populations are still growing at 2.5 to 3.5 percent per year (doubling in roughly 20 to 30 years). It was something of a mystery that some countries by 1975 had succeeded in reducing their birth rates to around 25 to 30 per 1,000 (almost approaching the levels that had prevailed in overdeveloped countries a decade or two ago), while other countries, apparently equally well "developed," experienced no significant change, their birth rates remaining at approximately 35 to 45 per 1,000.

Then, in 1972, some light was shed on the mystery. The People's Republic of China joined the United Nations and began to disclose previously secret information about its population and its own activities in "birth planning." While externally blasting Malthusian ideas and the family planning efforts of other nations, China had been carrying on what is probably the world's most vigorous population control program—and possibly the most successful. The U.S. Census Bureau estimates that China's 1975 population was about 935 million and that its growth rate is about 1.5 per-

cent and declining. The available demographic information on China is, however, by no means solid. Some demographers estimate that both total size and growth rates are somewhat lower; others believe they are higher.

The secret of success in reducing birth rates now appears not to be a high level of industrial development, as was previously thought. An essential factor seems simply to be equity. When people are given access to the basics of life—adequate food, shelter, clothing, health care, education (particularly for women), and an opportunity to improve their well-being—they seem to be more willing to limit the size of their families. Viewed in this light, it becomes clear why the family planning efforts of many "relatively advanced" less developed countries seem to get nowhere; often only the highest income groups (perhaps a quarter or less of the population) are benefiting from "development." The poor usually are excluded, and in many countries their condition is even deteriorating. This situation unfortunately prevails in numerous less developed countries, including several of the largest and fastest growing, for instance, Brazil, Mexico, and to some extent India.

Because of population momentum, all less developed countries must look forward to vastly increased populations over the next century and to the array of horrendous problems that such growth entails. Doubling a population in a generation implies that all resources (food, energy, raw materials), services, and facilities must also be doubled in that time. Those less developed countries whose growth has begun to slow may have somewhat brighter prospects (depending in part on their resources and political leadership) than countries where birth rates remain high.

All of the standard demographic projections contain the assumption that death rates can only remain constant or decline; they cannot rise. That this assumption is absurd is made clear by the rises in death rates due to famines that in the 1970s afflicted the Sahel and parts of southern Asia. It is made more absurd by even the briefest consideration of the state of Earth's ecosystems and of our social-political-economic systems.

Most people who try to monitor the functioning of these systems agree that the likeliest source of an unpleasant demographic surprise in the next decade or so is a massive famine. The global agricultural system, in combination with the world's fisheries, must provide almost 2 percent more food each year in order to keep up with population growth. In this decade, on the average, agricultural productivity has barely managed to do that and there have been several rather severe setbacks. This would be serious enough if the world's food were reasonably well distributed. But it is not; the rich, especially in overdeveloped countries, are if anything overfed, while the poor, especially in less developed countries, are chronically underfed. There has been no serious attempt at redistribution. The proportion of humanity that is hungry is usually estimated to be about 15 to 25 percent, and this probably has remained roughly constant over the years.

Considering the constant *proportion* of hungry people, however, tends to conceal a vast tragedy that is exposed by a look at the increasing *numbers* of the undernourished. One sometimes hears statements of the following sort: "The poor are always with us—the proportion of hungry people is no greater today than in 1850." Perhaps that is true (frankly we doubt it). But if so, it means the absolute number of those who go to bed each night inadequately fed has increased from perhaps 250 million to one billion. And a billion people is just about what the *total* population of the earth was in 1850.

Unfortunately, world fisheries production shows every sign of running up against biological limits. In decades to come it may be necessary for agricultural production not only to hold its place in the race with population growth, but also to take up the slack left by faltering fisheries production. There is good reason to believe that it will not be able to do so. The hoped-for transformations in the economics and sociology of agriculture, so widely discussed at the time of the World Food Conference in 1974, are not materializing. The weather has been generally favorable for the past few years, and famines have largely dropped from the headlines. Partly as a result, pressure to create an institution to hold world grain reserves, to institute other distribution reforms, and to improve agricultural productivity on a long-term basis in less developed countries has died away.

In the absence of a large-scale famine, such urgent tasks as land and tenancy reform in the poor nations continue to be neglected, and in the rich ones ecologically unsound agro-ecosystems and dietary habits are perpetuated. Meanwhile those in power can easily ignore the inequities and hazards of the present world food supply system. Widespread famine could, however, be just around the corner. An extended period of bad weather (which is thought to be quite possible by the most knowledgeable meteorologists), combined with environmental deterioration resulting from inadequate land management and ecologically unsound agricultural practices, could precipitate massive famines. This would provide a tragic "solution" to the population problem through a rapid rise in death rates.

There are other routes to such a "solution," routes we travel in part because of population pressures. One might be a pandemic, leading to a breakdown in the world health system. Crowding and malnutrition—common in poor countries—would be major contributors to such a disaster.

Nuclear war could bring about an even more efficient "solution." This route is made more likely by the spread of nuclear power, which we are told (erroneously) is necessary to keep up with a demand for more energy resources and raw materials. Or a war could be precipitated simply by some nation's perceived need for *Lebensraum*. Some of the stickiest international wickets are made even stickier by unequal rates of population growth between adversaries: The Arabs and Israelis and the Chinese and Russians are outstanding examples.

We must emphasize that the rapidly increasing level of overpopulation on our planet is only one element in the human predicament—albeit a major one. Achieving a birth-rate solution to the population explosion—one that would, we hope, lead to a gradual population decline—will not solve all our problems. We must also have profound transformations in our systems of economics and social justice, transformations that above all will permit Earth's ecosystems to continue to supply their indispensable, but little recognized, services to civilization. Hope that such transformations are possible can be taken from the dramatic and unexpected declines of birth rates in the United States and a number of other overdeveloped countries. However, this hope must be balanced by overall trends that remain gloomy. The staggering projected increase in the number of human beings overhangs all of our other problems, threatening not just the functioning of essential ecological systems but of human institutions as well. The old saying remains truer today than ever before:

"Whatever your cause, it's a lost cause without population control."

FOR FURTHER INFORMATION:

Bouvier, Leon F. "U.S. Population in 2000: Zero Growth or Not?" *Population Bulletin,* Vol. 30, No. 5, 1975.

Ehrlich, Paul R. *The Population Bomb.* Ballantine Books, 1968.

Ehrlich, Paul R., Anne H. Ehrlich, and John P. Holdren. *Ecoscience: Population, Resources, Environment.* W. H. Freeman, 1977.

Freedman, Ronald and Bernard Berelson. "The Human Population." *Scientific American,* September, 1974.

Keyfitz, Nathan. "On the Momentum of Population Growth." *Demography,* Vol. 8, No. 1, 1971.

United Nations. *Concise Report on the World Population Situation, 1970–1975, and Its Long-Range Implications, 1974.*

Westoff, C. F. "The Populations of the Developed Countries." *Scientific American,* September, 1974.

TAKING ANOTHER LOOK

1 What factors contributed to the declining birthrate and net reproductive rate of the United States during the 1970s?

2 What is meant by the term "the momentum of population growth"?

3 In the view of Ehrlich and Ehrlich, why is it that the family planning efforts of many "relatively advanced," less developed countries prove to be unsuccessful?

4 Why do Ehrlich and Ehrlich challenge the assumption that death rates can only remain constant or decline and cannot rise?

5 What factors contribute to the danger of a serious famine?

6 Do you agree with the "old saying" that "whatever your cause, it's a lost cause without population control"? Discuss.

7 How would conflict theorists be likely to view the assessment of the world's systems of economics and social justice offered by Ehrlich and Ehrlich?

A Critical Examination of the Social Contagion Image of Collective Behavior: The Case of the Enfield Monster

David L. Miller, Kenneth J. Mietus, and Richard A. Mathers

Practically all group activity can be thought of as collective behavior, but sociologists have given a distinct meaning to the term. Neil Smelser, a sociologist who specializes in this field of study, has defined *collective behavior* as the "relatively spontaneous and unstructured behavior of a group of people who are reacting to a common influence in an ambiguous situation." Among the forms of collective behavior identified by sociologists are crowd behavior, disaster behavior, fads and fashions, panics and crazes, rumors, public opinion, and social movements.

The earliest theories of collective behavior often suggested that people engaging in such spontaneous conduct are overcome, at least momentarily, by irrational impulses. For example, French scholar Gustave LeBon (1841–1931) argued that members of crowds give up their rational values for a contagious emotional fervor that is generally destructive. This characterization may have validity in describing crowds that turn into lynch mobs, but it fails to help us understand peaceful protest marches, pep rallies, and a host of other collective gatherings. Contemporary sociologists have recognized the limitations of LeBon's work and have offered alternative ways of viewing collective behavior.

In the following selection, sociologists David L. Miller, Kenneth J. Mietus, and Richard A. Mathers critically examine the "social contagion" approach to collective behavior offered by Herbert Blumer. This approach, similar in important respects to that of LeBon, assumes that under certain conditions, large numbers of people will quickly and unanimously adopt intense, irrational patterns of behavior. Drawing on alleged sightings of a monster in 1973 in the town of Enfield, Illinois, the researchers argue that the social contagion approach is unable to account adequately for differential participation in various events that followed. Both the type of participation in post-sighting events (such as a mobilization to hunt the monster) and the extent of participation varied significantly. Miller, Mietus, and Mathers conclude that communication processes, availability of the population for participation, and institutional demands are all key factors that influence this differential participation.

The aftermath of the *War of the Worlds* broadcast, religious revivals, financial panics and mass preoccupations have been recurring topics in the collective behavior literature. We will use Blumer's (1939) term "social contagion" to refer to this class of phenomena throughout this study.

Our discussion will be addressed to the following questions:

1 How accurate is the social contagion image of behavior?

Author's Note: This is a revised version of a paper that was presented at the 1976 Midwest Sociological Association Meetings, St. Louis. We gratefully acknowledge the critical comments of Clark McPhail, Carl J. Couch and Suzanne Prescott. We further acknowledge the assistance of Steve Brusko and Larry Althoff.

2 How theoretically sound are social contagion explanations of behavior?

3 What alternative foci can be employed to further our understanding of events which traditionally have been studied from the social contagion perspective?

THE SOCIAL CONTAGION IMAGE

The social contagion image of behavior includes the assumption that under certain conditions, widespread masses of people rapidly and unanimously adopt patterns of behavior that are intense, unwitting and non-rational (Blumer, 1939:230). Putatively descriptive accounts of events, such as the eighteenth century "tulip mania" in Holland, are cited as evidence for this assertion (cf. Lang and Lang, 1961:88–92; Turner and Killian, 1972:12; Klapp, 1972:113–36).

Critical examination of the quantitative literature, however, tends to undercut the social contagion characterization of behavior. The proportion of those in the available population who adopt patterns of behavior described as "social contagion" ranges from less than one third (Moss and McEvedy, 1967) to less than one percent (Johnson, 1945). Cantril's (1940) classic study of the *War of the Worlds* broadcast presents evidence that most fright reactions occurred during the first half of the broadcast and were of momentary duration. When the routine activities of the majority of the population become disrupted or held in abeyance, it is often the result of the intervention of institutionalized authorities. For example, disgruntled managers temporarily evacuated a factory when one fifth of the workers became upset (Kerckhoff and Back, 1968). In such instances, it is the directives of authorities, rather than "social contagion" which enlarges the scope of the event. . . .

THE ENFIELD MONSTER: A CHRONOLOGY OF EVENTS

On Thursday, April 26, 1973, the *Carmi Times* (Carmi, Illinois) published an account provided by a resident of the nearby town of Enfield (pop. 760) describing a face-to-face encounter with a "weird creature."[1] The informant, Mr. M., stated that about 9:00 p.m. the previous evening he had heard scratching at his front door. When Mr. M. opened the door to investigate he confronted a creature ". . . about five feet tall, with a flat body, grayish in color, . . . with a strange appearing head at least twelve inches across." The creature was further described as having ". . . three legs and two pink eyes the size of flashlight lenses." Mr. M. reported that he fired a pistol at the visitor which then ". . . hissed like a wildcat . . .," bounded away from the house, ran northward through some brush and out of sight along the railroad tracks near his house. The account also noted that Mrs. M. telephoned the state police who responded promptly and claimed to have discovered some unusual animal tracks near Mr. M.'s house. During this early evening disturbance, approximately 50–75 residents of Enfield converged near Mr. M.'s home, and discussed the event.

In addition to this newspaper coverage, the news director of radio station WWKI, Kokomo, Indiana had been dispatched to Enfield. The radio station broadcast their reporter's statement that at least three other residents of Enfield had seen "something strange." Among those residents was a ten-year-old boy (who lived near Mr. M.'s house) who claimed that about an hour prior to Mr. M.'s sighting of the creature, it had "jumped out of some bushes, stomped on his feet and had torn his tennis shoes to shreds." Newspaper accounts reported that the boy ran to his house "in hysteria."

By Friday, April 27, stories of the Enfield mon-

---

[1] With the assistance of the editor of the *Carmi Times*, (circulation of 5,000), we obtained copies of all their articles relating to the monster sightings. In addition, we sampled major newspapers in the state to obtain wire service releases concerning the event. While the format of these releases varied slightly, the essential content and wording of these articles remained consistent in both UPI and AP reports.

ster had been released to both AP and UPI News services and were being printed in newspapers thoughout the state. For example, the Champaign-Urbana *News Gazette* carried an article about the incident which stated that the investigating officers had described Mr. M. as a "rational and sober" person. The article quoted the officers' description of the creature's tracks as being "shaped like a dog's, but having six toe pads." The article also noted that school children had told Mr. M. that they had seen a similar creature near the school ballpark. The article concluded with Mr. M.'s statement that there was probably more than one creature, and that "they were not from this planet."

By Monday, April 30, the *Carmi Times* reported that Mr. M. had received approximately 250 telephone calls since the 26th, including a call from a "government representative" who told him that the incident was similar to others occurring since 1967, and that these incidents had been associated with UFO sightings. Monday's article noted that during the weekend, an anthropologist had interviewed Mr. M., examined the tracks of the creature, and had pronounced them as definitely *not* the tracks of a kangaroo. In addition, plaster casts of the tracks had been sent to an undisclosed laboratory for "closer examination," and two local hunters had engaged in a weekend search for the creature. The article concluded by suggesting that a bear was wandering about the Enfield area.

From Tuesday, May 1, until Saturday, May 5, there was minimal media discussion of the Enfield incident. Renewed interest was generated, however, when on Sunday, May 6, Mr. M. reported to radio station WWKI (Kokomo) that he had again sighted the creature at 3:00 a.m. on the railroad tracks near his house. Later that Sunday, WWKI's news director and three of his companions revisited Enfield. This search party reported that they had observed an "ape-like" creature standing in an abandoned barn near Mr. M.'s house. They claimed to have recorded some vocalizations of the creature and fired a shot at it

before it ran off.

By Monday morning, May 7, the events at Enfield were again on the wire service network. Mr. M. was interviewed by Wally Phillips of radio station WGN, Chicago and this telephone interview was broadcast live throughout the midwest. By Monday evening, stories of the Enfield incident were being cited in newspapers throughout the state, e.g., in the *Chicago Daily News,* the *Moline Dispatch,* Champaign-Urbana *Courier* and the Alton *Telegraph.*

Tuesday, May 8, the White County law enforcement officers arrested five young men from outlying communities after Enfield residents complained of gun fire. The men stated that after hearing radio reports about the monster, they had come to Enfield to photograph the creature. They brought shotguns and rifles with them for "protection" and claimed to have sighted a creature and fired at it. The hunters were charged with violating hunting regulations, fined and released.

Wednesday, May 9, accounts of the arrests appeared in many Illinois newspapers. The *Carmi Times* accompanied descriptions of the arrests with statements from Enfield residents expressing fears that monster hunters might shoot people by accident. It was also suggested that many of the "experts" visiting Enfield to examine tracks and gather other facts were "no more anthropologists than [were] any [of the] local citizens." The article concluded by noting that local newspeople and law enforcement agencies continue to receive telephone calls from various publications, television and radio stations.

On Thursday morning, May 10, our research team, consisting of five people, arrived and began to conduct interviews throughout Enfield and outlying communities. The following Sunday, a graduate student in anthropology from the University of Illinois arrived in Enfield. Later that day, UPI releases quoted this student as suggesting that in all likelihood, the Enfield monster was a wild ape, such animals having been reported sporadically throughout the Mississippi watershed since 1941.

Monday morning, May 14, Wally Phillips of

WGN contacted us by phone to inquire about our investigation. In the interview (which was broadcast live) we did not speculate as to the identity of the monster, but we did note the potential danger that "monster hunters" posed for local residents.

By Tuesday, May 15, almost three weeks since the first monster sighting, and a week after the arrest of the five monster hunters, the *Carmi Times* included two items: one discussed the building of a calf pen by an Enfield resident who, in response to his neighbor's inquiries, claimed he was constructing a "monster pen." The other item reported that an Ohio resident was offering a $500 reward for information as to the whereabouts of her kangaroo, missing for over a year. The Ohio woman was sure that the Enfield monster was her pet kangaroo. The Enfield incident ended on these whimsical notes. . . .

THE ENFIELD MONSTER: AN ANALYSIS

The Enfield monster sightings evidenced "classic" features of social contagion: (a) unverified and unusual sensory experiences, (b) mobilization processes, and (c) mass preoccupations. As noted, the social contagion orientation has failed to theoretically and empirically differentiate these phenomena. These distinctions provide a basis for assessing people's differential involvement across the time frame of the event, how the event grows (and recedes) in scope, and the event's impact on institutionalized patterns of behavior. In large measure, this approach follows from McPhail's (1971) discussion of civil disorders and McPhail and Miller's (1973) analysis of assembling processes.

UNVERIFIED AND UNUSUAL SENSORY EXPERIENCES

Social contagion explanations have been utilized following episodes wherein ordinary people report unusual sensory experiences, but most official investigators (e.g., law enforcement officers or medical examiners) debunk, or at least provide no

additional verification of these experiences. These investigators usually are acting with respect to immediate, practical problems (e.g., re-establishing work routines or domestic tranquility) rather than gathering data for sociologists. When the findings of these investigators are employed as the primary means of ascertaining the "hysterical" nature of the reported experience, social contagion explanations may be rendered suspect. For example, Johnson (1945) reported that the Mattoon police received approximately seventy telephone reports of prowlers during the week of the "hysteria." The conclusion that there were no reasonable grounds for these calls is reached primarily because the police did not apprehend any prowlers. Johnson does not indicate that systematic attempts were made to ascertain the particular sequences of events, nor the possible sights and sounds that lead various people to call the police. Such an investigation might have led to the conclusion that many of the calls were made under "reasonable" circumstances.

In our investigation of the Enfield event, we attempted to determine the number of monster sighting reports at issue. The number of these reports was considerably smaller than one would assume from journalistic accounts of the event. A portion of the "reports" were simply Mr. M.'s claim that others in his community had seen monsters. One report turned out to be an ill-advised practical joke, i.e., the boy's report that the monster tore his shoes. Our interview with the boy and his parents disclosed that they invented the "shoe tearing" episode to "tease" their eccentric neighbor and to have some fun with an out of town newsman.

The White County Sheriff told us that the five hunters who were arrested on May 8 were in various stages of intoxication and had alluded to the monster in the context of being arrested on charges of out of season hunting and improper use of weapons within the city limits.

Of the several monster reports discussed, only Mr. M.'s firsthand reports and the May 6 report of the WWKI party were made by people who, in all likelihood, thought that they "saw something." These three events hardly constitute a "social contagion" of monster sightings.

MOBILIZATION PROCESSES

The convergence of people toward, or dispersal from, scenes of unverified and unusual sensory experiences, the formation of vigilante groups and the gathering and subsequent movements of celebrating or hostile throngs of people have been cited as evidence of social contagion. These mobilization processes frequently consist of, or at least preceded by, *assembling processes* wherein people are notified of an event that is transpiring at some alternate location and subsequently they converge upon that location. A facilitating condition for the initiation of assembling processes is a large number of people in general proximity to one another, with a period of unscheduled or uncommitted time at their disposal. These time frames generally correspond to early evening, or "after work" hours, weekends, and holidays. [2] For example, the first monster sighting occurred about 9:30 p.m. and was accompanied by pistol shots and the arrival of state police vehicles. Subsequently, about 50–75 neighbors gathered at the site of the disturbance. In contrast, no assembling processes accompanied Mr. M.'s second monster report. This event occurred at a less opportune time (3:00 a.m.), no pistol shots were fired, nor were state police vehicles dispatched.

Increasing distance from the location of an event decreases sensory access to cues that something is occurring. Persons who can neither see nor hear the event are dependent upon others for instructions, face-to-face communications, phone calls, or mass media announcements, to establish the existence of the event or to specify movement toward (or away from) the event location. Newspaper stories and radio dispatches appraised persons throughout Illinois and parts of Indiana, Ohio, Missouri, and Kentucky of happenings at Enfield.

An issue that must be addressed is how such extensive notification of the event is produced. In this instance, notification of the event was facilitated by Mr. M.'s active pursuit of newspeople. For example, following the second sighting, Mr. M. called an Indiana radio station rather than the state police. Further, Enfield events may have been given play in media because the monster stories provided substantive contrast to other more ominous issues. Late April and early May of 1973 was a particularly gloomy period for people in southern Illinois. Severe flooding was seriously delaying spring planting, the Vietnam War was still to be resolved, the economy was beginning to slide into a recession, and Watergate disclosures were beginning to surface. Editors and station managers may have welcomed these monster stories for their contrast to an unusually long and depressing series of events.

Once people throughout Illinois and adjoining states had been informed of the Enfield events, mobilization processes occurred across this larger area. In general, most of these mobilization processes occurred on weekends (April 27–29, May 4–6) and/or involved people who were relatively unencumbered by immediate commitments. For example, one of the five hunters arrested May 8 was on military leave, and the others were unemployed.

While mobilization processes previously have been acknowledged only to the extent that they evidence social contagion, we suggest an alterna-

---

[2] We suggest that the availability of persons is a critical factor in determining the scope and temporal features of collective behavior events. McPhail and Miller (1973, 726) note that a majority of the disorders examined by the National Advisory Commission on Civil Disorders (1968) began and/or "peaked out" on weekends and evenings when the majority of people were free from the competing claims of work obliga-

tions and commitments. In addition, we suggest that authorities produced such availability when they closed schools, businesses and places of employment in "incipient" riot areas. While the availability of persons is a critical factor, it has not received the systematic attention warranted by its apparent importance.

tive interpretation. Temporal variations and participation in mobilization processes can be accounted for with reference to processes of *notification of the event and differential availability*, i.e., people's differential access to periods of negotiable, or uncommitted time within which participation in mobilization processes can be scheduled.

MASS PREOCCUPATIONS

Face-to-face and electronically mediated communication systems can disseminate vast amounts of information—fiction, trivia, and important news —to large numbers of people in short periods of time.[3] Given the existence of such effective communication systems in the United States, it is problematic to view the rapid and widespread dissemination of reports of events as a distinctive feature of social contagion. Rather, the rapid and widespread dissemination of information is a pervasive feature of contemporary social life.

The social contagion framework has been used to account for the dissemination of reports of unusual and unverified events and the belief or disbelief of these reports (e.g., Medalia and Larsen, 1958). The news of past or pending events and their location may "sensitize" or otherwise orient people with respect to such events (e.g., "A state police car just parked in front of Harry's house"). Such necessary information does not constitute sufficient conditions for the organization of innovative or disruptive activities. At a minimum, additional *specifications of action* such as those prescribing movements toward the location of the event (e.g., "Let's go see what is happening") must occur before activities are organized with respect to these events (McPhail and Miller, 1973:724).

The social contagion approach gives attention to the dissemination of information, but has failed to acknowledge whether, or examine how, this information is used to construct activity divergent from the usual. Residents of Enfield seemed to be well appraised of recent happenings in their vicinity. Their frequent discussions of these events, however were restricted to casual conversations, jokes and inconsequential bull sessions in homes, cafes, and other meeting places.

The only discussions we observed which disrupted usual kinds of activity were the interviews we conducted. Residents reported that because of their conversations, some young children were "afraid to go out at night," "became frightened by small noises," and "had bad dreams." One respondent said that after the hunters had been arrested, he instructed his children to stay away from the area near Mr. M.'s house, because they might be shot by "some fool."

In the studies cited throughout this paper, more attention has been given to the "belief" of information than the scope of attending disruptions of social behavior. In presenting an alternate approach to such events we posit that "belief" or "disbelief" of information may be quite inconsequential for immediate or subsequent activity. Of all our respondents, the White County Sheriff was perhaps the most vehement in his denial that a monster had been sighted. Yet because of the organizational position he occupied, his routine activities had been disrupted more than any other person we interviewed. He stated that the arrests and legal dealings with the hunters, telephone calls from newspapers across the nation, and incidental complaints from county residents had greatly hindered him and his staff in carrying out other duties. A key consideration in accounting for how routine activities are disrupted is not who believes information and who doesn't, but the preestablished, or institutionalized relationships between people.

---

[3] It is difficult empirically to assess the capacity of this communication network. Sheatsley and Feldman (1964) determined that virtually all (99.8 percent) of the people residing in the United States heard of the assassination of President Kennedy within six hours of the assassination. One half of these people heard of the event by word of mouth, the other half by radio, television, telephone and newspapers.

DISCUSSION

The social contagion orientation sets forth an undifferentiated view of social behavior by accepting the "illusion of unanimity" as social fact. Unverified and unusual sensory experiences, and the concomitant mobilization processes and mass preoccupations that accompany them, consistently have been treated as *equivalent* products of social contagion. Alternatively, we suggest that communications processes, availability of the population for participation, and institutional demands, result in differential participation in the event. These variables often are ignored in favor of more elaborate discussions that attempt to account for uniform states of aroused emotions.

Our analysis of a monster sighting in Enfield, Illinois illustrates the utility of this alternate approach when attempting to understand the dynamics of unusual events that typically have been cited as social contagions. This approach begins by ascertaining, from firsthand investigation, the general character of *differential participation* in this episode. In Enfield, only three instances of unusual and unverified sensory experience (monster sightings) had occurred. With respect to mobilization, respondents reported that approximately 50–75 people converged upon Mr. M's house *after* state troopers arrived. Less than ten persons actually mobilized for the purpose of hunting the monster. Regarding mass preoccupations, virtually everyone in the community discussed the event with friends and neighbors, at various times. In short, our data reveal that the type, as well as the extent of participation, varied considerably.

We did not interpret these events as evidence that everyone "took leave of their senses" or abandoned the forms of conduct that are employed in dealing with more familiar problems. The processes of notification of events that accompanied the monster reports were analogous to the sights, sounds, and media announcements that accompany street accidents, civil disorders, sports rallys, and public meetings. Mobilization processes tended to occur in the evenings or on weekends, and involved those who were relatively unencumbered by competing institutional demands. The pervasive, community-wide, discussion of monster events during this time frame did not preclude the continuation of most preestablished, or routine, behavior. The implication of this observation is that *notification of events* and *mobilization* are more likely to disrupt routine behavior than subsequent "mass preoccupations."

The occupants of institutionalized positions traditionally are approached by locals and outsiders to determine "what is happening" in a community. Consequently, monster sighting events created major problems of accommodation for local law enforcement agencies. Nevertheless, similar "overload" problems frequently are encountered by police following disasters, spectacular crimes, or during presidential visits and holiday celebrations. An examination of formal procedures of communication seems more appropriate to this issue than the emotions allegedly generated by social contagions.

We acknowledge that peoples' behavior with respect to strange millennial movement, and reports of monsters, flying saucers, and flying saucer abductions traditionally have been assigned to the "back wards" of sociological investigation. When discussed, these events usually are casually attributed to the workings of social contagion. In contrast, we suggest that events of this order occur quite frequently in all parts of the United States, and are constituted by processes common to other more familiar social phenomena. The analysis of these processes can be considered as legitimate sociological problems, whether they are transpiring in such diverse contexts as formalized work settings, or during monster sighting episodes. We concur with one of our reviewers who notes:

> To be wrong about collective behavior....is to be wrong about society as a whole. The study of such seemingly strange events as monster sightings is important, I think, precisely because such phenomena must cause us to examine more closely our assumptions about ordinary everyday life.

REFERENCES

Blumer, Herbert. 1939. "Collective behavior." in Robert E. Park (ed), An Outline of the Principles of Sociology. New York: Barnes & Noble.

Cantril, Hadley. 1940. The Invasion From Mars. New York: Harper & Row.

Chitamber, J. B. 1973. Introductory Rural Sociology. New York: Halsted Press. John Wiley & Sons, Inc.

Couch, Carl J. 1968. "Collective behavior: An examination of some stereotypes." Social Problems 15:310–22.

Hunter, Floyd. 1963. Community Power Structure, A Study of Decision Makers. Garden City, New York: Doubleday.

Johnson, Donald M. 1945. "The 'phantom anesthetist' of Mattoon: A field study of mass hysteria." Journal of Abnormal and Social Psychology 40:175–86.

Kerckhoff, Alan C. and Kurt W. Back. 1968. The June Bug: A Study of Hysterical Contagion. New York: Appleton-Century-Crofts.

Klapp, Orin E. 1972. Currents of Unrest: An Introduction to Collective Behavior. New York: Holt, Rinehart & Winston.

Lang, Kurt and Gladys Engel Lang. 1961. Collective Dynamics. New York: Thomas Y. Crowell Co.

McPhail, S. Clark. 1971. "Civil disorder participation: A critical examination of recent research." American Sociological Review 36:1058–71.

————. and David L. Miller. 1973. "The assembling process: A theoretical and empirical examination." American Sociological Review 38: 721–35.

————. and Ernest G. Rigney. 1973. "Instructions and behavioral alterations: A reinterpretation of the 'demand characteristics' of experiments and other social encounters." Paper presented at the 1973 meetings of the Midwest Sociological Society, Milwaukee, Wisconsin.

Medalia, Nahum Z. and Otto N. Larsen. 1958. "Diffusion and belief in a collective delusion: The Seattle windshield pitting epidemic." American Sociological Review 23:180–6.

Moss, Peter D. and Colin McEvedy. 1967. "Mass hysteria." Scientific American 216 (February):58.

National Advisory Commission on Civil Disorders. 1968. Report of the National Advising Committee on Civil Disorders. Washington: U.S. Government Printing Office.

Sheatsley, Paul B. and Jacob J. Feldman. 1964. "The assassination of President Kennedy: A preliminary report on public reactions and behavior." Public Opinion Quarterly 28:189–215.

Shibutani, Tamotsu. 1966. Improvised News: A Sociological Study of Rumor. New York: Bobbs-Merrill Company, Inc.

Spilerman, Seymour. 1976. "Structural characteristics of cities and the severity of racial disorders." American Sociological Review 41:771-93.

Turner, Ralph H. 1964. "New theoretical frameworks." Sociological Quarterly:122–32.

————. and Lewis M. Killian. 1972. Collective Behavior. Englewood Cliffs: Prentice-Hall, Inc.

TAKING ANOTHER LOOK

1 To what extent does quantitative social science research tend to support the social contagion approach to collective behavior?

2 What are *assembling processes*?

3 What role did the media play in the mobilization process described in this study?

4 On what grounds do Miller, Mietus, and Mathers criticize the social contagion approach's view of the dissemination of information?

5 Which research techniques were used by Miller, Meitus, and Mathers in studying "the case of the Enfield Monster"?

The Origins of the Women's Liberation Movement

Jo Freeman

Social movements are the most all-encompassing type of collective behavior because they may include aspects of other types such as crowds, rumors, publics, and public opinion. While such factors as physical environment, population, technology, and social inequality serve as sources of change, it is the collective effort of individuals organized in social movements that ultimately leads to social change. Sociologists use the term *social movements* to refer to organized collective activities to bring about or to resist fundamental change in existing society. Herbert Blumer, a theorist of collective behavior, recognized the special importance of social movements when he defined them as "collective enterprises to establish a new order of life."

It is important to distinguish between social movements and pressure groups that may belong to a movement. For example, the civil rights movement of the 1960s consisted of many diverse groups with differing strategies for social change, including the National Association for the Advancement of Colored People (NAACP), Dr. Martin Luther King's Southern Christian Leadership Conference (SCLC), and the more radical Student Nonviolent Coordinating Committee (SNCC). Each of these groups was part of a broad social movement advocating equality and justice for blacks, yet none would be viewed as constituting a movement in itself.

In many nations, including the United States, social movements have had a dramatic impact on the course of history and the evolution of social structure. It would be naive to ignore the actions of abolitionists, suffragists, civil rights workers, and activists opposed to the war in Vietnam. Members of each social movement stepped outside traditional channels for bringing about social change and yet had a noticeable impact on American public policy. Interestingly, while taking on a "cause," activists in a social movement assume new statuses and social roles. An individual can be transformed from an "average citizen" into a well-publicized, respected, or controversial community leader.

In the following selection, first published in 1973, political scientist Jo Freeman traces the origins of the feminist movement during the late 1960s and early 1970s. Freeman points out that sociologists have given little attention to the mechanisms of how a social movement is constructed. Drawing on her own participant-observation in women's liberation activities in Chicago and on interviews with early feminist activists, Freeman traces the evolution of two important branches of the women's movement: the "older branch" (whose most prominent core group is the National Organization for Women) and the "younger branch" (which included many radicals previously active in the civil rights movement and the New Left). She concludes by identifying "four essential elements contributing to the emergence of the women's liberation movement in the mid-sixties: (1) the growth of a preexisting communications network which was (2) cooptable to the ideas of the new movement; (3) a

Author's Note: I would like to thank Richard Albares and Florence Levinsohn for having read and criticized earlier versions of this paper.

series of crises that galvanized into action people involved in this network, and/or (4) subsequent organizing effort to weld the spontaneous groups together into a movement."

The emergence in the last few years of a feminist movement caught most thoughtful observers by surprise. Women had "come a long way," had they not? What could they want to be liberated from? The new movement generated much speculation about the sources of female discontent and why it was articulated at this particular time. But these speculators usually asked the wrong questions. Most attempts to analyze the sources of social strain have had to conclude with Ferriss (1971, p. 1) that, "from the close perspective of 1970, events of the past decade provide evidence of no compelling cause of the rise of the new feminist movement." His examination of time-series data over the previous 20 years did not reveal any significant changes in socioeconomic variables which could account for the emergence of a women's movement at the time it was created. From such strain indicators, one could surmise that any time in the last two decades was as conducive as any other to movement formation.

I

The sociological literature is not of much help: the study of social movements "has been a neglected area of sociology" (Killian 1964, p. 426), and, within that field, virtually no theorists have dealt with movement origins. The *causes* of social movements have been analyzed (Gurr 1970; Davies 1962), and the *motivations* of participants have been investigated (Toch 1965; Cantril 1941; Hoffer 1951; Adorno et al. 1950; but the mechanisms of "how" a movement is constructed have received scant attention.[1] As Dahrendorf (1959, p. 64) commented, "The sociologist is generally

interested not so much in the origin of social phenomena as in their spread and rise to wider significance." This interest is derived from an emphasis on cultural processes rather than on people as the major dynamic of social change (Killian 1964, p. 426). Consequently, even the "natural history" theorists have delineated the stages of development in a way that is too vague to tell us much about how movements actually start (Dawson and Gettys 1929, pp. 787–803; Lowi 1971, p. 39; Blumer 1951; King 1956), and a theory as comprehensive as Smelser's (1963) is postulated on too abstract a level to be of microsociological value (for a good critique, see Currie and Skolnick [1970]).

Part of the problem results from extreme confusion about what a social movement really is. Movements are rarely studied as distinct social phenomena but are usually subsumed under one of two theoretical traditions: that of "collective behavior" (see, especially, Smelser 1963; Lang and Lang 1961; Turner and Killian 1957) and that of interest-group and party formation (Heberle 1951; King 1956; Lowi 1971). The former emphasizes the spontaneous aspects of a movement; and the latter, the structured ones. Yet movements are neither fully collective behavior nor incipient interest groups except in the broadest sense of these terms. Rather, they contain essential elements of both. It is "the dual imperative of spontaneity and organization [that] . . . sets them apart from pressure groups and other types of voluntary associations, which lack their spontaneity, and from mass behavior, which is altogether devoid of even the rudiments of organization" (Lang and Lang 1961, p. 497).

---

[1] "A consciously directed and organized movement cannot be explained merely in terms of the psychological disposition or motivation of people, or in terms of a diffusion of an ideology. Explanations of this sort have a deceptive plausibility, but overlook the fact that *a movement has to be constructed* and has to carve out a career in what is practically always an opposed, resistant or at least indifferent world" (Blumer 1957, p. 147; italics mine).

Recognizing with Heberle (1951, p. 8) that "movements *as such* are not organized groups," it is still the structured aspects which are more amenable to study, if not always the most salient. Turner and Killian (1957, p. 307) have argued that it is when "members of a public who share a common position concerning the issue at hand supplement their informal person-to-person discussion with some organization to promote their convictions more effectively and insure more sustained activity, a social movement is incipient" (see also Killian 1964, p. 426). Such organization(s) and other core groups of a movement not only determine much of its conscious policy but serve as foci for its values and activities. Just as it has been argued that society as a whole has a cultural and structural "center" about which most members of the society are more or less "peripheral" (Shils 1970), so, too, can a social movement be conceived of as having a center and a periphery. An investigation into a movement's origins must be concerned with the microstructural preconditions for the emergence of such a movement center. From where do the people come who make up the initial, organizing cadre of a movement? How do they come together, and how do they come to share a similar view of the world in circumstances which compel them to political action? In what ways does the nature of the original center affect the future development of the movement?

II

Most movements have very inconspicuous beginnings. The significant elements of their origins are usually forgotten or distorted by the time a trained observer seeks to trace them out, making retroactive analyses difficult. Thus, a detailed investigation of a single movement at the time it is forming can add much to what little is known about movement origins. Such an examination cannot uncover all of the conditions and ingredients of movement formation, but it can aptly illustrate both weaknesses in the theoretical literature and new directions for research. During the formative period of the women's liberation movement, I had many opportunities to observe, log, and interview most of the principals involved in the early movement.[2] The descriptive material in Section III is based on that data. This analysis, supplemented by five other origin studies made by me, would support the following three propositions:

Proposition 1: The need for a preexisting communications network or infrastructure within the social base of a movement is a primary prerequisite for "spontaneous" activity. Masses alone don't form movements, however discontented they may be. Groups of previously unorganized individuals may spontaneously form into small local associations—usually along the lines of informal social networks—in response to a specific strain or crisis, but, if they are not linked in some manner, the protest does not become generalized: it remains a local irritant or dissolves completely. If a movement is to spread rapidly, the communications network must already exist. If only the rudiments of one exist, movement formation requires a high input of "organizing" activity.

Proposition 2: Not just any communications network will do. It must be a network that is *co-optable* to the new ideas of the incipient movement.[3] To be co-optable, it must be composed of

---

[2] As a founder and participant in the younger branch of the Chicago women's liberation movement from 1967 through 1969 and editor of the first (at that time, only) national newsletter, I was able, through extensive correspondence and interviews, to keep a record of each group around the country first started, where the organizers got the idea from, who they had talked to, what conferences were held and who attended, the political affiliations (or lack of them) of the first members, etc. Although I was a member of Chicago NOW, information on the origins of it and of the other older branch organizations comes entirely through ex post facto interviews of the principals and examination of early papers in preparation for my dissertation on the women's liberation movement. Most of my informants requested that their contribution remain confidential.

[3] The only use of this significant word appears rather incidentally in Turner (1964, p. 123).

like-minded people whose background, experiences, or location in the social structure make them receptive to the ideas of a specific new movement.

Proposition 3: Given the existence of a co-optable communications network, or at least the rudimentary development of a potential one, and a situation of strain, one or more precipitants are required. Here, two distinct patterns emerge that often overlap. In one, a crisis galvanizes the network into spontaneous action in a new direction. In the other, one or more persons begin organizing a new organization or disseminating a new idea. For spontaneous action to occur, the communications network must be well formed or the initial protest will not survive the incipient stage. If it is not well formed, organizing efforts must occur; that is, one or more persons must specifically attempt to construct a movement. To be successful, organizers must be skilled and must have a fertile field in which to work. If no communications network already exists, there must at least be emerging spontaneous groups which are acutely attuned to the issue, albeit uncoordinated. To sum up, if a co-optable communications network is already established, a crisis is all that is necessary to galvanize it. If it is rudimentary, an organizing cadre of one or more persons is necessary. Such a cadre is superfluous if the former conditions fully exist, but it is essential if they do not.

Before examining these propositions in detail, let us look at the structure and origins of the women's liberation movement.

III

The women's liberation movement manifests itself in an almost infinite variety of groups, styles, and organizations. Yet, this diversity has sprung from only two distinct origins whose numerous offspring remain clustered largely around these two sources. The two branches are often called "reform" and "radical," or, as the sole authoritative book on the movement describes them, "women's rights" and "women's liberation" (Hole and Le-

vine 1971). Unfortunately, these terms actually tell us very little, since feminists do not fit into the traditional Left/Right spectrum. In fact, if an ideological typography were possible, it would show minimal consistency with any other characteristic. Structure and style rather than ideology more accurately differentiate the two branches, and, even here, there has been much borrowing on both sides.

I prefer simpler designations: the first of the branches will be referred to as the older branch of the movement, partly because it began first and partly because the median age of its activists is higher. It contains numerous organizations, including the lobbyist group (Women's Equity Action League), a legal foundation (Human Rights for Women), over 20 caucuses in professional organizations, and separate organizations of women in the professions and other occupations. Its most prominent "core group" is the National Organization for Women (NOW), which was also the first to be formed.

While the written programs and aims of the older branch span a wide spectrum, their activities tend to be concentrated on legal and economic problems. These groups are primarily made up of women—and men—who work, and they are substantially concerned with the problems of working women. The style of organization of the older branch tends to be traditionally formal, with elected officers, boards of directors, bylaws, and the other trappings of democratic procedure. All started as top-down national organizations, lacking in a mass base. Some have subsequently developed a mass base, some have not yet done so, and others do not want to.

Conversely, the younger branch consists of innumerable small groups—engaged in a variety of activities—whose contact with each other is, at best, tenuous. Contrary to popular myth, it did not begin on the campus nor was it started by the Students for a Democratic Society (SDS). However, its activators were, to be trite, on the other side of the generation gap. While few were students, all were "under 30" and had received their political education as participants or concerned observers of the social action projects of the last decade. Many came direct from New Left and civil rights organizations. Others had attended various courses on women in the multitude of free universities springing up around the country during those years.

The expansion of these groups has appeared more amoebic than organized, because the younger branch of the movement prides itself on its lack of organization. From its radical roots, it inherited the idea that structures were always conservative and confining, and leaders, isolated and elitist. Thus, eschewing structure and damning the idea of leadership, it has carried the concept of "everyone doing her own thing" to the point where communication is haphazard and coordination is almost nonexistent. The thousands of sister chapters around the country are virtually independent of each other, linked only by numerous underground papers, journals, newsletters, and cross-country travelers. A national conference was held over Thanksgiving in 1968 but, although considered successful, has not yet been repeated. Before the 1968 conference, the movement did not have the sense of national unity which emerged after the conference. Since then, young feminists have made no attempt to call another national conference. There have been a few regional conferences, but no permanent consequences resulted. At most, some cities have a coordinating committee which attempts to maintain communication among local groups and to channel newcomers into appropriate ones, but these committees have no power over any group's activities, let alone its ideas. Even local activists do not know how big the movement is in their own city. While it cannot be said to have no organization at all, this branch of the movement has informally adopted a general policy of "structurelessness."

Despite a lack of a formal policy encouraging it, there is a great deal of homogeneity within the younger branch of the movement. Like the older branch, it tends to be predominantly white, middle class, and college educated. But it is much more homogenous and, unlike the older branch, has been unable to diversify. This is largely because most small groups tend to form among friendship networks. Most groups have no requirements for membership (other than female sex), no dues, no written and agreed-upon structure, and no elected leaders. Because of this lack of structure, it is often easier for an individual to form a new group than to find and join an older one. This encourages group formation but discourages individual diversification. Even contacts among groups tend to be along friendship lines.

In general, the different style and organization of the two branches was largely derived from the different kind of political education and experiences of each group of women. Women of the older branch were trained in and had used the traditional forms of political action, while the younger branch has inherited the loose, flexible, person-oriented attitude of the youth and student movements. The different structures that have evolved from these two distinctly different kinds of experience have, in turn, largely determined the strategy of the two branches, irrespective of any conscious intentions of their participants. These different structures and strategies have each posed different problems and possibilities. Intra-movement differences are often perceived by the participants as conflicting, but it is their essential complementarity which has been one of the strengths of the movement.

Despite the multitude of differences, there are very strong similarities in the way the two branches came into being. These similarities serve to illuminate some of the microsociological factors involved in movement formation. The forces which led to NOW's formation were first set in motion in 1961 when President Kennedy established the President's Commission on the Status of Women at the behest of Esther Petersen,[4] to be

[4]Then director of the Women's Bureau.

chaired by Eleanor Roosevelt. Operating under a broad mandate, its 1963 report (*American Women*) and subsequent committee publications documented just how thoroughly women are still denied many rights and opportunities. The most concrete response to the activity of the president's commission was the eventual establishment of 50 state commissions to do similar research on a state level. These commissions were often urged by politically active women and were composed primarily of women. Nonetheless, many believe the main stimulus behind their formation was the alleged view of the governors that the commissions were excellent opportunities to pay political debts without giving women more influential positions.

The activity of the federal and state commissions laid the groundwork for the future movement in three significant ways: (1) it brought together many knowledgeable, politically active women who otherwise would not have worked together around matters of direct concern to women; (2) the investigations unearthed ample evidence of women's unequal status, especially their legal and economic difficulties, in the process convincing many previously uninterested women that something should be done; (3) the reports created a climate of expectation that something would be done. The women of the federal and state commissions who were exposed to these influences exchanged visits, correspondence, and staff and met with each other at an annual commission convention. Thus, they were in a position to share and mutually reinforce their growing awareness and concern over women's issues. These commissions thus created an embryonic communications network among people with similar concerns.

During this time, two other events of significance occurred. The first was the publication of Betty Friedan's (1963) book, *The Feminine Mystique*. An immediate best seller, it stimulated many women to question the status quo and some to suggest to Friedan that a new organization be formed to attack their problems. The second

event was the addition of "sex" to Title VII of the 1964 Civil Rights Act. Many men thought the "sex" provision was a joke (Bird 1968, chap. 1). The Equal Employment Opportunity Commission (EEOC) certainly treated it as one and refused to adequately enforce it. The first EEOC executive director even stated publicly that the provision was a "fluke" that was "conceived out of wedlock" (Edelsberg 1965). But, within the EEOC, there was a "pro-woman" coterie which argued that "sex" would be taken more seriously if there were "some sort of NAACP for women" to put pressure on the government. As government employees, they couldn't organize such a group, but they spoke privately with those whom they thought might be able to do so. One who shared their views was Rep. Martha Griffiths of Michigan. She blasted the EEOC's attitude in a June 20, 1966 speech on the House floor (Griffiths 1966) declaring that the agency had "started out by casting disrespect and ridicule on the law" but that their "wholly negative attitude had changed —for the worse."

On June 30, 1966, these three strands of incipient feminism were knotted together to form NOW. The occasion was the last day of the Third National Conference of Commissions on the Status of Women, ironically titled "Targets for Action." The participants had all received copies of Rep. Griffith's remarks. The opportunity came with a refusal by conference officials to bring to the floor a proposed resolution that urged the EEOC to give equal enforcement to the sex provision of Title VII as was given to the race provision. Despite the fact that these state commissions were not federal agencies, officials replied that one government agency could not be allowed to pressure another. The small group of women who had desired the resolution had met the night before in Friedan's hotel room to discuss the possibility of a civil rights organization for women. Not convinced of its need, they chose instead to propose the resolution. When the resolution was vetoed, the women held a whispered conversation over lunch and agreed to form an action organization "to bring women into full participation in the mainstream of American society now, assuming all the privileges and responsibilities thereof in truly equal partnership with men." The name NOW was coined by Friedan, who was at the conference researching her second book. Before the day was over, 28 women paid $5.00 each to join (Friedan 1967).

By the time the organizing conference was held the following October 29–30, over 300 men and women had become charter members. It is impossible to do a breakdown on the composition of the charter membership, but one of the first officers and board is possible. Such a breakdown accurately reflected NOW's origins. Friedan was president, two former EEOC commissioners were vice-presidents, a representative of the United Auto Workers Women's Committee was secretary-treasurer, and there were seven past and present members of the State Commissions on the Status of Women on the 20-member board. Of the charter members, 126 were Wisconsin residents—and Wisconsin had the most active state commission. Occupationally, the board and officers were primarily from the professions, labor, government, and the communications industry. Of these, only those from labor had any experience in organizing, and they resigned a year later in a dispute over support of the Equal Rights Amendment. Instead of organizational expertise, what the early NOW members had was media experience, and it was here that their early efforts were aimed.

As a result, NOW often gave the impression of being larger than it was. It was highly successful in getting publicity, much less so in bringing about concrete changes or organizing itself. Thus, it was not until 1969, when several national news media simultaneously decided to do major stories on the women's liberation movement, that NOW's membership increased significantly. Even today, there are only 8,000 members, and the chapters are still in an incipient stage of development.

In the meantime, unaware of and unknown to

NOW, the EEOC, or to the state commissions, younger women began forming their own movement. Here, too, the groundwork had been laid some years before. Social action projects of recent years had attracted many women, who were quickly shunted into traditional roles and faced with the self-evident contradiction of working in a "freedom movement" without being very free. No single "youth movement" activity or organization is responsible for the younger branch of the women's liberation movement; together they created a "radical community" in which like-minded people continually interacted with each other. This community consisted largely of those who had participated in one or more of the many protest activities of the sixties and had established its own ethos and its own institutions. Thus, the women in it thought of themselves as "movement people" and had incorporated the adjective "radical" into their personal identities. The values of their radical identity and the style to which they had been trained by their movement participation directed them to approach most problems as political ones which could be solved by organizing. What remained was to translate their individual feelings of "unfreedom" into a collective consciousness. Thus, the radical community provided not only the necessary network of communication; its radical ideas formed the framework of analysis which "explained" the dismal situation in which radical women found themselves.

Papers had been circulated on women,[5] and temporary women's caucuses had been held as early as 1964, when Stokely Carmichael made his infamous remark that "the only position for women in SNCC is prone." But it was not until late 1967 and 1968 that the groups developed a determined, if cautious, continuity and began to consciously expand themselves. At least five groups in five different cities (Chicago, Toronto, Detroit, Seattle, and Gainesville, Florida) formed sponta-

---

[5] "A Kind of Memo," by Hayden and King (1966, p. 35) circulated in the fall of 1965 (and eventually published), was the first such paper.

neously, independent of each other. They came at a very auspicious moment. The year 1967 was the one in which the blacks kicked the whites out of the civil rights movement, student power had been discredited by SDS, and the organized New Left was on the wane. Only draft-resistance activities were on the increase, and this movement more than any other exemplified the social inequities of the sexes. Men could resist the draft; women could only counsel resistance.

What was significant about this point in time was that there was a lack of available opportunities for political work. Some women fit well into the "secondary role" of draft counseling. Many did not. For years, their complaints of unfair treatment had been ignored by movement men with the dictum that those things could wait until after the revolution. Now these movement women found time on their hands, but the men would still not listen.

A typical example was the event which precipitated the formation of the Chicago group, the first independent group in this country. At the August 1967 National Conference for New Politics convention, a women's caucus met for days but was told its resolution wasn't significant enough to merit a floor discussion. By threatening to tie up the convention with procedural motions, the women succeeded in having their statement tacked to the end of the agenda. It was never discussed. The chair refused to recognize any of the many women standing by the microphone, their hands straining upward. When he instead called on someone to speak on "the forgotten American, the American Indian," five women rushed the podium to demand an explanation. But the chairman just patted one of them on the head (literally) and told her, "Cool down little girl. We have more important things to talk about than women's problems."

The "little girl" was Shulamith Firestone, future author of *The Dialectic of Sex* (1971), and she didn't cool down. Instead, she joined with another Chicago woman, who had been trying to organize a women's group that summer, to call a meeting of those women who had half-heartedly attended the summer meetings. Telling their stories to those women, they stimulated sufficient rage to carry the group for three months, and by that time it was a permanent institution.

Another somewhat similar event occurred in Seattle the following winter. At the University of Washington, an SDS organizer was explaining to a large meeting how white college youth established rapport with the poor whites with whom they were working. "He noted that sometimes after analyzing societal ills, the men shared leisure time by 'balling a chick together.' He pointed out that such activities did much to enhance the political consciousness of the poor white youth. A woman in the audience asked, 'And what did it do for the consciousness of the chick?'" (Hole and Levine 1971, p. 120). After the meeting, a handful of enraged women formed Seattle's first group.

Groups subsequent to the initial five were largely organized rather than emerging spontaneously out of recent events. In particular, the Chicago group was responsible for the creation of many new groups in that city and elsewhere and started the first national newsletter. The 1968 conference was organized by the Washington D.C. group from resources provided by the Center for Policy Studies (CPS), a radical research organization. Using CPS facilities, this group subsequently became a main literature-distribution center. Although New York groups organized early and were featured in the 1969–70 media blitz, New York was not a source of early organizers.[6]

---

[6] The movement in New York has been more diverse than other cities and has made many major ideological contributions, but, contrary to popular belief, it did not begin in New York. In putting together their stories, the news media, concentrated as they are in New York, rarely looked past the Hudson for their information. This eastern bias is exemplified by the fact that, although the younger branch of the movement has no national organization and abjures leadership, all but one of those women designated by the press as movement leaders live in New York.

Unlike NOW, the women in the first groups had had years of experience as local-level organizers. They did not have the resources, or the desire, to form a national organization, but they knew how to utilize the infrastructure of the radical community, the underground press, and the free universities to disseminate ideas on women's liberation. Chicago, as a center of New Left activity, had the largest number of politically conscious organizers. Many traveled widely to Left conferences and demonstrations, and most used the opportunity to talk with other women about the new movement. In spite of public derision by radical men, or perhaps because of it, young women steadily formed new groups around the country.

Initially, the new movement found it hard to organize on the campus, but, as a major congregating area of women and, in particular, of women with political awareness, campus women's liberation groups eventually became ubiquitous. While the younger branch of the movement never formed any organization larger or more extensive than a city-wide coordinating committee, it would be fair to say that it has a larger "participationship" than NOW and the other older branch organizations. While the members of the older branch knew how to use the media and how to form national structures, the women of the younger branch were skilled in local community organizing.

IV

From this description, there appear to be four essential elements contributing to the emergence of the women's liberation movement in the mid-sixties: (1) the growth of a preexisting communications network which was (2) co-optable to the ideas of the new movement; (3) a series of crises that galvanized into action people involved in this network, and/or (4) subsequent organizing effort to weld the spontaneous groups together into a movement. To further understand these factors, let us examine them in detail with reference to other relevant studies.

1 Both the Commissions on the Status of Women and the "radical community" created a communications network through which those women initially interested in creating an organization could easily reach others. Such a network had not previously existed among women. Historically tied to the family and isolated from their own kind, women are perhaps the most organizationally underdeveloped social category in Western civilization. By 1950, the 19th-century organizations which had been the basis of the suffrage movement—the Women's Trade Union League, the General Federation of Women's Clubs, the Women's Christian Temperance Union, the National American Women's Suffrage Association—were all either dead or a pale shadow of their former selves. The closest exception was the National Women's Party (NWP), which has remained dedicated to feminist concerns since its inception in 1916. However, since 1923, it has been essentially a lobbying group for the Equal Rights Amendment. The NWP, having always believed that a small group of women concentrating their efforts in the right places was more effective than a mass appeal, was not appalled that, as late as 1969, even the majority of avowed feminists in this country had never heard of the NWP or the ERA.

References to the salience of a preexisting communications network appear frequently in the case studies of social movements, but it has been given little attention in the theoretical literature. It is essentially contrary to the mass-society theory which "for many . . . is . . . the most pertinent and comprehensive statement of the genesis of modern mass movements" (Pinard 1968, p. 682). This theory hypothesizes that those most likely to join a mass movement are those who are atomized and isolated from "a structure of groups intermediate between the family and the nation" (Kornhauser 1959, p. 93). However, the lack of such intermediate structures among women has proved more of a hindrance than a help in movement formation. Even today, it is those women who are most atomized, the housewives, who are least likely to join a feminist group.

The most serious attack on mass-society theory was made by Pinard (1971) in his study of the Social Credit Party of Quebec. He concluded that intermediate structures exerted *mobilizing* as well as restraining effects on individuals' participation in social movements because they formed communications networks that assisted in the rapid spread of new ideas. "When strains are severe and widespread," he contended, "a new movement is more likely to meet its early success among the more strongly integrated citizens" (Pinard 1971, p. 192).

Other evidence also attests to the role of previously organized networks in the rise and spread of a social movement. According to Buck (1920, pp. 43–44), the Grange established a degree of organization among American farmers in the 19th century which greatly facilitated the spread of future farmers' protests. In Saskatchewan, Lipset (1959) has asserted, "The rapid acceptance of new ideas and movements . . . can be attributed mainly to the high degree of organization. . . . The role of the social structure of the western wheat belt in facilitating the rise of new movements has never been sufficiently appreciated by historians and sociologists. Repeated challenges and crises forced the western farmers to create many more community institutions . . . than are necessary in a more stable area. These groups in turn provided a structural basis for immediate action in critical situations. [Therefore] though it was a new radical party, the C.C.F. did not have to build up an organization from scratch." More recently, the civil rights movement was built upon the infrastructure of the Southern black church (King 1958), and early SDS organizers made ready use of the National Student Association (Kissinger and Ross 1968, p. 16).

Indirect evidence of the essential role of formal and informal communications networks is found in diffusion theory, which emphasizes the importance of personal interaction rather than imper-

sonal media communication in the spread of ideas (Rogers 1962; Lionberger 1960), and in Coleman's (1957) investigations of prior organizations in the initial development of conflict.

Such preexisting communications networks appear to be not merely valuable but prerequisites, as one study on "The Failure of an Incipient Social Movement" (Jackson, Peterson, Bull, Monsen, and Richmond 1960) made quite clear. In 1957, a potential tax-protest movement in Los Angeles generated considerable interest and public notice for a little over a month but was dead within a year. According to the authors, its failure to sustain itself beyond initial spontaneous protest was largely due to "the lack of a pre-existing network of communications linking those groups of citizens most likely to support the movement" (Jackson et al. 1960, p. 40). They said (p. 37) that "if a movement is to grow rapidly, it cannot rely upon its own network of communications, but must capitalize on networks already in existence."

The development of the women's liberation movement highlights the salience of such a network precisely because the conditions for a movement existed *before* a network came into being, but the movement didn't exist until afterward. Socioeconomic strain did not change for women significantly during a 20-year period. It was as great in 1955 as in 1965. What changed was the organizational situation. It was not until a communications network developed among like-minded people beyond local boundaries that the movement could emerge and develop past the point of occasional, spontaneous uprising.

2 However, not just any network would do; it had to be one which was co-optable by the incipient movement because it linked like-minded people likely to be predisposed to the new ideas of the movement. The 180,000-member Federation of Business and Professional Women's (BPW) Clubs would appear to be a likely base for a new feminist movement but in fact was unable to assume this role. It had steadily lobbied for legislation of importance to women, yet as late as "1966 BPW rejected a number of suggestions that it redefine . . . goals and tactics and become a kind of 'NAACP for women' . . . out of fear of being labeled 'feminist' " (Hole and Levine 1971, p. 81). While its membership has become a recruiting ground for feminism, it could not initially overcome the ideological barrier to a new type of political action.

On the other hand, the women of the President's and State Commissions on the Status of Women and the feminist coterie of the EEOC were co-optable, largely because their immersion into the facts of female status and the details of sex-discrimination cases made them very conscious of the need for change. Likewise, the young women of the "radical community" lived in an atmosphere of questioning, confrontation, and change. They absorbed an ideology of "freedom" and "liberation" far more potent than any latent "antifeminism" might have been. The repeated contradictions between these ideas and the actions of their male colleagues created a compulsion for action which only required an opportunity to erupt. This was provided by the "vacuum of political activity" of 1967–68.

The nature of co-optability is much more difficult to elucidate. Heretofore, it has been dealt with only tangentially. Pinard (1971, p. 186) noted the necessity for groups to "*possess* or *develop* an ideology or simply subjective interests congruent with that of a new movement" for them to "act as mobilizing rather than restraining agents toward that movement" but did not further explore what affected the "primary group climate." More illumination is provided by the diffusion of innovation studies which point out the necessity for new ideas to fit in with already-established norms for changes to happen easily. Furthermore, a social system which has as a value "innovativeness" itself (as the radical community did) will more rapidly adopt ideas than one which looks upon the habitual performance of traditional practices as the ideal (as most organized women's groups did in the fifties). Usually, as Lionberger (1960, p. 91) points out, "people act in terms of past experience and knowledge." People who have

had similar experiences are likely to share similar perceptions of a situation and to mutually reinforce those perceptions as well as their subsequent interpretation.

A co-optable network, therefore, is one whose members have had common experiences which predispose them to be receptive to the particular new ideas of the incipient movement and who are not faced with structural or ideological barriers to action. If the new movement as an "innovation" can interpret these experiences and perceptions in ways that point out channels for social action, then participation in social movement becomes the logical thing to do.

3 As our examples have illustrated, these similar perceptions must be translated into action. This is the role of the "crisis." For women of the older branch of the movement, the impetus to organize was the refusal of the EEOC to enforce the sex provision of Title VII, precipitated by the concomitant refusal of federal officials at the conference to allow a supportive resolution. For younger women, there were a series of minor crises. Such precipitating events are common to most movements. They serve to crystallize and focus discontent. From their own experiences, directly and concretely, people feel the need for change in a situation that allows for an exchange of feelings with others, mutual validation, and a subsequent reinforcement of innovative interpretation. Perception of an immediate need for change is a major factor in predisposing people to accept new ideas (Rogers 1962, p. 280). Nothing makes desire for change more acute than a crisis. If the strain is great enough, such a crisis need not be a major one; it need only embody symbolically collective discontent.

4 However, a crisis will only catalyze a well-formed communications network. If such networks are only embryonically developed or only partially co-optable, the potentially active individuals in them must be linked together by someone. As Jackson et al. (1960, p. 37) stated, "Some protest may persist where the source of trouble is constantly present. But interest ordinarily cannot be maintained unless there is a welding of spontaneous groups into some stable organization." In other words, people must be organized. Social movements do not simply occur.

The role of the organizer in movement formation is another neglected aspect of the theoretical literature. There has been great concern with leadership, but the two roles are distinct and not always performed by the same individual. In the early stages of a movement, it is the organizer much more than any "leader" who is important, and such an individual or cadre must often operate behind the scenes.[7] Certainly, the "organizing cadre" that young women in the radical community came to be was key to the growth of that branch of the women's liberation movement, despite the fact that no "leaders" were produced (and were actively discouraged). The existence of many leaders but no organizers in the older branch of the women's liberation movement and its subsequent slow development would tend to substantiate this hypothesis.

The crucial function of the organizer has been explored indirectly in other areas of sociology. Rogers (1962) devotes many pages to the "change agent" who, while he does not necessarily weld a group together or "construct" a movement, does do many of the same things for agricultural innovation that an organizer does for political change. Mass-society theory makes reference to the "agitator" but fails to do so in any kind of truly informative way. A study of farmer's movements indicates that many core organizations were organized by a single individual before the spontaneous aspects of the movement predominated. Further, many other core groups were subsidized by older organizations, federal and state governments, and even by local businessmen (Salisbury 1969, p. 13). These organizations often served as training centers for organizers and sources of material support to aid in the formation of new interest groups and movements.

Similarly, the civil rights movement provided the training for many another movement's organizers, including the young women of the women's liberation movement. It would appear that the art of "constructing" a social movement is something that requires considerable skill and experience. Even in the supposedly spontaneous social movement, the professional is more valuable than the amateur. . . .

REFERENCES

Adorno, L. W., et al. 1950. *The Authoritarian Personality.* New York: Harper.

Bird, Caroline. 1968. *Born Female: The High Cost of Keeping Women Down.* New York: David, McKay.

Blumer, Herbert. 1951. "Social Movements." In *New Outline of the Principles of Sociology.* edited by A. M. Lee. New York: Barnes & Noble.

————. 1957. "Collective Behavior." *Review of Sociology: Analysis of a Decade,* edited by Joseph B. Gittler. New York: Wiley.

Buck, Solon J. *The Agrarian Crusade.* 1920. New Haven, Conn.: Yale University Press.

Cantril, Hadley. 1941. *The Psychology of Social Movements.* New York: Wiley.

Coleman, James. 1957. *Community Conflict.* Glencoe, Ill.: Free Press.

Currie, Elliott, and Jerome H. Skolnick. 1970. "A Critical Note on Conceptions of Collective Behavior." *Annals of the American Academy of Political and Social Science* 391 (September): 34–45.

Dahrendorf, Ralf. 1959. *Class and Class Conflict in Industrial Society.* Palo Alto, Calif: Stanford University Press.

Davies, James C. 1962. "Toward A Theory of Revolution." *American Sociological Review* 27 (1): 5–19.

Dawson, C. A., and W. E. Gettys. 1929. *An Introduction to Sociology.* New York: Ronald.

Edelsberg, Herman. 1965. "N.Y.U. 18th Conference on Labor." *Labor Relations Reporter* 61 (August): 253–55.

---

[7] The nature and function of these two roles was most clearly evident in the Townsend old-age movement of the thirties. Townsend was the "charismatic" leader, but the movement was organized by his partner, real estate promoter Robert Clements. Townsend himself acknowledges that, without Clement's help, the movement would never have gone beyond the idea stage (see Holzman 1963).

Ferriss, Abbott L. 1971. *Indicators of Trends in the Status of American Women.* New York: Russell Sage.

Firestone, Shulamith. 1971. *The Dialectic of Sex.* New York: Morrow.

Friedan, Betty. 1963. *The Feminine Mystique.* New York: Dell.

———. 1967. "N.O.W.: How It Began." *Women Speaking* (April).

Griffiths, Martha. 1966. Speech of June 20, *Congressional Record.*

Gurr, Ted. 1970. *Why Men Rebel.* Princeton, N.J.: Princeton University Press.

Hayden, Casey, and Mary King. 1966. "A Kind of Memo." *Liberation* (April).

Heberle, Rudolph. 1951. *Social Movements.* New York: Appleton-Century-Crofts.

Hoffer, Eric. 1951. *The True Believer.* New York: Harper.

Hole, Judith, and Ellen Levine. 1971. *Rebirth of Feminism.* New York: Quadrangle.

Holzman, Abraham. 1963. *The Townsend Movement: A Political Study.* New York: Bookman.

Jackson, Maurice, Eleanora Petersen, James Bull, Sverre Monsen, and Patricia Richmond. "The Failure of an Incipient Social Movement." *Pacific Sociological Reivew 3,* no. 1 (Spring): 40.

Killian, Lewis M. 1964. "Social Movements." In *Handbook of Modern Sociology,* edited by R. E. L. Faris. Chicago: Rand McNally.

King, C. Wendell, 1956. *Social Movements in the United States.* New York: Random House.

King, Martin Luther, Jr. 1958. *Stride toward Freedom.* New York: Harper.

Kissinger, C. Clark, and Bob Ross. 1968. "Starting in '60: Or From SLID to Resistance." *New Left Notes,* June 10.

Kornhauser, William. 1959. *The Politics of Mass Society.* Glencoe, Ill.: Free Press.

Lang, Kurt, and Gladys Engle Lang. 1961. *Collective Dynamics.* New York: Cromwell.

Lionberger, Herbert F. 1960. *Adoption of New Ideas and Practices.* Ames: Iowa State University Press.

Lipset, Seymour M. *Agrarian Socialism.* Berkeley: University of California Press, 1959.

Lowi, Theodore J. 1971. *The Politics of Disorder.* New York: Basic.

Pinard, Maurice. 1968. "Mass Society and Political Movements: A New Formulation." *American Journal of Sociology* 73, no. 6 (May): 682–90.

———. 1971. *The Rise of a Third Party: A Study in Crisis Politics.* Englewood Cliffs, N.J.: Prentice-Hall.

Rogers, Everett M. 1962. *Diffusion of Innovations.* New York: Free Press.

Salisbury, Robert H. 1969. "An Exchange Theory of Interest Groups." *Midwest Journal of Political Science,* vol. 13, no. 1 (February).

Shils, Edward. 1970. "Center and Periphery." in *Selected Essays.* Center for Social Organization Studies. Department of Sociology, University of Chicago.

Smelser, Neil J. 1963. *Theory of Collective Behavior.* Glencoe, Ill.: Free Press.

Toch, Hans. 1965. *The Social Psychology of Social Movements.* Indianapolis: Bobbs-Merrill.

Turner, Ralph H. 1964. "Collective Behavior and Conflict: New Theoretical Frameworks." *Sociological Quarterly.*

Turner, Ralph H., and Lewis M. Killian. 1957. *Collective Behavior.* Englewood Cliffs, N.J.: Prentice-Hall.

TAKING ANOTHER LOOK

1 Summarize Freeman's critique of the sociological literature that focuses on social movements.

2 How did the "older branch" of the early women's liberation movement differ from the "younger branch"?

3 How did the activities of federal and state commissions lay the groundwork for the women's liberation movement?

4 On what grounds is Freeman critical of mass-society theory?

5 According to Freeman, what factors make a preexisting communications network "cooptable" to the ideas of a new social movement?

6 According to Freeman, what is the role of the "crisis" in the evolution of a social movement?

Resistance and Social Movements

James W. Vander Zanden

Efforts to promote social change are likely to be met with resistance. Almost inevitably, powerful individuals and groups in a society have a vested interest in opposing change. (Social economist Thorstein Veblen coined the term *vested interests* to refer to those persons or groups who will suffer in the event of social change.) While members of a social movement attempt to mobilize their resources, the powerful do the same—and often have more money, more political influence, and greater access to the media.

In the following selection, written in the late 1950s, sociologist James W. Vander Zanden focuses on resistance to social change and emphasizes that "movement frequently begets countermovement." Vander Zanden criticizes traditional definitions of the term *social movement* that automatically exclude movements resisting social change. Through examination of the southern white resistance movement to school integration, which arose following the Supreme Court's 1954 desegregation ruling, he suggests that such countermovements should indeed be viewed as social movements because of their efforts to preserve the status quo and *prevent* social change.

Sociologists and anthropologists have long been interested in the tenacity of culture and its slowness to change. Representative of this concern are Tylor's "survivals," Bagehot's "cake of custom," Tönnies' "sitte," Sumner's "mores and folkways," Boas' "cultural inertia," and Ogburn's "cultural lag." Common to these concepts is the notion that once a pattern of social relationships has been established, it tends to carry on unchanged, except as the dynamics of other social forces operate to undermine it.

Closely associated with the study of cultural persistence is the study of resistance to social change. The one, however, should not be confused with the other. Resistance is not simply a function of cultural persistence. Resistance implies behavior on the part of some or all of the members of society, either passive or active, which is directed toward the rejection or circumvention of a social change.

Except perhaps for Bernhard J. Stern in his studies of resistance to medical and technological change,[1] writers have concerned themselves with resistance primarily as a by-product of other work and interests. Thus Veblen and Marx in their respective analyses of "vested interests" and the "bourgeoisie" treated resistance to social change as it originated from particular groups within soci-

[1]Bernhard J. Stern, *Social Factors in Medical Progress* (New York: Columbia University Press, 1927); Bernhard J. Stern, "Resistance to the Adoption of Technological Innovations," in *Technological Trends and National Policy*, Report of the Subcommittee on Technology to the National Resources Committee (Washington: Government Printing Office, 1937), pp. 39–66; and Bernhard J. Stern, *Society and Medical Progress* (Princeton: Princeton University Press,

1941). In these works Stern is primarily concerned with the social factors impeding medical and technological progress. Theodore K. Noss has sought to apply the Stern analysis in the resistance to social innovations. See: Theodore K. Noss , Resistance to Social Innovations as Found in the Literature Regarding Innovations which Have Proved Successful (unpublished doctoral dissertation, University of Chicago, Chicago, 1940).

Author's note: I have profited considerably in discussing the ideas in this paper with Dr. Guy B. Johnson and Dr. Rupert B. Vance of the University of North Carolina.

ety. There have also appeared various descriptive accounts of social movements with a predominantly resistance orientation.[2] And some aspects of nativistic phenomena studied by anthropologists have possessed characteristics of resistance movements.[3] However, in most nativistic movements the revivalistic rather than the perpetualistic component appears to be the dominant theme, e.g., the Ghost Dance among the Plains Indians.[4]

Unfortunately sociologists in the field of social movements have tended to neglect these materials and the phenomenon of resistance in their studies. "Social movement" traditionally has been defined in a manner which would automatically exclude movements resisting social change. This has been the product of either explicitly or implicitly treating social movements as agencies seeking to bring about social change, often of a fundamental sort.[5] Thus the work which has emerged in the field is a study of reformistic and revolutionary movements.

Representative of the reformistic orientation are the following concepts of a social movement:

The main criterion of a social movement. . . .is that it aims to bring about *fundamental changes in the social order,* especially in the basic institutions of property and labor relationships.—*Rudolf Heberle.*[6]

Social movements can be viewed as collective enterprises to establish a new order of life.—*Herbert Blumer.*[7]

. . . a social movement is circumscribed by pluristic behavior functioning as organized mass-effort directed toward *a change of established folkways or institutions.—Theodore Abel.*[8]

. . . social movements may be distinguished from other phenomena on the basis of the kind of goal to which they are committed. Unlike social institutions, their purpose is *change,* whether of relationships, norms, beliefs, or all of these. . . . But without some change in view there is no social movement.— *C. Wendell King.*[9]

To narrow the concept of a social movement in this manner is to preclude an area of fruitful research and to close the door upon a good deal of the social dynamics in movement and social change. In fact, the study of social movement within such a context becomes to a considerable degree sterile. Little more is involved than a struggle on the part of the reform effort to overcome cultural persistence. Very often there is more involved than the mere tenacity of culture. Movement frequently begets countermovement. Between the two a dynamic interrelation occurs.

In short, social movements do not initiate social change merely because they arise. They often stimulate the rise of movements opposed to the change, and between the two a more or less prolonged struggle takes place. Thus in order to understand the ultimate outcome, itself a transitory phase, it is not enough to study the change-

---

[2] See for example: Guy B. Johnson, "A Sociological Interpretation of the New Ku Klux Movement," *The Journal of Social Forces,* 1 (May 1923), pp. 440–45.

[3] Ralph Linton, "Nativistic Movements," *American Anthropologist* (n.s.), 45 (April–June 1943), pp. 230–40.

[4] Bernard Barber, "Acculturation and Messianic Movements," *American Sociological Review,* 6 (October 1941), pp. 663–69; Alexander Lesser, *The Pawnee Ghost Dance Hand Game* (New York: Columbia University Press, 1933); and Melville J. Herskovits, *Acculturation* (New York: J. J. Augustin Publisher, 1938), pp. 75–103.

[5] Some writers also include here the effort to revive or restore social forms that have existed in the past. See, for example, Seba Eldridge and Associates, *Fundamentals of Sociology* (New York: Thomas Y. Crowell Company, 1950), pp. 426–7. But to revive or restore a moribund mode is quite different from the effort to preserve and prevent changes in

existing patterns and institutions.

[6] Rudolf Heberle, *Social Movements* (New York: Appleton-Century-Crofts, Inc., 1951), p. 6. Italics mine.

[7] Herbert Blumer, "Social Movements," in A. M. Lee (ed.), *New Outline of the Principles of Sociology* (New York: Barnes & Noble, 1946), p. 199. Italics mine.

[8] Theodore Abel, "The Pattern of a Successful Political Movement," in Logan Wilson and William L. Kolb, *Sociological Analysis* (New York: Harcourt, Brace and Company, 1949), p. 828. Italics mine.

[9] C. Wendell King, *Social Movements in the United States* (New York: Random House, 1956), pp. 25–6. For other similar concepts see Eldridge and Associates, *op. cit.,* pp. 425–6; Hans Gerth and C. Wright Mills, *Character and Social Structure* (New York: Harcourt, Brace and Company, 1953), p. 438; and Arnold W. Green, *Sociology* (2nd ed.; New York: McGraw-Hill Book Company, 1956), p. 530.

oriented movement. A study of the countermovement and the resultant interaction of the movements is essential to such analysis.

Countermovement frequently influences the speed, degree, and nature of the social change. In fact as a consequence of the interaction between the movements and the processes which flow from it, the net result or product is rarely the complete fulfillment of the goal or goals of the parties involved. In some instances the outcome is totally different from the originally conceived goals, i.e., it is not a mere quantitative mixing of aspects of the opposing programs but a completely new qualitative entity. Likewise the resistance often serves to gradualize the process of social change. In so doing it functions to prevent sharp and sudden social dislocations within a society and to provide for a less traumatic or precipitous transition and adjustment to the new.

Illustrative of the phenomena of movement and countermovement is the southern white resistance movement to integration which arose following the Supreme Court's May 17, 1954, school desegregation ruling. It is a countermovement which has arisen in defense of southern race patterns in the wake of the challenge from the integration movement, a movement which in its organized aspect includes the National Association for the Advancement of Colored People, the united AFL-CIO labor movement, the nation's major church bodies (although a few southern denominations are at most only lukewarm supporters), the major political parties through their platform statements and the declarations of their spokesmen, various minority organizations such as B'nai B'rith, many civic organizations, and probably most formidable of all, the federal government via the national administration and the judiciary.

Some may question whether the southern white resistance in fact constitutes a social movement. In dealing with this matter the most satis-

factory and definitive criteria of a social movement are probably those which can be abstracted from Rudolf Heberle's work.[10] They are the following:

1 "... it aims to bring about fundamental changes in the social order, especially in the basic institutions of property and labor relationships."

2 A consciousness of group identity and solidarity is necessary along with an awareness of common sentiments and goals.

3 It is "always integrated by a set of constitutive ideas, or an ideology ..."

4 They contain among their members groups that are formally organized, but the movements *as such* are not organized groups.

5 "... they are, as a rule, large enough to continue their existence even if there should be a change in the composition of the membership."

6 They are not short-lived but have duration.

Let us apply these criteria to the present southern white resistance. First, Heberle's "main criterion"[11] is that a social movement aims to bring about fundamental changes in the social order. This criterion of course is not met by the southern white resistance. Some may argue, however, that it is applicable, there being merely a question of semantics at issue. Thus it may be argued that in effect the southern whites are seeking to alter the *status quo,* i.e., the Supreme Court school ruling constitutes for the nation the new *status quo,* a *status quo* which the South is attempting to overturn.

But to argue in this manner is to obscure the picture and to lose sight of what is actually taking place. First, segregation *is* the pattern of race relations in the South and the Court's ruling where effected will *alter* this pattern, i.e., in some areas one will find desegregated schools. Secondly, the southern movement is essentially "resistance" oriented. This is how it conceives of itself and in turn is perceived by the nation.[12]

---

[10] Heberle, *op. cit.,* pp. 6, 7, 8, 11, 269.

[11] *Ibid.,* p. 6.

[12] Frequent use is made of the terms "resist" and "resis-

tance" by white southerners in speeches, resolutions, publications, articles, etc.

The second feature suggested by Heberle is that a social movement possesses a consciousness of group identity and solidarity along with an awareness of common sentiments and goals. Involved here is the existence of a "we-feeling" among the members of the movement. Without making an attempt to delineate any degree of the intensity of the "we-feeling,"[13] the southern white resistance qualifies as a social movement under this criterion on two counts: first, the consciousness of identity and solidarity of the white southerner as a "white" distinguished from the subordinately defined "Negro" and the awareness of the common goal of preserving white supremacy; and secondly, the consciousness of identity and solidarity of the white southerner as a "Southerner" distinguished from the "Yankee" and the awareness of the common goal of "defending the southern way of life." The struggles waged in the past four years by the South, together with a number of sharp, well-publicized encounters between the forces of integration and segregation have undoubtedly served to intensify and heighten this southern white consciousness and awareness. Its highest form of expression has been in the organized activities of southern governmental leaders and resistance organizations.

Heberle's third criterion of a social movement is that it possesses an ideology. The body of ideas giving the southern white resistance its intellectual and ideological cohesion revolve about the Negro (white supremacy) and states' rights. It is epitomized by the two mottoes found in the emblem of the Citizens Councils: "STATES RIGHTS —RACIAL INTEGRITY."

The fourth characteristic is that although containing groups which are formally organized, the movement as such is not an organized group. More than 90 resistance organizations[14] have sprung up in the South in the wake of the Supreme Court ruling, some such as the Mississippi Association of Citizens Councils claiming 65 chapters and 80,000 members. But the movement is more inclusive than organized groups in the customary usage of the term, i.e., structured, formalized organizations. Included have been a wide variety of activities ranging from the legal maneuverings of state governors and legislators to mass petition signings and letters to the editors.

With regard to Heberle's fifth characteristic, size, the southern resistance again qualifies as a social movement. The resistance forces are large enough to continue the movement's existence even if there should be a change in the composition of the membership. Technically "membership" here could be construed to be applicable to only the organized aspects of the movement, but to do so would seem to be contradictory to the fourth feature. Here the question of sufficient size will be interpreted to mean that there is a collective effort on the part of a *considerable number of persons within a given society* to deal with a situation which they perceive to be a problem and that this number is sufficient to give the movement durability. In this instance the southern white resistance is a regional movement with deep historical roots and traditions embracing wide sections of its white population.

Finally, according to Heberle, a social movement is not short-lived but has duration, a feature closely related to the previous one. The present resistance qualifies with regard to this criterion on two counts. First, the movement is already four-and-a-half-years old and gives every promise of continuing vitality in the years ahead. Second, the present resistance cannot be divorced from its history with roots extending to the foundation of our nation. It can best be understood as merely one

---

[13] Heberle never makes the degree explicit although he cites one reason for excluding "short-lived group actions, such as a 'wildcat strike,' a race riot or *coup d'etat*" from the social movement category as lacking a sufficient "intensity of the we-feeling." Rudolf Heberle, "Observations on the Sociology of Social Movements," *American Sociological Review,* 14 (June 1949), p. 350.

[14] James W. Vander Zanden, The Southern White Resistance Movement to Integration (unpublished doctoral dissertation, University of North Carolina, Chapel Hill, 1958), pp. 437–40.

episode in a social movement embracing some 150 years. During this time it has gone through many forms in terms of organized expressions, issues, tactics, and leadership. Over the years it has repeatedly risen and ebbed. But knitting the whole together over time have been the two central questions: the Negro and states' rights.

Thus the southern white resistance qualifies as a social movement with regard to all Heberle's criteria but the first, namely it does not seek to *initiate* social change. But if a social movement is defined and approached exclusively in terms of its altering the *status quo*, what is to be done with those "movements" which seek to preserve the *status quo*? It is suggested that a more satisfactory definition of a social movement would be the following: *A social movement is a more or less persistent and organized effort on the part of a considerable number of members of a given society either to change a situation which they define as unsatisfactory or to prevent change in a situation which they define as satisfactory.*

The southern white resistance which has developed in the past few years and its historical predecessors probably are not unique or peculiar phenomena. A scanning of the pages of history reveal many others, e.g., the movement in opposition to the Roosevelt New Deal, the bootlegging and speak-easy movement during Prohibition, and the resistance movements in Nazi-occupied countries.

It should be noted that occasionally movements begin with a predominantly resistance orientation but as time progresses, particularly as a consequence of the dynamic interplay of movement and countermovement, become transformed into offensive, anti-*status quo* movements. This appears to be especially characteristic of nationalistic movements. Thus, for example, such Irish secret societies of the seventeenth, eighteenth, and early nineteenth centuries as the Defenders, White Boys, and Ribbonmen, oriented toward resistance of various British colonial measures and to the abuses of British landlords, were the precursors of the Irish independence movement represented organizationally by groups such as the Irish Republican Brotherhood, Fenians and Sinn Fein. By the same token, anti-*status quo* movements may have become transformed into movements with considerable defensive, resistance qualities as witness the case of the Hungarian Communists, especially during late 1956 and early 1957.

The study of resistance to social change is undoubtedly one which offers great promise for further sociological research and study. In a world characterized by tremendous social change and upheavals, in which the dynamics of movement and countermovement have become increasingly inescapable in their day-by-day consequences, it becomes a phenomenon with a growing challenge for sociologists.

TAKING ANOTHER LOOK

1 According to Vander Zanden, why is the study of countermovements essential in analyzing the struggle for social change?

2 Summarize the six criteria of a social movement that Vander Zanden abstracts from the work of Rudolf Heberle.

3 According to Vander Zanden, does the southern white resistance movement qualify as a social movement with regard to Heberle's criteria? Discuss.

4 In Vander Zanden's view, how should sociologists define the term *social movement*?

5 How might functionalist theorists be likely to view the existence of countermovements dedicated to resisting social change?

6 How might conflict theorists be likely to view the existence of countermovements dedicated to resisting social change?

The American Family in the Year 2000

Andrew Cherlin and Frank F. Furstenberg, Jr.

Sociologist William F. Ogburn prepared a report in 1934 for a Presidential
Research Committee on Social Trends that dealt with the effects of social
change on the functions of the family. Ogburn pointed out that many functions
once performed solely or primarily by the family, such as the economic
function, the protective function, the religious function, the educational
function, and the recreational function, have been turned over to other
institutions such as corporations, hospitals, churches, and schools. Ogburn
pointed to the process of "family defunctionalization"—loss of functions by the
family unit—as a factor contributing to marital unhappiness and divorce.
However, he stressed that the family maintains responsibility for the function of
providing affection, thereby reducing social isolation and serving the interests of
the larger society.

    In the following selection, written about 50 years after Ogburn's report,
sociologists Andrew Cherlin and Frank F. Furstenberg, Jr., examine the future
of the American family as a social institution. They point out that, by the year
2000, "what we have come to view as the 'traditional' family will no longer
predominate." Yet, while there will be far more single-parent families and
families of remarriage than in the 1980s, family ties will remain an important
part of American life.

    • At current rates, half of all American marriages begun in the early 1980s will end in divorce.

    • The number of unmarried couples living together has more than tripled since 1970.

    • One out of four children is not living with both parents.

    The list could go on and on. Teenage pregnancies: up. Adolescent suicides: up. The birthrate: down. Over the past decade, popular and scholarly commentators have cited a seemingly endless wave of grim statistics about the shape of the American family. The trends have caused a number of concerned Americans to wonder if the family, as we know it, will survive the twentieth century. And yet other observers ask us to consider more positive developments:

    • Seventy-eight percent of all adults in a recent national survey said they get "a great deal" of satisfaction from their family lives; only 3% said "a little" or "none."

    • Two thirds of the married adults in the same survey said they were "very happy" with their marriages; only 3% said "not too happy."

    • In another recent survey of parents of children in their middle years, 88% said that if they had to do it over, they would choose to have children again.

    • The vast majority of the children (71%) characterized their family life as "close and intimate."

    Family ties are still important and strong, the optimists argue, and the predictions of the demise of the family are greatly exaggerated.

    Neither the dire pessimists who believe that the family is falling apart nor the unbridled optimists who claim that the family has never been in better shape provide an accurate picture of family life in the near future. But these trends indicate that what we have come to view as the "traditional" family will no longer predominate.

DIVERSE FAMILY FORMS

In the future, we should expect to see a growing amount of diversity in family forms, with fewer Americans spending most of their life in a simple "nuclear" family consisting of husband, wife, and children. By the year 2000, three kinds of families will dominate the personal lives of most Americans: families of first marriages, single-parent families, and families of remarriages.

In first-marriage families, both spouses will be in a first marriage, frequently begun after living alone for a time or following a period of cohabitation. Most of these couples will have one, two, or, less frequently, three children.

A sizable minority, however, will remain childless. Demographer Charles F. Westoff predicts that about one-fourth of all women currently in their childbearing years will never bear children, a greater number of childless women than at any time in U.S. history.

One other important shift: in a large majority of these families, both the husband and the wife will be employed outside the home. In 1940, only about one out of seven married women worked outside the home; today the proportion is one out of two. We expect this proportion to continue to rise, although not as fast as it did in the past decade or two.

SINGLE-PARENT FAMILIES

The second major type of family can be formed in two ways. Most are formed by a marital separation, and the rest by births to unmarried women. About half of all marriages will end in divorce at current rates, and we doubt that the rates will fall substantially in the near future.

When the couple is childless, the formerly married partners are likely to set up independent households and resume life as singles. The high rate of divorce is one of the reasons why more men and women are living in single-person households than ever before.

But three-fifths of all divorces involve couples with children living at home. In at least nine out of ten cases, the wife retains custody of the children after a separation.

Although joint custody has received a lot of attention in the press and in legal circles, national data show that it is still uncommon. Moreover, it is likely to remain the exception rather than the rule because most ex-spouses can't get along well enough to manage raising their children together. In fact, a national survey of children aged 11 to 16 conducted by one of the authors demonstrated that fathers have little contact with their children after a divorce. About half of the children whose parents had divorced hadn't seen their father in the last year; only one out of six had managed to see their father an average of once a week. If the current rate of divorce persists, about half of all children will spend some time in a single-parent family before they reach 18.

Much has been written about the psychological effects on children of living with one parent, but the literature has not yet proven that any lasting negative effects occur. One effect, however, does occur with regularity: women who head single-parent families typically experience a sharp decline in their income relative to before their divorce. Husbands usually do not experience a decline. Many divorced women have difficulty reentering the job market after a long absence; others find that their low-paying clerical or service-worker jobs aren't adequate to support a family.

Of course, absent fathers are supposed to make child-support payments, but only a minority do. In a 1979 U.S. Bureau of the Census survey, 43% of all divorced and separated women with children present reported receiving child-support payments during the previous year, and the average annual payment was about $1,900. Thus, the most detrimental effect for children living in a single-parent family is not the lack of a male presence but the lack of a male income.

FAMILIES OF REMARRIAGES

The experience of living as a single parent is temporary for many divorced women, especially in the middle class. Three out of four divorced people remarry, and about half of these marriages occur within three years of the divorce.

Remarriage does much to solve the economic problems that many single-parent families face because it typically adds a male income. Remarriage also relieves a single parent of the multiple burdens of running and supporting a household by herself.

But remarriage also frequently involves blending together two families into one, a difficult process that is complicated by the absence of clearcut ground rules for how to accomplish the merger. Families formed by remarriages can become quite complex, with children from either spouse's previous marriage or from the new marriage and with numerous sets of grandparents, stepgrandparents, and other kin and quasi-kin.

The divorce rate for remarriages is modestly higher than for first marriages, but many couples and their children adjust successfully to their remarriage and, when asked, consider their new marriage to be a big improvement over their previous one.

THE LIFE COURSE: A SCENARIO FOR THE NEXT TWO DECADES

Because of the recent sharp changes in marriage and family life, the life course of children and young adults today is likely to be far different from what a person growing up earlier in this century experienced. It will not be uncommon, for instance, for children born in the 1980s to follow this sequence of living arrangements: live with both parents for several years, live with their mothers after their parents divorce, live with their mothers and stepfathers, live alone for a time when in their early twenties, live with someone of the opposite sex without marrying, get married, get divorced, live alone again, get remarried, and end up living alone once more following the death of their spouses.

Not everyone will have a family history this complex, but it is likely that a substantial minority of the population will. And many more will have family histories only slightly less complex.

Overall, we estimate that about half of the young children alive today will spend some time in a single-parent family before they reach 18; about nine out of ten will eventually marry; about one out of two will marry and then divorce; and about one out of three will marry, divorce, and then remarry. In contrast, only about one out of six women born in the period 1910 to 1914 married and divorced and only about one in eight married, divorced, and remarried.

Without doubt, Americans today are living in a much larger number of family settings during their lives than was the case a few generations ago.

The life-course changes have been even greater for women than for men because of the far greater likelihood of employment during the childbearing years for middle-class women today compared with their mothers and grandmothers. Moreover, the increase in life expectancy has increased the difference between men's and women's family lives. Women now tend to outlive men by a wide margin, a development that is new in this century. Consequently, many more women face a long period of living without a spouse at the end of their lives, either as a widow or as a divorced person who never remarried.

Long-lived men, in contrast, often find that their position in the marriage market is excellent, and they are much more likely to remain married (or remarried) until they die.

CONVERGENCE AND DIVERGENCE

The family lives of Americans vary according to such factors as class, ethnicity, religion, and region. But recent evidence suggests a convergence among these groups in many features of family life. The clearest example is in childbearing, where the differences between Catholics and non-

Catholics or between Southerners and Northerners are much smaller than they were 20 years ago. We expect this process of convergence to continue, although it will fall far short of eliminating all social class and subcultural differences.

The experiences of blacks and whites also have converged in many respects, such as in fertility and in patterns of premarital sexual behavior, over the past few decades. But with respect to marriage, blacks and whites have diverged markedly since about 1960.

Black families in the United States always have had strong ties to a large network of extended kin. But in addition, blacks, like whites, relied on a relatively stable bond between husbands and wives. But over the past several decades—and especially since 1960—the proportion of black families maintained by a woman has increased sharply; currently, the proportion exceeds four in ten. In addition, more young black women are having children out of wedlock; in the late 1970s, about two out of three black women who gave birth to a first child were unmarried.

These trends mean that we must qualify our previously stated conclusion that marriage will remain central to family life. This conclusion holds for Americans in general. For many low-income blacks, however, marriage is likely to be less important than the continuing ties to a larger network of kin.

Marriage is simply less attractive to a young black woman from a low-income family because of the poor prospects many young black men have for steady employment and because of the availability of alternative sources of support from public-assistance payments and kin. Even though most black women eventually marry, their marriages have a very high probability of ending in separation or divorce. Moreover, they have a lower likelihood of remarrying.

Black single-parent families sometimes have been criticized as being "disorganized" or even "pathological." What the critics fail to note is that black single mothers usually are embedded in stable, functioning kin networks. These networks tend to center around female kin—mothers, grandmothers, aunts—but brothers, fathers, and other male kin also may be active. The members of these networks share and exchange goods and services, thus helping to share the burdens of poverty. The lower-class black extended family, then, is characterized by strong ties among a network of kin but fragile ties between husband and wife. The negative aspects of this family system have been exaggerated greatly; yet it need not be romanticized, either. It can be difficult and risky for individuals to leave the network in order to try to make it on their own; thus, it may be hard for individuals to raise themselves out of poverty until the whole network is raised.

THE DISINTEGRATING FAMILY?

By now, predictions of the demise of the family are familiar to everyone. Yet the family is a resilient institution that still retains more strength than its harshest critics maintain. There is, for example, no evidence of a large-scale rejection of marriage among Americans. To be sure, many young adults are living together outside of marriage, but the evidence we have about cohabitation suggests that it is not a lifelong alternative to marriage; rather, it appears to be either another stage in the process of courtship and marriage or a transition between first and second marriages.

The so-called "alternative lifestyles" that received so much attention in the late 1960s, such as communes and lifelong singlehood, are still very uncommon when we look at the nation as a whole.

Young adults today do marry at a somewhat older age, on average, than their parents did. But the average age at marriage today is very similar to what it was throughout the period from 1890 to 1940.

To be sure, many of these marriages will end in divorce, but three out of four people who divorce eventually remarry. Americans still seem to desire the intimacy and security that a marital relationship provides.

Much of the alarm about the family comes

from reactions to the sheer speed at which the institution changed in the last two decades. Between the early 1960s and the mid-1970s, the divorce rate doubled, the marriage rate plunged, the birthrate dropped from a twentieth-century high to an all-time low, premarital sex became accepted, and married women poured into the labor force. But since the mid-1970s, the pace of change has slowed. The divorce rate has risen modestly and the birthrate even has increased a bit. We may have entered a period in which American families can adjust to the sharp changes that occurred in the 1960s and early 1970s. We think that, by and large, accommodations will be made as expectations change and institutions are redesigned to take account of changing family practices.

Despite the recent difficulties, family ties remain a central part of American life. Many of the changes in family life in the 1960s and 1970s were simply a continuation of long-term trends that have been with us for generations.

The birthrate has been declining since the 1820s, the divorce rate has been climbing since at least the Civil War, and over the last half century a growing number of married women have taken paying jobs. Employment outside the home has been gradually eroding the patriarchial system of values that was a part of our early history, replacing it with a more egalitarian set of values.

The only exception occurred during the late 1940s and the 1950s. After World War II, Americans raised during the austerity of depression and war entered adulthood at a time of sustained prosperity. The sudden turnabout in their fortunes led them to marry earlier and have more children than any generation before or since in this century. Because many of us were either parents or children in the baby-boom years following the war, we tend to think that the 1950s typify the way twentieth-century families used to be. But the patterns of marriage and childbearing in the 1950s were an aberration resulting from special historical circumstances; the patterns of the 1960s and 1970s better fit the long-term trends. Barring

unforeseen major disruptions, small families, working wives, and impermanent marital ties are likely to remain with us indefinitely.

A range of possible developments could throw our forecasts off the mark. We do not know, for example, how the economy will behave over the next 20 years, or how the family will be affected by technological innovations still at the conception stage. But, we do not envision any dramatic changes in family life resulting solely from technological innovations in the next two decades.

Having sketched our view of the most probable future, we will consider three of the most important implications of the kind of future we see.

GROWING UP IN CHANGING FAMILIES

Children growing up in the past two decades have faced a maelstrom of social change. As we have pointed out, family life is likely to become even more complex, diverse, unpredictable, and uncertain in the next two decades.

Even children who grow up in stable family environments will probably have to get along with a lot less care from parents (mothers in particular) than children received early in this century. Ever since the 1950s, there has been a marked and continuous increase in the proportion of working mothers whose preschool children are cared for outside the home, rising from 31% in 1958 to 62% in 1977. The upward trend is likely to continue until it becomes standard practice for very young children to receive care either in someone else's home or in a group setting. There has been a distinct drop in the care of children by relatives, as fewer aunts, grandmothers, or adult children are available to supplement the care provided by parents. Increasingly, the government at all levels will be pressured to provide more support for out-of-home daycare.

How are children responding to the shifting circumstances of family life today? Are we raising a generation of young people who, by virtue of their own family experiences, lack the desire and skill to raise the next generation? As we indicated earlier, existing evidence has not demonstrated that marital disruption creates lasting personality damage or instills a distinctly different set of values about family life.

Similarly, a recent review on children of working mothers conducted by the National Research Council of the National Academy of Sciences concludes:

> If there is only one message that emerges from this study, it is that parental employment in and of itself —mothers' employment or fathers' or both parents' —is not necessarily good or bad for children.

The fact that both parents work *per se* does not adversely affect the well-being of children.

Currently, most fathers whose wives are employed do little childcare. Today, most working mothers have two jobs: they work for pay and then come home to do most of the childcare and housework. Pressure from a growing number of harried working wives could prod fathers to watch less television and change more diapers. But this change in fathers' roles is proceeding much more slowly than the recent spate of articles about the "new father" would lead one to expect. The strain that working while raising a family places on working couples, and especially on working mothers, will likely make childcare and a more equitable sharing of housework prominent issues in the 1980s and 1990s.

FAMILY OBLIGATIONS

Many of the one out of three Americans who, we estimate, will enter a second marriage will do so after having children in a first marriage. Others may enter into a first marriage with a partner who has a family from a previous marriage. It is not clear in these families what obligations remain after divorce or are created after remarriage. For one thing, no clear set of norms exists specifying how people in remarriages are supposed to act toward each other. Stepfathers don't know how much to discipline their stepchildren; second wives don't know what they're supposed to say when they meet their husbands' first wives; stepchildren don't know what to call their absent father's new wife.

The ambiguity about family relations after divorce and remarriage also extends to economic support. There are no clear-cut guidelines to tell adults how to balance the claims of children from previous marriages versus children from their current marriages. Suppose a divorced man who has been making regular payments to support his two small children from a previous marriage marries a woman with children from her previous marriage. Suppose her husband isn't paying any child support. Suppose further that the remarried couple have a child of their own. Which children should have first claim on the husband's income? Legally, he is obligated to pay child support to his ex-wife, but in practice he is likely to feel that his primary obligation is to his stepchildren, whose father isn't helping, and to his own children from his remarriage.

Our guess, supported by some preliminary evidence from national studies, is that remarriage will tend to further reduce the amount of child support that a man pays, particularly if the man's new family includes children from his new wife's previous marriage or from the current marriage. What appears to be occurring in many cases is a form of "childswapping," with men exchanging an old set of children from a prior marriage for a new set from their new wife's prior marriage and from the remarriage.

Sociologist Lenore J. Weitzman provides a related example in her book *The Marriage Contract*. Suppose, she writes, a 58-year-old corporate vice president with two grown children divorces his wife to marry his young secretary. He agrees to adopt the secretary's two young children. If he dies of a heart attack the following year:

> In most states, a third to half of his estate would go to his new wife, with the remainder divided among the four children (two from his last marriage, and his new wife's two children). His first wife will receive nothing—neither survivors' insurance nor a survivors' pension nor a share of the estate—and

both she and his natural children are likely to feel that they have been treated unjustly.

Since the rate of mid-life divorce has been increasing nearly as rapidly as that of divorce at younger ages, this type of financial problem will become increasingly common. It would seem likely that there will be substantial pressure for changes in family law and in income security systems to provide more to the ex-wife and natural children in such circumstances.

INTERGENERATIONAL RELATIONS

A similar lack of clarity about who should support whom may affect an increasing number of elderly persons. Let us consider the case of an elderly man who long ago divorced his first wife and, as is fairly typical, retained only sporadic contact with his children. If his health deteriorates in old age and he needs help, will his children provide it? In many cases, the relationship would seem so distant that the children would not be willing to provide major assistance. To be sure, in most instances the elderly man would have remarried, possibly acquiring stepchildren, and it may be these stepchildren who feel the responsibility to provide assistance. Possibly the two sets of children may be called upon to cooperate in lending support, even when they have had little or no contact while growing up. Currently, there are no clear guidelines for assigning kinship responsibilities in this new type of extended family.

Even without considering divorce, the issue of support to the elderly is likely to bring problems that are new and widespread. As is well known, the low fertility in the United States, which we think will continue to be low, means that the population is becoming older. The difficulties that this change in age structure poses for the Social Security system are so well known that we need not discuss them here. Let us merely note that any substantial weakening of the Social Security system would put the elderly at a great disadvantage with regard to their families, for older Americans increasingly rely on Social Security and

other pensions and insurance plans to provide support. A collapse of Social Security would result in a large decrease in the standard of living among older Americans and a return to the situation prevailing a few decades ago in which the elderly were disproportionately poor.

The relations between older people and their children and grandchildren are typically close, intimate, and warm. Most people live apart from their children, but they generally live close by one or more of them. Both generations prefer the autonomy that the increased affluence of the older generation has recently made possible. Older people see family members quite often, and they report that family members are their major source of support. A survey by Louis Harris of older Americans revealed that more than half of those with children had seen them in the past day, and close to half had seen a grandchild. We expect close family ties between the elderly and their kin to continue to be widespread. If, however, the economic autonomy of the elderly is weakened, say, by a drop in Social Security, the kind of friendly equality that now characterizes intergenerational relations could be threatened.

One additional comment about the elderly: Almost everyone is aware that the declining birthrate means that the elderly will have fewer children in the future on whom they can rely for support. But although this is true in the long run, it will not be true in the next few decades. In fact, beginning soon, the elderly will have more children, on average, than they do today. The reason is the postwar baby boom of the late 1940s and 1950s. As the parents of these large families begin to reach retirement age near the end of this century, more children will be available to help their elderly parents. Once the next generation—the baby-boom children—begins to reach retirement age after about 2010, the long-term trend toward fewer available children will sharply reassert itself.

Were we to be transported suddenly to the year 2000, the families we would see would look very recognizable. There would be few unfamiliar forms—not many communes or group marriages, and probably not a large proportion of lifelong singles. Instead, families by and large would continue to center around the bonds between husbands and wives and between parents and children. One could say the same about today's families relative to the 1960s: the forms are not new. What is quite different, comparing the 1960s with the 1980s, or the 1980s with a hypothetical 2000, is the distribution of these forms.

In the early 1960s, there were far fewer single-parent families and families formed by remarriages after divorce than is the case today; and in the year 2000 there are likely to be far more single-parent families and families of remarriage than we see now. Moreover, in the early 1960s both spouses were employed in a much smaller percentage of two-parent families; in the year 2000, the percentage with two earners will be greater still. Cohabitation before marriage existed in the 1960s, but it was a frowned-upon, bohemian style of life. Today, it has become widely accepted; it will likely become more common in the future. Yet we have argued that cohabitation is less an alternative to marriage than a precursor to marriage, though we expect to see a modest rise in the number of people who never marry.

TAKING ANOTHER LOOK

1 According to Cherlin and Furstenberg, what three types of families will dominate the personal lives of most Americans by the year 2000?
2 In the view of Cherlin and Furstenberg, what is the most detrimental effect for children in a single-parent family?
3 How has the overall increase in life expectancy in the United States increased the difference between men's and women's family lives?
4 According to Cherlin and Furstenberg, what are the strengths and limitations of the lower-class black extended family?
5 According to the National Research Council of the National Academy of Sciences, what is the impact of parental employment—mothers' employment or fathers' employment, or both parents' employment—upon children?
6 Why is the issue of support for the elderly likely to bring new problems by the year 2000?

After the Missiles: Sociopsychological Effects of Nuclear War

Bem P. Allen

It may seem strange to conclude a section on social change with an examination of the sociopyschological effects of nuclear war. But we live in a time in which governmental leaders continue to "think the unthinkable"—even going so far as to suggest that a nuclear confrontation could be "winnable." Consequently, the question arises: if there were a nuclear battle between the superpowers, if all human life were not extinguished rather quickly, what could survivors expect after this devastating experience of "social change"?

In the following selection, social psychologist Bem P. Allen speculates on the physical, medical, and emotional effects of a nuclear holocaust. Allen draws on the experiences of Japanese survivors of the American bombings of Hiroshima and Nagasaki in 1945; he also describes the impact of a hypothetical attack on the city of Boston. With painful and frightening detail, he reminds us that "nuclear war would not just destroy buildings and people; it would shatter the lives of those who remained."

As July 16, 1945, approached, the countdown to the explosion of the first nuclear weapon proceeded near Alamagordo, New Mexico, amid frantic activity. Physicist Robert Krohn remarked, "Now prior to the shot, back in the lab there had been some speculation that it might be possible to explode the atmosphere—in which case the world disappears" (quoted in Else, 1980, p. 16). Fellow scientist Robert Wilson said, "There was building up tremendous, almost hysterical anxiety . . . Things did not appear to be ready" (quoted in Else, 1980, p. 17). A dispassionate narrator described the scene:

> Fourteen July, seventeen hundred hours. Gadget complete. Should we have a chaplain here? . . . The betting pool cost a dollar. Edward Teller bet on a blast equal to 45,000 tons of TNT. Oppenheimer bet low, 3,000 tons. I. I. Rabi put his money on twenty kilotons. Young technicians were horrified to overhear Enrico Fermi taking side bets on the possibility of incinerating the State of New Mexico. (Else, 1980, pp. 17–18)

Obviously, the world's most brilliant scientists were quite uncertain as to what their efforts would bring.

Commenting on the myopic judgments made by scientists concerning the physical effects of modern nuclear explosions, astronomer Carl Sagan wondered, "What else have we overlooked?" (Sagan, 1983, p. 7). The question applies to the sociopsychological effects of a nuclear holocaust with even greater force. Although the extreme importance of sociopsychological factors has been clearly recognized (Office of Technology Assessment [OTA], 1979; National Academy of Sciences [NAS], 1975), there has been little speculation concerning sociopsychological results of a present-day nuclear exchange between the superpowers. Nuclear war would not just destroy buildings and people; it would shatter the lives of those who remained. This article is an attempt to anticipate social, cognitive, and emotional outcomes following multiple nuclear explosions.

Author's Note: Thanks are due Paula Allen for her helpful comments on earlier drafts of this article, as well as to colleague Gene Smith, editor Peter Nathan, and three anonymous reviewers for their help and encouragement.

Medical and physical effects of a major exchange are covered first, because these will be precursors of and partial determinants of sociopsychological effects.

MEDICAL AND PHYSICAL EFFECTS

Hiroshima

At 8:15 a.m. on August 6, 1945, a nuclear bomb variously rated at from 12,500 to 20,000 tons of TNT was detonated 1,850 feet above downtown Hiroshima, Japan. Two miles from the hypocenter, people saw the flash and had time to duck before being showered with debris (Hersey, 1946). At one mile, an office building was splintered. Victims located three fourths of a mile from the hypocenter had time to take one step and then were hurled through space. Near the hypocenter, people were vaporized, leaving only shadows imprinted on stone (Hersey, 1946). Others within a half mile of the hypocenter were destroyed by the force of the blast, burned to death by temperatures ranging up to several thousand degrees or shredded by flying masonry, steel, or glass. It was estimated that 95% of sheltered victims within one-half mile of the hypocenter who did not die of blast, burns, or shrapnel succumbed to radiation. The often slow and agonizing death by radiation was preceded by nausea, vomiting, diarrhea, loss of hair, bleeding gums, and discolored skin.

Heat at ground zero matched the solar surface. Two and one-half miles from the hypocenter, exposed victims were subjected to thermal radiation at 240°C (460°F). Burn victims appeared to be covered with soot. They walked like zombies, with arms outstretched to avoid contacting the burned skin that hung from their bodies (Lifton, 1967). A witness reported, "Many of them died along the road—I can still picture them in my mind—like walking ghosts . . . They didn't look like people of this world . . . They had a special way of walking —very slowly . . . I myself was one of them" (Lifton, 1967, p. 27).

Of Hiroshima's 340,000 residents, 130,000 died by November 1945 and 70,000 more by 1950 (Silberner, 1981a). That they are still dying today is recognized by U.S. insurance companies that cover Americans of Japanese descent who were present at Hiroshima and Nagasaki (National Public Radio [NPR], 1981). Although the U.S. government has flatly denied any responsibility for Japanese-American victims (NPR, 1981), it is preparing to recognize radiation effects that are delayed even for years (Raloff, 1983a). Leukemia has been the major cause of death for those victims who survived the first few months after the blast (Lifton, 1967). By the late 1950s, the rate of leukemia had dropped considerably, but as of 1971, it was still five times normal (Silberner, 1981a). Just as the threat of leukemia subsided, solid tumors began to be reported. Cancer of the stomach, lung, thyroid, ovary, uterine cervix, and breast have shown increases (Lifton, 1967; Silberner, 1981a). There have also been noncarcinogenic effects. In some instances, cataracts developed one to two years after the attack (Lifton, 1967). Though victims and unborn children have suffered genetic defects, it has been reported that none have been passed on to the offspring of victims (Silberner, 1981a).

A Hypothetical Attack on Boston

By today's standards, the weapons used on the Japanese were minute. Many modern warheads have at least a thousand times the power of the bomb dropped on Hiroshima, and single warheads ranging up to several thousand times the potency of the Hiroshima weapon probably exist (NPR, 1981). A meaningful comparison to the Hiroshima attack to a modern nuclear exchange would be Ervin et al.'s (1962) speculation concerning a 20-megaton (MT) ground blast over the center of metropolitan Boston; 20 MT would equal the blast of about 1,000 Hiroshima bombs. (Two MT is approximately equal to the explosive output of all the bombs dropped during World War II; Sagan, 1983.)

At just under a radius of 30 miles from the hypocenter of a 20-MT attack on Boston, exposed persons would receive first-degree burns, and synthetic cloth would ignite. At 21 miles from the center, people in the open would suffer second-degree burns and injuries due to flying debris driven by winds of up to 1,000 mph. At about 18 miles, third-degree burns would be sustained. Twelve and a half miles from the center, auto upholstery would catch fire. People 11 miles from the hypocenter would be imperiled by the collapse of frame houses and trees. Fallout shelters would be useless. Ten miles from the hypocenter or closer, a reflex glance at the fireball would burn the retina, resulting in blindness. Seven to eight miles from the center, power and telephone lines would be down, and people would sustain ear drum damage. At about five and a half miles, auto sheet metal would melt, and reinforced concrete structures would be damaged. Between three and four miles from the hypocenter, auto sheet metal would vaporize. Individuals who somehow escaped blast and thermal effects would succumb to lung injuries due to a shock wave traveling from the hypocenter faster than sound. Streets would be impassable.

Burning of various structures and fuels would generate a huge firestorm, initially sweeping toward the hypocenter at from 150 to 200 mph and eventually consuming everything in its path out to 16 to 21 miles from the center. Experience with such conflagrations during World War II indicates that fallout shelters and even bomb shelters near the center could be subjected to such high temperatures that no one would survive. For example, days after a fire bomb raid on Hamburg during 1943, shelters burst into flame when opened, because of contact between oxygen and trapped heat (Ervin et al., 1962).

If the 20-MT attack on Boston were an air rather than a ground blast, the damage would be nearly doubled, with each effect listed above extending out from the center almost twice as far. However, ground attacks generate maximum fallout. Ervin et al. (1962) estimated that within 48

hours of the attack, fallout would extend over a 4000-square-mile area, with exposed persons at the fringe receiving a dose sufficient to kill half of the *healthy* recipients (400 to 450 rads, units of radiation dosage). In all, it was hypothesized that of the nearly 2,900,000 persons in the metropolitan area at the time the scenario was posed, 739,000 within five miles would die of blast effects alone, and an additional 1,501,000 within 16 miles would fall victim to blast and thermal effects (Ervin et al., 1962). These figures assume that victims were sheltered from radiation.

Uncertainties

The hypothetical attack on Boston described above assumes a single 20-MT blast. It is possible that the metropolitan area would be subjected to 10 or more smaller explosions (Knox, 1980). The effects of such attacks are very difficult to predict (Ervin et al., 1962). To further complicate estimations, attacks might come in waves. Bunn and Tsipis (1983) suggested that first waves might be off their marks by some margin of error, and because of residual effects of first waves, second waves might be off even more or might be destroyed by lingering effects of first waves. Such inaccuracy could have the effect of scattering warheads, with many dropping in suburban and rural areas, generating interactions with unknown effects. Bunn and Tsipis assumed that most missiles, though perhaps inaccurate, would at least make it to target areas. Marshall (1983) went further by arguing that even the most modern of missiles have some appreciable probability of not working at all (see Associated Press, 1983). In case of misfires or inaccuracy, the superpowers might "unload their guns" on each other for fear that unreliable missiles would leave enemy silos intact and able to retaliate. The result would be Armageddon.

Controversies have always existed concerning the data from the Hiroshima attack (Marshall, 1981). Now, nearly 40 years later, new analyses of that data are fueling fresh debates. For example, it is entirely possible that the form of radiation causing cancer was not the uncommon high linear energy transfer (LET, e.g., neutron), as originally believed. Rather, cancer effects among victims at Hiroshima may have been due largely to low LET radiation (e.g., gamma). As well as indicating uncertainty about radiation effects after almost four decades of study, this possibility bodes ill for persons working around sources of the relatively common low LET radiation. Even more surprising are questions raised about standards of radiation dosage (Marshall, 1981). Such standards form the basis for advice concerning safe dosages of radiation. In fact, there may be no safe dosage. Rather than there being a maximum dosage of radiation per unit of time that yields no ill effects, a linear relationship might hold between dosage above natural background level and probability of ill effects (Marshall, 1981). Thus, even low dosages may increase the likelihood of harmful outcomes. Knox (1980) indicated that a dosage as low as 20 rads increased the incidence of leukemia among exposed Japanese children, and dosages of 50 to 100 rads increased birth and growth defects for offspring exposed in utero at the time of the blast.

The likelihood of surviving radiation is also uncertain. If only the healthiest residents of Hiroshima and Nagasaki escaped with their lives, estimates of radiation hazards based on survivors' data may be seriously in error (Raloff, 1982). Epidemiologist Alice Stewart estimated the "healthy survivor effect" while controlling for "residual disability effects" by studying the incidence of sudden deaths from cerebral hemorrhage among survivors. Many apparently unscathed survivors would have been exposed to low level radiation, which would show up only in "residual disability effects," such as bone marrow damage, that would result in decreased immunity to disease. Since cerebral hemorrhage would be relatively uninfluenced by such damage, investigating strokes in survivors controls for residual disabilities due to low level radiation exposure. Stewart showed that

survivors were only 70% as likely as normals to die of a stroke (cited in Raloff, 1982). Thus, "healthy survivors" may be more resistant to radiation effects than most people, which means that normal people may be more likely to die of exposure to radiation than was previously recognized.

The Nuclear Winter

Perhaps the most catastrophic effect of a major nuclear exchange would be what scientist Richard Turco and colleagues have called the "nuclear winter" (Turco, Toon, Ackerman, Pollack, & Sagan, 1983). If only 38% of the combined Soviet-U.S. arsenals (5,000 MT) were used, fires and ground blasts would drive so much smoke (as well as soot) and dust into the lower and upper levels of the atmosphere, respectively, that sunlight would drop to 5% to 10% of normal. Within days, temperatures in the northern hemispheres would begin to fall, reaching a low of about $-25°C$ ($-13°F$; Turco et al., 1983). The subzero weather could last for months. Reservoirs might freeze solid. If it were summer, plants would die; if it were winter, residual effects of the cold might undermine the spring planting. Plants that survived the cold and radiation would emerge to an environment infested with chemical smog (Ehrlich et al., 1983). Due to the low level of sunlight, it is even possible that photosynthesis would be insufficient to sustain plant life (Turco et al., 1983). Anyone who wishes to learn what it would be like to live through an approximation of the nuclear winter could consult the survivors of the battle of Leningrad during World War II (Bethell, 1980). Leningrad was besieged by the Germans for 900 days. The city was isolated during the infamous Russian winter, and life was much like that which might exist during the nuclear winter. Other recent work indicates that constant, gale-force winds might plague coastal areas as a result of the land-ocean temperature differential (Ehrlich et al., 1983), and certain mountainous areas might be warmer than usual, melting the snows and glaciers and leading to post-winter floods of continental proportions (Raloff, 1983b).

After particles had fallen from the atmosphere, the shroud would be lifted from the earth, but a new danger would arise. Depletion of the ozone layer would expose life to abnormally high levels of ultraviolet radiation (Ehrlich et al., 1983; NAS, 1975; Turco et al., 1983). The result would be the demise of many plants and animals, suppression of the immune system in humans and other mammals (Ehrlich et al., 1983), as well as an increased incidence of skin cancer and eye damage in humans (NAS, 1975). Of course, a larger exchange would yield more disastrous effects, and even megatonage as low as 100 could create nearly as bad a scenario (Turco et al., 1983). In any case, there might be no place to hide, as effects in the southern hemispheres could be somewhat attenuated versions of those in the northern counterpart (Ehrlich et al., 1983).

SOCIOPSYCHOLOGICAL EFFECTS

The behavioral results of nuclear war that are surveyed below are not presented as necessarily representative and certainly not as exhaustive. The focus is on behaviors likely to be associated with the expected physical and physiological effects cited above.

Psychologists have emphasized prevention of nuclear war through attempts to influence policy, rather than prediction of behavioral effects following an exchange (Morawski & Goldstein, 1985). Their efforts were largely confined to the 1940s, 1950s, and early 1960s, a period yielding so little relevant data on which to base advice on policy that frustration was virtually guaranteed (Morawski & Goldstein, 1985). However, today there is sufficient evidence to allow speculation about sociopsychological effects of modern nuclear war. As mentioned throughout this article, physical scientists have been able only to speculate about the effects of a modern nuclear exchange. Because massive nuclear war is a potential rather than actual event, neither they

nor we can do more than conjecture about its effects. However, psychologists are no more restricted to past research than physical scientists. As is done in the remainder of this article, psychologists can begin to draw analogies between projected environmental effects of a nuclear war and the determinants of known psychological phenomena, but that is not all that can be done. Studies that indirectly address psychological effects of nuclear war can be conducted. For example, present available psychological research techniques could be used to investigate the joint effects of low temperature and low illumination, conditions that would prevail after a nuclear exchange (Baron & Byrne, 1984). In addition, the exploration in this article of nuclear and nonnuclear events that occurred during World War II could be expanded to include additional analogies to conditions that would exist after a modern nuclear war. In any case, the involvement of psychology and related disciplines in the investigation of life after the missiles is crucial. The behavioral effects of multiple nuclear explosions would be one of several critical factors determining the continuing existence of humanity (Ehrlich et al., 1983; OTA, 1979; NAS, 1975). Behavioral scientists are by definition the most qualified to study those effects.

Generalizing research results to circumstances that have not yet occurred is always risky. In psychology, projecting from laboratory results to outcomes in "real life" must be done with great caution (Baron & Byrne, 1984). Even more care must be exercised in generalizing from psychological outcomes in the lab to "real life" in the future. Once again, though, the situation of behavioral scientists is quite similar to that of physical scientists. The possibility of the nuclear winter was in large part extrapolated from data yielded by Martian dust storms and volcanic eruptions on the Earth (Sagan, 1983; Turco et al., 1983). Similarly, psychologists can generalize from known behavioral effects of crowding to postexchange behaviors associated with that condition.

As physical scientists dwell on the uncertainties of their work (A. Erlich, 1984), so must we consider the imprecision of our efforts. Nevertheless, uncertainties must be tolerated when the fate of all humanity hangs in the balance. To know of the horror that might be is to prevent it.

It is hoped that the account of sociopsychological effects will apply to the United States, the U.S.S.R., and Europe. However, because much of it is based on data collected in this country and, therefore, bound to this culture, caution should be exercised in generalizing beyond these borders (OTA, 1979). As attacks would be concentrated in urban regions, except for a few rural areas near missile silos, effects for the two arenas will be considered separately. More general, long-term effects are covered next, with uncertainties discussed at the end. The worst-case scenario involving a 5,000 to 10,000-MT exchange is assumed and considered plausible. It is difficult to imagine that whoever strikes first will limit the attack in the belief that the target of their deceitful assault will also limit theirs.

Urban Areas

If nuclear war seemed imminent, the superpowers could empty their cities, but that maneuver appears unlikely. Should the side that hoped to attack first clear its cities, it would be telegraphing its move. If, in a crisis, both sides successfully emptied their cities, each could simply reprogram warheads to strike new population centers (Lamperti, 1983). In any case, should either side begin to clear its cities, it might provoke the other side (OTA, 1979). All this assumes that citizens would cooperate and leave the cities in a reasonable amount of time or leave at all and that millions could be somehow accommodated in outlying areas (Leaning & Leighton, 1983). More likely, the cities would not be evacuated. The side attacking first could not issue warnings to its citizens until detection by the target occurred a couple of minutes after launch, otherwise any hope of stopping the target's intercontinental ballistic missiles (ICBMs) would be lost (Steinbruner, 1984). Be-

cause about 30 minutes would lapse between launch and detonation of ICBM warheads, if the attacker warned its citizens at the earliest opportunity and the target counterattacked immediately, the attacker's citizens would have at most 28 minutes to escape the cities or seek shelter (missiles launched from submarines and aircraft would leave a shorter warning time; Bunn & Tsipis, 1983). Unless they were anticipating an attack under a "launch on warning" plan (Steinbruner, 1984), targeted officials might waste so much time funneling information of detection through channels that a warning would leave citizens almost no time to act. Although they could have as much as 28 minutes to act (Steinbruner, 1984), targeted heads of state might have as little as 10 minutes (Zacharias, Gordon, & Davis, 1983), leaving targeted citizens no more than 25 minutes to escape. However, there is no need to dwell on the difference between the amount of time the attacker would have to issue a warning and the warning time available to the target. Given too little space in deep underground shelters, warnings would cause monumental traffic jams and ensure that city-dwellers would be trapped in the open when the warheads fell (OTA, 1979). The cramming of shelters and freeways would also set the stage for the panic reactions that would destroy rational, adaptive behavior (Kelley, Condry, Dahlke, & Hill, 1965). To avoid panic, leaders of the U.S.S.R. and the United States might elect not to warn their citizens at all.

Lieutenant General Brent Scowcroft (U.S. Air Force Retired) has argued that an attack would probably not be "a bolt out of the blue" but would nevertheless be a surprise (Zacharias et al., 1983). A public that does not understand the consequences of nuclear war and is full of denial with regard to its occurrence is not likely to believe that it will happen (Lifton, 1967; Nash, 1983). In any case, the differences in the initial reactions of persons having absolutely no warning, those warned of severe international tensions via the media, and those crammed on the freeways attempting to flee the cities are too small to mention further. For most individuals within the borders of large cities, the transformation from conditions that are recognizable to ultimate chaos would be stunning. In the case of a daylight attack, people might one moment be going about their business, walking down familiar halls or seated next to friends or colleagues, and a fraction of a second later they might be flung into a nearby body of water, suspended between shattered support beams, or groping in a dark abyss formed by debris (Hersey, 1946). They would look about, only to find a wasteland where a house or an office building once stood. A few feet away they might discover the dismembered, bloodied, or badly burned bodies of people with whom they had just been conversing. The horror of viewing mangled bodies may alone be enough to severely and permanently traumatize survivors (Hebb, 1966). Even members of the Nazi SS, who apparently enjoyed annihilation of humans, recoiled at the sight of disintegrated corpses (Dawidowicz, 1975). The shock may be impossible to understand by those who have not experienced it (Lifton, 1967). Apparently, some victims of Hiroshima later showed psychotic symptoms at least in part traceable to the transition from everyday reality to ultimate chaos (Lifton, 1967).

After the initial shock, reactions of some may be tainted with selfishness (Leiderman & Mendelson, 1962; Lifton, 1967; NPR, 1981). People who are severely wounded do not think of loved ones or small children in their charge: They blindly seek comfort. A number of victims at Hiroshima spoke of leaving family members behind as they fled the terror of pain or fire (Lifton, 1967). Needless to say, their guilt never subsided. At Hiroshima and Nagasaki, there were a few heroic exceptions to self-centeredness and some profound tributes to the capacity of humans to deny. Some people picked themselves up and went about their daily tasks amid the rubble, although their endeavors had totally lost meaning. A messenger received such severe burns on the back that he later spent months on his abdomen

begging to die, yet he paused to pick up his mail (Silberner, 1981b). A soldier carefully gathered up the ashes of official papers in his possession, so that he could obediently return them to superiors (Lifton, 1967). But most Japanese victims simply made their way from the center of the disaster, or begged for help, or died where they lay.

City dwellers who initially survived would find that all they took for granted about modern urban living had been obliterated in a single stroke. A turn of the water faucet would produce a diminishing dribble; a flick of the light switch would not alter the darkness; no reassuring dial tone would emanate from the receiver; TV and radio would probably be off the air; and transportation would be at a standstill (Sidel, Geiger, & Lown, 1962; Zacharias et al., 1983). Stores might not be open, even if they were accessible over streets littered with debris. Police and firefighters who remained would be overwhelmed, but more important, medical facilities and personnel would be extraordinarily deficient. The entire United States contains facilities for only 1,300 burn victims and fewer than 65,000 intensive care patients (Adams, 1983). The former would be grossly inadequate even for one large city, and the latter probably would not accommodate a targeted city the size of Chicago. It was estimated that of 6,500 physicians and 128 hospitals in the Boston metropolitan area during the early 1960s, only 640 and 24, respectively, would survive (Sidel et al., 1962). In a desperate attempt to provide beds for the injured, physicians might seek evacuation of psychiatric institutions (Sidel et al., 1962) and even prisons. If they succeeded, persons who were dangerous or unable to care for themselves would be left to roam the streets. Remaining medical personnel would be under unimaginable pressure. Physicians and perhaps even laypersons would hurriedly inspect the injured lining hospital halls and make snap judgments as to whether they might survive if given medical attention (Hersey, 1946). Many who might have otherwise had a chance would be passed over as a result of inadequate diagnosis or would not even receive a look.

Conditions would be ripe for the practice of euthanasia (Strieber & Kunetka, 1984). Thousands would stream into hospitals daily, and thousands would leave as corpses (NPR, 1981). Sidel and colleagues (1962) have suggested that Boston is potentially a giant mausoleum. The bodies would be only one of the more severe health problems (Bethell, 1980). Stress generated by these conditions would take a heavy toll of physicians and other medical personnel, making many suicides likely. In fact, experience with total disaster during World War II makes it seem probable that numerous suicides would occur among even healthy survivors (Ryan, 1966). But some individuals would live to face the nuclear winter.

As the pall of near total darkness enshrouded large portions of targeted areas, surviving victims would begin the search for food and fuel. Acting under the assumption that radioactivity in the environment had diminished to safe levels, or being willing to risk contamination to avoid starvation, individuals would leave enclosures to scavenge for what they could find (OTA, 1979). At first, there would be food left in stores that had escaped destruction, wood for fires, and perhaps, in some areas, coal or fuel oil. Money would be the medium of exchange in the beginning, but the disruption or closing of financial institutions and the absence of help from local or national governments would soon destroy faith in dollars or the equivalent (Zacharias et al., 1983). Bartering would become the way of the marketplace, with food being the most valued commodity. Under these circumstances, looting would be the order of the day; citizens would even prey on corpses (Lifton, 1967). A burgeoning underground would develop to feed on the inevitable black market. It might be led by former criminals, but ordinary people would be hard-pressed to resist the relative luxury it would offer. The actual "merchants" in this enterprise might be children, urchins forever denied socialization by the loss of their parents (Lifton, 1967).

The hospitals would continue to overflow, but the people queuing outside would contain a new element. Thousands would view the symptoms of radiation victims, and they would see themselves as suffering from a dreaded new affliction, called "A-bomb disease" by residents of Hiroshima (Lifton, 1967). The neurosis that would result has been termed *hysterical contagion* (Wheeler, Deci, Reis, & Zuckerman, 1978). Because only a minimal stimulus seems needed to trigger epidemic conversion reaction even in the absence of a universal crisis, it is easy to imagine the reaction that widespread radiation sickness would instigate following the devastation of the northern hemisphere. As the number of people stricken with this neurosis would be extremely large, psychologists and psychiatrists could be as overwhelmed as medical personnel. This would be especially true because psychological personnel tend to be heavily concentrated in the cities, and therefore they would be greatly reduced in numbers.

The filth in the air and on the ground, the lack of water for bathing, the lack of fresh clothing, the tendency to form gangs for support and sustenance (OTA, 1979), the prevalence of facial injuries in burn victims, and the existence of perpetual night might reduce many people to a state of *deindividuation.* Deindividuation is the loss of individuality or sense of uniqueness and is often accompanied by bizarre, antisocial behavior (Diener, 1980; Zimbardo, 1970). Anonymity due to "being lost in the crowd" or to being indistinguishable from other burned and soiled people can be precursors of deindividuation. Lifton (1967) reported that some victims at Hiroshima were so badly burned about the face that even immediate family could not recognize them. The continued darkness of the nuclear winter could alone be a powerful and general determinant of deindividuation (Mann, 1981). Behavior resulting from deindividuation would range from simple aggression to wild, frenzied attacks, sometimes perpetrated on individuals by mobs (Zimbardo, 1970). It is even possible that psychotic symptoms would result from the sensory deprivation accompanying chronic darkness (Bexton, Heron, & Scott, 1954). If humanity is not "bombed back to the stone age," it might nevertheless regress to the savagery of the medieval period.

Because earlier and later in this article many analogies are drawn to the reactions of people at Hiroshima and Nagasaki, the reader should remember that conditions following a multimegaton exchange of nuclear weapons are likely to be drastically different from those at the two Japanese cities. Hiroshima and Nagasaki were two small sites of nuclear disaster. Unaffected areas quickly furnished help. The outside world provided a stimulus and model for return to normality, as well as untainted environs to which victims could escape. Adjustment was facilitated by the positive attention provided to the relatively few victims of an unusual weapon. Such conditions would not prevail if the superpowers launched a major attack on one another.

Rural Areas

Although some rural areas near missile silos would be destroyed (Bunn & Tsipis, 1983), many others would be initially unscathed. However, destruction of communication centers and the electromagnetic pulse generated by high altitude explosions would lead to a cutoff of electronic communications (Steinbrunner, 1984). The major networks would be off the air, and long-distance telephone service would terminate. The latter would be a source of most immediate stress, as it would be impossible to contact friends and relatives living in cities. Mail services would stop, and trains, buses, and other forms of supply and transportation would cease. Although the nuclear winter would not arrive for a number of days after the blasts (Turco et al., 1983), a feeling of impending doom would grip rural areas. Normal life would continue for a time, but it would be in the back of people's minds that everything would soon change (OTA, 1979).

Among the first evidence of imminent disaster would be hoarding. People would swamp stores, buying up everything, especially food. Huge quantities of gasoline and fuel for heat would be purchased and stored in personal residences. Soon store shelves and fuel tanks would be empty, as neither would be replenished by supplies from the outside. However, as there is evidence that people in rural areas might be more likely to show altruistic behaviors than their urban counterparts (Byrne & Kelly, 1981), it is possible that initially people would share. Co-ops might even be set up to help the poor and disadvantaged. Certainly, neighbors would help neighbors, and family members would aid one another. In fact, "the spirit of community" might never be stronger than just after the missiles, but it would surely die in time. As supplies dried up and exposure to fallout created much sickness and death, people would begin to think only of the next meal and enough fuel to blunt the cold of the nuclear winter.

Individuals would continue to work for some time after missiles fell, but eventually it would be obvious that their efforts were meaningless (Lifton, 1967). Needed supplies would not arrive, and products could not be shipped to market. For people employed by national firms, pay might be suspended. As writers like Erskine Caldwell (1962; *God's Little Acre*) and Studs Terkel (1975; *Working*) have illustrated, jobs are essential to feelings of identity. Without them people's sense of self would begin to deteriorate (Allen & Potkay, 1983). However, these effects would be evidenced for only a few weeks after the missiles. Later, people would descend Maslow's hierarchy of needs and be concerned only with bare survival (Potkay & Allen, in press).

Confinement indoors would begin with the first evidence of fallout and continue for months because of the cold. Inevitably, people would venture out, thus exposing themselves to radiation and later to the effects of freezing weather, but most hours would be spent inside. Anne Frank's (1952) *Diary of a Young Girl*, experiences in the Jewish ghettos of World War II (Dawidowicz, 1975), and considerable research (Baron & Byrne, 1984; Brigham, in press; Paulus & McCain, 1983) all indicate that crowding people together in cramped space for long periods generates depression and conflict. Adding starvation and sickness to this scenario would make matters much worse (Dawidowicz, 1975).

In a few days or weeks, people in rural areas would be faced with a new threat (OTA, 1979). Survivors from urban areas would start to arrive. Migration would begin because of depletion of supplies in the cities and because city dwellers would, like ghetto residents, assume that life anywhere else would be better (Dawidowicz, 1975). Massive conflict over limited supplies would accompany the hordes of dirty, injured, and degenerated infiltrators from the cities. Rural residents might begin to feel they were living the legend of frontier people besieged by hostile "natives," but they would be without the glory of winning in the end. Paranoia would be widespread, and violence would be common. Within a few months after the missiles, rural and urban areas would be indistinguishable in terms of inhabitants' behaviors.

Long-Term Effects

The 5,000-to-10,000-megaton nuclear exchange envisioned by those who postulate the nuclear winter would kill about 1.1 billion people almost immediately and would leave a like number stricken with serious injury and radiation sickness (Sagan, 1983). Months later, as many as two billion people—half of the world's population—might be dead as a result of the war (Raloff, 1983b). However, many might live until some semblance of stability, if not normality, returned. These people would suffer the guilt that is common in survivors (Lifton, 1967). They would ask, "Why was I spared?" Many would remember friends and loved ones that they failed to help or could not help sufficiently. Even if they could have done nothing for intimates who perished, they might suffer the continual nightmare of having somehow contributed to the demise of family members and colleagues (Lifton, 1967). Special guilt would characterize scientists and government officials who failed to anticipate or prevent nuclear war (Lifton, 1967). It would be guilt nurtured by loss of status. Because government and

other institutions would have failed, respect for people associated with these institutions might diminish to near zero. Being located close to the centers of large cities where even deep shelters might be inadequate (Ervin et al., 1962), many high government officials would die, but those who remained would face humiliation or worse. Individuals who were powerful and esteemed before the missiles might become scapegoats afterward.

Status differentials would largely disappear, with former possessors of rank, name, and/or wealth joining the rest (Strieber & Kinetka, 1984). The collapse of the social ladder would destroy the power of status. Stripped of their usual sources of influence, people would be left with mainly one method of getting their way, aggression (Tedeschi, Smith, & Brown, 1974). Life in the mythical "wild west" would seem lawful and tame by comparison (Strieber & Kunetka, 1984).

The United States and the U.S.S.R. would suffer severe loss of status. In a just world "you get what you deserve and deserve what you get" (Lerner, Miller, & Holmes, 1975). The people of other nations might well see the Americans and the Soviets as getting what they deserved. The status of the two countries would be lowered even further because each would have to accept aid, given that there were enough people left to help. More likely, both former superpowers would disintegrate into a multitude of states, some controlled by foreigners (Strieber & Kunetka, 1984).

Democracy would be an early casualty of a major exchange (Office of Technology Assessment, 1979). In relatively undamaged areas and during recovery, governments would likely take over with a vengeance (OTA, 1979). In such cases, blind obedience to omnipotent authority would be common (Milgram, 1974). After Pearl Harbor, Hawaiians surrendered their individual rights to military authorities, even going so far as to obey when ordered to give blood in "payment" of traffic fines (Zich, 1977). In the long run, authoritarian rule would dominate in the northern hemispheres (OTA, 1979). One gets the picture of automatons all marching to the same drummer. By contrast, immediately after the attack in areas where damage and death were high, authority would be undermined and its credibility lost (Allen, 1978). At that time in those locations, people would be unlikely to obey anyone. Chaos would be the result.

With the enormous reduction of population, small pockets of humanity might be formed, each cut off from the others. The result could be widespread intermarriage, including incest. Such behaviors would lead to loss of genetic diversity, resulting in the deterioration of the human species (Ehrlich et al., 1983).

The number of serious and permanent scars resulting from burn wounds would be enormous. Keloid tumors, ugly reddish, swollen areas, were common among survivors of the attacks on the Japanese cities (Lifton, 1967). Aside from physical problems, such as inability to gain weight due to painful stretching of scars, disfigurement would create serious social and psychological problems (Lifton, 1967; also see Walster, Walster, & Berscheid, 1978). Severely disfigured persons, especially those burned on the face, would be shunned by some and would suffer a crippling loss of self-esteem (Lifton, 1967; NPR, 1981). The premium that Westerners place on physical attractiveness might be enhanced if it continued after the missiles (Allen, 1978). Burn scars could create a wide gulf and a strong contrast between those who are and those who are not attractive, to the advantage of the former and the detriment of the latter. This tragic aftermath of blast and fire could become one of three prime sources of prejudice against victims of the missiles. A second would be the belief that all burned people were exposed to high radiation and that the resultant genetic damage could be passed to future generations. Although such transmission might be slight (NAS, 1975) or nonexistent (Siberner, 1981a), the belief would very likely be propagated anyway (Lifton, 1967). A third source of prejudice would be the "just world" belief that disfigured individuals suffered victimization because they were

"bad people" (Lerner et al., 1975). One important practical result of prejudice against victims would be extreme frustration in their pursuit of suitable marital partners (Lifton, 1967; NPR, 1981). Even more serious would be the day-to-day agony suffered by objects of prejudice (Brigham, in press; NPR, 1981). Anger and frustration result from persecution and can lead to hostility toward those even lower in the social ladder (Byrne & Kelly, 1981; NPR, 1981). Lifton (1967) reported that some Japanese victims did turn on those at the bottom of their country's social stratum. Prejudice breeds prejudice, a fact of social life that might be more prominent after the missiles than before.

Lifton (1967) conveyed the impression that nearly all of those who were victims of the atom bomb bore its stigma indefinitely. Those who coped best were individuals who campaigned against nuclear weapons. However, this source of adaptation and relief would not be available to victims of a modern nuclear exchange. Working to rid the world of nuclear arms would not make sense after Armageddon had already occurred.

Uncertainties

The "total war" conditions described above might not occur. Of course, one would like to believe that any level of nuclear exchange is improbable. On the one hand, a disaster the magnitude of that proposed here is unprecedented in the history of humanity. On the other hand, just as it is likely that there are other intelligent beings in this universe or another, it is probable that the perpetual buildup of weapons in the context of international tension will eventually result in an exchange, if only by accident (Zacharias et al., 1983). Should that happen, it is possible that the exchange would be limited (Hackett, 1978; Zacharias et al., 1983). If a future nuclear war were so small in scale that it was below the threshold for the nuclear winter (Sagan, 1983), humanity would survive. Further, if one is willing to forget that thousands, even millions, would die if only a few missiles were fired (OTA, 1979), there could be possible positive results of a limited war. Favorable outcomes might include markedly fewer automobiles, and, thus, fewer accidents, less fuel consumption, and more physical exercise (OTA, 1979). There would be little meat and, therefore, less of the cancer thought to be caused by it (OTA, 1979). The need to be near jobs would end the flight from and decay of the cities (OTA, 1979). Those who dislike technology would be pleased to find it diminished in importance in the relatively primitive existence that would characterize life after a small exchange (OTA, 1979). Computers, telephone equipment, and other electronic systems would be scarce, because many such units would be destroyed by electromagnetic pulse (Steinbruner, 1984). Replacement would be haphazard due to the lack of components for repair and for construction of new equipment (Strieber & Kunetka, 1984). With the demise of technology would come the downfall of its citadel, the university. If technology is the bone structure of higher education, the arts and humanities are its flesh. However, the latter two might seem trivial when the theme of life had become mere survival. Obviously, preservation and transmission of knowledge would be in jeopardy.

Even in a limited exchange, almost every family in the United States and the U.S.S.R. would lose members. A death in the family might have salutary effects on surviving members. Families might become closer, and members might experience psychological growth (Moriarty, 1967). However, it is unfortunately also possible that families might deteriorate due to loss of members (Moriarty, 1967). Adults might be too grief-stricken to function as parents, and children would be likely to show aggression, withdrawal, denial, destructiveness, and preoccupation with death (Moriarty, 1967).

As indicated earlier, people might initially be devastated by the ubiquity of death and suffering manifested in piles of bodies and the commonness of unrelieved pain. In time, desensitization might diminish the reaction of horror, facilitating adap-

tation. If multiple murders and assaults per hour of television programming can desensitize children to violence, people can get used to death and suffering (Baron & Byrne, 1984). However, this loss of sensitivity would be a mixed blessing. It would lower stress but would also numb survivors to the suffering of others and to the value of life.

Finally, it is likely that the world would come to the aid of the relatively few victims; circumstances would be more like those at Hiroshima and Nagasaki than those depicted earlier in this article. Also, it is possible that humans might learn their lesson—people everywhere might finally rise up and destroy nuclear weapons. However, one would not want to bet heavily on a positive outcome of a small exchange. After all, the lessons of Hiroshima and Nagasaki were not learned.

It is possible that, should a major exchange occur, the aftermath would not be so extreme as indicated in this article. People might take adequate shelter or even be absent from the cities. Climatic conditions might make fallout effects less severe than expected (Ervin et al., 1962), and the ravages of the nuclear winter might be less severe than predicted. Total disaster might cause people to rally around one another. Altruism might characterize behavior, and people might forever swear off the evil precursors of war, aggressiveness and prejudice. At the minimum, the world after a major exchange might be just what the survivalists want, a chance to struggle for existence and emerge the "fittest." After all, postulations about a future nuclear war are all speculations, open to debate (Raloff, 1983b). No wholly adequate experiments can be conducted, and there is no precedent for such a war (Turco et al., 1983). Unfortunately, it is also possible that the dire outcome presented above underestimates the horror that would descend with the warheads (Sagan, 1983). If this article is an understatement, instead of gloriously besting others in the struggle for meager resources, the few remaining survivalists would be groping in the frigid opacity of the nuclear winter, scratching for food and fuel and awaiting almost certain death.

Should favorable behavior characterize responses to nuclear disaster, it would be because the widespread ignorance and denial of nuclear war that now prevails would have been eliminated before the warheads fell (Nash, 1983). More important, such a cure for our intellect and psyche would be an important factor in preventing disaster. The seriousness of the failure to think of or collect information about nuclear catastrophe can be seen in the responses of first-year university students. Out of 25 multiple-choice questions about nuclear war, only an average of 11 were answered correctly, with a fourth of the respondents being unable to identify "Hiroshima" and less than 30% correctly selecting the date of the first nuclear explosion. Zweingenhaft (1984) reported similar results for a nonuniversity population.

Even if the horror described in the first part of this article were replaced by the more favorable scenario presented in this section, the difference would be only a matter of degree. The contrast is in the comparison between one of the worst tragedies in recorded history and the end of humankind. If any degree between the two extremes should occur, many if not most survivors would find life after the missiles not worth living.

EPILOGUE

In a now famous lamentation, J. Robert Oppenheimer, director of the project to develop the first nuclear weapons, spoke on film about the feelings he and his colleagues experienced after witnessing the awesome destructiveness of their invention:

> We knew the world would not be the same. A few people laughed, a few people cried. Most people were silent. I remembered the line from the Hindu scripture, the Bhagavad Gita. Vishnu is trying to persuade the prince that he should do his duty, and to impress him, takes on his multi-armed form and says: "Now I am become death, the destroyer of worlds."
>
> In one way or another, we all felt that way. (Else, 1980, p. 30)

Perhaps, like Vishnu, we have been transformed, albeit not by our own volition. Although once we were preservers of the world, passive acceptance of weapons we do not understand threatens to make destroyers of us.

REFERENCES

Adams, H. (1983, June/July). Preparing for "the highest rate of casualities in history." *Bulletin of the Atomic Scientists, 39,* 11S–16S.

Allen. B. (1978). *Social behavior.* Chicago: Nelson Hall.

Allen. B., & Potkay, C. (1983). *Adjective Generation Technique (AGT): Research and applications.* New York: Irvington.

Associated Press. (1983, December 19). Cruise missile crashes in test. *Peoria Journal Star,* p. 2.

Baron, R., & Byrne, D. (1984). *Social psychology: Understanding human interaction* (4th ed.). Boston: Allyn & Bacon.

Bethell, N. (1980). *Russia besieged.* Alexandria, VA: Time-Life.

Bexton, W., Heron, W., & Scott, T. (1954). The effects of decreased variation in the sensory environment. *Canadian Journal of Psychology: 8.* 70–76.

Brigham, J. (in press). *Social psychology.* Boston: Little, Brown.

Bunn, M., & Tsipis, K. (1983). The uncertainties of a preemptive nuclear attack. *Scientific American, 249.* 38–47.

Byrne, D., & Kelly, K. (1981). *An introduction to personality.* Englewood Cliffs, NJ: Prentice-Hall.

Caldwell, E. (1962). *God's little acre.* New York: New American Library.

Dawidowicz, L. (1975). *The war against the Jews 1933–1945.* New York: Bantam Books.

Diener, E. (1980). Deindividuation: The absence of self-awareness and self-regulation in group members. In P. Paulus (Ed.), *The psychology of group influence.* Hillsdale, NJ: Erlbaum.

Ehrlich, A. (1984, April). Nuclear winter. *Bulletin of the Atomic Scientists, 40,* 1S–14S.

Ehrlich, P., Harte, J., Harwell, H., Raven, P., Sagan, C., Woodwell, G., Berry, J., Ayensu, E., Ehrlich, A., Eisner, T., Gould, S., Grover, H., Herrera, R., May, R., Mayr, E., McKay, C., Mooney, H., Myers, N., Pimentel, D., & Teal, J. (1983). Long-term biological consequences of nuclear war. *Science, 222,* 1293–1300.

Else, J. (Director-Producer). (1980). *The day after of Trinity: J. Robert Oppenheimer and the atomic bomb* [film transcript]. Kent, OH: PTV Publications.

Ervin, F., Glazier, J., Aronow, S., Nathan, D., Coleman, R., Avery, N., Shohet, S., & Leeman, C. (1962). Human and ecologic effects in Massachusetts of an assumed thermonuclear attack on the U.S. *The New England Journal of Medicine, 266,* 1127–1137.

Frank, A. (1952). *The diary of a young girl.* Garden City, NY: Doubleday.

Hackett, J. (1978). *The third world war: August 1985.* New York: Macmillan.

Hebb, D. (1966). *Psychology* (2nd ed.). Philadelphia: Saunders.

Hersey, J. (1946). *Hiroshima.* New York: Bantam Books.

Kelley, H., Condry, J., Dahlke, A., & Hill, A. (1965). Collective behavior in a simulated panic situation. *Journal of Experimental Social Psychology, 1,* 20–54.

Knox, R. (1980, May/June). Nuclear war: What if? *Science 80,* pp. 32–34.

Lamperti, J. (1983, June/July). What harm can it do? *Bulletin of the Atomic Scientists, 39,* 7S–10S.

Leaning, J., & Leighton, M. (1983, June/July). The world according to FEMA. *Bulletin of the Atomic Scientists, 39.* 2S–7S.

Lerner, M., Miller, D., & Holmes, J. (1975). Deserving versus justice: A contemporary dilemma. In L. Berkowitz & E. Walster (Eds.), *Advances in experimental social psychology* (Vol. 12). New York: Academic Press.

Leiderman, P., & Mendelson, J. (1962). Some psychiatric and social aspects of the defense-shelter program. *The New England Journal of Medicine, 266,* 1149–1155.

Lifton, R. (1967). *Death in life: Survivors of Hiroshima.* New York: Random House.

Mann, L. (1981). The baiting crowd in episodes of threatened suicide. *Journal of Personality and Social Psychology: 41,* 703–709.

Marshall, E. (1981). New A-bomb studies alter radiation estimates. *Science, 212,* 900–903.

Marshall, J. (1983, October). The missiles of December. *Inquiry,* pp. 16–19.

Milgram, S. (1974). *Obedience to authority:* New York: Harper & Row.

Morawski, J., & Goldstein, S. (1985). Psychology and nuclear war: A chapter in our legacy of social responsibility, *American Psychologist, 40.* 276–284.

Moriarty, D. (1967). *The loss of loved ones.* Springfield, IL: Charles C Thomas.

Nash, H. (1983, October). Thinking about thinking about the unthinkable. *Bulletin of the Atomic Scientists, 39,* pp. 39–42.

National Academy of Sciences. (1975). *Long-term worldwide effects of multiple nuclear-weapons detonations.* Washington, DC: Author.

National Public Radio. (1981). *Japanese-American Survivors of the atom bomb* [audio tape]. Washington, DC: Author.

Office of Technology Assessment. (1979). *The effects of nuclear war* (OTA Publication No. 052-003-00668-5). Washington, DC: U.S. Government Printing Office.

Paulus, P., & McCain, G. (1983). Crowding in jails. *Basic and Applied Social Psychology, 4.* 89–107.

Potkay, C., & Allen, B. (in press). *Personality.* Monterey, CA: Brooks/Cole.

Raloff, J. (1982). A-bomb survivor risks are revised upward. *Science News, 123,* 405.

Raloff, J. (1983a). Compensating radiation victims. *Science News, 124,* 330–331.

Raloff, J. (1983b). Beyond Armageddon. *Science News, 124,* 314–317.

Ryan, C. (1966). *The last battle.* New York: Simon & Schuster.

Sagan, C. (1983, October 30). The nuclear winter. *Parade,* pp. 4–7.

Sidel, V., Geiger, J., & Lown, B. (1962). The physician's role in the postattack period. *New England Journal of Medicine, 266,* 1137–1145.

Silberner, J. (1981a). Hiroshima & Nagasaki: Thirty-six years later, the struggle continues. *Science News, 120,* 284–287.

Silberner, J. (1981b). Psychological A-bomb wounds. *Science News, 120,* 296–298.

Steinbruner, J. (1984). Launch under attack. *Scientific American, 250,* 37–47.

Strieber, W., & Kunetka, J. (1984). *War day.* New York: Holt.

Tedeschi, J., Smith, R., & Brown, R. (1974). A reinterpretation of research on aggression. *Psychological Bulletin, 81,* 540–562.

Terkel, S. (1975). *Working.* New York: Avon.

Turco, R., Toon, T., Ackerman, T., Pollack, J., & Sagan, C. (1983). Nuclear winter: Global consequences of multiple nuclear explosions. *Science, 222,* 1283–1292.

Walster, E., Walster, G., & Berscheid, E. (1978). *Equity theory and research.* Boston: Allyn & Bacon.

Wheeler, L., Deci, E., Reis, H., & Zuckerman, M. (1978). *Interpersonal influence.* Boston: Allyn & Bacon.

Zacharias, J., Gordon, M., & Davis, S. (1983). *Common sense and nuclear peace.* (Available from Educational Development Center, 55 Chapel Street, Newton, MA 02160)

Zich, A. (1977). *The rising sun.* Alexandria, VA: Time-Life Books.

Zimbardo, P. (1970). The human choice. In W. Arnold & D. Levine (Eds.), *Nebraska Symposium on Motivation: The human choice: Individuation, reason, and order versus deindividuation, impulse, and chaos.* Lincoln: University Nebraska Press.

Zweigenhaft, R. (1984). What do Americans know about nuclear weapons? *Bulletin of the Atomic Scientists, 40,* 48–50.

TAKING ANOTHER LOOK

1 Briefly describe the impact of the 1945 bombing of Hiroshima.

2 According to Allen, how would the impact of a 20-megaton ground blast over the center of metropolitan Boston compare to the impact of the bomb dropped on Hiroshima?

3 Briefly discuss the possible effects of the "nuclear winter."

4 According to Allen, what would be the sociopsychological effects of a nuclear attack on urban residents?

5 How would rural areas be affected by a nuclear attack on cities?

6 According to Allen, what forms of prejudice would be likely to emerge against victims of nuclear attacks?

7 How would family life be affected by a nuclear confrontation?

ACKNOWLEDGMENTS

Kingsley Davis, "The Sociology of Prostitution," from *American Sociological Review*, 2 (October 1937), pp. 744–755. Reprinted by permission of the American Sociological Association.

Lewis Coser, "The Functions of Social Conflict," from *The Functions of Social Conflict*. Copyright © 1956 by The Free Press, renewed 1984 by Lewis A. Coser. Reprinted with permission of The Free Press, a Division of Macmillan, Inc.

Erving Goffman, "Presentation of Self in Everyday Life," from *Presentation of Self in Everyday Life*. Copyright © 1959 by Erving Goffman. Reprinted by permission of Doubleday & Company, Inc.

Murray Melbin, "Night as Frontier," from *American Sociological Review*, 43 (February 1978), pages 3, 5–7, 9–13, and 17–22. Reprinted by permission of the American Sociological Association.

Robert Ferber, Paul Sheatsley, Anthony Turner, and Joseph Waksberg, "What Is a Survey?," from *What is a Survey*. Reprinted by permission of the American Statistical Association.

Richard L. Baxter, Cynthia De Riemer, Ann Landini, Larry Leslie, and Michael W. Singletary, "A Content Analysis of Music Videos," from *Journal of Broadcasting and Electronic Media*, Vol. 29, Summer 1985, pages 333–340. Copyrighted by the Broadcast Education Association. Reprinted by permission of the Journal of Broadcasting & Electronic Media.

Anson D. Shupe, Jr. and David G. Bromley, "Walking a Tightrope," from Qualitative Sociology, 2 (1980), pp. 8–21. Published by Human Sciences Press, Inc., New York. Reprinted by permission of Human Sciences Press, Inc.

Laud Humphreys, "Tearoom Trade: Impersonal Sex in Public Places." Published by permission of Transaction, Inc. from *Transaction*, Vol. 7, No. 3. Copyright © 1970 by Transaction, Inc.

Clyde Kluckhohn, "Queer Customs," from *Mirror for Man*. Copyright © 1949 by the author. Reprinted by permission of Florence R. Taylor.

Eldon E. Snyder and Elmer A. Spreitzer, "Baseball in Japan," from *Social Aspects of Sport*, pp. 53–56. Copyright © 1983 by E. E. Snyder and E. A. Spreitzer. Reprinted by permission of Prentice-Hall, Englewood Cliffs, New Jersey.

Edward T. Hall and Mildred Reed Hall, "The Sounds of Silence," from *Playboy*, June 1971. Copyright © 1971 by Edward T. Hall and Mildred Reed Hall. Reprinted by permission of the authors.

Myra Sadker and David Sadker, "Sexism in the Schoolroom of the '80s," from *Psychology Today*, 19 (March 1985), pp. 54–57. Copyright © 1985 by American Psychological Association. Reprinted with permission from *Psychology Today* magazine.

Howard S. Becker and Blanche Geer, "The Fate of Idealism in Medical School," from *American Sociological Review*, 23 (February 1958), pp. 50–56. Reprinted by permission of American Sociological Association.

Peter Berger, "The Importance of Role," from *Invitation to Sociology*, pp. 95–100 and 105. Copyright © 1963 by Peter L. Berger. Reprinted by permission of Doubleday & Company, Inc.

David L. Rosenhan, "On Being Sane in Insane Places," from *Science*, 179 (January 19, 1973), pp. 250–252 and 256–258. Copyright © 1973 by *Science* magazine and D. L. Rosenhan. Reprinted by permission of *Science* and the author.

Jean Bethke Elshtain, "A Key to Unlock the Asylum,"

from *Nation*, May 16, 1981, pp. 602–604. Reprinted by permission of the *Nation*.

Irving L. Janis, "Groupthink," from *Yale Alumni Magazine*, January 1973, pp. 16–19. Reprinted with permission from the January 1973 issue of the *Yale Alumni Magazine*; copyright by Yale Alumni Publications, Inc.

Peter M. Blau and Marshall W. Meyer, "The Concept of Bureaucracy," from *Bureaucracy in Modern Society*, Second Edition. Copyright © 1956, 1971 by Random House, Inc. Reprinted by permission of the publisher.

Martin S. Weinberg, "Sexual Modesty, Social Meanings, and the Nudist Camp," from *Social Problems*, 12:3 (Winter, 1965), pp. 311, 314–318. Reprinted by permission of the Society for the Study of Social Problems and the author.

William J. Chambliss, "The Saints and the Roughnecks," from *Society*, Vol. 11, No. 1, 1973. Published by permission of Transaction, Inc. Copyright © 1973 by Transaction, Inc.

Mark Fishman, "Crime Waves as Ideology," from *Social Problems*, 25 (June, 1978), pp. 531–543. Reprinted by permission of the Society for the Study of Social Problems and the author.

Charles H. Anderson, "Social Class and the Proletariat," from *The Political Economy of Social Class*, copyright © 1974, pp. 49–56. Reprinted by permission of Prentice-Hall, Englewood Cliffs, New Jersey.

James R. Millar and Peter Donhowe, "The Classless Society has a Wide Gap Between Rich and Poor," from the *Washington Post National Weekly*, Edition 3, February 17, 1986, pp. 16–17. Copyright 1986 by James R. Millar and Peter Donhowe. Reprinted by permission of the authors.

Richard T. Schaefer, "Racial Prejudice in a Capitalist State: What Has Happened to the American Creed" from *Phylon*, 47, 3 (September, 1986). Reprinted with the permission of *Phylon*, the Atlanta University Review of Race and Culture.

Harry Edwards, "The Black 'Dumb Jock'." Reprinted with permission from *The College Board Review*, No. 131, Spring 1984. Copyright © 1984 by College Entrance Examination Board, New York. Also reprinted by permission of the author.

Tim Giago and Sharon Illoway, "Dying Too Young," from *Civil Rights Quarterly Perspectives*, 14 (Fall 1982), pp. 29, 31, and 33.

Gene Oishi, "The Anxiety of Being a Japanese-American," from *New York Times Magazine*, April 28, 1985, pp. 58–60 and 65. Copyright © 1985 by The New York Times Company. Reprinted by permission.

Libby Slate, "The Able Disabled: The Media Office Promotes the Country's Largest Minority," from *Emmy Magazine*, November/December 1985, pp. 28–33. Copyright 1985 by Libby Slate. Reprinted by permission of the author.

Sandra L. Bem and Daryl J. Bem, "Case Study of a Nonconscious Ideology: Training the Woman to Know Her Place," from *Beliefs, Attitudes and Human Affairs*, Daryl J. Bem, Editor. Belmont, California: Brooks/Cole, copyright © 1970, pp. 89–99. Reprinted by permission of Sandra L. Bem.

Sharon Tucker, "Careers of Men and Women MBAs, 1950-1980," from *Work and Occupations*, 12 (May 1985), pp. 166–185. Copyright 1985 by Sage Publications, Inc. Reprinted by permission of Sage Publications, Inc.

Samuel H. Preston, "Children and the Elderly in the U.S.," From the *Scientific American*, December 1984, pp. 44–49. Copyright © 1984 by Scientific American, Inc. Reprinted with permission. All rights reserved.

Philip Blumstein and Pepper Schwartz, "Job Satisfaction, Ambition, and Success," pp. 154–164, and Notes pp. 566–567, from *American Couples*. Copyright © 1983 by Philip Blumstein, Ph.D. and Pepper W. Schwartz, Ph.D. By permission of William Morrow & Company.

Letty Cottin Pogrebin, "Are Men Discovering the Joys of Parenthood?" from *Ms.* magazine, February 1982, pp. 41, 43–44, and 46. Excerpted with permission from *Growing Up Free* by Letty Cottin Pogrebin, copyright © 1980 by Letty Cottin Pogrebin.

Linda Haas, "Role-Sharing Couples: A Study of Egalitarian Marriages," from *Family Relations*, July 1980. Reprinted by permission of National Council on Family Relations.

James M. Makepeace, "Courtship Violence Among College Students," from *Family Relations*, 30 (January 1981), pp. 97–102. Reprinted by permission of National Council on Family Relations.

Saul V. Levine, "Radical Departures," from *Psychology Today*, August 1984, pp. 20–27. Reprinted by permission of the author.

Dean M. Kelley, "Why Conservative Churches are Still Growing," from *Journal for the Scientific Study of Religion*, 17 (June 1978), pp. 165–172. Reprinted by permission of National Council of Churches and the author.

Calvin Goldscheider, "Social Change and Jewish

Continuity," from *Jewish Continuity and Change*. Copyright © 1986 by Indiana University Press. Reprinted by permission of the publisher.

Max Weber, "On Authority," from *From Max Weber: Essays in Sociology*, by Hans H. Gerth, and C. Wright Mills. Copyright © 1946, 1973 by Oxford University Press, Inc. Reprinted by permission.

Harold R. Kerbo and L. Richard Della Fave, "The Empirical Side of the Power Elite Debate: An Assessment of Critique of Recent Research," from *Sociological Quarterly*, 20 (Winter 1979), pp. 5–22. Reprinted by permission of The Sociological Quarterly.

Donald F. Roy, " 'Banana Time': Job Satisfaction and Informal Interaction," from *Human Organization*, 18 (Winter 1959–1960), pp. 158–168. Reproduced by permission of the Society for Applied Anthropology and Dr. Joy K. Roy, executor.

Christopher J. Hurn, "Theories of Schooling and Society: The Functional and Radical Paradigms," from *The Limits and Possibilities of Schooling*. Copyright © 1978 by Allyn and Bacon, Inc. Reprinted with permission.

Jomills Henry Braddock II, Robert L. Crain, and James M. McPartland, "A Long-Term View of School Desegregation: Some Recent Studies of Graduates as Adults." Copyright © 1984 by Phi Delta Kappa.

Reprinted by permission of the authors.

C. R. Creekmore, "Cities Won't Drive You Crazy," from *Psychology Today*, January 1985, pp. 46–50 and 52–53. Copyright © 1985, American Psychological Association. Reprinted with permission from *Psychology Today* magazine.

Joseph A. McFalls, Jr., "Where Have All the Children Gone?," from *USA Today*, March 1981. Copyright © 1981 by Society for the Advancement of Education. Reprinted with permission.

Paul R. Ehrlich and Anne H. Ehrlich, "What Happened to the Population Bomb," from *Human Nature*, January 1979, pp. 88–92. Copyright © 1979 by Human Nature, Inc. Reprinted by permission of the publisher.

David L. Miller, Kenneth J. Mietus, Richard A. Mathers, "A Critical Examination of the Social Contagion Image of Collective Behavior: The Case of the Enfield Monster," from *The Sociological Quarterly*, 19 (Winter 1978), pp. 129–130 and 132–140. Reprinted by permission of The Sociological Quarterly.

Jo Freeman, "The Origins of the Women's Liberation Movement" from *American Journal of Sociology*, 78 (January 73), pp. 792–807 and 810–811. Copyright © 1973 by Jo Freeman. Reprinted by permission of the author.

INDEX